THE

WILLARD J. GRAHAM SERIES

IN ACCOUNTING

BOOKS IN
THE WILLARD J. GRAHAM SERIES IN ACCOUNTING

CONSULTING EDITOR   ROBERT N. ANTHONY   *Harvard University*

ADVANCED ACCOUNTING

ADVANCED ACCOUNTING

CHARLES H. GRIFFIN
Professor of Accounting

THOMAS H. WILLIAMS
Professor of Accounting

KERMIT D. LARSON
Professor of Accounting

All of the Graduate School of Business
The University of Texas at Austin

1971
Revised Edition

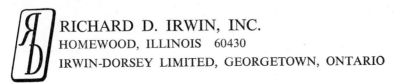RICHARD D. IRWIN, INC.
HOMEWOOD, ILLINOIS   60430
IRWIN-DORSEY LIMITED, GEORGETOWN, ONTARIO

REVISED EDITION
First Printing, May, 1971
Second Printing, September, 1971

Library of Congress Catalog Card No. 71–149896
PRINTED IN THE UNITED STATES OF AMERICA

Preface

This revised edition of *Advanced Accounting* is designed to maximize the instructor's flexibility in selecting subject matter to be covered in an advanced accounting course. Consistent with this aim, the content of the text is classified into the following seven unit divisions:

  I. Prologue (Chapter 1)
 II. Accounting for Partnerships (Chapters 2 through 4)
III. Accounting for Combined Corporate Entities (Chapters 5 through 10)
 IV. Consolidated Statements: An Expanded Analysis (Chapters 11 through 17)
  V. Fiduciary Accounting (Chapters 18 and 19)
 VI. Institutional and Social Accounting (Chapters 20 through 22)
VII. Special Sales Contracts (Chapters 23 and 24)

Two appendixes are provided to complement and to enlarge upon the analyses of individual chapters. The appendixes are:

Mathematical Notes and Tables

A Summary of Recommended Governmental Accounting Principles

Each of the units in the book, with the exception of Unit IV, can be treated as an *independent* topical division in planning the subject matter coverage of an advanced accounting course. Unit IV (Consolidated Statements: An Expanded Analysis) assumes previous study of Chapters 7 through 9 of Unit III.

In addition to the new, more flexible organization of material, the revised edition incorporates several significant expansions of topical coverage and a substantial increase in the number of problems provided at the end of each chapter. The entire book has been critically reviewed and revised to include the latest pronouncements of authoritative bodies (such as the Accounting Principles Board), and to provide a complete examination and illustration of them.

Chapter 1, Accounting Measurement, is presented as a separate unit, the Prologue, to emphasize its general applicability to the entire range of subjects dealt with in the book.

The revision of Unit II has maintained the basic approach of providing a summarized treatment of the more elementary problems of partnership formation and operations; thereafter attention focuses on the more complex problems of ownership realignment and the processes of dissolution and liquidation.

vii

Unit III represents the most striking expansion and reorganization of material in the revised edition. This unit consists of an analytical overview of the accounting problems associated with mergers, acquisitions, and the preparation and interpretation of financial reports in respect to the resultant combined corporate entities. Chapters 5 and 6 emphasize the importance of providing relevant information to the negotiators of corporate mergers and acquisitions. New material includes a historic, economic, and legal analysis of corporate combinations; alternative ways of classifying combinations; the development of information deemed relevant to the negotiation of stock exchange ratios; and a summary of tax factors which affect mergers and acquisitions. Chapters 7 through 9 provide an introductory treatment of the consolidated balance sheet, income statement, statement of retained earnings, and statement of sources and applications of funds. Chapter 10 includes: (1) a complete examination of the purchase and pooling of interests methods of accounting for corporate combinations; (2) the preparation of historical financial summaries and financial analyses (including a comprehensive treatment of earnings-per-share calculations) when the relevant time periods include corporate combinations; and (3) the preparation of segmental (or divisional) reports. A brief summary of additional problem areas in consolidated statement preparation is provided at the close of Chapter 10. This concluding section of the chapter is designed to complete the introduction to consolidated statements, developed in the context of the major accounting problems which relate to mergers, acquisitions, and the resultant combined corporate entities. For the instructor who prefers to abbreviate the coverage of consolidated statements in order to facilitate the study of other current topics, this unit provides unique textual coverage.

Unit IV is an expanded analysis of consolidated financial statements. It is designed to accommodate those advanced accounting courses which contemplate a comprehensive examination of this area and which accordingly require a more intensive treatment than is presented in Unit III. Chapters 11–15 provide an exhaustive and rigorous analysis of the more technical problems associated with the preparation of consolidated financial statements (intercompany inventory profits, changes in ownership interests, etc.). Accounting for branches is presented in Chapter 16 with a miscellany of items related to consolidations. Chapter 17, a significant new addition to this unit, provides an analysis of the problems of accounting for international operations.

The revised edition presents corporate liquidation and reorganization (Chapter 18) and accounting for estates and trusts (Chapter 19) in a separate unit (Unit V) devoted to fiduciary accounting. Unit VI comprises the chapters which relate to institutional and social accounting. Chapter 20, which provides a discussion of the principles of governmental accounting, has been revised to reflect the recent recommendations of the National Committee on Governmental Accounting as well as the President's Commission on Budget Concepts. The chapter applies basic fund accounting concepts to municipal, federal, and regulatory agency accounting. Chapters 21 and 22 utilize the techniques of preparing consolidated financial statements to develop an understanding of national income accounting. These chapters have been revised to reflect current definitional changes in basic national income concepts.

Unit VII, Special Sales Contracts, includes two chapters (23 and 24) related to consignment and installment sales transactions. These chapters illustrate special modifications in the conventions of income determination.

This revised edition of *Advanced Accounting* does not include one unit which was presented in the first edition. A series of three chapters, which examined the role of quantitative analysis in accounting, has been excluded. As the increasing importance of these topics to accounting has become more widely recognized, they generally have been incorporated appropriately in lower level courses, thereby eliminating the need for their inclusion in an advanced course.

The authors wish to gratefully acknowledge the many individuals who contributed to this book through their comments, constructive criticisms, and support in preparing the manuscript. Special appreciation is due to Professor Emeritus G. H. Newlove of The University of Texas, whose lifelong example as a scholarly researcher has been an inspiration to the authors. Professor Newlove has generously allowed the authors to appropriate and adapt for their use a variety of schedular forms and analyses which he developed in earlier works on consolidated financial statements. We are indebted to Dayton H. Simms for his contribution of problem material and assistance in the final preparation and review of the manuscript. Our appreciation is also extended to Professor Robert D. Mettlen of The University of Texas, who made numerous suggestions in respect to the material on national income accounting, and to Professor Raynard M. Sommerfeld of The University of Texas for his critical review of the sections related to taxation.

The authors also wish to recognize the cooperation of the American Institute of Certified Public Accountants in permitting the reproduction of selected portions of research bulletins and studies, Accounting Principles Board Opinions, and the use of relevant C.P.A. questions and problems.

May, 1971   C.H.G.
                                                                        T.H.W.
                                                                        K.D.L.

Contents

Balances. Partners' Loans. Liquidation Expenses. INSTALLMENT (PERI-ODIC) PAYMENTS: Basic Accounting Problem. Periodic Computation of Safe Payments to Partners. Partners' Loans. Cash Predistribution Plan. Liquidation Expenses and Unrecorded Liabilities. INSOLVENT PARTNER-SHIP: Basic Rights. Accounting Analysis of the Insolvent Partnership.

UNIT III.   ACCOUNTING FOR COMBINED CORPORATE ENTITIES

Special Problems. Extended Usefulness of the Statement of Affairs. RE-
ORGANIZATION: Nonjudicial Remedies. Judicial Remedies. RECEIVERS'
ACCOUNTS. REALIZATION AND LIQUIDATION ACCOUNT: Statement Annota-
tions. Special Problems. Illustrative Problem—Alternative Statement
Form.

ADMINISTRATION BY A FIDUCIARY: Introduction. Role of the Fiduciary in
Estate Administration. Inventory of Assets. Claims against the Estate.
Bequests of Personal Property. Role of the Fiduciary in Trust Administra-
tion. DUAL BASES OF ACCOUNTABILITY: Principal (Corpus) and Income
Distinguished. Special Problems. FIDUCIARY ACCOUNTS AND REPORTS:
Accounting Procedures and Entry Sequence for an Estate. Illustrative
Problem. Charge and Discharge Statement. Closing Entries. Properties
Transferred to Trustee.

UNIT VI.   INSTITUTIONAL AND SOCIAL ACCOUNTING

BASIC CONCEPTS OF GOVERNMENTAL ACCOUNTING: The Nature of Funds.
Expendable and Nonexpendable Funds. The Budget and Budgetary Ac-
counting. Encumbrances and Obligations. Appropriations. Allotments
and Apportionments. STATE AND LOCAL GOVERNMENTAL UNITS: General
Fund. Special Revenue Funds. Intragovernmental Service Funds. Special
Assessment Funds. Capital Projects Funds. Debt Service Funds. Trusts
and Agency Funds. Enterprise Funds. General Fixed Assets—A Self-
Balancing Group of Accounts. General Long-Term Debt—A Self-Balanc-
ing Group of Accounts. Summary. FEDERAL GOVERNMENT: Introduction.
Basic Objectives. Basic Accounting Procedures. Federal Agency Account-
ing—An Illustrative Example. REGULATORY ACCOUNTING: Prescribed
Accounts and Reports. Theoretical Framework. GOVERNMENTAL AC-
COUNTING SYSTEMS RECONSIDERED: Federal and Nonfederal Systems
Compared. Governmental and Commercial Accounting Compared.

INTRODUCTION. BASIC OBJECTIVE. BASIC DEFINITIONS. THE BUSINESS
SECTOR—A SINGLE FIRM ILLUSTRATION. CONSOLIDATION OF THE BUSI-
NESS SECTOR. SPECIAL PROBLEMS IN THE BUSINESS SECTOR: Inventory
Valuation Adjustment. Imputed Values. Governmental Operating Enter-
prises and Subsidies to Business. Classification of Taxes. A COMPREHEN-
SIVE EXAMPLE.

OTHER SECTOR ACCOUNTS: Household (Personal) Sector. Government
Sector. Rest of World Sector—Foreign Transactions Account. Gross
Saving and Investment Account. INTEGRATION OF ACCOUNTS. THE NA-

TIONAL INCOME AND PRODUCT ACCOUNT. RESTATEMENT OF GUIDING CONCEPTS: National Income and Product Aggregates. Components of National Income and Product Aggregates. SUMMARY.

UNIT VII.   SPECIAL SALES CONTRACTS

UNIT I | PROLOGUE

Chapter 1 | Accounting Measurement

DEFINITION AND MEASUREMENT

Accounting is essentially an applied science concerned with the measurement of selected economic data for the benefit of many and diverse business users. An appreciation of the problems of accounting measurement, however, begins with the ability to distinguish between *definition* and *valuation*. "Valuation" is generally used in accounting in reference to the process of applying specifiable methods which result in the assignment of numbers to represent economic properties. Thus perceived, the term valuation is essentially synonymous with the term measurement.

A prescription of measurement procedures can be appropriately identified as an *operational definition*. Taken alone, however, such definitions leave unanswered the critical question of the basic nature and significance of the properties being measured. Without such understanding, it is meaningless to assign magnitudes to the properties. Terms such as *asset, equity, revenue,* and *expense* are significant identifying expressions only to the extent that their basic properties and characteristics are clearly understood. The process of isolating and stipulating the essential qualities and relational significance of economic phenomena is appropriately referred to as *constitutive definition*. It is this form of definition that must be clearly distinguished from valuation. Relevant discourse presumes a recognition that accounting concepts are essentially qualitative; quantification is a process of translation, or reduction, of economic phenomena to numerical terms.

With its heritage firmly established historically in business practice, the accounting discipline has been slow to react to the need for investigating and refining the formulation of basic concepts. Yet, continuous reexamination and appraisal are prerequisite to a progressive evolution of any scientific and intellectual discipline. Although precise, unambiguous definitions are virtually impossible in the early development of any science, a failure to emphasize basic definitions signals a fundamental deficiency in the underlying structure of accounting theory. Wherever possible, theoretical consistency and basic logic should be preserved and protected; they should not be compromised merely to accommodate an existing measurement methodology. Sidney S. Alexander comments in this regard:

3

Faced with a choice between precision of operation and precision of concept, the accountant has chosen the former, the economist the latter. That is, the accountant has chosen a concept of income which permits precise measurements but which yields misleading results under conditions of fluctuation and uncertainty. The economist has sought to construct a concept that would stand up under fluctuating conditions but such a concept cannot easily be applied in practice.[1]

Although these essentially polar positions may be inadequate reflections of accounting and economics, they do reveal a fundamental difference in orientation. Accountants have tended to define basic concepts in terms of methods of measurement. This operational approach to definition, rigorously applied, is consonant with many scientific disciplines. In accounting, however, it may be criticized in many cases as being merely a rationale of existing practice. Whereas accounting theory must necessarily remain responsive to the needs of current practice, it should not eschew attempts to refine and extend formulations of underlying concepts.

The distinction between definition and measurement was clearly recognized in the American Accounting Association's 1957 revision of *Accounting and Reporting Standards for Corporate Financial Statements*. In a prefatory remark, the authoring committee indicated that "accounting procedures and reports are based on the premise that quantitative data provide an effective means of description and are basic to the communication of qualitative information about the enterprise."[2] Assets, for example, are *defined* as economic resources, the *values* of which are expressed in terms of money equivalents, variously determined. The ascription of value is clearly a measurement process. Similar distinctions are drawn with respect to equities, expenses, and other significant concepts. The discussion to follow will emphasize both the definitional and measurement aspects of a number of important accounting concepts. Additionally, the authors propose to give attention to the *fundamental role of definitions* in the development of the various topics throughout this text.

THE MEASUREMENT OF ASSETS

The assets of a business enterprise, given numerical measurement, indicate in their static state the value of resources employed in a profit-making endeavor; in their dynamic state, i.e., as value increments and expirations, they are fundamental to the process of net income measurement. Yet, assets are variously defined in accounting literature. Signifi-

---

[1] Sidney S. Alexander, "Income Measurement in a Dynamic Economy," *Five Monographs on Business Income* (New York: Institute of Certified Public Accountants, 1950), p. 9.

[2] Committee on Accounting Concepts and Standards, American Accounting Association, *Accounting and Reporting Standards for Corporate Financial Statements* (Evanston, Ill., 1957), p. 1.

cantly, most definitions are minor variants on the following two different emphases:

[An asset is] something represented by a debit balance that is or would be properly carried forward upon a closing of books of account according to the rules or principles of accounting (provided such debit balance is not in effect a negative balance applicable to a liability), on the basis that it represents either a property right or value acquired, or an expenditure made which has created a property right or is properly applicable to the future. Thus, plant, accounts receivable, inventory, and a deferred charge are all assets in balance-sheet classification.[3]

Assets are economic resources devoted to business purposes within a specific accounting entity; they are aggregates of service-potentials available for or beneficial to expected operations. The significance of some assets may be uniquely related to the objectives of the business entity and will depend upon enterprise continuity.[4]

The first statement is in part a definition (property right or value acquired) and in part a description of the measurement process (debit balance properly carried forward upon a closing of the books of account), with principal emphasis given to measurement characteristics. In fact, the "definition" presumes, in large part, that the measurement function is predetermined. Contrariwise, the second citation is an attempt to define a basic concept which may accommodate to various value assignments. Assets are valuable to an enterprise because they represent aggregates of service-potentials expected to benefit future operations. This expression is clearly more definitive and provides a more useful basis for accounting classification.

Given the second definition and assuming a value expression in terms of dollars, the measurement process focuses upon the translation of the service-potentials into dollar-equivalents. The Committee on Accounting Concepts and Standards (American Accounting Association) appraises the valuation process as follows:

Conceptually, this [the value measure of an asset] is the sum of the future market prices of all streams of service to be derived, discounted by probability and interest factors to their present worths. However, this conception of value is an abstraction which yields but limited practical basis for quantification. Consequently, the measurement of assets is commonly made by other more feasible methods.[5]

Notwithstanding the practical impediments to this discounting type of measurement, it will be discussed in summary manner in the following

---

[3] Committee on Terminology, American Institute of Certified Public Accountants, "Review and Résumé," *Accounting Terminology Bulletin No. 1* (New York, 1953), p. 13.

[4] Committee on Accounting Concepts and Standards, *op. cit.,* p. 3.

[5] *Ibid.,* p. 4.

paragraphs, as it represents a method of valuation theoretically to be preferred (see Appendix 1 for a review of compound interest).

The evaluation of an investment in corporate bonds provides a useful illustrative model of discount measurement. In *Intermediate Accounting* of this series, it was pointed out that in respect to bond investments, two distinct revenue flows may be isolated: (1) the cash interest to be received at specified intervals of time; and (2) the principal, or face, of the bond to be collected at maturity. In measuring investment value, therefore, both future sources of revenue must be discounted, at an appropriate interest rate, for relevant periods of time. That is, a specified dollar amount of future revenue is equivalent to a sum which if presently invested at the current or investment interest rate would accumulate to the given amount at compound interest. Consider a $1,000, 5 percent, five-year bond investment. If the current investment rate is 6 percent and if interest is paid annually, the current *value* of this asset may be computed as follows:

$$\text{Present value of future interest receipts} = \text{Cash interest} \times \text{Present value of annuity of \$1 for five periods at } 6\%$$
$$(a_{\overline{5}|6\%})$$
$$= \$50 \, (4.2123638)$$
$$= \$210.62 \, .$$

$$\text{Present value of bond principal} = \text{Face amount of bond} \times \text{Present value of \$1 for five periods at } 6\%$$
$$[(1.06)^{-5}]$$
$$= \$1,000 \, (.74725817)$$
$$= \$747.26 \, .$$

$$\text{Total present value of bond} = \$210.62 + \$747.26$$
$$= \$957.88 \, .$$

The underlying assumptions implicit in these computations are indicated in the following analysis:

End of Period	Accumulated Amount of Present Value	Future Revenue	
		Receipts	Accumulated Amount
0.............	$ 957.88	$ 0.00	$ 0.00
1.............	1,015.35	50.00	50.00
2.............	1,076.27	50.00	103.00
3.............	1,140.85	50.00	159.18
4.............	1,209.30	50.00	218.73
5.............	1,281.85	1,050.00	1,281.85

Several important observations can be made from the above analysis:

1.   The present value of the bond is less than the face amount of the bond. This condition exists where the prevailing effective interest rate (6 percent) is greater than the nominal interest rate (5 percent); the investment base must accordingly be lower than the face amount of the bond if a recovery of an amount certain in dollars is to represent a 6 percent return. The present value will equal the face amount of the bond only if the effective interest rate is at that time equal to the nominal interest rate.

2.   The value of the asset of the start of the first period, $957.88, is based upon a discounting of future revenue. The amount to which this present value will accumulate in five years, $1,281.85, reflects the application of 6 percent compound interest. Thus, it must be implicitly assumed that future revenue receipts may be *reinvested* at the same interest rate and thereafter generate additional interest increments. At the end of five years, the two amounts are then necessarily equal.

3.   In respect to a bond investment, the original cost is usually determined on the basis of a discount rate equivalent to the then prevailing current rate of interest. The discount or premium is thereafter amortized in a manner to reflect the given yield (or investment return) for each period during the life of the bond (using scientific, or compound interest, amortization). If the effective interest rate remains constant, the adjusted cost will continue to equal the current value. If the effective interest rate should change, however, the two values will diverge. Consequently, one must elect between a measurement which either reflects income on *invested* capital, with an asset value based thereon, *or* a measurement which emphasizes *current* asset value, with income therefrom a composite of interest calculated on the basis of this value and the change in market value during the current period.

Another example of this theoretically preferred method of asset valuation is provided by an investment in capital equipment. Assume that a business owns a machine which is expected to produce over a period of three years, annual revenue of $11,000, with associated annual out-of-pocket costs of $1,000; the machine has an expected salvage value of $2,000 at the end of its useful life. If an investment return of 5 percent is assumed, the *present value* of this asset may be computed as follows:

$$\text{Present value of future net revenues} = \$10,000 \times a_{\overline{3}|5\%}$$
$$= \$27,232.48 \, .$$

$$\text{Present value of salvage value} = \$2,000 \times (1.05)^{-3}$$
$$= \$1,727.68 \, .$$

$$\text{Total present value of equipment} = \$27,232.48 + \$1,727.68$$
$$= \$28,960.16 \, .$$

From this illustration, one may draw additional conclusions respecting compound discount and asset valuation:

1.   Selection of an appropriate discount rate is an important factor in asset measurement. Conceptually, it is that rate at which capital can be employed in available, alternative investment projects of comparable risk. Manifestly, equating risk factors is a difficult practical problem. In the case of bond investments, the effective interest rate for specific bonds is an appropriate index of the discount rate. Apropos of fixed assets, however, such a rate is not available. Although the current cost of borrowing funds to finance the purchase of property and equipment is occasionally used, this is not a theoretical equivalent of the discount rate; a preferable rate is the rate of return on funds *loaned,* or moneys *invested* in assets other than in the asset to be valued, i.e., the *opportunity rate* for money.

2.   This second illustration, as in the case of the first, assumes a *certain* and *constant* dollar return over the life of the asset. These assumptions accommodate the use of present value of annuity tables. However, the asset may be assigned a present value even if these assumptions are relaxed. If the dollars returned are certain but of unequal amounts, each partial return can be individually discounted back to the date of measurement and the respective present values summed. Furthermore, if the dollars returned are uncertain in amount, as they often are, it is possible to use probability theory to determine an *expected* return, after which discounting may proceed as before.

3.   The approach illustrated here assumes a return on investment at *discrete* points in time. This method is modeled after interest-bearing obligations which exhibit this behavior pattern. For other investments, however, a *continuous* return on investment may provide a more refined measurement of the current value of the asset. This may be accomplished with only a minor modification to the basic method.

4.   Finally, it should be observed that the *net dollar return* (rather than net income) is used to evaluate the current value of an asset. It is important that depreciation be excluded from this computation, as the present value of net future revenues assumes that each "rent" represents both a return *of* capital and a return *on* capital. The inclusion of depreciation would render invalid the underlying assumptions of the method. Yet a more subtle consideration relates to the question of expense recognition and revenue realization. Ideally, a cash basis of accounting should be used in this type of discount measurement, since the discount rate explicitly measures the opportunity cost of the previously committed cash. Where the accrual method is used, however, and when revenue generated from an investment in equipment is converted into an investment in receivables (claims against customers), a different, and much smaller, discount rate is appropriate because the risk factor is frequently reduced. For practical purposes, net income plus depreciation represents a reasonable approximation of the appropriate value for net revenue.

A more precise analysis than the separate evaluation of each asset involves the calculation of a single value expression for the aggregate resources of the enterprise. The measurement process remains essentially the same as in the application of the discount concept to individual assets, except that the net receipts of the enterprise *in total* are discounted. If the expected returns are unequal, the previously indicated method of separately discounting each period's return may be applied. However, if the enterprise is expected to have an indefinite life, this procedure may be approximated by means of the following technique:

1. Compute the *average* net receipts expected in each future period.
2. Capitalize this amount by using an appropriate discount factor, i.e.,

$$\text{Present value} = \frac{\text{Average net receipts}}{\text{Discount factor}}.$$

Use of this capitalization procedure, as a substitute for discounting in respect to separate, annual returns, is easily verified mathematically.[6]

This procedure not only results in an assignment of an implicit value to the tangible assets, it also necessarily includes intangibles such as organizational efficiency, customer goodwill, etc. Consequently, the present value calculated is a quantitative expression of total enterprise value. There remain, however, difficult problems of assigning values to the several equities in the enterprise and, if necessary, specific values to each of the asset components. This latter assignment to individual assets may be conceptually inconsistent, however, as the total value of the enterprise often represents an indivisible combination of the firm's resources.

A method of asset valuation which has much theoretical merit has been illustrated by two relevant examples. If accepted, this discount method quantifies a definition of assets that is relatively independent of other assumptions; the resulting value expression is a function of the intrinsic service value of the asset when employed in the manner indicated by the measurement calculation. As previously noted, practical limitations currently militate against this valuation process; and other, more objective, methods of quantifying assets are often used. The traditional method is based upon a dichotomy of assets into monetary and nonmonetary assets:

Monetary assets—cash or claims to cash—should be expressed in terms of expected cash receipts adjusted for collection delay where significant.

Non-monetary assets—inventories, plant, long-term investments, and deferred items generally—are not as amenable to money measurement. Such assets are typically stated at acquisition cost or some derivative thereof. Assuming a free

---

[6] Given an average annual return, the present value for a specified number of years is computed using the present value of an annuity factor, i.e., $a_{\overline{n}|i} = \dfrac{1 - \dfrac{1}{(1+i)^n}}{i}$. The approximation asserts that as the number of time periods increases $(n \to \infty)$, then $\dfrac{1 - \dfrac{1}{(1+i)^n}}{i} \to \dfrac{1}{i}$.

market, acquisition cost expressed in the bargained price of an asset is presumed to be a satisfactory quantification of future service expectations at the time of acquisition. . . . Modification of acquisition cost may be occasioned by recognition of such factors as depreciation, depletion, or obsolescence.

The aim of all measurement of assets is to state the amount of available service potential in the most objective and realistic terms.[7]

This approach to measurement clearly has more moderate implications for accounting practice than does the discounting approach. However, for reasons of materiality, objectivity, conservatism, or otherwise, existing accounting practice does not yet evidence *all* of the measurement principles implicit in the moderate "monetary-nonmonetary" approach.

Another approach to the valuation of assets has received attention in accounting literature for many years and is expected to be used by many firms in the near future to prepare supplementary financial statements. This approach involves adjustment of cost valuations for general monetary unit fluctuations, in order that the underlying measuring unit will have a constant unit dimension.[8]

Other proposals for valuing assets have also attracted the attention of accountants and have provoked some measure of support. Some of these diverge sharply from the long-established cost principle. Sprouse and Moonitz, in a comprehensive study of accounting principles for business enterprises, recommend as appropriate asset valuations a combination of acquisition costs, current exchange prices, and future exchange prices.[9] This effort at formulating a tentative set of theoretically consistent and useful principles superimposed upon a framework of basic accounting postulates is a progressive forward look at theory construction. A proposal of more limited scope by the Committee on Inventory Pricing of the American Accounting Association recommends that inventories be valued at current replacement cost.[10] This study in inventory pricing harmonizes in important particulars with the Sprouse-Moonitz conclusions.

R. J. Chambers has proposed an interesting theory of accounting measurement in which the essential property of assets to be measured is identified as current cash equivalent (exit price).[11] However, the measurement methods advocated by Chambers involve a variety of those already in use

---

[7] Committee on Accounting Concepts and Standards, *op. cit.*, pp. 4–5.

[8] Staff of the Accounting Research Division, American Institute of Certified Public Accountants, "Reporting the Financial Effects of Price-Level Changes," *Accounting Research Study No. 6* (New York, 1963).

[9] Robert T. Sprouse and Maurice Moonitz, "A Tentative Set of Broad Accounting Principles for Business Enterprises," *Accounting Research Study No. 3* (New York, 1962).

[10] Committee on Concepts and Standards—Inventory Measurement, American Accounting Association, "A Discussion of Various Approaches to Inventory Measurement," Supplementary Statement No. 2, *The Accounting Review*, July, 1964. pp. 700–714.

[11] Raymond J. Chambers, *Accounting Evaluation and Economic Behavior* (Englewood Cliffs, N.J.: Prentice-Hall, Inc., 1966).

or previously espoused as part of other theories. Thus, his analysis is not so distinctly different in terms of measurement methods as it is in terms of the development of definitions to explain the significance of the measurements.

The pervasive element in most of these recommendations as to asset measurement is the attempt to quantitatively express the essence of the basic definition of assets. In most of the recent proposals, the concept of a bundle of future economic benefits, or services, is implicitly or explicitly accepted as a guiding objective.

THE MEASUREMENT OF EQUITIES

Equity interests are traditionally classified into two principal groups: liabilities and ownership interests. From an entity point of view, however, the interest groups are essentially indistinguishable, without rank or preference; included therein are creditors, shareholders, and the entity's equity in itself.

Although the accounting "entity" status is frequently cited as defense for specific accounting actions in respect to assets, the proprietary argument is more often used with regard to equities, in which the two basic equity components are separately defined. The AICPA casts its definitions of liabilities and stockholders' equity in a format similar to its definition of assets. The definitions of the Committee on Accounting Concepts and Standards of the American Accounting Association are as follows:

The interests or equities of creditors (liabilities) are claims against the entity arising from past activities or events which, in the usual case, require for their satisfaction the expenditure of corporate [business] resources. The interests or equities of stockholders [owners] represent residual claims to corporate [business] assets. . . .[12]

These definitions are, to a large degree, a reflection of existing accounting practices. It should be noted that reference to *past* events or activities effectively eliminates from the liability classification such items as future wage payments—which often are committed by implication if not legally guaranteed. Contrariwise, future payments to be made on notes or bonds payable are included in the definition because of the occurrence of a prior event which created a current and/or future claim against entity resources. The merit of this position must ultimately meet the test of usefulness to justify its acceptance as a guide to practice. Additionally, the ownership interest is described as a residual interest and thus is implicitly defined in terms of the algebraic sum of assets and liabilities.

Creditor Interests

The measurement process must express the interests or equities of creditors in enterprise assets in quantitative terms. If measured in a manner

---

[12] Committee on Accounting Concepts and Standards, *op. cit.*, p. 7.

similar to assets, the value of creditor claims at a given point in time would reflect the cash, or its equivalent, required to discharge the liability then existing. Sprouse and Moonitz defend this position.

To measure a liability is to determine the "weight" or the "burden" of the obligation on the balance sheet date. This "burden" is the lowest amount for which the obligation could be effectively discharged. If, for example, payment in cash now will discharge the liability, that amount of cash is the measure of the liability, even though in fact payment is delayed. If the creditor will not or cannot accept cash now in discharge of the liability, the appropriate amount is that sum which, if invested now (e.g., in a sinking fund), will provide the sums needed at maturity, even though in fact no explicit sinking fund or other investment device is actually used.[13]

Although this position differs materially from generally accepted procedures for the evaluation and disclosure of liabilities, it can be shown that liability measurements, particularly long-term liabilities, frequently approximate this value closely.

As a first example, consider a bond liability. Assume an outstanding 6 percent, five-year, $100,000 bond, interest payable annually, with an effective interest rate of 5 percent. The present value of the bond liability is calculated in the same manner as for the corresponding bond investment:

$$\text{Present value of principal} = \$100,000 \times (1.05)^{-5}$$
$$= \$78,352.62 .$$

$$\text{Present value of interest payments} = \$6,000 \times a_{\overline{5}|5\%}$$
$$= \$25,976.86 .$$

$$\text{Total present value of bond} = \$104,329.48 .$$

If this determination relates to the date of issue, the proceeds received from the sale would be $104,329.48. Thus, the typical accounting measurement of the bond liability at issue date, i.e., principal, or face amount, plus premium, yields a result equivalent to the "burden or weight of the obligation" concept. As in the case of a bond investment, however, fluctuations in the effective interest rate during the period the bond remains outstanding will cause the current "burden" of the obligation to assume new values. In the traditional accounting sense, the difference between this adjusted "burden" and the "burden" assumed at date of issue represents an *unrealized* gain or loss. For example, if in the previous illustration, the effective interest rate subsequent to the date of issue increased to 6 percent, the present value of the bond would be $100,000, and the gain could accordingly be *realized* by redeeming or refunding the bond issue. Similarly, if the effective interest rate subsequently decreased below the original 5 percent rate, the present value of the bond issue would be correspondingly greater than the recorded amount (assuming compound interest amortization in the interim), and the *unrealized loss* might again be *realized* by

---

[13] Sprouse and Moonitz, *op. cit.,* p. 39.

retirement or refunding. If liability measurement is to be consistent with the discount method of asset valuation, however, an adjustment of the value of the liability to correspond to the weight of the obligation as of the date of the financial statements is required; manifestly, this new point of reference injects the *current* values of the relevant variables—time and interest rate—into the valuation of liabilities. Accountants traditionally compensate for the passage of time with periodic amortization (preferably compound interest amortization); they usually neglect, however, to adjust for variations in interest rates during the holding period.

This concept of value is equally applicable to short-term obligations. If the time interval between the creation of a liability and its subsequent payment is relatively short, the practical benefits derived from a present value measurement of the obligation may be negligible, or immaterial. This should not be construed as a refutation of the guiding philosophy of discount measurement but rather a recognition of the influence of the materiality concept in the transition from theory to practice. As vehicles for measurement become more precise and resulting differences more meaningful, the disparity between theory and practice may be reduced accordingly.

Ownership Interests

Ownership interests have been previously described as the equity of residual claimants to enterprise assets. Consequently, if a method of measurement is accepted for the fundamental notions of asset and liability, the ownership interest is implicitly determined. A commitment to another basis of measurement need not be made.

Once assets and liabilities are given value assignments, there still remains the problem of explaining quantitatively the net *change* in the ownership interest during an interval of time. Consonant with the proprietary theory, this variation can be explained in terms of transactions between the owners and the enterprise *and* gains or losses on transactions with independent parties. Distinguishing between classes of transactions in this manner is, of course, only one of several possible explanations for changes in residual equity. If the entity definition of an equity interest is accepted, such a distinction is not relevant.

Assignment of specific values to the ownership interest is based primarily on legal considerations. For example, the distinction between invested capital and accumulated earnings and the differences in status accorded to classes of invested capital derive principally from statutory provisions. There are, however, certain accounting problems involving these interests, such as treasury stock transactions and defaulted subscriptions, which require the exercise of accounting judgment and accordingly merit consideration on theoretical bases. These topics have been considered in detail in *Intermediate Accounting* of this series. It is important to recognize, however, that solutions to these problems, as well as the problems of asset and liability measurement, are dependent upon current concepts of enterprise net income. With a primary emphasis on asset-liability measurement, net income is implicitly determined (subject to the choice between the entity and proprietary theories) and requires classification only in terms of important, or significant, components. If, on the other hand, net income is defined and measured as the first objective of the accounting process, asset and liability measurements are reckoned as residuals. Although prevailing concepts of enterprise net income have been previously alluded to, a more general abstraction of business net income will be now considered.

NATURE OF BUSINESS INCOME

Net income has been defined in numerous ways. Conceptually, it implies an increase in well-being, or in net worth, over a period of time. Sprouse and Moonitz reflect this basic position in their statement that "net profit (earnings, income) or net loss for an accounting period is the increase (decrease) in owners' equity, assuming no changes in the amount of invested capital either from price-level changes or from additional investments and no distribution to the owners."[14] This is, of course, consistent with the method of asset and liability valuation described previously as theoretically preferred. The wealth positions of a business at two points in time are compared to determine the incremental change. Classification of this net change, however, into net income from operations, changes in future expectations (price and quantity), uncontrollable fluctuations in environmental factors (e.g., opportunity rates of investment), etc., currently remains an unresolved practical problem.

Some accountants have "defined" income in what they believe to be a more objective and operational manner. The following is representative of such a "definition":

The realized net income of an enterprise measures its effectiveness as an operating unit and is the change in its net assets arising out of (a) the excess or deficiency of revenue compared with related expired cost and (b) other gains or losses to the enterprise from sales, exchanges, or other conversions of assets. Interest charges, income taxes and true profit-sharing distributions are not determinants of *enterprise* net income.[15]

It should be evident that this definition of net income is essentially a description of the measurement process. Such an operational definition is characteristic of many accounting treatises on income. For example, in one authoritative statement of accounting theory, which enjoys wide acceptance, the process of measuring net income in terms of associating relevant costs and revenues is justified as follows: "With acquisition and

---

[14] *Ibid.,* p. 9.

[15] Committee on Accounting Concepts and Standards, *op. cit.,* p. 5.

disposition prices measuring both the efforts to produce results and the results produced, the principal concern of accounting is the periodic matching of costs and revenues as a test reading by which to gauge the effect of the efforts expended."[16] Herein, explicit reference is made to the matching concept—a matching of related disposition prices and acquisition costs. If this concept of net income is accepted, a commitment to a given measurement methodology for assets and liabilities has already been made. It should be additionally noted that the aforementioned operational definition indicates that *enterprise* net income is computed before deduction of any distributions to the various equity interests. An appendage thereto, however, acknowledges that *net income to shareholders* is calculated after deduction of amounts distributed to nonshareholders.[17] This reference to two types of income additionally confirms the importance of adopting a basic approach to conventional income determination—either an entity theory or a proprietary theory.

Revenue

A principal determinant of net income is revenue; its recognition in the accounts provides a basis for subsequent matching against expired costs. Revenue is traditionally defined as follows:

Revenue, the principal source of realized net income, is the monetary expression of the aggregate of products or services transferred by an enterprise to its customers during a period of time.[18]

This definition effectively sets the transaction of sale or the rendering of service as the realization criterion for the timing of revenue recognition, although there exists a number of departures from this standard that are acceptable under special conditions, e.g., the installment sales method and the percentage of completion method.

Sprouse and Moonitz define revenue in more general terms:

Revenue is the increase in net assets of an enterprise as a result of the production or delivery of goods and the rendering of services.[19]

This definition anticipates the use of detailed guidelines for determining when revenue emerges during the production process and when it is generated upon the completion of a sale transaction. Once the basic properties of revenue are thus exposed, the collateral problem of revenue measurement follows.

---

[16] W. A. Paton and A. C. Littleton, *An Introduction to Corporate Accounting Standards* (Evanston, Ill.: American Accounting Association, 1940), p. 7.

[17] Committee on Accounting Concepts and Standards, *op. cit.* Thus, bond interest would be deducted from enterprise net income in the calculation of net income to shareholders.

[18] *Ibid.*

[19] Sprouse and Moonitz, *op. cit.,* p. 9.

Expired Costs

The dual aspect of the net income determination process is the matching of expired costs (efforts expended) with revenue realized (measured accomplishments):

Expired costs are those having no discernible benefit to future operations. They may be classified as "expense" or "loss." Expense is the expired cost, directly or indirectly related to a given fiscal period, of the flow of goods and services into the market and of related operations. Loss is expired cost not beneficial to the revenue producing activities of the enterprise.[20]

Expired costs are thus defined in general terms and classified as either expenses or losses. Sprouse and Moonitz similarly define them.

Given this conceptual framework in which to record an expiration of costs, it is important to determine that critical point (or period) in time when the inherent services of an asset have been consumed, and accordingly in what amount consumption shall be recognized. As a fundamental first consideration, accountants have generally accepted acquisition cost as the initial measurement. This acceptance does not, however, eliminate or even greatly alleviate other facets of the measurement problem. For example, the available alternatives in inventory pricing are a specific instance of a collection of procedures (perhaps too many!) developed and used over a comparatively long period of time to allocate acquisition costs between units sold and units unsold. Similar problems exist in respect to other areas of accounting, such as bond refunding costs, product guaranty costs, depreciation, and income tax expense. However, given a definitional framework, the accountant has a useful point of departure in terms of which he may analyze a given problem.

The precise nature of business income, like that of assets and equities, is an elusive concept, subject to numerous interpretations. Accountants' recent efforts to define basic concepts and to reappraise the fundamental propositions of accounting therefore deserve special commendation, even though they appear only to render complex what seems to be a simple accounting structure.

ALTERNATIVE COST CONCEPTS FOR REPORTING AND ANALYSIS

The previous discussion has indicated the accountant's election of acquisition cost as the underlying basis for subsequent processes of valuation and allocation. Cost is, however, a generic term which is variously interpreted and is frequently found in company with such qualifying adjectives as "standard," "replacement," "imputed," and "decision." These many cost references punctuate accounting expression so completely as to

---

[20] Committee on Accounting Concepts and Standards, *op. cit.,* p. 6.

warrant additional comment. There are numerous "costs" which are reasonably independent of acquisition cost but are nonetheless important to decision functions. A selected group of alternative cost concepts for reporting and/or analysis will be subsequently reviewed not within a general theoretical framework but in the context of their relevance to various accounting functions.

This abbreviated discussion of cost concepts is manifestly not intended to be exhaustive in scope, nor is it concerned with detailed illustrations. Rather, it merely identifies and distinguishes between some of the large number of cost concepts which find various applications in both financial statement presentations and accounting analyses for the decision function.

Acquisition and Aboriginal Costs

Acquisition, or invested, cost is a monetary measurement of the economic sacrifice incurred to acquire an asset. Aboriginal cost is the acquisition cost of an asset to the *first purchaser*. The term original cost is frequently used in accounting literature to refer to either of these cost concepts.

The aboriginal cost concept has special usefulness in respect to public utilities, where it is defined, for rate purposes, as the acquisition cost to that individual or business first committing resources to public service. For example, a value increment indicated by the sale of an operating unit of one utility to a second does not justify an increase in rates for the purchaser. The rate base remains the acquisition cost to the selling utility, notwithstanding the higher acquisition cost to the purchasing utility.

Fixed and Variable Costs

A dichotomy of acquisition costs is frequently made on a fixed-variable classification. Fixed costs are defined as those costs which remain invariant and unaffected by changes in the volume of production, while variable costs are those that vary directly in response to changes in the volume of production. This definition implies that whereas total fixed costs will remain constant during an interval of time, unit fixed costs vary with production; contrariwise, total variable costs vary with production, while unit variable costs remain constant. It is this distinction between fixed and variable costs that is the essence of the absorption costing–direct costing controversy—not the distinction between direct and indirect costs.

In a practical application, one must be careful to delimit the *revelant production range* before attempting to measure the fixed and variable costs. This is important because over the total productive capacity, there are distinct irregularities or steps in the cost function (increases in fixed costs) as well as occasional changes in the slope of the function curve (shift in variable cost). Once defined and measured for a relevant range, however, this classification continues to be useful for both reporting purposes (inventory valuation) and analytical studies (cost-volume-profit comparisons).

Direct and Indirect Costs

Direct costs are those costs which have a plausible identification with a specific product or business activity; indirect costs are those costs that cannot be so associated. It is important to establish a frame of reference in terms of which directness of association may be determined.

For example, with respect to specific units of product, materials that enter into the physical product are typically direct costs, i.e., they can be associated directly with each unit; in contrast, taxes levied on plant properties are usually regarded as indirect costs. Whereas units of product ultimately derive benefit from the expenditure in respect to taxes, the association of the cost with specific units is not so evident. In this instance, the variable cost is direct and the fixed cost is indirect. It would be inaccurate, however, to generalize from this illustration. For example, if the focal point or frame of reference were the plant, the taxes would represent direct, albeit still fixed, costs. However, in most product-costing applications, fixed costs are indirect costs and variable costs are correctly regarded as direct costs.

Controllable and Uncontrollable Costs

The fixed-variable and the direct-indirect classifications have been used in the past to assign responsibility to departments or individuals for cost incurrence. This assignment produced, in many instances, an inefficient, and inequitable, method of evaluating performance. Presently, performance indexes more often relate to *controllable* costs, i.e., costs which within a given time frame are solely a function of the decisions and actions of the individual or department being evaluated. All other costs—direct or indirect, variable or fixed—which are assigned to the department are viewed as uncontrollable, and accordingly are unrelated to performance efficiency. Such cost assignments, however, are important for other purposes, including inventory valuation, break-even analyses, product make-or-buy decisions, etc.

Consider the foreman who by his decisions directly influences the quantity of material and labor consumed in his operating subdivision of the enterprise. It may be useful to evaluate his actual achievements in terms of projected or standard quantities of labor and material (excluding "price" shifts in most cases). Significantly, however, he cannot alter or otherwise affect that portion of the total plant rental or ownership charge that is allocated to his department. This expense is an uncontrollable cost in respect to his authority. From the point of view of the manufacturing vice president, however, within a time frame of perhaps three to five years, the decision to rent or to purchase a plant is a controllable cost. Similar analyses of other costs indicate that an increasing amount of controllability frequently exists with the increase in managerial authority, although not necessarily within a single operating period.

It is apparent that a controllable cost may be classified as some type of direct cost; however, not all direct costs are controllable at the same organizational level. For example, the depreciation on a machine utilized solely in a department producing one product may be identified directly with the department or the product; yet it is not controllable by the departmental supervisor. On the other hand, a controllable cost may be either fixed or variable, depending upon the level of management under consideration.

Product Cost and Period Cost

Costs which can be associated directly or indirectly with the current *production* of goods are designated product costs and accordingly are allocated between inventory and cost of sales at the end of the accounting period. All other noncapital expenditures of the current period are regarded as period costs. With the exception of a few conventionally classified prepaid expenses, such as unexpired insurance and office supplies, these period costs are regarded as expired costs not subject to deferral. Viewed somewhat differently, product costs are usually a consequence of manufacturing and storage activities, while period costs reflect the functions of administration, distribution, and financing.

This traditional distinction between product and period costs is essentially a compromise made in the interest of practicality. Theoretically, many costs that are treated as period expenses, such as advertising and selected elements of administrative overhead, are incurred primarily to stimulate future product sales, and thus should not be wholly matched against current revenue. The difficulty in establishing a basis for making this association, however, militates against further refinement in cost assignment to periods or units of product.

Replacement Cost and Economic Cost

The volatile nature of the accounting measuring unit has stimulated numerous proposals for a restatement of the accounts in "current" dollars. Although this general problem is multi-faceted, it will be sufficient here to clarify the nature of two related, but conceptually quite different, cost concepts—replacement cost and economic cost.

Replacement cost is the outlay required to replace an asset in kind at current market prices. If accumulated depreciation on depreciable fixed property is computed on the basis of replacement cost and for a period of revised service life, the resulting value (sound value) may be compared with existing book value to determine the net increase or decrease generated by recording *current* cost. Manifestly, a rapidly changing state of the arts, or technological level, may render difficult the computation of the current cost of the *same* asset at different points in time.

On the other hand, economic cost is more directly related to a system of accounting based on acquisition cost. Since it is assumed that acquisition cost expresses the economic sacrifice, measured in dollars, incurred to obtain an asset, future measurements of the asset should denote the same economic sacrifice. Therefore, if the value of the medium of exchange or measurement standard has fluctuated, the recorded asset cost should be adjusted to reflect acquisition cost, or economic cost, in terms of constant dollars. Such an adjustment is generally approximated by using index number multipliers which indicate changes in the value of the measuring unit—viz., a general price-level index.

After Costs

After costs represent the dollar expression of efforts to be expended subsequent to the period in which related revenue was received, i.e., the benefits precede, to a greater or lesser degree, the expenditure of effort. Two types of after costs deserve specific mention. One general type relates to the clerical and risk function involved in the processing and collection of trade accounts receivable. Since this cost is alleged to have direct association with the total revenue-producing effort, the argument is made that it should be accrued and matched against revenues currently recognized. While an estimate of bad debts is conventionally accrued, other portions of the group of after costs (e.g., clerical expenses) in respect to trade receivables are treated as expired costs in the period of outlay. By comparison, the other type of after cost relates to an outlay that can be more directly associated with a measurable amount of revenue. In respect to some product warranties, the obligation to perform future services is compensated for by related service revenue. In this instance, it seems preferable to defer revenue recognition until the warranty obligation is actually discharged, when the period's service costs may be matched appropriately against the revenue.

Imputed Costs

Imputed costs are those costs that relate to a particular economic event, or commitment, although no conventionally accepted exchange transaction has then occurred. For example, some economists argue that one of the costs of an enterprise to be accounted for is the implicit interest (or cost of capital) on the owner's investment. Although there is no cash or price-oriented transaction which is evidence of this commitment, an acceptance of the entity theory implies an independence of the business entity and the owners. Therefore, it follows that as between the entity and its owners, an implicit transaction may be imputed. Total costs would be increased by such imputed interest; necessarily the cost increase is also indicated by a contra increase in the equity of the owners. The residual profit after all expenses are considered (including the cost of each equity element) represents excess profits which accrue to the entity itself. Since the objectivity of such an imputation does not accord with present accounting standards, this type of cost is not currently recognized for reporting purposes.

The calculation of imputed costs for purposes of accounting and economic analysis, however, is often recommended. These costs may be important determinants in the management decision process. One of the most important applications of imputed costs in analytical studies relates to *opportunity cost*. Opportunity cost is the value of resources (money or otherwise) in available alternative uses. In deciding whether to commit funds to an investment project, management should compare critically the expected rate of return from the project contemplated with the return that may be realized on alternative uses of these funds (including low-risk, savings opportunities). Similarly, a business that has a vertically integrated production sequence may use the opportunity cost concept in evaluating each of the related functional activities. For example, if an automobile manufacturer also produces its own steel, the opportunity cost of the steel consumed in automobile production is *not* the sum of acquisition costs directly attributable to the manufacturing process but rather the value at which the steel could presumably be sold if it were not internally consumed. Thus, in the determination of efficiency indexes, the opportunity cost should be charged to the automobile manufacturing operations and credited to the steel mill. Furthermore, the decision whether or not to continue manufacturing steel can be aided by a comparison of opportunity cost with production cost.

Differential (Incremental) Cost

Some accountants take the position that differential, or incremental, costs are perhaps the most fundamental elements underlying the majority of managerial decisions based upon accounting analyses. Differential cost is the variation in cost incurred in electing between two alternative courses of action. Thus, differential cost is essentially the accounting equivalent of the economist's *marginal* cost, where the addition of one more unit of output is the alternative course of action under consideration.

Differential cost analysis and the related concept of differential revenue relate to virtually every financial management decision. Each decision normally involves a commitment to invest or not to invest funds; to make a specific investment in preference to another; to continue an old process or to institute an improved, modernized one; to make or to buy a particular product; etc. Whether the analysis is expressed in terms of total projected costs and revenues or the incremental amounts, it is the increased (decreased) cost and revenue generated by the decision that is relevant to the analysis. This differential cost concept does not necessarily negate the basic assumption presently implicit in accounting practice that total general overhead attaches to, or benefits, all of the activities of an enterprise. For inventory valuation and net income determination, the allocation of overhead is a tenable position. However, for decision-making purposes, the allocation of existing fixed costs to proposed projects is often unrealistic.

Differential cost analysis relies fundamentally upon several other cost concepts. For example, the concept of direct costs is involved in identifying a given cost with a particular project, and fixed-variable cost classifications are used to estimate differential costs. Additionally, opportunity costs are often an important element of the total differential cost. Thus, a synthesis of cost concepts independent of financial accounting is frequently indicated.

Two more specific examples of differential cost analysis are illustrated following. Should there exist an opportunity to sell a given quantity of merchandise at a specified price (usually below the customary selling price), the decision to sell depends upon a comparison of the additional revenue provided with the additional costs to produce and distribute the units. General factory overhead presently incurred, although allocable to all units produced, should not be included in the analysis if the production of the additional units will not cause a change in the amount of this overhead, i.e., if production stays in the same relevant range. Contrariwise, if additional fixed costs will be incurred, they should be allocated in total to the new production proposed. Thus, existing fixed costs not subject to change with production of additional units are considered *sunk costs* and are not germane to the decision; additional fixed costs generated by accepting the proposal must be related, together with additional variable costs, to the anticipated revenue from the proposal. If the anticipated (differential) revenue exceeds the differential cost, the project is assumed to augment the total net income of the enterprise. A final decision must necessarily weigh this value increment against certain qualitative and long-run considerations.

Another example of differential cost analysis is illustrated by a decision in respect to refunding outstanding bonds. The relevant factors to be compared are the present values of the total cash outlays to be made on each of the two bond issues, viz., the outstanding bond issue and the proposed refunding issue. In addition to cash interest payments, the total outlay to refund the old issue will necessarily include any required call premium and issue costs; any discount or premium on the old issue is a sunk cost (or cost adjustment factor), and while an integral element in income determination, it is not relevant to this decision process. Although this approach is based upon total projected outlays under both circumstances, a more refined, but equivalent, analysis would focus on differential outlays.

Each of these examples emphasizes the wide applicability of differential cost analysis. The accountant should be especially alert to its uses in decision processes concerned with profit maximization.

QUESTIONS

1. Distinguish between *definition* (constitutive definition) and *measurement* (valuation).
2. What is the principal difference between the AAA's definition of assets and that of the AICPA's Committee on Terminology?
3. Conceptually, what discount rate is preferred in the "present value" measurement of assets?

4. Using the discount concept, describe the basic process involved in valuing a firm's aggregate resources.

5. Explain the "monetary-nonmonetary" approach to asset valuation.

6. Briefly describe the "weight" or "burden" method of measuring a liability and indicate how it would be applied to long- and short-term liabilities.

7. What are expired costs and how may they be classified? In what manner does an expired cost affect the determination of periodic net income?

8. Distinguish between—
   a) Acquisition and aboriginal costs.
   b) Fixed and variable costs.
   c) Direct and indirect costs.
   d) Controllable and uncontrollable costs.
   e) Product and period costs.
   f) Replacement and economic cost.

9. What are "after costs"? Give an example.

10. Define imputed cost, opportunity cost, and sunk cost.

11. What are differential or incremental costs? What significance do these concepts have for management?

PROBLEMS

Problem 1–1

A State Turnpike Commission contracts with a construction firm to build a limited access highway for $60,000,000, for which payment is to be made in 20-year, 3 percent bonds of the Commission. Additionally, it is expected that approximately $40,000,000 will be expended for right-of-way and other costs; these outlays will also be financed with the bond issue referred to above. Bond interest is payable annually. The bond indenture provides that semiannual payments are to be made to a sinking fund for the eventual retirement of the bonds. It is estimated that the sinking fund will earn 4 percent, compounded annually; however, interest will accrue from the date each sinking fund deposit is made. Annual maintenance and operating costs on the turnpike are expected to average $200,000.

It is desired that tolls be sufficient to fund the debt and cover all financial and operating costs. The schedule of tolls calls for automobiles to be charged $1 for each vehicle, and trucks, $3. It is expected that automobile tolls will be 20 times as numerous as truck tolls.

Required:

How many tolls are necessary each year to enable the Turnpike Commission to accomplish its financial "break-even" objective?

Problem 1–2

(i) Your client has agreed to sell a property for $60,000. He is to receive $20,000 cash at date of sale and 20 notes of equal amount which will not bear interest. The notes are due serially, one each six months starting six months from date of sale. It is agreed that the notes will include in their face an amount which will equal 5 percent interest to be compounded semiannually.

Compute to the nearest dollar the amount of each note. Show your computation in good form, with each part explained or labeled.

(ii) Smith, an employee of the Jones Company, asks your advice on the following matter:

He is eligible to participate in a company insurance and retirement plan. His payment into the company plan would amount to $500 each six months for the next 10 years, and starting with the 11th year he would receive an annual payment of $1,080 for life. He does not need insurance protection and states that he can save and invest each six months the amounts to be paid into the company plan so that he will earn 6 percent compounded semiannually. Also, he can continue to earn the same rate on his capital after retirement. He would like to have an equal amount per year of funds for 15 years after retirement.

Assuming that he can carry out his personal saving and investing plan, how much can he expect to have available *each six months* for the 15 years following his retirement? Compute to the nearest dollar and show your computations in good form. (Note: The present value of an annuity of $1 for 30 periods at 3 percent per period is 19.6004.)

(iii) (*a*) The X Company has outstanding $2,000,000 of 20-year, 5 percent bonds which were issued 10 years ago. Unamortized discount and expense of $100,000 remains on the books. The bonds are callable at 105. The company has the opportunity to refinance by issuing at par, $2,150,000 of 4 percent, 10-year bonds. Expenses which would be incurred in connection with the issue are estimated to be $50,000. Interest on both issues is payable semiannually.

Determine whether the refinancing would be desirable. Show your computations in good form and explain the basis used in reaching your conclusion. Ignore any tax difference which might arise out of the refinancing.

(*b*) Assuming the X Company refunds this bond issue, prepare journal entries for the refunding and the first interest payment using the AICPA preferred method of amortization of unamortized discount and refunding cost.

(AICPA adapted)

Problem 1–3

The Midwest Cosmetics Company is an established manufacturer and mail-order retailer of women's cosmetics. The company manufactures and markets a complete line of products under the trade name of "Sta Young." Three years ago a new management group assumed administrative responsibility of Midwest Cosmetics. One of the strategies of the new management team was the development and introduction of a face cream for women to be used as a complexion aid and skin softener. The product was developed and marketed under the name of "Sta Young Wrinkle Preventing Face Cream."

Due, in part, to an imprudent marketing policy, the company has suffered financial distress. A federal regulatory commission issued an order preventing further distribution of the new product in interstate commerce because of improper and misleading labeling; consequently, the new management currently is confronted with litigation in respect to "using the U.S. mails to defraud." Midwest Cosmetics has accordingly been adjudged bankrupt and is awaiting liquidation. Benjamin Miller and Associates, CPAs, have been asked by the Referee in Bankruptcy to counsel with him in respect to certain aspects of the liquidation. Specifically, the Referee wishes to be advised whether to attempt to sell the total cosmetic operation as a going concern or to sell the individual assets separately.

The accountants' preliminary work has enabled them to construct the following current balance sheet reflecting all accounting adjustments:

MIDWEST COSMETICS COMPANY
Balance Sheet

ASSETS

Cash...	$ 300,000
Land...	900,000
Building, less accumulated depreciation.................	400,000
Cosmetic manufacturing, packaging and shipping equipment, less accumulated depreciation...................	500,000
	$2,100,000

EQUITIES

Liability..	$ 500,000
Capital stock...	2,500,000
Deficit..	[900,000]
	$2,100,000

The liability is a term loan from Midwestern Heritage Insurance Company, secured by a first mortgage on the land and buildings, and would require immediate settlement on liquidation.

Best available estimates are that if the business is allowed to continue as an operating unit, its net receipts (net income plus depreciation) would average $110,000 per year for an indefinite period.

It is estimated that if the assets are employed by different companies in their most efficient applications, the land and building (exclusive of the equipment) will provide an average *net income* of $100,000 per year for 14 years, at which time the salvage value of the building will be approximately $50,000; at that same time, the value of the land is estimated to be $1,200,000. It is further estimated that the various units of equipment will provide *net income* of approximately $7,500 a year for eight years, at which time they will have to be scrapped.

Required:

(i) Assuming that the average rate of return on capital in the cosmetics industry is 8 percent, develop a recommendation to the Referee in Bankruptcy which incorporates the following:

(*a*) The value of the owners' equity in the enterprise, as a going concern, by capitalizing its anticipated flow of net receipts.

(*b*) The value of the owners' equity in the enterprise, as a collection of properties and debts, by assigning a value to each asset through the process of finding the present value of estimated flow of net receipts.

(c)   Assuming present sales values are equal to the present values of the assets and/or the enterprise computed in (a) and (b), make your recommendation to the Referee.

(ii)   Offer an explanation why the above divergence exists between the overall enterprise value and the sum of the values of the individual assets.

Problem 1–4

In 1971 The Hays Company entered into an agreement with a bank for an unsecured long-term loan of $2,000,000. The loan agreement provides for interest at 5 percent and lump-sum repayment in 1981. Certain terms of the loan agreement placing restrictions on incurring additional long-term debt and payment of dividends are presented in summary:

a)   Additional long-term debt shall not be incurred unless the net tangible assets (investments, plant, and equipment), adjusted to include the proceeds of such additional long-term debt, will be at least 225 percent of the total long-term debt after incurring such additional debt.

b)   Long-term debt shall mean the total of all debt outstanding for a period of one year or longer plus an amount equal to the "Capitalized Rent" on unexpired long-term leases of real property. "Capitalized Rent" shall be computed by discounting the aggregate rental obligations under the long-term lease, by years, to the date of the computation at the rate of 5 percent per annum.

c)   Payment of cash dividends during the period of the loan shall be subject to the following limitations:

(1)   Working capital of at least $6,500,000 shall be maintained.

(2)   Cash dividends shall not exceed earnings subsequent to December 31, 1970, except that the payment of cash dividends in 1971 may exceed 1971 net income by an amount which is not more than 50 percent of the net income for 1970.

(3)   In 1972 and subsequent years, cash dividends shall be limited to 25 percent of the prior year's net income.

(4)   The total annual cash dividends shall not exceed $2 per share of stock outstanding at the end of any year.

(5)   Should cash dividends be paid in excess of restrictions, such excess shall be applied in determining the amounts of dividends which may be paid in subsequent years.

The condensed balance sheet of The Hays Company at December 31, 1972, follows:

ASSETS

Current assets	$16,787,000
Investments	300,000
Plant and equipment	5,000,000
Goodwill and patents	400,000
	$22,487,000

LIABILITIES AND OWNERS' EQUITY

Current liabilities	$ 8,290,000
Note payable to bank	2,000,000
Capital stock (par value, $50)	3,131,000
Contributed capital in excess of par value	2,485,000
Retained earnings	6,581,000
	$22,487,000

An analysis of the company's retained earnings for 1970, 1971, and 1972 discloses the following:

Balance, December 31, 1969	$5,445,000
Net income for 1970	422,000
Balance, December 31, 1970	$5,867,000
Net income for 1971	507,000
Cash dividends paid in 1971	[98,000]
Balance, December 31, 1971	$6,276,000
Net income for 1972	522,000
Cash dividends paid in 1972	[124,000]
1 percent stock dividend—at market value of shares issued	[93,000]
Balance, December 31, 1972	$6,581,000

The company has a 10-year lease for a warehouse which expires December 31, 1976. The annual rental is $40,000 until December 31, 1973, and $50,000 thereafter. Under an option, the lease may be extended for another 10 years, or a portion thereof, at an annual rental of $60,000.

Required:

(i) Determine the maximum amount of cash dividends which may be paid under the loan agreement in 1973, including an indication of the application of each of the limitations contained in the loan agreement.
(ii) Determine the maximum amount of additional long-term debt which may be incurred under the loan agreement as of December 31, 1972. (Round present value factors to three places.)

(AICPA adapted)

Problem 1–5

The controller of the Broad Manufacturing Company asks for your advice and assistance regarding the problem of whether or not they should replace their A machines with new and advanced B machines. B machines are capable of doubling the present annual capacity of the A machines. At the present time the annual finished production of the A machines is 2,500,000 good units. You are to assume that the increased production can be sold at the same profitable price.

The A machines are being depreciated by the Broad Manufacturing Company under the straight-line method using a salvage value of 10 percent and a useful life of eight years. The A machines cost the Broad Manufacturing Company $175,000 plus freight and insurance of $25,000. The raw materials as they are fed into the machines are subject to heavy pressure; because of this there is a 20 percent waste factor on an annual basis. The waste materials have no value and are scrapped for nominal value. Direct labor costs are equal to 60 percent of prime costs at the present time (labor and materials are considered prime costs). The company has been purchasing its raw materials in small lots at a cost of $50 per 1,000 units. Factory overhead, exclusive of depreciation, is applied to the manufacturing process at the rate of 20 percent of direct labor costs.

If the company purchases the B machines, certain economies will be gained. Material costs will decrease 20 percent because the company will be able to buy in larger quantities. In addition, the new machines have been perfected to such an extent that the waste factor will be reduced by 50 percent. However, because the B machine is much larger than the A machine, direct labor cost will be expected to increase by 20 percent of itself. Direct labor will continue to be 60 percent of prime cost before the increase of 20 percent in direct labor cost is applied. In addition to this, it is expected that the factory overhead rate will increase by 10 percent of itself. The life of the new machines is expected to exceed the life of the A machines by one fourth, and the salvage value of the B machines will be in the same ratio as the salvage value of the A machines. The cost of the B machines, including freight and insurance of $35,000, will amount to $500,000. The company is aware of the fact that dismantling costs and installation costs will be involved; however, they do not wish to consider this factor at the present time.

Required:

(i) A statement of estimated cost comparisons on an annual basis. (Round to the nearest dollar.)
(ii) List additional factors that should be considered in deciding upon the replacement.
(iii) Comment briefly on the usefulness and validity of the comparisons made in (i).

(AICPA adapted)

Problem 1–6

The Largo Manufacturing Company makes and sells a single product, VOSTEX, through normal marketing channels. You have been asked by its president to assist in determining the proper bid to submit for a special manufacturing job for the Aztec Sales Company. Below is the information you have collected:

a) The special job is for MOFAC, a product unlike VOSTEX, even though the manufacturing processes are similar.
b) Additional sales of MOFAC to the Aztec Sales Company are not expected.
c) The bid is for 20,000 pounds of MOFAC. Each 1,000 pounds of MOFAC requires 500 pounds of material A, 250 pounds of material B, and 250 pounds of material C.
d) Largo's materials inventory data follow:

Material	Pounds in Inventory	Acquisition Cost per Pound	Current Replacement Cost per Pound
A................	24,000	$.40	$.48
B................	4,000	.25	.27
C................	17,500	.90	.97
X................	7,000	.80	.85

Material X may be substituted for material A in MOFAC. Material X, made especially for Largo under a patent owned by Largo, is left over from the manufacture of a discontinued product, is not usable in VOSTEX, and has a current salvage value of $180.

e) Each 1,000 pounds of MOFAC requires 180 direct labor hours at $3 per hour (overtime is charged at time and one half). However, Largo is working near its two-shift capacity and has only 1,600 hours of regular time available. The production manager indicates that he can keep the special job on regular time by shifting the production of VOSTEX to overtime if necessary.

f) Largo's cost clerk informs you that the hourly burden rate at normal production is as follows:

Fixed element....................	$ .20 per direct labor hour
Variable element..................	.80 per direct labor hour
Total hourly burden rate...........	$1.00 per direct labor hour

g) The bid invitation states that a performance bond must be submitted with the bid. A local agent will bond Largo's performance for 1 percent of the total bid.

Required:

(i) Compute the minimum bid (i.e., the bid that would neither increase nor decrease total profits) that Largo Manufacturing Company may submit.

(ii) Largo's president also wants to know what his now competitor, Melton Manufacturing Company, probably will bid. You assume that Melton's material inventory has been acquired very recently and that Melton's cost behavior is similar to Largo's. You know that Melton has ample productive capacity to handle the special job on regular time. Compute the minimum bid (i.e., the bid that would neither increase nor decrease total profits) that Melton Manufacturing Company might submit.

(AICPA adapted)

Problem 1–7

Niebuhr Corporation is beginning its first capital budgeting program and has retained you to assist the budget committee in the evaluation of a project to expand operations designated as Proposed Expansion Project No. 12 (PEP No. 12).

a) The following capital expenditures are under consideration:

Fire sprinkler system..............................	$ 300,000
Landscaping.......................................	100,000
Replacement of old machines.......................	600,000
Projects to expand operations (including PEP No. 12).....	800,000
	$1,800,000

b) The corporation requires no minimum return on the sprinkler system or the landscaping. However, it expects a minimum return of 6 percent on all investments to replace old machinery. It also expects investments in expansion projects to yield a return that will exceed the average cost of the capital required to finance the sprinkler system and the landscaping in addition to the expansion projects.

c) Under Proposed Expansion Project No. 12 (PEP No. 12), a cash investment of $75,000 will be made one year before operations begin. The investment will be depreciated by the sum-of-the-years'-digits method over a three-year period and is expected to have a salvage value of $15,000. Additional financial data for PEP No. 12 follow:

Time Period	Revenue	Variable Costs	Maintenance, Property Taxes, and Insurance
0–1..................	$80,000	$35,000	$ 8,000
1–2..................	95,000	41,000	11,000
2–3..................	60,000	25,000	12,000

The amount of the investment recovered during each of the three years can be reinvested immediately at a rate of return approximating 15 percent. Each year's recovery of investment, then, will have been reinvested at 15 percent for an average of six months at the end of the year.

d) The present value of $1 due at the end of each year and discounted at 15 percent is:

End of Year	Present Value
2 years before 0..............	$1.32
1 year before 0..............	1.15
0.............	1.00
1 year after 0.............	.87
2 years after 0.	.76
3 years after 0.	.66

e) The present values of $1 earned uniformly throughout the year and dis-
counted at 15 percent follow:

Year	Present Value
0–1.	$0.93
1–2.	0.80
2–3.	0.69

Required:

(i) Assume that the cutoff rate for considering expansion projects is 15 percent. Prepare a schedule calculating the—
  (a) Annual cash flows from operations for PEP No. 12.
  (b) Present value of the net cash flows for PEP No. 12.

(ii) (a) Assume that the average cost of capital computed in (b) is 9
percent. Prepare a schedule to compute the minimum return (in
dollars) required on expansion projects to cover the average cost
of capital for financing the sprinkler system and the landscaping
in addition to expansion projects. Assume that it is necessary to
replace the old machines.
  (b) Assume that the minimum return computed in (ii) (a) is $150,-
000. Calculate the cutoff rate on expansion projects.

(AICPA adapted)

Problem 1–8

You are to match each of the 10 numbered items with the *one* term listed
below (*a* through *r*) which *most specifically* identifies the cost concept indicated
parenthetically.

(*Hint:* An item of cost may be classified in several ways, depending on the
purpose of the classification. For example, the commissions on sales of a proposed new product line might be classified as direct, variable, and marginal,
among others. However, if such costs are being considered specifically as to the
amount of *cash outlay* required in making a decision concerning adoption of
the new line, the commissions are out-of-pocket costs. That would be the most
appropriate answer in the context.)

a)	By-product costs	*g*)	Historical costs	*m*)	Out-of-pocket costs
b)	Common or joint costs	*h*)	Imputed costs	*n*)	Prime costs
c)	Controllable costs	*i*)	Differential costs	*o*)	Replacement costs
d)	Direct costs	*j*)	Indirect costs	*p*)	Standard costs
e)	Estimated costs	*k*)	Opportunity costs	*q*)	Sunk costs
f)	Fixed costs	*l*)	Original costs	*r*)	Variable costs

ITEMS

1. The management of a corporation is considering replacing a machine
which is operating satisfactorily with a more efficient new model. De-

preciation on the cost of the existing machine is omitted from the data used in judging the proposal because it has little or no significance with respect to such decision. (The omitted cost.)

2. In public utility accounting, regulatory bodies require that assets be carried at the cost to those owners who *first devoted the assets to public use.* (The cost described.)

3. One of the problems encountered by a bank in attempting to establish the cost of a commercial-deposit account is the fact that many facilities and services are shared by many revenue-producing activities. (Costs of the shared facilities and services.)

4. A company declined an offer received to rent one of its warehouses and elected to use the warehouse for storage of extra raw materials to insure uninterrupted production. Storage cost has been charged with *the monthly amount of the rental offered.* (This cost is known as ?)

5. A manufacturing company excludes all "fixed" costs from its valuation of inventories, assigning to inventory only *applicable portions of costs which vary with changes in volume of product.* (The term employed for the variable costs in this context by advocates of this costing procedure.)

6. The sales department urges an increase in production of a product and as part of the data presented in support of its proposal indicates the *total additional cost involved for the volume level it proposes.* (The increase in total cost.)

7. A CPA takes exception to his client's inclusion in the cost of a fixed asset of an "interest" charge based on *the client's own funds* invested in the asset. The client states the charge was intended to obtain a cost comparable to that which would have been the case if funds had been borrowed to finance the acquisition. (The term which describes such interest charges.)

8. The "direct" production cost of a unit includes those portions of factory overhead, *labor, and materials* which are obviously traceable directly to the unit. (The term used to specify the last *two* of the named components.)

9. Calling upon the special facilities of the production, planning, personnel, and other departments, a firm estimated its future unit cost of production and used this cost (analyzed by cost elements) in its accounts. (The term used to specify this scientifically predetermined estimate.)

10. A chemical manufacturing company produces three products originating in a common initial material mix. Each product gains a separate identity part way through processing and requires additional processing after the "split." Each contributes a significant share of revenue. The company plans to spread the costs up to the "split" among the three products by the use of relative market values. (The term used to specify the costs accumulated up to the point of the split.)

(AICPA adapted)

Problem 1–9

Included in the tabular presentation which follows are selected managerial (financial) data relating to the projected operations of The Duke Company:

THE DUKE COMPANY
Selected Operating Statistics

Units Produced	Product A Raw Material (per Unit)	Product B Raw Material (per Unit)	Estimated Cost of Product Warranty (per Unit)	Depreciation	Maintenance	Supervisory Labor	Nonsupervisory Labor	Insurance	Taxes on Plant	Imputed Interest on Capital Invested
10,000–10,999.....	$20.00	$35.00	$1.00	$100,000	$ 50,000	$130,000	$300,000	$12,000	$11,000	$60,000
11,000–11,999.....	19.80	35.00	1.00	100,000	52,000	135,000	300,000	12,000	11,000	62,000
12,000–13,999.....	19.50	34.00	1.00	100,000	54,000	135,000	310,000	12,000	11,000	64,000
14,000–16,999.....	19.40	34.00	1.00	100,000	60,000	140,000	320,000	12,000	11,000	65,000
17,000–17,999.....	19.60	34.00	1.00	100,000	70,000	150,000	340,000	14,000	11,000	66,000
18,000–18,999.....	20.00	33.00	1.10	100,000	85,000	160,000	370,000	14,000	11,000	68,000
19,000–19,500.....	21.00	33.00	1.15	100,000	100,000	160,000	400,000	14,000	11,000	70,000

The Duke Company is faced with an important election in respect to production. *Either* product A *or* product B may be produced. Costs other than raw material costs are the same for both products. Each unit produced includes one unit of raw material. The raw material cost per unit is the cost of placing one unit at the starting point of the production process. The selling price of product A is $200 per unit, and the selling price of product B is $212 per unit. The level of production does not affect the selling price. If new equipment is purchased, the amounts in the Depreciation column will increase by 100 percent and the amounts in the Nonsupervisory Labor column will decrease by 50 percent. The minimum production period is one year. All data and requested information refer to the operations of the ensuing year, and it may be assumed that all production can be sold. Selling and administrative expenses are to be ignored in the analyses.

Required:

(i)   Which costs are fixed over the entire production range?
       Which costs vary moderately with the production level?
       Which costs vary most directly with the production level?

(ii)   Which costs are directly associated with product A?
       With product B? Of these costs, which costs differ depending on which product is produced?
       Which costs are not directly associated with either product?

(iii) Which costs are controllable by the authority responsible for setting the production level?
       By the authority responsible for deciding which product to produce?
       By the authority responsible for supervising production?

(iv)   Which costs are period costs?
       Which costs are product costs?
       Which costs are likely to be a mixture of both?
       Are any costs not classifiable as either period or product costs? If so, what are they?

(v)   On what basis does the schedule of depreciation amounts depend?
       Is any other basis acceptable?

(vi)   Are any "after costs" associated with either product A or product B? If so, give two possible methods for accounting for these costs.

(vii) What are the imputed costs of plant operation in this problem? Do they represent a cash outlay? An amortization of some past investment?

Are these costs included in financial reports to third parties?

(viii) Assuming that all possible alternatives are represented by the given data, compute the opportunity cost of producing product A *without* purchasing new equipment at the 10,000 and 19,500 production levels; compute the opportunity cost of producing product B *with* the use of new equipment at the 15,000 production level. Ignore all other production levels.

(ix)   If product A is being produced at the 15,000 production level now, what is the differential cost of producing product B at the same level *with* the new equipment? The net differential profit of such a change?

Problem 1–10

The Millar Company was formed on January 1, 1971, at which time common stock was issued for $100,000. In addition, $100,000 of 5 percent, five-year bonds were concurrently issued for $95,735; this price provides an effective annual yield rate of interest of 6 percent. Interest on the bonds is payable semiannually.

Two investments were made on January 1, 1971. Investment A is undeveloped real estate, and investment B is mineral-producing property. The cost of each investment was based upon expected net cash inflows for the five-year period following January 1, 1971 (10 six-month periods), discounted at appropriate interest rates; the discount rates reflect both the type of investment and the risk involved. All of the real estate acquired in investment A will be sold during years 3 through 5; investment B, which will produce income over the five-year period, will be valueless at the end of this interval. The expected net cash inflows and the *semiannual* discount rates are given below:

	Investment A	Investment B
Discount rate......................	6%	5%
Period 1.........................	$–0–	$10,000
2.........................	–0–	10,000
3.........................	–0–	10,000
4.........................	–0–	10,000
5.........................	10,000	10,000
6.........................	10,000	10,000
7.........................	10,000	10,000
8.........................	10,000	10,000
9.........................	10,000	10,000
10.........................	10,000	10,000

Assume that expected net cash inflows become available as of the end of each six-month period. As of January 1, 1971, the present value of the expected net cash inflows from investment A is $38,950 and the present value of the expected net cash inflows from investment B is $77,217. Thus, the balance sheet of the Millar Company as of January 1, 1971, is as follows:

MILLAR COMPANY

Balance Sheet

As of January 1, 1971

ASSETS

Cash..	$ 79,568
Investment A...	38,950
Investment B...	77,217
Total Assets..	$195,735

LIABILITIES AND CAPITAL

Bonds payable.............................	$100,000	
Less: Unamortized discount..............	4,265	$ 95,735
Capital stock..............................		100,000
Total Liabilities and capital............		$195,735

On December 31, 1971, the Millar Company again estimated future expected net cash inflows for each investment. It was also decided at this time that a semiannual discount rate of 8 percent was now appropriate for investment A because of new business developments. The revised expected net cash inflows and discount rates are as follows:

	Investment A	Investment B
Discount rate........................	8%	5%
Period 1*.........................	$–0–	$12,000
2*.........................	–0–	12,000
3..........................	–0–	12,000
4..........................	–0–	12,000
5..........................	10,000	12,000
6..........................	10,000	12,000
7..........................	10,000	12,000
8..........................	10,000	12,000
9..........................	10,000	12,000
10.........................	10,000	12,000

* Data for these periods are not estimates but are actual net cash inflows during 1971.

The market rate of interest for long-term debt is 5 percent as of December 31, 1971.

Ignore income taxes in all calculations.

Required:

(i) Determine net income for 1971 and construct a balance sheet as of December 31, 1971, using conventional accounting procedures. Assume that current assets consist only of cash, that the discount on bonds is amortized on a compound interest basis, and that depletion is calculated on a straight-line basis.

(ii) Construct a balance sheet as of December 31, 1971, with assets and liabilities valued at the present value of all future net cash inflows and outflows, respectively, under each of the following independent assumptions:

    (*a*)   Assume that the revised interest rates and estimates are used for valuation purposes as of December 31, 1971.

    (*b*)   Assume that the discount and bond interest rates and the estimates of *future* net cash inflows and outflows remain unchanged, i.e., current excesses of actual cash inflows over expectations are considered random fluctuations identifiable with the current period.

    Hint: Read requirement (iii) (*d*) before constructing the statements; strive to integrate the *realization concept* into your classification of value increments (decrements) for the period.

(iii)   In a concise manner, answer each of the following questions:

    (*a*)   Would any entry normally be made under conventional accounting procedures to record any change in the value of investment A as of December 31, 1971? The net change in the present value of future net cash inflows for investment A as of December 31, 1971, consists of what two elements under assumption (ii) (*a*)?

    (*b*)   Would any entry be made under conventional accounting procedures to record any change in the value of investment B as of December 31, 1971? The net change in the present value of future net cash inflows for investment B as of December 31, 1971, consists of what two elements under assumption (ii) (*a*)?

    (*c*)   If an entry were made [assumption (ii) (*a*)] to record the change in the value of the bonds (other than normal amortization), what rationale supports this entry? If the market rate were 7 percent instead of 5 percent, what would be your answer? Should these changes be reported as interest expense, if they are included at all? What would be the effect on net income if the entries to record the change in value were made?

    (*d*)   If present values are used for accounting valuation purposes, may the difference between net worth as of January 1, 1971, and net worth as computed for (ii) (*a*) be considered as net income for 1971? If not, how would you describe this value difference? What about the difference between net worth as of January 1, 1971, and net worth as computed for (ii) (*b*)? If "capital" accounts other than retained earnings are used, when are the balances of these accounts "absorbed" into net income, if at any time?

    (*e*)   What may be concluded from a comparison of accumulated retained earnings as computed for (ii) (*a*) and (ii) (*b*)?

    (*f*)   What explanation may be offered for the difference between retained earnings as computed for (i) and retained earnings as computed for (ii) (*b*)?

UNIT II

ACCOUNTING FOR PARTNERSHIPS

Chapter 2

Formation and Operation of Partnerships

The partnership is a form of business affiliation involving two or more individuals associated in a joint profit-making endeavor. A number of problems peculiar to this type of organization structure have generated unique accounting procedures for reporting on partnership operations and for disclosing the economic and legal equities of various interested parties in partnership assets. These accounting techniques will be the focus of attention in the following three chapters.

NATURE OF A PARTNERSHIP

Although the common law originally provided the legal framework within which partnership operations were generally conducted, most states have now adopted the Uniform Partnership Act, or some variant thereof, as the controlling statutory authority. Emphasis will hereafter be directed toward relevant provisions of this Act.

Aggregative versus Entity Concept

Section 6 of the Uniform Partnership Act defines a partnership as "an association of two or more persons to carry on as co-owners a business for profit."[1] This definition suggests an aggregative, or proprietary, concept of the partnership as the underlying legal philosophy; a partnership is perceived as being nothing more than an aggregation of the rights and responsibilities of the individual partners. Such a notion was fundamental to the structure of the common law and has been extended in the Uniform Partnership Act in the provision that the individual partners are jointly liable for all debts and obligations of the partnership (Section 15). Yet, the dominant theme of the Act nonetheless appears to rest upon a concept of the partnership as a legal entity, separate and distinct from the individual partners. This point of view is implicit in numerous provisions, among which are the following:

---

[1] Section 2 defines the terms person and business as they are used in the definition of a partnership; Section 6 provides criteria for the legal determination of the *existence* of a partnership.

1. In the event of liquidation, partnership creditors have priority in respect to the assets of the partnership and creditors of the individual partners are given priority in respect to the partners' personal assets (Section 40).
2. Title to partnership assets may be vested in the name of the partnership (Section 8).
3. A clear distinction is drawn between the partners' rights to partnership assets and their interests in the partnership (Sections 25 and 26).
4. A continuity of partnership organization may exist under circumstances which formerly, under the common law, would have caused a dissolution of the partnership (see, for example, Section 23, continuation of the partnership beyond a fixed term, and Section 27, assignment of a partner's interest in the partnership).

Notwithstanding this evolving legal conception of the partnership organization, many current accounting practices continue to emphasize the aggregative aspects of the partnership. Although this circumstance is no doubt due in large measure to an inheritance of the proprietary emphasis from both accounting and law, it does derive additional support from current provisions of the Internal Revenue Code. The following two examples illustrate the basic proprietary emphasis of the Code:

1. The tax basis of assets contributed by individual partners to the partnership transfers to the partnership, regardless of market values existing at the time of the contribution.
2. The income tax is levied on the individual partners' shares of periodic net income of the partnership and is reported in their separate returns; it is not assessed on the net income of the partnership.

The existence of such tax legislation partially explains the continuing infusion of the aggregative notion in partnership accounting; it does not, however, provide strong theoretical justification for the practice.

Specific manifestations of the aggregative and entity concepts of the partnership will be referred to subsequently in this chapter.

Partnership Agreement

Before a particular form of organizational structure is selected for a business activity, the various parties at interest should carefully analyze the advantages and disadvantages of alternative types of organizations—the corporation, general partnership, limited partnership, etc. If a general partnership is regarded as the suitable choice, an important first step in the organization sequence is to formulate basic provisions within which the partners elect to operate—from initial formation, through operating routines and realignment of ownership interests, to eventual dissolution of the partnership. Appropriate attention to the details of these provisions at the time the partnership is initially formed will minimize or eliminate the subsequent emergence of possible inequities and legal uncertainties regarding the relationships between partners and their relations with outside parties. The partnership agreement may be either a written or an oral contract. A formal, written agreement between the partners, often called the articles of partnership, or copartnership, is perhaps the most effective method of delineating the desired relationships in respect to individual partners' rights and responsibilities. The importance of this agreement should be emphasized. Although the Uniform Partnership Act imposes certain obligations upon the partnership which may not be avoided or overcome, such as joint liability for all partnership debts, most of the provisions of this act control *only* in the absence of an express agreement to the contrary between the partners. Indeed, judicial remedy is often based upon the court's interpretation of what the partners *intended,* when in fact the partners may not have anticipated a particular problem currently in dispute. Consequently, partners would be wise to seek the counsel of both an accountant and an attorney in formulating a comprehensive, *written* agreement indicating their intentions in various areas of partners' responsibilities and interests which if omitted or ambiguously conceived may subsequently generate dispute and possibly litigation.

Important provisions in the articles of partnership, including the purpose of the partnership, management rights and authority, and causes of dissolution, should reflect clearly the partners' intentions in terms of prevailing legal doctrine. Yet, there are a number of legally unregulated areas of mutual interest to the several partners which have important accounting (and equity) implications concerning which the accountant may offer valuable counsel. Among these interest areas are the following:

1. The assets which the partners initially are to contribute to the partnership and the monetary value to be ascribed thereto should be itemized.
2. A clear distinction should be drawn between the individual partners' initial interests in partnership capital and their interests in subsequent profits or losses. If the initial interest in capital is not consistent with a summation of the agreed-upon values for the contributed assets, the articles should be specific in regard to the treatment of this difference. For example, if the partners insist upon an equal dollar interest in capital, even though the valuations of their contributed assets are not equal, two possible accounting solutions are possible: (*a*) either a bonus, or capital transfer, may be effected between the partners in order to equalize their capital credits; or (*b*) intangible assets, which may derive from unusual managerial ability or widespread customer appeal and which apparently are implicit in such an agreement, may be recognized in the accounts. Although the judgment of the partners should not be the principal criterion for recognizing intangible assets in the partnership books, an explicit indication in the partnership agreement of the purported existence of such intangibles does provide an initial argument for account recognition.

3. The basis for dividing partnership profits should be expressly stated. In the absence of a contrary agreement, Section 18 of the Uniform Partnership Act provides that the partners shall share equally in profits. If it is desired that individual partners be rewarded for their separate capital contributions and/or services to the partnership before a distribution of the residual profits in the profit-sharing ratios, the basis or monetary value for this distribution should be specified.

4. If contributed capital is to be a basis for distributing partnership profits, the agreement should normally be responsive to the following questions:

    a) Is the distribution to be based on initial capital contributions or capital as adjusted by subsequent contributions, profits, and/or withdrawals?

    b) If the distribution is computed upon adjusted capital, is it to be based upon beginning, average, or ending capital balances for the year?

    c) In the event average or ending capital balances are used, what treatment should be accorded current withdrawals? In particular, if it is desired to distinguish between capital withdrawals and withdrawals in anticipation of the current period's profits, the basis for the distinction should be expressly stated. Moreover, where the distinction is made, the accounting treatment of amounts available for withdrawal but permitted to remain in the business must be established.

5. Section 18 of the Act further provides that losses are to be shared in the profit-sharing ratio. Thus, if it is desired to protect a partner, whose principal contribution is service, from incurring a disproportionate share of possible losses, special loss-sharing ratios should be indicated.

6. The bases for calculating the monetary equity of a withdrawing partner, either through retirement or death, should be outlined. A withdrawal may involve consideration of such factors as the possible revaluation of tangible assets and the recognition of implicit intangible asset values.

7. If net income and the partners' drawing accounts are to be closed to the capital accounts at the end of the accounting period, thereby increasing or decreasing the total contributed capital, this closing sequence should be indicated. Such a provision may be important in the event the partnership is dissolved and assets are distributed to the retiring partners.

Although this list of significant provisions is necessarily incomplete, it does indicate the *type* of accounting considerations which are important in a careful formulation of the partnership agreement.

PARTNERSHIP FORMATION

Recording the Initial Contributions

The initial formation of a partnership presents relatively few difficult accounting problems. In the event that there exists a predecessor business, an election must be made as to whether its records are to be preserved; if not, new books must be opened. In the former case, only those entries necessary to record the contributions of partners not previously affiliated with the predecessor are required; in the latter case, all contributions must be entered in the new records. Based upon the provisions of the articles of partnership, the opening journal entries for the new partnership record the several assets contributed and the liabilities assumed. Necessarily, the partners' respective dollar interests in the initial capital of the organization are appropriately entered as credits to their individual capital accounts. The following two cases illustrate typical accounting entries to open the books of a new partnership.

Case 1. The partnership agreement of X and Y lists the following assets which are to constitute the resources of the new XY Partnership:

	Contributed by—	
	X	Y
Cash...........................	$10,000	$20,000
Merchandise.....................		10,000
Building........................		30,000
Furniture and equipment.........	5,000	

The building is subject to a mortgage loan of $25,000, which is to be assumed by the partnership.

The journal entry to open the books of the partnership is as follows:

Cash..	30,000	
Inventory...	10,000	
Building..	30,000	
Furniture and equipment..............................	5,000	
Mortgage payable.....................................		25,000
X, capital...		15,000
Y, capital...		35,000

In this case, the partners' capital credits are based upon the net assets contributed by each partner.

Case 2. Assume that in the previous illustration, the partnership agreement provided that the partners initially should have an equal interest in partnership capital (or partnership net assets).

Two accounting solutions are possible. If it is the intent of the partners that the capital accounts be equalized by means of a bonus—transferring capital equity from Y to X—the assets and liabilities would be recorded as before; however, each partner would receive a capital credit of $25,000 (one half of $50,000 net assets). Under these circumstances, Y essentially pays a bonus of $10,000 to X, in the form of an increased monetary equity in the firm, as an inducement to enter the partnership venture.

A second solution is predicated on the assumption that X contributes to the partnership an additional asset, intangible in character but having value to the partnership. Based upon the requirement of equalizing capital balances, it can be inferred that this asset has a value of approximately $20,000. The entry under these conditions is:

Cash.	30,000	
Inventory.	10,000	
Building.	30,000	
Furniture and equipment.	5,000	
Goodwill (or some other intangible asset).	20,000	
Mortgage payable.		25,000
X, capital.		35,000
Y, capital.		35,000

The net assets of the business with this assumption are $70,000, of which $50,000 are represented by net tangible assets.

If the partners' future interests in partnership profits and losses are also to be equal, the choice of either solution method will produce no inequity in the relative monetary interest of the two partners, as they will share equally in the subsequent gain or loss, of whatever amount, on the realization of the intangible asset. However, recording the goodwill in the partnership books will have a significant effect on the balance sheet of the partnership; accordingly, the measurement of goodwill must be carefully determined, as the reported valuation of this intangible asset will make an impression upon the reader of the partnership balance sheet.

The above examples refer to the source of new partnership assets in terms of the contributing partners. On occasions one or more of the new partners may contribute the assets and liabilities of an existing business to the new partnership. In such a circumstance, it is important that the assets be appraised at the time the new partnership is formed; existing book values of the contributed assets may be grossly inadequate as a measure of the relative capital investments of the partners in the new venture.

Income Tax Considerations

Although the problems in income tax accounting are not a principal concern of this text, certain *fundamental* income tax concepts related to partnerships are briefly considered within the context of partnership accounting. Basically the Internal Revenue Code adopts the aggregative theory and treats the partnership as a conduit through which net income of the firm is allocated to the partners *as if* they had individually earned it. With this partnership conception, two value bases are particularly relevant to initial formation of the firm:

1. The tax "basis" of the *assets* contributed to the partnership.
2. The tax "basis" of the partners' dollar *interest* in the partnership.

No taxable gain or loss is assumed to result from the contribution of property to a partnership by an individual partner. Rather, the partnership adopts the same *asset* basis, or unamortized cost, for income tax purposes as applied to the individual partner in respect to the calculation of his personal tax liability. It is unlikely that this value will be equivalent to the fair market value of the asset at the date of contribution. Although the market valuation of contributed assets is an important determinant in computing the dollar interest of the partners in the capital of the new firm, the tax-basis valuation will necessarily modify the relative interests of the partners for income tax purposes.

The tax "basis" of a partner's *interest* in the firm is defined as *the sum of the bases of the individual assets he contributes to the firm, increased by any liabilities of other partners which he assumes, and decreased by his personal liabilities, if any, which are assumed by other partners*. Thus, the accounting equation for the tax bases of the partners' interests in the firm takes the following form: the sum of the bases of the contributed assets is equal to the sum of the bases of the partners' separate interests in the partnership. It should be noted that partnership liabilities are excluded from this basic equation, as they are implicitly included in the bases of the partners' separate interests.

The following case illustrates these provisions:

Case 3. Using the data of Case 1 and assuming that the basis of the building to Y is $20,000, that other assets have a tax basis equal to their present market values, and that X agrees to accept joint liability for the mortgage on the building, the income tax implications of the initial formation may be reflected in the following journal entry form:[2]

Cash..	30,000	
Merchandise................................	10,000	
Building....................................	20,000	
Furniture and equipment....................	5,000	
Basis of X's interest..................		27,500
Basis of Y's interest..................		37,500

Significantly, this entry is *not* made in the partnership books; it is simply a convenient way of expressing the tax bases of the contributed assets and the partners' tax basis interests in the partnership. The journalizing form of expression may be utilized in supporting tax records or working papers.

---

[2] This method of analyzing the tax bases of partners' interests is described more completely in Richard H. Homburger, "Tax Basis of Partner's Interest Explained by Double Entry," *The Accounting Review*, January, 1960, pp. 132–34.

In the above entry, it is evident that the basis equation is satisfied, as the sum of the asset bases, $65,000, equals the sum of the bases of the partners' interests. The computation of the interests of X and Y is made as follows:

	X	Y
Bases of assets contributed:		
Cash...................................	$10,000	$20,000
Inventory.............................		10,000
Building..............................		20,000
Furniture and equipment..................	5,000	
	$15,000	$50,000
Add: Liabilities assumed by X (½ of $25,000 mortgage)................................	12,500	
Deduct: Personal liability transferred to X......		[12,500]
	$27,500	$37,500

The implications of the partnership formation entry *on a tax basis* are to reduce, for tax purposes, the depreciable cost of partnership assets by $10,000 and to alter the relative monetary interests of the individual partners. The ultimate effect of these changes will be reflected in the periodic determination of taxable net income for the partnership to be allocated to the individual partners and in the computation of taxable gain or loss in the event one or both partners elect to dispose of their interests in the firm. This problem will be considered again following the discussion of partnership operations.

PARTNERSHIP OPERATIONS

Accounting for the operations of a partnership is not essentially unlike accounting for other profit-oriented businesses. The objective of the accounting process continues to focus on the determination of periodic net income. To this end, a partnership is perceived as a separate and distinct accounting entity. Net income is calculated in the traditional manner, i.e., by relating periodic revenues and expenses, with only the accounting treatment of salary payments to the partners and interest on capital investments subject to theoretical dispute.

The special problems of accounting for partnership operations are classified for discussion purposes as follows:

1. Establishing the nature and determining the amount of the relative interests of the partners in the firm.

2. Determining the proper distribution of partnership net income between the partners.

3. Examining special problems in the allocation of *taxable* net income to the partners.
4. Preparing financial statements for the partnership: the balance sheet, income statement, and statement of partners' net worth.

Nature and Amount of Relative Interests

The partners' interests in, and obligations to, the partnership may be dichotomized initially into (1) debtor-creditor relationships and (2) capital equities and/or deficiencies. In many cases, these divisions are essentially arbitrary in nature, but in light of generally accepted accounting practices, they may materially influence the financial statements of the partnership.

Debtor-Creditor Relationships. If in addition to contributions to the capital of the firm, a partner advances money to the partnership in the form of a loan, with provision that it be repaid within a specified period of time, appropriate recognition of the separateness of the accounting entity and the nature of the transaction requires that such an advance be recorded as a partnership liability. Similarly, advances to individual partners, which are to be repaid subsequently to the partnership, are properly classified as partnership receivables. Interest expense and/or income generated by these explicitly conceived contractual obligations are normally considered in the periodic computation of partnership net income. This treatment is consistent with the classification of the originating transaction as a business loan and with the acceptance of the separate entity status of the partnership.

Capital Equities and/or Deficiencies. The total capital equity of the partnership is, of course, the amount of partnership assets which are in excess of partnership liabilities. It is necessary, however, that the amount of each partner's capital credit in the firm be independently calculated and recorded. Normally, two accounts are maintained for each partner: (1) a drawing, or personal, account; and (2) a capital account. The drawing account is debited with the partner's withdrawals of cash or other assets during the period in anticipation of his interest in partnership net income, and is credited subsequently with his equity in the final distribution of partnership net income. The capital account, as previously mentioned, initially reflects the dollar investment of each partner at the date of formation of the partnership. Subsequently, additional investments or withdrawals which are believed to be relatively permanent in character are entered in the account; if the partners should so elect, the balance of the drawing account may be periodically transferred to the capital account. In the event of such a transfer, accumulated profits in excess of current withdrawals are effectively capitalized. As will be discussed later, it is possible that a more informative statement of financial position may result from segregating capital transactions from those which summarize profits; where the transactions are thus separated, the closing of the drawing accounts to capital accounts may prove undesirable.

Conventionally, interest credits on capital equities are not accounted for as partnership expenses, chargeable against partnership revenues in determining net income. Interest credits on partners' loans, however, are deducted as a determinant of partnership net income. Thus, the objectivity of net income determination is at least partially compromised if the partners, at their discretion, can control whether additional equity shall be provided by partners' loans or accumulated profits. However, in this connection, a subtlety often overlooked relates to the implicit interest on "excessive" capital contributions. In the absence of a contrary agreement, Section 18 (c) of the Act provides that a partner, who in aid of the partnership makes any payment or advance beyond the amount of capital which he agreed to contribute, shall be paid interest from the date of the payment or advance. An extension of this argument implies that from a legal point of view, profit accumulations of the partnership *may* be the basis of interest payments to individual partners. In point of fact, little substantive difference exists between accumulated profits and loans to the partnership. It would appear that the accounting problem is eliminated only where there is a complete acceptance of the proprietary theory, wherein no expense or income may be generated in transactions with the owners, *or* by a complete acceptance of the entity theory, wherein the expense of total capital (creditors' and owners') is recognized.

Determining Distributive Shares of Net Income

Some of the fundamental problems underlying the distribution of partnership net income were discussed earlier in terms of eliminating unnecessary ambiguity from the partnership agreement. The three most commonly used bases for allocating partnership net income are:

1. Specified ratios.
2. Relative capital investments of the partners.
3. Service contributions of the partners.

Frequently, some combination of these several bases is used to reward the partners, appropriate weight being given each factor contributed by an individual partner in respect to partnership profitability.

Specified Ratios. As noted before, the Uniform Partnership Act provides that in the absence of an explicit contrary agreement, profits are to be allocated equally (equal ratios) among the partners. If the partners prefer some other uniform basis of distribution, negotiated ratios may be specified in the partnership agreement.

Case 4. Assume that X and Y agree to divide profits from their partnership operations in a ratio of 3:1, that is, 75 percent to X and 25 percent to Y. If net income for the year is $60,000, the following journal entry indicates the allocation of profits:

Income summary	60,000	
X, drawing ($\frac{3}{4} \times$ $60,000)		45,000
Y, drawing ($\frac{1}{4} \times$ $60,000)		15,000

In the absence of this specific profit-sharing agreement, each partner would have received $30,000. In both cases, the allocation of profits is uniform; each partner receives a predetermined percentage of profits, without regard to the magnitude of such profits.

Relative Capital Investments.   Because capital is an income-producing factor, it may be important to consider the partners' respective capital investments in allocating partnership net income. If partners are to be rewarded, in part at least, in proportion to the relative magnitudes of their investments of capital, it is imperative that there be an unequivocal statement in the partnership agreement concerning the computation of these capital balances. As indicated earlier, if average or ending capital balances are to be used, the treatment of withdrawals, or amounts available for withdrawal, may pose a problem.

The following data will be used in Cases 5 and 6 to illustrate alternative approaches to the allocation of net income when it is based upon the partners' relative capital investments.

X, Capital

2/1	10,000	1/1 Balance	50,000
		4/1	10,000
		8/1	20,000
		11/1	20,000

X, Drawing

1/1–12/1 ($1,000/month, per agreement)	12,000

Y, Capital

4/1	5,000	1/1 Balance	25,000
7/1	10,000	9/1	15,000

Y, Drawing

1/1–12/1 ($1,000/month, per agreement)	12,000

Income Summary

12/31	50,000

It is assumed that withdrawals *in excess of* the $1,000 monthly allowance (withdrawals in anticipation of profits) are to be accounted for as permanent reductions in capital; accordingly, they are entered as debits to the partners' capital accounts.

Case 5.   Interest on Beginning Capital Balances.   In this example, it is assumed that each partner is to receive a 6 percent return (interest) on his capital investment, calculated in terms of the capital balances at the beginning of the year, with the remaining profit (or loss) to be distributed in a ratio of 4:6 to X and Y respectively. Computation of the allocated partnership net income is as follows:

	X	Y	Total
Interest:			
6% × $50,000	$ 3,000		$ 3,000
6% × $25,000		$ 1,500	1,500
Remainder (in residual profit-sharing ratio):			
4/10 × $45,500	18,200		18,200
6/10 × $45,500		27,300	27,300
	$21,200	$28,800	$50,000

Case 6. Interest on Average Capital Balances.   In this example, each partner is assumed to receive a 6 percent return (interest) on his *average* capital investment, utilizing the basis previously described for determining capital withdrawals. Since each partner withdrew the total amount allowable each month, no problem arises concerning amounts available for withdrawal but not actually withdrawn. After interest allowances, the residual profit element is again to be allocated in the ratio 4:6.

The first step in determining profit allocations is to calculate the average capital balance for each partner. This may be accomplished by weighting each new capital balance by the number of months (or other appropriate time interval) that the balance remains unchanged; by adding each of these products and dividing by the sum of weights, an average balance is determined. Calculation for the data in this example is made as follows:

	Capital Balance	Weighting Factor— Number of Months	Weighted Product
X's capital balance:			
January 1–February 1	$50,000	1	$ 50,000
February 1–April 1	40,000	2	80,000
April 1–August 1	50,000	4	200,000
August 1–November 1	70,000	3	210,000
November 1–December 31	90,000	2	180,000
		12	$720,000
Average capital balance ($720,000 ÷ 12)			$ 60,000
Y's capital balance:			
January 1–April 1	$25,000	3	$ 75,000
April 1–July 1	20,000	3	60,000
July 1–September 1	10,000	2	20,000
September 1–December 31	25,000	4	100,000
		12	$255,000
Average capital balance ($255,000 ÷ 12)			$ 21,250

Following the calculation of average capital balances, the several profit elements are allocated as follows:

	X	Y	Total
Interest:			
6% × $60,000.....................	$ 3,600		$ 3,600
6% × $21,250.....................		$ 1,275	1,275
Remainder (in residual profit-sharing ratio):			
4/10 × $45,125....................	18,050		18,050
6/10 × $45,125....................		27,075	27,075
	$21,650	$28,350	$50,000

The ending capital balances of the partners may be used also as a basis for interest allowances in net profit distribution. Or, alternatively, the total net profit for the accounting period may be allocated on the basis of relative capital investments. However, it is perhaps more usual for partnership agreements to specify that only a *reasonable* return should accrue from the investment of capital and that additional excess earnings of the partnership should be divided in some specified ratio to compensate the partners for the disproportionate risks they assume in the operation of the business. Furthermore, in determining the base to be used in computing the return on investments, the beginning or average capital balances are frequently preferred—the beginning balance because of the simplicity of interest calculation, or the average capital balance because it provides a more refined measurement of the actual capital available to the firm *during* the accounting period.

Services Rendered. In order to reward the individual partners for their different service contributions to the operation of the partnership, salary allowances are often provided as an additional basis for distributing partnership net income. This basis, as in the case of interest allowances on capital investments, is frequently used in combination with negotiated ratios or other allocation bases. Where the partners contribute a disproportionate amount of time and talent to partnership activities, inclusion of a provision for salaries in the allocation basis may contribute to a more equitable distribution of the net income of the business.

Case 7. Using the data of Case 6, with the additional provision that salaries of $6,000 and $12,000 are to be awarded to X and Y respectively. the net profit is distributed as follows:

	X	Y	Total
Salary allowances.......................	$ 6,000	$12,000	$18,000
Interest credits.......................	3,600	1,275	4,875
Remainder:			
4/10 × $27,125...................	10,850		10,850
6/10 × $27,125...................		16,275	16,275
	$20,450	$29,550	$50,000

If the proprietary theory is literally accepted, salary allowances should be considered a *distribution* of net income rather than a *determinant* of net income. Although this position has no effect upon the ultimate capital accumulations of the various partners, it results in an amount of partnership net income which is in excess of that calculated for a corporate enterprise wherein officer-shareholders have a status comparable to that of partners in a partnership. For this reason, the argument is frequently made that if it is desirable to make net income comparisons with other similar types of businesses, some of which may be incorporated, *or* if the partners are examining the feasibility of incorporating, partners' salaries should be accounted for as an expense. Notwithstanding the value of these comparisons, this position would seem to avoid a basic issue. If the salary of an officer-stockholder of a closely held corporation is treated as an expense when it meets the test of reasonableness, why is not the salary of a partner similarly a factor in net income determination if it satisfies the same criterion? If the entity theory is adopted in accounting for one type of transaction between the partners and the firm (debtor-creditor relationships), why is it denied in other types of business transactions which appear to be equally valid? While little theoretical support can be marshalled for this traditional accounting distinction between salaries of officers of corporations (expenses) and salaries of partners (distribution of income), it currently remains dominant in accounting practice.

Order of Distribution.   If the net income is insufficient to cover the prescribed distributions for salaries and/or interest on capital balances, two alternatives are available. First, the partners may elect that the distribution for salaries and interest on investment be made and that the earnings deficiency produced by these allocations be allocated in the residual profit- and loss-sharing ratio, or loss-sharing ratio if separate ratios exist. Second, a sequence of distributions may be specified, with the provision that available net income is to be distributed to the fullest extent possible. This necessarily requires that the relative ratio of the partners' earned salaries or interest on investment be used to distribute that amount of net income remaining after prior distributions, if any, which is insufficient to make a total distribution for a profit-sharing factor. Consider the following data:

	X	Y	Total
Earned salaries.	$10,000	$5,000	$15,000
Earned interest.	4,000	6,000	10,000

If X and Y agreed that available earnings are to be distributed first for salaries, then for interest on capital investment, and finally in the residual profit-sharing ratio, this second method yields the following types of distributions of earnings when there are insufficient profits to make total distributions for both salaries and interest:

	X	Y	Total
Case I. (Net income, $9,000):			
Salaries:			
X (10/15 × $9,000).	$ 6,000		$ 6,000
Y (5/15 × $9,000).		$3,000	3,000
	$ 6,000	$3,000	$ 9,000
Case II. (Net income, $20,000):			
Salaries.	$10,000	$5,000	$15,000
Interest:			
X (4/10 × $5,000).	2,000		2,000
Y (6/10 × $5,000).		3,000	3,000
	$12,000	$8,000	$20,000

The net income would be distributed differently if the first method were employed, i.e., salaries and interest would be first allocated, after which the resulting deficiency would be distributed.

This situation reflects yet another instance requiring adequate forward planning in the formulation of the partnership agreement. In the absence of such an agreement, or where the agreement is silent as to the order of earnings distribution, the first method discussed is generally followed. Apropos of this selection, it should be observed that this method implicitly treats the salaries and interest on capital investments as a partnership expense, and thus makes but one actual distribution of net income, viz., partnership net income after partners' salaries and interest on their investments. If the entity theory is otherwise adopted, this method further confirms the commitment to the entity concept.

Correction of Prior Years' Net Income. Whereas the correction of prior years' net income has important reporting implications for virtually all forms of business organization, there exists in respect to the partnership an additional problem of allocating adjustments and corrections of net income among the partners. If the identity of the partners is the same as in the year to which the adjustments or corrections relate and the profit- and loss-sharing ratios remain unchanged, with no special constraints on allocations of salaries and/or interest, no special complication is met in respect to the earnings correction of prior years.

If these rather restrictive conditions are not fully satisfied, however, the accountant must examine more carefully a proposed correction or adjustment of prior years' net income. In general, three alternatives exist:

1. The amount of the adjustment is minor, and it may be absorbed in the current period's net income without material effect on the partners' capital balances (subject to their approval).
2. The adjustment is material in amount but is not easily identified with a specific period or periods. An example of such an adjustment is one involving the correction of the allowance for uncollectible accounts. In this case, the gain or loss resulting from over- or under-allowances in prior periods may be absorbed in the current period, or an arbitrary allocation to prior periods may be made, depending upon the decision of the partners.
3. The adjustment is material in amount and is identifiable with specific accounting periods. This condition may obtain where clerical or bookkeeping errors are discovered, or where adjustments are necessary to reflect a revision of the estimated service life of depreciable assets. In this type of circumstance, equity would seem to call for a recomputation of the allocations of adjusted net incomes for the affected periods.

Of course, corrections of prior periods' net incomes may not be the only, nor the most significant, adjustments which affect an equitable distribution of partnership net income. The existence of material, extraordinary or nonrecurring gains or losses raises the question as to the specific period or periods to which they properly relate. Where this problem exists, the traditional realization criterion should be applied until further refinements in accounting methodology permit a more accurate determination of periodic net income.

Special Tax Problems

As a general rule, the tax basis of a partner's interest in the partnership is increased by his share of recognized partnership net income and decreased by his share of recognized net losses. Section 704 of the Internal Revenue Code provides that for income tax purposes, partnership net income may be allocated in any consistent manner specified in the partnership agreement, *except* that the allocation shall not be made for the manifest purpose of avoiding the tax burden. Specifically, there is evidence that the framers of the Code intended to prohibit such distributions as allocating all capital losses to partners without personal capital gains, and ordinary losses or expenses to those partners with capital gains, in order to avoid the relevant offset provisions. With this general exception, the provisions of the Code seem sufficiently broad to permit a unique allocation agreement for *each item* of partnership revenue and expense. In most cases, however, more general distribution agreements prevail, and the same distribution agreement is usually applicable for both financial accounting and income tax purposes.

One problem that may warrant special treatment in the allocation agreement has been previously mentioned. When the property contributed by a partner has a tax basis that is less than its market value at the date it is contributed to the partnership, the depreciation deduction for tax purposes is necessarily reduced.[3] Usually, this depreciation deduction is allocated in the same manner as are other partnership expenses. As a result of this allocation, the *other* (noncontributing) partners must report larger taxable net incomes than they would have reported if the property's tax basis had been equal to its market value. Also, if the property is subsequently sold with a taxable gain recognized, an additional tax burden is assumed by these noncontributing partners.[4] Although the inequity of this allocation can be very significant, the long-run inequity is ultimately reduced; since the larger relative taxable net incomes of the noncontributing partners increase the tax bases of their interests in the partnership, these partners' taxable gains at the time their partnership interests are sold or liquidated will be accordingly reduced.

A second solution, more equitable in the short run to the noncontributing partners, calls for the assignment of the difference between the fair market value and the tax basis of the property as a potential gain to the contributing partner, to be realized at the time the property is sold.[5] The periodic depreciation deductions for the noncontributing partners are then determined on the basis of their ratable interests in the fair market value of the assets, subject to the constraint that the sum of these deductions cannot exceed the allowable depreciation computed on the tax basis of the property. In effect, a portion of the contributing partner's deduction for depreciation is allocated to the noncontributing partners. If the constraint is operative, due to a material difference between the fair market value and the tax basis of depreciable property, it is possible that the contributing partner will be unable to claim any amount of depreciation for income tax purposes, as the total allowable depreciation deduction is allocated between the noncontributing partners.

---

[3] Under certain circumstances, Section 707 of the Code does permit the partners to sell rather than contribute assets to the partnership, with gain or loss recognized by the selling partner and a current market value established as the tax basis for the partnership. Notwithstanding this unique entity aspect of the Code, it is here assumed that the partners elect to contribute assets to the partnership.

[4] If the property is subject to the recapture provisions in Sections 1245 and/or 1250, the rate differential is eliminated in large measure, and the timing problem is the only one that remains. Hereafter, it will be assumed that the recapture provisions are not operative.

[5] The potential gain is reduced proratably over the life of the asset, and any actual recognized gain in excess of this adjusted amount is then allocated between all of the partners in the profit-sharing ratio.

Case 8. Assume X, Y, and Z are partners sharing profits and losses equally. X and Y each contributed cash of $30,000 to the partnership, and Z contributed depreciable property having a fair market value of $30,000, with a tax basis of $12,000. The estimated life of the asset is 10 years; salvage value is estimated to be negligible.

Method 1. Following the general method of allocating taxable deductions in the same manner as net income is distributed for financial accounting purposes, each partner will report a periodic deduction of $400 ($\frac{1}{3} \times \frac{1}{10} \times$ $12,000) for depreciation, and the tax basis of his partnership interest is accordingly reduced by this amount.

Method 2. If the potential gain of $18,000 (the difference between the fair market value and the tax basis of the depreciable property contributed by Z) is initially ascribed to Z, partners X and Y may calculate depreciation deductions on the basis of their respective interests in the fair market value of the property—$10,000 for each. Since these interests exceed the tax basis of the asset, the limiting constraint applies and X and Y are each allowed deductions for depreciation in the amount of only $600 per year ($\frac{1}{2} \times \frac{1}{10} \times$ $12,000). The tax bases of the partnership interests of X and Y are accordingly reduced $600 each per year, while Z's basis remains unchanged.

In order to project the ultimate effects of these two methods, assume additionally that the depreciable property is sold after five years for $15,000; although there is no gain or loss recorded by the partnership, there is a $9,000 gain ($15,000 − $6,000) for tax purposes. Financial and tax accounting treatments for depreciation and the property disposal are compared in Illustration 2–1. In Method 2, it is evident that the loss of $2,000 in annual depreciation deductions for X and Y ($5,000 in financial accounting, and $3,000 in tax accounting) is offset by their increased tax bases ($27,000 in tax accounting, as compared to $25,000 in financial accounting); although of different amount, this offsetting phenomenon exists also in Method 1. Sale or liquidation of the interests of X, Y, and Z in the partnership will ultimately "equalize" a partner's total recognized net income as reported under financial and both methods of tax accounting.[6] Due to the disparity between the rates for ordinary income and capital gains, however, complete equity is seldom realized; Method 2 would seem to approximate the most equitable consequence. The accountant should stand ready to advise the partners on the tax implications of electing either of these tax methods for depreciable property.

Financial Statement Presentation

Income Statement. As previously indicated, accounting practice conventionally regards interest on partners' loans as a partnership expense, while it excludes partners' salaries and interest on capital as factors in profit

---

[6] Total recognized net income consists of operating net income, gain or loss on the sale of fixed assets, and gain or loss on the sale of an interest in the partnership.

Illustration 2–1

| | Financial Accounting | | | Tax Accounting | | | | | | | | |
| | | | | Method 1 | | | Method 2 | | | | | |
	X	Y	Z	X	Y	Z	X	Y	Z
Interest in partnership..........	$30,000	$30,000	$30,000	$30,000	$30,000	$12,000	$30,000	$30,000	$12,000
Deductions for depreciation (five years)...........	5,000	5,000	5,000	2,000	2,000	2,000	3,000	3,000	-0-
Adjusted interest in the partnership.......	$25,000	$25,000	$25,000	$28,000	$28,000	$10,000	$27,000	$27,000	$12,000
Gain on sale of property.........	-0-	-0-	-0-	3,000	3,000	3,000	-0-	-0-	9,000
Adjusted interest in the partnership after sale......	$25,000	$25,000	$25,000	$31,000	$31,000	$13,000	$27,000	$27,000	$21,000

Note: Under method 2, potential gain allocable to Z at the time of the sale of the property is $9,000 (5/10 × $18,000). Therefore, the entire recognized gain of $9,000 is allocated to Z.

determination. The exclusions are normally cited in an appendage to the income statement, which contains the distribution of the net income elements. The following income statement makes use of the traditional format:

XY PARTNERSHIP
Income Statement
For Year Ended December 31, 1971

Sales..............................		$100,000
Cost of goods sold.................		60,000
Gross profit.......................		$ 40,000
Operating expenses:		
Interest on partners' loans........	$ 1,000	
Other expenses....................	19,000	20,000
Net Income........................		$ 20,000

Allocated as follows:

	X	Y	Total
Partners' salaries................	$ 8,000	$4,000	$12,000
Interest on capital...............	-0-	2,000	2,000
Remainder equally................	3,000	3,000	6,000
	$11,000	$9,000	$20,000

If the position is taken that partners' salaries are "reasonable compensation for services rendered," consistent reporting would require disclosure of the $12,000 as an operating expense, with a corresponding reduction of net income to $8,000.

Statement of Partners' Capital. In the same manner that the activity in respect to changes in corporate retained earnings are excluded from the balance sheet and are reported separately in a statement of retained earnings, so are the changes (both increases and decreases) in the partners' equity reported separately in a statement of partners' capital. This statement typically assumes the following form:

XY PARTNERSHIP
Statement of Partners' Capital
For Year Ended December 31, 1971

	X	Y	Total
Capital, January 1...............	$10,000	$20,000	$30,000
Net income for the year.........	11,000	9,000	20,000
	$21,000	$29,000	$50,000
Withdrawals....................	12,000	10,000	22,000
Capital, December 31...........	$ 9,000	$19,000	$28,000

Balance Sheet. The usual partnership balance sheet reflects the proprietary concept in its equity section, as the capital accounts of the partners are given separate and prominent attention. Following is an abbreviated example of this format:

XY PARTNERSHIP

Balance Sheet
December 31, 1971

Cash....................	$ 6,000	Current liabilities..	$30,000
Accounts receivable.........	12,000	Loans payable....	25,000
Inventory................	20,000	Capital:	
Fixed assets (net)..........	40,000	X............. $ 9,000	
Other assets..............	5,000	Y............. 19,000	28,000
	$83,000		$83,000

Possibly, a more meaningful disclosure may result if the equity section were divided into capital and accumulated profits divisions. In addition to the fact that Section 40 of the Uniform Partnership Act makes such a distinction, albeit a vague one, between partners' capital and accumulated partnership profits, valuable additional information respecting the financial management of the business is provided if this distinction is maintained in the balance sheet. Also, for credit purposes, the balances of the individual partners' accounts are relatively unimportant, as the partners remain jointly liable for partnership obligations, settlement to be made from their personal assets should this be necessary. Additionally, the information relating to the individual partners' equities in the business is reported in detail in the statement of partners' capital. It is to be regretted that the conventional partnership balance sheet conceals, by integration, the separate net worth elements—partners' capital and accumulated profits.

QUESTIONS

1. What is the essential nature of a partnership? What distinguishes it from other forms of business organization?
2. Enumerate five important provisions which should be explicitly considered in the partnership agreement.
3. The partnership agreement of the XYZ partnership provides that "profits and losses shall be shared in the ratio of the partners' capital balances." Can you foresee any problems with the language of this profit-sharing arrangement? Should such an agreement be in writing to have full legal effect on the parties?
4. How is the tax "basis" of a partner's interest in the partnership defined? Is this concept different from the tax basis of the assets a partner contributes?
5. What are three commonly used bases for allocating partnership net income to the partners?

6. What is the justification for salary allowances in a partnership agreement? Why is interest on capital balances frequently included in a partnership agreement as a basis for profits distribution?

7. What are two possible solutions to the problem arising from the inequity that results from a partner contributing to the partnership depreciable property with a tax basis less than the property's market value?

8. If by agreement the partners wish to begin with equal interests in the partnership net assets yet do not contribute assets of equal value, what methods exist to enable them to accomplish their objective?

9. What alternatives exist for correction of prior years' net income when (a) the amount of the adjustment is minor; (b) the adjustment is material in amount but is not easily identifiable with a specific period or periods; (c) the adjustment is material in amount and is identifiable with specific accounting periods?

10. What advantages may derive from reporting partners' capital accounts on the balance sheet *divided between contributed capital and accumulated profits?* Does present practice more closely approximate the proprietary or entity concept of the partnership?

11. What advantage would result from reporting the salaries and interest paid on partners' capital balances as *expenses* on the income statement rather than recognizing them as earnings distributions?

PROBLEMS

Problem 2–1

Higley and Schlosser organize the H & S partnership on January 1, 1971, with capital contributions of $40,000 and $55,000 respectively. It is agreed that each will be allowed a salary credit of $5,000 annually plus an additional 5 percent credit for interest on the beginning-of-year capital balances. Residual profits are to be divided equally.

| | | Cash Withdrawals | |
Year	Profits before Interest and Salaries	Higley	Schlosser
1971	$22,750	$3,000	$4,750
1972	17,500	4,500	6,250

Required:

(i) Prepare a statement of partners' capital accounts for the two years ended December 31, 1972.

(ii) Prepare closing entries as of December 31, 1972.

Problem 2–2

Brock and Barnes are partners in the BB Confectionery. Their capital account balances on January 1, 1971, are $40,000 and $25,000 respectively. They agree that partnership profits are to be distributed as follows:

	Brock	Barnes
Salary......................	$4,000	$6,000
Interest on beginning capital balances.................	5%	5%
Bonus.....................	20% of net income *after* salaries and bonus *but before* interest has been deducted	None
Residual profits or losses.....	40%	60%

Required:

Calculate the distribution of 1971 partnership profits (identifying the profit elements separately) if the partnership net income before salaries, interest, and bonus is $22,000.

Problem 2–3

Kelly and Anderson organized the KA partnership on January 1, 1971. The following entries were made in their capital accounts during 1971.

	Debit	Credit	Balance
Kelly, capital:			
January 1......................		$30,000	$30,000
April 1........................	$2,000		28,000
October 1......................		4,000	32,000
Anderson, capital:			
January 1......................		15,000	15,000
March 1.......................		3,000	18,000
September 1....................	1,000		17,000
November 1....................		500	17,500

Required:

If the partnership net income, computed without regard to salaries or interest, is $14,000 for 1971, indicate its division between the partners under the following independent profit-sharing conditions:

(i)   Interest at 4 percent is allowed on average capital investments, and the reminder is divided equally.

(ii) A salary of $6,000 is to be credited to Anderson; 4 percent interest is allowed each partner on his ending capital balance.

(iii) Salaries are allowed Kelly and Anderson in amounts of $8,500 and

$9,500 respectively, and residual profits or losses are divided in the ratio of average capital balances.

(iv)   A bonus of 10 percent of partnership net income is credited to Kelly, a salary of $4,000 is allowed to Anderson, and residual profits or losses are shared equally. (The bonus is regarded as an "expense" for purposes of calculating its amount.)

Problem 2–4

(i)   McGuire and Harrell share profits 5:2 after annual salary allowances of $5,000 and $9,000 respectively; however, if partnership net income is insufficient to make these distributions in full amount, net income shall be divided equally between the partners. In 1971 the following errors were discovered:

(a)   Depreciation for 1970 was understated by $4,200.

(b)   Inventory on December 31, 1970, was overvalued by $1,400.

The partnership net income for 1970 was reported to be $17,500. Indicate the correcting entry or entries necessary upon discovery of these errors.

(ii)   Allen, Baker, and Cardwell are partners sharing profits and losses as follows:

Salaries:

Allen..	$ 5,000
Baker......................................	3,000
Cardwell..................................	2,000

Interest (6 percent) on the following average capital balances:

Allen, capital............................	10,000
Baker, capital...........................	15,000
Cardwell, capital.......................	20,000

Residual profits and losses divided equally.

Required:

If the partnership net income for 1971 is reported to be $6,100, indicate the distribution to each partner. Identify the profit and loss elements separately.

Problem 2–5

Jack and Sam are partners, sharing profits equally. In 1971 the partnership had net income before depreciation of $30,000. The only depreciable asset was contributed by Sam on January 1, 1968. It had a $75,000 market value at that date and a tax basis of $50,000. Remaining useful life on January 1, 1968, was 25 years.

Required:

(i)   Compute the depreciation expense allocable to Jack on his 1971 tax return, assuming that the partnership adopted the tax alternative method which attempts to mitigate the inequities beween partners associated with one partner contributing a depreciable asset with less basis than fair market value.

(ii) Prepare the closing journal entry to transfer the income summary balance to the partners' capital accounts.

(iii) What amount of depreciation expense would be allocable to Jack's 1971 tax return if the depreciable asset had a tax basis of only $25,000 on January 1, 1968?

Problem 2–6

Raymond Wintertown developed an interesting idea for marketing sport coats in Alaska. He interested Ednard Fallfield in joining him in a partnership. Following is the information you have collected relative to their original contributions.

Ednard contributed $50,000 cash, a tract of land, and three units of delivery equipment. Raymond contributed $90,000 cash. After giving special consideration to the tax bases of the assets contributed, the relative usefulness of the assets to the partnership versus the problems of finding buyers for the assets and contributing cash, and other such factors, the partners agreed that Raymond's contribution was equal to 45 percent of the partnership's tangible assets, measured in terms of the fair value of the assets *to the partnership*. However, in that the marketing idea originated with Raymond, it was agreed that he should receive credit for 50 percent of the recorded capital. Recent sales of land similar to that contributed by Ednard suggested a market value of $45,000. Likewise, recent sales of delivery equipment similar to that contributed by Ednard suggest $45,000 as the market value of the equipment. These sales, of course, were not entirely representative of the particular assets contributed by Ednard and therefore may be a better indicator of their relative values than their absolute values. In reflecting on their venture, the partners agree that it is a rather risky affair in respect to anticipated profits. Hopefully, however, they will be able to build good customer relations over the long run and establish a permanent business with an attractive long-run rate of return.

Required:

(i) Journalize the partners' contributions under the most appropriate method, given the circumstances.

(ii) Journalize their contributions under another method, probably less appropriate.

(iii) State why you think method (i) is better than (ii) in this situation.

Problem 2–7

On January 1, 1971, the XYZ Partnership was formed with each partner making the following contributions:

	Asset Valuations	
	Fair Market Value	Tax Basis
X: Cash of $50,000	$50,000	$50,000
Y: (1) Machinery and equipment currently valued at $60,000 with a $21,000 mortgage thereagainst	60,000	34,000
(2) Cash of $4,000	4,000	4,000
Z: Building valued at $50,000	50,000	30,000

The mortgage on the machinery and equipment contributed by Y is assumed by the partnership.

Required:

(i) Prepare the journal entry for the formation of the XYZ Partnership using financial accounting procedures.
(ii) Prepare the journal entry for the formation of the XYZ Partnership using tax accounting procedures.

Problem 2–8

Partnership contracts usually specify a profit and loss ratio. They may also provide for such additional profit- and loss-sharing features as salaries, bonuses, and interest allowances on invested capital.

Required:

(i)   What is the objective of profit- and loss-sharing arrangements? Why may there be a need for features in addition to the profit and loss ratio? Discuss.
(ii) Discuss the arguments for recording salary and bonus allowances to partners as charges to operations.
(iii) What are the arguments against treating partnership salary and bonus allowances as expenses? Discuss.
(iv) In addition to its other profit- and loss-sharing features, a partnership agreement may state that "interest is to be allowed on invested capital." List the additional provision that should be included in the partnership agreement so that "interest to be allowed on invested capital" can be computed.

(AICPA adapted)

Problem 2–9

A, B, and C have been partners throughout the year 1971. The average balances for the year and their balances at the end of the year before closing the nominal accounts are as follows:

	Average Balances		Balances, Dec. 31, 1971	
A.	Cr.	$90,000	Cr.	$60,000
B.	Cr.	3,000	Dr.	1,000
C.	Cr.	7,000	Cr.	10,000

The profit for 1971 is $75,000 before charging partners' drawing allowances (salaries) and before interest on average balances at the agreed rate of 4 percent per annum. A is entitled to a drawing account credit of $10,000, B of $7,000, and C of $5,000 per annum. The balance of the profit is to be distributed at the rate of 60 percent to A, 30 percent to B, and 10 percent to C.

It is intended to distribute amounts of cash to the partners so that after credits and distributions as indicated in the preceding paragraph, the balances in the partners' accounts will be proportionate to their profit-sharing ratio. None of the partners is to pay in any money, but it is desired to distribute the lowest possible amount of cash.

Required:

Prepare a schedule of the partners' capital accounts, showing balances at the end of 1971 before closing, the allocations of the net profit for 1971, the cash distributed, and the closing balances.

(AICPA adapted)

Problem 2–10

On January 1, 1971, the XYZ partnership was organized with the following contributions:

Contributor	Assets	Tax Basis	Fair Market Value
X	Building (10-year remaining life)	$24,000	$60,000
Y	Cash	60,000	60,000
Z	Miscellaneous assets with mortgage of $21,000 thereagainst, which is assumed by the partnership	80,000	80,000

Net income (excluding the effects of depreciation and capital gains) for each of the first five years of the partnership life was $30,000. Withdrawals of $5,000 each year were made by each of the partners.

On December 31, 1975, the building contributed by X was sold for $30,000. The gain on sale is taxable as a capital gain.

It is assumed that the combined normal and surtax rate for each partner is 60 percent, while the capital gain tax rate is 30 percent.

Required:

(i) Journalize the original investment of each partner using financial accounting methods.

(ii) Journalize the original investment of each partner reflecting the effects of income tax provisions.

(iii) Prepare a schedule showing the comparative *adjusted* interests of the partners after the sale of the building, using both financial accounting and tax accounting methods.

(iv) Compute the total tax liability for each partner by each of the alternative tax methods for the five-year period.

(v) Discuss the relative equities in respect to the tax obligation of each partner under the two alternative tax methods.

Problem 2–11

The Gottheiner-Robinson-Johnson partnership was formed in 1970, Gottheiner contributing a major portion of the capital, with Robinson and Johnson to provide important management skills and experience. The partnership agreement specifies that the accounting records shall be maintained on the accrual basis and that the net income shall be distributed to the partners as follows:

a) Each partner shall receive 5 percent interest on the balance in his capital account at the beginning of the year.

b) Robinson and Johnson shall each receive a commission of 20 percent of an amount representing net income determined under cash basis accounting after deducting the normal allowance for depreciation and the interest on capital. For this purpose all merchandise purchased is to be regarded as an expense.

c) The net income remaining after deducting the interest on capital and commissions due to Robinson and Johnson shall be distributed equally, except that the total portion of net income to Gottheiner must not be less than 50 percent of the net income determined under accrual accounting.

During 1971, $150 of accounts receivable were considered uncollectable and charged off to the allowance for doubtful accounts, and $10 were collected on accounts which had been charged off to the allowance for doubtful accounts in prior years.

There were no changes in the partners' capital accounts during 1971.

Required:

Given the balance sheets below, prepare—

(i) A schedule, supported by computational detail, showing the adjustments necessary to convert the net income for 1971 from an accrual basis to a cash basis.

(ii) A statement, supported by computational detail, indicating the distribution of 1971 net income to the partners.

GOTTHEINER-ROBINSON-JOHNSON
Comparative Balance Sheet

	December 31, 1970		December 31, 1971	
ASSETS				
Cash....................................		$ 7,000		$ 11,120
Accounts receivable—customers.........	$ 5,000		$ 6,000	
Allowance for doubtful accounts........	100	4,900	120	5,880
Inventory............................		26,000		24,000
U.S. government bonds (at cost)........				8,000
Fixed assets (at cost).................	$120,000		$220,000	
Accumulated depreciation..............	42,500	77,500	46,300	173,700
Prepaid expenses.....................		1,000		800
Total Assets....................		$116,400		$223,500
LIABILITIES AND CAPITAL				
Accounts payable—trade..............		$ 7,000		$ 4,000
Accrued wages.......................		3,000		5,000
Accrued taxes........................		500		500
Deferred income......................		5,900		
Bonds payable.......................				100,000
Net income, 1971....................				14,000
Partners' capitals:				
Gottheiner.......................	$ 80,000		$ 80,000	
Robinson........................	12,500		12,500	
Johnson.........................	7,500	100,000	7,500	100,000
Total Liabilities and Capital......		$116,400		$223,500

(AICPA adapted)

Problem 2–12

Lynn and Kay, architectural designers and interior decorators, combined May 1, 1971, agreeing to share profits: Lynn, two thirds; Kay, one third. Lynn contributed furniture and fixtures, $3,000, and cash, $2,000; Kay contributed cash, $500.

They plan to submit monthly bills and make the following arrangements with their clients:

a) The salaries of draftsmen and shoppers, who are paid on an hourly basis, shall be billed to clients at the hourly rate for time spent on each job, plus 125 percent for overhead and profit and plus 4½ percent for all payroll taxes.

b) Partners' time on jobs shall be billed at $10 an hour.

c) A 10 percent service fee shall be charged on purchases of furniture, drapes, etc., installed on the jobs. (Lynn and Kay will pay the vendors and charge their clients for these purchases but would like to have their operating statements reflect only revenue from services.)

d) There will be no service fee on taxis, telephone, and other expenses identifiable to jobs and charged to clients.

Voucher register totals for May are given below:

Credits:

Vouchers payable....................................	$3,469
Taxes withheld—federal income......................	93
Taxes withheld—FICA..............................	27
Income from charges to jobs for partners' time........	790
Total..	$4,379

Debits:

Purchases and expenses chargeable to clients...........	$1,615
Partners' drawings (Lynn, $100; Kay, $125)...........	225
General expenses...................................	784
Jobs in process:	
Draftsmen's salaries............................	940
Partners' time..................................	790
Petty cash fund....................................	25
Total..	$4,379

The first debit column is analyzed in the voucher register as follows:

Purchases subject to 10 percent fee:

Client M, Job 51.....................................	$1,210	
Client H, Job 52.....................................	320	$1,530

Expenses chargeable to clients:

Client M 51...	$ 23	
Client M 54...	7	
Client H 52...	19	
Client L 53...	36	85
		$1,615

The client has not yet authorized them to do Job M 54. The partners are confident, however, that the job will be authorized and the above expenses, as well as charges for time spent by a draftsman and Mr. Lynn on preliminary designs, will be billed and collected.

The payroll analysis is summarized below. Partners' time on jobs, charged to the jobs at $5 an hour, is summarized in the payroll analysis for convenience in posting costs to job sheets, although the partners are not paid for direct time on jobs.

	Secretary	Draftsmen	Lynn	Kay
Job:				
M 51..................... ...	...	$ 312	$120	$150
H 52..................... ...	...	276	60	115
L 53..................... ...	...	304	65	160
M 54..................... ...	...	48	120	
		$ 940	$365	$425
General Expenses:				
General office............	$160	40		
Idle time................	...	60		
Total payroll............	$160	$1,040		

Journal entries recorded depreciation on furniture and fixtures of $25 and the employer's share of federal and state taxes of $54.

There were no cash receipts other than the original investment. The cash disbursements book shows the following totals:

Debit	Vouchers payable	$2,373
Credit:	Cash	2,358
Credit:	Discount on purchases	15

Required:

(i)   Compute billings to clients for May.

(ii) Prepare a work sheet showing the balance sheet, profit and loss general ledger accounts, and the profit allocation at May 31, 1971. Show how you arrive at these balances by entering all May transactions on the work sheet. Use the accounts indicated in the voucher register.

(AICPA adapted)

Problem 2–13

The Kelley-Thomas Company is a partnership that has not maintained adequate accounting records because it has been unable to employ a competent bookkeeper. The company sells hardware items to the retail trade and also wholesales to builders and contractors. As the company's CPA, you have been asked to prepare the company's financial statements as of June 30, 1971.

Your work papers provide the following postclosing trial balance at December 31, 1970:

THE KELLEY-THOMAS COMPANY

Postclosing Trial Balance
December 31, 1970

	Debit	Credit
Cash...	$10,000	
Accounts receivable................................	8,000	
Allowance for bad debts............................		$ 600
Merchandise inventory..............................	35,000	
Prepaid insurance..................................	150	
Automobiles.......................................	7,800	
Allowance for depreciation—automobiles..............		4,250
Furniture and fixtures..............................	2,200	
Allowance for depreciation—furniture and fixtures......		650
Accounts payable..................................		13,800
Bank loan payable.................................		8,000
Accrued expenses..................................		200
Kelley, capital....................................		17,500
Thomas, capital...................................		18,150
Total..	$63,150	$63,150

You are able to collect the following information at June 30, 1971.

a) Your analysis of cash transactions, derived from the company's bank statements and checkbook stubs, is as follows:

Deposits:

Cash receipts from customers ($40,000 of this amount represents collections on receivables including redeposited protested checks totaling $600)....................................	$65,000
Bank loan, 1/2/71 (due 5/1/71, 5%).......................	7,867
Bank loan, 5/1/71 (due 9/1/71, 5%).......................	8,850
Sale of old automobile...................................	20
Total deposits......................................	$81,737

Disbursements:

Payments to merchandise creditors........................	$45,000
Payment to Internal Revenue Service on Thomas' 1971 declaration of estimated income tax...........................	3,000
General expenses.......................................	7,000
Bank loan, 1/2/71......................................	8,000
Bank loan, 5/2/71......................................	8,000
Payment for new automobile.............................	2,400
Protested checks.......................................	900
Kelley withdrawals.....................................	5,000
Thomas withdrawals....................................	2,500
Total disbursements.................................	$81,800

b) The protested checks include customers' checks totaling $600 that were redeposited and a $300 check from an employee that is still on hand.

c) Accounts receivable from customers for merchandise sales amount to $18,000 and include accounts totaling $800 that have been placed with an attorney for collection. Correspondence with the client's attorney reveals that one of the accounts for $175 is uncollectible. Experience indicates that 1 percent of credit sales will prove uncollectible.

d)   On April 1 a new automobile was purchased. The list price of the automobile was $2,700, and $300 was allowed for the trade-in of an old automobile, even though the dealer stated that its condition was so poor that he did not want it. The client sold the old automobile, which cost $1,800 and was fully depreciated at December 31, 1970, to an auto wrecker for $20. The old automobile was in use up to the date of its sale.

e)   Depreciation is recorded by the straight-line method and is computed on acquisitions to the nearest full month. The estimated life for furniture and fixtures is 10 years and for automobiles is three years. (Salvage value is to be ignored in computing depreciation. No asset other than the car in item [d] was fully depreciated prior to June 30, 1971.)

f)   Other data as of June 30, 1971, include the following:

Merchandise inventory	$37,500
Prepaid insurance	80
Accrued expenses	166

g)   Accounts payable to merchandise vendors total $18,750. There is on hand a $750 credit memorandum from a merchandise vendor for returned merchandise; the company will apply the credit to July merchandise purchases. Neither the credit memorandum nor the return of the merchandise had been recorded on the books.

h)   Profits and losses are divided equally between the partners.

Required:

Prepare a work sheet that provides on the accrual basis information regarding transactions for the six months ended June 30, 1971, the results of the partnership operations for the period, and the financial position of the partnership at June 30, 1971.

(AICPA adapted)

Problem 2–14

The partnership of King, Gill, and Fisher engaged you to adjust its accounting records and convert them uniformly to the accrual basis in anticipation of admitting Wagner as a new partner. Some accounts are on the accrual basis and others are on the cash basis. The partnership's books were closed at December 31, 1971, by the bookkeeper who prepared the general ledger trial balance that appears below:

KING, GILL AND FISHER

General Ledger Trial Balance
December 31, 1971

	Debit	Credit
Cash...	$ 10,000	
Accounts receivable...........................	40,000	
Inventory.....................................	26,000	
Land...	9,000	
Buildings.....................................	50,000	
Allowance for depreciation of buildings..............		$ 2,000
Equipment....................................	56,000	
Allowance for depreciation of equipment.............		6,000
Goodwill......................................	5,000	
Accounts payable..............................		55,000
Allowance for future inventory losses...............		3,000
King, capital..................................		40,000
Gill, capital...................................		60,000
Fisher, capital................................		30,000
Total.....................................	$196,000	$196,000

Your inquiries disclosed the following:

a) The partnership was organized on January 1, 1970, with no provision in the partnership agreement for the distribution of partnership profits and losses. During 1971 profits were distributed equally among the partners. The partnership agreement was amended effective January 1, 1971, to provide for the following profit and loss ratio: King, 50 percent; Gill, 30 percent; and Fisher, 20 percent. The amended partnership agreement also stated that the accounting records were to be maintained on the accrual basis and that any adjustments necessary for 1970 should be allocated according to the 1970 distribution of profits.

b) The following amounts were not recorded as prepayments or accruals:

	December 31	
	1971	1970
Prepaid insurance..................	$700	$ 650
Advances from customers...........	200	1,100
Accrued interest expense............		450

The advances from customers were recorded as sales in the year the cash was received.

c) In 1971 the partnership recorded a provision of $3,000 for anticipated declines in inventory prices. You convinced the partners that the provision was unnecessary and should be removed from the books.

d) The partnership charged equipment purchased for $4,400 on January 3, 1971, to expense. This equipment has an estimated life of 10 years and an estimated salvage value of $400. The partnership depreciates its capitalized equipment under the income tax declining balance method at twice the straight-line depreciation rate.

e) The partners agreed to establish an allowance for doubtful accounts at 2 percent of current accounts receivable and 5 percent of past-due accounts. At December 31, 1970, the partnership had $54,000 of accounts receivable, of which only $4,000 was past due. At December 31, 1971, 15 percent of accounts receivable was past due, of which $4,000 represented sales made in 1970 and was generally considered collectible. The partnership had written off uncollectible accounts in the year the accounts became worthless as follows:

	Account Written Off in—	
	1971	*1970*
1971 accounts....................	$ 800	
1970 accounts....................	1,000	$250

f) Goodwill was recorded on the books in 1971 and credited to the partners' capital accounts in the profit and loss ratio in recognition of an increase in the value of the business resulting from improved sales volume. The partners agreed to write off the goodwill before admitting the new partner.

Required:

Prepare a work sheet showing the adjustments and the adjusted trial balance for the partnership on the accrual basis at December 31, 1971. All adjustments affecting income should be made directly to partners' capital accounts. Number your adjusting entries. Supporting computations should be in good form.

(AICPA adapted)

Chapter 3

Legal Dissolution: Realignment of Ownership Structure

NATURE OF REALIGNMENT

Basic Legal Provisions

Under the common law, any change in the ownership structure of a partnership resulted in its dissolution, although concurrently a new partnership was often formed. In many instances the legal dissolution was not a reflection of an overt intention to interrupt the continuity of partnership operations. However, the existence of this common law provision, together with numerous concepts concerning the nature of partnership dissolution, often created problems the effect of which was to disrupt, and sometimes terminate, the operations of the business. Problems often created by this legal dissolution include, among others, the determination of equitable settlements to the partners and the computation of their taxable net income. Provisions of the Uniform Partnership Act partially ameliorate the dangers of an unexpected dissolution by stating more precisely the nature of a dissolution, and also by reducing the number of conditions under which the partnership may be dissolved.

Section 29 of the Act defines dissolution of a partnership as "the change in the relation of the partners caused by any partner ceasing to be associated in the carrying on as distinguished from the winding up of the business." The following partial enumeration from Sections 31 and 32 indicates the various types of conditions which constitute a legal dissolution of a partnership:

1. By completion of a definite term of existence (or a particular undertaking) specified in the partnership agreement.
2. By the express will of any partner when no definite term of existence is specified in the agreement.
3. By the death of a partner.
4. By decree of a court for various reasons.
5. By the bankruptcy of any partner or the partnership.

It should be noted, however, that conveyance of an interest in the partnership does not of itself constitute a dissolution (Section 27), and although the admission or retirement of a partner by implication dissolves the partnership, according to Section 41 (1), this provision has little *functional* significance if the partnership is immediately reestablished without actually terminating its operations. Furthermore, various states have adapted for their own purposes certain provisions of the Uniform Partnership Act such that the partners are permitted to include in the articles of copartnership further restrictions on dissolution; for example, the Texas Uniform Partnership Act allows a provision to be included in the partnership agreement prescribing that the death of a partner is not a cause of dissolution. In view of this trend toward greater permanency in the partnership structure, it is not especially important to emphasize the *legal* problems coextensive with the types of ownership realignment herein considered.

Types of Realignment

In order to facilitate a systematic review of the accounting problems involved in changes in the ownership structure, three general classes of realignment will be considered:

1.   Admission of a new partner.
2.   Retirement of a partner.
3.   Death of a partner.

These classes are obviously not mutually exclusive; for example, a new partner may be admitted to an existing partnership by purchasing the interest, or partial interest, of a retiring partner. Nonetheless, the above classes do provide an operational framework for the analysis of most of the basic accounting problems associated with the realignment of ownership interests.

ADMISSION OF A NEW PARTNER

There are two principal bases upon which a new partner may be admitted to an existing partnership. Either the new partner may invest cash or other assets in the business, the net assets of the partnership being enlarged by his contribution, or he may purchase an interest directly from one or more of the existing partners. In the latter case, the consideration merely passes between the partners, acting as individuals, and partnership net assets are usually not altered. The firm's potential need for additional resources is often an important determining factor as to the method elected to admit a new partner; for example, a deficiency in current working capital may be the compelling initial motivation for the admission of a new partner. Once the partners have selected a basis for admitting a new partner, his capital credit must be duly recorded, as well as any necessary adjustments to the capital accounts of the existing partners and/or the assets of the partnership.

The problem of assigning appropriate values to partnership assets is especially important in accounting for the admission of a new partner. Three separate asset classes require analysis in this valuation process:

1. Existing assets, tangible and intangible, presently recorded in the books of the partnership should be appraised and their current market values established. Although the accountant may elect not to record appraisal increments, these values should nonetheless be considered in analyzing the basis of the admission "price" imposed upon the new partner.
2. Unrecorded partnership assets, particularly intangible assets, may be inferred from a comparison of the price paid by the new partner for an interest in the partnership and the preexistent capital after adjustment for appraisal increments.
3. Values must be assigned to the declared assets, both tangible and intangible, contributed by the new partner. Additional value may also be inferred for undeclared intangible assets.

After these analyses have been completed, assignment of value measurements to the respective partners' capital accounts is merely a derivative, routine calculation.

Admission by Investment

As previously mentioned, the resource requirements of the firm may indicate a need for an enlargement of the ownership structure. In this event, it is appropriate that assets be contributed to augment present partnership capital. The procedure for recording the admission of a new partner under this condition will be illustrated by considering the unique aspects of each of the possible valuation conditions referred to in the previous paragraph.

Case 1. Assume that X and Y are partners with capital balances of $7,000 and $3,000 respectively. The profit- and loss-sharing ratio is 60:40. Z invests tangible assets valued at $15,000 for a 50 percent interest in the capital of the partnership. Concurrently, an appraisal of existing partnership net assets reveals a current market valuation of $15,000.

An analysis of these data indicates that Z is investing $15,000 for a one-half interest in partnership net assets, which after the investment total $30,000. The data further imply that additional unrecorded assets do not exist. However, the accountant must elect whether or not to record the appraisal increment for existing partnership assets. The alternative entries to record the admission of Z are as follows:

1. *Appraisal increment recorded:*

Assets	5,000	
X, capital		3,000
Y, capital		2,000
Assets	15,000	
Z, capital		15,000

2. *Appraisal increment not recorded:*

Assets..	15,000	
X, capital (60% × $2,500)......................		1,500
Y, capital (40% × $2,500)......................		1,000
Z, capital.....................................		12,500

In the first entry, the interests of the old partners in the existing assets are adjusted for value increments of these assets suggested by the appraisal; this valuation is a basis for determining the contribution to be made by Z. Accordingly, Z is given credit for the total amount of his investment. The acknowledgment of capital credit in the full amount of the contribution is believed to have psychological appeal which argues for the use of this method. In the second entry, Z is merely given a 50 percent interest in the *recorded values* of the net assets (without appraisal increment adjustments) of the new partnership, and X and Y are awarded capital credits as consideration for Z's newly acquired, implicit interest in the *unrecorded values* of these assets. In effect, X and Y transfer to Z $2,500 of their preexisting interests in these unrecorded values ($5,000 appraisal increment) when Z is given a 50 percent interest in partnership assets, and they are accordingly rewarded therefor in their capital accounts. This method is frequently referred to as the *bonus method,* and it yields equivalent results to the first method only under certain restrictive conditions to be considered later. Hereafter, it will be assumed that the recorded assets of the firm are properly valued, or that an adjustment for current market values has previously been recorded in the old partners' capital accounts.

Case 2.   X and Y are partners with capital balances of $40,000 and $10,000 respectively. Profits and losses are shared in the ratio of 80:20. Z invests tangible assets valued at $30,000 for a 25 percent interest in the capital of the new partnership.

Analysis of this condition of entry indicates that Z has acquired a $20,000 (25% × $80,000) interest in the tangible net assets of the firm, inclusive of Z's contribution, at a cost of $30,000. Since it is assumed that all tangible assets are properly valued, Z is apparently paying $10,000 for a one-fourth interest in *unrecorded* intangible assets of the partnership. Conventionally, this type of intangible asset is assumed to be partnership "goodwill." The amount of the goodwill is easily determined by applying the following rule:

1. Let *C* equal the total new capital of the firm, including the as yet undetermined goodwill, and solve the following two equations:
   a) (Fractional interest in capital retained by the old partners) × C = Total recorded capital balances of old partners.
   b) (Fractional interest in capital obtained by the new partner) × C = Investment of the new partner.
2. Determine the amount of implied goodwill by subtracting the total recorded net assets of the *new* firm (including the tangible assets con-

tributed by the new partner) from the larger amount computed for *C* in (1) above. If (*a*) is larger, the new partner contributes goodwill; if (*b*) is larger, the goodwill identifies with the old partners.[1]

This technique may be applied to the data of Case 2 in the following manner:

1. Computation of alternative capital balances:

   a) .75 (*C*) = $ 50,000 ,
   $\qquad$ *C* = $ 66,667 .
   b) .25 (*C*) = $ 30,000 ,
   $\qquad$ *C* = $120,000 .

2. Computation of goodwill:

   $\qquad$ Goodwill = $120,000 − $80,000
   $\qquad\qquad$ = $ 40,000 .

The above valuation for goodwill may be analyzed and rendered more plausible by reconsidering the details of the investment transaction. It was noted that Z paid $10,000 more than his acquired capital interest in the net tangible assets of the new firm. It is now evident that this $10,000 was a payment for a one-fourth interest in the unrecorded goodwill of $40,000.

$\qquad$ There are two alternative methods for recording the entry of the new partner into the partnership:

1. *Bonus method:*

Assets..	30,000	
$\qquad$ X, capital (4/5 × $10,000).....................		8,000
$\qquad$ Y, capital (1/5 × $10,000).....................		2,000
$\qquad$ Z, capital (1/4 $80,000).....................		20,000

2. *Goodwill method:*

Goodwill.......................................	40,000	
$\qquad$ X, capital (4/5 × $40,000).....................		32,000
$\qquad$ Y, capital (1/5 × $40,000).....................		8,000
Assets...	30,000	
$\qquad$ Z, capital.......................................		30,000

These two methods are, in substance, identical with the alternative methods employed in the previous case. In this illustration, however, the account-ant's election relates to the propriety of recording implicit goodwill rather than of recording appraisal increments (or decrements). Generally, the evidence adduced for the existence and amount of "goodwill" is less per-suasive than that provided by an appraisal which indicates the market replacement values of tangible assets. As indicated before, the motivational impetus provided by giving the new partner credit for his *total* investment

---

[1] See the Note at the end of this chapter.

often overcomes the disadvantage of the indefiniteness of the amount of goodwill. The equivalance of the two methods with respect to the relative equities of the partners is, as before, subject to certain constraints to be investigated after considering the following case.

Case 3. X and Y are partners with capital balances of $50,000 and $30,000, respectively. Profits and losses are shared in the ratio of 70:30. Z invests tangible assets valued at $15,000 for a 20 percent interest in the capital of the new partnership.

In this instance, Z acquires an interest of $19,000 ($\frac{1}{5} \times \$95,000$) in the net tangible assets of the firm at a cost of $15,000. By implication Z has contributed an additional, undeclared asset to the partnership for which he receives additional capital credit. The undeclared asset is usually described as goodwill (unusual managerial ability, special customer appeal, etc.). The rule cited earlier may again be applied to estimate the amount of the implicit goodwill:

1. Computation of alternative capital balances:

   a) $.80\,(C) = \$\ 80,000$,
        $C = \$100,000$.
   b) $.20\,(C) = \$\ 15,000$,
        $C = \$\ 75,000$.

2. Computation of goodwill:

   Goodwill $= \$100,000 - \$95,000$
             $= \$\ \ 5,000$.

A heuristic argument similar to that offered above may again be cited to justify the appropriateness of this amount. The existing partners have acquired an 80 percent interest in the implicit goodwill contributed by Z when it accrues to the benefit of the partnership. For this interest, they have given to Z a $4,000 interest in partnership assets in excess of the tangible assets he contributed to the firm ($19,000 - $15,000). Therefore, the amount of the goodwill, as measured by the price imposed upon Z for his interest in net tangible assets, is $5,000 ($4,000 ÷ .80).

Either the goodwill or the bonus method may again be used to record this transaction:

1. *Bonus method:*

Assets...	15,000	
X, capital (70% × $4,000)............................	2,800	
Y, capital (30% × $4,000)............................	1,200	
Z, capital (20% × $95,000)........................		19,000

2. *Goodwill method:*

Assets...	15,000	
Goodwill...	5,000	
Z, capital...		20,000

An Appraisal of the Bonus and Goodwill Methods— Quantitative Implications

Accounting problems of recording asset revaluations or implicit good-will have been considered relative to the alternative *bonus* method of re-cording a new partner's admission by investment. However, an understand-ing of the implications of selecting one method or the other requires further analysis of the conditions under which the two methods are ultimately equivalent in terms of their effects on the relative equities of the individual partners.

Assume that goodwill is recorded and subsequently proves to have been overstated. A condition of equivalence would require that after the write-down adjustment to eliminate the recorded goodwill (loss realization), the individual partners' capital accounts should be equivalent to those balances that would have resulted had the bonus method been originally used. Con-trariwise, if the bonus method is initially employed and subsequently a determinable amount of goodwill is confirmed by an objective transaction of the partnership, a similar requirement of equality is imposed to establish equivalence.

The conditions necessary to achieve equivalence of these alternative methods will be introduced by means of an example. Using the data of Case 3, the effect of recording the admission of Z with goodwill recognized, and subsequently writing off the total amount of this intangible, is con-trasted with the capital balances obtained by initially applying the bonus method (see Illustration 3–1). Interim transactions are ignored in order

Illustration 3–1

	X	Y	Z	Total
Bonus method—capital balances.....	$47,200	$28,800	$19,000	$ 95,000
Goodwill method:				
Situation (1):				
Initial capital balances........	$50,000	$30,000	$20,000	$100,000
Write-off of goodwill..........	[2,800]	[1,200]	[1,000]	[5,000]
Ending capital balances.......	$47,200	$28,800	$19,000	$ 95,000
Difference between methods after writeoff..............	$ –0–	$ –0–	$ –0–	$ –0–
Situation (2):				
Initial capital balances........	$50,000	$30,000	$20,000	$100,000
Write-off of goodwill..........	[2,450]	[1,050]	[1,500]	[5,000]
Ending capital balances.......	$47,550	$28,950	$18,500	$ 95,000
Difference between methods after write-off..............	$ 350	$ 150	$ [500]	$ –0–
Situation (3):				
Initial capital balances........	$50,000	$30,000	$20,000	$100,000
Write-off of goodwill..........	[3,000]	[1,000]	[1,000]	[5,000]
Ending capital balances.......	$47,000	$29,000	$19,000	$ 95,000
Difference between methods after write-off..............	$ [200]	$ 200	$ –0–	$ –0–

to isolate the equity effects of the two methods. Three different profit and loss ratios are assumed:

	Profit and Loss Ratios		
	X	Y	Z
Situation (1).....................	56%	24%	20%
Situation (2).....................	49	21	30
Situation (3).....................	60	20	20

Illustration 3–1 isolates in situation (1) the two conditions necessary for the equivalence of the bonus and goodwill methods, viz.:

1. The percentage interest in profits and losses of the new partner must be the same as his initial fractional interest in the partnership capital; *and*
2. The new (or adjusted) percentage interests in profits and losses of the old partners must be in the same relative proportion as their old percentage interests.

In situation (1), Z has a 20 percent interest in profits and losses, which is equal to his initial fractional interest in partnership capital, and the new percentage interests in profits and losses of X and Y are in the same relative proportion as their prior percentage interests—80 percent of 70 percent for X, and 80 percent of 30 percent for Y, or 70:30 = 56.24. In situation (2), the new percentage interests in profits and losses of the old partners are in the same relative proportion, but the interest of Z in profits and losses exceeds his initial fractional interest in capital; consequently, an advantage accrues to X and Y equivalent in amount to the disadvantage to Z. In situation (3), the new percentage interests of X and Y are in a different proportion than existed prior to the admission of Z, i.e., 70:30 $\neq$ 60:20; this condition results in an advantage to Y, and a disadvantage to X.

Purchase of a Partial Interest

A second basic method of acquiring an interest in a partnership is to purchase a capital equity directly from one or more of the old partners, without an increase in partnership assets. In this section, two cases will be distinguished:

1. Purchase of a portion of one partner's interest, and
2. Purchase of a partial interest uniformly from all of the existing partners.

In both instances, the ownership structure is numerically enlarged by the conveyance of an interest in the existing partnership to a new member. In the discussion of retirement of partners, the sale by one partner of his *total* interest in the partnership will be described briefly.

If an existing partner sells a portion of his interest in capital and profits to another individual, the only entry *required* on the books of the partnership is one which establishes the new partner's capital credit by a transfer of the amount of the purchased interest from the capital account of the selling partner. For example, if X and Y are partners, with capital balances of $60,000 and $40,000 respectively, and Y sells one fourth of his interest to Z for $12,000, the only entry required on the partnership books is:

Y, capital (1/4 × $40,000)............................. 10,000
    Z, capital..   10,000

The cash consideration which passes between the old and new partner is established independently by Y and Z and need not be reflected in the above entry on the partnership books. From the point of view of the partnership entity, Y has merely transferred a personal asset to a new partner, viz., one fourth of his *recorded* interest in partnership capital; only this fact need be recognized in the partnership accounts.

If in the preceding illustration Z had purchased a one-fourth interest in the partnership by means of a direct purchase from *both* X and Y for $30,000 (a ratable transfer of one fourth of the monetary interest of each in the partnership), the accounting entry to record the capital transfer is essentially the same. Each partner conveys to Z one fourth of his interest in the *recorded* capital of the firm.

X, capital (1/4 × $60,000)............................. 15,000
Y, capital (1/4 × $40,000)............................. 10,000
    Z, capital..   25,000

Again, the cash price for the purchased interests is not a compelling factor affecting the partnership accounts, as the sale represents an *independent* transaction between the existing partners and the incoming partner. The transaction may be compared to the sale of shares of corporate stock in the open market subsequent to their original issuance; the total net worth of the corporate entity remains unaffected by the sale—only the identity and the relative interests of the various owners are changed.

Two problems intrude upon this relatively simple accounting framework for recording the purchase of a partnership interest directly from one or more partners. First, an argument can be made that the cash price established in the sale of an interest should be used as an independent index of the current value of the partnership net assets. If this premise is accepted and if the tangible net assets of the partnership are assumed to reflect current market values, the purchase price may be used to estimate the amount of goodwill possessed by the preexistent partnership. Returning to the previous example in which Z purchased a one-fourth ratable interest from X and Y for $30,000, there is an indication that the total value of the partnership net assets may be $120,000 (one fourth of the total value = $30,000). Since the recorded net worth presently is only $100,000, implicit goodwill of $20,000 may be inferred from this purchase. If the goodwill were recorded, and assuming X and Y share profits and losses equally, the entries to record the admission of Z are:

Goodwill.	20,000	
X, capital.		10,000
Y, capital.		10,000

X, capital (1/4 × $70,000).	17,500	
Y, capital (1/4 × $50,000).	12,500	
Z, capital.		30,000

In an analogous manner, goodwill identified with the new partner may be computed. The advantages and disadvantages of recording the implicit goodwill in either case, and the requisite conditions for the equivalence of this and the preceding method, are the same as those discussed earlier in this chapter.

A second problem arising from the purchase of an interest from more than one existing partner concerns the distribution settlement of cash to the selling partners. This is ultimately a matter of negotiation between the new partner and each of the old partners or between the old partners. Frequently, however, the accountant is consulted and asked to suggest a basis for distributing the cash contributed by the new partner. Using the above data, the following tabulation is the conventional approach:

	X	Y	Total
Capital balances, as recorded.	$60,000	$40,000	$100,000
Implicit goodwill—allocated in profit and loss ratio.	10,000	10,000	20,000
Adjusted capital balances.	$70,000	$50,000	$120,000
Retained capital—three fourths of adjusted balances.	52,500	37,500	90,000
Capital transferred to Z—basis for allocation of cash.	$17,500	$12,500	$ 30,000

An analysis of this schedule of cash distribution raises several questions concerning its general validity. Since the sale was assumed to be independent of the partnership entity, one may take the position that it is inappropriate to utilize present partners' capital balances and provisions of the partnership agreement (i.e., the profit and loss ratios of X and Y) as a basis for determining the cash allocations. In this case, the capital balances are not in the profit- and loss-sharing ratios; consequently, X and Y are surrendering an interest in recorded net worth according to one ratio, 60:40, and they are forsaking an interest in future profits in yet another ratio, 50:50. The above schedule indicates the accepted method of recording, on the partnership books, the existence of implicit goodwill, and the resulting transfers of capital from X and Y to Z. The schedule, however, may not represent the most appropriate allocation of the $30,000 as between the amount paid for an interest in present net worth. and that amount which is paid for an interest in future changes in net worth. Clearly, the ultimate decision in respect to cash distributions remains with the old partners. The above solution may or may not represent an acceptable settlement; their preferences should and will control.

One may also appropriately question the basic premise underlying the conventional computation of implicit goodwill. It is tacitly assumed that the amount of invested assets or the purchase price of a partner's interest may be capitalized to the extent of the fractional interest in capital acquired by the new partner, and that this value may be compared with the recorded net worth of the partnership to infer the existence of unrecorded goodwill. However, as noted above, the new partner is, in fact, buying an interest in both present net worth *and* future profits; accordingly, it is questionable whether only one of these components should be used in computing the amount of goodwill. For example, the price paid for a partnership interest which is in excess of net tangible assets acquired may be a payment for the excess earning capacity of the business (goodwill); however, it may represent rather the purchase of a greater interest in profits than in capital. If this interpretation prevails, the existence and amount of goodwill is an indeterminate element and should be recorded only when supporting evidence is compelling.

Legal Status of a New Partner

Section 27 of the Uniform Partnership Act confers upon any partner the right to convey by assignment to a third party his interest in the partnership —which is, as previously noted, personal property. This assignment does not, however, give the assignee authority to participate in the management of the business. Rather, it entitles him merely to receive the profits and in the case of dissolution to receive an interest in net assets which would normally accrue to the assignor.

If the existing partners agree to admit by assignment a new partner to the ownership structure, as is implicitly done when a prospective partner invests assets in the business, the new partner assumes the same rights and obligations as the old partners; this assumption is modified somewhat in Section 17 of the Act, in which it is provided that the new partner is personally liable for only those liabilities created subsequent to his admission to the firm. Thus, if dissolution should occur shortly after the admission of a new partner, it is necessary to distinguish between "old" and "new" liabilities of the partnership. The reader will note that the accounting treatment previously discussed for the "purchase of an interest" implicitly assumes that the assignee is admitted to the partnership with the status of a new partner, i.e., no special equity status is identified.

Tax Basis of a New Partner

The tax basis of a new partner admitted by investing assets in the business is determined in the same manner as was outlined in the preceding chapter, viz., his basis is the sum of the bases of the contributed assets plus the amount of any partnership liabilities assumed by the new partner, and less the amount of any personal liabilities of the new partner which is assumed by the existing partners.

Case 4. Assume the following data is given for the XY Partnership:

	Tax Basis	Book Value
Assets.	$50,000	$60,000
Liabilities.	18,000	18,000
Capital (interest) of partners:		
X.	30,000	25,000
Y.	20,000	17,000

Z is admitted to a one-fourth interest in the capital, profits, and losses of XY Parnership by contributing $14,000 (one fourth of the net tangible assets of the new firm), and he assumes a one-fourth responsibility for present partnership obligations.

Assuming X and Y have equal interests in profits and losses, the tax bases of the contributed assets and relevant capital adjustments are given as follows:

Basis of assets.	14,000	
Basis of X's interest.	2,250	
Basis of Y's interest.	2,250	
Basis of Z's interest.		18,500

The basis of Z's interest can be proved:

Basis of assets contributed.	$14,000
Partnership liabilities assumed (¼ × $18,000).	4,500
	$18,500

Although Z acquired a one-fourth interest in future profits and losses of the partnership, he also assumed responsibility for one fourth of the existing partnership liabilities. This is recognized in the reduction of X's and Y's tax bases by $2,250 each, the amount of partnership liabilities transferred to Z. Importantly, the sum of the asset tax bases, $64,000 ($50,000 + $14,000), is equal to the sum of the bases of the partners' capital interests in the firm, $64,000 ($27,750 + $17,750 + $18,500).

When a new partner purchases an interest *directly* from one or more of the existing partners, Section 742 of the Internal Revenue Code states that the basis of the new partner's interest in the firm is determined in a manner similar to Case 4. In essence, his basis is the price paid to acquire the interest, adjusted for liabilities which he assumes and/or liabilities which the other partners assume. Obviously, the tax basis of the new partner's interest can be different from the tax basis of the old partners' interests. This difference is subject to alternative tax treatments. The following case illustrates this point.

Case 5. Z purchases one half of Y's interest in the XY Partnership for $10,000 when the tax basis of Y's total interest is $16,000.

Manifestly the tax basis of the interest transferred to Z is $8,000; and subject to certain specified conditions, Y must recognize a capital gain on the sale. Based upon the provision that the tax basis of Z's interest is the cost of acquisition, or $10,000, an examination of the separate tax bases of Y and Z indicates the following:

Basis of Y's interest	8,000
Differential	2,000
Basis of Z's interest	10,000

If additional adjustments are not made, this differential measures the extent to which the sum of the partners' interests in the firm exceeds the sum of the bases of the assets. The differential will remain until either Z transfers his interest to some new partner (at which time it may simply be confirmed by that transaction and continue to exist) or until the partnership is liquidated. However, Section 754 of the Code provides that the partnership may *elect* to increase the bases of its assets by an amount equal to this excess payment (differential), as it is assumed that it measures and confirms an increase in the market value of partnership assets over their tax bases. If this election is made, the differential is allocated to the various partnership assets in relation to the relative increase in fair market value over the tax basis of each asset category.[2] Importantly, however, the adjustment of the assets' bases only affects the subsequent tax position of the new partner Z. If the assets are subsequently sold, the taxable gain is then allocated to the partners, with the increased basis of $2,000 in the partnership assets being applied to reduce Z's portion of the gain. In other words, the taxable gain allocated to Z at the time of sale will be *less* than if the adjustment had not been made.

RETIREMENT OF A PARTNER

If one of the partners desires to withdraw from the partnership and he is not in violation of the agreement between the partners (Section 31),[3] two sections of the Uniform Partnership Act are relevant. As noted previously, Section 27 permits a partner to convey his interest in the partnership either to the existing partners or to a third party. If sold to a third party, the assignee is admitted to the partnership and is accorded the status of partner, *only* with the consent of the continuing partners; if they should disapprove, the assignee is entitled to receive the profits which would have accrued to the assignor; he is not otherwise entitled to management privileges.

If there is no express agreement in respect to settlement of accounts with a retiring partner, Section 42 provides that the retiring partner is entitled to have the value of his equity at the date of retirement ascertained, and to

---

[2] If goodwill is revealed by this transaction, the allocation must include this partnership asset.

[3] If the withdrawal and the resulting partnership dissolution is in contravention of the articles of copartnership, the retiring partner is liable for damages suffered by the innocent partners (Section 38).

receive, as an ordinary creditor, an amount equal to this value plus an interest credit on this amount. However, at his option, he may retain a passive interest in the firm and receive, in lieu of interest, the "profits attributable to the use of his right in the property of the dissolved partnership." Determining the value of a retiring partner's equity is often a basic issue in the settlement arrangement. The accounting problems of reclassifying the retiring partner's capital equity as a liability and the treatment of any assigned value increment in excess of recorded capital will be considered in the following discussion.

Sale of an Interest to a New Partner

The sale of a retiring partner's interest to a new partner introduces no special problems other than those which relate to a conveyance of a partial interest. The admission of the new partner is recorded merely by transferring the recorded capital interest of the retiring partner to the new partner; however, the conditions of admission may indicate the presence of partnership goodwill. If goodwill is to be formally recognized in the accounts, the recorded amount is normally the *total* amount of goodwill attaching to the partnership entity, not merely the amount which relates to the retiring partner. However, in the event goodwill previously existed in the partnership books and is reduced as a consequence of the retirement of a partner, i.e., the goodwill attaches primarily to the retiring partner as a separate individual, the purchase transaction may indicate the amount of "lost" goodwill.

Sale of an Interest to Continuing Partners

If the continuing partners acquire the interest of a retiring partner, whether negotiating jointly or separately *outside* the partnership or jointly *within* and *through* the partnership entity, the essence of the accounting problem remains substantially unchanged. If the purchase is completed independently of the partnership, the transaction is analogous to the sale of an interest to a third party; if the retiring partner sells his interest to the partnership entity, the substance of the transaction is unchanged but the partnership assumes the obligation to make payment to the retiring partner —essentially a liquidating distribution. As before, partnership goodwill may be inferred if the purchase price (or the computed amount of a liquidating settlement) exceeds the recorded capital of the retiring partner. In this case, however, the evaluation of goodwill is subject to greater question, as the parties to the transaction are not mutually independent. The accountant, therefore, should be especially circumspect in recording partnership goodwill in this instance. The following case illustrates the sale of interest of a retiring partner to the partnership.

Case 6. Z elects to retire from the XYZ Partnership, and the remaining partners agree to purchase his interest for and through the partnership. The partners share profits and losses equally. On this date, the balance sheet of the partnership is as follows:

XYZ PARTNERSHIP

Balance Sheet
Date of Proposed Retirement

ASSETS		EQUITIES	
Assets....................	$110,000	Liabilities.................	$ 10,000
		X, capital..................	30,000
		Y, capital..................	30,000
		Z, capital..................	40,000
	$110,000		$110,000

An examination of the values of existing assets and an estimate of prospective earnings for future years indicate that Z's interest is worth considerably more than his recorded capital credit. It is determined that the current market value of the partnership assets is $140,000. After negotiation with Z and in consideration of the demonstrated excess earnings potential of the partnership, it is agreed that Z shall receive $60,000 for his capital interest, payment to be made in four annual installments, with interest of 4 percent accruing annually on the unpaid balance.

As a consequence of Z's retirement, the partnership is legally dissolved; the first accounting objective, therefore, is to determine and record the status of the retiring partner and to establish a proper basis of accounting for the partnership as a continuing entity. From this point of view, it is appropriate to adjust the assets to their current market values. Accordingly, the entry to record the value adjustments is as follows (assuming profits and losses are shared equally):

Assets......	30,000	
X, capital.......		10,000
Y, capital.......		10,000
Z, capital.......		10,000

The entry to adjust the equity of the retiring partner in the continuing partnership may be made in either of two ways. Using a method similar to the bonus method previously discussed, the entry may take the following form:

Method 1:

Z, capital......	50,000	
X, capital......		5,000
Y, capital......		5,000
Notes payable to Z......		60,000

Since Z received $10,000 more than his recorded capital interest after adjustments were made for asset revaluations, there is evidence that the partnership has unrecorded goodwill. Should the partners elect to recognize a value for goodwill, it may be recorded in the following manner:

Method 2:

Z, capital...	50,000	
Goodwill...	10,000	
Notes payable to Z.................................		60,000

The entry is based upon the long-established accounting precept that only *purchased* goodwill should be expressed quantitatively in the accounts.

However, the reader will recognize that this precept, even if valid or useful, is inappropriate when applied in this instance. There has been no purchase of goodwill. The goodwill, if it exists, is an asset of the partnership, a measurement of which has been established independently of the settlement with the retiring partner. Clearly, the partnership did not acquire its own goodwill, nor did it transfer a portion of it to the retiring partner. If the goodwill identifies with Z, no payment would be made therefor, as its value to the partnership would necessarily dissipate with the withdrawal of the retiring partner. Rather, the transaction merely offers evidence, however cogent, as to the existence and amount of partnership goodwill. If the accountant is persuaded that the $10,000 excess payment does, in fact, represent a valid measure of a one-third interest in the unrecorded goodwill—giving due attention to the imponderables of such a calculation—then either the total amount of goodwill ($30,000) should be recorded, or none should be recorded with the bonus method used to record the retirement. It appears inconsistent to recognize the existence of intangibles and then to record but a fraction of their value. If the total amount of goodwill is to be recorded, the following entries should be made:

Method 2 (as modified):

Goodwill..	30,000	
X, capital...		10,000
Y, capital...		10,000
Z, capital...		10,000
Z, capital...	60,000	
Notes payable to Z................................		60,000

These two methods may be analyzed as before for equivalence in respect to their effects on the partners' equities. Regardless of the method employed, the interest on the unpaid liability to the retiring partner remains an expense in determining the periodic net income of the partnership.

DEATH OF A PARTNER

Partnership Agreement

The death of a partner dissolves a partnership under provisions of the Uniform Partnership Act (Section 31). However, modifications of the Act adopted by a number of states permit the partners to prevent dissolution by including a contrary provision in the partnership agreement. For tax and other reasons, a provision of this type may be desirable.

It is important that the partnership agreement specify the procedures to be followed upon the death of a partner whether or not legal dissolution is a consequence of the death. Whether the surviving partners acting separately or the partnership entity purchases the interest of the deceased partner, a determination of the value of this equity at the date of death is an important first consideration. Where the partnership continues as an operating entity under the control of the surviving partners, the agreement may provide that payments for this interest be based upon recorded partnership values, or that a revaluation of assets be made and the adjusted capital interests be based thereon.[4] Where the agreement is silent in respect to payments made for a deceased partner's interest, the amount of settlement is the result of negotiations between the estate of the deceased partner and the surviving partners. The estate is accorded the same status under Section 42 as a retiring partner, viz., the option to receive either interest on an unliquidated capital balance, or profits attributable to the use of this equity.

Once the capital interest of the deceased partner is determined, the remaining partners must agree upon an acceptable means of settlement. Life insurance coverage in respect to individual partners is one commonly employed method of meeting this contingency. Two types of life insurance are often used: (1) cross-insurance and (2) entity insurance. If cross-insurance is utilized, the lives of individual partners are insured by the other partners independently of the partnership. Where this type of coverage exists, the partnership does not incur an expense. If entity insurance is used, the partnership insures the lives of each of the partners, and although nondeductible for income tax purposes, the premium payments represent proper expense charges in determining periodic partnership net income.

If insurance is evaluated as a low-return investment as compared to alternative types of investment and accordingly is rejected as the vehicle to provide a means of settlement, the partners must decide whether to make a liquidating payment in cash or to make distributions of assets in kind. If the partnership is to be terminated, it is probable that distribution will be made in specific assets, although it is unlikely that the assets will be those originally contributed. However, if it is anticipated that partnership operations will continue, a method of installment payments, with interest, is a common method of discharging the obligation to the estate of the deceased partner.

---

[4] Again, the problem of determining the amount of goodwill to be recognized may arise. The argument for recording only the "purchased" goodwill is subject to the same limitation as in the case of a retiring partner.

LEGAL AND TAX STATUS OF A RETIRING OR DECEASED PARTNER

Legal Status

The fact of partnership dissolution does not of itself result in the discharge of individual partners from unpaid partnership debts. However, Section 36 provides that "a partner is discharged from any existing liability upon dissolution of the partnership by an agreement to that effect between himself, the partnership creditors and the person or partnership continuing the business." Assuming proper notice is given past and prospective creditors, the retiring or deceased partner is, at most, liable for only those obligations existing at the date of dissolution.

Tax Basis

If a retiring partner or the estate of a deceased partner *sells* his interest to an individual, capital gain or loss is usually recognized in the amount of the difference between the proceeds of sale and the tax basis of the converted interest in the partnership. This favorable tax treatment is not extended, however, to payments which are received by the retiring partner directly from the partnership for other than his interest in partnership property. If a payment is interpreted as consideration for other than this interest, it is treated either as a distributive share of net income or as a guaranteed payment (salary); both of these types of payment are accordingly taxable as ordinary income.[5]

If the retiring partner receives property in the form of a liquidating distribution, generally gain or loss is not recognized at the time of distribution, except to the extent of cash distributions which are in excess of the tax basis of the partner's interest in the partnership. In such a calculation, the retiring partner's share of partnership liabilities which are assumed by the remaining partners are equivalent to the receipt of a cash distribution. Upon receipt of the distributed assets, the partner, or his estate, must deduct the amount of cash distributed from his basis, and then allocate his remaining basis to the individual noncash assets in the ratio of their relative tax bases to the partnership.

Case 7. In the following example, which ignores the special provisions applicable to unrealized receivables and substantially appreciated inventory items, the balance sheet of the XYZ Partnership at the date of Z's death is:

---

[5] Unless a "reasonable" payment for goodwill was previously specified in the partnership agreement, such a payment is also taxable as ordinary income.

XYZ PARTNERSHIP

Balance Sheet
Deceased Partner's Date of Death

ASSETS	Tax Basis	Market Value	EQUITIES	Tax Basis	Market Value
Cash..........	$20,000	$20,000	Liabilities.......	$15,000	$15,000
Receivables.....	15,000	15,000	Capital:		
Inventory.......	20,000	20,000	X..........	$20,000	17,500
Land..........	10,000	22,000	Y..........	20,000	17,500
Other assets.....	5,000	8,000	Z..........	30,000	35,000
	$70,000	$85,000		$70,000	$85,000

It is agreed that Z's estate shall receive $5,000 cash, the "other assets," and the land in exchange for his partnership interest. The partnership agrees to assume Z's share of partnership liabilities. Additionally, the estate is to receive 5 percent of partnership net income for the next five years.

The adjusted basis of Z's estate is computed as follows:

Unadjusted partnership basis of Z..........		$30,000
Deduct:		
Distribution of cash....................	$5,000	
Assumption of liabilities...............	5,000	10,000
Adjusted basis to the estate...............		$20,000

The unadjusted basis includes Z's share of partnership liabilities; the adjustments include the distribution of $5,000 cash and the assumption by the partnership of Z's share of liabilities—$5,000. Since the "cash" distributed ($10,000) does not exceed Z's unadjusted basis, gain or loss is not recognized on the distribution of assets in consideration for Z's interest. However, his adjusted basis must now be allocated to the land and other assets in the ratio of the relative tax bases of these assets to the partnership:

	Basis to Partnership	Ratio	Basis to Estate
Land........................	$10,000	2/3	$13,333
Other assets.................	5,000	1/3	6,667
	$15,000		$20,000

Thus, Z's adjusted basis in the partnership transfers to the distributed property, and capital gain or loss will be recognized when these assets are sold. The annual payments of partnership net income to the estate will be taxed as ordinary income during the next five years as this payment is a distributive share of net income rather than payment for the deceased partner's current interest in partnership property.

This illustration is also relevant in principle to a retiring partner. Additionally, the procedures here described for a liquidating distribution to one partner may be extended to a liquidating distribution to all partners at the time the partnership is dissolved. However, it must be recognized that many subtle options and exceptions have not been considered in favor of exposing only the basic tax implications involved in the distribution of assets.

NOTE

The validity of the rule for determining new capital of a partnership following an expansion in the ownership structure (pages 76 and 77) is confirmed as follows:

Let A = capital of old partners before investment,
B = tangible assets invested by new partner,
α = percent interest in capital retained by the old partners,
β = percent interest in capital acquired by the new partner,
G = goodwill implicit in the transaction,
C = total capital, including goodwill, after the investment,
D = capital of old partners after the investment, and
E = capital of the new partner after the investment.

By definition, the following equations are valid:

$$C = A + B + G,$$
$$C = D + E,$$
$$G > 0 \text{ (the assumption is that goodwill exists)}.$$

Case 1. Goodwill Identified with Existing Partners. This requires that $C = B \div \beta > A \div \alpha$. It is assumed that the old partners possess a yet undetermined amount of goodwill and the following equations are valid:

$$D = A + G = \alpha C,$$
$$E = B = \beta C.$$

Therefore,

$$C = B \div \beta = (A + G) \div \alpha.$$

Since $G > 0$,

$$B \div \beta > A \div \alpha.$$

Case 2. Goodwill Identified with New Partner. This requires that $C = A \div \alpha > B \div \beta$. Again, by the assumptions stated, the following equations are appropriate:

$$D = A = \alpha C,$$
$$E = B + G = \beta C.$$

Therefore,

$$C = A \div \alpha = (B + G) \div \beta.$$

Since $G > 0$,

$$A \div \alpha > B \div \beta .$$

From the above calculations, it is obvious that *if* goodwill does not exist $(G = 0)$,

$$C = A \div \alpha = B \div \beta ,$$

and the amounts of capital computed under each of the alternatives specified by the rule described on pages 76 and 77 are equal.

QUESTIONS

1. What circumstances or conditions effect a legal dissolution of a partnership?

2. Discuss three alternative explanations and related accounting treatments of the following situation. A new partner is admitted to a partnership on the basis of contributing additional assets. Further, the new partner's agreed upon interest in the previously recorded equity of the partnership plus the tangible assets he contributed is smaller than the value of the assets he contributed.

3. What is the usual accounting procedure for calculating the value of unrecorded intangibles ("goodwill") implied in the transactions surrounding the admission of a new partner?

4. What two conditions are necessary for the bonus method and goodwill method to have equivalent effects on the relative balances in the capital accounts?

5. If a partner sells part of his interest in the partnership to another individual, is the purchase price reflected on the books of the partnership? Why or why not?

6. What special problems may arise when a new partner acquires a partnership interest directly from one or more partners?

7. If goodwill is to be recognized at the time of a partner's retirement, should the partnership recognize the entire amount of goodwill or merely that portion of the intangible associated with the retiring partner? Explain.

8. In the event of a partner's death, is there concurrent dissolution of the partnership or may the enterprise continue in existence?

9. What is the general method for determining the tax basis of a new partner's interest in a partnership?

10. Enumerate several important factors which the accountant should consider in evaluating the appropriateness of recognizing implied goodwill upon the retirement and/or withdrawal of a partner from a partnership.

PROBLEMS

Problem 3–1

Journalize the admission of Skadden to the Zimmerman-Wyatt partnership in each of the following independent cases. The capital balances of Zimmerman and Wyatt are $12,000 and $8,000 respectively; they share profits and losses equally.

a) Skadden is admitted to a one-third interest in capital with a contribution of $10,000.
b) Skadden is admitted to a one-fourth interest in capital with a contribution of $8,000. Total capital of the new partnership is to be $28,000.
c) Skadden is admitted to a one-fifth interest in capital upon contributing $4,000. Total capital of the new partnership is to be $25,000.
d) Skadden is admitted to a one-fourth interest in capital by the purchase of one fourth of the interests of Zimmerman and Wyatt for $5,500. Total capital of the new partnership is to be $20,000.
e) Same conditions as in (d), except that the new partnership capital is to be $22,000.
f) Skadden is admitted to a one-third interest in capital upon contributing $7,000, after which each partner is to have an equal capital equity in the new partnership.
g) Skadden is admitted to a one-fifth interest in capital upon contributing $6,000. Total capital of the new partnership is to be $30,000.

Problem 3–2

Amstead and Bruegman are partners. They share profits equally and have equal investments. The partnership's net assets are carried on the books at $20,000. Geis is admitted to the partnership with a one-third interest in profits and net assets. Geis pays $9,000 cash into the partnership for his interest.

Prepare journal entries to show three possible methods of recording on the partnership books the admission of Geis. State the conditions under which each method would be appropriate.

(AICPA adapted)

Problem 3–3

Spaulding and Patterson are partners in the SP Company sharing profits and losses 60:40 respectively. Their capital account balances are: Spaulding, $21,000; and Patterson, $15,000. Journalize the admission of Coffin to the partnership under the following independent conditions:

a) Coffin invests $13,000 for a one-fourth interest in partnership capital. Goodwill implicit in the investment is to be recorded.
b) Coffin invests $8,000 for a one-fifth interest in partnership capital. Total capital after the admission of Coffin is to be $44,000.
c) Coffin purchases one third of the interests of the existing partners, paying $7,500 to each partner. Goodwill implied by the purchase price is to be recorded.

Problem 3–4

John retired from the Dynamic Partnership on January 1, 1971. In accordance with the provisions of the partnership agreement, John was paid $45,000 from the partnership assets in satisfaction of his one-third interest. This amount was based on a formula that was specified in the original partnership agreement. It was determined by such factors as number of years of service to the partnership, capital contributed, and recent years' sales and earnings performance of the partnership. John's capital balance on January 1, 1971, was $30,000. Bud and Hank, the other partners, each have one-third interests and $30,000 capital balances. Assume that the tangible assets of the partnership are correctly valued.

Required:

(i)   Journalize John's retirement under each of the three alternative methods.

(ii) Discuss the relative merits of each method, noting the conditions under which each may draw the greatest support. As a part of your answer, state which method appears least appropriate under the circumstances.

Problem 3–5

Stum, Best, and Ross are partners in a construction company. Their profit-sharing ratio and capital balances at December 31, 1971, are as follows:

Partners	Profit-Sharing Ratio	Capital Balance
Stum.....................	60%	$97,000
Best.....................	30	65,000
Ross.....................	10	38,000

Frazier is admitted to the partnership on January 2, 1972, by investing $45,000 for a 20 percent interest in capital and profits.

Required:

(i)   Prepare journal entries for each of three alternative methods of recording the admission of the new partner.

(ii) Assume that Frazier purchased an interest in the partnership ratably from the existing partners. Prepare a schedule of cash transfers to Stum, Best, and Ross.

(iii) Under assumption (ii), prepare journal entries for each of two alternative methods of recording the admission of Frazier.

Problem 3–6

Dickason and Yeardon are partners in the Vermillion Company and have capital balances of $128,000 and $112,000 respectively on December 31, 1971. Profits and losses are shared 60:40. Jones is admitted to the partnership on January 2, 1972, by investing $100,000 for a one-fourth interest in capital and profits.

Required:

(i)   Prepare journal entries to record the admission of Jones under both the bonus and goodwill methods.

(ii) Assuming the goodwill method is used to record the admission of Jones *and* that subsequently the goodwill is written off, compare the effect of this treatment on the partners' capitals with that of the bonus method under the following three independent conditions (ignore the effects of other changes in capital):

	Percentage Interest in Profits		
	Dickason	Yeardon	Jones
Case 1...................... 45%		30%	25%
Case 2...................... 50		25	25
Case 3...................... 42		28	30

Problem 3–7

A, B, and C decide to practice law together as of January 1, 1971. They enter into an agreement under which they share profits and losses in the proportion of 50 percent, 25 percent, and 25 percent, respectively, and agree to contribute $50,000 in cash in these same proportions to provide working capital. They decide to keep their books on a cash basis.

On January 1, 1972, B died and the remaining partners agreed to admit D, giving him a 20 percent share in the profits with a minimum guarantee of $10,000 per year whether operations are profitable or not. A and C have percentages of 45 and 35 respectively. This partnership is of one year's duration, and at the end of this period C decides to retire but permits the use of his name in future partnerships subject to the payment to him of $5,000 per annum to be treated as an expense of the partnership.

As of January 1, 1973, a partnership is formed in which C's name is utilized in accordance with his proposal and to which E is admitted. The partners' interests in this partnership are as follows: A, 55 percent; D, 30 percent; E, 15 percent.

Since there were no substantial accruals at the end of the year, disbursements for expenses made during any one period were treated as expenses of the then current partnership. These disbursements were $70,000 in 1971, $80,000 in 1972, and $90,000 in 1973.

Receipts of fees were as follows:

	Earned by Partnership		
	No. 1	No. 2	No. 3
1971....................	$ 80,000		
1972....................	145,000	$40,000	
1973....................		50,000	$70,000

Each new partnership agreement provided for the newly created partnership to purchase from the old partnership the $50,000 capital originally paid in by A, B, and C. The agreements also provided that the partners should bear the cost of acquisition of this amount in the proportion which they shared profits (and losses). However, it was agreed that an incoming partner, or one acquiring an increased percentage, need not make his contribution in cash immediately but could have the same charged to his drawing account. All such partners availed themselves of this privilege. Partners selling all or a part of their interest in capital are credited through their drawing accounts and immediately withdraw the amount of such credit. In addition to drawings made under this agreement, the partners or their heirs made cash drawings as follows:

	A	B	C	D	E
1971.........	$10,500	$27,750	$13,750		
1972.........	40,000	4,750	5,000	$7,000	
1973.........	10,000	5,000	15,000	2,500	$5,000

Required:

Prepare schedules or statements showing the details of transactions in the partners' drawing accounts and capital accounts for each of the years involved. These accounts should be in such form that the balance at the end of each year which was available for withdrawal by each partner is shown in that partner's drawing account. The capital accounts are to reflect only the $50,000 original investment.

(AICPA adapted)

Problem 3–8

Abbott and Barnes, equal partners in the A & B Grocery Stores, sold a one-third interest in Store No. 3 to Costello, manager of that store, on January 1, 1972. The new partnership will operate as the A.B.C. Grocery Company. Abbott and Barnes will continue to operate other stores. The balance sheet of Store No. 3 at January 1, 1972, was as follows:

ASSETS			EQUITIES		
Merchandise............		$63,000	Accounts payable........		$20,000
Fixtures and equipment...	$22,000				
Allowance for deprecia-			Capital:		
tion...............	10,000	12,000			
Prepaid expenses........		3,900	Abbott..............	$30,000	
Utility deposits.........		1,100	Barnes..............	30,000	60,000
		$80,000			$80,000

Furniture and fixtures, which have an estimated remaining life of five years, were revalued at $18,000, according to the agreement of sale. Each partner contributed $1,000 as working capital, which was credited to his drawing account. The following transactions for the year 1972 were all in cash:

Sales..	$620,000
Merchandise purchases......................................	493,000
Salaries and wages (including salary of $9,000 to Costello, as manager)...	77,000
Expenses...	25,400
New equipment purchased 7/1/72 (estimated life—10 years).....	3,000

You are also given the following information:

Merchandise inventory, December 31, 1972.................... $60,000
Prepaid expenses, December 31, 1972........................   3,000

The check record was kept open until all 1972 bills were paid before closing the books as of December 31, 1972.

The partnership agreement provides for a salary of $750 monthly to Costello. All remaining profits are divided equally.

Partners' drawing accounts each show a net debit balance of $3,000.

	Abbott	Barnes
Income from A & B Grocery Stores (all ordinary income).......	$55,000	$55,000
Interest income..	4,000	3,000
Long-term capital gains [losses]—does not include anything from A.B.C. partnership transactions.....................	4,000	[3,000]
	$63,000	$55,000

Required:

(i)   Prepare a schedule showing the cash payment which Costello made to Abbott and Barnes.

(ii) Prepare an income statement of the A.B.C. Grocery Company for the year ended December 31, 1972, including a schedule showing the distribution of profit and loss to the partners.

(iii) Prepare a statement showing the total taxable income of Abbott and of Barnes before personal deductions. (Assume their original contributions were equal amounts of cash.)

(iv) Compute the tax basis of the partners' interests in the new partnership on December 31, 1972.

(AICPA adapted)

Problem 3–9

Smith and Company is a family partnership engaged in the wholesale trade. It closes its books at December 31. During the year, all transactions are recorded on a cash receipts and disbursements basis. However, at the end of the fiscal year, adjustment is made to what was termed the "inventory account" for all items necessary to reflect operations and financial position on an accrual basis.

Partner E died on October 31, 1971. His will left equal shares in his estate to partners A and C and an outsider, F. For purposes of this problem, assume no probate period and that E's estate was distributed immediately. All remaining partners, together with F, agreed that the business of Smith and Company would continue as a partnership of A, B, C, D, and F, with beginning interest on November 1, 1971, as computed on a proper accrual basis to October 31, and after distribution of E's interest on that date.

Depreciation of fixed assets may be ignored.

Balances as shown by the books of the firm were as follows:

	January 1, 1971	October 31, 1971
Cash......................	$ 42,000	$ 55,000
Inventory account...........	195,000	195,000
Fixed assets................	60,000	59,000
Accruals...................	29,000	16,000
Notes payable..............	100,000	60,000
Partners' equity.............	168,000	168,000
Sales......................	...	2,000,000
Purchases..................	...	1,725,000
Operating expenses..........	...	210,000

In addition to the above, the following information concerning the inventory account was available:

At January 1, 1971: accounts receivable, $80,000; merchandise, $200,000; freight claims (on incoming merchandise), $2,000; prepaid operating expenses, $10,000; accounts payable, $90,000; allowances due customers, $7,000. At October 31, 1971: accounts receivable, $83,300; merchandise, $221,000; freight claims (on incoming merchandise), $1,500; prepaid operating expenses, $6,000; accounts payable, $85,000; allowances due customers, $8,000.

Partners' equities and profit- and loss-sharing ratio:

	Equities	Profit and Loss Ratio
A.............................	$ 10,500	6.25%
B.............................	52,500	31.25
C.............................	77,000	37.50
D.............................	7,000	12.50
E.............................	21,000	12.50
	$168,000	100.00%

Required:

(i) Prepare an income statement for the period January 1 to October 31, 1971.

(ii) Prepare a statement of financial position on November 1, 1971.

(AICPA adapted)

Problem 3–10

The trial balance of AB, a partnership, on January 1, 1971 is shown on page 100.

Profits and losses were to be shared equally by A and B.

As of December 31, 1971, C purchased for $125,000 in cash from partners A and B a one-third interest in the partnership; each partner agreed to transfer one third of his individual capital account to C. Prior to C's admission, it was decided that a valuation reserve of $5,000 should be provided with respect to the investments; that an allowance for bad debts should be established in the amount of $10,000; and that the valuation of buildings and equipment should be reduced to $11,000. Profit sharing by C commenced on January 1, 1972.

As of December 31, 1972, D was admitted to a one-fourth interest in the

	Debit	Credit
Cash.....	$ 70,000	
Accounts receivable.....	50,000	
Notes receivable.....	40,000	
Merchandise inventories.....	35,000	
Land.....	85,000	
Buildings and equipment—less allowance for depreciation......	15,000	
Investments—at cost.....	35,000	
Prepaid insurance.....	4,500	
Office supplies.....	3,000	
Bank loans.....		$ 45,000
Accounts payable.....		60,000
Accrued taxes.....		2,500
First-mortgage 7 percent long-term notes.....		55,000
Capital accounts:		
A.....		100,000
B.....		75,000
	$337,500	$337,500

partnership and contributed the following assets from a business previously operated by him as a sole proprietor:

Cash.....	$80,000
Accounts receivable.....	70,000
Investments.....	10,000

The following liabilities incurred by D in his previous business were assumed by the new partnership:

Accounts payable.....	$20,000
Bank loans.....	30,000

As an inducement to merge his enterprise with the ABC partnership, D was allowed goodwill of $25,000. Profits were to be shared equally by A, B, C, and D in the new firm, commencing January 1, 1973.

Additional data to be used in the solution of this problem are as follows:

	Year Ended December 31	
	1971	1972
Profit of the firm.....	$19,000	$27,000
Drawings:		
A.....	10,000	7,500
B.....	7,000	6,000
C.....	—	14,000

For the purposes of simplicity, it is assumed that profits for each year were realized in cash and that the balance sheet of the firm on January 1, 1971, did not change during the two-year period, except as indicated in the terms of this problem.

Required:

(i) Prepare an interim work sheet for the two-year period from January 1, 1971, through December 31, 1972.

(ii) Prepare journal entries to record the admission of C and D, assuming goodwill is implicitly determined.

(AICPA adapted)

Problem 3–11

P and R have been operating a business for several years as partners, during which time they have divided profits equally. They need additional capital to expand their business and have agreed to admit B to the partnership as of January 1, 1971, with a one-third interest in profits and in the capital; B is to pay cash into the business as additional capital in an amount equal to one half of the combined capital of the present two partners, redetermined as follows:

The average partnership profits, after partners' salaries, for the past two years are to be capitalized at the rate of 10 percent per annum, which will redetermine the aggregate capital of the two present partners. Before such capitalization of profits, the accounts are to be adjusted for errors and omissions.

The business has not followed a strict accrual basis of accounting. As a result the following items have been omitted from the books:

Item	Balance 12/31/68	Balance 12/31/69	Balance 12/31/70
Accrued expenses...................	$3,201	$2,472	$4,360
Prepaid expenses..................	1,010	1,226	872
Accrued income...................	—	250	475

In addition, no provision has been made for loss on uncollectible accounts. It is agreed that a provision of $4,500 is needed as of December 31, 1970, of which $600 is for 1969 accounts. Charge-offs have been made to expense in 1968 of 1967 and prior accounts—$1,200; in 1969 of 1968 accounts—$3,100, and of 1969 accounts—$400; in 1970 of 1969 accounts—$2,280, and of 1970 accounts—$525.

The inventory at December 31, 1970, contains some obsolete goods carried at cost of $4,300. A 20 percent write-down is to be made to reduce these items to their present value.

In 1969 and 1970, salaries of $3,000 for each partner were taken out of the business and charged to expense before determining profits. It has been agreed that the salaries should have been $4,000 each.

The following financial data are available:

Balance Sheet
December 31, 1970

ASSETS		EQUITIES	
Cash......................	$ 7,000	Accounts payable...........	$ 43,200
Accounts receivable..........	42,500	Notes payable..............	25,000
Notes receivable.............	6,000	Accumulated depreciation—	
Merchandise................	64,000	fixtures...................	5,300
Store fixtures...............	12,400	P, capital...................	22,000
		R, capital..................	36,400
	$131,900		$131,900

	1968	1969	1970
Profit per books...................	$ 8,364	$ 8,585	$10,497
P, capital........................	20,000	24,000	22,000
R, capital.......................	25,000	33,000	36,400

Required:

Show the computation of the amount that B will pay into the partnership, and prepare a balance sheet as it would appear after adjustment for errors and omissions and after redetermination of capital accounts and receipt of B's capital contribution as of January 1, 1971.

(AICPA adapted)

Problem 3–12

Following is the balance sheet of the Martin, Thomas, and Martin partnership as of December 31, 1970:

	Tax Basis	Market Value
Cash................................	$50,000	$ 50,000
Receivables.........................	10,000	10,000
Inventory...........................	5,000	5,000
Land................................	5,000	10,000
Building............................	15,000	20,000
Other assets........................	10,000	15,000
	$95,000	$110,000
Liabilities..........................	$12,000	$ 12,000
Capital:		
Martin, Senior......................	41,000	50,000
Thomas............................	22,000	25,000
Martin, Junior......................	20,000	23,000
	$95,000	$110,000

Martin, Senior wishes to retire from the partnership. Accordingly, it is agreed that he may receive a liquidating distribution consisting of: cash, $5,000; other assets; and the land and building (remaining service life, 10 years), which he will make available to Thomas and Martin, Junior at an annual rental of 5 percent of future annual gross revenues. It is further agreed that the new Thomas and Martin partnership will assume Martin, Senior's share of partnership liabilities on December 31, 1970.

For the year ended December 31, 1971, the following information is made available:

a)   Gross revenue of the Thomas and Martin partnership, $200,000.
b)   Net proceeds from sale of "other assets" by Martin, Senior, $16,000.
c)   Expenses incurred by Martin, Senior in respect to the maintenance of the building, $2,000.

Required:

(i)   Determine the gain or loss to be recognized by Martin, Senior on the liquidating distribution and his tax basis for the noncash assets received.
(ii)   Calculate the taxable income to be reported by Martin, Senior from his 1971 transactions.

Problem 3–13

The partnership agreement of Jones, McDill, Gilrey, Carter, and Adams contained a buy and sell agreement, among numerous other provisions, which would become operative in case of the death of any partner. Some provisions contained in the buy and sell agreement were as follows:

ARTICLE V. *Buy and Sell Agreement*

1. Purposes of the Buy and Sell Agreement.

(*a*) The partners mutually desire that the business shall be continued by the survivors without interruption or liquidation upon the death of one of the partners.

(*b*) The partners also mutually desire that the deceased partner's estate shall receive the full value of the deceased partner's interest in the partnership and that the estate shall share in the earnings of the partnership until the deceased partner's interest shall be fully purchased by the surviving partners.

2. Purchase and Sale of Deceased Partner's Interest.

(*a*) Upon the death of the partner first to die, the partnership shall continue to operate without dissolution.

(*b*) Upon the decedents' death, the survivors shall purchase and the executor or administrator of the deceased partner's estate shall sell to the surviving partners the deceased partner's interest in the partnership for the price and upon the terms and conditions hereinafter set forth.

(*c*) The deceased partner's estate shall retain the deceased partner's interest until the amount specified in the next paragraph shall be paid in full by the surviving partners.

(*d*) The parties agree that the purchase price for the partnership interest shall be an amount equal to the deceased partner's capital account at the date of death. Said amount shall be paid to the legal representative of decedent as follows:

(i) The first installment of 30 percent of said capital account shall be paid within 60 days from the date of death of the partner or within 30 days from the date on which the personal representative of decedent becomes qualified by law, whichever date is later, and

(ii) The balance shall be due in four equal installments which shall be due and payable annually on the anniversary date of said death.

3. Deceased Partner's Estate's Share of the Earnings.

(*a*) The partners mutually desire that the deceased partner's estate shall be guaranteed a share in the earnings of the partnership over the period said estate retains an interest in the partnership. Said estate shall not be deemed to have an interest in the partnership after the final installment for the deceased partner's capital account is paid even though a portion of the guaranteed payments specified below may be unpaid and may be due and owing.

(*b*) The deceased partner's estate's guaranteed share of the earnings of the partnership shall be determined from two items and shall be paid at different times as follows:

(i) First, interest shall be paid on the unpaid balance of the deceased partner's capital account at the same date the installment on the purchase price is paid. The amount to be paid shall be an amount equal to accrued interest at the rate of 6 percent per annum on the unpaid balance of the purchase price for the deceased partner's capital account.

(ii) Second, the parties agree that the balance of the guaranteed payment from the partnership earnings shall be an amount equal to 25 percent of the deceased partner's share of the aggregate gross receipts of the partnership for the full 36 months preceding the month of the partner's death. Said amount shall be payable in 48 equal monthly installments without interest, and the first payment shall be made within 60 days following the death of the partner or within 30 days from the date on which the personal representative of deceased becomes qualified, whichever date is later; provided, however, that the payments so made under this provision during any 12-month period shall not exceed the highest annual salary on a calendar-year basis received by the partner for the three calendar years immediately preceding the date of his death. In the event that said payment would exceed said salary, then an amount per month shall be paid which does not so exceed said highest monthly salary, and the term over which payments shall be paid to the beneficiary shall be lengthened out beyond the said 48 months in order to complete said payments.

Jones and Adams were both killed simultaneously in an automobile accident on January 10, 1971. The surviving partners notified the executors of both estates that the first payment due under the buy and sell agreement would be paid on March 10, 1971, and that subsequent payments would be paid on the 10th day of each month as due.

The following information was determined from the partnership's records:

Partner	Profit- and Loss-Sharing Ratio	Capital Account on January 10, 1971	Annual Salaries to Partners by Years		
			1968	1969	1970
Jones...........	30	$25,140	$16,500	$17,000	$17,400
McDill..........	25	21,970	15,000	15,750	16,500
Gilrey..........	20	4,780	12,000	13,000	14,000
Carter..........	15	5,860	9,600	10,800	12,000
Adams..........	10	2,540	8,400	9,600	10,800

The partnership's gross receipts for the three prior years were:

1968.....................	$296,470
1969.....................	325,310
1970.....................	363,220

Required:

Prepare a schedule of the amounts to be paid to the Jones Estate and to the Adams Estate in March, 1971; December, 1971; and January, 1972. The schedule should identify the amounts attributable to earnings and to interest in the guaranteed payments and to capital. Supporting computation should be in good form.

(AICPA adapted)

Chapter 4

Partnership Dissolution and Liquidation

INTRODUCTION

The Liquidation Process

The nature of partnership dissolution, viz., "the change in the relation of the partners caused by any partner ceasing to be associated in the carrying on as distinguished from the winding up of the business" (Section 29), was discussed in the previous chapter where attention focused on the continuity of partnership operations. In this chapter, emphasis will be directed toward those accounting problems and procedures involved in the winding up (liquidation) of partnership affairs—that interval of time between legal *dissolution* and effective *termination* of partnership operations.

Accounting Problems in Partnership Liquidation

The basic objectives of the partnership during the liquidation process are to convert the firm's assets to cash with minimum loss in value (*realization of assets*), to discharge valid partnership liabilities, and to distribute cash and any unrealized assets to the individual partners in an equitable manner. The primary objective underlying the accounting function during the liquidation process is to provide information adequate for an equitable disbursement of the partnership assets to creditors and partners, in compliance with the law. The accounting focus is therefore shifted from the measurement of periodic income to the determination of realization gains and losses, the allocation of these gains and losses among the partners, the payment of partnership creditors, and the planning and recording of asset distributions to partners. Careful attention must be given to relevant provisions of the Uniform Partnership Act, the partnership agreement, and in some instances, state and federal insolvency (bankruptcy) statutes. It is especially important that the accounting process be guided primarily by legal rights and obligations.

Basic Dichotomy—Partnership Solvency and Insolvency

Since the liquidation of solvent and insolvent partnerships introduces essentially different problems, each condition will be separately considered.

105

For purposes of the following discussion, a partnership is regarded as insolvent when its recorded assets are of insufficient amount to discharge existing partnership liabilities, i.e., an entity approach to the condition of insolvency. From a purely legal point of view, however, partnership insolvency is defined in terms of the underlying aggregative concept: "The new settled view is that a partnership is insolvent only when the surplus of *individual* assets over *non-partnership debts* is insufficient, together with partnership assets to pay partnership obligations."[1] This more restrictive definition of partnership insolvency need not stultify the value of the entity definition which is used in subsequent discussion. The aggregative (or legal) notion of partnership insolvency will be illustrated as a special condition of entity insolvency, viz., that circumstance where the separate net assets of individual partners are inadequate to discharge the partnership obligations not paid with partnership assets.

In the process of liquidating a partnership which is solvent by the entity definition, two alternative ways of proceeding with the liquidation may be identified. First, under the "simple liquidation" process, all of the partnership assets are realized or converted *before* any distributions are made to the partners. In this case, the accounting treatment is relatively simple. Since the amount of the total liquidation gain or loss is known before asset distributions to partners, the accountant needs only to indicate a distribution of assets which complies with the order of priority established by existing statutes.

Second, under the "installment payments" approach to liquidation, the partners elect to receive liquidating payments in a series of installments *prior* to the point in time at which partnership assets are completely realized or converted. In this case, the accountant must develop a plan of settlement which will produce the same ultimate distribution as if payments had been deferred until all of the noncash assets were converted.

Following an examination of simple liquidations, the accounting problems associated with installment payments will be analyzed; separate consideration will be given to situations in which there exists one insolvent partner, so long as all are not insolvent. In the final section of this chapter, the accounting problems associated with insolvent partnerships will be analyzed. The rights of both partnership creditors and individual creditors will be examined with reference to provisions of the Uniform Partnership Act, the Federal Bankruptcy Act, and selected decisions of the common law.

SIMPLE LIQUIDATION

Basic Distributive Rights

If all of the partnership assets are converted into cash before any distribution is made to creditors or to individual partners, a condition of

---

[1] Reed Rowley, *Rowley on Partnership* (New York: The Bobbs-Merrill Co., Inc., 1960), Vol. II, p. 85 (emphasis supplied).

simple liquidation exists. In this circumstance, the distribution of assets will be made in the order of priority established in the Uniform Partnership Act where that Act is operative. Section 40 (B) of the Act provides:

The liabilities of the partnership shall rank in order of payment, as follows:
(I)   Those owing to creditors other than partners,
(II)   Those owing to partners other than for capital and profits,
(III)   Those owing to partners in respect of capital,
(IV)   Those owing to partners in respect of profits.

Since the conversion of all noncash assets precedes the distribution of cash to the partners, the total amount of gain or loss on realization is known at the time of distribution. Unless a specific liquidation gain and loss ratio is indicated in the partnership agreement, the gain or loss should be allocated to the partners in the current profit and loss residual ratio, i.e., salary and interest factors are disregarded. This basis for distribution appears equitable, as realization gains or losses frequently reflect, in large part, adjustments of prior years' reported profits, which were distributed on this basis. Additionally, gains or losses which can be attributed to the *fact* of liquidation are in essence components of the overall profitability of the business, and thus should relate to individual partners in the same ratio as normal periodic earnings and losses of the partnership. The position taken by some accountants that liquidation losses are capital losses, and thus distributable in the relative ratios of the partners' capital balances, would appear to have no greater validity in the period of liquidation than during the period of normal operations.

Where current profits are transferred in the closing entry sequence to the partners' capital accounts, priorities (III) and (IV) of Section 40 (B) coalesce. In any event, however, the distinction between capital and profits is of no practical consequence, unless a "deficit" in the profits account is not absorbed by, or offset against, capital balances before distribution of cash to individual partners. Since an "equitable" settlement is the controlling consideration in most partnership law, the existence of a nonabsorbed deficit condition seems unlikely, unless expressly anticipated and provided for in the partnership agreement. Consequently, elements (III) and (IV) will hereafter be considered as one priority status.

The basic rights of creditors and partners in a simple liquidation are illustrated in the paragraphs which follow.

Case 1. The balance sheet of the XYZ Company at the date of dissolution is as follows:

ASSETS		EQUITIES	
Cash....................	$10,000	Liabilities............	$12,000
Noncash assets...........	80,000	Capital:	
		X.................	31,000
		Y.................	20,000
		Z.................	27,000
	$90,000		$90,000

During liquidation, $50,000 is realized from the conversion of the noncash assets. The partners share profits and losses in the ratio 5:3:2.

Given these data, a *partnership liquidation schedule* may be prepared as in Illustration 4–1.

Illustration 4–1

XYZ COMPANY

Schedule of Partnership Liquidation

Dr. [Cr.]

	Assets		Claimants			
					Residual Equities	
	Cash	Noncash	Priority Claims	X	Y	Z
Profit and loss ratio...				50%	30%	20%
Preliquidation balances..........	$ 10,000	$ 80,000	$[12,000]	$[31,000]	$[20,000]	$[27,000]
Realization of assets and allocation of loss............	50,000	[80,000]		15,000	9,000	6,000
Predistribution balances..........	$ 60,000	$ -0-	$[12,000]	$[16,000]	$[11,000]	$[21,000]
Cash distribution: Priority claims......	[12,000]		12,000			
Partners' residual equities.........	[48,000]			16,000	11,000	21,000
Termination of partnership........	$ -0-	$ -0-	$ -0-	$ -0-	$ -0-	$ -0-

The schedule of partnership liquidation is the primary historical statement which reflects partnership transactions during the period of liquidation. The schedule indicates the condition of the partnership at the date of dissolution (preliquidation balances), losses sustained in the conversion of noncash assets, the allocation of losses to the partners in their profit and loss ratio, and the distribution of cash in the order of payment specified in Section 40 (B). The same schedular format may be expanded to include other significant events during the liquidation process.

Partners' Debit Balances

In the previous illustration, each of the partners had a sufficiently large credit balance in his capital account to absorb his proportionate share of the realization loss. However, such a favorable circumstance does not always exist. Frequently, an individual partner's share of the realization loss will exceed his capital credit, producing a *debit balance* in his capital account. This capital deficiency creates a valid claim of the partnership against the partner; Section 18 (A) specifies that "each partner . . . must contribute toward the losses, whether of capital or otherwise, sustained by the partnership according to his share in the profits." Additionally, Section

40 (D) provides that "the partners shall contribute, as provided by Section 18 (A), the amount necessary to satisfy the liabilities; but if any, but not all, of the partners are insolvent, or, not being subject to process, refuse to contribute, the other partners shall contribute their share of the liabilities, and, in the relative proportions in which they share the profits, the additional amount necessary to pay the liabilities." Since Section 40 relates to the sequence of distribution of partnership assets in settlement of partnership liabilities, it is important that the term "liability" in this particular usage be fully understood. This section of the Act contemplates that liabilities may be generated either by accumulated losses from operations, realization losses, or the *loss* incurred when a partner with a debit balance in his capital account fails to contribute personal assets sufficient in amount to remove this deficit. In fact, Section 40 (A) defines the assets of a partnership to include contributions due from the partners for this cause;[2] consequently, a partner's failure to contribute to the extent of his capital deficiency is equivalent essentially to a realization loss for the remaining partners. Thus, if an amount equal to a debit balance is not collected from the delinquent partner, it is allocated in total to the remaining partners as if it were a realization loss; the allocation is made in the ratio of the remaining partners' original shares of profits and losses. For example, assume X, Y, and Z share profits and losses in the ratio 5:3:2. If Y should fail to contribute to the partnership the amount of a debit balance in his capital account, X and Z will share this loss (a capital deficiency) in the ratio 5:2, i.e., 5/7 to X and 2/7 to Z; if X should fail to contribute for a pre-existent capital deficiency, Y and Z would share this loss in the ratio 3:2, i.e., 3/5 to Y and 2/5 to Z.

The effects of partners' debit balances on the liquidation process and their treatment in the partnership liquidation schedule are illustrated in the following case.

Case 2. The balance sheet of XYZ Company immediately prior to the liquidation of the partnership is given below:

ASSETS		EQUITIES	
Cash....................	$ 5,000	Liabilities............	$15,000
Noncash assets...........	45,000	Capital:	
		X.................	9,000
		Y.................	6,000
		Z.................	20,000
	$50,000		$50,000

The partners share profits and losses in the ratio 4:4:2. It is assumed that X and Z have personal resources sufficient in amount to "make good" capital debit balances which may be created during the liquidation process.

---

[2] The discerning reader will note that this provision is consistent with the legal definition of partnership insolvency, whereby insolvency is impossible unless the claims against the individual partners are uncollectible due to a condition of personal insolvency.

Y has no available personal assets. The noncash assets of the partnership are realized in the amount of $15,000.

A partnership liquidation schedule based upon these data is shown in Illustration 4–2.

Illustration 4–2

XYZ COMPANY
Schedule of Partnership Liquidation
Dr. [Cr.]

	Assets		Claimants			
					Residual Equities	
	Cash	Noncash	Priority Claims	X	Y	Z
Profit and loss ratio...				40%	40%	20%
Preliquidation balances.........	$ 5,000	$ 45,000	$[15,000]	$[9,000]	$[6,000]	$[20,000]
Realization of assets and allocation of loss............	15,000	[45,000]		12,000	12,000	6,000
Balances............	$ 20,000	$ –0–	$[15,000]	$ 3,000	$ 6,000	$[14,000]
Absorption of Y's balance (4:2).......				4,000	[6,000]	2,000
Balances............	$ 20,000	$ –0–	$[15,000]	$ 7,000	$ –0–	$[12,000]
Contribution by X....	7,000			[7,000]		
Predistribution balances..........	$ 27,000	$ –0–	$[15,000]	$ –0–	$ –0–	$[12,000]
Cash distribution: Priority claims......	[15,000]		15,000			
Partners' residual equities.........	[12,000]					12,000
Termination of partnership........	$ –0–	$ –0–	$ –0–	$ –0–	$ –0–	$ –0–

In this instance, Y's uncollectible debit balance generates an additional "realization loss" to be absorbed by X and Z in their relative profit and loss ratio, whereas X contributes personal assets to restore the debit balance in his capital account to zero. It should be noted that if X had failed to contribute personal assets, the partnership would have remained solvent, since cash was otherwise available to discharge liabilities to partnership creditors.

Partners' Loans

In the distribution of partnership assets, the Uniform Partnership Act ranks payments to partners in respect to loans ahead of payments on their capital accounts. However, this priority has functional significance *only* if it is contemplated that payments are to be made to partners with capital deficiencies. And, as a matter of fact, repayment of a partner's loan is not generally made where the partner has a capital deficiency. If in liquidation a partner's capital account has a debit balance, the partner is required by Section 18 of the Act to contribute an amount equal to his debit balance. Of course, the partnership may be unable to collect this amount from the delinquent partner. Under these circumstances, if partnership assets are first distributed to the partner in repayment of his loan, the assets may be permanently lost. In effect, the distribution in repayment of a (deficient) partner's loan increases the partnership losses to be allocated to the remaining (solvent) partners, assuming the deficient partner does not satisfy his obligation. To prevent this sequence of events, the rule of *setoff* has been generally accepted by the courts as a means of achieving an equitable settlement; accordingly, debit balances are offset against partners' loans to the fullest extent possible, *before* any cash distribution is made.[3]

Application of the rule of setoff is illustrated in the following case.

Case 3. The preliquidation balances of the assets and equities of the Fortune Partnership are given below:

ASSETS		EQUITIES		
Cash	$ 20,000	Liabilities		$ 40,000
Noncash assets	80,000	Partners' loans:		
		W	$ 4,000	
		X	5,000	
		Y	7,000	16,000
		Partners' capital:		
		W	$10,000	
		X	12,000	
		Y	16,000	
		Z	6,000	44,000
	$100,000			$100,000

The partners share profits and losses in the ratio 3:3:2:2. W, X, and Y are committed to making contributions for any debit balances which may be created by loss absorption and are assumed to have sufficient personal assets for this purpose; Z has only $2,000 of available personal assets. The noncash assets are realized during liquidation for $30,000.

A partnership liquidation schedule for this case is given in Illustration 4–3.

This case illustrates the offset principle as it relates to the loans of two partners (W and X), a partial contribution by Z in reduction of a capital deficiency, the absorption of the capital debit residue of Z by the remaining partners (W, X, and Y), and a full contribution by a partner (W) in respect to an existing debit balance. The occurrence of two separate offsets

[3] This general provision may be challenged by the individual creditors of an insolvent partner; in the event of such a challenge, the accountant should advise the withholding of cash in an amount equal to the loan balance pending a final determination of priorities.

Illustration 4–3
FORTUNE PARTNERSHIP
Schedule of Partnership Liquidation
Dr. [Cr.]

	Assets			Claimants						
					Residual Equities					
				W		X		Y		Z
	Cash	Noncash	Priority Claims	Loan	Capital	Loan	Capital	Loan	Capital	Capital
Profit and loss ratio					30%		30%		20%	20%
Preliquidation balances	$20,000	$80,000	$[40,000]	$[4,000]	$[10,000]	$[5,000]	$[12,000]	$[7,000]	$[16,000]	$[6,000]
Realization of assets and allocation of loss	30,000	[80,000]			15,000		15,000		10,000	10,000
Balances	$50,000	$ –0–	$[40,000]	$[4,000]	$ 5,000	$[5,000]	$ 3,000	$[7,000]	$ [6,000]	$ 4,000
Offset of loans against debit balances:										
W				4,000	[4,000]					
X						3,000	[3,000]			
Balances	$50,000	$ –0–	$[40,000]	$ –0–	$ 1,000	$[2,000]	$ –0–	$[7,000]	$ [6,000]	$ 4,000
Contribution by Z	2,000									[2,000]
Balances	$52,000	$ –0–	$[40,000]	$ –0–	$ 1,000	$[2,000]	$ –0–	$[7,000]	$ [6,000]	$ 2,000
Absorption of Z's debit balance (3:3:2)					750		750		500	[2,000]
Balances	$52,000	$ –0–	$[40,000]	$ –0–	$ 1,750	$[2,000]	$ 750	$[7,000]	$ [5,500]	$ –0–
Additional offset against X's loan balance						750	[750]			
Balances	$52,000	$ –0–	$[40,000]	$ –0–	$ 1,750	$[1,250]	$ –0–	$[7,000]	$ [5,500]	$ –0–
Contribution by W for debit balance	1,750				[1,750]					
Predistribution balances	$53,750	$ –0–	$[40,000]	$ –0–	$ –0–	$[1,250]	$ –0–	$[7,000]	$ [5,500]	$ –0–
Cash distribution:										
Priority claims	[40,000]		40,000							
Partners' loans	[8,250]					1,250		7,000		
Partner's residual equity	[5,500]								5,500	
Termination of partnership	$ –0–	$ –0–	$ –0–	$ –0–	$ –0–	$ –0–	$ –0–	$ –0–	$ –0–	$ –0–

of X's loan against a debit balance in his capital account was merely a consequence of the schedular sequence. If the complete liquidation relationship between Z and the partnership (partial contribution and absorption of residue debit balance) had been first established, only one setoff—$3,750 in amount—would have been required in respect to X. Of course, the total effect would remain unchanged.

Liquidation Expenses

In each of the previous cases, the reference to "realization of assets and allocation of loss" indicated the *net* proceeds realized on the disposition of noncash assets. Such a description is appropriate when an item of expense is directly related to the sale of an asset, e.g., commissions on sales. If, however, expenses are incurred during the liquidation process which are not directly associated with specific assets but rather are identifiable only with the liquidation process or period, it may be preferable to separately disclose such expenses in the liquidation schedule. Whatever the treatment, no substantive change will result in the distribution of partnership assets. The "residual" profit and loss ratio properly relates to the allocation of expenses as well as to gains and losses from realization of assets. If one of the partners assumes sole responsibility for managing or directing the liquidation activities and is accorded a specific fee for such service, this cost should be clearly disclosed as a separate liquidation expense, with a corresponding increase in the relevant partner's capital account. Such an assignment discloses more completely the effect of the expense on the liquidation process, and it effectively precludes a premature distribution of cash to this managing partner, a distribution subject to legal challenge should a debit balance ultimately exist in his capital account.

INSTALLMENT (PERIODIC) PAYMENTS

Basic Accounting Problem

Under conditions of simple liquidation, the total gain or loss on the realization of assets, including the effects of liquidation expenses, is known before distribution of cash is made to individual partners. However, if the liquidation period should extend over a prolonged period of time, it may be appropriate to make partial distributions of cash periodically to the partners *before* all of the assets have been realized, provided certain precautions are taken. In this regard, the accountant often assumes a special fiduciary status with respect to the ultimate claims of both partnership creditors and the individual partners against the available cash accumulation of the partnership. Therefore, he must be particularly circumspect in determining the amount of each installment payment in order to avoid an overdistribution to one or more of the partners. Necessarily, liability attaches to the fiduciary for losses which proceed from excessive distributions. Thus, a distribution procedure is needed which will enable the accountant to compute periodic payments which may be made safely without undue risk of personal liability.

As an underlying basis, the accountant first must estimate the *largest potential loss* that may be incurred in future realizations of noncash assets. Since the equities of the partners are based upon the book values of the partnership assets, the total recorded value of the noncash assets approximates the maximum potential loss to the partnership.[4] If the accountant *assumes* the actual incurrence of the maximum potential loss, he may easily compute its hypothetical effect on the individual partners' capital balances. Any debit balance in a partner's capital account that results from this loss allocation process represents still another *potential* loss to the other partners in that it may not be satisfied by contributions of the deficient partner. Accordingly, it should be allocated to the remaining partners—in effect, it is a reallocation of a portion of the maximum potential loss to the partnership. This sequence of hypothetical loss absorptions will result in one or more partners' capital accounts having credit balances which, in total, are equal to the cash available for distribution to partners. Initially, this amount is the total cash less claims of outside creditors. After obligations to creditors are discharged, the residual amount of cash on hand may be distributed in amounts equal to these adjusted credit balances. Then, if the noncash assets in fact prove worthless and if all debit balances are absorbed in sequence, a zero balance will necessarily exist in each of the partners' capital accounts.

Periodic Computation of Safe Payments to Partners

The procedure outlined above, expressed in the form of a *partnership liquidation schedule* and supported by a *schedule of safe installment payments,* is illustrated in Case 4 which follows.

Case 4. On January 1, 1971, X, Y, and Z agree to dissolve their partnership. Their preliquidation capital balances and percentage interests in profits and losses are:

Partner	Capital	Ratio
X........................	$25,000	50%
Y........................	45,000	30
Z........................	15,000	20

The partnership has cash of $5,000 and noncash assets of $85,000; liabilities to outside creditors amount to $5,000. The partners elect to make periodic distributions of all accumulated cash at the end of each month

---

[4] See page 123 for a more precise statement of the maximum potential loss.

during the liquidation process. The following data relate to the realization of assets:

	Book Values	Net Proceeds
January	$25,000	$20,000
February	40,000	20,000
March	10,000	5,000
April	10,000	2,000

The partnership liquidation schedule and the supporting schedule of safe installment payments are shown in illustrations 4–4 and 4–5. Several important conclusions can be drawn from an analysis of the schedules in this case:

1. The total cash payments to each partner are equivalent to the amount of a single payment computed under a simple liquidation procedure. This is illustrated as follows:

Simple Liquidation Method

	X	Y	Z
Preliquidation balances	$25,000	$45,000	$15,000
Realization loss ($85,000–			
$47,000)	19,000	11,400	7,600
Partners' claims	$ 6,000	$33,600	$ 7,400

Installment Payments Method

	X	Y	Z
January	$ –0–	$20,000	$ –0–
February	2,500	11,500	6,000
March	2,500	1,500	1,000
April	1,000	600	400
Total payments	$ 6,000	$33,600	$ 7,400

2. The ratio of the partners' capital balances at the end of February exhibits a significant relationship, viz., the ratio of capital balances is equal to the profit and loss ratio. When this condition exists, all subsequent installment distributions are based upon the profit and loss ratio (see March and April installment payments in Illustration 4–4). Future losses, should they occur, are allocated on this basis, and thus the availability of cash for distribution to partners indicates that the total equity of the partners exceeds the total potential loss. The computation of safe payments is, in

Illustration 4–4

XYZ PARTNERSHIP
Schedule of Partnership Liquidation
Dr. [Cr.]

	Assets		Priority Claims	Claimants Residual Equities		
	Cash	Noncash		X	Y	Z
Profit and loss ratio............................				50%	30%	20%
Preliquidation balances......................	$ 5,000	$ 85,000	$[5,000]	$[25,000]	$[45,000]	$[15,000]
Realization of assets and allocation of loss...	20,000	[25,000]		2,500	1,500	1,000
Balances.......................................	$ 25,000	$ 60,000	$[5,000]	$[22,500]	$[43,500]	$[14,000]
Payment of liabilities..........................	[5,000]		5,000			
Balances.......................................	$ 20,000	$ 60,000	$ -0-	$[22,500]	$[43,500]	$[14,000]
January installment payment (see supporting schedule—Illustration 4–5)...............	[20,000]				20,000	
Balances.......................................	$ -0-	$ 60,000	$ -0-	$[22,500]	$[23,500]	$[14,000]
Realization of assets and allocation of loss...	20,000	[40,000]		10,000	6,000	4,000
Balances.......................................	$ 20,000	$ 20,000	$ -0-	$[12,500]	$[17,500]	$[10,000]
February installment payment (see supporting schedule—Illustration 4–5)............	[20,000]			2,500	11,500	6,000
Balances.......................................	$ -0-	$ 20,000	$ -0-	$[10,000]	$[6,000]	$[4,000]
Realization of assets and allocation of loss...	5,000	[10,000]		2,500	1,500	1,000
Balances.......................................	$ 5,000	$ 10,000	$ -0-	$[7,500]	$[4,500]	$[3,000]
March installment payment (see supporting schedule—Illustration 4–5)...............	[5,000]			2,500	1,500	1,000
Balances.......................................	$ -0-	$ 10,000	$ -0-	$[5,000]	$[3,000]	$[2,000]
Realization of assets and allocation of loss...	2,000	[10,000]		4,000	2,400	1,600
Balances.......................................	$ 2,000	$ -0-	$ -0-	$[1,000]	$[600]	$[400]
Final payment to partners......................	[2,000]			1,000	600	400
Termination of partnership.....................	$ -0-	$ -0-	$ -0-	$ -0-	$ -0-	$ -0-

Illustration 4–5

XYZ PARTNERSHIP

Schedule of Safe Installment Payments
Dr. [Cr.]

	Residual Equities		
	X	Y	Z
Profit and loss ratio....................	50%	30%	20%
Computation of January installment:			
Predistribution balances..................	$[22,500]	$[43,500]	$[14,000]
Potential loss—noncash assets—$60,000.....	30,000	18,000	12,000
Balances..............................	$ 7,500	$[25,500]	$ [2,000]
Potential loss—X's debit balance..........	[7,500]	4,500	3,000
Balances..............................	$ –0–	$[21,000]	$ 1,000
Potential loss—Z's debit balance..........		1,000	[1,000]
Safe payments to partners................	$ –0–	$[20,000]	$ –0–
Computation of February installment:			
Predistribution balances..................	$[12,500]	$[17,500]	$[10,000]
Potential loss—noncash assets—$20,000.....	10,000	6,000	4,000
Safe payments to partners................	$ [2,500]	$[11,500]	$ [6,000]
Computation of March installment:			
Predistribution balances..................	$ [7,500]	$ [4,500]	$ [3,000]
Potential loss—noncash assets—$10,000.....	5,000	3,000	2,000
Safe payments to partners................	$ [2,500]	$ [1,500]	$ [1,000]

fact, an iterative process that systematically causes the ratio of partners' equities to converge to the profit and loss ratio as rapidly as can be accomplished by controlling cash distributions to partners. Therefore, after one payment is allocated among two or more partners, subsequent distributions to these partners will be in the same ratio as their relative profit and loss ratio. Additionally, after a payment has been made to all partners, the ratio of the partners' equities will be equal to the profit and loss ratio. This fact is confirmed by the data of Case 4 with the February installment payment. In this case, a supporting schedule to determine safe payments to partners is unnecessary after the February distribution.

3. The order of payments in the schedule of partnership liquidation is consistent with the order of priority established in the Uniform Partnership Act, i.e., distributions are first made to creditors; subsequent payments, as cash becomes available, are to partners.

Partners' Loans

It has been noted previously that in partnership liquidation a partner's loan balance should be offset against a debit balance in his capital account; accordingly, liquidating payments are based upon each partner's total equity (or net equity in the event of a capital deficit) in the partnership. This principle is equally valid in the case of installment payments made to partners during the period of liquidation. The total equity of each partner (the sum of both loan and capital balances) should be entered in the schedule of safe installment payments. Entering the total equity implicitly recognizes the relevance of setoff in the event a partner's capital balance is completely absorbed in the process of allocating potential losses. In the schedule of partnership liquidation, however, indicated payments to each partner are traditionally reported as first in abatement of loans and second in reduction of capital balances.

The addition of this variable, partners' loans, to a liquidation process involving installment distributions is illustrated in the following case.

Case 5. The partners of the Sutlif Company agree to dissolve their partnership on March 31, 1971. Their preliquidation capital and loan account balances and the profit and loss ratio are:

Partner	Capital	Loan	Ratio
W..........................	$16,000	$4,000	50%
X..........................	29,000	2,000	20
Y..........................	23,000		20
Z..........................	9,000	1,000	10

The partnership has a cash balance of $10,000 and noncash assets of $80,000; obligations to outside creditors amount to $6,000. Available cash is to be distributed at the end of each month during the period of liquidation. Assets were realized as follows:

	Book Values	Net Proceeds
April.	$54,000	$30,000
May......................	24,000	18,000
June......................	2,000	–0–

The partnership liquidation schedule is given in Illustration 4–6, and the supporting schedule of safe installment payments is given in Illustration 4–7.

The schedules for Case 5 accent several concepts previously discussed:

1. Although the total equity (capital and loan balance) of each partner is used in the schedule of safe installment payments, any cash distribution to a partner is assumed to apply first against the partner's loan account, with any remaining payment made against his capital balance.

2. Since installment payments were made to X, Y, and Z in April, the ratio of their *total equities* should be equal to their relative profit and loss ratio at the end of April. This equality is confirmed by the schedule of partnership liquidation (7200:7200:3600 = 20:20:10). The schedule ad-

Illustration 4–6

SUTLIF COMPANY
Schedule of Partnership Liquidation
Dr. [Cr.]

	Assets			Claimants						
						Residual Equities				
			Priority	W		X		Y	Z	
	Cash	Noncash	Claims	Loan	Capital	Loan	Capital	Capital	Loan	Capital
Profit and loss ratio					50%		20%	20%		10%
Preliquidation balances	$10,000	$80,000	$[6,000]	$[4,000]	$[16,000]	$[2,000]	$[29,000]	$[23,000]	$[1,000]	$[9,000]
Realization of assets and allocation of loss	30,000	[54,000]			12,000		4,800	4,800		2,400
Balances	$40,000	$26,000	$[6,000]	$[4,000]	$[4,000]	$[2,000]	$[24,200]	$[18,200]	$[1,000]	$[6,600]
Payment to creditors	[6,000]		6,000							
Balances	$34,000	$26,000	$ -0-	$[4,000]	$[4,000]	$[2,000]	$[24,200]	$[18,200]	$[1,000]	$[6,600]
April installment payment (see supporting schedule—Illustration 4–7)	[34,000]				3,000	2,000	17,000	11,000	1,000	3,000
Balances	$ -0-	$26,000	$ -0-	$[4,000]	$[4,000]	$ -0-	$[7,200]	$[7,200]	$ -0-	$[3,600]
Realization of assets and allocation of loss	18,000	[24,000]			3,000		1,200	1,200		600
Balances	$18,000	$ 2,000	$ -0-	$[4,000]	$[1,000]	$ -0-	$[6,000]	$[6,000]	$ -0-	$[3,000]
May installment payment (see supporting schedule—Illustration 4–7)	[18,000]			4,000			5,600	5,600		2,800
Balances	$ -0-	$ 2,000	$ -0-	$ -0-	$[1,000]	$ -0-	$ [400]	$ [400]	$ -0-	$ [200]
Realization of assets and allocation of loss		[2,000]			1,000		400	400		200
Termination of partnership	$ -0-	$ -0-		$ -0-	$ -0-	$ -0-	$ -0-	$ -0-	$ -0-	$ -0-

Illustration 4–7

SUTLIF COMPANY
Schedule of Safe Installment Payments
Dr. [Cr.]

	Residual Equities *(Capital and Loan Balances)*			
	W	X	Y	Z
Profit and loss ratio.............	50%	20%	20%	10%
Computation of April installment:				
Predistribution balances........	$[8,000]	$[26,200]	$[18,200]	$[7,600]
Potential loss—noncash assets—$26,000.............	13,000	5,200	5,200	2,600
Balances....................	$ 5,000	$[21,000]	$[13,000]	$[5,000]
Potential loss—W's debit balance..................	[5,000]	2,000	2,000	1,000
Safe payments to partners......	$ –0–	$[19,000]	$[11,000]	$[4,000]
Computation of May installment:				
Predistribution balances........	$[5,000]	$ [6,000]	$ [6,000]	$[3,000]
Potential loss—noncash assets—$2,000...............	1,000	400	400	200
Safe payments to partners......	$[4,000]	$ [5,600]	$ [5,600]	$[2,800]

ditionally indicates that subsequent distributions to these partners are made in their relative profit and loss ratio (e.g., in May, 1200:1200:600 = 20:20:10). Since an installment payment is made to W in May, all of the partners' equities at May 31 are in their respective profit- and loss-sharing ratio; subsequent distributions, if any, would be made on the basis of this ratio.

Cash Predistribution Plan

In the partnership liquidation schedule and supporting schedule of safe installment payments, a new and separate calculation is required each time an installment distribution is contemplated—at least until such time as the partners' equities are in their relative profit and loss ratio. Yet, it may be desirable to establish a systematic plan for distributing partnership assets in advance of the start of the liquidation process. Such a cash *predistribution plan* must anticipate the determination of the amount of safe payments to the partners at any point in time.

The following sequence of operations is used in establishing the predetermined order and amount of distribution payments:

1. Using each partner's residual equity (combined capital and loan balances) and percentage interest in profits and losses, compute the partners' *loss-absorption potentials*. The amount of this potential for each partner is the amount of possible loss the partnership may incur before the

partner is obliged to contribute new assets to the partnership, i.e., his residual equity divided by his percentage interest in profits and losses.

For example, if X and Y have equities (including loans) of $48,000 and $40,000, respectively, and share profits and losses in the ratio 6:4, a table of loss-absorption potentials may take the following form:

XY PARTNERSHIP
Loss Absorption Potentials

Partner	Equities	Profit and Loss Ratio	Loss-Absorption Potentials	Order of Equity Absorption
X...............	$48,000	60%	$80,000($48,000 ÷ .60)	1
Y...............	40,000	40	100,000($40,000 ÷ .40)	2

A loss of $80,000 would totally absorb X's equity in the partnership (including any possible offset of a loan balance should one exist), whereas a loss of $100,000 would be required before Y's total equity would be absorbed.

2. After calculating the loss-absorption potential of each partner, prepare a schedule which assumes potential losses in sequence such that the amount of each assumed loss is sufficient to absorb the equity of exactly one partner, beginning with the partner having the smallest loss-absorption potential. The order of this equity absorption is indicated in the table of loss-absorption potentials, i.e., in the order of ascending amounts of loss-absorption potentials.

If the XY Partnership has cash of $7,000, noncash assets of $93,000, and liabilities of $12,000, such a schedule would assume the following form:

XY PARTNERSHIP
Schedule of Loss Absorption
Dr. [Cr.]

	Assets		Claimants		
			Priority	Residual Equities	
	Cash	Noncash	Claims	Y	X
Profit and loss ratio......				40%	60%
Preliquidation balances....	$7,000	$ 93,000	$[12,000]	$[40,000]	$[48,000]
Potential loss to absorb X's equity.............		[80,000]		32,000	48,000
Balances...............	$7,000	$ 13,000	$[12,000]	$ [8,000]	$ –0–
Potential loss to absorb Y's remaining equity....		[8,000]		8,000	
Balances...............	$7,000	$ 5,000	$[12,000]	$ –0–	

In this simple case the total potential loss is attributed to the degree of realization of noncash assets; therefore, as noted before, the book value of noncash assets is assumed to establish a maximum possible loss. This case illustrates the important principle that after one partner's equity has been totally eliminated, additional losses are absorbed by the remaining partners in their relative profit and loss ratio. Given the assumption that debit balances will *not* be restored to zero by contributions, no benefit is to be derived by allocating subsequent assumed losses to all partners; doing so would simply require a reallocation of the debit balances created in the first allocation. In this example, Y is the only remaining partner with an equity; consequently he must absorb 100 percent of all additional losses, and a loss of $8,000 would thus completely absorb his $8,000 equity. In the schedule, the sequence progresses until all partners' equities have been reduced to zero, unless the cash on hand exceeds the claims of outside creditors; in this event, the schedule should be continued until a balance remains in but one partner's capital account.

3. Using the above schedule, which indicates the effect of loss absorption on the several equities, construct a predistribution plan indicating in sequence the distribution of cash as it is made available to the partnership. This is accomplished by reverse movement through the loss-absorption schedule, as the continued availability of cash systematically negates the assumption of potential losses:

XY PARTNERSHIP
Cash Predistribution Plan

		Distributions		
		Priority Claims	X	Y
Preliquidation cash balance............	$ 7,000	$7,000		
Subsequent collections (on realization of noncash assets):				
First..............................	$ 5,000	5,000		
Next..............................	8,000			100%
Next..............................	80,000		60%	40
Noncash assets.................	$93,000			
Any additional cash collected...........			60	40

It should be observed that any available cash in excess of the $93,000 book value of noncash assets implies a net realization gain, which must be credited to the partners in accordance with the partners' profit- and loss-sharing ratio. The percentages in the schedule may be easily converted to dollar amounts and also included in the cash predistribution plan; however, this translation would not indicate explicitly the proper distribution if only a portion of the indicated cash were made available.

The cash predistribution plan is applied in the following case to a more complex collection of data.

Case 6. Using the data of Case 5, the series of predistribution schedules assume forms as indicated in Illustrations 4–8, 4–9, and 4–10.

Illustration 4–8

SUTLIF COMPANY

Loss Absorption Potentials

Partner	Partners' Equities			Profit and Loss Ratio	Loss-Absorption Potentials	Order of Equity Absorption
	Capital	Loan	Total			
W.........................	$16,000	$4,000	$20,000	.50	$ 40,000	1
X.........................	29,000	2,000	31,000	.20	155,000	4
Y.........................	23,000		23,000	.20	115,000	3
Z.........................	9,000	1,000	10,000	.10	100,000	2

This plan is easily reconciled with the more conventional partnership liquidation schedule and supporting schedule of safe installment payments. Using the data of Case 5, the amounts of cash distributed in accordance with the predistribution plan are as shown in Illustration 4–11. It is evident that these installment payments are equivalent to those calculated in Illustration 4–6. Necessarily, the earliest payments to partners are applied in reduction of any existing loan balances.

Liquidation Expenses and Unrecorded Liabilities

The total potential loss of a partnership has heretofore been assumed to be equal to the book value of noncash assets. This assumption is true *only* if the assets are determined to be completely worthless, *and* if *additional* expenses are not incurred in the process of liquidation, and if all partnership liabilities have been properly recorded. However, if liquidation expenses, including disposal costs for noncash assets, should exceed the proceeds from asset realization, the actual loss suffered will be greater than the assumed loss. Additionally, unrecorded liabilities to outside creditors may be discovered during the period of liquidation; necessarily, these claims will rank ahead of the residual claims of partners. Therefore, in order to avoid personal liability, the fiduciary should explicitly recognize these items in the liquidation schedule where the amounts are predictable with reasonable accuracy. In the schedule of safe installment payments, provision may be made for estimated future liquidation expenses and unrecorded liabilities by treating them as additions to the potential loss as previously determined. This adjustment has the effect of reserving cash in an amount equal to the total of anticipated liquidation expenses and unrecorded liabilities. In the event a cash predistribution plan is used, adjustments for estimated liquidation expenses and unrecorded liabilities should be indicated by withholding cash available for distribution; the plan will then provide for the distribution of the remaining cash in the prescribed manner.

Illustration 4-9

SUTLIF COMPANY
Schedule of Loss Absorption
Dr. [Cr.]

	Assets		Priority Claims	Claimants			
					Residual Equities		
	Cash	Noncash		X	Y	Z	W
Profit and loss ratio				20%	20%	10%	50%
Preliquidation balances	$10,000	$ 80,000	$[6,000]	$[31,000]	$[23,000]	$[10,000]	$[20,000]
Potential loss to absorb W's equity		[40,000]		8,000	8,000	4,000	20,000
Balances	$10,000	$ 40,000	$[6,000]	$[23,000]	$[15,000]	$ [6,000]	$ -0-
Potential loss to absorb Z's equity		[30,000]		12,000	12,000	6,000	
Balances	$10,000	$ 10,000	$[6,000]	$[11,000]	$ [3,000]	$ -0-	
Potential loss to absorb Y's equity		[6,000]		3,000	3,000		
Balances	$10,000	$ 4,000	$[6,000]	$ [8,000]	$ -0-		
Remaining potential loss		[4,000]		4,000			
Balances	$10,000	$ -0-	$[6,000]	$ [4,000]			

Illustration 4–10

SUTLIF COMPANY
Cash Predistribution Plan

		Distributions			
	Priority Claims	W	X	Y	Z
Preliquidation cash balance..........	$10,000	$6,000	$4,000		
Subsequent collections (on realizations of noncash assets):					
First...........................	$ 4,000		100%		
Next...........................	6,000		50	50%	
Next...........................	30,000		40	40	20%
Next...........................	40,000	50%	20	20	10
Noncash assets...............	$80,000				
Any additional cash collected.........		50	20	20	10

Illustration 4–11

SUTLIF COMPANY
Actual Distribution of Cash

	Priority Claims	Partners' Equities			
		W	X	Y	Z
April installment distribution....	$40,000				
First......................	$10,000	$6,000	$ 4,000		
Next......................	4,000		4,000		
Next......................	6,000		3,000	$ 3,000	
Next......................	20,000		8,000	8,000	$4,000
Total..................	$40,000	$6,000	$ –0–	$19,000	$11,000	$4,000
May installment distribution.....	$18,000				
First......................	$10,000		$ 4,000	$ 4,000	$2,000
Next......................	8,000	$4,000	1,600	1,600	800
Total..................	$18,000	$4,000	$ 5,600	$ 5,600	$2,800

INSOLVENT PARTNERSHIP

Basic Rights

In an earlier discussion, partnership insolvency was said to exist where recorded partnership assets are insufficient to discharge partnership liabilities. As noted, this definition emphasizes the financial condition of the partnership, viewed as a separate and distinct entity. It thereby ignores the existence and potential value of the partnership claim against the individual partners for debit balances in their capital accounts; at least one such debit balance must exist if partnership liabilities exceed partnership assets. In the discussion to follow, it is initially assumed that the partnership creditors first exhaust partnership assets in discharging partnership liabilities, and thereafter make claims against the partners jointly for any remaining unpaid balances of partnership debts. Two conditions are possible:

1. One or more of the individual partners possesses separate net assets sufficient to meet the claims of the partnership creditors (i.e., legally, the partnership is not insolvent).

2. The partners individually do not have sufficient assets to discharge all existing partnership debts (i.e., the partnership is legally insolvent, and considering the claims of partnership creditors, all of the partners are individually insolvent). Manifestly, the order of distributing the partners' individually owned assets depends upon the relative rights of partnership and individual creditors.

To determine the basic rights of creditors, it is important first to marshal the assets of both the partnership and the several partners. This legal doctrine, *marshaling of assets,* prescribes that partnership assets and individual assets constitute separate pools of resources against which partnership creditors and individual creditors, respectively, have initial and separate recourse. If the partnership is insolvent, partnership assets are completely exhausted in the *partial* settlement of partnership debts. If the partnership is solvent, creditors of individual partners have a claim against the remaining partnership assets to the extent of the partner's residual interest therein. Once individual creditors have satisfied their claims against individual assets, the partnership creditors may recover from the partners' separately owned assets to the extent of their unsatisfied claims, *regardless of the equity status of the partner in the firm* (debit or credit balance). A special point of interest in this allocation process is the definition of individual and partnership assets and liabilities. A difficult and legally unresolved problem relates to a debit balance existing in an insolvent partner's capital account (whether or not the *other* partners are insolvent). Section 40 (i) of the Uniform Partnership Act is explicit on this point:

Where a partner has become bankrupt or his estate is insolvent the claims against his separate property shall rank in the following order:
    (I)   Those owing to separate creditors,
    (II) Those owing to partnership creditors,
    (III) Those owing to partners by way of contribution.

Under this Act, the obligation to the partnership, and the remaining partners, for a debit balance does not constitute a *separate* or *individual* liability of the insolvent partner. The language of the Federal Bankruptcy Act, which emphasizes the marshaling principle, would also appear to support this position. There exists, however, a possible legal *interpretation* of the "contribution obligation" as constituting an individual liability of the partner. In this regard, the following observations made at the time the Uniform Partnership Act was formulated are relevant:

> It is to be hoped that eventually in all our courts of insolvency the liability of the partner to contribute to the payment of partnership liabilities, correctly described by the Act as a partnership asset, will be treated as on a parity with his other liabilities for purpose of distribution of his insolvent estate.[5]

> This [Section 40 (i)] however introduces several changes into the law as it is established by the weight of authority. A partner who has paid the partnership debts can at present [prior to passage of the Act] prove for contribution against the insolvent partner's estate and share *pari passu* with his other separate creditors.[6]

A contrary opinion is expressed in the following terms:

> It is submitted that the partner, by paying the partnership debts, should be held to have stepped into the right of the partnership creditors against the assets of the insolvent partner. He should not obtain, however, in respect to that estate a better position than the person whose claim he has paid. Indeed, if he were allowed to do so, the rule giving priority to separate creditors on the separate estate would be to that extent nullified.[7]

The first opinion (Crane) appears to support the position that a partner's debit balance in his capital account, particularly if it represents an obligation to a solvent partner who has personally discharged the total claims of partnership creditors, constitutes a separate liability of the insolvent partner. The counterargument, however, focuses on the apparent *equity* of the provision in the Uniform Partnership Act. It may be concluded, therefore, that in those states which have not adopted the Uniform Partnership Act, or in federal bankruptcy cases, it is possible that the individual partner's estate may be prorated among his separate creditors and his obligation to the partnership.[8]

The basic rights of creditors, apropos of the underlying principle in respect to the marshaling of assets, may then be summarized as follows:

1. Partnership creditors should seek the discharge of partnership debts by first exhausting partnership assets (exclusive of contributions of partners) to the extent of their claims.

2. A partner's individual creditors should first seek recourse against his separate assets to the extent of their claims. Under the Uniform Partner-

---

[5] Judson A. Crane, "The Uniform Partnership Act—A Criticism," *Harvard Law Review*, June, 1915, pp. 784–85.

[6] *Ibid.*, p. 786.

[7] William Draper Lewis, "The Uniform Partnership Act," *Harvard Law Review*, January, 1916, pp. 307–8.

[8] Even other interpretations have been made. In *Robinson* v. *Security Co.*, Ann Cas 1915C, 1170, it was held that a judgment should be rendered "dividing the distributable assets belonging to the estate of each partner ratably among the separate creditors of such partners together with the partnership creditors." Marshaling of assets was not applied even *in form* in this case.

ship Act, amounts due to the partnership by way of contribution do not constitute individual liabilities; under common law, or in federal bankruptcy cases, the contribution requirement *may* be construed as an individual liability sharing *pari passu* with other individual liabilities.

3. To the extent of their unsatisfied claims, partnership creditors may prove against the residual assets of an individual partner after his separate creditors have been satisfied, regardless of the amount of his residual interest in the partnership.

4. To the extent of their unsatisfied claims, a partner's individual creditors may prove against the *recorded* interest of the individual partner in the residual assets of a solvent partnership.

5. If a partner pays more than his share of partnership liabilities, he has a claim, as measured by the resulting credit balance in his account, against those partners with debit balances (representing their unrequited share of partnership losses).

Accounting Analysis of the Insolvent Partnership

Determination of amounts to be allocated to the various creditor and equity interests will be illustrated under each of the two conditions of insolvency: (1) an insolvent partnership with at least one solvent partner, and (2) an insolvent partnership with all partners insolvent.

Case 7. At Least One Solvent Partner. The trial balance of the XYZ Partnership, after realization of assets but before distribution of cash to either creditors or partners, is as follows:

	Debit	Credit
Cash	$20,000	
Liabilities		$30,000
X, capital		10,000
Y, capital	5,000	
Z, capital	15,000	
	$40,000	$40,000

X, Y, and Z share profits and losses in the ratio 2:4:4. The separate financial status of each individual partner, excluding his interest in, or obligation to, the partnership, is as follows:

	Assets (Realizable Value)	Liabilities
X	$ 5,000	$20,000
Y	6,000	4,000
Z	30,000	10,000

Given these data, it is apparent that both X and Y are insolvent. X's individual liabilities exceed his individual assets and his interest in the firm (even assuming his partnership interest is recoverable at book value), and Y's obligations to individual creditors ($4,000) and to the partnership

($5,000) exceed his individual assets. It is assumed further that partnership creditors obtain a judgment against Z and that he makes full payment of the partnership obligations to its outside creditors, using his separate assets as necessary. Schedules of partnership liquidation and distribution of separate assets of the individual partners under the provisions of the Uniform Partnership Act are given in Illustrations 4–12 and 4–13.

Illustration 4–12

XYZ PARTNERSHIP
Schedule of Partnership Liquidation
Dr. [Cr.]

	Assets		Claimants		
				Residual Equities	
	Cash	Priority Claims	X	Y	Z
Profit and loss ratio............			20%	40%	40%
Balances......................	$ 20,000	$[30,000]	$[10,000]	$ 5,000	$ 15,000
Payment of liabilities...........	[20,000]	20,000			
Balances......................	$ –0–	$[10,000]	$[10,000]	$ 5,000	$ 15,000
Establish status of partner's personal solvency. Record payment of partnership liabilities by Z from his separate assets....		10,000			[10,000]
Balances......................	$ –0–	$ –0–	$[10,000]	$ 5,000	$ 5,000
Contribution by Y.............	2,000			[2,000]	
Balance.......................	$ 2,000	$ –0–	$[10,000]	$ 3,000	$ 5,000
Allocation of Y's debit balance...			1,000	[3,000]	2,000
Balances......................	$ 2,000	$ –0–	$ [9,000]	$ –0–	$ 7,000
Contribution by Z.............	7,000				$ [7,000]
Balances......................	$ 9,000	$ –0–	$ [9,000]	$ –0–	$ –0–
Distribution of cash............	[9,000]		9,000		
Termination of partnership......	$ –0–	$ –0–	$ –0–	$ –0–	$ –0–

If the Uniform Partnership Act is not controlling in this case *and* if the partners' obligations to the firm are adjudged individual liabilities sharing *pari passu* with other individual obligations, the schedule will be modified only by the amount of Y's contribution to the firm (since X, the second insolvent partner, does not have an obligation to contribute to the partnership). The amount of Y's contribution is calculated as follows:

	Y		
	Liabilities	Ratio of Assets to Liabilities	Asset Settlement
To partnership.................	$5,000	2/3	$3,334
Separate creditors..............	4,000	2/3	2,666
	$9,000		$6,000

Illustration 4–13

X, Y, AND Z
Schedule of Distribution of Separate Assets

	X	Y	Z
Separate assets................................	$ 5,000	$ 6,000	$ 30,000
Separate liabilities (Rank I)...................	[20,000]	[4,000]	[10,000]
Separate capital [deficit].....................	$[15,000]	$ 2,000	$ 20,000
Payment of partnership debts (Rank II)........			[10,000]
Separate capital [deficit].....................	$[15,000]	$ 2,000	$ 10,000
Payment of debt to partnership (Rank III).......		[2,000]	[7,000]
Separate capital [deficit].....................	$[15,000]	$ –0–	$ 3,000
Distribution of cash by partnership............	9,000		
Separate capital [deficit].....................	$ [6,000]	$ –0–	$ 3,000
Obligations of Y to X and Z through the			
partnership................................	1,000	[3,000]	2,000
Separate capital [deficit].....................	$ [5,000]	$[3,000]	$ 5,000

Under these conditions, X, the only partner with a credit balance, will receive $445 more than under the provisions of the Uniform Partnership Act, Z will contribute $889 less to the partnership, and Y's personal creditors will receive $1,334 less.

Case 8. All Partners Insolvent. Assume the same information of Case 7, except that Z has separate assets of $10,000 rather than $30,000. In this circumstance, the partnership is legally insolvent, as it will be shown that there are insufficient partnership assets and net assets of individual partners to make a full settlement with partnership creditors.

Under the provisions of the Uniform Partnership Act, the partnership creditors will receive the $20,000 of partnership cash and the $2,000 excess assets of Y (those not required to discharge separate debts), leaving a deficiency in payments to partnership creditors of $8,000. The $22,000 distribution to these creditors will necessarily be made according to priorities established by law.[9]

If the partners' obligations to the partnership are considered separate (individual) liabilities and are accorded the same status as other separate liabilities, the distribution of separate property is calculated as follows:

	Y		
	Liabilities	Ratio of Assets to Liabilities	Asset Settlement
To partnership.................	$5,000	2/3	$3,334
Separate creditors..............	4,000	2/3	2,666
	$9,000		$6,000

---

[9] These priorities are discussed in Chapter 18.

	Liabilities	Z Ratio of Assets to Liabilities	Asset Settlement
To partnership...............	$15,000	2/5	$ 6,000
Separate creditors.............	10,000	2/5	4,000
	$25,000		$10,000

The allocation of Y's separate assets remains unchanged in this case, as there is no adjustment of Y's financial status. Consequently, where the partners' obligations to contribute to the firm for debit balances are confirmed legally and given an equal status with their separate liabilities, the partnership creditors will receive an additional $7,334 ($1,334 + $6,000) from the partnership, $1,334 being contributed by Y and $6,000 being contributed by Z. It should be noted, however, that this calculational technique ignores the subtlety introduced by the inherent variability of the obligation to the partnership when two or more partners are involved, i.e., the undischarged balance must be absorbed by the remaining partners, which accordingly alters the relative ratio of liabilities to separate creditors and to the partnership.

QUESTIONS

1. What are the principal activities of a partnership during the liquidation process?

2. What is the order of priority for the distribution of assets under Section 40 (B) of the Uniform Partnership Act?

3. If after liquidation of the partnership assets, a partner has a debit balance in his capital account, what procedure would be followed if the partner is solvent (i.e., he holds personal assets sufficient to cover the capital deficiency)? What if the partner is insolvent?

4. Explain the rule of "setoff"?

5. If one partner is assigned the role of managing the liquidation process and is to be compensated for this service by the partnership, how should the compensation be recorded in the records of the partnership?

6. If installment (periodic) payments are to be made during the course of liquidation, what factors might the accountant be concerned with in determining the amounts of cash or other assets to be distributed?

7. Describe the role and usefulness of a schedule of safe (installment) payments?

8. How are loans from partners accounted for in the schedule of partnership liquidation and in the schedule of safe (installment) payments?

9. What is a "cash predistribution plan"? What are "loss-absorption potentials"?

10. How should expected liquidation expenses and/or unrecorded liabilities be treated in proceeding with the process of liquidation by installments?
11. Briefly explain the "marshaling of assets" principle.

PROBLEMS

Problem 4–1

Ball, Ludick, and Thatcher are partners in the BLT Company and have capital balances on January 1, 1971, of $50,000, $35,000, and $72,000 respectively. After electing to liquidate the business, the partners convert the non-cash assets of $117,000 into $92,000 cash. All the liabilities, totaling $15,000, are paid; and the remaining cash is distributed among the partners. They share profits and losses: Ball, 60 percent; Ludick, 30 percent; Thatcher, 10 percent.

Required:

Prepare a partnership liquidation schedule showing how cash is distributed.

Problem 4–2

You are engaged to assist in terminating the affairs of the T and A Discount Store, a partnership undergoing liquidation. Chamblin, who owns Toy Distributors Company, contributed $10,000 in inventory for a 50 percent interest in T and A Discount Store on January 2, 1971. McIntosh, who owns Appliance Distributors Company, contributed $2,000 cash and $8,000 in inventory for a 50 percent interest on the same date. All profits and losses are shared equally.

The T and A Discount Store proved to be an unsuccessful venture, and the partners decided to dissolve the business after the Christmas shopping season.

In the course of your examination you determine the following facts:

a) An incompetent part-time bookkeeper had discarded all cash register tapes and invoices for expenses and purchases. He also served as bookkeeper for the Appliance Distributors Company.
b) The partners state that the only existing payables are to themselves and are as follows:

Toy Distributors Company..................	$ 9,740
Appliance Distributors Company.............	5,260
	$15,000

c) You prepare the following summary of cash transactions from bank statements and canceled checks:

Cash balance, January 2, 1971.......................		$ 2,000
Receipts:		
Sales..	$70,000	
Inventory liquidation............................	7,000	77,000
		$79,000

Disbursements:

Purchases....................................	$36,000	
Operating expenses.............................	26,000	
Leasehold improvements (five year lease)............	6,000	
Liquidating expenses...........................	4,000	72,000
Cash balance, December 31, 1971....................		$ 7,000

d) On December 31, 1971, each partner was paid $3,500 in partial settlement of the $15,000 liability.

e) The partners indicate that the dollar amounts of regular sales of toys and appliances were approximately equal, and that the dollar amounts of liquidation sales of toys and appliances were also approximately equal. There was a uniform markup of 40 percent on cost of toys and 25 percent on cost of appliances. All sales were for cash. The ending inventory of shopworn merchandise was liquidated on December 31, 1971, for 50 percent of the retail sales price.

f) The partners believe that some appliances may have been returned to Appliance Distributors Company; there is no record of such returns, however, on the books of either company.

Required:

(i) Estimate the unrecorded amount of appliances returned to Appliance Distributors Company, if any.

(ii) Prepare an income statement for the partnership for 1971.

(iii) Prepare a statement of changes in partners' capital accounts in 1971.

(AICPA adapted)

Problem 4–3

A, B, C, and D agree to dissolve their partnership. Their preliquidation capital and loan account balances are:

	Capital	Loan
A.................	$28,000	$7,000
B.................	41,000	2,000
C.................	18,000	
D.................	12,000	2,000

They share profits and losses 40:30:20:10. Unpaid liabilities at date of dissolution amount to $10,000; noncash assets total $105,000.

During the first month of liquidation, assets having a book value of $55,000 were sold for $31,000. During the second month, assets recorded at $32,000 were sold for $28,000. During the third month, the remaining unsold assets were determined to be worthless.

Required:

Prepare a schedule of liquidation indicating the cash distribution which is made at the end of each month of the liquidation period.

Problem 4–4

The XYZ Partnership is being dissolved. All liabilities have been liquidated. The balance of assets on hand are being realized by a comparatively slow conversion schedule. The following are details of partners' accounts:

Partners	Capital Account (Original Investment)	Current Account (Undistributed Earnings Net of Drawings)	Loans to Partnership	Profit and Loss Ratio
X................	$20,000	$1,500 credit	$15,000	40%
Y................	25,000	2,000 debit		40
Z................	10,000	1,000 credit	5,000	20

Required:

Prepare a predistribution plan showing how cash payments should be made to the partners as assets are realized.

(AICPA adapted)

Problem 4–5

X, Y, and Z, partners in the Ace Hardware Company, prepare to liquidate their business. On December 31, 1971, the partnership account balances are:

Cash....................	$ 5,430	Trade payables............	$12,892
Other assets.............	61,870	Loans from partners:	
		X....................	8,000
		Y....................	4,000
		Z....................	14,000
		Capital balances:	
		X....................	16,402
		Y....................	1,469
		Z....................	10,537
	$67,300		$67,300

X, Y, and Z share profits and losses 50:30:20.

It is agreed that cash made available during liquidation shall be distributed to the partners at the end of each month. However, an amount sufficient to provide for anticipated future expenses and unrecorded liabilities is to be withheld.

A summary of transactions for the three-month liquidation period is as follows:

	Liquidation of Noncash Assets		Liquidation Expenses	Newly Discovered Unrecorded Partnership Liability	Estimated Future Expenses and Unrecorded Liabilities
	Book Value	Cash Realized			
January.............	$24,700	$20,120	$1,200	$ –0–	$3,000
February...........	33,170	28,400	1,400	1,550*	800
March..............	4,000	3,700	200	–0–	–0–

*The partnership bookkeeper failed to record the real property tax liability in December, 1971.

Required:

Prepare a partnership liquidation schedule indicating amounts of periodic cash distributions.

Problem 4–6

Part A

The partnership of Adams, Baker, and Crane have called upon you to assist them in winding up the affairs of their partnership.

You are able to compile the following information:

a) The trial balance of the partnership at June 30, 1971, is as follows:

	Debit	Credit
Cash................................	$ 6,000	
Accounts receivable.................	22,000	
Inventory...........................	14,000	
Plant and equipment (net)...........	99,000	
Adams, loan........................	12,000	
Crane, loan........................	7,500	
Accounts payable...................		$ 17,000
Adams, capital.....................		67,000
Baker, capital.....................		45,000
Crane, capital.....................		31,500
	$160,500	$160,500

b) The partners share profits and losses as follows: Adams, 50 percent; Baker, 30 percent; and Crane, 20 percent .

c) The partners are considering an offer of $100,000 for the accounts receivable, inventory, and plant and equipment as of June 30. The $100,000 would be paid to the partners in installments, the number and amounts of which are to be negotiated.

Required:

Prepare a partnership distribution schedule as of June 30, 1971, showing how the $100,000 cash would be distributed as it becomes available.

Part B

Assume the same facts as in Part A, except that the partners have decided to liquidate their partnership instead of accepting the offer of $100,000. Cash is distributed to the partners at the end of each month.

A summary of the liquidation transactions follows:

July:
$16,500—collected on accounts receivable; balance is uncollectible.
$10,000—received for the entire inventory.
$ 1,000—liquidation expenses paid.
$ 8,000—cash retained in the business at end of the month.

August:
$1,500 liquidation expenses paid.
As part payment of his capital, Crane accepted an item of special

equipment that he developed which had a book value of $4,000. The partners agreed that a value of $10,000 should be placed on this item for liquidation purposes.

$2,500—cash retained in the business at end of the month.

September:

$75,000—received on sale of remaining plant and equipment.

$ 1,000—liquidation expenses paid.

No cash retained in the business.

Required:

Prepare a schedule of cash payments as of September 30, 1971, showing how the cash was distributed.

(AICPA adapted)

Problem 4–7

On August 25, 1971, Norton, Olson, and Parker entered into a partnership agreement to acquire a speculative second mortgage on undeveloped real estate. They invested $55,500, $32,000, and $12,500 respectively. They agreed on a profit and loss ratio of 4:2:1 respectively.

On September 1, 1971, they purchased for $100,000 a mortgage note with an unpaid balance of $120,000. The amount paid included interest accrued from June 30, 1971. The note principal matures at the rate of $2,000 each quarter. Interest at the annual rate of 8 percent computed on the unpaid balance is also due quarterly.

Regular interest and principal payments were received on September 30 and December 31, 1971. A working capital imprest fund of $150 was established, and collection expenses of $70 were paid in December.

In addition to the regular September payment on September 30 the mortgagor made a lump-sum principal reduction payment of $10,000 plus a penalty of 2 percent for prepayment.

Because of the speculative nature of the note, the partners agree to defer recognition of the discount until their cost has been fully recovered.

Required:

(i)   Assuming that no cash distributions were made to the partners, prepare a schedule computing the cash balance available for distribution to the partners on December 31, 1971.

(ii) After payment of collection expenses the partners expect to have cash in the total amount of $170,000 available for distribution to themselves for interest and return of principal. They plan to distribute the cash as soon as possible so that they can individually reinvest the cash.

Prepare a schedule as of September 1 showing how the total cash of $170,000 should be distributed to the individual partners by installments as it becomes available.

(AICPA adapted)

Problem 4–8

Partners A, B, and C who share profits and losses 50:30:20 elect to liquidate the partnership business. Their preliquidation capital balances are: A, $40,000; B, $30,000; and C, $15,000. Partnership unpaid liabilities amount to $6,500.

Required:

Prepare a schedule indicating the distribution of cash as it becomes available in the realization process.

Problem 4–9

Edmondson, Richey, Smith, and Pinson decide to dissolve their partnership; accordingly they plan a program of piecemeal conversion of assets in order to minimize liquidation losses. Partners share profits and losses as follows: Edmonson, 40 percent; Richey, 35 percent; Smith, 15 percent; and Pinson, 10 percent. The period of liquidation begins on June 1, 1971, when the trial balance of the partnership is as follows:

	Debit	*Credit*
Cash..	$ 200	
Receivables.............................	25,900	
Inventory, June 1, 1971..................	42,600	
Equipment (net)........................	19,800	
Accounts payable.......................		$ 3,000
Edmondson, loan........................		6,000
Richey, loan............................		10,000
Edmondson, capital.....................		20,000
Richey, capital.........................		21,500
Smith, capital..........................		18,000
Pinson, capital.........................		10,000
	$88,500	$88,500

Required:

(i)   Prepare a schedule as of June 1, 1971, showing how cash will be distributed among partners as it becomes available.

(ii) On July 31, 1971, cash of $12,700 is available for payment to creditors and partners. How should it be distributed?

(iii) Assume that the partnership elects to continue operations rather than suffer liquidation. Subsequent to this decision, the partnership earns profits of $23,625. How should the profits be distributed if in addition to the aforementioned profit-sharing arrangement, it was provided that Pinson receive a bonus of 5 percent of the net income from operations, such bonus to be treated as a partnership expense?

(AICPA adapted)

Problem 4–10

Blake, Carson, and Davis are partners in the Carson Supply Company and share profits and losses 50:30:20. Their capital balances on January 1, 1971, are:

Blake.....................	$ 5,000 debit
Carson...................	39,000 credit
Davis....................	24,000 debit

The partnership liabilities are $15,000.

On liquidation, the noncash assets of $18,000 are converted into $4,000 cash.

The nonbusiness (personal) assets and liabilities of each partner are:

Partner	Assets	Liabilities
Blake..................	$13,000	$14,000
Carson................	17,000	6,400
Davis.................	21,000	3,200

Required:

Prepare a partnership liquidation schedule according to provisions of—
(i)   Bankruptcy law.
(ii) Uniform Partnership Act.

Problem 4–11

The United Service Company, a partnership, prepared the following trial balance after realization of noncash assets but before distribution of cash to creditors or partners:

	Debit	Credit
Cash..................................	$10,000	
Liabilities............................		$40,000
Ficken, capital........................	20,000	
Powell, capital........................		30,000
Carlson, capital.......................	40,000	
	$70,000	$70,000

The individual financial status of each partner, excluding his relationship to the partnership, is:

	Assets	Liabilities
Ficken............................	$40,000	$ 30,000
Powell............................	50,000	100,000
Carlson...........................	80,000	30,000

Required:

(i)   Prepare a schedule of partnership liquidation and a schedule indicating the partners' personal financial status under the provisions of the Uniform Partnership Act.
(ii) Calculate the amounts the partnership and the creditors of the separate partners would receive if the partners' obligations to the firm were adjudged individual liabilities.

Problem 4–12

Hadler, Mashburn, and Quest are partners sharing profits in the ratio of 4:3:2 respectively. The partnership and two of the partners are currently unable to make full payment of their obligations to creditors. The balance sheet of the partnership and an enumeration of the assets and liabilities of the separate partners are as follows:

HMQ PARTNERSHIP
Balance Sheet
(Date)

ASSETS		EQUITIES		
Cash........................	$ 500	Accounts		
Other assets................	60,500	payable......		$37,000
		Capital:		
		Hadler........	$10,000	
		Mashburn.....	6,000	
		Quest........	8,000	24,000
	$61,000			$61,000

Assets and Liabilities of Partners H, M, and Q
Excluding Partnership Interests

Partner	Cash and Cash Value of Personal Assets	Liabilities
Hadler............................	$31,000	$20,000
Mashburn.........................	9,450	11,900
Quest............................	4,000	5,000

Required:

(i) Assuming that "other assets" are converted into $33,500 cash, prepare a partnership liquidation schedule *and* a complementary schedule indicating the distribution of partners' personal assets according to the provisions of the Uniform Partnership Act.

(ii) Calculate the minimum amount which must be realized from the sale of noncash partnership assets in order that the personal creditors of Mashburn will receive full settlement of their claims.

(AICPA adapted)

Problem 4–13

You are the CPA retained by Smith, Charles, and Black who are in business together. Answer the following questions as true or false.

i) If the partners have made no agreement to the contrary—

(a) A majority vote of the partners may control decisions connected with the ordinary partnership business.

(b) All partners have equal rights in the management and conduct of the business regardless of the amount of experience or talent each may have.

(c)   No partner is entitled to receive interest on monies lent by him to the partnership.

(d)   Each partner must contribute to losses according to his share of profits.

(e)   Profits will be divided in proportion to the amount of each partner's capital investment in the partnership.

ii)   If a new partner is to be admitted to the firm—

(a)   All present partners must agree that he is to be admitted.

(b)   The old partnership is dissolved.

(c)   The old partnership must be wound up and liquidated.

(d)   The new partner is not liable in any manner for any preexisting obligations of the partnership.

(e)   The new partner is liable for preexisting obligations of the partnernership to the same extent as the other partners.

iii)   If a partnership agreement provides that the partnership is to remain in force for a definite term—

(a)   The partnership cannot be dissolved before the expiration of that term.

(b)   The partnership may only be dissolved by the unanimous consent of all of the partners.

(c)   The death of any partner dissolves the partnership.

(d)   Any partner has the power to dissolve the partnership at any time.

(e)   Repudiation of the partnership by a partner before the end of the stipulated term may subject the partner to an action for breach of contract.

iv)   In settling accounts between partners and creditors upon dissolution, among the items to be paid prior to satisfying the general creditors are—

(a)   Debts of creditors entitled to a preference.

(b)   Debts owing to partners on account of loans made to the partnership.

(c)   Amounts owing to partners in respect of capital investments.

(d)   Debts of secured creditors which remain after exhausting any available security.

(e)   Back salaries due to partners.

v)   The partnership is to be liquidated. Smith has contributed $6,000 to capital; Charles $3,000 to capital; and Black has made no contribution to capital but has merely contributed his services. Liabilities of the partnership exceed assets by $9,000. The following contributions must be made by the partners from their personal assets if there is no prior agreement on sharing losses:

(a)   Smith need not make a contribution.

(b)   Smith must contribute $3,000.

(c)   Charles must contribute $3,000.

(d)   Black must contribute $6,000.

(e)   Black must contribute $3,000.

(AICPA adapted)

Problem 4–14

A, B, and C formed the ABC Company, a partnership, with A contributing $12,000 of capital, B contributing $8,000, and C contributing $6,000. In their partnership agreement, A, B, and C provided that the partnership was to exist for 20 years, but the partners made no provision as to the proportions in which profits and losses were to be shared. During the course of operating the partnership, A made a loan of $1,000 to the partnership which has not been repaid, and the partnership also owes outside creditors additional amounts which exceed the value of partnership assets by $3,000.

Required:

(i) Under the Uniform Partnership Act, in absence of a specific agreement between the parties, how is the compensation and profit for each partner determined during the course of operating the partnership?

(ii) Under the Uniform Partnership Act—

    (*a*) If A wishes to terminate the partnership but B and C do not, does A have the right to withdraw from the partnership? *Explain.*

    (*b*) If A, B, and C agree to terminate the partnership, how will losses be divided?

(iii) Discuss—

    (*a*) The role of marshaling of assets.

    (*b*) The distinction between the "dissolution" of the partnership and the "winding up" of partnership affairs.

(iv) If D becomes a partner in ABC Company and replaces A, what is D's liability with respect to obligations arising before his admission to the partnership?

(AICPA adapted)

UNIT III

ACCOUNTING FOR COMBINED CORPORATE ENTITIES

Chapter 5

Mergers and Acquisitions—I

HISTORICAL, ECONOMIC, AND LEGAL CONSIDERATIONS

"For nearly a decade, a great corporate merger game has generated more excitement, more glamour—and probably more fortunes—than any other phenomenon in the business scene."[1] The corporate growth objective, which underlies this merger movement, has apparently become increasingly important relative to other business goals. One major corporation summarizes its objectives in terms of successive three-year plans to double sales and earnings per share.[2] Another corporation began its annual report as follows:

Tenneco Inc. is unique. It is the first and only industrial corporation ever to pass the $3 billion mark in assets while still under 25 years old.

Obviously, this is the result of planned growth, of diligently pursuing a business objective. And purposeful growth, within the confines of good business judgment, remains the goal.[3]

The significance of growth is perhaps stated most clearly in the 1968 annual report of Teledyne, Inc. The following statements were included in the letter to shareholders:

These sustained results reflect our purpose—sound and healthy growth in assets and earnings per share, on both a short-term and a long-term basis, with current gains providing the basis for long-term growth in the future.

Teledyne has been systematically organized around a plan designed to produce sustained growth, and its assets are continuously deployed and redeployed with the goal of growth in mind.[4]

Notwithstanding its apparent dominance as an objective of many corporations, growth must be weighed with myriad other objectives as corporate policy is formulated. The decision to engage in a significant business expansion has an obvious effect on the size of operations. But it also may have a material impact on liquidity, risk, and efficiency, as well as many

---

[1] "Time of Testing for Conglomerates," *Business Week,* March 2, 1968, p. 38.

[2] "Successful People United for Greater Growth," U.S. Industries, Inc., *Annual Report 1968,* p. 3.

[3] Tenneco Inc., *1967 Annual Report,* p. 1.

[4] Teledyne, Inc., *1968 Annual Report,* p. 2.

other management objectives. Further, the form within which the business expansion is accomplished may substantially alter the expansion's effect.

All business expansions can be broadly classified as either internal or external. *Internal* business expansion includes the normal increase in operations arising from increasing demand for a firm's products and services. It also includes the establishment of new product lines and geographic sales areas, so long as these activities are financed through the normal corporate means of earnings retention and issuances of debt and/or residual equities. The primary distinguishing characteristic of internal expansion is that it does not involve the acquisition of preexisting business operations from other business units. *External* business expansion, on the other hand, is achieved by the acquisition of established business operations. Indeed, it frequently may involve the acquisition of an *entire* business entity. Subsequent to acquisition, the operations of the acquired firm may be integrated with operating divisions of the purchasing firm; or they may be left intact, leaving the acquired unit to operate as a distinct division or subsidiary corporation of the acquiring firm.

"Business combination" is the general term applied to external expansions in which all, or substantially all, of the operations of two or more firms are brought under centralized control. Depending upon the relative sizes of the constituent companies in an external business expansion, it may be somewhat inappropriate to refer to them as "acquiring" or "acquired" firms. The managements of the constituent firms may in fact continue with the combined unit in positions of responsibility similar to their roles previous to the combination. The stockholders of both constituents may be stockholders in the combined unit. A new corporation may even be formed to replace the legal structures of the combining entities. Nonetheless, such combinations have similar attributes as does the more typical external business expansion, in which one dominant enterprise *acquires* another. Correspondingly, such amalgamations (poolings) of business units bear a similar relationship to the variety of business objectives mentioned earlier. Even a company that anticipates being acquired and losing its corporate identity must relate the prospect of business combination to objectives such as growth, diversification, and minimization of risk.

Historical Significance of Business Combinations

Business combinations are not a recent phenomenon, notwithstanding the widespread significance they have attained in recent years. The formal combination of established business operations under centralized control has undoubtedly existed since the earliest days of organized commercial activity. However, since the first great wave of combination activity in the United States, which took place at the turn of the 20th century, business combinations have gone through cyclical periods of greater and lesser importance. Table 5–1 indicates the sharply varying number of firms that disappeared as a result of mergers during the years 1895 to 1908. The

Table 5–1

Time Period	Firm Disappearances by Merger or Acquisitions
1895–96	69
1897–98	372
1899–1900	1,548
1901–2	802
1903–4	221
1905–6	354
1907–8	137

Source: Ralph L. Nelson, *Merger Movements in American Industry 1895–1956* (Princeton, N.J.: Princeton University Press for the National Bureau of Economic Research, 1959), table B-7, pp. 153–54.

total number of firms disappearing in any year as a result of mergers or acquisitions did not again reach 200 until 1920.

Table 5–2 indicates business combination activity during the period

Table 5–2

Time Period	Mergers and Acquisitions in Mining and Manufacturing
1920–24	2,235
1925–29	4,583
1930–34	1,687
1935–39	577
1940–44	906
1945–49	1,505
1950–54	1,424
1955–59	3,365
1960–64	4,366

Source: U.S. Department of Commerce, Bureau of the Census, *Statistical Abstract of the United States 1966* (87th ed.; Washington, D.C.: U.S. Government Printing Office, 1966), table No. 707, p. 501.

1920–64. Two additional peaks of business combination activity are clearly evidenced during 1925–29 and during 1955–64. Of interest is the fact that the most recent period of peak combination activity, beginning in 1955, has continued throughout the 1960s. Business combinations in mining and manufacturing during the period 1965–68 were reported by the Federal Trade Commission as follows:[5]

1965	1,125
1966	1,106
1967	1,639
1968	2,655

[5] Bureau of Economics, Federal Trade Commission, *Current Trends in Merger Activity, 1968* (Washington, D.C., March, 1969). Although these data are somewhat more comprehensive than those presented in Table 5–2 and therefore do not provide a precise comparison with the earlier years, they do clearly indicate the continued swell of merger activity.

The two early periods of high-combination activity were characterized by the formation of industrial giants representing important and continuing industries in the United States economy. By comparison, the most recent surge of combination activity suggests a desire on the part of management to overcome the risk and general attributes of being limited to any specific industry. Many of the recent business combinations have resulted in the widest possible diversification of business operations being centrally controlled by one corporate parent. For example, operations during 1968 that were controlled by Ling-Temco-Vought, Inc., included aerospace, electronics, meat products, cable and wire, sporting goods, chemicals, airlines, services, banking, and insurance. In 1968, Tenneco Inc. classified its diverse operations as natural gas pipelines, oil production and refining, marketing, chemicals, packaging, manufacturing, land use, and investments (in insurance, banking, etc.).

The problems of accounting for combined business units are becoming increasingly *significant* to the business community, investors, and government. The student will intuitively recognize that the problems of accounting for such combined units are also becoming more *complex*. Much of the discussion in this and several following chapters relates directly to such accounting problems.

The significance of business combinations to the financial and investing community is highlighted most dramatically in terms of its effect upon particular corporations. In 1958, Ling Electronics reported consolidated operating revenue of less than $8,000,000. Ling-Temco-Vought, Inc., the firm resulting from many business combinations between Ling Electronics and other firms, reported 1968 consolidated sales as $2,769,700,000. It must be understood, of course, that Ling Electronic sales did not grow from $8 million to $2.7 billion in 10 years. The 1968 sales represents the operations of *many* business units that operated separately in 1958. It is the unusual concentration of control over what was once a large variety of separate business entities that is indicated by comparing 1958 sales of Ling Electronics with 1967 sales of Ling-Temco-Vought, Inc. Similar statistics depict the histories of several other corporate giants, e.g., Litton Industries, Inc., and Gulf & Western Industries.

A proper conception of the accounting problems associated with combined business units requires, in part, an appreciation for the tremendous alterations in economic characteristics of firms that can result from business combinations. Understanding these accounting problems is also facilitated by a recognition of the motives which underlie business combinations and the constraints associated therewith. These subjects are examined in the following discussion.

Impetus for Business Combinations

Many of the motives underlying business combinations also tend to induce internal business expansion. Thus, it is important to recognize the forces that lead to business combination as a unique form of expansion. Presuming a preexisting desire of management to begin or enlarge a particular set of operations in a given market area, the approach of business combination may have several advantages over internal expansion.

1. Business combination provides the management of the acquiring company the opportunity of utilizing the acquired company's historical data on operations and sales effectiveness. Thus, projections concerning profitability, cash requirements, and many other significant operating factors can be based upon the reality of historical operations. Internal expansion into new product lines, by comparison, is similar to establishing an entirely new business. An adequate historical basis for planning projections may be derived from other operations of the firm. But they are, at best, only analogous to the proposed expansion.

2. Combination provides the expanding company the immediate availability of suppliers, productive facilities (including operating management), and an established channel of distribution. Internal expansion provides few or none of these resources, thereby requiring a lengthy start-up period before the new operations evidence an adequate return on investment. This necessary start-up period not only defers the expected return on investment but also increases the risk associated with expansion.

3. Internal expansion into a particular market nearly always involves the interjection of an additional competitor (the expanding firm) into the market, thereby tending to enhance price and service competition. It may also tend to increase production costs by increasing competition in factor markets. Combination, on the other hand, merely alters the organizational structure and the control of an existing competitor, leaving the market's competing forces essentially unchanged.

4. Tax considerations, as in most major business decisions, are significant in evaluating alternative forms of business expansion. Special tax characteristics of a firm, such as the existence of unused operating loss carry forwards, may be transferable to an acquiring firm. Such tax benefits may provide a significant impetus for business combination. Alternatively, internal expansion may have preferential tax implications in certain instances. Nevertheless, tax factors have frequently led to combinations. Evidence in many situations suggest that the crucial decision in management's election to expand was not between alternative *forms* of expansion (internal versus external); rather, it was whether or not a combination with a *specific* company should be pursued, the dominant benefit of which would be the effect on the tax status of the constituent firms.

The student should not infer that business combination always provides a superior means of expansion. There may be no existing firms that are willing to combine. Also, these which are available, may not be suitable from the acquiring firm's point of view. While business combination provides numerous advantages, it also burdens the expansion effort with any inefficiencies that are characteristic of the acquired firm, such as an old plant, ineffective management, and marketing deficiencies.

Other factors which give rise to business combinations also tend to support internal expansion.

1. A traditional motive underlying business expansion is to develop a fully integrated operation in a particular product line. Acquisition of supplier and customer entities, or internal expansion into their fields of operation, leads to centralized control over the productive and distributive channel of a product. This type of expansion reduces the risk of dependence upon particular suppliers and customers, as well as permitting the firm to avail itself of the profit associated with the new operations.

2. Another traditional motive for expansion is to broaden the market area covered by the firm. While this typically implies geographical expansion, it may also involve the addition of related product lines. The expected result is a reduction in the risk associated with the economic vagaries of a narrow product line or limited market area.

3. A more general motive for expansion is to afford the firm economies of large scale. Financial economies are at least as significant in this regard as are the possibilities of increased productive efficiencies. The variety of financing methods, as well as the expense of financing, are usually more favorable for large firms than for small firms. Service or overhead functions such as are provided by corporate management and computer installations are also subject to economies of scale. Thus, expansion may accomplish the employment of what were previously idle resources.

4. The desire to increase the earnings growth rate is an additional stimulus for business combinations. The effect of increasing earnings growth through business combination is frequently referred to as "synergism." To the extent such growth derives from improvements in efficiency or other factors mentioned in this discussion, the synergistic motive is redundant. However, later discussion will disclose how certain business combinations can result in significant increases in reported earnings per share without any real gains in efficiency. Managerial motives for growth of the latter nature may be of questionable propriety, although their existence should be recognized.

5. Business operations that are especially sensitive to cyclical profit patterns frequently lead to expansion in the attempt to stabilize profits. Successful expansion, in these terms, requires that the historical profit pattern of the expanding company be counter cyclical to that of the new operations. A noncyclical or relatively stable profit pattern is generally evaluated by the investing community as being less risky.

6. Another impetus to expansion and business combination might be referred to as the psychology of scale. Aside from consequences of economic efficiencies or inefficiencies, there is an apparent desire on the part of many managements for bigness per se. Management prestige and realm of

authority tend to be enhanced as a firm becomes larger. Without rendering a judgment on the appropriateness or quality of such goals, it is important to recognize their existence.

Constraints upon Business Combinations

Various branches of the United States government have exhibited a concern with the movement toward economic concentration that results from business combinations. The Sherman Act and the Clayton Act (as amended) provide the statutory framework with which the Department of Justice and Federal Trade Commission have prevented the formation or continuation of numerous combinations. The Clayton Act was enacted to strengthen the Sherman Act, and it allows government to challenge some mergers that are not yet in violation of the Sherman Act. In general, Section 7 of the Clayton Act disallows any corporate combination the effect of which may be substantially to lessen competition or tend to create a monopoly. The thrust of Section 7 is to deal with monopolistic tendencies before significant injury has been incurred.

Horizontal Combinations. Three general types of combinations have been interpreted by the courts. Firms that perform similar functions in the production or sale of comparable products are horizontal in relationship.[6] Thus, if the acquiring firm and the acquired firm have been competitors or are potential competitors, the combination is referred to as "horizontal." In the process of analyzing horizontal mergers to determine whether they may substantially lessen competition or tend to create monopoly, the courts have considered several factors of varying significance, depending upon the case. After designating the "relevant market" within which the firms in question have influence, courts have considered: (1) the level of concentration in that market; (2) the rank of the acquiring and acquired firms in the market and their shares of the market; (3) any change in the number of companies operating in the market; (4) any changes in barriers to entering the market; and (5) the elimination of a large independent firm from an oligopolistic market. In general, horizontal mergers are vulnerable ". . . if the acquiring company is a major company and if the acquired company is a strong competitor in its own right and concentration in the relevant market is high; nor can a viable independent with relatively low market shares be acquired if concentration in the relevant market is high, the number of companies is declining in the face of expanding demand, and the acquiring company is a dominant one in the market affected."[7]

Vertical Combinations. The second general (economic) type of business combination may be referred to as "vertical." In a vertical merger, the combining firms have a supplier-customer relationship. Vertical mergers

---

[6] *Brown Shoe Co.* v. *United States,* 370 U.S. 294, p. 334 (1962).

[7] Betty Bock, *Mergers and Markets on Economic Analysis of Developments on the Mid-1960's under the Merger Act of 1950* (New York: National Industrial Conference Board, Inc., 1968), p. 7.

are especially sensitive to challenge if as a result of the merger, a substantial share of the relevant market will be foreclosed from other firms. In terms of more specific tests, such a combination is likely to be litigated if the market of either constituent is concentrated and if there is a history of similar combinations that have increased the risk of independent firms, making it difficult for them to find suppliers or customers that are not competitors.[8]

Conglomerate Combinations. A third category of business combinations that has received congressional and judiciary attention is referred to as "conglomerate." Notwithstanding the widespread use of the term "conglomerate" to describe certain combination processes as well as the resulting business entities, there remains considerable disagreement as to what constitutes a conglomerate combination. Part of the confusion stems from somewhat differing usage of the term in the worlds of finance vis-à-vis antitrust law. In a financial context, conglomerate combination tends to imply a union of business units which have little if any production or market similarities. Translated into terms of antitrust significance, this would mean that the products of the combining firms are unrelated and therefore do not compete—for buyers or for raw materials. Given the present antitrust laws and court interpretations thereof, such a definition of conglomerate combination would essentially exclude such mergers from possible prosecution.

However, in framing the 1950 amendments to Section 7 of the Clayton Act, Congress notes that the law applies to all types of combinations, including conglomerates.[9] Apparently, the legislative intent was to include combinations that do not evidence traditional competing patterns in terms of suppliers, products, or customers.[10] The propriety of a conglomerate combination depends largely upon its effect on *potential* competition. Thus, if the acquiring and acquired firms probably would have become competitors (through internal expansion of either one or both), the combination may be viewed as an arrangement which may eliminate a potential competitor. Even if probable *internal* expansion into a competitive position is unsupported by the evidence, it is possible for the combination to be challenged. Some combinations could discourage further entry into a market even though a potential entrant is not in sight.[11]

The basic antitrust laws affecting contemporary business activity were enacted prior to the emergence of conglomerate combinations as a prevalent

---

[8] *Ibid.,* p. 7.

[9] U.S. House, 81st Cong. 1st sess. (1949), H. R. 1191, p. 11.

[10] Robert A. Bicks, "Corporate Mergers and the Antitrust Laws: Clayton Act, Section 7" in William W. Alberts and Joel E. Segall, *The Corporate Merger* (Chicago, Ill.: The University of Chicago Press, 1966), p. 85.

[11] Betty Bock "Conglomerate Mergers, Joint Ventures and Potential Competition," *The Conference Board Record* (February, 1968), p. 6.

type of business expansion. Correspondingly, combinations that exhibit vertical or horizontal characteristics are less likely to succeed than are conglomerate mergers. Many lawmakers have expressed opposition to the long-term trend toward increasing concentration of control in business. But it has been difficult to structure laws that would forestall this trend (in its conglomerate form) and remain within the traditional bounds of attacking monopolistic tendencies and competitive restraining forces. Conglomerate entities have been subjected to increased scrutiny by Congress, the Department of Justice, and the Federal Trade Commission. On another front, the Securities Exchange Commission and the Accounting Principles Board have cast a critical eye on the reporting practices of conglomerates, many of which relate to the problems of accounting for highly diversified operations. Currently, however, the amount and types of constraints that should be appropriately placed upon conglomerate combination activity remain unsettled questions.

METHODS OF CLASSIFYING BUSINESS COMBINATIONS

An examination of business combinations is generally facilitated by an attempt to devise classes or categories of combinations. The scheme of classification selected necessarily depends on the purpose of the examination. One of the most frequently used methods of classifying combinations has already been discussed; horizontal, vertical, and conglomerate are expressions which convey certain economic characteristics of the combination classes in question. This economic perspective of business combinations finds significance in studies of the legal implications of combinations. It is also relevant to economists' investigations relating to economic trends and federal policies.

Legal Perspective

A traditional method of classifying business combinations focuses upon the corporate structures involved. Thus, combinations are labeled as mergers, consolidations, or acquisitions. If the only surviving company is one of the original group of companies, the union is termed a *merger;* if a new corporate enterprise is organized for the purpose of acquiring the net assets of other companies, the combination is termed a *consolidation.* In both forms of combination, the legal entity status of each of the controlled companies is normally terminated. The term *acquisition* is applied to a combination in which one firm exchanges its ownership securities for the ownership securities of another firm, and both continue their legal existence. A parent-subsidiary relationship results from this form of combination.

Notwithstanding the distinctions that can be drawn between the terms merger, consolidation, and acquisition, contemporary usage of the terms frequently disregards these definitional refinements. One may expect to find *merger, consolidation, acquisition,* and *business combination* used interchangeably in normal business discourse unless, of course, the objective is to concentrate on the distinctions outlined above.

Tax Perspective

According to the "tax-free reorganization" provisions of the Internal Revenue Code, certain business combinations can be accomplished without requiring that new valuations be determined and income taxes assessed. Business combinations can therefore be classified as taxable exchanges or tax-free reorganizations. The criteria and attributes of both categories will be examined in later discussion.

Financial Perspective

The method of financing used by an acquiring firm to accomplish a combination is significant in several types of analyses. The selection of a financing method, for example, may determine the tax status of the combination. It may also determine the method of accounting for the combination, a selection that can have material effects upon operating reports for future periods. Without attempting to specify all of the problems and analyses for which a financing method has relevance, alternative financing arrangements should be recognized as a means of classifying corporate combinations. Payment methods include the transfer of cash or other assets as well as the issuance of common stock, preferred stock, bonds, and convertible securities. Classifying combinations by financing method does not allow the determination of mutually exclusive and collectively exhaustive classes. Business combinations often involve a mixing of payment methods. Further, the use of treasury stock, or payment by cash shortly following a stock issuance, allows management to accomplish one particular payment form while giving the impression of another. If an acquiring company has available cash with which to make payment but wishes to have the combination classified as an "exchange of stock," it can use the cash to buy treasury stock and then issue the treasury stock to consummate the combination. Conversely, a company can issue stock for cash and use the cash in settlement. Such transactions may allow the firm to benefit from some of the desirable attributes of both payment methods.

An added complexity in financing combinations is sometimes evidenced by firms that have a history of successful acquisitions. Paradoxically, this complexity involves the use of *divisive* reorganizations as a means of financing combinations. A controlling interest in the acquired firm is established by any one of the payment methods mentioned earlier. Assume, for example, that an acquiring corporation issues notes payable and uses the cash proceeds to buy the stock of the acquired firm. The acquired firm is then merged into the acquiring firm, which eliminates the separate corporate existence of the subsidiary, thereby also eliminating any minority (outside) interest in the subsidiary. Outsiders are forced to accept cash in exchange for the fair value of their minority interest in the liquidated subsidiary corporation. Next, the controlling firm organizes a new corporation, the stock of which is issued to the controlling firm in exchange for the assets of the acquired (and now liquidated) firm. Generally, the name selected for the *new* subsidiary corporation will identify it with the successful history of the parent firm. Finally, the parent offers to the public approximately 20 percent of the new corporation's stock. Cash proceeds can be used either to repay the original notes payable issued by the parent or to make unrelated acquisitions.

If the divisive reorganization method of financing is successful, the "new image" of the acquired corporation will substantially increase its market value. As a consequence, the proceeds from issuing a small portion of the new stock to the public will be large enough to defray a substantial portion of the original outlay to acquire the company. In a few recent examples, the proceeds were almost equal to the original expenditure. Thus, the parent acquired a controlling interest in another firm at a net cost that was relatively insignificant.

Case 1.   Conglom-Glammer Company issued $50,000,000 of three-year, 6 percent, notes payable on January 1, 1971. During January 15–30, it acquired 920,000 shares of Slow Company at an average per share cost of $50. During May, 1971, Slow Company was merged into Conglom-Glammer Company. The 80,000 shares held by minority interests were surrendered for $54 per share. Additional costs associated with the merger were $180,000. In October, 1971, a new corporation, Conglom-Shimmer, Inc., issued 3,500,000 of its 4,000,000 authorized common shares to Conglom-Glammer Company in exchange for the operating assets originally belonging to Slow Company. On November 1, 1971, Conglom-Glammer Company sold 875,000 shares of Conglom-Shimmer, Inc., for $30 per share.

Net Cash Outlay of Conglom-Glammer Company
As of November 1, 1971

Purchases of stock:	920,000 × 50 =	$46,000,000
	80,000 × 54 =	4,320,000
Costs of merger	=	180,000
Interest on debt	(50,000,000 × .06 × 10/12) =	2,500,000
Total......................................		$53,000,000
Proceeds from stock sale	875,000 × 30 =	26,250,000
Net cash outlay on November 1, 1971..............		$26,750,000

Shares owned:		
By Conglom-Glammer Company........	2,625,000	75%
By minority interest..................	875,000	25
	3,500,000	100%

Current value of Conglom-Glammer Company's investment:
2,625,000 × 30 = $78,750,000

Accounting Perspective

There are two strikingly different sets of accounting procedures which are used to record business combinations on the books of the combined business entity; these differing accounting procedures are referred to as the *purchase* method and the *pooling of interests* method. In the case of any specific business combination, the question of which method of accounting will be utilized is resolved by analyzing the provisions of the combination agreement and the factual characteristics of the combining companies. In the event a business combination and the combining companies exhibit 12 specific factual conditions, the pooling of interests method of accounting is used to record the combination. Correspondingly, such a combination is referred to as a *pooling of interests* combination. In the event the business combination fails to satisfy any one of the specified 12 conditions, the purchase method of accounting is employed and the combination is referred to as a *purchase* combination. Chapter 10 includes a detailed examination of the criteria that are used to classify business combinations as purchases or poolings of interests and the corresponding sets of procedures that are used to account for these classes. As a consequence, the present discussion is intended only to emphasize the general characteristics of each class.

In general, a business combination is classified as a purchase if the facts of the combination agreement suggest that one of the combining companies, especially its stockholder group, emerges as the dominant, controlling interest; the combining agreement is in substance a purchase-sale transaction in which the dominant company acquires the assets and assumes the liabilities of the other combining firm(s). In contradistinction to a purchase, a business combination is classified as a pooling of interests if none of the combining companies, especially the constituent stockholder groups, assume a position of dominance in the combined entity; the common stockholders of each combining company become common stockholders in the combined entity, thereby retaining their relative ownership positions.

CLASSICAL VALUE ANALYSIS: A NORMATIVE APPROACH

The negotiating participants in a business combination must reach agreement on several fundamental considerations. The provisions of the combination agreement must be approved by the boards of directors of the constituent companies; and in many instances, the agreement must also be ratified by the shareholders of the selling and/or the purchasing companies.

Determination of Price

Of primary importance to the negotiators is the determination of a mutually agreeable exchange price for the transferred net assets of the acquired company. The most obvious indicator of an equitable price would be the current market quotation of the acquired firm's outstanding equity securities. However, one cannot presume that the negotiated exchange price will equate with this current market value. If the firm to be acquired is closely held, a current market value is probably not available. Even in those cases where a current market price for the acquired company's stock is available, the potential gain to be realized by refusing a specific offer, in expectation of rising stock prices, usually provokes the acquiring company to offer a premium over the current price. Thus, the determination of an exchange price demands a careful analysis of relevant accounting and statistical data, current market circumstances, and business expectations. The book values of recorded assets seldom provide an equitable basis for settlement; at best, these amounts, together with the earnings history of each company, merely provide a convenient point of departure for a more refined evaluation.

It is important that the accounts of constituent companies be free of significant accounting errors and omissions, and that they reflect comparable underlying measurement processes; accordingly, adjustment should be made, where appropriate, to provide uniform valuation. There are often significant accounting differences between companies regarding inventory pricing, depreciation policies, criteria for distinguishing between capital and revenue expenditures, appraisal of long-lived assets, recognition of contingent liabilities and losses, and policies for deferral and accrual of revenues and expenses. The accountant may offer valuable counsel in reconciling such differences and in translating the accounting data to comparable bases.

While uniform accounting data are important, they are not sufficient to provide a complete basis for an equitable settlement value. The adjusted net asset book values are usually inadequate indexes of the earning power of the contributing companies; in particular, they fail to reflect increasing technological obsolescence. Replacement costs of individual assets, or their fair appraised values, frequently indicate the earnings prospects of the assets more accurately than do acquisition costs less amortization. Additionally, the valuations of the individual assets may be deficient in disclosing a value increment which attaches to a collection of functionally related assets; i.e., the asset collection often has an earning capacity greater than the sum of the profit projections for the component asset elements. Correspondingly, the current value of the asset collection often exceeds the sum of the current values of the individual assets. An estimate of the future earnings of the constituent companies for which there is no apparent identification with tangible assets is frequently ascribed to unrecorded intangibles, or "goodwill." In assessing the value of these future earnings, however, there should exist persuasive evidence that the earnings projected for individual companies will identify with the combination of companies.

Consistent with the discussion above, the price negotiations of the parties to the combination can be focused on two contributions of the acquired companies—the value of transferred net assets *and* the capitalized value of projected earnings.

Methods of Payment

Once the exchange price is established, an acceptable *method* of payment must be determined. A number of alternatives are available. The acquiring corporation may either issue its own securities directly to the individual shareholders of the acquired companies *or* to the respective corporations for distribution as a liquidating settlement with their shareholders. As previously discussed, the shares to be issued may be either common or preferred stock, or a combination of the two security types. Payment may also be made in cash, other assets, or bonds. Clearly, the method of payment which is chosen is subject to negotiation and will normally reflect the underlying motivations of those who have initiated the proposal for consolidation.

Many business combinations are predicated upon the desire of the constituents to merge their controlling and ownership interests so that the control and ownership of the new combined entity will reflect the relative positions of the constituent firms' ownership interests. Voting stock must be a primary method of payment in these situations. However, the preservation of interests may also require the distribution of senior securities as well as common stock. The idea of preserving the interests of the various shareholder groups in the new or surviving company is essentially an attempt to make the stock distribution plan *equitable*. Although equity is in the final analysis a subjective concept, the following two criteria are proposed as essential elements of an equitable stock distribution plan.

1. Equity would suggest that the income generated by any one constituent in a combination should be allocated to those who held shares in that constituent. Thus, if 60 percent of the combined entity's income will be generated by the assets and operations contributed by constituent firm A, the stock distribution plan should allocate approximately 60 percent of the combined entity's income to shares held by those who were precombination firm A stockholders. As a matter of practicality, the percentage of profits contributed by each constituent is usually approximated by comparing the recent historical earnings records of the combining firms.

2. Equity would also appear to be served if the stockholders in a combined entity are given a preference position, as to liquidation and income distribution, for the net tangible assets contributed by their respective firms. If a firm contributes goodwill to the combination in the form of earning power above the normal rate of return on net tangible assets, this firm's stockholders will be adequately compensated for the goodwill as those above-normal earnings are allocated to them. This is the essence of the equity requirement discussed under 1 above. Goodwill is at times, however, a most illusive asset. It generally disappears if the asset collection is

dispersed in liquidation. Thus, the net tangible assets contributed should dominate over goodwill contributions, given subsequent liquidation of the combined entity.[12] Furthermore, the market values of net tangible assets contributed are presumed to reflect the present value of a normal earnings stream attributable to those assets. Unlike the more subjective return on goodwill—that above-normal portion of total earnings that derives solely from the present asset combination—normal earnings on net tangible assets presumably could be totally realized at any time by simply selling those assets. Equity therefore requires a preference position as to normal earnings on tangible assets contributed. Of course, if common stock (only) is distributed in the same proportion that net tangible assets were contributed, this "preference" is automatically satisfied.

The inequity which results from the issuance of *only* the common stock of the new or surviving company will be illustrated as follows:

Assume that the R Corporation is organized with common stock authorized in the amount of $1,200,000 ($100 par); it is anticipated that the R Corporation will consolidate the operations and resources of companies X, Y, and Z. A summary of selected net asset and earnings data for the combination participants is given in the following table:

Company	Net Assets	Relative Interest in the Combined Net Assets	Average Earnings —Past Five Years	Relative Interest in the Combined Average Earnings	Percentage Return on Net Assets
X............	$ 120,000	10%	$ 20,000	20%	16.7%
Y............	480,000	40	35,000	35	7.3
Z............	600,000	50	45,000	45	7.5
	$1,200,000	100%	$100,000	100%	

The 12,000 shares of R Corporation stock may be allocated among the several companies on the basis of the contributed net assets of each. In this

---

[12] Although recognizing preferred stock to be the normal method of satisfying this equity requirement, a strong case can nonetheless be made for the use of *convertible* bonds or *convertible* preferred stock. As the combined entity's life begins to extend beyond the remaining useful lives of net tangible assets existing at acquisition, internally financed new investments will derive from *actual* earnings (before depreciation)—not from *normal* earnings. If actual earnings include a return associated with goodwill at acquisition, this goodwill eventually becomes transformed into tangible assets. This transformation is no less real than is the transformation of net tangible assets at acquisition into *new* tangible assets. Therefore, the preference position associated with tangible assets contributed should eventually relate to the total historical earnings of the combined entity. As the proportion of tangible assets contributed and the proportion of total earnings contributed approach equality, equity requirements can be fulfilled with common stock. The conversion of senior securities would facilitate this objective.

case the equitable interest of the former shareholders of the constituent companies in net assets are preserved; yet, the interest of each shareholder group in the earnings of the consolidation are altered in the following respects:

| Company | Percentage Interest in Earnings | | |
	Before Consolidation	After Consolidation	Advantage [Disadvantage]
X....................	20%	10%	[10%]
Y....................	35	40	5
Z....................	45	50	5
	100%	100%	

Alternatively, the 12,000 shares of R Corporation may be issued to each company on the basis of the relative interest of each in their combined average earnings. If this plan of stock distribution were adopted, the interest in earnings before and after consolidation necessarily would remain unchanged; yet, the relative interest of each company in the combined net assets of the affiliation would be modified in the following respects:

| Company | Percentage Interest in Net Assets | | |
	Before Consolidation	After Consolidation	Advantage [Disadvantage]
X....................	10%	20%	10%
Y....................	40	35	[5]
Z....................	50	45	[5]
	100%	100%	

These alternative methods of payment demonstrate that where only shares of common stock of the new enterprise are issued to the several combination participants, the equitable interest of each in either the net assets or the future earnings of the consolidation may be altered from previous interests. Such an alteration occurs whenever the ratios of assets and earnings contributions are originally unequal. This condition of inequity will persist even when the capitalized values of average earnings are used as the basis for stock distribution, since the capitalized values will necessarily be in the same ratio as the average earnings of the constituents.

Distribution Formula

It is apparent from the previous discussion that protection of the equitable interests of the various shareholder groups frequently requires issuing other than common shares of stock of the new or surviving enterprise. The following formula has often been recommended as the most effective mechanism for determining the appropriate combination of security values:

1. Preferred stock (cumulative, fully participating) should be issued in the amount of the existing net tangible assets contributed by each of the constituents. This amount should be equivalent to the sum of the capitalized values of the normal earnings of the several companies. The dividend preference rate should equal a normal rate of return on tangible assets.
2. Common stock should be issued for goodwill or other intangibles of the contributors. The value of contributed intangibles is assumed to be equivalent in amount to the capitalized values of above-normal, or excess, earnings of each company.

This formula is implicitly based upon a single capitalization rate for earnings returned on net tangible assets and unrecorded intangibles; however, the combination participants may agree to the use of different rates, and the effect of this decision on the formula will be considered later.

When the earnings of the new enterprise subsequent to the combination are at least as large as the sum of the projected earnings of the individual constituents before consolidation, the effect of the above plan is to reward the shareholders of the consolidated entity in the same ratio as their percentage interests in contributed earnings. In the event the postconsolidation earnings are less than the sum of the earnings of the separate companies before consolidation, however, inequity frequently results, since issuance of the common stock was predicated upon an anticipation of above-normal earnings which were not realized.

As mentioned above, this plan assumes that preferred stock is not only preferred as to assets but is also fully participating with common stock in "excess" earnings. The formula also requires that the *total* stated value of all shares to be issued to combination participants be based upon their relative earnings contributions. The rate to be used in capitalizing earnings should not be greater than the lowest rate of return earned by any of the participants on their contributed net assets, nor less than the dividend rate on the preferred stock to be issued therefor. Accordingly, in the example on page 159, the capitalization rate should not be greater than 7.3 percent. Subject to these constraints, any rate agreed to by the negotiators will yield an equitable result.

Consider the reasoning underlying the constraints upon the choice of a capitalization rate. The expected earnings of each constituent (usually approximated with historical data) are capitalized with the selected rate to determine the total value of stock to be issued in payment for that firm's net assets. If the capitalization rate exceeds the historical rate of return on tangible assets, the resulting total value to be paid for the firm will be less than net tangible assets contributed. Thus, the equitable preference position for net tangible assets contributed would require more stated value of stock than the entire value to be paid for the firm. Consequently, the capitalization rate should be no higher than the *lowest* rate of return on net tangible assets earned by any one of the constituents.

On the other hand, if the selected capitalization rate is less than the preferred dividend rate, an inequitable distribution of earnings will probably result. An equitable earnings allocation demands that *all* outstanding shares receive the same rate of return. Given the existence of some preferred stock, the lowest postcombination income level at which equity occurs is that which provides the preferred rate to all outstanding shares. If a capitalization rate (e.g., 4 percent) that is less than the preferred dividend rate (e.g., 5 percent) is applied to expected postcombination earnings to determine the total stock outstanding, the minimum equitable earnings level (5 percent × par or stated value of outstanding stock) will exceed *expected* earnings (4 percent × par or stated value of outstanding stock).

The above formula is recommended for its structural simplicity; yet, it nonetheless may be modified to compromise the diverse interests of the several negotiators, and additional types of securities may be issued to resolve these interests, as necessary. In the two cases which follow, this formula is tested using different capitalization rates and levels of postconsolidation net income. In each case, the calculation is simplified by assuming that all earnings of the new enterprise are distributed currently as cash dividends. In respect to a given year, this procedure is equivalent to calculating total equity interests in undistributed earnings.

Case 2. Earnings Capitalized at 5 Percent. The R Corporation is organized with authorized capital stock of 20,000 shares of $100 par value common stock and 10,000 shares of $100 par value, 5 percent fully participating, preferred stock. The R Corporation proposes to consolidate the resources of companies X, Y, and Z to which the following summary information relates:

	Company		
	X	*Y*	*Z*
Net tangible assets....................	$150,000	$250,000	$400,000
Five years' average annual earnings......	15,000	20,000	60,000
Rate of return on net tangible assets.....	10%	8%	15%
Ratio of earnings distribution..........	15.79%	21.05%	63.16%

The average annual earnings for the preceding five years may reflect a weighting process which emphasizes net incomes of the most recent years. Whether or not weighted, however, the average earnings are regarded as indexes of prospective earnings contributed to the combination.

The division of the expected earnings into the return on net tangible assets and the return on unrecorded intangible assets, and the proposed stock distribution plan resulting therefrom, are as follows:

		Company	
	X	Y	Z
Five years' average annual earnings..........	$ 15,000	$ 20,000	$ 60,000
Return on net tangible assets contributed:			
5% of $150,000.......................	7,500		
5% of $250,000.......................		12,500	
5% of $400,000.......................			20,000
Return on unrecorded intangibles............	$ 7,500	$ 7,500	$ 40,000
Stock distribution plan:			
*Preferred shares (5%, fully participating)			
for net tangible assets..............	$150,000	$250,000	$ 400,000
Common shares for unrecorded intangibles:			
$ 7,500 ÷ .05........................	150,000		
$ 7,500 ÷ .05........................		150,000	
$40,000 ÷ .05........................			800,000
*Total........................	$300,000	$400,000	$1,200,000

* The amount of preferred shares to be issued to each company may also be determined by capitalizing at 5 percent the earnings return on net tangible assets. Therefore, since the amount of common shares are calculated in this same manner, the total value of both preferred and common shares is equal to the capitalized value of the five years' average annual earnings.

The proposed plan of distribution is tested for its equitable consequence on each combination participant assuming three different levels of post-consolidation earnings.

Assumption 1. If the first year's net income of the consolidated entity is $95,000, an amount equal to the sum of the estimated net incomes contributed by the participants, the earnings distribution is as follows:

		Company	
	X	Y	Z
Preferred shares:			
5% of $150,000................	$ 7,500		
5% of $250,000................		$12,500	
5% of $400,000................			$20,000
Common shares:			
5% of $150,000................	7,500		
5% of $150,000................		7,500	
5% of $800,000................			40,000
Total....................	$15,000	$20,000	$60,000
Ratio of earnings distribution be-			
fore consolidation............	15.79%	21.05%	63.16%
Ratio of earnings distribution after			
consolidation................	15.79%	21.05%	63.16%

Assumption 2. If the first year's earnings following the consolidation are greater than the estimated earnings contributions, in this instance $190,000, the earnings distribution is made as follows:

	Company		
	X	Y	Z
Preferred shares:			
10% of $150,000.............	$15,000		
10% of $250,000.............		$25,000	
10% of $400,000.............			$ 40,000
Common shares:			
10% of $150,000.............	15,000		
10% of $150,000.............		15,000	
10% of $800,000.............			80,000
Total...................	$30,000	$40,000	$120,000
Ratio of earnings distribution before consolidation...........	15.79%	21.05%	63.16%
Ratio of earnings distribution after consolidation..............	15.79%	21.05%	63.16%

Assumption 3. If the first year's earnings following the consolidation are less than net income projections, $62,000, then the earnings distribution is made as follows:

	Company		
	X	Y	Z
Preferred shares:			
5% of $150,000.............	$ 7,500		
5% of $250,000.............		$12,500	
5% of $400,000.............			$20,000
Common shares:			
2% of $150,000.............	3,000		
2% of $150,000.............		3,000	
2% of $800,000.............			16,000
Total...................	$10,500	$15,500	$36,000
Ratio of earnings distribution before consolidation...........	15.79%	21.05%	63.16%
Ratio of earnings distribution after consolidation...........	16.94	25.00	58.06
Earnings advantage [disadvantage] after consolidation..........	1.15%	3.95%	[5.10%]

In Assumptions 1 and 2, it is apparent that the equitable interests of the former shareholders of companies X, Y, and Z have not been altered as a result of consolidation. Where earnings of the new enterprise are thus equal to or greater than those accumulated by the separate companies, previously operating independently, equitable interests in earnings are not distorted. However, in Assumption 3, where earnings of the consolidated entity are not so great as the earnings of the individual constituents before consolidation, the former shareholders of companies X and Y gain an earnings advantage to the disadvantage of the former shareholders of

Z Company. The discerning reader may wish to consider the underlying characteristics producing this particular condition of inequity.

Case 3. Earnings Capitalized at 4 Percent. The data in respect to net tangible assets and average annual earnings for each company presented in Case 2 are combined here, with the lower capitalization rate (4 percent):

	Company		
	X	Y	Z
Five years' average annual earnings..........	$ 15,000	$ 20,000	$ 60,000
Return on net tangible assets contributed:			
4% of $150,000.......................	6,000		
4% of $250,000.......................		10,000	
4% of $400,000.......................			16,000
Return on unrecorded intangibles............	$ 9,000	$ 10,000	$ 44,000
Stock distribution plan:			
Preferred shares (5%, fully participating) for net tangible assets................	$150,000	$250,000	$ 400,000
Common shares for unrecorded intangibles:			
$ 9,000 ÷ .04........................	225,000		
$10,000 ÷ .04........................		250,000	
$44,000 ÷ .04........................			1,100,000
Total...........................	$375,000	$500,000	$1,500,000

The above proposed plan of distribution is tested for its equitable consequence on each combination participant assuming two levels of postconsolidation earnings.

Assumption 1. If the first year's earnings subsequent to consolidation are $95,000, the distribution to shareholders would be made as follows:

	Company		
	X	Y	Z
Preferred shares:			
5% of $150,000...............	$ 7,500		
5% of $250,000...............		$12,500	
5% of $400,000...............			$20,000
Common shares:			
3.492% of $225,000............	7,857		
3.492% of $250,000............		8,730	
3.492% of $1,100,000..........			38,413
Total....................	$15,357	$21,230	$58,413
Ratio of earnings distribution before consolidation...........	15.79%	21.05%	63.16%
Ratio of earnings distribution after consolidation...............	16.16	22.35	61.49
Earnings advantage [disadvantage] after consolidation...........	.37%	1.30%	[1.67%]

It is evident that an inequitable condition results even though postconsolidation earnings are equal to the projected net incomes. This derives from the use of a capitalization rate (4 percent) less than the preferred dividend rate. The condition of inequity, however, does not obtain for all levels of net incomes, as demonstrated in Assumption 2 which follows.

Assumption 2. If the first year's earnings subsequent to consolidation are $118,750 (5 percent return on total shares outstanding), the distribution to shareholders would be made as follows:

	Company		
	X	Y	Z
Preferred shares:			
5% of $150,000	$ 7,500		
5% of $250,000		$12,500	
5% of $400,000			$20,000
Common shares:			
5% of $225,000	11,250		
5% of $250,000		12,500	
5% of $1,100,000			55,000
Total	$18,750	$25,000	$75,000
Ratio of earnings distribution before consolidation	15.79%	21.05%	63.16%
Ratio of earnings distribution after consolidation	15.79%	21.05%	63.16%

Thus, if the net income reflects a rate of return on all shares equal to the preferred dividend rate, equity is restored. Furthermore, any net income level in excess of this amount will preserve the equitable relationship.

These illustrations confirm that the equity or inequity of the stock distribution formula is dependent upon the postconsolidation level of earnings *and* the rate used to capitalize the earnings of the constituent companies. Given a capitalization rate equal to, or larger than, the preferred stock dividend rate, but less than the aforementioned upper constraint, an equitable distribution will always exist when consolidation earnings are equal to or greater than the sum of the earnings of the separate companies before consolidation. Where the preferred stock dividend rate is greater than the capitalization rate, an equitable distribution will exist when earnings reach that level which represents a return equal to the preferred dividend rate on *all* shares issued and outstanding. This earnings plateau will be greater than the sum of the earnings of the individual constituents before consolidation. The equity implications of choosing a capitalization rate greater than the upper constraint on such rates will be illustrated in the following graphic presentation.

Graphic Illustration—Two Combination Participants

The importance of the capitalization rate and the postconsolidation level of earnings to the equity of the distribution is sharply outlined in the following graphic presentation. Assume that the R Corporation is organized with authorized capital stock of 20,000 shares of $100 par value common stock and 10,000 shares of 5 percent, fully participating $100 par value preferred stock. It is proposed that the R Corporation consolidate the resources of X Company and Y Company. The following data relate to these constituents:

	Company	
	X	Y
Net tangible assets...........................	$200,000	$600,000
Five years' average annual earnings.............	30,000	60,000
Rate of return on net tangible assets............	15%	10%
Ratio of earnings distribution.................	33⅓%	66⅔%

First, an "equitable" stock distribution plan will be formulated. The returns on net tangible assets and unrecorded intangibles, assuming an 8 percent capitalization rate, and the resulting stock distribution plan are determined to be:

	Company	
	X	Y
Five years' average annual earnings................	$ 30,000	$ 60,000
Return on net tangible assets contributed:		
8% of $200,000..............................	16,000	
8% of $600,000..............................		48,000
Return on unrecorded intangibles..................	$ 14,000	$ 12,000
Stock distribution Plan 1:		
Preferred stock (5%, fully participating) for net tangible assets.............................	$200,000	$600.000
Common stock for unrecorded intangibles:		
$14,000 ÷ .08..............................	175,000	
$12,000 ÷ .08..............................		150,000
Total......................................	$375,000	$705,000

Two additional plans, both "inequitable" according to the conventionai distribution formula, are presented (without supporting calculations):

	Company	
	X	Y
Stock distribution Plan 2:		
Capitalization rate...................	4%	
Preferred stock.....................	$200,000	$ 600,000
Common stock.....................	550,000	900,000
Total........................	$750,000	$1,500,000
Stock distribution Plan 3:		
Capitalization rate...................	12%	
Preferred stock.....................	$200,000	$ 600,000
Common stock.....................	50,000	-0-
Total........................	$250,000	$ 600,000

In Plan 3, preferred stock is issued to Y Company for the total amount of net tangible assets without penalty for the deficiency in "normal" earnings thereon. In this case, the total value of shares issued exceeds the capitalized value of the total contributed net incomes.

There follows in Illustration 5–1 a tabular enumeration of postconsolidation earnings of the R Corporation for both "equitable" and "inequitable" distribution formulae. Observe that in the first plan (outlined above), the capitalization rate lies between the recommended earnings rate constraints; in the second plan, the capitalization rate falls below the lower constraint; in the third, the capitalization rate exceeds the upper constraint.

The graphic representation of each plan (Illustration 5–2) emphasizes that inequity (or the degree of inequity) is relevant only in the context of a specific postconsolidation level of earnings of the new or surviving enterprise. However, it is evident that a careful selection of capitalization rates within the constraints previously given may expedite the stabilizing of the ratio of earnings distribution among the participants. In respect to the first plan (the "equitable" plan), inequity is observed to decrease as postconsolidation earnings move from $40,000 to $56,250, at which point inequity is eliminated. In the second plan, the inequity decreases at a slower rate as postconsolidation earnings increase, and in the third plan the degree of inequity sharply declines as earnings exceed $40,000 and becomes stable again when earnings reach $42,500; the inequity is not thereafter decreased. The inequity implicit in the third plan may be further reduced, however, by making the preferred stock nonparticipating, or possibly by issuing bonds as a substitute therefor.

Dual Capitalization Rates

The previous examples have illustrated the use of a single capitalization rate for both normal and above-normal earnings. However, the combination participants may elect to use different rates for each class of earnings.

Illustration 5-1

"EQUITABLE PLAN" POSTCONSOLIDATION EARNINGS DISTRIBUTION (PLAN 1)

The capitalization rate (8 percent) is greater than the preferred dividend rate and is less than the lower earnings rate on net assets of either combination constituent.

Rate of Return	Postconsolidation Earnings	Earnings Distribution X	Earnings Distribution Y	Ratio of Earnings Distribution before Consolidation X/Y	Ratio of Earnings Distribution after Consolidation X/Y	Percent Advantage [Disadvantage] X/Y
3.0%	$ 33,750	$ 8,437.50	$ 25,312.50	33.3%/66.7%	25.0%/75.0%	[8.3%]/8.3%
4.0	45,000	12,692.00	32,308.00	33.3 /66.7	28.2 /71.8	[5.1]/5.1
5.0	56,250	18,750.00	37,500.00	33.3 /66.7	33.3 /66.7	0.0 /0.0
8.0	90,000	30,000.00	60,000.00	33.3 /66.7	33.3 /66.7	0.0 /0.0
10.0	112,500	37,500.00	75,000.00	33.3 /66.7	33.3 /66.7	0.0 /0.0
15.0	168,750	56,250.00	112,500.00	33.3 /66.7	33.3 /66.7	0.0 /0.0

"INEQUITABLE PLAN" POSTCONSOLIDATION EARNINGS DISTRIBUTION (PLAN 2)

The capitalization rate (4 percent) is less than the preferred dividend rate.

Rate of Return	Postconsolidation Earnings	Earnings Distribution X	Earnings Distribution Y	Ratio of Earnings Distribution before Consolidation X/Y	Ratio of Earnings Distribution after Consolidation X/Y	Percent Advantage [Disadvantage] X/Y
2.0%	$ 45,000	$11,897	$ 33,103	33.3%/66.7%	26.4%/73.6%	[6.9%]/6.9%
3.0	67,500	20,431	47,069	33.3 /66.7	30.3 /69.7	[3.0]/3.0
4.0	90,000	28,965	61,035	33.3 /66.7	32.2 /67.8	[1.1]/1.1
5.0	112,500	37,500	75,000	33.3 /66.7	33.3 /66.7	0.0 /0.0
6.0	135,000	45,000	90,000	33.3 /66.7	33.3 /66.7	0.0 /0.0

"INEQUITABLE PLAN" POSTCONSOLIDATION EARNINGS DISTRIBUTION (PLAN 3)

The capitalization rate (12 percent) is greater than the lowest earnings rate on net assets of any constituent.

Rate of Return	Postconsolidation Earnings	Earnings Distribution X	Earnings Distribution Y	Ratio of Earnings Distribution before Consolidation X/Y	Ratio of Earnings Distribution after Consolidation X/Y	Percent Advantage [Disadvantage] X/Y
4.5%	$ 38,250	$ 9,562.50	$ 28,687.50	33.3%/66.7%	25.0%/75.0%	[8.3%]/8.3%
4.7	40,000	10,000.00	30,000.00	33.3 /66.7	25.0 /75.0	[8.3]/8.3
4.8	40,800	10,800.00	30,000.00	33.3 /66.7	26.5 /73.5	[6.8]/6.8
5.0	42,500	12,500.00	30,000.00	33.3 /66.7	29.4 /70.6	[3.9]/3.9
10.0	85,000	25,000.00	60,000.00	33.3 /66.7	29.4 /70.6	[3.9]/3.9
15.0	127,500	37,500.00	90,000.00	33.3 /66.7	29.4 /70.6	[3.9]/3.9
20.0	170,000	50,000.00	120,000.00	33.3 /66.7	29.4 /70.6	[3.9]/3.9

NOTE: These data are graphically depicted in Illustration 5–2.

Illustration 5–2

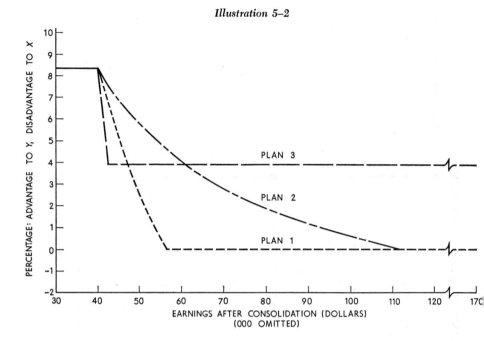

In the event a unique capitalization rate is used for excess profits, it should reflect the increased risk normally associated with the above-normal earnings; accordingly, it should be higher than the rate used to capitalize normal earnings.

Where two capitalization rates are used, the rate used for normal earnings should be the preferred dividend rate. It appears reasonable that the preferred stock issued in payment for the net tangible assets should carry a dividend rate equal to the normal rate of return on these assets. Additionally, preferred shares should be nonparticipating in that the above-normal (excess) profits are attributed exclusively to the unrecorded intangibles contributed by the combination participants, for which common stock is given in payment.

Case 4. Normal Earnings Capitalized at 5 Percent; Excess Earnings Capitalized at 10 Percent. The R Corporation is organized to consolidate the resources and operations of companies X and Y. The charter provides for authorized capital stock of 10,000 shares of 5 percent, nonparticipating preferred stock (par, $100) and 10,000 shares of common stock (par, $100). Selected financial data in respect to these companies are as follows:

	Company	
	X	Y
Net tangible assets............................	$200,000	$600,000
Five years' average annual earnings............	30,000	60,000
Rate of return on net tangible assets............	15%	10%

The calculations of earnings returned on net tangible and intangible assets and the stock distribution plan are given below:

	Company	
	X	Y
Five years' average annual earnings....................	$ 30,000	$ 60,000
Return on net tangible assets contributed:		
5% of $200,000...	10,000	
5% of $600,000...		30,000
Return on unrecorded intangibles.....................	$ 20,000	$ 30,000
Ratio of earnings distribution returned on net tangible assets..	25%	75%
Ratio of earnings distribution returned on intangible assets..	40%	60%
Composite ratio of earnings distribution...............	33⅓%	66⅔%
Stock distribution plan:		
Preferred shares (5%, nonparticipating) for net tangible assets..	$200,000	$600,000
Common shares for unrecorded intangibles:		
$20,000 ÷ .10..	200,000	
$30,000 ÷ .10..		300,000
Total...	$400,000	$900,000

The equity or inequity of this plan is tested in Illustration 5–3 for different levels of earnings for the new enterprise. Although dual capitalization rates are used in respect to earnings segments, tests for equity in the distribution formula are based upon a composite rate for normal and above-normal earnings, i.e., earnings attributed to net tangible assets and earnings attributed to unrecorded intangibles. This composite of the two earnings distribution ratios will then indicate a condition of equity at only one level of postconsolidation earnings—a level represented by the sum of the earnings of the individual companies before consolidation.

The graphic representation in Illustration 5–4 indicates that until post-consolidation earnings reach the level of $40,000, dividend distributions are possible only on the preferred shares of the new enterprise. These distributions are made in the ratio of 25:75 to the former shareholders of X Company and Y Company, the ratio of normal earnings on net tangible assets. Thus, within the range of earnings between $0 and $40,000, the preconsolidation normal rate and the postconsolidation composite rate are the same, and the two composite rates differ by a constant amount. Earnings which are accumulated in excess of $40,000—defined as above-normal, or excess, earnings—are distributed on the common shares, 40 percent to the former shareholders of X Company and 60 percent to the former shareholders of Y Company. It is evident that the postconsolidation composite rate is thereafter equal to the preconsolidation composite rate only at the $90,000 earnings level. This is an inherent characteristic of this type of stock distribution plan. Earnings in excess of $40,000, but less than $90,000, as

Illustration 5–3

POSTCONSOLIDATION EARNINGS DISTRIBUTION

Rate of Return (Composite)	Post-consolidation Earnings	Earnings Distribution		Composite Ratio of Earnings Distribution before Consolidation X/Y	Composite Ratio of Earnings Distribution after Consolidation X/Y	Percent Advantage [Disadvantage] X/Y
		X	Y			
1.000%	$ 13,000	$ 3,250	$ 9,750	33.3%/66.7%	25.0%/75.0%	[8.3%]/ 8.3 %
2.000	26,000	6,500	19,500	33.3 /66.7	25.0 /75.0	[8.3]/ 8.3
3.077	40,000	10,000	30,000	33.3 /66.7	25.0 /75.0	[8.3]/ 8.3
4.000	52,000	14,800	37,200	33.3 /66.7	28.5 /71.5	[4.8]/ 4.8
5.000	65,000	20,000	45,000	33.3 /66.7	30.8 /69.2	[2.5]/ 2.5
6.923	90,000	30,000	60,000	33.3 /66.7	33.3 /66.7	0.0 / 0.0
8.000	104,000	35,600	68,400	33.3 /66.7	34.2 /65.8	0.9 /[0.9]
9.000	117,000	40,800	76,200	33.3 /66.7	35.0 /65.0	1.7 /[1.7]
10.000	130,000	46,000	84,000	33.3 /66.7	35.4 /64.6	2.1 /[2.1]

NOTE: These data are graphically depicted in Illustration 5–4.

Illustration 5-4

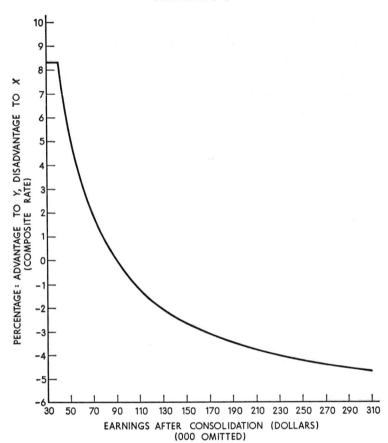

well as those in excess of $90,000, should, therefore, be further tested for equity in terms of the separate ratios for normal and excess earnings segments before and after consolidation. This may produce an even more reliable index of the equity of stock distribution plans when excess earnings have been capitalized at a different rate than the composite rate reflected in the graphic analysis.

QUESTIONS

1. Distinguish between internal and external expansion in business enterprises.
2. Enumerate and briefly discuss several cogent reasons why a company might wish to acquire control of another company. Additionally, suggest reasons an enterprise might wish to be acquired.
3. What is "synergism" in the context of corporate combination?

4. Describe three general types of business combinations as they have been interpreted by the courts. Give an example of each.

5. What factors do the courts cite as relevant considerations in determining whether horizontal mergers violate antitrust laws?

6. Distinguish between "merger," "consolidation," and "acquisition."

7. Describe briefly the technique involved in financing corporate combinations through divisive reorganizations.

8. In general, there are two classes of financial contributions made by the parties to a combination. What are they?

9. Discuss the problems of measuring the financial contributions made by the parties to a combination, indicating the role of the accountant in resolving these problems.

10. Are there equitable limitations imposed by the issuance of a single class of stock to the parties in a consolidation? If so, what are they? Under what circumstances would the issuance of a single class of stock be as equitable as the issuance of several classes?

11. Describe the procedure involved in issuing securities to the several participants in a consolidation if both the relative net asset and the relative earnings contributions are to be preserved.

12. "The degree of inequity associated with a stock distribution plan is determinant only in the context of a specific postconsolidation level of earnings of the new or surviving enterprise." Explain.

13. If two capitalization rates are used to provide an "equitable" stock distribution plan, what determines the selection of these two rates?

PROBLEMS

Problem 5–1

The Never-Fail Electronics Company has been in operation for the past 10 years making circuit boards. Feeling the need to diversify, the board of directors decides to gain control of the Ever-Brite Plastics Company. Thus, on February 1, 1971, Never-Fail issued $3,000,000 in two-year, 7 percent notes payable. In March the company purchased in the open market 72,000 shares (90 percent) of Ever-Brite at an average per share cost of $35. During June, 1971 Ever-Brite was merged into Never-Fail. At this time the 10 percent (8,000 shares) minority interest in Ever-Brite was purchased for $40 per share. Miscellaneous legal and other costs associated with the merger were $60,000. In September, 1971, a new corporation, Never-Ever, Inc., issued 300,000 of its 350,000 authorized shares to Never-Fail Company in exchange for the operating assets originally belonging to Ever-Brite. On December 1, 1971, Never-Fail Company sold 80,000 shares of Never-Ever, Inc., for $25 per share.

Required:

(i) Prepare a schedule showing the net cash outlay for Never-Fail Electronics as of December 1, 1971, resulting from the above transactions.

(ii) What is the implied value of Never-Fail's interest in Never-Ever?

Problem 5–2

Identify the appropriate terms that are used in reference to the following descriptions:

(i) The combining of two, or more, previously independent business enterprises in such a manner that the stockholder interests in the combining companies are maintained in the surviving company and none of the participants emerges as a dominant party.

(ii) A business combination in which the participants perform similar functions in the production or sale of comparable products.

(iii) An increase in business operations, derived from increasing demand for a firm's products and services and the establishment of new product lines and geographic sales areas, so long as these expansions are financed through the normal corporate means of earnings retention and issuances of debt and/or equity securities and the expansion does not involve the acquisition of preexisting business operations from another business unit.

(iv) A combination between two business enterprises in which one of the companies, especially its common stockholder group, emerges as the dominant, controlling interest in the combined enterprise.

(v) A business combination in which the surviving corporation is one of the original group of combining companies.

(vi) A business combination which results in a parent-subsidiary relationship between the combining companies.

(vii) A business combination in which the combining firms have a supplier-customer relationship.

(viii) An expansion in business operations that is accomplished by acquiring a preexisting business unit.

(ix) A business combination in which a new corporate enterprise is organized for the purpose of acquiring the net assets of the combining companies.

(x) A business combination in which the combining companies have little if any production or market similarities.

Problem 5–3

Swing, Inc., a new corporation, is authorized to issue 100,000 shares of 5 percent, fully participating, $100 par, preferred stock and 100,000 shares of common stock, $10 par. Swing, Inc., was organized for the purpose of combining High Company and Low Company, about which you have determined the following:

	High Company	Low Company
Net tangible assets	$100,000	$90,000
Expected annual earnings	15,000	9,000

Required:

(i)   Utilizing a 6 percent capitalization rate, determine an equitable allocation of Swing, Inc.'s preferred stock and common stock to the shareholders of High Company and Low Company.

(ii) Determine the minimum annual net income of Swing, Inc., that would allow an equitable distribution of earnings under the conditions outlined above (including the data provided in requirement [i]).

(iii) Determine the maximum capitalization rate that could be utilized to provide an equitable allocation of stock. Disregard any facts given in requirements (i) and (ii).

(iv) Given the 5 percent preference rate on preferred stock, could a 4 percent capitalization rate ever result in an equitable allocation of earnings? If yes, at what income level?

Problem 5–4

The Bryant Company was organized on January 1, 1971, to purchase the properties and assume the liabilities of Wilton Games and Webster Novelties, toy manufacturers. The Bryant Company issued its 5 percent preferred stock (par, $100) in exchange for the net assets of each company and additionally issued common stock (par, $100) for projected excess earnings contributed. The following data are relevant to the stock distribution plan:

	Wilton Games	Webster Novelties
Assets....................................	$190,000	$118,000
Liabilities...............................	40,000	8,000
Capital stock...........................	120,000	93,000
Retained earnings......................	30,000	7,000
Average net income (1966–70 inclusive).........	24,300	2,700

Required:

Indicate the types and amounts of Bryant Company shares to be issued Wilton Games and Webster Novelties. In calculating the amount of common stock to be distributed it is agreed that the *sum* of the excess earnings of the contributing companies should be capitalized at—

(i)   Five percent.

(ii) Ten percent.

Problem 5–5

S Company wishes to purchase the assets of X Company and Y Company, which total $900,000. In exchange for these assets, S Company is willing to give 9,000 shares of its common stock ($100 par). X Company will contribute twice as much in asset value as Y Company. For the last five years, the average percentage return on assets of the individual companies has been 15 percent for X Company and 20 percent for Y Company.

Required:

(i)   Assume that the earnings streams of X Company and Y Company are not expected to change, and that S Company wishes to distribute the 9,000 shares on the basis of each firm's relative percentage in the combined earnings before consolidation. How much stock will each company receive?

(ii) If after the consolidation, Y Company's earnings are expected to increase by 50 percent while X Company's earnings are not expected to change, how would the 9,000 shares of S Company's stock be distributed if the distribution is to be based on each company's relative interest in combined anticipated earnings.

(iii) Refer to requirement (i), in which the earnings of each company do not change. Stated in terms of the percentage return on assets of each constituent company, what condition must exist for the relative net incomes of the constituents to be a fully equitable basis of stock distribution?

Problem 5–6

Syndicate A controls B Company through the ownership of 75,600 shares of the latter's capital stock, out of a total of 96,000 shares outstanding at June 30, 1971. The authorized capital stock of B Company is 150,000 shares, all of one class.

B Company controls C Company through the ownership of 6,250 shares of the latter's capital stock out of a total of 10,000 shares outstanding at June 30, 1971.

The sum of the capital stock and surplus of B Company at June 30, 1971, is $5,894,706, and of C Company, $2,132,470.

B Company wishes to acquire the minority interest in C Company through the issuance of shares of its capital stock at a value equal to its book value at June 30, 1971, taking into account the book value of capital stock of C Company, B Company's investment in which is carried on B Company's books at a total cost of $687,500.

Required:

(i)   You are to determine the number of shares to be issued by B Company, ignoring fractional shares.

(ii) You are to compute the percentage of control held by Syndicate A after such shares have been issued.

(AICPA adapted)

Problem 5–7

The R Corporation is organized with authorized capital stock of 30,000 shares of $100 par value common stock and 20,000 shares of $100 par value, 5 percent fully participating, preferred stock. The R Corporation proposes to consolidate companies A, B, and C to which the following information relates:

		Company		
	A	B	C	Total
Net tangible assets........	$200,000	$300,000	$500,000	$1,000,000
Five years average annual earnings.............	30,000	20,000	50,000	100,000
Rate of return on net tangible assets...........	15%	6⅔%	10%	
Ratio of earnings distribution before consolidation..............	———	———	———	———
Stock distribution (earnings capitalized at 5%):				
Preferred stock (5%, fully participating, $100 par).................	———	———	———	———
Common stock ($100 par).................	———	———	———	———
Earnings distribution:				
Preferred.............. (a)	———	———	———	———
(b)	———	———	———	———
(c)	———	———	———	———
Common............. (a)	———	———	———	———
(b)	———	———	———	———
(c)	———	———	———	———
Total............... (a)	———	———	———	———
(b)	———	———	———	———
(c)	———	———	———	———
Ratio of earnings distribution after consolidation............... (a)	———	———	———	———
(b)	———	———	———	———
(c)	———	———	———	———

Required:

Fill in the blanks for the following postcombination earnings levels:

(a) $100,000.
(b) $90,000.
(c) $120,000.

Problem 5–8

Companies X and Y agree to consolidate their assets and liabilities into newly formed Z Company. At the time of the proposed consolidation, the following data are relevant.

	X Company	Y Company
Net assets..$180,000		$120,000
Average net income............................... 14,000		14,000

Required:

(i) Demonstrate the inequity of Z Company's issuing shares of $100 par value, common stock to companies X and Y in the ratio of their contributions of—

    (*a*) Net assets.

    (*b*) Average net income.

(ii) If Z Company's 6 percent fully participating, $100 par value, preferred stock is issued for the net assets contributed, and $100 par value, common stock is issued for the difference between each company's average earnings capitalized at 7 percent and the net assets contributed, demonstrate the equity of this distribution. Additionally, indicate the inequitable consequence of using the following capitalization rates:

    (*a*) Five percent.

    (*b*) Ten percent.

Problem 5–9

The W Corporation was chartered on July 1, 1971, for the purpose of consolidating the resources and operations of companies X, Y, and Z.

The balance sheets of the affiliates on June 30, 1971, are as follows:

	Company		
	X	Y	Z
Tangible fixed assets—at cost................	$500,000	$400,000	$300,000
Goodwill.....................................		60,000	
Other assets.................................	200,000	280,000	85,000
	$700,000	$740,000	$385,000
Liabilities...................................	$ 80,000	$130,000	$ 35,000
Capital stock (par, $100)....................	400,000	500,000	250,000
Other contributed capital....................	70,000		40,000
Retained earnings...........................	150,000	110,000	60,000
	$700,000	$740,000	$385,000
Average profits (7/1/66–6/30/71 inclusive).....	$ 90,000	$120,000	$ 50,000
Appraised valuation of tangible fixed assets on June 15, 1971.........................	$620,000	$480,000	$360,000

Conferees to consolidation negotiations are agreed that the recorded goodwill of Y Company is valueless and that the "Other assets" of X Company are inflated to the extent of $50,000. The appraisal report of June 15 in respect to tangible fixed assets is accepted. These adjustments are to be made preliminary to the completion of formal consolidation.

The consolidation agreement calls for the exchange of W Corporation's 6 percent, $100 par value, cumulative and fully participating preferred stock for the net assets of companies X, Y, and Z, and for the issuance of its $50 par value common stock for the capitalized average earnings of each acquired company in excess of net tangible assets contributed. The capitalization rate is established at 10 percent.

Required:

(i)   Calculate the amounts of W Corporation's preferred and common shares to be issued to companies X, Y, and Z.

(ii) Indicate the equity or inequity of this plan of stock distribution if the earnings of W Corporation for the year ended June 30, 1972, are—

(*a*) $520,000.

(*b*) $130,000.

Problem 5–10

The stockholders of companies Alpha, Beta, and Gamma have decided to consolidate. The net assets and average earnings (for the past five years) are given below:

	Company			
	Alpha	*Beta*	*Gamma*	*Total*
Net assets.............	$1,200,000	$600,000	$1,200,000	$3,000,000
Average earnings........	100,000	100,000	100,000	300,000

Companies Alpha and Gamma suggest the issuance of a single class of stock based upon net asset contributions. Beta, however, suggests basing any stock issuance on average earnings.

Required:

(i)   Discuss these two proposals as to the fairness for all three parties.

(ii) Can you suggest a plan using more than one class of stock which would be more equitable than either of the two proposed plans?

Chapter 6

Mergers and Acquisitions—II

MODERN VALUE ANALYSIS: A NEGOTIATING APPROACH

Earlier discussion recognized the primary importance in combination negotiations of determining the price to be paid for the net assets of an acquired company. The payment frequently involves exchanging common stock. Thus, the stockholders of the acquired company receive common shares of the acquiring company; in return they transfer to the acquiring company shares of the acquired company.

Determination of Stock Exchange Ratios

Given a business combination which involves a stock for stock exchange, the price to be paid for the acquired firm's net assets is usually expressed in terms of a *stock exchange ratio*. This ratio may be defined as the number of shares of the acquiring firm to be given in exchange for one share of the acquired entity.

The stock exchange ratio is, of course, a *negotiated* price. However, that does not mean its determination is beyond analysis. An important category of relevant information that accountants can provide to the negotiators of business combinations relates directly to the determination of a stock exchange ratio.

Assuming that neither party to a combination agreement is willing to accept a reduction in the total market value of its stock holdings as a result of combination, the accountant can provide information which incorporates the negotiator's expectations and which approximates the range of potential exchange ratios within which negotiation should take place. In the present discussion, a common for common stock exchange is assumed. However, if the transfer plan includes other means of payment, the information regarding common stock (only) can often be adjusted so as to retain its relevance.

Significance of Price/Earnings Ratios

The stock exchange ratio is directly related to the expected price/earnings ratio[1] of the combined entity. To understand this relationship, it should

---

[1] Price/earnings ratio is defined as the market price per common share divided by the earnings per common share. Refinements in the earnings per share calculation which result from complex capital structures (including convertible securities) are analyzed in Chapter 10.

prove beneficial to consider first the general significance of price/earnings ratios within the context of business combinations.

Case 1. The following data relate to the constituents in a proposed combination which will involve a common for common stock exchange:

	Acquiring Firm A	*Acquired Firm B*
Net income.	$1,000,000	$1,000,000
Common shares outstanding.	1,000,000	1,000,000
Earnings per share.	$ 1	$ 1
Common stock market price.	$30	$10
Price/earnings ratio.	30:1	10:1

Given no additional information, the most intuitively obvious exchange ratio to effect this combination is 1/3:1, the ratio of current stock prices. Thus, a person holding one share of B stock, worth $10, would exchange it for one-third share of A stock, worth $10. If the combination is consummated under these conditions, the combined entity will exhibit the following characteristics:

	Combined Firm AB
Net income.	$2,000,000
Common shares outstanding.	1,333,333
Earnings per share.	$1.50

Assuming that no special efficiencies, inefficiencies, or risk changes are wrought by the combination, the price/earnings ratio of the combined entity should be the average of the constituents' ratios, weighted by the earnings streams they represent. This calculation is presented in Illustration 6–1.

A price/earnings ratio of 20 for the combined firm would result in a market price of $30, which is equal to the old market price of firm A. This

Illustration 6–1

	Price/ Earnings Ratio (1)	*Earnings Stream (2)*	*Weighted Factors (1) × (2)*
Firm A.	30	$1,000,000	30,000,000
Firm B.	10	1,000,000	10,000,000
Total.		$2,000,000	40,000,000
Firm AB.	20 = 40,000,000 ÷ 2,000,000		

price confirms the reasonableness of a 1/3:1 stock exchange ratio. The total market value of AB shares held by former stockholders of A is $30,000 which is equal to the value of their former holdings in firm A. Similarly, the market value of the shares held by the former stockholders of firm B remains the same. Neither group enjoys an advantage over the other as a consequence of the combination.

Given an exchange ratio of 1/3:1, consider the effect of a change in the expected price/earnings ratio of AB from the weighted average (20) to the level of old firm A (30).

	Combined Firm AB
Price/earnings ratio......................	30
Net income............................	$2,000,000
Common shares outstanding................	1,333,333
Earnings per share.......................	$ 1.50
Common stock price will be...............	$45.00

Should these facts occur, a holder of three shares of B Company stock (worth $30) would now gain possession of one share of AB stock (worth $45). Similarly, a holder of one share of A Company stock (worth $30) would now find his share[2] worth $45.

Several conclusions may be drawn from the foregoing discussion. First, if the price/earnings ratio of the combined entity equals a weighted average of the constituents' ratios, total wealth is not altered as a result of the combination. However, if the combined entity's price/earnings ratio exceeds the constituents' ratios' weighted average, total stockholders' wealth will be enhanced by the combination.

Second, given an increase in total stockholders' wealth resulting from a business combination, the allocation of this increment between the stockholder groups representing each combining firm is determined by the stock exchange ratio. As the ratio increases (in Case 1, for example, if the ratio were 1:1 instead of 1/3:1), the amount of wealth increment allocated to the former stockholders of the acquired firm will also increase. Conversely, as the ratio decreases, more of the wealth increment is allocated to the former stockholders of the acquiring firm.

Third, any wealth increment will be shared in proportion to the relative precombination stock values of the constituent firms if the exchange ratio equals the inverse of the ratio of the constituents' precombination share

---

[2] The new combined entity, which has been referred to as AB, may exist in several alternative forms. B may continue to exist as a separate corporate subsidiary to A. Or, a new legal corporation may be formed which replaces both A and B. Also, B may cease to exist, leaving A as the surviving corporation. In any case, and regardless of the surviving corporate name, the combined entity includes the operations of A and B. Thus it is described as AB.

prices. In Case 1, when the price/earnings ratio of the combined firm was assumed to be 30, the total market value of the combined firm was $60,000,000 (2,000,000 × 30). This constituted a total wealth increment of 50 percent. Given the exchange ratio of 1/3:1, which is the inverse of the precombination stock prices of $30 and $10, the wealth increment of *each* constituent stockholder group was 50 percent. Thus the total wealth increment was shared in the same proportion as the relative precombination stock values of the constituents.

Fourth, it may be noted that earnings per share of the combined entity is not the same as it was for either of the precombination constituents. In Case 1, the combined entity's earnings per share is $1.50, whereas it was $1 for each constituent firm. This difference can be explained by the variation in size of the constituents' earnings streams and by the fact that the combining firms had different price/earnings ratios. Whenever a combined entity reports earnings per share that is different from those of the constituents, it can be established that the negotiated exchange ratio reflects a difference in the combining firms' price/earnings ratios.[3] The amount by which the combined entity's earnings per share deviates from the constituents' earnings per shares is dependent upon (1) the amount of the difference in the constituents' negotiated price/earnings ratios; and (2) the relative size of their income streams and number of shares outstanding. Illustration 6–2 displays the kinds of changes in earnings per share that result from introducing changes in the variables discussed above.

The problem of evaluating earnings per share when it has been materially affected by a business combination is part of the more general problem category of interpretive accounting. Several aspects of this accounting function will be analyzed in Chapter 10.

Exchange Ratio Negotiating Range

A reasonable assumption underlying combination negotiations is that neither negotiating party would accept terms which would tend to result in that party having to incur a diminution in wealth. One can point to several factors which might promote a combination even if reasonable expectations did not include a wealth increment. But it is unlikely that any stockholder group would accept a loss of wealth as an appropriate price for participating in a corporate combination. As discussed earlier, the total stockholders' wealth (market value) of the combined entity will equal the sum of the constituent firms' stockholders' wealth *if* the combined entity's price/earnings ratio equals a weighted average of the combining firms' price/earnings ratios. This sets a minimum expected price/earnings ratio for the combined entity, below which the combination will probably not be consummated. If

---

[3] This generalization refers only to common for common stock exchanges and assumes that total combined earnings in the period immediately following combination is equal to the sum of the constituents' total earnings in the period immediately preceding combination.

Illustration 6-2

	Net Income (1)	Shares Outstanding (2)	Stock Market Price (3)	Price/ Earnings Ratio (4)	Exchange Ratio Implied by (3) and (4) (5)	Earnings per Share (6)	Compared to Case A, the Variables Altered Were—
Case A:							
Acquiring firm A........	$1,000,000	1,000,000	$30	30:1		$1.00	
Acquired firm B........	1,000,000	1,000,000	10	10:1		1.00	
Combined firm AB......	2,000,000	1,333,333			1/3:1	1.50	
Case B:							
Acquiring firm A........	1,000,000	1,000,000	30	30:1		$1.00	Total earnings and
Acquired firm B........	500,000	500,000	10	10:1		1.00	shares of B
Combined firm AB......	1,500,000	1,166,667			1/3:1	1.28	
Case C:							
Acquiring firm A........	1,000,000	1,000,000	20	20:1		$1.00	Price/earnings ratio
Acquired firm B........	1,000,000	1,000,000	10	10:1		1.00	of A (and, there-
Combined firm AB......	2,000,000	1,500,000			1/2:1	1.33	fore, the exchange ratio)
Case D:							
Acquiring firm A........	1,000,000	1,000,000	30	30:1		$1.00	Price/earnings ratio
Acquired firm B........	1,000,000	1,000,000	60	60:1		1.00	of B (and, there-
Combined firm AB......	2,000,000	3,000,000			2:1	.67	fore, the exchange ratio)
Case E:							
Acquiring firm A........	1,000,000	1,000,000	30	30:1		$1.00	Price/earnings ratio
Acquired firm B........	1,000,000	1,000,000	30	30:1		1.00	of B, altered so
Combined firm AB......	2,000,000	2,000,000			1:1	1.00	that it would equal A's price/ earnings ratio

the expected price/earnings ratio of the combined entity were lower, at least one of the constituent firms would be forced by the combination to incur a loss of stockholder wealth.

Case 2. The analysis of Case 1 showed that the combined entity's expected price/earnings ratio of 20 equaled the weighted average of the constituents' price/earnings ratios. Utilizing the expected price/earnings ratio of AB (20) and a stock exchange ratio of one third, the wealth of all stockholders remained unchanged. Assume now that AB's expected price/earnings ratio is only 15. Illustration 6–3 depicts a $10,000,000 re-

Illustration 6–3

	Outstanding Shares	Price/ Earnings Ratio	Earnings/ Share	Total Stockholder Wealth
Firm A...............	1,000,000	30	$1.00	$30,000,000
Firm B...............	1,000,000	10	1.00	10,000,000
Total.............				$40,000,000
Firm AB.............	1,333,333	15	1.50	$30,000,000

duction in total stockholders' wealth when the expected price/earnings ratio falls from the weighted average (20) to 15. Having established the minimum acceptable combined entity price/earnings ratio, it is important to note that given this price/earnings ratio, only one exchange ratio is acceptable. It is the inverse of the ratio of the constituent firms' stock prices. Case 3 discloses the effects of assuming exchange ratios that are either equal to, greater than, or less than the unique ratio which leaves the wealth positions of each stockholder group unchanged.

Illustration 6–4

	Combined Firm AB	Number and Total Value of Firm AB Shares Held by—	
		Stockholders from Firm A	Stockholders from Firm B
Net income..................	$ 2,000,000		
Shares outstanding............	1,333,333	1,000,000	333,333
Earnings/share...............	$ 1.50		
Price/earnings ratio...........	20		
Stock price..................	$30	$30	$30
Total stock value..........	$40,000,000	$30,000,000	$10,000,000
Wealth positions prior to combination...............		30,000,000	10,000,000
Gain or [loss] on combination...............		$ 0	$ 0

Case 3. Given the data of Case 1, consider the effects of alternative stock exchange ratios.

Assumption 1. Given a stock exchange ratio of 1/3:1, the equities in firm AB are displayed in Illustration 6–4.

Assumption 2. Given a stock exchange ratio of 1/2:1, the equities in firm AB are presented in Illustration 6–5.

Assumption 3. Given a stock exchange ratio of 1/4:1, the equities in firm AB are presented in Illustration 6–6.

Illustration 6–5

	Combined Firm AB	Number and Total Value of Firm AB Shares Held by—	
		Stockholders from Firm A	Stockholders from Firm B
Net income...................	$ 2,000,000		
Shares outstanding............	1,500,000	1,000,000	500,000
Earnings/share...............	$ 1.33		
Price/earnings ratio...........	20		
Stock price..................	$26.67	$26.67	$26.67
Total stock value..........	$40,000,000	$26,666,667	$13,333,333
Wealth positions prior to combination...............		30,000,000	10,000,000
Gain or [loss] on combination................		[$ 3,333,333]	$ 3,333,333

Illustration 6–6

	Combined Firm AB	Number and Total Value of Firm AB Shares Held by—	
		Stockholders from Firm A	Stockholders from Firm B
Net income...................	$ 2,000,000		
Shares outstanding............	1,250,000	1,000,000	250,000
Earnings/share...............	$ 1.60		
Price/earnings ratio...........	20		
Stock price..................	$32	$32	$32
Total stock value..........	$40,000,000	$32,000,000	$ 8,000,000
Wealth positions prior to combination...............		30,000,000	10,000,000
Gain or [loss] on combination................		$ 2,000,000	[$ 2,000,000]

In Case 3, it is important to recognize that the price/earnings ratio of the combined firm was held constant at 20:1, the weighted average of the constituents' price/earnings ratios. Thus, the total stock value of AB was equal to the sum of the stock values of A and B. The assumed changes in the exchange ratio resulted in differing allocations of this value between the stockholder groups. Since the total wealth did not change as a result of the combination, the allocations on the basis of exchange ratios other than 1/3:1 resulted in the two stockholder groups realizing counterbalancing gains and losses. It should be apparent that if the expected price/earnings ratio of AB increases (above the minimum level), total stockholders' wealth also increases (above the precombination level). Correspondingly, as the expected price/earnings ratio increases, the exchange ratio is subject to increasing variability without forcing a loss on either stockholder group.

General Formulation of the Model

Consider the limit on the exchange ratio that would be imposed by an acquiring firm (A). This limit is the maximum exchange ratio that is acceptable to A, given a specific expected price/earnings ratio of the combined entity (AB). In other words, it is the exchange ratio that will leave the wealth positions of firm A stockholders undiminished. Assume the following notation:

W_A = total wealth (market value) of firm A stock.
S_A = firm A outstanding shares.
S_B = firm B outstanding shares.
W_{AB} = total wealth (market value) of firm AB stock.
ER = common stock exchange ratio, i.e., the number of shares of firm A (the acquiring firm) given in exchange for 1 share of (acquired) firm B.
ER_A = maximum exchange ratio acceptable to firm A stockholders.
NI_{AB} = total earnings of firm AB in the first postcombination period. It is assumed that these earnings equal the sum of A's and B's total earnings in the last precombination period.
PE_{AB} = expected price/earnings ratio of firm AB.

From the definitions given above, it may be noted that—

$$\frac{S_A}{S_A + ER(S_B)}$$

equals the equity percentage of firm A stockholders in firm AB. Further, $W_{AB} = NI_{AB} (PE_{AB})$. Thus, to equate the firm A stockholders' precombination wealth with the value of their equity in firm AB:

$$W_A = \frac{S_A}{S_A + ER(S_B)} [NI_{AB}(PE_{AB})].$$

To solve for the maximum exchange ratio acceptable to firm A stockholders:

(1) $$ER_A = \frac{(S_A/W_A)NI_{AB}(PE_{AB}) - S_A}{S_B}.$$

Within the context of a particular business combination, the values of all terms in equation (1) are constant, except for ER_A and PE_{AB}. Thus, it can be demonstrated that as the expected price/earnings ratio of the combined entity increases, the maximum exchange ratio acceptable to acquiring firm stockholders also increases. Illustration 6–7 depicts the nature of this relationship.

Illustration 6–7

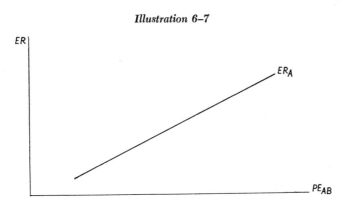

Next, consider the limit on the exchange ratio that would be imposed by an acquired firm B. This limit takes the form of a minimum exchange ratio. It is the ratio that will leave the wealth positions of firm B stockholders undiminished. Assume the notation presented previously and the following:

W_B = total wealth (market value) of firm B stock.

ER_B = minimum exchange ratio acceptable to firm B stockholders.

The equity percentage of firm B stockholders in firm AB is

$$\frac{ER(S_B)}{S_A + ER(S_B)} \, .$$

Firm B stockholders' precombination wealth is equated with the value of their equity in firm AB as follows:

$$W_B = \frac{ER(S_B)}{S_A + ER(S_B)} \, [NI_{AB}(PE_{AB})] \, .$$

Substituting appropriate values in equation (2), which follows, will yield the minimum exchange ratio acceptable to firm B stockholders.

(2)
$$ER_B = \frac{S_A}{(S_B/W_B)NI_{AB}(PE_{AB}) - S_B} \, .$$

Within the context of a particular corporate combination, the values of all terms in equation (2) are constant, except for ER_B and PE_{AB}. Thus, as the expected price/earnings ratio of the combined entity increases, the minimum exchange ratio acceptable to the acquired firm's stockholders decreases (at a decreasing rate). Illustration 6–8 graphically indicates the nature of this relationship.

The negotiated exchange ratio of a business combination must be consistent with the boundary conditions (equations 1 and 2) imposed by both negotiating parties. The field of exchange ratios that are consistent with both limits can be portrayed by superimposing the minimum exchange ratio acceptable to the acquired firm (ER_B) on the maximum exchange ratio acceptable to the acquiring firm (ER_A). This field is shown in Illustration 6–9. Thus, the exchange ratio used to execute the combination must

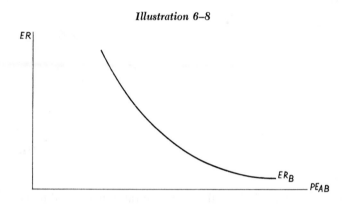

Illustration 6–8

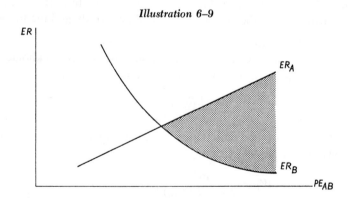

Illustration 6–9

fall within the shaded area of the illustration. Upon specifying an expected price/earnings ratio of the combined entity, a negotiator can use the above analysis to assess a reasonable bargaining range. The unique point of intersection between ER_A and ER_B (Illustration 6–9) specifies the only acceptable exchange ratio in the event that the expected price/earnings ratio of AB equals the weighted average of the constituent firms' price/earnings ratios. As previously discussed, this unique exchange ratio is equal to the inverse of the ratio of the constituent firms' stock prices.

   Case 4.   Utilizing the data of Case 1, the stock exchange ratio negotiating ranges are as follows:

Expected Price/Earnings Ratio of Firm AB	Maximum Exchange Ratio (1)	Minimum Exchange Ratio (2)
10	−1/3	1
15	0	1/2
20	1/3	1/3
25	2/3	1/4
30	1	1/5

(1)
$$ER_A = \frac{(S_A/W_A)NI_{AB}(PE_{AB}) - S_A}{S_B}$$

$$ER_A = \frac{(1/30)2{,}000{,}000(PE_{AB}) - 1{,}000{,}000}{1{,}000{,}000}$$

(2)
$$ER_B = \frac{S_A}{(S_B/W_B)NI_{AB}(PE_{AB}) - S_B}$$

$$ER_B = \frac{1{,}000{,}000}{(1/10)2{,}000{,}000(PE_{AB}) - 1{,}000{,}000}$$

The negotiating field is presented graphically in Illustration 6–10.

It must be emphasized that the exchange ratio to be used in a specific combination remains a negotiated price; it is not subject to precise determination through logical analysis. The agreed-upon ratio will depend on the relative bargaining powers of the combination participants as well as

Illustration 6–10

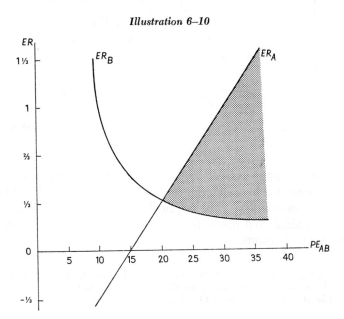

the estimated contributions of each constituent to the profitability of the combined entity. The above analysis can only provide information which may facilitate the negotiating process.

Parameter Changes

A firm that exhibits an interest in expansion via the process of acquisition may wish to compare alternative prospective combination participants. By inspecting the general form of the equation for determining its maximum acceptable exchange ratio, an acquiring firm can note the effects (upon ER_A) of firms being considered for combination which have different net income levels or different amounts of outstanding stock.

The income of a potential combination participant, for example, naturally affects the income of the potential combined entity (NI). Given the position of NI_{AB} (in the numerator), it is obvious that the ER_A is directly related to changes in NI. Thus, if firm A is considering three alternative firms to acquire (B, C, D) and if $NI_B > NI_C > NI_D$, the comparative ER curves will have relationships as shown in Illustration 6–11.

Illustration 6–11

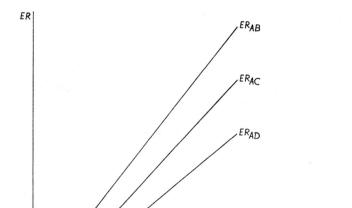

A similar kind of analysis can be made to show the effects of considering alternative firms that have differing amounts of common stock outstanding. By the same token a firm to be acquired can analyze the difference in its boundary condition that results from differing characteristics of alternative combination participants.[4]

---

[4] For further consideration of the exchange ratio model, see Kermit D. Larson and Nicholas J. Gonedes, "Business Combinations: An Exchange Ratio Determination Model," *The Accounting Review,* October, 1969, pp. 720–28.

PRO FORMA FINANCIAL STATEMENTS

The previous analyses of Chapters 5 and 6 have exposed a variety of factors that must be evaluated and/or negotiated before a corporate combination is completed. Several additional factors will be treated in subsequent chapters. Yet, it should already be apparent that the *combined* effects of each constituent's unique characteristics as well as the alternative means by which a combination might be completed and accounted for are not easily perceived. To overcome this problem, it is often useful to prepare financial statements which assume the completion of specific business transactions that have not yet been executed. Such statements which "give effect to" anticipated or contemplated transactions are commonly referred to as *pro forma* statements.

Pro forma statements may be especially informative in the preliminary negotiations of combination agreements. For example, in devising equitable settlement arrangements with several combination participants, it may be useful to construct a series of pro forma statements, each reflecting the effect of an alternative stock distribution plan. The financial implications of each proposed course of action are then exposed in a similar comparative format for the consideration of management.

Pro forma financial statements are frequently used *after* the combination agreement has been tentatively accepted by the corporate officers of the combining firms. After the agreement between corporate officers, it is frequently necessary to obtain the approval of a specified majority of the stockholders of one or both of the combining firms before a combination can be finalized. Pro forma statements, which portray the tentatively accepted combination conditions, are typically included in the report to stockholders. Further, if the combination involves the issuance of new securities which must be approved by the Securities and Exchange Commission, pro forma statements are generally a required inclusion in the registration statement.[5]

In preparing a pro forma statement, the hypothetical nature of the statement should be clearly disclosed. The title of the statement should carry a reference to its pro forma character and should clearly state the proposed or assumed condition. Furthermore, elaboration of the types of adjustments embodied in the statement should be provided, either in the body or in related footnotes.

A typical pro forma balance sheet is represented in columnar format with entries for the hypothetical transactions juxtaposed against audited balance sheet classifications. Of course, this basic format may also be utilized for pro forma income statement presentations.

Case 5 includes a pro forma balance sheet that was extracted from a

---

[5] It should be clear that pro forma statements can be used in a wide variety of situations other than in anticipation of a business combination. Wherever it is desirable to observe the financial statement effects of hypothetical transactions, pro forma statements may be prepared.

prospectus issued by Ling-Temco-Vought, Inc. The case is an illustration of the usefulness of pro forma statement in circumstances where the anticipated transactions are very complex, thereby making it difficult to perceive their financial statement implications.

Case 5. During 1968, Ling-Temco-Vought, Inc., offered the holders of certain LTV securities the opportunity to exchange those securities for a "package" of different securities. The "package" was defined in terms of *Units,* as follows:

Each Unit will consist of 1.0 share of Braniff Special Stock, Class A, 0.6 share of National Common Stock, 1.0 share of National Special Stock, Class A, 0.33 share of Computer Technology Common Stock and 1.1 LTV Common Stock Purchase Warrants.[6]

The corporations mentioned in the package, other than LTV, were subsidiaries of LTV. The exchange offer was extended to the holders of the following LTV securities:

1.10 Units for 1 share of LTV Common Stock
9.75 Units for $1,000 principal amount of 6½ % Notes
10.00 Units for $1,000 principal amount of 6¾ % Debentures
6.70 Units for $1,000 principal amount of 5% Debentures
9.50 Units for $1,000 principal amount of 5¾ % Debentures[7]

In preparing pro forma financial statements to show the effects of the exchange offer, LTV first had to prepare a pro forma statement to record the consequences of certain transactions which had actually taken place at the date the prospectus was issued (October 31, 1968) but had not taken place in time to be included in the June 30, 1968, balance sheet. These transactions included the acquisition of Greatamerica Corporation. Illustration 6–12 presents this portion of the complete pro forma balance sheet. Illustration 6–13 continues the pro forma presentation by showing the effects of the securities exchange offer, assuming 100 percent and 50 percent acceptances of the exchange offer.

TAX FACTORS AFFECTING CORPORATE COMBINATIONS

Various business objectives which may lead to expansion through combination were discussed in Chapter 5. The provisions of the Internal Revenue Code were recognized as significant factors in the decision as to whether a contemplated combination should be pursued. Tax consequences are equally significant in determining the methods to be used to pay for the acquired firm. In fact, the influence of taxes on one aspect of a combination often has a simultaneous impact on other aspects of the combination. For example, the tax implications of available payment methods may

---

[6] Prospectus of Ling-Temco-Vought, Inc., October 31, 1968, p. 1.
[7] *Ibid.,* p. 1.

Illustration 6–12

LING-TEMCO-VOUGHT, INC. AND SUBSIDIARIES
PRO FORMA BALANCE SHEET

The following pro forma balance sheet at June 30, 1968, gives effect to (1) the issuance of debentures and warrants of Ling-Temco-Vought, Inc. in the acquisition of the assets of Greatamerica, (2) the assumption of liabilities of Greatamerica, and (3) certain other transactions described in Note (1) below. The statement should be read in conjunction with the financial statements and related notes of Ling-Temco-Vought, Inc. included elsewhere herein.

In Thousands

ASSETS	LTV	Pro Forma Adjust- ments(2)	Great- america	As Adjusted before Exchange Offer
Current assets	$1,047,151	$ ...	$ 18,695	$1,065,846
Investment in Greatamerica(1)	475,145	25,166	(500,311)	...
Investment in Braniff Airways(1)	...	...	338,736	338,736
Investment in National Car Rental(1)	...	...	134,756	134,756
Other assets	41,151	15,476	37,353	93,980
Fixed assets	960,505	...	455	960,960
Intangibles	48,051	1,500	...	49,551
	$2,572,003	$42,142	$ 29,684	$2,643,829

LIABILITIES AND STOCKHOLDERS' EQUITY				
Current liabilities	$ 627,333	$ ...	$ 77,876	$ 705,209
Long-term debt	1,194,001	25,166 / 16,976	40,005	1,276,148
Due Greatamerica Corporation	88,500	...	(88,500)	...
Deferrals	46,293	...	303	46,596
Minority interests	350,681	...	...	350,681
Stockholders' equity:				
Series A preferred stock	2,962	...	...	2,962
Special stock, class AA	786	...	...	786
Common stock	1,991	...	...	1,991
Capital surplus	168,014	...	...	168,014
Earned surplus	91,442	...	...	91,442
Total Stockholders' Equity	265,195	...	...	265,195
	$2,572,003	$42,142	$ 29,684	$2,643,829

(1) The acquisition of the capital stock of Braniff and National through the purchase of assets of Greatamerica will be carried on the books of LTV as investments in an unconsolidated subsidiary or affiliate. Reference is made to the balance sheets of Braniff and National included elsewhere herein. Paragraphs 8 and 9 of *Opinion No. 10* of the Accounting Principles Board of the American Institute of Certified Public Accountants, which recommends that a portion of the proceeds received for debentures issued with warrants to purchase stock be attributed to such warrants, have been temporarily suspended for further study by the Board. In the event the accounting principles set out in these paragraphs are made effective retroactively to cover transactions in fiscal years beginning after December 31, 1966, and if accounting principles as there stated are applicable to the issuance of securities with conversion rights or warrants in an acquisition of this type, the Company will establish an amount representing the value of the warrants as deferred debt discount to be amortized over the life of the debentures. This value is estimated at approximately $50,000,000 which, if amortized on a straight line basis, would amount to $2,500,000 annually (subject to adjustment for retirements and use of such debentures in the exercise of warrants), equal after tax reduction to $0.23 per share based on the average number of shares outstanding (including residual securities) during the six month period ended June 30, 1968.

See also Note B—Long-Term Debt in Notes to Financial Statements of LTV included elsewhere herein.

(2) The following transactions are reflected in the pro forma adjustments:

    (a) The sale by LTV International, N.V. in July, 1968, of $77,380,000 of 5% guaranteed (subordinated) debentures, less discount of $1,500,000, the borrowing by LTV of $15,476,000 from a foreign bank and contribution of such amount to the capital of LTV International, the deposit by LTV International of such $15,476,000 in a foreign bank, the repurchase by LTV of $17,380,000 of 6½% notes payable June 1, 1973, and the partial prepayment by LTV of $58,500,000 of bank loans due July 31, 1969, borrowed in connection with the acquisition of Jones & Laughlin.

    (b) The issuance by LTV of $25,166,000 of its 5% debentures due January 15, 1988, in the purchase of the assets of Greatamerica.

Illustration 6–13

The following sets forth the effects of the Exchange Offer on the above pro forma balance sheet assuming (1) the exchange of 100% of the Eligible Securities in the Exchange Offer, and (2) the exchange of 50% of the Eligible Securities in the Exchange Offer.

In Thousands

	Pro Forma	100% Exchange Effect on Accounts	100% Exchange Balances after Exchange	50% Exchange Effect on Accounts	50% Exchange Balances after Exchange
ASSETS					
Current assets	$1,065,846	$ (7,836) (3) 6,260 (4)	$1,064,270	$ (4,305) (3) 3,192 (4)	$1,064,733
Investment in Braniff	338,736	(103,321) (1)	235,415	(51,660) (1)	287,076
Investment in National Car Rental	134,756	(128,961) (1)	5,795	(64,480) (1)	70,276
Other assets	93,980	.....	93,980	.....	93,980
Fixed assets	960,960	.....	960,960	.....	960,960
Intangibles	49,551	(936) (2)	48,615	(468) (2)	49,083
	2,643,829	(234,794)	2,409,035	(117,721)	2,526,108
LIABILITIES AND STOCKHOLDER'S EQUITY					
Current liabilities	$ 705,209	$	$ 705,209	$	$ 705,209
Long-term debt	1,276,148	(248,361) (6)	1,027,787	(124,180) (6)	1,151,968
Deferrals	46,596	3,573 (5)	50,169	1,770 (5)	48,366
Minority interests	350,681	1,830 (7)	352,511	915 (7)	351,596
Stockholders' equity:					
Series A preferred stock	2,962	.....	2,962	.....	2,962
Special stock, class AA	786	.....	786	.....	786
Common stock	1,991	(1,000) (8)	991	(500) (8)	1,491
Capital surplus	168,014	(3,989) (3) 34,722 (9)	198,747	(2,191) (3) 17,361 (9)	183,184

Earned surplus............	91,442	(3,847) (3) (20,409) (10) 6,260 (4) (3,573) (5)		69,873	(2,114) (3) (10,204) (10) 3,192 (4) (1,770) (5)	80,546
	265,195	8,164		273,359	3,774	268,969
Total Stockholders' Equity......	$2,643,829	($234,794)		$2,409,035	($117,721)	$2,526,108

The effects of the Exchange Offer on the accounts as reflected in the above statement are explained below:

(1) Reduction in carrying value of investments in Braniff and National applicable to shares exchanged.
(2) Write-off of unamortized discount and expense on debt reduced.
(3) Estimated expenses in connection with Exchange Offer ($7,836,000 in 100% exchange and $4,305,000 in 50% exchange), allocated to capital surplus with respect to common stock reacquired and to gain on debt retired with respect to debt retired.
(4) Estimated current income taxes refundable resulting from loss on retirement of 6½%, 6¾%, and 5¾% debt issues.
(5) Estimated deferred income tax applicable to gain on retirement of 5% debentures.
(6) Face value of debt retired.
(7) Minority interest in CT applicable to shares to be issued.
(8) Par value of common stock to be reacquired.
(9) Capital surplus credit for market value of warrants issued in connection with debt retired ($117,162,000 in 100% exchange and $58,581,000 in 50% exchange), less capital surplus applicable to shares reacquired ($82,440,000 on 2,000,000 shares and $41,220,000 on 1,000,000 shares).
(10) Earned surplus credit for excess of face value of debt retired over carrying value of securities and market value of warrants issued in debt retirement ($15,-390,000 in 100% exchange and $7,696,000 in 50% exchange), less retained earnings applicable to shares reacquired ($35,799,000 on 2,000,000 shares and $17,900,000 on 1,000,000 shares).

dominate the final decision as to whether a combination will be completed or abandoned. Furthermore, potential income tax benefits, such as operating loss carryovers, may be a principal motivation underlying a proposed merger; and the transaction must therefore be carefully formulated to conform with relevant tax provisions.

Tax-Free Reorganizations

A critical tax factor in planning a corporate combination involves the taxable or tax-free status of the transaction between the acquiring corporation and the acquired corporation and/or its stockholders. In general, exchanges of assets (including securities such as stock) are recognized by the Code as the appropriate point in time at which to assign new bases to the transferred items and to assess tax. However, corporate combinations may be either taxable or tax-free, depending upon the nature of the agreement and the payments made to the combination participants (or their shareholders).

If a combination qualifies as a tax-free "reorganization," the acquired corporation may, in whole or in part, escape recognition of gain or loss on the transfer of its property to the acquiring corporation; and the existing bases of the assets are carried forward without change in amount to the acquiring corporation. The shareholders of the acquired corporation also may exchange their shares for stock of the acquiring corporation without the recognition of gain or loss. On the other hand, in a taxable combination, gain or loss is recognized by the selling party, and the acquiring corporation usually establishes new (current) bases in the assets acquired.[8]

Criteria for Assessing Tax Status

Tax-free acquisitions are usually effected under one of three basic forms of reorganization defined in Section 368 of the Internal Revenue Code. In general terms, the following alternatives are available:

1. Statutory mergers and consolidations, i.e., a merger or consolidation consummated in accordance with a state statute (type A).
2. Acquisition of stock in exchange for *voting* shares of stock, subject to the requirement that the acquiring corporation must then hold a controlling interest (a minimum of 80 percent) in the acquired corporation (type B).
3. Acquisition of assets in exchange for *voting* stock where "substantially all" of the assets of the selling corporation are transferred to the purchasing corporation (type C).

The type A business combination refers to situations in which the acquiring and the acquired corporations are combined into one corporation (the acquiring, the acquired, or a new corporation) and the combination is ef-

---

[8] Boris I. Bittker and James E. Eustice, *Federal Income Taxation of Corporations and Shareholders* (2d ed., Hamden, Conn.: Federal Tax Press, 1966), chap. xii.

fected in compliance with state statutes which specify the procedures to be followed. Such a transaction may qualify as a tax-free reorganization even if preferred stock and nonvoting stock are issued in payment for the acquired corporation. Depending on the relevant state statutes, the use of some limited amounts of cash and debt securities may also be permitted. However, an additional requirement imposed by the courts is that continuity of equity interests be maintained. For example, if debt regarded as excessive in amount is used as part payment, the courts may rule that a continuity of equity interests has not been maintained and accordingly refuse to accord tax-free status to the combination. Thus, it is possible for a combination to comply fully with the appropriate state merger laws and with the mechanics of the Code, and yet be disallowed as a tax-free reorganization.

To qualify as a type B reorganization, the means of payment is limited to voting stock of the acquiring corporation. However, past cash purchases of stock by the acquiring corporation of a minority interest in the acquired corporation do not necessarily disqualify the eventual tax-free status of the combination. Moreover, the *acquired* corporation may purchase (for cash) the shares of those stockholders who are unwilling to accept voting stock in the acquiring corporation.

Under a type C reorganization, the question as to what constitutes "substantially all" of the selling corporation's properties is subject to varied interpretation. Final determination depends on the nature of the assets retained, the purposes of retention, and the dollar amount of such assets (measured in terms of fair market value). In general, if the assets retained by the seller are not essential to the past operations of the seller, if retention is not for the purposes of continuing operations or for sales to another purchaser, and if the amount does not exceed the retained liabilities of the seller, the acquisition will satisfy type C requirements.

The type C requirement that payment be made with voting shares is not absolute. If at least 80 percent of the selling firm's assets are acquired in this manner, cash or other forms of consideration may be used to acquire the remaining 20 percent. Finally, the voting shares issued in payment may be shares in the acquiring firm's parent corporation.

Although the voting stock requirements of type B or C combinations are not absolute, it may be observed that the continuity of equity interests problem that may arise under a type A combination is always overcome as a natural consequence by the high voting stock requirements of types B and C reorganizations.

It should be noted that the distinguishable characteristics of the three reorganization types are difficult to isolate in many combination arrangements. What first appears as a type B reorganization may, if the acquired subsidiary is liquidated, have the substance of a type A or type C reorganization. This can be accomplished because the liquidation of a subsidiary into a parent is also tax free. Also, types A and C reorganizations may be essentially equivalent in terms of their final equity arrangements.

Implications for Equitable Distribution Plans

The implications of these alternative "reorganization" forms on the securities distribution plan are important. In the case of a statutory merger or consolidation, cash, bonds, nonvoting preferred stock, and/or common stock may be distributed, all of which may be utilized to fulfill the type of equitable distribution plan previously outlined. In the other two cases (types B and C), however, only voting stock may be distributed. Although shares of *voting* preferred stock are not preemptorily excluded from the package of securities that may be issued, their use may produce other undesirable income tax consequences (see Section 306). Hence, if a tax-free reorganization is the controlling objective, the criteria for an equitable distribution plan (Chapter 5) may have to be largely ignored.

Motives for Planning Tax Status

Whether a corporate combination will be deemed a taxable exchange or a tax-free reorganization is obviously susceptible to planning by combination participants. In this regard, a major concern of the acquiring corporation is the bases of the assets to be acquired. If the assets' current fair market values exceed their bases to the acquired firm, a taxable transaction is desirable (other things being equal). Establishing a taxable status to the combination would assign the current fair market values of the assets as the acquiring corporation's bases, thus increasing future period's tax deductions. Conversely, if current fair market values are less than the acquired corporation's bases in assets, the acquiring corporation should prefer a tax-free combination.

The acquired firm and/or its stockholders will generally prefer a tax-free combination status so long as the fair market value of securities received exceeds their bases in properties and/or shares given up. The general motive is, of course, to defer tax payments. Conversely, should the bases of properties and/or securities given up exceed their fair market value, a taxable exchange status would facilitate early recognition of losses.

Tax Attribute Carryovers

When a tax-free reorganization is accomplished as a type A or type C (as defined in Section 368), certain tax benefits, rights, and obligations of the acquired corporation may carry over to the surviving firm. Subject to specified conditions and limitations, the accounting methods employed by the acquired firm, net operating losses, unused investment credits, unexhausted capital loss carryovers, and other tax attributes generally are applicable to the calculation of income tax for the surviving firm. However, numerous additional restrictions are imposed (e.g., Sections 269, 381, and 382) to prevent special advantages from carrying over if the combination serves no sound business purpose other than to gain the benefit of the acquired corporation's favorable tax attributes.

If a combination involves the establishment of a parent-subsidiary relationship (type B), the tax attributes of the acquired-subsidiary corporation typically remain with the subsidiary corporation. Should the constituents of the combination qualify for, and elect to file, a consolidated return, the subsidiary's unique attributes are generally applicable to that return only to the extent that they would be effective on a separate return. If the subsidiary is subsequently liquidated into the parent corporation, the same provisions which provide a carryover (of tax attributes) in a type A or type C reorganization provide a carryover of the liquidated subsidiary's attributes.

QUESTIONS

1. In respect to a corporate combination, how is a "stock exchange ratio" generally expressed?

2. If the price/earnings ratio of the combined entity is equivalent to a weighted average of the constituent companies' ratios, is the total wealth of the several companies (increased, decreased, or not altered) as a direct result of the combination?

3. Consider a combination which is accomplished via a common for common stock exchange and which is not expected to result in economies or diseconomies of scale. If the combined entity's price/earnings ratio exceeds a weighted average of the constituent companies' ratios, total shareholders' wealth will be (increased, decreased, or not altered) by the combination?

4. Mr. Algoe compiles the following information concerning companies A and B:

	A Company	B Company
Net income....................	$2,000,000	$1,500,000
Common shares outstanding......	1,000,000	750,000
Earnings per share.............	$ 2	$ 2
Common stock price...........	$40	$20
P/E ratio.....................	20:1	10:1

Mr. Algoe concludes: "If A Company and B Company are combined to form AB Company, the restated earnings per share will be $2. Since it is $2 for A and for B, it obviously will not change." Is Algoe correct? If not, what factors determine the deviation of the earnings per share for the combined entity from the earnings per share of each participant?

5. "If the expected price/earnings ratio of a proposed combined entity were lower than a weighted average of the combining firms' price/earnings ratios, the combination probably would not take place." Comment on the validity of this statement.

6. Two companies, A and B, are contemplating a combination. A Company's corporate management projects a price/earnings ratio for the combined

entity of 20. However, B Company's officials are somewhat more optimistic and project a ratio of 30. Which forecast would allow the greatest flexibility in establishing a specific stock exchange ratio? Why?

7. What are *pro forma* statements and how do they assist corporate managements in deciding on the provisions of a combination agreement?

8. Briefly describe what is meant by type A, type B, and type C reorganizations under Section 368 of the Internal Revenue Code.

9. Under a type B reorganization, is it possible for minority interests to be purchased for cash and yet preserve a tax-free status?

10. Under a type C reorganization, would it be possible to exchange some security other than *voting* shares? If so, is there any practical limit to the use of other types of securities?

11. Would a type B or type C reorganization impose limits on the type of "equitable" distribution plan used for a combination?

PROBLEMS

Problem 6–1

L Corporation plans to acquire a television manufacturing company (abbreviated TV). The president of L Corporation wants to calculate the earnings per share and the expected P/E ratio of the proposed combination. He believes that no special efficiencies or inefficiencies will accrue to the new entity as a result of the combination.

Required:

(i) Using the notation below, present *general* formulas for calculating E/S_{LTV} and P/E_{LTV} ratio for the new combination.

Let S_L = L Corporation outstanding shares (common),
S_{TV} = firm TV outstanding shares (common),
P_L = current market price of L Corporation stock,
P_{TV} = current market price of firm TV stock,
NI_L = average net income of L Corporation,
NI_{TV} = average net income of firm TV, and
E/R = the exchange ratio determined by taking the inverse of the constituent firms' stock prices.

(ii) After the combination, the earnings of the new firm equal the combined average precombination earnings of the separate firms; however, the market reacts favorably to the new combination and the price per share increases to P_{LTV}. Present a general formula for computing the P/E ratio at the new price. Use the same notation as above.

Problem 6–2

Harley Corporation is planning to negotiate a stock for stock purchase of Summers, Inc. The following information is available about the two firms:

	Market Price	No. Shares Outstanding	Average Net Income
Harley......................	$20	6,000,000	$7,500,000
Summers..................	25	4,000,000	5,000,000

Required:

(i) Determine the values for minimum and maximum exchange ratios as the expected P/E_{HS} varies from 10 to 40 using increments of 5.

(ii) Graph the minimum and maximum curves obtained from the calculation in part (i) and shade the area within which negotiations between Harley Corporation and Summers, Inc., will take place.

Problem 6–3

The following information is for companies A and B and the proposed combination AB:

	A	B	AB
Net income...........................	$1,000,000	$2,000,000	$3,000,000
Common shares outstanding............	1,000,000	1,000,000	1,333,000
Earnings per share....................	$ 1	$ 2	$ 2.25
Common stock market price............	$40	$20	$45
P/E ratio............................	40:1	10:1	20:1
Stock exchange ratio, 1/3:1			

	Number and Total Value of Firm AB Shares Held by—	
	Shareholders Firm A	Shareholders Firm B
Number of shares held....................	1,000,000	333,333
Price per share.........................	$45	$45
Total stock value.......................	$45,000,000	$15,000,000
Value prior to combination...............	40,000,000	20,000,000
Gain or [loss] on combination............	$ 5,000,000	$ [5,000,000]

Required:

Prepare similar schedules to illustrate the value of AB shares issued to the shareholders of A and B if the stock exchange ratio were instead (i) 1/2:1 and (ii) 1:1. Assume the P/E ratio of AB to be 20:1 in both cases.

Problem 6–4

Assume the same facts as in Problem 6–3 where the stock exchange ratio is 1/3:1.

Required:

Prepare schedules similar to the one in Problem 6–3 where the stock exchange ratio remains at 1/3:1 if the expected P/E ratio for the combined entity were instead (i) 30:1 and (ii) 15:1.

Problem 6–5

The balance sheets for companies A and B appear as follows as of December 31, 1971.

ASSETS	A Company	B Company
Cash.....................................	$ 250,000	$ 400,000
Receivables..............................	350,000	575,000
Inventories..............................	450,000	625,000
Total Current Assets...................	$1,050,000	$1,600,000
Fixed assets (net).........................	2,000,000	3,000,000
Total Assets........................	$3,050,000	$4,600,000

LIABILITIES AND STOCKHOLDERS' EQUITY		
Current liabilities..........................	$ 500,000	$ 650,000
Long-term debt...........................	375,000	450,000
Total Liabilities......................	$ 875,000	$1,100,000
Capital stock ($10 par)....................	$1,000,000	$2,000,000
Other contributed capital..................	550,000	750,000
Retained earnings.........................	625,000	750,000
Total Stockholders' Equity..............	$2,175,000	$3,500,000
Total Liabilities and Stockholders' Equity...........................	$3,050,000	$4,600,000

A Company plans to issue 400,000 shares ($10 par) which can be sold for $15 per share less commissions and other legal costs of $2 per share. A Company then proposes to acquire the capital stock of B Company in exchange for $3,000,000 cash and the balance of the $4,000,000 selling price in long-term notes payable. A Company receivables include $200,000 owed by B Company.

Required:

Prepare a pro forma balance sheet that shows the effect of these transactions.

Problem 6–6

R Corporation plans to acquire one of three firms: S, T, or V. The possible resulting combinations would be RS, RT, or RV. In each case, it is believed that first postcombination period earnings will equal the combined precombination earnings of the two constituent firms. (For example, the first period expected net income of firm RS would be the average precombination net income of R plus the average precombination net income of S.)

The following data have been collected during negotiations with each firm:

	Earnings/ Share	Price/ Earnings	No. Shares Outstanding	Par Value	Negotiated ER
Firm R.............	$4.00	15	2,000,000	$100	
Firm S.............	.75	20	8,000,000	50	1/4:1
Firm T.............	2.40	20	5,000,000	100	1/2:1
Firm V.............	1.50	18	4,000,000	25	1:1

Required:

Present all answers in good form with supporting calculations.

(i)   Which combination will produce the largest postcombination P/E ratio, assuming the market attributes no special advantages or disadvantages to the combination?

(ii) Which combination will result in the largest postcombination net income?

(iii) Which combination(s) will result in a loss to R Corporation stockholders?

(iv) Which of the three firms would you recommend R Corporation purchase? What was the basis of your evaluation?

Problem 6–7

Firm G plans to acquire firm H. The following data are available regarding the companies and the negotiations before combination:

$$
\begin{array}{llll}
P/E_G & = \text{Price earnings ratio of firm G} & = & 15 \\
P/E_H & = \text{Price earnings ratio of firm H} & = & 20 \\
S_G & = \text{Number of G shares outstanding} & = & 4{,}500{,}000 \\
S_H & = \text{Number of H shares outstanding} & = & 2{,}000{,}000 \\
NI_G & = \text{Average net income of firm G} & = & \$9{,}000{,}000 \\
NI_H & = \text{Average net income of firm H} & = & \$3{,}000{,}000 \\
E/R & = \text{Negotiated exchange ratio} & = & 1\tfrac{1}{2}{:}1
\end{array}
$$

Required:

(i)   If the E/R of $1\tfrac{1}{2}$ for 1 is the maximum price that firm G was willing to pay, what is the implied P/E_{GH} expected by firm G?

(ii) If the E/R of $1\tfrac{1}{2}$ to 1 was the minimum price acceptable to firm H, what is the implied P/E_{GH} expected by firm H?

(iii) Assume that the combination does not increase or decrease the aggregate wealth of firms G and H. Will either firm incur a diminution in stockholder wealth, given an E/R of $1\tfrac{1}{2}$ to 1? If so, which firm and in what amount?

Problem 6–8

The Ecton Company proposes to sell all of its assets except cash and receivables to the Jones Company on July 31, 1971. The sales price shall be $10,000,000, adjusted by the change in book value from December 31, 1970, to May 31, 1971, for inventories and property. The May 31 book values of prepaid expenses and other assets are to be added to the sales price.

The settlement shall be:

a)   Jones Company 4 percent note for $3,000,000 payable in semiannual installments of $150,000 commencing January 31, 1972.

b)   Assumption of all liabilities except the estimated federal income taxes payable and long-term debt.

c)   Balance payable in cash immediately.

The company intends to retire the preferred stock and establish a $300,000 reserve for contingencies. The net profit for June and July is estimated at $150,-

000 before taxes (assume that a 50 percent tax rate has been in effect since 1966).

The last preferred stock dividend was declared on December 31, 1970. The regular common stock dividend was paid on June 15, 1971.

Taxable income for the past four years follows:

1967	$1,481,000
1968	412,400
1969	639,600
1970	842,500

ECTON COMPANY
Balance Sheets

	December 31, 1970	May 31, 1971
ASSETS		
Cash	$ 1,038,000	$ 472,000
Receivables	2,550,000	3,105,000
Inventories	5,592,000	6,028,000
Prepaid expenses	308,000	297,000
Total Current Assets	$ 9,488,000	$ 9,902,000
Property (net)	6,927,000	6,804,000
Other assets	635,000	604,000
Total Assets	$17,050,000	$17,310,000
LIABILITIES AND CAPITAL		
Accounts payable	$ 2,427,000	$ 3,052,500
Current maturities—long-term debt	600,000	600,000
Accrued liabilities	1,096,000	922,000
Dividends payable—preferred stock	63,000	
Estimated federal income taxes	417,000	333,500
Total Current Liabilities	$ 4,603,000	$ 4,908,000
Long-term debt	4,200,000	4,050,000
Stockholders' equity:		
Preferred cumulative stock— 21,000 shares of $100 par, 3%, outstanding, redeemable at $102	2,100,000	2,100,000
Common stock—100,000 shares of $10 par outstanding	1,000,000	1,000,000
Capital contributed in excess of par value of common stock	587,000	587,000
Retained earnings	4,560,000	4,665,000
Total Liabilities and Capital	$17,050,000	$17,310,000

Note: The increase in retained earnings is net of a dividend of $.20 per share paid March 15, 1971, on common stock.

Required:

(i)   Compute the total sales price and settlement to be made.

(ii) Compute Ecton Company's gain or loss on the sale, giving effect to income taxes.

(iii) Prepare a working paper with column headings "Per Books," "Adjustments," and "Estimated Balance Sheet, July 31, 1971" giving effect to the proposed sale and other information given. Support your adjustments with schedules or computations you deem necessary.

(AICPA adapted)

Problem 6–9

The Holt Company was organized on January 1, 1971, to consolidate the resources and operations of three farm equipment manufacturers. Shares of Holt Company stock are to be issued in payment for the net assets acquired from each company. Authorized capitalization of the Holt Company consisted of 10,000 shares of $100 par value common stock and 6,000 shares of 6 percent fully participating preferred stock (par, $100). The number of shares to be issued in payment is to be based upon property values established by independent appraisal. An appraisal report, dated January 5, 1971, contains the following information:

	Roto Company	Exco Company	Till Company
Cash...............................	$ 40,000	$ 20,000	$ 80,000
Receivables........................	30,000	25,000	25,000
Merchandise.......................	60,000	18,000	22,000
Plant and equipment.................	145,000	132,000	191,000
Accumulated depreciation.............	35,000	19,000	26,000
Accounts payable...................	25,000	6,000	12,000
Accrued liabilities..................	15,000	20,000	30,000
Eight-year average annual profits.......	25,000	50,000	15,000

Required:

(i) Prepare an equitable capitalization plan for the Holt Company, indicating the amounts of common and preferred shares to be issued to Roto, Exco, and Till. It may be assumed for purposes of this calculation that the earnings rate of return on tangible and intangible assets is the same.

(ii) Prepare a pro forma balance sheet for the Holt Company as of January 1, 1971, giving effect to the consolidation plan developed in (i) above.

Problem 6–10

You have just commenced your audit of Shaky Company for the year ended December 31, 1971. The president advises you that the company is insolvent and must declare bankruptcy unless a large loan can be obtained immediately. A lender who is willing to advance $450,000 to the company has been located, but he will only make the loan subject to the following conditions:

a) A $600,000 6 percent mortgage payable on the company's land and buildings held by a major stockholder will be canceled along with four months' accrued interest. The mortgage will be replaced by 5,000 shares of $100 par value, 6 percent, cumulative if earned, nonparticipating, preferred stock.

b) A $450,000 8 percent mortgage payable over 15 years on the land and buildings will be given as security on the new loan.

c) On May 1, 1970, the company's trade creditors accepted $360,000 in notes payable on demand at 6 percent interest in settlement of all past-due accounts. No payment has been made to date. The company will offer to settle these liabilities at $.75 per $1 owed or to replace the notes payable on demand with new notes payable for full indebtedness over five years at 6 percent interest. It is estimated that $200,000 of the demand notes will be exchanged for the longer term notes and that the remaining creditors which hold notes will accept the offer of a reduced cash settlement.

d) A new issue of 500 shares of $100 par value, 5 percent, noncumulative, nonparticipating, preferred stock will replace 500 outstanding shares of $100 par value, 7 percent, cumulative, participating preferred stock. Preferred stockholders will repudiate all claims to $21,000 of dividends in arrears. The company has never formally declared the dividends.

e) A new issue of 600 shares of $50 par value, class A common stock will replace 600 outstanding shares of $100 par value, class A common stock.

f) A new issue of 650 shares of $40 par value, class B common stock will replace 650 outstanding shares of $100 par value, class B common stock.

g) The deficit in retained earnings should be eliminated, if possible, as a result of the entire plan.

The president of the Shaky Company requests that you determine the effect of the foregoing on the company and furnishes the following condensed account balances, which you believe are fairly presented:

Bank overdraft	$ 15,000
Other current assets	410,000
Fixed assets	840,000
Trade accounts payable	235,000
Other current liabilities	85,000
Contributed capital in excess of par value	125,000
Retained earnings deficit	345,000

Required:

Prepare a pro forma balance sheet for the Shaky Company at January 1, 1972, as if the recapitalization plan had taken affect. The statement should have one column for the balance sheet prior to the assumed events, two columns in which to journalize the changes, and one column in which to present the pro forma results.

(AICPA adapted)

Chapter 7

Consolidated Financial Reports—Date of Acquisition

Corporate Affiliations

In Chapter 5, corporate combinations were categorized as *mergers, consolidations,* and *acquisitions.* In the present chapter (and Chapters 8 and 9), attention is focused on the financial reports of the economic entity which results from the acquisition form of combination. Following an acquisition, the acquiring company owns a majority of the acquired firm's voting stock. The acquiring company is frequently identified as the *parent;* the acquired company is described as a *subsidiary.* Their joint status is called a corporate *affiliation.* Of course, a corporate affiliation may include more than two corporations. The parent may hold a majority of the voting shares of many subsidiaries. Additionally, a chain of majority ownership may be established in which a parent (P) owns a majority interest in the stock of a subsidiary (S_1) which, in turn, owns a majority interest in another subsidiary (S_2), etc. Such multilevel affiliations commonly extend from three to five levels. In fact, the history of United States business evidences some multilevel affiliations which included up to 60 levels in the parent-subsidiary chain. It is not uncommon for some corporations at each level to engage in separate business operations in addition to holding stock in subsidiaries. Alternatively, other corporations are organized for the sole purpose of holding stock in subsidiaries, in which case the parent may be referred to as a *holding company.*

Reasons for Corporate Affiliations

There are numerous reasons why a corporate enterprise may select *acquisition* as a form of corporate combination, in contrast to mergers and consolidations. Stock acquisition is relatively simple, and it usually provides financial control with minimal difficulty. The continuity of legal life of each of the affiliated companies also serves to protect the group assets from possible attachment by creditors of individual subsidiaries. Acquisition may be achieved at substantially less cost than the processes of merger and consolidation. The latter forms of combination require 100 percent ownership by the acquiring firm, whereas the former permits the execution of control with any amount of voting stock in excess of 50 percent. Also, the legal and processing costs of mergers or consolidations are typically avoided by the acquisition method. Further, the asset acquired by the parent—subsidiary stock—may provide collateral to support additional debt financing above the traditionally acceptable levels that would apply to the combined entity existing in the form of one corporate structure. After a formal merger or consolidation, the subsidiary corporation stock that is acquired by the parent is retired or canceled, and therefore is not available for use as collateral. For these and other reasons, control achieved by stock acquisition may produce significant rewards for the parent company, frequently at less cost than would be possible through other forms of business amalgamation.

Consolidated Statements

The primary financial reports of corporate affiliations are described as *consolidated* financial statements. These statements are essentially summations of the assets, liabilities, revenues, and expenses of the individual affiliates, calculated on the basis of transactions with nonaffiliates; the statement formats and the account classifications parallel those of a single corporation. Consolidated statements are prepared because the *unconsolidated* reports of a parent do not provide sufficient information on the financial position and operations under the parent's control. Indeed, the published financial reports of a parent corporation typically do not include the unconsolidated statements of the parent company.

Consolidated statements reflect a single entity perspective of the affiliated companies, from which many of the legal distinctions between the affiliates are ignored as being a matter of form rather than of substance. The overriding objective in consolidated statement preparation is to reflect the operations and financial position of the single *economic* entity. In the event that a minority portion of the subsidiary's stock is owned by parties that are unrelated to the parent, a special equity position must be established in the consolidated statements so that the unique interest of these outside parties will be appropriately disclosed.

While consolidated statements constitute the primary source of financial information regarding corporate affiliations, they should not be viewed as the only source of such information. Some parties, such as minority interest stockholders in a subsidiary and the outside creditors of a subsidiary, are primarily concerned with the separate financial reports of the subsidiary. Thus, the need for separate financial statements of each individual subsidiary corporation is not necessarily eliminated by the preparation of consolidated statements.

Parties whose primary interest is in the parent corporation may find that consolidated statements are not an adequate basis for making detailed analyses of operations. Thus, it is becoming increasingly common to provide, in addition to consolidated statements, supplementary reports which relate to defined segments of the consolidated entity. Such reports may consist of statements for each subsidiary or they may be prepared on other bases, such as product lines. Further consideration of these segmental reports is deferred until Chapter 10.

Criteria for Inclusion in Consolidated Statements

The criteria for including a subsidiary in consolidated statements are typically stated in terms of the degree of control the parent exercises over the subsidiary. There are two essential attributes of this concept of control, neither of which alone provides sufficient ground for inclusion in the consolidated statement. (1) The parent corporation must have the ability to govern, or effectively regulate, the subsidiary corporation's managerial decisions. (2) The parent corporation must be so related to the subsidiary that the economic results of subsidiary operations will accrue to the parent, allowing, of course, for the necessity of making appropriate allocations to reflect the interests of minority (outside, noncontrolling) parties.

Reference has been made to the necessity for owning more than 50 percent of the voting stock of a subsidiary—either directly or indirectly—in order to justify inclusion in consolidated financial statements. Yet, in point of fact, effective *managerial* control may well exist short of this critical percentage. Accountants are generally agreed, however, that it is usually unwise to include in consolidated financial statements those corporations for which this majority ownership condition is not satisfied. On occasions, effective managerial control may exist without the ownership of *any* voting shares. For example, the presence of a lease arrangement, whereby the lessor retains control of leased property, may indicate effective managerial control. Normally, however, situations of this kind do not evidence sufficient control in terms of the second attribute stated above.

It should not be inferred that voting control necessarily implies managerial (administrative) control. "Administrative control implies that each constituent unit is operated as if it were a department or branch of a larger entity."[1]

Other factors which merit attention in determining the admissibility of a subsidiary in consolidated statements are (1) the expectation of continuity in control; (2) the degree of existing restrictions upon the availability of assets and earnings of a subsidiary (an item of special importance regarding foreign subsidiaries); (3) the general coincidence of accounting periods; and (4) the degree of heterogeneity in the assets and operations of the affiliates. As currently interpreted, the last factor precludes consolidating the accounts of insurance companies, banks, and finance companies with the accounts of entities that are primarily engaged in manufacturing. At one time this factor was interpreted more rigidly, placing in doubt the inclusion of firms that operated in different manufacturing industries. Currently, how-

---

[1] Committee on Accounting Concepts and Standards, American Accounting Association, "Consolidated Financial Statements," *Supplementary Statement No. 7* (Evanston, Ill., 1954), p. 43.

ever, the heterogeneity of assets and operations criterion is not generally applied except for the exclusion of financial institutions mentioned above.

The Securities and Exchange Commission is explicit in respect to the conditions which must be satisfied by a registrant in preparing consolidated financial statements:

a) The registrant shall not consolidate any subsidiary which is not a majority-owned subsidiary;

b) If the statements of a subsidiary are as of a date or for periods different from those of the registrant, such subsidiary may be consolidated only if all the following conditions exist: (1) such difference is not more than 93 days; (2) the closing date of the subsidiary is expressly indicated; (3) the necessity for the use of different closing dates is briefly explained; and (4) any changes in the respective fiscal periods of the registrant and the subsidiary made during the period of report are clearly indicated, together with the manner of treatment.[2]

Disclosure of Consolidation Policy

The consolidation policy adopted by the parent company is important to a complete understanding of consolidated statements and it should be disclosed in the financial reports. A statement of policy normally refers to such matters as the degree of stock control required of the parent company, the accounting methods that were used to record the acquisition of subsidiary stock (alternative methods are examined in Chapter 10), and the status of a subsidiary as either a domestic or a foreign corporate entity. In the event that a subsidiary is excluded from consolidated statements, it is important that the exclusion be noted in the statements and the justifying reasons given therefor. This information may be provided in the body of the report, in footnote notation, or by parenthetical statement. It is important that the users of financial reports be provided with all relevant information; yet they should not be burdened with an over elaboration of detail.

Precautions in the Evaluation of Consolidated Statements

The summarizing character of consolidated statements provides them with special qualities of strength and usefulness; however, this attribute demands that special precautions be taken in evaluating these statements. Among the factors which require special care in the evaluation process are the following:

1. Consolidated statements create numerous and complex problems in statistical analyses, the apparent solutions to which may be misleading. For example, ratios prepared from consolidated account information are weighted averages. As such, their reliability is dependent upon the degree of variability among the account balances of the individual affiliates. A

---

[2] United States Securities and Exchange Commission, *Regulation S-X, Form and Content of Financial Statements* (Washington, D.C.: U.S. Government Printing Office, 1961), p. 7.

weak position of one company may be balanced, in the process of summation, by an especially strong position of an affiliate. In such an instance, an average may be an inaccurate descriptive index.

2. Differences in the bases of classification and valuation of accounts of the constituent companies may distort the meaning of composite statements. The unique accounting systems of the affiliates cannot easily be transformed so that the classifications and valuations of each affiliate will be entirely consistent. Further, the differing industry identifications of the affiliates limit the meaning that can be attributed to the aggregated account balances.

3. The monetary equities assigned to both creditors and owners may be misinterpreted in the evaluation of consolidated statements. This is particularly true in respect to the seeming availability of retained earnings for dividend distributions. The earnings of subsidiaries are not actually available for parent company distributions until formally declared as dividends by the subsidiaries. In regard to liabilities, the result of summation often is to obscure the special legal status of those individual creditors having liens on specific assets. Additionally, minority stockholders must continue to look to the subsidiary's separate financial statements to determine accurately the status of their investment. Their shareholder status relates *only* to the legal entity to which they have committed resources.

4. Consolidated statements involving foreign subsidiaries may be misleading if foreign exchange rates are subject to unusual fluctuations, or if foreign assets are unduly restricted as to their availability to a domestic parent company.

Notwithstanding these limitations, consolidated statements continue to grow in significance and number. Accumulating evidence suggests that they now assume a role of *primary* importance, with the separate statements of affiliates and other segmental reports relegated to a secondary or supplementary position.

Consolidated Balance Sheet

Where the dates of investment in subsidiary stock and consolidated statement preparation coincide, attention may be confined to the consolidated balance sheet only. This financial report is a summary enumeration of the assets and liabilities of the various affiliates, calculated without regard to their separate corporate identities. Because majority stock ownership is tantamount to control over the assets of a subsidiary, it is meaningful to substitute the subsidiary's net assets for the stock investment account of the parent company. Traditionally, this substitution is accomplished in consolidated statement working papers by eliminating the parent company's investment account against its equity in the stockholders' equity accounts of the subsidiary. Following this elimination, it is then appropriate to combine the assets and liabilities of the affiliate companies. It is, of course, important that the amounts of other accounts resulting from intercompany transactions, e.g., intercompany receivable-payable balances, also be eliminated, in order that the consolidated balance sheet reflect the assets and equities of the affiliation perceived as a single economic entity. It may be observed that the *total* net assets of the subsidiary are substituted for the contra investment account, notwithstanding the existence of minority shareholders. This accords with the accounting view that each group of shareholders has a fractional interest in the undivided net assets of the subsidiary. Accordingly, it is appropriate to indicate the value of minority interests in terms of the aggregate net assets rather than in terms of a fractional equity in specific assets and liabilities of a subsidiary.

The form and arrangement of these accumulated data follow the usual statement classifications. Where minority shareholders exist, their rights must be clearly disclosed together with those of other claimants. However, in that the consolidated statement is often presumed to be oriented toward the dominant shareholders (those of the parent company), the rights and equities of minority interests assume—at least partially—the character of liabilities. Yet, significantly, because the evidences of this type of equity are ownership certificates, they also have a certain quality of proprietorship. Accountants are not generally agreed as to the most appropriate balance sheet disposition of this category; often a compromise position is that of a separate identification between liabilities and stockholders' equity.

Procedural details for the preparation of consolidated balance sheet working papers are described and illustrated in the pages which follow.

Investment at Book Value of Subsidiary Stock

In the cases which follow, it is assumed that concurrent with the acquisition of a subsidiary's capital stock, a consolidated balance sheet is prepared. The stockholders' equity accounts of the subsidiary are reflected in the working paper accompanying each case, and it is assumed that the parent company's investment cost is equal to the book value of the subsidiary stock acquired.

Case 1. Total (100 Percent) Acquisition of Subsidiary Stock. It is useful, preliminary to the preparation of a consolidated working paper, to prepare an *investment elimination schedule*. This is merely a columnar description of the elimination elements represented by the investment account of the parent and the related book value of the subsidiary's capital stock. In the present case, such a schedule may take the following form:

Investment Elimination Schedule

	Dr. [Cr.]
Capital stock—Y Company	$ 40,000
Retained earnings—Y Company	10,000
Investment in Y Company stock	$[50,000]

It may be observed that the amounts are identified as either debits or credits, and are easily posted to the working paper in Illustration 7–1.

It is useful to relate the contra elements of eliminating entries with some connective notation; in this instance, arabic numerals are used.

An examination of this consolidated working paper will confirm that the net assets of Y Company have, in fact, been substituted for the investment account of X Company, and that the amounts extended to the "consolidated" column are merely a result of a summation process. It may also be

Illustration 7–1

X COMPANY AND SUBSIDIARY Y COMPANY
Consolidated Balance Sheet Working Paper
(Acquisition Date)

	X Company	Y Company	Eliminations		Consolidated
			Dr.	Cr.	
ASSETS					
Cash................	15,000	4,000			19,000
Receivables...........	30,000	16,000			46,000
Merchandise..........	25,000	35,000			60,000
Investment in Y Company stock........	50,000			(1) 50,000	
	120,000	55,000			125,000
EQUITIES					
Payables.............	10,000	5,000			15,000
Capital stock:					
X Company........	90,000				90,000
Y Company........		40,000	(1) 40,000		
Retained earnings:					
X Company........	20,000				20,000
Y Company........		10,000	(1) 10,000		
	120,000	55,000	50,000	50,000	125,000

noted that consolidated capital stock and retained earnings at date of acquisition are the balances in the parent company's accounts, the total amount of the subsidiary's capital stock and retained earnings having been eliminated. Consolidated retained earnings are defined to be the parent company's retained earnings increased by its interest in subsidiary profits or decreased by its interest in subsidiary losses since acquisition; accordingly, the balance of consolidated retained earnings at date of acquisition will be the amount of the parent company's own retained earnings. Although the stockholders' equity of Y Company in this illustration was limited to capital stock and retained earnings accounts, no special problems would have arisen had there been other stockholders' equity accumulations, such as amounts of contributed capital in excess of par value, unrealized increments from appraisals, or earnings appropriations. Each of these elements would have been additional determinants in the calculation of book value, and subsequently eliminated in the investment elimination schedule in the consolidation process.

Case 2. Acquisition of a Majority (90 Percent) of Subsidiary Stock (Subsidiary Deficit). This case illustrates the elimination procedures to be followed in the event the parent acquires a controlling interest in the voting shares of a subsidiary by purchasing less than 100 percent of the outstanding stock. Additionally, the case indicates the elimination when the subsidiary has a retained earnings deficit at the acquisition date. It is assumed that 90 percent of a subsidiary's capital stock is acquired at a cost of $45,000. The stockholders' equity account balances of the subsidiary at the acquisition date are capital stock, $60,000 (Cr.); and retained earnings, $10,000 (Dr.). The investment elimination schedule is as follows:

Investment Elimination Schedule

	Dr. [Cr.]
Capital stock—Y company..........................	$ 54,000
Retained earnings—Y Company...................	[9,000]
Investment in Y Company stock..................	$[45,000]

The deficit is eliminated by a credit to the retained earnings of Y Company. It may be noted in Illustration 7–2 that the extended amounts of capital stock and retained earnings of Y Company are marked with the letter "M" denoting that these amounts represent the value interests of minority shareholders. Such a notation serves as an appropriate reminder concerning the classification of these amounts in the preparation of formal statements. This working paper illustrates the importance of substituting the *total* net assets of the subsidiary for the investment account of the parent company, even where there exist minority shareholders, and extending the interest of these minority shareholders on the basis of their fractional interest in the recorded stockholders' equity accounts of the subsidiary company. Calculation of the minority interest is made in the same manner, whether the subsidiary has an accumulated earnings balance or a deficit. Manifestly, there is no dilution in minority interests in the consolidation process, as the equity of this group (10 percent of $50,000) is clearly indicated in the enumeration of the various equities.

Investment Cost More than Book Value of Subsidiary Stock

Frequently, it will be necessary for the investing company to pay more than the book value of the subsidiary's capital stock. Costs of investment in excess of book value may be defended with the argument that there is an understatement of a subsidiary's assets, that there exist unrecorded subsidi-

Illustration 7–2

X COMPANY AND SUBSIDIARY Y COMPANY
Consolidated Balance Sheet Working Paper
(Acquisition Date)

	X Company	Y Company	Eliminations Dr.	Eliminations Cr.	Consolidated
ASSETS					
Cash...............	15,000	4,000			19,000
Receivables..........	30,000	16,000			46,000
Merchandise.........	25,000	35,000			60,000
Investment in Y Company stock.......	45,000			(1) 45,000	
	115,000	55,000			125,000
EQUITIES					
Payables.............	5,000	5,000			10,000
Capital stock:					
X Company........	90,000				90,000
Y Company........		60,000	(1) 54,000		6,000 M
Retained earnings:					
X Company........	20,000				20,000
Y Company........		[10,000]		(1) 9,000	[1,000]M
	115,000	55,000	54,000	54,000	125,000

ary assets, or for other less apparent reasons. In such instances it is necessary to recognize and identify this variation, or *differential,* in the consolidated statements.

Case 3. The data of the previous case are repeated here, with the exception that the cost of X Company's 90 percent investment in the capital stock of Y Company is assumed to be $50,000. In this instance, the investment elimination schedule indicates the presence of a *debit differential.*

Investment Elimination Schedule

	Dr. [Cr.]
Capital stock—Y Company...................	$ 54,000
Retained earnings—Y Company..............	[9,000]
Differential...............................	5,000
Investment in Y Company stock.............	$[50,000]

At this point the differential does not require more complete identification; it is sufficient to note that it represents the excess of the cost of the investment over the parent's interest in the book value of subsidiary stock at date of acquisition. The working paper treatment of a debit differential is given in Illustration 7–3.

Illustration 7–3

X COMPANY AND SUBSIDIARY Y COMPANY
Consolidated Balance Sheet Working Paper
(Acquisition Date)

	X Company	Y Company	Eliminations Dr.	Eliminations Cr.	Consolidated
ASSETS					
Cash..............	15,000	4,000			19,000
Receivables..........	30,000	16,000			46,000
Merchandise........	25,000	35,000			60,000
Investment in Y Company stock........	50,000			(1) 50,000	
Differential..........			(1) 5,000		5,000
	120,000	55,000			130,000
EQUITIES					
Payables.............	10,000	5,000			15,000
Capital stock:					
X Company........	90,000				90,000
Y Company........		60,000	(1) 54,000		6,000 M
Retained earnings:					
X Company........	20,000				20,000
Y Company........		[10,000]		(1) 9,000	[1,000]M
	120,000	55,000	59,000	59,000	130,000

Investment Cost Less than Book Value of Subsidiary Stock

In the event that the investment cost is less than the book value of a subsidiary's capital stock at acquisition, there exists a *credit* differential. This circumstance is illustrated in Case 4. The sources of debit and credit differentials will be developed more completely following this case illustration.

Case 4. Using the basic data of Case 2, it is assumed that X Company acquires 90 percent of the capital stock of Y Company at a cost of $40,000. The investment elimination schedule follows.

Investment Elimination Schedule

	Dr. [Cr.]
Capital stock—Y Company..................	$ 54,000
Retained earnings—Y Company..............	[9,000]
Differential......................	[5,000]
Investment in Y Company stock.............	$[40,000]

These data confirm that there exists a credit differential, and that its amount is measured by the amount of the parent's interest in the book value of subsidiary stock at date of acquisition which is in excess of the cost of the investment (see Illustration 7–4).

Illustration 7–4

X COMPANY AND SUBSIDIARY Y COMPANY
Consolidated Balance Sheet Working Paper
(Acquisition Date)

	X Company	Y Company	Eliminations Dr.	Eliminations Cr.	Consolidated
ASSETS					
Cash..................	25,000	4,000			29,000
Receivables...........	30,000	16,000			46,000
Merchandise..........	25,000	35,000			60,000
Investment in Y Company stock........	40,000			(1) 40,000	
Differential...........				(1) 5,000	[5,000]
	120,000	55,000			130,000
EQUITIES					
Payables..............	10,000	5,000			15,000
Capital stock:					
X Company........	90,000				90,000
Y Company........		60,000	(1) 54,000		6,000 M
Retained earnings:					
X Company........	20,000				20,000
Y Company........		[10,000]		(1) 9,000	[1,000] M
	120,000	55,000	54,000	54,000	130,000

Debit and Credit Differentials

In the previous two cases, it was demonstrated that investment cost may exceed, or be less than, the parent's interest in the book value of a subsidiary's capital stock at date of acquisition. In the consolidated working papers, these differences may be described merely as debit or credit differentials, depending upon the relative magnitude of the contra elements. However, in a formal consolidated balance sheet, the identifying reference should contain a more complete and informative description.

Investment Cost in Excess of Book Value. Among the possible explanations why the cost of investment may exceed the parent's interest in the book value of a subsidiary's capital stock at date of acquisition are the following:

1. The accounts of the subsidiary may reflect inaccurate underlying valuations. Either assets or liabilities, or both, may be incorrectly measured. For example, past failures to capitalize appropriate costs, or excessive provisions for depreciation or doubtful accounts, create a net understatement in asset values. Accelerated amortization of intangibles or deferred charges may also contribute to asset understatement. To the extent that the improper valuations may be isolated in this manner, it is appropriate to

assign the debit differential to the relevant account or accounts improperly measured.

2. Even when the accuracy of book valuation is not in dispute, the accounts are usually deficient in reflecting the current market influences which are important determinants of investment cost. Clearly an investment decision presumes an evaluation of existing market variables, as well as various economic and business anticipations. Any of these considerations may induce an investing corporation to expend more than subsidiary book value. In that the purchase of a controlling interest in subsidiary capital stock is not essentially unlike the acquisition of its assets, a confirmation of asset valuations by appraisal may be appropriate. In the event of an appraisal, increments in the value of specific assets may be formally entered in the accounts of the subsidiary by adjustment, or reported only in the consolidated statements of the affiliation.

3. The willingness of an investing company to pay an amount in excess of the book value of a subsidiary's stock may indicate that there exist intangibles which are not recorded in the subsidiary's accounts, or that measurements of recorded intangibles are understated. In the latter instance, adjustment is required as previously noted. However, if there is evidence that the purchase cost is predicated—in part—on the above-normal earning capacity of the purchased affiliate, "goodwill from consolidation" is indicated. Above-normal earnings of the subsidiary affiliate often identify with special managerial skills; additionally excess earning capacity is frequently implicit in centralized administrative control achieved by consolidation. Differential payments may be made in recognition of these attributes, advantages of which are expected to accrue to the affiliation.

4. A debit differential may exist merely because of an unfavorable purchase commitment of the parent company. If it is established that the parent sustains such a loss on the purchase of subsidiary shares, it should be reported in the consolidated income statement. However, it is often difficult to confirm the fact of such a loss, and accountants are accordingly reluctant to make this assumption.

5. Where the parent company issues its own stock in exchange for that of the subsidiary and records the investment at the par or stated value of the issued capital stock, the amount which is in excess of the book value of the acquired shares may represent an issuance discount to the parent. In the event that there are no corporate legal barriers to a discount on the issuance of capital stock, the differential may be recognized as a discount in the books of the parent company.

6. In the event that the excess payment is not attributable to net asset understatement, the presence of unrecorded intangibles, or other identifiable resources, the expression "cost of investment in subsidiary stock in excess of book value" may be the most meaningful, albeit lengthy, description of a debit differential. More frequently, however, it is reported as "goodwill."

Book Value in Excess of Investment Cost. Among the reasons why investment cost may be less than the parent's equity in the book value of subsidiary stock at acquisition are the following:

1. Net asset values of a subsidiary may be overstated. Adjustments therefor may be recorded in the subsidiary's books, or compensation for the overstatement may be made in the consolidated working paper by applying the credit differential to the relevant account(s).

2. Book valuations may fail to reflect a depressed market in which current exchange values are less than existing book values. Where this condition obtains, the credit differential should be applied, as before, to a reduction in the overvalued account(s). Where there exists a credit differential in respect to a subsidiary whose books contain "goodwill," it is usual to apply the differential in reduction of the balance of this account. Where there are several subsidiaries, accountants are not agreed as to the propriety of offsetting the credit differential arising from the acquisition of one subsidiary's stock against the recorded goodwill of a second subsidiary. Some assume that the convenience of the single economic entity perspective of the affiliation justifies such a treatment. The authors, however, take the position that the differentials have relevance only in respect to the company whose stock is acquired, and that to associate a differential arising from the purchase of one subsidiary's stock with the accounts of a second subsidiary is to confuse the character of intercompany transactions.

3. Where the parent company issues its own capital stock in payment for subsidiary shares, the excess of the book value of the shares acquired over the par or stated value of the issued shares may be treated as a premium on the parent's capital stock issue.

4. Where the evidence is inconclusive as to the reason for a credit differential, or where the allocation of a differential to net assets results in a residual (unallocated) credit, the Accounting Principles Board has articulated a specific treatment of the unallocated residual credit. In accordance with *Opinion No. 16,* the credit should be allocated among the subsidiary's noncurrent assets (except long-term investments in marketable securities) in relation to the fair values of these items. Only after noncurrent assets are reduced to zero valuations should a remaining credit differential be treated as a deferred credit.[3]

Some accountants are disposed to favor immediate recognition of gains or losses on transactions involving the purchase of assets. As a consequence, they would give immediate income statement recognition to an unallocated credit differential. Such an argument denies the validity of the valuation established by the current investment transaction and therefore contradicts the general valuation basis of accounting. One of the fundamental assumptions underlying accounting practice is that the amount of considera-

---

[3] Accounting Principles Board, American Institute of Certified Public Accountants, "Business Combinations," *Opinion No. 16* (New York, 1970), para. 91.

tion exchanged in a purchase transaction represents the best acquisition date valuation of the assets received. Recording a gain or loss at the time of purchase would violate this fundamental assumption.

Other Intercompany Transactions

Emphasis has thus far been directed to the intercompany transaction establishing the parent-subsidiary relationship. However, other intercompany transactions may be reflected in the accounts of the various affiliates, and their effects also must be eliminated in the consolidated statement working papers. All accounts classified as assets on one affiliate's books for which the originating transaction created a liability on the books of a second affiliate must be totally eliminated. The amount of the elimination is not dependent upon the percentage of stock control. Intercompany accounts receivable are eliminated against related accounts payable; intercompany notes receivable are eliminated against the related notes payable; and the intercompany portion of accrued expenses are eliminated against the corresponding accrued incomes. It is only necessary to establish the intercompany character of the originating transaction. Failure to eliminate the total amount of these accounts—whatever the percentage of stock ownership—will result in a type of transaction circularity in which there are included in the consolidated balance sheet claims to and from the same entity—the economic entity for which the consolidated balance sheet is prepared.

Unpaid Subsidiary Dividends at Acquisition

Should the parent become a stockholder of record after the declaration of subsidiary dividends but before the record date for payment, such dividends merely serve to reduce the cost of the investment shares. As such, they are classified as Dividends Receivable; the remainder of the investment outlay is debited to the Investment account. Subsequent collection of this receivable balance by the parent is recorded in the conventional manner. In the preparation of a consolidated balance sheet at the date of acquisition, Dividends Payable must be eliminated against Dividends Receivable to the extent that the subsidiary's declared dividend will accrue to the shares held by the parent. If the parent failed to record the dividend receivable upon making the investment, an adjustment is necessary to correct this omission.

In the case that a subsidiary declares dividends prior to the parent's purchase of shares and the record date also occurs prior to acquisition of subsidiary stock by the parent, Dividends Payable represents a liability to outside interests. Thus, no adjustment to the investment elimination is necessary and there exists no payable-receivable relationship to be eliminated in the consolidated working paper.

Adjustments

On occasion, it may be necessary to adjust the account data after the preparation of consolidated working papers has begun. In such cases, adjusting entries may be entered in the "eliminations" column of the working paper. To distinguish adjusting and eliminating entries, it is desirable to adopt an appropriate system of notation. The authors prefer to use numeral prefixes as connectives for eliminating entries, with lowercase letters used to indicate adjustments. The consolidated working paper in Case 5 uses this notation. Frequently, confusion may be avoided if the statements of the constituent companies are adjusted previous to entering the account information in the consolidated working paper.

Illustrative Problem

It may now be useful to illustrate the preparation of a consolidated balance sheet working paper involving several subsidiaries, where there is a necessity for recording both adjusting and eliminating entries.

Case 5. Assume the following data with respect to affiliate companies X, Y, and Z:

	January 1, 1971		
	X Company	*Y Company*	*Z Company*
Capital stock (par, $100).......	$100,000	$50,000	$40,000
Retained earnings..............	20,000	5,000	4,000

On January 1, 1971, X Company purchased 90 percent of the capital stock of Y Company for $50,000, and 80 percent of the capital stock of Z Company for $36,000. The notes receivable listed among the assets of Y Company are the result of a loan to Z Company, on which the January 1, 1971, accrued interest is $60. The interest is as yet unrecorded by Z Company.

The process of constructing a consolidated balance sheet should begin with the preparation of an investment elimination schedule and an affiliation diagram indicating percentages and directions of share ownership.

Affiliation Diagram	**Investment Elimination Schedule** **Dr. [Cr.]**		

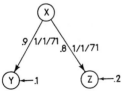

		Y Company	*Z Company*
Capital stock........		$ 45,000	$ 32,000
Retained earnings..............	(1)	4,500	(2) 3,152
Differential.........		500	848
Investment.........		$[50,000]	$[36,000]

(1) .9 ($5,000) = $4,500.
(2) .8 ($4,000 − $60) = $3,152.

It may be noted that the retained earnings of Z Company on January 1, 1971, are overstated by the amount of the omission of accrued interest

Illustration 7-5

X COMPANY AND SUBSIDIARIES
Consolidated Balance Sheet Working Paper
January 1, 1971

	X Company	Y Company	Z Company	Eliminations Dr.	Eliminations Cr.	Consolidated
ASSETS						
Cash	4,000	4,940	3,000			11,940
Accounts receivable	5,000	19,000	15,000			39,000
Notes receivable		1,000			(3) 1,000	
Merchandise	25,000	15,000	10,000			50,000
Interest receivable		60			(4) 60	
Investment in Y Company stock	50,000				(1) 50,000	
Investment in Z Company stock	36,000				(2) 36,000	
Fixed assets (net)	15,000	25,000	21,000			61,000
Differential—Y Company				(1) 500		500
Differential—Z Company				(2) 848		848
	135,000	65,000	49,000			163,288
EQUITIES						
Accounts payable	5,000	10,000	4,000			19,000
Notes payable	10,000		1,000	(3) 1,000		10,000
Accrued interest payable				(4) 60	(a) 60	
Capital stock:						
X Company	100,000					100,000
Y Company		50,000		(1) 45,000		5,000 M
Z Company			40,000	(2) 32,000		8,000 M
Retained earnings:						
X Company	20,000			(1) 4,500		20,000
Y Company		5,000		(a) 60		500 M
Z Company			4,000	(2) 3,152		788 M
	135,000	65,000	49,000	87,120	87,120	163,288

Explanations of adjustments and eliminations:

(a) Adjustment to record the accrual of interest expense by Z Company.
(1) Elimination of investment in Y Company.
(2) Elimination of investment in Z Company.
(3) Elimination of intercompany notes.
(4) Elimination of intercompany accrued interest.

expense. The 80 percent elimination is made against the balance of this account *as adjusted.*

The consolidated working paper is shown in Illustration 7–5.

The preparation of the formal consolidated balance sheet is completed by recasting the account information from the "consolidated" column of the working paper in traditional statement form (see Illustration 7–6).

Illustration 7–6

X COMPANY AND SUBSIDIARY COMPANIES Y AND Z
Consolidated Balance Sheet
January 1, 1971

ASSETS		EQUITIES		
Cash....................	$ 11,940	Accounts payable...		$ 19,000
Accounts receivable...........	39,000	Notes payable......		10,000
Merchandise................	50,000	Minority interest in—		
Fixed assets (net)............	61,000	Subsidiary Y		
Excess of investment cost over		Company......	$ 5,500	
book value of capital stock,		Subsidiary Z		
subsidiary Y Company......	500	Company......	8,788	14,288
Excess of investment cost over		Stockholders' equity:		
book value of capital stock,		Capital stock.....	$100,000	
subsidiary Z Company.......	848	Retained earnings.	20,000	120,000
	$163,288			$163,288

As mentioned earlier, these data are classified according to usual balance sheet arrangements, with the minority interests given separate status between the liability and owners' equity classifications.

The equity of minority shareholders is sometimes presented together with that of the controlling interest; more frequently, however, it is interposed between the liabilities and the majority stockholders' equity. The traditional emphasis of consolidated statements on the dominant shareholder group would appear to support this latter position. Those who favor the "entity theory" of consolidated statements, about which more will be said later, would prefer to cite only one category of shareholders' equity, consisting of both majority and minority interest groups.

While it is a common practice to assign a single value to minority shareholder interests in each subsidiary company, it is clearly more informative to detail the separate credits of which it consists. The Securities and Exchange Commission insists that "separation shall be made between the minority interest in the capital and in the surplus."[4]

More Informative Disclosure

Complete reporting in respect to corporate affiliations requires the use of a series of financial reports, including the statements of the parent company, subsidiary affiliates, and the consolidated entity. Each statement should

---

[4] United States Securities and Exchange Commission, *op. cit.,* p. 8.

articulate with and complement others in the series. The separate statements of the subsidiaries are of primary importance to the minority shareholders. These statements also have special significance to those interested in the legal relationships existing between various members of the affiliation. Consolidated statements, however, emphasize the economic union of the affiliated companies and accordingly seek to disclose significant financial information about the entity in summary terms.

QUESTIONS

1. What is the appropriate designation of a company that is organized for the sole purpose of holding shares of stock in subsidiaries?
2. Why might a corporation prefer to use the acquisition form of corporate combination as opposed to the merger or consolidation forms?
3. What is the principal motivation in preparing consolidated financial statements of affiliated companies?
4. What are the essential elements of parental control over a subsidiary which must exist if consolidated statements are to be prepared?
5. Is it necessary to own 50 percent of a company's voting stock in order to maintain effective control over the company? Explain.
6. What factors (other than voting control) are important determinants in electing whether or not to include a specific subsidiary in consolidated statements?
7. Interpretation of consolidated statements requires careful consideration of the inherent limitations of these statements. What are some of these inherent limitations?
8. Given a situation in which a parent owns less than 100 percent of a subsidiary's stock, the consolidated balance sheet nevertheless includes 100 percent of the subsidiary's assets. Explain the reasoning which supports this method of presentation.
9. For what reasons may a parent's cost of investment exceed or be less than its interest in the book value of the subsidiary's capital stock?
10. Explain how cash dividends of a subsidiary, which was acquired after the date of declaration but before the date of record, affect the cost of the investment as recorded by the parent company.

PROBLEMS

Problem 7–1

On January 1, 1971, Lincoln Corporation exchanged 10,000 shares of its own $20 par value common stock for 90 percent of the capital stock of the Juilliard Company.

Required:

(i) The principal limitation of consolidated financial statements is their lack of separate information about the assets, liabilities, revenues, and expenses of the individual companies included in the consolidation. List the problems which the reader of consolidated financial statements encounters as a result of the limitation.

(ii)   The minority interest in Juilliard Company can be presented several ways on the consolidated balance sheet. Discuss the propriety of reporting the minority interest on the consolidated balance sheet

   (*a*)   As a liability.

   (*b*)   As a part of stockholders' equity.

   (*c*)   In a separate classification between liabilities and the equity of the Lincoln Corporation.

(AICPA adapted)

Problem 7–2

In the preparation of the consolidated balance sheet of a parent corporation and its subsidiaries, a decision must be reached concerning the inclusion or exclusion of each of them as a member of the consolidated group. A common criterion is the percentage of voting stock owned by the parent company.

Required:

(i)   What is the significance of the percentage of voting stock ownership in justifying the inclusion of a subsidiary company in a consolidated statement?

(ii)   List other criteria upon which the decision to consolidate or not may also rest.

(AICPA adapted)

Problem 7–3

Prepare investment elimination schedules for the Texton Company and its subsidiary, Valley-View Company, for each of the conditions listed below:

			Valley-View Capital Balances		
	Acquired Interest	*Amount Paid*	*Capital Stock*	*Other Contributed Capital*	*Retained Earnings [Deficit]*
(i)	100%	1,450,000	1,000,000	250,000	300,000
(ii)	90	1,125,000	1,000,000	325,000	[100,000]
(iii)	75	1,000,000	1,000,000	200,000	120,000

Problem 7–4

An examination of the December 31, 1971, balance sheet of Y Company revealed the following account balances:

Capital stock (100,000 shares, $10 par)	$1,000,000
Other contributed capital	275,000
Donated capital	125,000
Reserve for future inventory losses	100,000
Retained earnings	300,000
Estimated 1971 federal income tax liability	200,000

Prepare an investment elimination schedule immediately following the December 31, 1971, open-market purchases of Y Company's capital stock by X Company in each of the following independent conditions:

i)   100,000 shares; per share cost, $20.
ii)   100,000 shares; per share cost, $18.
iii) 80,000 shares; total cost, $1,540,000.
iv)   80,000 shares; total cost, $1,400,000.
v)   40,000 shares; per share cost, $20⅝.
vi)   300,000 shares (authorized, but previously unissued) purchased *directly* from Y Company; per share cost, $20.

Problem 7–5

On December 1, 1971, B Company declares a dividend of $2.50 per share on its outstanding 100,000 shares for shareholders of record, January 10, 1972. On December 31, 1971, A Company acquires a 90 percent interest in B for a cash outlay of $2,000,000. B Company has the following balances in its capital accounts:

Capital stock ($10 par)	$1,000,000
Other contributed capital	500,000
Retained earnings	400,000

Required:

(i)   Prepare an investment elimination schedule for A Company as of December 31, 1971.
(ii) Give the journal entries A Company would make to record the acquisition.

Problem 7–6

The following data relate to companies X, Y, and Z on February 1, 1971:

	X Company	Y Company	Z Company
Capital stock (par, $100)	$10,000	$10,000	$10,000
Retained earnings [deficit]	4,000	[2,000]	–0–

Prepare an investment elimination schedule on February 2, 1971, following the purchase of stock *from the subsidiary* as indicated in the following independent cases:

Case A: P Company purchased 800 shares of X Company stock; 100 shares were issued concurrently to minority shareholders. Sales price per share for each stockholder group was—

(1) $140.
(2) $160.
(3) $120.

Case B: P Company purchased 800 shares of Y Company stock; 100 shares were issued concurrently to minority shareholders. Sales price per share for each stockholder group was—

(1) $80 to P Company.
     $74 to minority shareholders.
(2) $82 to P Company.
     $84 to minority shareholders.

Case C: P Company purchased 700 shares of Z Company stock; 200 shares were issued concurrently to minority shareholders. Sales price per share for each stockholder group was—
(1) $102 to P Company.
     $105 to minority shareholders.
(2) $ 93 to P Company.
     $ 91 to minority shareholders.

Problem 7–7

Given the following data, prepare an investment elimination schedule for each of the following independent, open-market, investment transactions:

	January 1, 1971, Balances				
	Capital Stock (Par Value, $100)	Retained Earnings [Deficit]	Other Contributed Capital	1971 Net Income [Loss]	1971 Cash Dividends
M Company.........	$50,000	$10,000	$6,000	$20,000	$8,000
W Company.........	40,000	[5,000]		15,000	5,000
Z Company.........	30,000	12,000	2,000	[5,000]	

For Consolidated Balance Sheet
January 1, 1971

P Company purchased on January 1, 1971:
Case A: 400 shares of M Company capital stock at book value.
Case B: 300 shares of W Company capital stock at 90.
Case C: 300 shares of M Company capital stock at 125.
Case D: 200 shares of M Company capital stock at 130.

For Consolidated Balance Sheet
January 1, 1971

P Company purchased on January 1, 1971:
Case E: 400 shares of M Company capital stock at 157.
Case F: 300 shares of M Company capital stock at 150.
Case G: 200 shares of Z Company capital stock at 125.
Case H: 300 shares of W Company capital stock at book value and 200 shares of Z Company capital stock at $3 per share less than book value.

Problem 7–8

On November 1, 1970, the Moore Company entered into negotiations with the Sydney Corporation to purchase a controlling interest in its capital stock. On December 1, it is mutually agreed that the assets of the Sydney Corporation should be appraised as a condition of final price determination. On December 31, the following data are available:

Fixed Assets:

Cost..	$100,000
Accumulated depreciation (based upon a 20-year life)........	50,000
Reproduction cost—new...............................	200,000
Estimated remaining life............................	15 years
Capital stock (par, $100)............................	$ 50,000
Retained earnings [deficit]...........................	[5,000]
Other contributed capital............................	10,000

Based on the above information, the Sydney Corporation recorded the appraisal on January 1, 1971, after which the Moore Company purchased 1,500 shares of its unissued capital stock at $300 per share.

Required:

(i) Record the appraisal on the books of the Sydney Corporation on January 1, 1971.
(ii) Prepare an investment elimination schedule for a consolidated balance sheet working paper as of January 1, 1971.

Problem 7–9

The June 1, 1971 balance sheets for A Company and B Company are as follows:

ASSETS	A Company	B Company
Cash..................................	$ 100,000	$ 52,000
Accounts receivable....................	200,000	125,000
Notes receivable.......................	300,000	100,000
Merchandise inventory..................	375,000	225,000
Investment in B Company stock..........	700,000	
Fixed assets (net).....................	825,000	700,000
Total Assets.....................	$2,500,000	$1,202,000

EQUITIES		
Accounts payable......................	$ 100,000	$ 150,000
Accrued interest payable...............		2,000
Notes payable.........................	500,000	300,000
Capital stock ($10, par)...............	1,500,000	500,000
Retained earnings.....................	400,000	250,000
Total Equities...................	$2,500,000	$1,202,000

On June 1, 1971, A Company purchased 80 percent of the capital stock of B Company for $700,000. Included in the accounts receivable for B Company is an account for $25,000 due from A Company. The notes receivable for A Company includes a loan to B Company for $50,000 on which the June 1 accrued interest is $2,000. The interest is unrecorded by A Company.

Required:

Prepare a consolidated balance sheet for A Company and its subsidiary as of June 1, 1971.

Problem 7–10

The Northern Company purchased 100 percent of the capital stock of the Atlantic Company on January 1, 1971, for $61,000. Immediately following the investment, the statements of financial position for the constituent companies are as follows:

ASSETS	Northern Company	Atlantic Company
Cash...	$ 8,000	$ 5,000
Accounts receivable.............................	16,000	15,000
Advances to Atlantic............................	5,000	
Investment in Atlantic Company stock.............	61,000	
Merchandise....................................	20,000	10,000
Other assets...................................	53,000	40,000
	$163,000	$70,000

EQUITIES		
Liabilities....................................	$ 8,000	$ 5,000
Due to Northern................................		5,000
Capital stock ($100 par)........................	100,000	50,000
Retained earnings..............................	55,000	10,000
	$163,000	$70,000

Required:

Prepare a consolidated balance sheet working paper as of January 1, 1971.

Problem 7–11

On April 1, 1971, the Pratt Company purchased a controlling interest in both the Trine Company and the Briski Corporation, after which the following balance sheet information is summarized:

ASSETS	Pratt	Trine	Briski
Cash..	$ 4,000	$ 1,500	$ 3,500
Accounts receivable.........................	11,000	9,000	12,500
Other current assets........................	8,000	4,500	10,000
Investment in corporate stock:			
320 shares in Trine Company..............	50,000		
540 shares in Briski Corporation...........	51,000		
Fixed assets (net).........................	30,000	41,000	54,000
Other assets...............................	26,000	24,000	10,000
	$180,000	$80,000	$90,000

EQUITIES			
Accounts payable...........................	$ 14,000	$ 5,000	$15,000
Other current liabilities....................	6,000	12,000	8,000
Fixed liabilities...........................	15,000	3,000	11,000
Capital stock (par, $100)...................	100,000	40,000	60,000
Retained earnings [deficit].................	41,000	18,000	[4,000]
Other contributed capital...................	4,000	2,000	
	$180,000	$80,000	$90,000

Required:

Prepare a consolidated balance sheet working paper as of April 1, 1971.

Problem 7–12

On October 1, 1971, the Dunhill Company purchased 960 shares of the King Company stock for $164,000 and $50,000 of King Company bonds at par plus accrued interest. Immediately after these transactions, the following trial balances were prepared:

	Dunhill Company	King Company
ASSETS		
Cash....................................	$ 15,250	$ 10,000
Accrued interest receivable..................	750	
Inventory..................................	120,000	100,000
Accounts receivable........................	80,000	50,000
Fixed assets (net)..........................	100,000	160,000
Other assets...............................	20,000	10,000
Investment in King Company stock............	164,000	
Investment in King Company bonds...........	50,000	
	$550,000	$330,000
EQUITIES		
Accounts payable...........................	$ 60,000	$ 21,500
Accrued interest payable....................		1,500
Accrued expenses...........................	10,000	7,000
Bonds payable, 6%, payable January 1 and July 1......................................		100,000
Capital stock ($100 par)....................	300,000	120,000
Retained earnings..........................	80,000	50,000
Other contributed capital...................	100,000	30,000
	$550,000	$330,000

Additionally, a $4,000 balance remains in the respective trade accounts receivable and payable from previous trading between the two companies.

Required:

(i) Prepare an investment elimination schedule on October 1, 1971.
(ii) Prepare a consolidated balance sheet working paper on October 1, 1971.

Problem 7–13

The December 31, 1971, trial balances of X Company, a petroleum refinery, and companies Y and Z, two of its crude oil suppliers, are as follows:

	X Company	Y Company	Z Company
ASSETS			
Cash....................	$ 10,400,000	$ 570,000	$ 1,100,000
Marketable securities........	27,300,000		
Accounts receivable.........	29,000,000	1,200,000	3,200,000
Notes receivable............			1,500,000
Inventory..................	55,900,000	2,240,000	10,800,000
Fixed assets (net)...........	187,000,000	3,900,000	14,600,000
Other assets...............	4,320,000	100,000	200,000
	$313,920,000	$8,010,000	$31,400,000
EQUITIES			
Accounts payable............	$ 36,900,000	$1,200,000	$ 1,800,000
Notes payable, Z Company...................		1,500,000	
Dividends payable (Note 1)................		100,000	
Accrued expenses...........	1,820,000	570,000	700,000
Bonds payable.............	100,000,000		10,000,000
Capital stock:			
$100 par.................	100,000,000		
$ 10 par.................		2,000,000	
No par (100,000 shares)....			17,400,000
Other contributed capital	47,800,000	1,800,000	
Retained earnings...........	27,400,000	840,000	1,500,000
	$313,920,000	$8,010,000	$31,400,000

Note 1: Cash dividends were declared December 28, 1971, payable on January 25, 1972, to stockholders of record, January 5, 1972.

On January 1, 1972, X Company purchased a controlling interest in the capital stock of companies Y and Z to assure continuity of supply of crude oil. The acquisition of stock was as follows:

a) 160,000 shares of Y Company's capital stock purchased in the open market for $25⅝.

b) 90,000 shares of Z Company's capital stock acquired by issuing 80,000 shares of X Company's stock to the individual stockholders of Z Company. On January 1, 1972, the capital stock of X Company is quoted at $250.

Required:

Prepare a consolidated balance sheet working paper as of January 1, 1972.

Problem 7–14

At December 31, 1971, the balance sheet of A Company was as follows:

ASSETS		EQUITIES	
Cash......................	$ 50,000	Payables...................	$1,750,000
Receivables (net)...........	300,000	Accruals..................	450,000
Inventories...............	1,600,000	Common stock, 10,000	
Prepayments..............	47,000	shares..................	1,000,000
Fixed assets (net)..........	2,003,000	Retained earnings..........	800,000
	$4,000,000		$4,000,000

An appraisal as of that date, which was carefully considered and approved by the boards of directors of A Company and B Company, placed a total replacement value, less sustained depreciation, of $3,203,000 on the fixed assets of A Company.

B Company offered to purchase all the assets of A Company, subject to its liabilities, as of December 31, 1971, for $3,000,000. However, 40 percent of the stockholders of A Company objected to the price on the ground that it did not include a consideration for goodwill, which they believed to be worth at least $500,000. A counterproposal was made, and final agreement was reached on the basis that B Company acquired 60 percent of the common stock of A Company at a price of $300 per share.

B Company's condensed balance sheet at December 31, 1971, following the acquisition of A Company's stock, showed:

ASSETS		EQUITIES	
Cash and investments (including stock of A)	$ 7,000,000	Payables	$ 7,872,000
Receivables (net)	2,400,000	Accruals	1,615,000
Inventories	11,200,000	Common stock, 100,000 shares	10,000,000
Prepayments	422,000	Retained earnings	20,513,000
Fixed assets (net)	18,978,000		
	$40,000,000		$40,000,000

Required:

Prepare a consolidated balance sheet working paper as of December 31, 1971, for the two companies.

(AICPA adapted)

Problem 7–15

Midway Sales, Inc., and Kent Realty Corporation are wholly owned subsidiaries of the Davis Manufacturing Company, Inc. The parent corporation manufactures electric refrigerators, electric ranges, and various other electric appliances. The refrigerators and ranges are sold only to Midway Sales, Inc., which acts as a distributor. Other appliances are sold directly to outside distributors.

The parent and the subsidiary sales corporation are tenants of property owned by Kent Realty Corporation.

The intercompany accounts on the books of each company as of December 31, 1971, are as shown below:

DAVIS MANUFACTURING COMPANY, INC.

	Debit	Credit
Investment in Midway Sales, Inc. (at cost)	$100,000.00	
Investment in Kent Realty Corporation (at cost)	175,000.00	
Due from Midway Sales, Inc.	86,175.97	
Due to Kent Realty Corporation		$ 1,475.00
Capital stock issued and outstanding, 100,000 shares, no-par value		1,000,000.00
Retained earnings		410,169.50

MIDWAY SALES, INC.

Due to Kent Realty Corporation.....................	$	800.00
Due to Davis Manufacturing Company, Inc............		33,910.00
Capital stock issued and outstanding, 1,000 shares,		
no-par value......................................		100,000.00
Retained earnings.................................		62,501.10

KENT REALTY CORPORATION

Due from Davis Manufacturing Company, Inc.........	$	6,575.00	
Due to Midway Sales, Inc..........................		$	2,800.00
Capital stock issued and outstanding, 1,000 shares,			
no-par value......................................			175,000.00
Retained earnings.................................			34,109.50

An audit of the books of the three companies for the year ended December 31, 1971, revealed the following:

a) The minute books of the three companies indicate the following with respect to dividends:

(1) The board of directors of Davis Manufacturing Company, Inc., at a meeting on January 4, 1972, declared a regular quarterly dividend of 50 cents per share, payable January 31, 1972, to stockholders of record on January 23, 1972.

(2) The board of directors of Midway Sales, Inc., at a meeting on December 28, 1971, declared a 1 percent dividend, payable in cash on January 15, 1972, to stockholders of record on December 31, 1971.

(3) The board of directors of Kent Realty Corporation at a meeting on December 1, 1971, declared a dividend of $1 per share, payable January 2, 1972, to stockholders of record on December 15, 1971.

No effect has been given to these dividend declarations on the books of the parent company as of December 31, 1971. The subsidiary companies recorded the dividend declarations pertaining to their respective companies at date of declaration.

b) Midway Sales received from one of its customers a check for $4,200 covering its own invoices aggregating $2,400 and invoices of Davis Manufacturing aggregating $1,800. The sales corporation recorded this transaction as follows:

Cash...	4,200	
Accounts receivable............................		4,200

c) Midway Sales, Inc., advanced $5,000 in cash to Kent Realty Corporation and made the following entry:

Due to Davis Manufacturing Company, Inc.............	5,000	
Cash.......................................		5,000

d) On September 15, 1971, Davis Manufacturing shipped 100 appliances of a new design on consignment at $20 each to Midway Sales. Midway made no entry upon receipt of the goods. During October, 1971, Midway sold all of these appliances at $25 each, crediting Sales for the total thereof. Davis Manufacturing made no entries on its books, but included the 100 appliances in its inventory at December 31, 1971, at its cost of $14 each.

e) The parent corporation filed a consolidated federal income tax return for the year ended December 31, 1970. The results of operations for the respective companies that year, before consolidation, were as follows:

Davis Manufacturing Company, Inc., net loss.......... $13,280
Midway Sales, Inc., net profit....................... 42,260
Kent Realty Corporation, net profit.................. 21,130

The federal income tax, amounting to $21,000, was paid by the parent corporation which recorded the transaction as follows:

Federal income taxes payable....................... 21,000
Cash...   21,000

An agreement in the files indicates that federal income taxes should be apportioned among the companies based upon unconsolidated net profits. A company having a loss year is to pay no tax nor charge the other companies for the benefit derived from the use of its loss in the return. The proper liability of each company was recorded as of December 31, 1970.

f) Kent Realty sold certain of its furniture to Midway Sales at current market value, which it was agreed should be 75 percent of net book value. The Kent Realty Corporation had purchased the furniture for $3,500 exactly two years prior to the date of sale and had taken depreciation at the rate of 10 percent per annum. It billed Midway Sales, Inc., for $2,800 and recorded the transaction as follows:

Due to Midway Sales, Inc............................ 2,800
Furniture and fixtures.............................   2,800

Midway Sales recorded the purchase as follows:

Furniture and fixtures............................... 2,800
Due to Kent Realty Corporation....................   2,800

g) As of December 31, 1971, the books of the parent corporation and the sales subsidiary do not reflect rent for the month of December, 1971, in the amounts of $6,100 and $1,400, respectively, due to Kent Realty Corporation.

h) Midway Sales, Inc., had not recorded December, 1971, purchase invoices submitted by the parent corporation in the amount of $48,265.97.

Required:

(i) Prepare an itemized reconciliation of the intercompany accounts.

(ii) Prepare the adjusting journal entries necessary to correct each set of books.

(AICPA adapted)

Chapter 8

Consolidated Financial Reports—Postacquisition

The preparation of consolidated statements following a period of subsidiary operations is complicated, at least in part, by the introduction of two new variables: the elapsed time since the acquisition of subsidiary shares *and* the parent company's method of accounting for the investment. At date of acquisition, the investment is recorded at total purchase cost; subsequently, an election must be made by the parent as to whether this measurement should be preserved without change *or* periodically adjusted to reflect the activities and operations of the subsidiary. The more conventional approach is the cost, or legal-basis, method. It will be considered in this chapter, with adjusted cost bases deferred for discussion in Chapter 9.

The Cost Method

The cost method of accounting for stock investments presumes that cost is an accurate reflection of the market at date of acquisition and that this valuation should remain undisturbed in most instances by the influence of subsequent operations of the company which issued the stock. Accordingly, under the cost method, subsidiary profits are not recorded by the parent when they are reported by the subsidiary; dividend receipts are instead credited to Dividend Income. Similarly, the losses sustained by a subsidiary are not recorded by the parent until there is convincing evidence which indicates the incurrence of a material and apparently permanent impairment of the value of the investment.

Chapter 9 includes a comparative analysis of the cost method and its principle alternative, the equity method. However, it may be noted at this point that regardless of which method is employed by the parent to account for its investment in a subsidiary that is to be included in the consolidation, the formal consolidated statements will remain unaffected. The working paper eliminations are designed to compensate for the differences between the two methods.

Statements of Consolidated Income and Retained Earnings

Following a period of subsidiary operations, it is important that consolidated statements of income and retained earnings be prepared in addition to the consolidated balance sheet. A consolidated income statement is essentially a summary enumeration of the revenues, expenses, gains, and losses of the allied companies after elimination of those account balances which result from transactions between the affiliates. The process of combination includes a deduction from the combined net incomes of all the affiliated companies, after eliminations, for the amounts of minority interests in the net incomes of the subsidiary affiliates. The residual, so determined, is then assignable to the majority shareholders and is designated *consolidated net income.*

An alternative definition of consolidated net income is based on the argument that the amount of income allocated to minority interests should be treated as a *distribution* of consolidated net income rather than a *deduction necessary to determine* consolidated net income. This view emphasizes the single entity concept of a corporate affiliation. It rests on the belief that the *determinants* of an entity's net income should not include allocations to any of the stockholders of the entity, notwithstanding the unique character of minority stockholders.

It should be emphasized that the nature of consolidated net income is essentially a definitional problem. The authors support the first definition presented above primarily because it emphasizes the equity of parent company stockholders. The significance of consolidated statements clearly stems from the informational needs of parties that have interests in the parent company, i.e., parent company creditors and stockholders. Defining consolidated net income as the portion of combined net income accruing to the parent is fully consistent with this dominant statement function. Thus, the preferred definition reflects the orientation of the users of consolidated statements. Subsequent development is based on this interpretation unless otherwise noted.

The consolidated statement of retained earnings is simply a sequential ordering of the consolidated retained earnings at the beginning of an accounting period, increased by consolidated net income, and reduced by the parent company's dividends declared; the algebraic sum of these amounts is the balance of consolidated retained earnings at the end of the accounting period.

In the preparation of the family of consolidated reports, it is useful to select a working paper, the organization of which accommodates the preparation of *all* statements in the series.

The Three-Division Horizontal Working Paper

Frequently, the source information for consolidated reports is to be found in the financial statements of the separate affiliates. Where the account data are thus conveniently prearranged in statement form, the three-division horizontal working paper is especially suitable for the preparation of the entire complement of consolidated reports. On other occasions, however, the trial balances of the affiliates are more accessible. In these instances, the trial balances must be reclassified in financial statement form to accommodate the three-division working paper analysis. In the remaining discussion of consolidated statements, trial balances of affiliated companies are given as the source information for consolidated working papers in order to minimize the space devoted to underlying detail; nonetheless, the three-division working paper analysis will usually be employed because it provides a logical framework for analysis.

In the illustrative examples which follow, the December 31, 1971, trial balances for companies X and Y will be used as basic source data, with minor adjustments as noted:

	—X Company—		—Y Company—	
Cash........................	$ 29,500		$ 8,000	
Accounts receivable..........	18,000		3,000	
Merchandise (1/1/71)........	16,000		4,000	
Investment in Y Company stock....................	61,000			
Other assets................	66,000		62,000	
Accounts payable............		$ 22,000		$ 5,000
Other liabilities..............		6,000		
Capital stock................		100,000		50,000
Retained earnings (1/1/71)..................		40,000		10,000
Dividends declared...........	10,000		5,000	
Sales.......................		78,000		40,000
Dividend income............		4,500		
Purchases..................	42,000		20,000	
Expenses..................	8,000		3,000	
	$250,500	$250,500	$105,000	$105,000
Merchandise (12/31/71)......	$ 10,000		$ 7,000	

The Dividends Declared account facilitates the analysis in the retained earnings statement division of the working paper, and it is assumed that this additional classificational refinement is usually practiced by the affiliates. Obviously, this account will be closed to Retained Earnings at the end of each accounting period.

Case 1. It is assumed that X Company acquired 90 percent of the capital stock of Y Company on January 1, 1971, at a cost of $61,000. Although consolidated statements are being prepared one year subsequent to the acquisition of a subsidiary's capital stock, the investment elimination schedule relates, as before, to subsidiary net worth balances existing at date of acquisition. The postacquisition earnings or losses of the subsidiary are not overlooked by this analysis; rather they are recognized as amounts to be extended to the "consolidated" column of the working paper. The extended values, representing changes in a subsidiary's retained earnings since acquisition, become important determinants of consolidated retained earnings.

Each division of the consolidated working paper (Illustration 8–2)

Affilation Diagram

Investment Elimination Schedule

Dr. [Cr.]

Capital stock—Y Company....	$ 45,000
Retained earnings—	
Y Company..............	9,000
Differential.................	7,000
Investment in Y Company	
stock....................	$[61,000]

provides the requisite data for the preparation of one of the series of con-solidated statements. While the working paper is subdivided for this pur-pose, the links which unite the various divisions are also clearly evident. All items on the "net income" line of the income statement division, including elimination debits and credits, are carried forward to the same line descrip-tion in the retained earnings statement division. Similarly, the several totals on the line of the final balance of retained earnings in this division are carried forward to the identical line description in the balance sheet di-vision. These divisions, each representing a formal consolidated statement, articulate with each other. It may be observed that equality of amounts of elimination debits and credits is not preserved in respect to a specific di-vision of the working paper; yet total elimination debits and credits for the three divisions are necessarily balanced. It is additionally important to note that consolidated dividends declared are the parent company's dividend declarations; to the extent that subsidiary dividends are intercompany, they are eliminated; remaining amounts of subsidiary dividends are distributed to nonaffiliate minority shareholders. Accordingly, the consolidated divi-dends declared represent the earnings distribution of the parent company. In this illustration, subsidiary dividends of $5,000 are distributed $4,500 to the parent and $500 to minority shareholders. The $4,500 payment to X Company is an intercompany transaction and is eliminated; the $500 payment to nonaffiliate shareholders is extended in the working papers as the minority interest in subsidiary dividends and is therefore deducted.

Observe that the minority interest is given separate column identification in each division of the consolidated working paper (Illustration 8–2). The amount of the minority interest in subsidiary net income is calculated on the basis of the subsidiary's recorded net income, without regard to elimi-nated revenue and expense items. This amount is deducted from the com-bined net incomes of the affiliates, after eliminations, in arriving at consoli-dated net income. The working paper discloses additionally how the equity of minority shareholders in retained earnings and capital stock is calculated in the normal progression from one working paper division to another.

The presence of minority shareholders requires special disclosure in the formal consolidated statements. Their equity in subsidiary net income is indicated in the consolidated income statement as a deduction from the combined net incomes, after eliminations, in arriving at consolidated net income. This is consistent with the usual interpretation of consolidated net income as an amount accruing to the majority shareholders. No explicit disclosure of minority interest is required in the consolidated retained earnings statement, and reference has previously been made to the alternative forms of disclosure for minority interests frequently found in consolidated balance sheets.

The formal consolidated statements for this case are shown in Illustration 8–1.

Illustration 8–1

X COMPANY AND SUBSIDIARY Y COMPANY
Consolidated Income Statement
For Year Ended December 31, 1971

Sales..		$118,000
Cost of sales:		
Merchandise inventory, January 1, 1971........	$20,000	
Purchases................................	62,000	
Total....................................	$82,000	
Merchandise inventory, December 31, 1971......	17,000	65,000
Gross profit.................................		$ 53,000
Expenses....................................		11,000
Combined net income........................		$ 42,000
Minority interest in subsidiary net income........		2,000
Consolidated net income......................		$ 40,000

X COMPANY AND SUBSIDIARY Y COMPANY
Consolidated Statement of Retained Earnings
For Year Ended December 31, 1971

Retained earnings, January 1, 1971...............	$40,000
Consolidated net income.......................	40,000
Total..	$80,000
Dividends declared...........................	10,000
Retained earnings, December 31, 1971.............	$70,000

X COMPANY AND SUBSIDIARY Y COMPANY
Consolidated Balance Sheet
December 31, 1971

ASSETS			EQUITIES		
Cash......................	$ 37,500		Liabilities:		
Accounts receivable..........	21,000		Accounts payable....		$ 27,000
Merchandise inventory........	17,000		Other liabilities......		6,000
Other assets................	128,000		Minority interest:		
Cost of subsidiary stock in			Capital stock.......	$5,000	
excess of book value at			Retained earnings...	2,500	7,500
acquisition................	7,000		Shareholders' equity:		
			Capital stock.......		100,000
			Retained earnings...		70,000
	$210,500				$210,500

Illustration 8-2

X COMPANY AND SUBSIDIARY Y COMPANY
Consolidated Statement Working Paper
For Year Ended December 31, 1971

	X Company	Y Company	Eliminations Dr.	Eliminations Cr.	Minority Interest	Consolidated
Income Statement:						
Sales....................	78,000	40,000				118,000
Dividend income.........	4,500		(2) 4,500			
Merchandise inventory (12/31/71).....	10,000	7,000				17,000
Total credits...........	92,500	47,000				135,000
Merchandise inventory (1/1/71).....	16,000	4,000				20,000
Purchases...............	42,000	20,000				62,000
Expenses................	8,000	3,000				11,000
Total debits............	66,000	27,000				93,000
	26,500	20,000				42,000
Minority interest in net income—Y Company......					°2,000	2,000
Net income—carried forward......	26,500	20,000	4,500	–0–	2,000	40,000
Retained Earnings Statement:						
Retained earnings, January 1, 1971:						
X Company................	40,000					40,000
Y Company................		10,000	(1) 9,000		†1,000	
Net income—brought forward.........	26,500	20,000	4,500		2,000	40,000
	66,500	30,000			3,000	80,000
Dividends declared:						
X Company................	10,000					10,000
Y Company................		5,000		(2) 4,500	500	
Retained earnings, December 31, 1971—carried forward......	56,500	25,000	13,500	4,500	2,500	70,000

Balance Sheet:

	X Company	Y Company	Eliminations Dr.	Eliminations Cr.	Minority	Consolidated
Cash	29,500	8,000				37,500
Accounts receivable	18,000	3,000				21,000
Merchandise inventory	10,000	7,000				17,000
Investment in Y Company stock	61,000			(1) 61,000		
Other assets	66,000	62,000				128,000
Differential			(1) 7,000			7,000
	184,500	80,000				210,500
Accounts payable	22,000	5,000				27,000
Other liabilities	6,000					6,000
Capital stock:						
X Company	100,000					100,000
Y Company		50,000	(1) 45,000		5,000	
Retained earnings—brought forward	56,500	25,000	13,500	4,500	2,500	70,000
Minority interest in Y Company					7,500	7,500 M
	184,500	80,000	65,500	65,500	7,500	210,500

* 10 percent of $20,000.
† 10 percent of $10,000.

Explanation of eliminations:
(1) Elimination of investment in subsidiary stock.
(2) Elimination of intercompany dividends.

The Three-Division Horizontal Working Paper (Subsequent Periods)

The income statement and balance sheet divisions of the consolidated working paper for periods subsequent to the first year after acquisition of subsidiary stock are essentially the same, in respect to details of format, eliminations, and extensions, as in the working paper for the year of acquisition. However, one significant difference should be noted in respect to the retained earnings division. The previous illustration clearly indicated that the amount of subsidiary retained earnings at acquisition is partially eliminated with the residual amount extended to the minority interest column. This accords with a firmly established accounting tenet that it is inappropriate to include any portion of the subsidiary's accumulated earnings at date of acquisition in consolidated retained earnings.

Earned surplus [retained earnings] of a subsidiary company created prior to acquisition does not form a part of the consolidated earned surplus [retained earnings] of the parent company and subsidiaries; nor can any dividend declared out of such surplus properly be credited to the income account of the parent company.[1]

In the consolidated working papers of subsequent years, however, it is necessary to recognize the parent company's equity in the *changes* in a subsidiary's retained earnings from the date of acquisition to the beginning of the current period. This recognition is indicated by merely extending to the "consolidated" column of the retained earnings working paper division that part of a subsidiary's retained earnings at the beginning of the year which is neither eliminated as "purchased" retained earnings nor extended to the "minority interest" column. This may be simply illustrated by enlarging the data for Case 1 to include changes in retained earnings of the affiliates for one additional year.

These additional data are incorporated in the retained earnings statement division of the consolidated working paper in Illustration 8–3:

	X Company	Y Company
Net income for 1972	$37,200	$15,000
Dividends declared, 1972	7,500	8,000

The reader will recognize that the amount of retained earnings of Y Company on January 1, 1972, to be extended, $16,000, is allocated $2,500 to the minority shareholders and $13,500 to the majority shareholders. The minority interest is 10 percent of the subsidiary's January 1 retained earnings balance, i.e., 10 percent of $25,000, or $2,500; the majority interest is

---

[1] Committee on Accounting Procedure, American Institute of Certified Public Accountants, *Accounting Research Bulletin No. 43* (1953), p. 11, in *Accounting Research and Terminology Bulletins,* Final Edition (New York, 1961).

Illustration 8-3

X COMPANY AND SUBSIDIARY Y COMPANY
Consolidated Statement Working Paper—Retained Earnings Division
For Year Ended December 13, 1972

	X Company	Y Company	Eliminations Dr.	Eliminations Cr.	Minority Interest	Consolidated
Retained Earnings Statement:						
Retained earnings, January 1, 1972:						
X Company..............................	56,500					56,500
Y Company..............................		25,000	(1) 9,000		2,500	13,500
Net income—brought forward......	37,200	15,000	7,200		1,500	43,500
	93,700	40,000			4,000	113,500
Dividends declared:						
X Company...........................	7,500					7,500
Y Company...........................		8,000		(2) 7,200	800	
Retained earnings, December 31, 1972—carried forward........	86,200	32,000	16,200	7,200	3,200	106,000

90 percent of the *undistributed* subsidiary earnings from the date of acquisition to the *beginning* of the current period, 90 percent of ($20,000 − $5,000), or $13,500.

Schedular Calculation of Consolidated Net Income and Retained Earnings

On occasion, it may be useful to determine the amounts of consolidated net income and/or retained earnings independently, without undertaking the often arduous task of completing lengthy consolidated working papers. A determination can be made using either of two schedular methods—by definition or by residual calculation. Since these two methods either explicitly articulate or implicitly reflect the basic concepts underlying consolidated statement preparation, the authors believe special attention should be devoted to the discussion which follows. Additionally, frequent references to these analyses, including several restatements of the fundamental definition, will be found in subsequent chapters.

By Definition.   This method presumes that it is appropriate to measure the various elements referred to in the definition of an accounting expression, and thereafter to algebraically sum these measurements. *Consolidated net income is defined as the parent company's net income, exclusive of subsidiary dividends, increased or decreased by its equity in subsidiary net profits or net losses for the period.* Using the data in Case 1, the amount of consolidated net income is determined *by definition* in the following schedule:

Parent company's net income for 1971 (exclusive of subsidiary dividends)—$26,500 − $4,500	$22,000
Increased by—	
Parent company's equity in subsidiary net income for 1971—90 percent of $20,000	18,000
Consolidated net income for 1971	$40,000

Consolidated retained earnings are defined as the aggregate of the parent company's retained earnings, exclusive of accumulated subsidiary dividends received, and its equity in the postacquisition, cumulative net profits, or net losses of its subsidiaries. Using again the data of Case 1, consolidated retained earnings on December 31, 1971, are calculated *by definition* to be:

Parent company's retained earnings, December 31, 1971 (exclusive of subsidiary dividends)—$56,500 − $4,500	$52,000
Increased by—	
Parent company's equity in cumulative subsidiary net income since acquisition—90 percent of $20,000	18,000
Consolidated retained earnings, December 31, 1971	$70,000

Since the accounts of the parent will customarily include intercompany dividend receipts from a subsidiary, it may be easier to begin the calculation of consolidated retained earnings with the parent company's retained earnings as actually recorded; thereafter, it is necessary to add the parent company's equity in the *net* increase or decrease in the subsidiary's retained earnings since acquisition. Where the parent company partially disposes of its shareholdings in a subsidiary company, it is especially useful to regard consolidated retained earnings as the parent company's recorded retained earnings, adjusted for the *undistributed* earnings or losses of the subsidiary since acquisition. Complications resulting from a reduction in the parent company's equity in subsidiary affiliates are discussed in Chapter 14. While both solution forms necessarily result in the same final measurement, the first calculation conforms more closely to the fundamental definition of consolidated retained earnings.

By Residual Calculation. This method employs the same arithmetic processes found in the previously illustrated working papers. Yet attention in this schedule focuses only on those data which relate to the calculation of either consolidated net income or consolidated retained earnings. In respect to the determination of consolidated net income, the calculation begins with the addition of the net incomes of the several affiliates; from this sum of net incomes is deducted the *net* elimination in the income statement division of the consolidated working paper, i.e., the excess of debit eliminations over credit eliminations. The combined net income *remainder* represents the value of the total equity of all shareholders—both majority and minority. The separation of their interests is accomplished by first calculating the value claim of the minority shareholders. After deducting this value from the total equity, there remains the residual claim of the majority shareholders, or consolidated net income.

Using the data of the previous illustration, consolidated net income is determined *by residual calculation* as follows:

Parent company's net income for 1971	$26,500
Subsidiary net income for 1971	20,000
	$46,500
Net elimination—intercompany dividends in 1971	4,500
Total equity	$42,000
Minority interest in subsidiary net income—10 percent of $20,000	2,000
Consolidated net income for 1971	$40,000

In a similar manner, the consolidated retained earnings may be determined

Retained earnings, December 31, 1971:	
Parent Company	$56,500
Subsidiary	25,000
	$81,500
Net elimination—90 percent of subsidiary retained earnings at acquisition	9,000
Total equity	$72,500
Minority interest in subsidiary retained earnings, December 31, 1971—10 percent of $25,000	2,500
Consolidated retained earnings, December 31, 1971	$70,000

Note that in the computation of consolidated retained earnings, the intercompany dividends no longer represent a net elimination, as the debit elimination in the income statement division is brought forward and offsets the credit elimination against Dividends Declared. Referring to Illustration 8–2, the reader will observe that the $9,000 net elimination is the excess of $13,500 debit eliminations over $4,500 credit eliminations on the "totals" line of the retained earnings division.

Other Intercompany Transactions

Discussion has heretofore centered on those intercompany transactions involving the purchase of subsidiary stock, reciprocal debtor-creditor relationships among affiliate companies, and the declaration of subsidiary dividends. If there are other intercompany transactions completed during a period of affiliation, their effects must also be eliminated. One such transaction, which occurs with relative frequency, is the sale of merchandise by one affiliate to another. Since the consolidated income statement should exhibit only those revenues and expenses which are confirmed by transactions with nonaffiliates, it is appropriate to eliminate the total amount of intercompany sales by a debit to Sales and a credit to Purchases (or Cost of Sales) in the consolidated working paper. Special elimination problems arise if some of the items in the intercompany merchandise shipments are not subsequently resold by the purchasing affiliate during the current period and are accordingly included in its final inventory. The complications created by the profit residue in the final inventory are dealt with in detail in Chapter 12.

Other types of intercompany revenue-expense transactions which must be similarly eliminated in the consolidated working papers include transactions arising from intercorporate financing, or the rendering of services by one affiliate to another. All evidences of these transactions must be removed from the consolidated statements to avoid duplicate measurement. Reciprocal accounts, for which eliminating entries must be made in the consolidated statement working paper, include interest income-interest expense, management fee income-management expense, commissions earned-commissions expense, and various others.

Note Receivable Discounted

If a nonaffiliate's note is held by one of the constituent companies and is discounted at a bank, or other financial institution, no elimination is required in the preparation of consolidated statements. Both the Note Receivable and the contingent liability thereon, Note Receivable Discounted, properly relate to the affiliation of companies. However, if the nonaffiliate's note is discounted with another member of the affiliation, Note Receivable will appear on the books of each affiliate, with Note Receivable Discounted also shown in the books of the discounting affiliate. Insofar as the economic entity is concerned, there is but one note receivable, without a contingent liability to a nonaffiliate; consequently, Note Receivable Discounted should be eliminated against the twice-recorded Note Receivable. Should this note be rediscounted with still another affiliate, only the amount of the original note should appear as an asset in consolidated statements, with all other amounts eliminated, since they are redundant in respect to the affiliation. However, in the event that the rediscounting is *not* intercompany, then both the amount of the original note and the amount of the contingent liability should be reported in consolidated statements, since a cause of action exists for which there is a secondary liability to an outside interest.

Where a note is drawn by one affiliate payable to a second affiliate, it is usual to eliminate both the Note Receivable and the contra Note Payable. Where the affiliate payee discounts the note with a third affiliate, it is also necessary to eliminate the Note Receivable Discounted against Note Receivable; however, if the payee affiliate discounts the note with a non-affiliate, the elimination should remove only the Note Receivable and Note Receivable Discounted. The Note Payable account in the amount recorded by the drawer should be extended to the "consolidated" column, as it now represents an obligation of the affiliation to an outside interest.

Multicompany Affiliations

The illustrative example presented previously focused on two-party affiliations, a parent company and a single subsidiary. However, the difficulty of consolidated statement preparation is compounded by an increase in the number of subsidiaries only to the extent of the necessity of dealing with a larger number of accounts and eliminations. Consider the following case of a three-party affiliation.

Case 2. The December 31, 1971, trial balances for companies X, Y, and Z are given in Illustration 8–4. The affiliation diagram and investment elimination schedule prepared from these data are shown following:

Affiliation Diagram

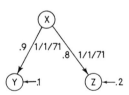

Investment Elimination Schedule
Dr. [Cr.]

	Y Company	Z Company
Capital stock......	$ 45,000	$ 32,000
Retained earnings....	9,000	4,000
Differential....	7,000	[3,000]
Investment....	$[61,000]	$[33,000]

The consolidated working paper for this case is presented in Illustration 8–5.

Proof of the consolidated net income and consolidated retained earnings amounts in Illustration 8–5 is established following by schedular compu-

Illustration 8-4

	X Company		Y Company		Z Company	
Cash	$ 34,300		$ 8,000		$ 4,000	
Accounts receivable	18,000		3,000		6,000	
Merchandise inventory (1/1/71)	16,000		4,000		3,000	
Investment in Y Company stock	61,000					
Investment in Z Company stock	33,000					
Other assets	31,700		62,000		44,000	
Accounts payable		$ 22,000		$ 5,000		$ 4,000
Other liabilities		6,000				1,000
Capital stock		100,000		50,000		40,000
Retained earnings (1/1/71)		40,000		10,000		5,000
Dividends declared	10,000		5,000		6,000	
Sales		78,000		40,000		30,000
Dividend income		9,300				
Purchases	42,000		20,000		12,000	
Expenses	9,300		3,000		5,000	
	$255,300	$255,300	$105,000	$105,000	$80,000	$80,000
Merchandise inventory (12/31/71)	$ 10,000		$ 7,000		$ 5,000	

Additional Information:

(1) X Company acquired 90 percent of the capital stock of Y Company on January 1, 1971, for $61,000. On the same date, X Company acquired 80 percent of the capital stock of Z Company for $33,000.

(2) On December 30, 1971, X Company transferred $1,000 cash to Z Company in partial settlement of a $3,000 obligation, classified by X Company as "other liabilities." As of December 31, this transfer was not yet recorded by Z Company.

(3) The sales of merchandise by Y Company to Z Company during 1971 were $5,000 (ignore the question of unconfirmed, or unrealized, inventory profit).

tations—one by definition, the other by residual calculation. Consolidated net income is computed *by definition* to be:

X Company's net income (exclusive of subsidiary dividends for 1971)—$30,000 − $9,300.........................	$20,700
Increased by—	
X Company's equity in subsidiary net income for 1971:	
Y Company—90 percent of $20,000...................	18,000
Z Company—80 percent of $15,000...................	12,000
Consolidated net income for 1971........................	$50,700

Consolidated retained earnings *by residual calculation* are as follows:

Retained earninings, December 31, 1971:		
X Company...		$60,000
Y Company...		25,000
Z Company...		14,000
		$99,000
Net eliminations:		
90 percent of Y Company's retained earnings at acquisition.....	$9,000	
80 percent of Z Company's retained earnings at acquisition......	4,000	13,000
Total equity...		$86,000
Minority interests in subsidiary retained earnings, December 31, 1971:		
Y Company—10 percent of $25,000.........................	$2,500	
Z Company—20 percent of $14,000.........................	2,800	5,300
Consolidated retained earnings, December 31, 1971..............		$80,700

Treasury Stock of the Subsidiary

On some occasions there may exist treasury stock on the books of a subsidiary when its outstanding shares are acquired by a parent company. In such instances, the presence of these shares must be appropriately accounted for in the investment elimination schedule. Consider the following example.

Case 3. X Company acquired 800 shares of the capital stock of Y Company on January 1, 1971, for $115,000 when the latter's net worth consisted of:

Capital stock (par, $100)...........................	$120,000
Treasury stock (recorded at par)....................	20,000
Retained earnings.................................	40,000

The investment elimination entry details are:

	Dr. [Cr.]
Capital stock....................................	$ 96,000
Treasury stock...................................	[16,000]
Retained earnings................................	32,000
Differential......................................	3,000
Investment......................................	$[115,000]

Alternatively, the treasury shares may be regarded as having been constructively retired, and accordingly are not identified as such in the financial

Illustration 8–5

X COMPANY AND SUBSIDIARIES
Consolidated Statement Working Paper
For Year Ended December 31, 1971

	X Company	Y Company	Z Company	Adjustments and Eliminations Dr.	Adjustments and Eliminations Cr.	Minority Interest Y Company	Minority Interest Z Company	Consolidated
Income Statement:								
Sales	78,000	40,000	30,000					143,000
Dividend income	9,300			(3) 5,000 (5) 9,300				22,000
Merchandise inventory (12/31/71)	10,000	7,000	5,000					22,000
Total credits	97,300	47,000	35,000					165,000
Merchandise inventory (1/1/71)	16,000	4,000	3,000		(3) 5,000			23,000
Purchases	42,000	20,000	12,000					69,000
Expenses	9,300	3,000	5,000					17,300
Total debits	67,300	27,000	20,000					109,300
Net income—carried forward	30,000	20,000	15,000					55,700
Minority interest in net income of:								
Y Company—10% of $20,000						2,000		[2,000]
Z Company—20% of $15,000							3,000	[3,000]
Net income—carried forward	30,000	20,000	15,000	14,300	5,000	2,000	3,000	50,700
Retained Earnings Statement:								
Retained earnings, January 1, 1971:								
X Company	40,000							40,000
Y Company		10,000		(1) 9,000		1,000		
Z Company			5,000	(2) 4,000			1,000	
Net income—brought forward	30,000	20,000	15,000	14,300	5,000	2,000	3,000	50,700
Dividend: declared:								
X Company	10,000							10,000
Y Company		5,000			(5) 4,500	500		
Z Company			6,000		(5) 4,800		1,200	
Retained earnings, December 31, 1971—ca'ried forward	60,000	25,000	14,000	27,300	14,300	2,500	2,800	80,700

Balance Sheet:

	X Company	Y Company	Z Company	Adjustments and Eliminations Dr.	Adjustments and Eliminations Cr.	Minority Interest (Y)	Minority Interest (Z)	Consolidated
Cash	34,300	8,000	4,000	(a) 1,000				47,300
Accounts receivable	18,000	3,000	6,000		(a) 1,000 / (4) 2,000			24,000
Merchandise inventory	10,000	7,000	5,000					22,000
Investment in Y Company stock	61,000				(1) 61,000			
Investment in Z Company stock	33,000				(2) 33,000			
Other assets	31,700	62,000	44,000					137,700
Differential—Y Company				(1) 7,000				7,000
Differential—Z Company					(2) 3,000			[3,000]
	188,000	80,000	59,000					235,000
Accounts payable	22,000	5,000	4,000					31,000
Other liabilities	6,000		1,000	(4) 2,000				5,000
Capital stock:								
X Company	100,000							100,000
Y Company		50,000		(1) 45,000		5,000		
Z Company			40,000	(2) 32,000			8,000	
Retained earnings—brought forward	60,000	25,000	14,000	27,300	14,300	2,500	2,800	80,700
Minority interest in Y Company						7,500		7,500 M
Minority interest in Z Company							10,800	10,800 M
	188,000	80,000	59,000	114,300	114,300	7,500	10,800	235,000

[deduction]

Explanation of adjustments and eliminations:

(a) Adjustment for unrecorded cash receipt by Z Company. The obligation from X Company is assumed to be reflected in the accounts receivable of Z Company.

(1) Elimination of investment in subsidiary stock—Y Company.

(2) Elimination of investment in subsidiary stock—Z Company.

(3) Elimination of intercompany sale.

(4) Elimination of intercompany debt.

(5) Elimination of intercompany dividends.

statements. In this event, a first elimination in the consolidated statement working paper is:

Capital stock	20,000	
Treasury stock		20,000

The investment elimination entry which follows is based upon the resulting account balances and takes the form:

	Dr. [*Cr.*]
Capital stock	$ 80,000
Retained earnings	32,000
Differential	3,000
Investment	$[115,000]

Note that in both cases the parent company's equity percentage in the subsidiary is based upon the number of shares *outstanding*.

Where the subsidiary's treasury shares are recorded at cost, and such cost is other than par value, an adjustment of its retained earnings accumulation and/or other contributed capital accounts is required before calculating the elimination elements. For example, if the treasury stock is carried at cost—$25,000—in the previous illustration, the first elimination is:

Capital stock	20,000	
Retained earnings	5,000	
Treasury stock		25,000

The investment elimination necessarily relates to the adjusted balances *after* this entry and is calculated in the same manner as before.

The reader is referred to *Intermediate Accounting* in this series for a detailed discussion of accounting for treasury shares.

Statement of Sources and Applications of Funds

An increasing number of companies are including a statement of sources and applications of funds in the group of financial statements published annually for stockholders and the public. The Accounting Principles Board, although not requiring the inclusion, has supported the presentation of this statement as follows:

The Board believes that a statement of source and application of funds should be presented as supplementary information in financial reports. The inclusion of such information is not mandatory, and it is optional as to whether it should be covered in the report of the independent accountant.[2]

In some instances, the decision as to how an item should be disclosed, if at all, in the funds statement depends on the concept of "funds" that is

---

[2] Accounting Principles Board, American Institute of Certified Public Accountants, "The Statement of Source and Application of Funds," *Opinion No. 3* (New York, 1963), p. 16.

adopted. One frequently adopted concept of "funds" has been (net) working capital, i.e., current assets less current liabilities. However, if this concept is adopted without exception, any transaction that affected *only* noncurrent accounts would not be disclosed and any transaction that affected *only* current accounts would not be disclosed.

The Accounting Principles Board has adopted a definition of funds which is of broader dimension. The Board's position, which the authors support as a sound resolution of the problem, is as follows:

> The concept of "funds" underlying the preparation of a statement of source and application of funds should be consistent with the purpose of the statement. In the case of statements prepared for presentation in annual reports, a concept broader than that of working capital should be used which can be characterized or defined as "all financial resources," so that the statement will include the financial aspects of all significant transactions, e.g., "non-fund" transaction such as the acquisition of property through the issue of securities.
>
> . . . .
>
> Related items should be shown together when the result contributes to the clarity of the statement, and less important items should be combined. Significant changes in individual current assets and current liabilities should be shown as separate items whenever they are not otherwise adequately disclosed in the financial statements; changes in the other current items may then be combined and shown as a single amount.[3]

The inclusion of a statement of sources and applications of funds in the series of consolidated financial statements presents no unusually difficult problems. However, the existence of minority stockholders requires a unique deduction in the consolidated income statement that must be properly analyzed to correctly determine the amount of funds provided by the operations of the consolidated entity.

Traditionally, the amount of "funds provided by operations" is calculated as the reported net income plus nonfund using expenses minus nonfund providing credits. The nonfund adjustments generally consist of current amortizations such as depreciation, bond discount, and bond premium. Following this approach to the calculation, the income statement deduction for minority interests is not a fund using item and must be added to consolidated net income to derive "funds provided by operations." The fact that the minority interest deduction in the income statement does not use funds is evidenced by the carry forward of this item to the retained earnings section of the working paper, and finally to the balance sheet as a long-term equity.

Subsidiary dividend payments to minority interest shareholders must be disclosed as an application of funds, since the income statement allocation to minority interests is treated as a nonfund using item. Adequate disclosure

---

[3] *Ibid.,* pp. 16–17.

in the statement requires that these payments, if material, be shown separately from parent company dividends paid to majority interest stockholders.

Transactions between affiliates are eliminated in the normal course of preparing a consolidated income statement, statement of retained earnings, and balance sheet. These eliminations are equally applicable to the statement of sources and applications of funds, since interaffiliate transactions do not affect the amount of working capital associated with the consolidated entity.

In the event the parent acquires additional shares of an existing subsidiary, the cost of the acquisition may or may not represent a use of funds. If the shares were purchased directly from the subsidiary corporation, the interaffiliate character of the transaction would eliminate any effect on consolidated funds. If the shares are purchased from outside (minority) interests and payment is made in cash or other assets, the acquisition represents an application of funds. On the other hand, if the acquisition of subsidiary shares from minority shareholders is paid for by issuing stock of the parent, the appropriate manner of disclosure is less clear. For the sake of clarity and in the interest of full disclosure, an informative presentation would be to list the acquisition of subsidiary stock and the issuance of the parent company's stock as contra items with any resulting differential extended as a positive or negative item in the application of funds category.

The problems of amortizing differentials are treated in Chapter 9. However, it may be noted that amortizations of differentials do not use funds. Thus, the income statement deductions for such amortizations must be added to consolidated net income to derive "funds provided by operations."

Case 4. The consolidated income statement and comparative balance sheets for A and its 80 percent owned subsidiary B are as shown in Illustration 8–6.

In preparing a statement of sources and applications of funds, several items of significance can be extracted from the above statement. These

Illustration 8–6

A COMPANY AND SUBSIDIARY B COMPANY

Consolidated Income Statement

For the Year Ended December 31, 1971

Sales.....................................		$171,000
Expenses:		
Cost of goods sold.....................	$ 60,000	
Depreciation..........................	15,000	
Other operating expenses...............	75,000	150,000
Income from operations..................		$ 21,000
Gain on sale of equipment...............		4,000
Combined net income....................		$ 25,000
Minority interest in net income...........		2,000
Consolidated net income.................		$ 23,000

Illustration 8–6 (Continued)

A COMPANY AND SUBSIDIARY B COMPANY

Consolidated Balance Sheets

December 31, 1971, and 1970

ASSETS	1971	1970
Cash....................................	$ 24,000	$ 25,000
Receivables.............................	55,000	60,000
Inventory...............................	105,000	75,000
Equipment (net of depreciation)............	155,000	150,000
Land...................................	40,000	40,000
Total Assets......................	$379,000	$350,000

EQUITIES		
Liabilities:		
Accounts payable........................	$ 46,000	$ 40,000
Accruals...............................	19,000	15,000
Bonds.................................	80,000	100,000
Total............................	$145,000	$155,000
Minority interest:		
Common stock.........................	$ 10,000	$ 10,000
Retained earnings......................	11,000	10,000
Total.............................	$ 21,000	$ 20,000
Stockholders' equity:		
Common stock.........................	$125,000	$100,000
Retained earnings......................	88,000	75,000
Total.............................	$213,000	$175,000
Total Equities....................	$379,000	$350,000

items, and additional information that is important to the statement preparation, are enumerated as follows:

1. The investment in inventory increased by $30,000 during 1971. The change in this item is substantially larger than the changes in the other elements of working capital; it is, in fact, as large as any other single application of funds. As a consequence, the change in inventory would appear to warrant separate disclosure as an application of funds.
2. Equipment (net of depreciation) increased by $5,000, notwithstanding the annual depreciation charge of $15,000. This increase resulted from a $30,000 purchase of equipment and a $14,000 sale of equipment which had a $10,000 book value at the date of sale.
3. Minority interest in net income was $2,000; however, minority interest in retained earnings increased by only $1,000. The $1,000 difference represents dividends paid by the subsidiary to minority shareholders. It may be noted that the subsidiary paid dividends of $4,000 to A Company, which amount was appropriately eliminated as an inter-affiliate transaction.
4. A Company common stock was increased by $25,000 during 1971. which represents a stock issuance to outside parties.

5. Consolidated retained earnings increased by $13,000, although consolidated net income was $23,000. The difference of $10,000 reflects dividends paid to A Company stockholders.

The formal statement of sources and applications of funds is presented in Illustration 8–7. Except for the separate disclosure of the change in the

Illustration 8–7

A COMPANY AND SUBSIDIARY B COMPANY

Consolidated Statement of Sources and Applications of Funds
For the Year Ended December 31, 1971

Sources of funds:
  Funds provided by operations:

Consolidated net income	$23,000	
Minority interest in net income	2,000	
Depreciation	15,000	
Gain on sale of equipment (included below)	(4,000)	$36,000

  Funds provided by other sources:

Issuance of stock	$25,000	
Sale of equipment	14,000	
Other items	16,000	55,000
Total funds provided		$91,000

Application of funds:

A Company dividends	$10,000
B Company dividends to minority interests	1,000
Purchase of equipment	30,000
Retirement of debt	20,000
Investment in inventory	30,000
Total funds applied	$91,000

inventory, the changes in current assets and current liabilities have been summarized as "Other items" ($16,000) and presented under "Funds provided by other sources." The amount of this item may be confirmed as follows:

Decrease in current assets (other than inventory):

Cash	$1,000	
Receivables	5,000	
		$ 6,000

Increase in current liabilities:

Accounts payable	$6,000	
Accruals	4,000	10,000
Funds provided by other items		$16,000

QUESTIONS

1. Suggest two variables which complicate the preparation of consolidated statements when the statements are prepared subsequent to the date of a subsidiary's acquisition by a parent.

2. What statements are generally included in the "family" of consolidated reports?

3. Indicate two alternative approaches to defining "consolidated net income."

4. What is the composition of the consolidated retained earnings statement?

5. When using the three-division horizontal working paper, do the "debits equal the credits" in *each* of the three sections of the "eliminations" columns? If so, why? If not, why not?

6. How is the minority interest in a subsidiary's net income calculated? Is this amount added to or substracted from the combined net incomes of the affiliates in order to determine "consolidated net income"?

7. Describe the determination of consolidated *net income* according to the definitional approach. The residual approach.

8. Indicate how consolidated *retained earnings* may be calculated using the definitional approach. The residual approach.

9. Suggest five types of intercompany transactions which generate elimination entries in the consolidation process.

10. Should a distinction be made in the preparation of consolidated statements between a note receivable discounted at a bank and one discounted by an affiliate? If so, why?

11. In the event a subsidiary has acquired treasury stock before its shares are acquired by a parent company, should the parent company's equity percentage in the subsidiary relate to the number of shares outstanding or to the total number of shares issued?

12. In the preparation of a consolidated statement of sources and applications of funds, what adjustments arise as a result of the existence of minority interests?

PROBLEMS

Problem 8–1

The consolidate income statement for 1971 of Clark Corporation and its 90 percent owned subsidiary is as follows:

Sales.	$85,000
Cost of goods sold.	30,000
Gross profit.	$55,000
Operating expenses.	25,000
Combined income.	$30,000
Minority interest.	1,000
Consolidated net income.	$29,000

Required:

(i) Is it possible to determine the amount of net income contributed by the parent's operations? If so, how much was contributed by Clark in 1971?

(ii) Assuming that none of the reported expenses represent noncash expenses (e.g., depreciation), what is your best estimate of the net amount of funds generated by operations during 1971 and therefore available for use by the consolidated entity?

Problem 8–2

On January 1, 1971, the Central Company purchased 80 percent of the capital stock of the Western Company for $51,000. On December 31, 1971, their trial balances are as follows:

	Central Company	Western Company
Cash.................................	$ 8,000	$ 5,000
Accounts receivable.....................	21,000	17,000
Merchandise—January 1.................	15,000	8,000
Investment in Western Company capital stock.......................	51,000	
Other assets...........................	54,000	48,000
Dividends declared.....................	10,000	5,000
Purchases.............................	90,000	20,000
Expenses..............................	10,000	7,000
	$259,000	$110,000
Accounts payable......................	$ 5,000	$ 6,000
Other liabilities.......................	5,000	
Advances from Central..................		4,000
Capital stock (par, $100)................	100,000	50,000
Retained earnings......................	40,000	10,000
Sales.................................	105,000	40,000
Dividend income.......................	4,000	
	$259,000	$110,000
Merchandise—December 31..............	$ 20,000	$ 10,000

Required:

On December 31, 1971, prepare consolidated statements supported by a three-division working paper.

Problem 8–3

The Cruse Company purchased 80 percent of the capital stock of Summers, Inc., on January 1, 1971, for $51,000. One year thereafter trial balances of the respective companies were:

	December 31, 1971	
	Cruse Company	Summers, Inc.
Cash.................................	$ 22,000	$ 12,500
Notes receivable.......................	5,000	2,000
Merchandise, January 1.................	28,000	11,000
Investment in Summers, Inc.............	51,000	
Other assets...........................	58,000	80,500
Dividends declared.....................	8,500	5,000
Purchases.............................	161,000	83,000
Freight-in.............................	1,000	200
Selling expenses.......................	18,000	11,100
Administrative expenses.................	9,300	5,700
	$361,800	$211,000

	—December 31, 1971—	
	Cruse Company	Summers, Inc.
Accounts payable..............................	$ 18,000	$ 12,000
Other liabilities............................	3,000	16,000
Capital stock (par, $100)...................	100,000	50,000
Retained earnings...........................	31,000	12,000
Sales......................................	205,000	121,000
Dividend income...........................	4,000	
Interest income............................	800	
	$361,800	$211,000
Merchandise, December 31.................	$ 41,000	$ 18,000

"Other liabilities" of Summers, Inc., include a $3,000 noninterest-bearing note payable to the Cruse Company.

Required:

Prepare a three-division consolidated statement working paper for the year ended December 31, 1971.

Problem 8–4

The following information is available for companies X and Y:

	December 31, 1971		December 31, 1972	
	X Company	Y Company	X Company	Y Company
Capital stock........................	$100,000	$50,000	$100,000	$50,000
Retained earnings (after closing)........	55,000	40,000	65,000	65,000
Net income (includes dividend income)............................			20,000	30,000

Additional Information:

X Company declared a $10,000 dividend in 1972, and Y Company declared a $5,000 dividend in 1972. X Company acquired 90 percent of Y Company for $75,000 on January 1, 1972.

Required:

(i) Prepare an investment elimination schedule as of January 1, 1972, the date of acquisition.
(ii) Calculate consolidated net income for 1972—
    (*a*) According to the definitional approach.
    (*b*) According to the residual approach.
(iii) Calculate consolidated retained earnings as of 12/31/72—
    (*a*) According to the definitional approach.
    (*b*) According to the residual approach.

Problem 8–5

P Company purchased a 90 percent interest in S Company on January 1, 1970. Given the following information regarding the two companies reported earnings and dividends record:

	Parent	Subsidiary
Retained earnings December 31, 1969.........	$100,000	$50,000
Net incomes reported on individual nonconsolidated income statements:		
1970....................................	30,400	10,000
1971....................................	35,400	10,000
Dividends declared and paid:		
1970....................................	–0–	6,000
1971....................................	–0–	6,000

Required:

(i)   Compute consolidated net income using the definitional approach: (*a*) for 1970 and (*b*) for 1971.

(ii) Compute consolidated net income in accordance with the residual approach: (*a*) for 1970 and (*b*) for 1971.

(iii) Compute consolidated retained earnings using the definitional approach: (*a*) as of December 31, 1970, and (*b*) as of December 31, 1971.

(iv) Compute consolidated retained earnings in accordance with the residual approach: (*a*) as of December 31, 1970, and (*b*) as of December 31, 1971.

Problem 8–6

X Company acquired a 90 percent interest in the capital stock of Y Company on January 1, 1971, and an 80 percent interest in the capital stock of Z Company on the same day.

Changes in the retained earnings of companies X, Y, and Z for the two-year period ended December 31, 1972, are summarized as follows:

	X Company	Y Company	Z Company
Retained earnings, 1/1/71............	$40,000	$30,000	$15,000
Net income [loss], 1971..............	15,000	8,000	[5,000]
Net income, 1972...................	10,000	4,000	7,000
Dividends paid, 1971...............	5,000	2,000	
Dividends paid, 1972...............			2,000
Retained earnings, 12/31/72.........	$60,000	$40,000	$15,000

Required:

(i)   Calculate the amount of consolidated net income for 1971 and 1972.

(ii) Calculate consolidated retained earnings as of January 1, 1971, December 31, 1971, and December 31, 1972.

Problem 8–7

On July 1, 1971, Jones Aluminum acquired a 90 percent interest in the capital stock of Harvey Transportation, Inc., for $265 per share. On December 31, 1971, consolidated statements were prepared and consolidated net income for the six-month period was reported to be $69,000. Net income for Jones Aluminum for the same period was $60,000. Dividends paid subsequent to the affiliation were Jones Aluminum, $20,000; and Harvey Transportation, Inc., $10,000. Interest payments of $5,000 were made by Jones Aluminum to Harvey Transportation, Inc., during this period.

	December 31, 1972	
	Jones Aluminum	Harvey Trans-portation, Inc.
Capital stock (par value, $100)..............	$800,000	$200,000
Paid-in surplus...........................	550,000	200,000
Retained earnings, January 1, 1972............	230,000	110,000
Net income...............................	90,000	30,000
Dividends paid...........................	40,000	20,000

Intercompany interest payments of $10,000 were made in 1972.
Jones Aluminum carries its investment in Harvey Transportation, Inc., at cost.

Required:

(i) As of December 31, 1972, prepare an investment elimination schedule for a consolidated statement working paper.
(ii) Compute the amount of consolidated net income for 1972.
(iii) Compute the amounts of consolidated retained earnings and minority interest in subsidiary net worth as of December 31, 1972.

Problem 8–8

A Company purchased 80 percent of the capital stock of B Company on January 1, 1969, and 90 percent of the capital stock of C Company on January 1, 1970.

The following two-year operating summary relates to the affiliated companies:

	A Company	B Company	C Company
Retained earnings, January 1, 1969............	$70,000	$40,000	$35,000
1969 net income (inclusive of subsidiary dividends)...............................	48,000	20,000	30,000
1969 cash dividends.......................		10,000	5,000
1970 net income (exclusive of subsidiary dividends)...............................	10,000	15,000	20,000
1970 cash dividends.......................	4,000	6,000	10,000

Required:

Calculate consolidated net income for 1969 and 1970 and consolidated retained earnings as of December 31, 1970—

(i) By definition.
(ii) By residual calculation.

Problem 8–9

On January 1, 1970, the Belt Company purchased in the open market 90 percent of the capital stock of the Kaplan Company for $140,000 *and* 70 percent of the capital stock of the Baxter Company for $35,000. On this date the following account balances of Kaplan and Baxter were:

	Kaplan	Baxter
Capital stock (par, $100).............	$100,000	$50,000
Retained earnings [deficit].............	50,000	[10,000]

A summary of changes in retained earnings for 1971 is as follows:

	Belt	Kaplan	Baxter
Retained earnings, January 1..........	$100,000	$60,000	$20,000
Net income, 1971....................	40,000	25,000	10,000
Dividends paid, 1971.................	5,000	8,000	4,000

Required:

If the investments in subsidiary stock are carried at cost—

(i)   Prepare on December 31, 1971, an investment elimination schedule for a consolidated statement working paper.

(ii) Prepare a consolidated retained earnings working paper for the year ended December 31, 1971.

(iii) Verify by schedule calculation the amount of consolidated retained earnings determined in (ii) above.

Problem 8–10

A summary of the changes in the stockholders' equity of the Dial Company and the Landry Company for the two-year period ending December 31, 1971, is given following:

	Dial Company	Landry Company
Capital stock (no-par value), January 1, 1970:		
Dial Company (20,000 shares).................	$120,000	
Landry Company (10,000 shares)..............		$80,000
Retained earnings, January 1, 1970...............	$ 60,000	$40,000
Net income, 1970............................	30,000	24,000
	$ 90,000	$64,000
Dividends paid (cash), November 15, 1970.........	10,000	8,000
Retained earnings, December 31, 1970............	$ 80,000	$56,000
Net income [loss], 1971.......................	18,000	[4,000]
	$ 98,000	$52,000
Dividends paid (cash), December 15, 1971..........	6,000	10,000
Retained earnings, December 31, 1971............	$ 92,000	$42,000

Dunham, Inc., purchased in the open market the following:

a)   8,000 shares of Landry Company stock on January 1, 1970, cost $110,000.
b)   18,000 shares of Dial Company stock on January 1, 1971, cost $185,000.

On December 31, 1971, Dunham, Inc., had retained earnings, exclusive of dividend income, of $50,000. The only present source of income for Dunham, Inc., is subsidiary dividends.

Required:

(i)   Prepare an investment elimination schedule for a consolidated statement working paper, December 31, 1971.
(ii)   Prepare a consolidated retained earnings statement working paper for the year ended December 31, 1971.
(iii) Verify by schedular analysis the amount of consolidated retained earnings, December 31, 1971, established in (ii) above.

Problem 8–11

The balance sheets of The Arnold Company and its 90 percent owned subsidiary, The Penney Company, acquired on January 1, 1971, are as follows:

	December 31, 1971	
ASSETS	Arnold Company	Penney Company
Cash..	$ 34,000	$ 24,500
Accounts receivable.......................................	85,000	47,000
The Penney Company.......................................	31,600	
Merchandise...	29,300	18,100
Investment in The Penney Company stock (at cost).........	65,000	
Long-lived assets...	88,000	41,700
Intangibles..	17,100	
	$350,000	$131,300

EQUITIES		
Notes payable...	$ 30,000	$ 10,000
Accounts payable...	68,900	26,300
The Arnold Company...		16,000
Capital stock (par, $100)...................................	150,000	50,000
Retained earnings...	93,000	29,000
Undistributed profits in The Penney Company since acquisition..	8,100	
	$350,000	$131,300

The variation in the reciprocal accounts can be accounted for as follows:

a)   The Arnold Company rendered a statement to the subsidiary for advertising beneficial to the subsidiary, $4,000. The billing remains unrecorded by The Penney Company.
b)   The Arnold Company shipped merchandise, at cost, $8,000 to The Penney Company. The merchandise is in-transit on December 31, is not included in The Penney Company's inventory, and no liability therefor has yet been recorded.
c)   The subsidiary paid a 10 percent cash dividend on December 28, 1971, crediting The Arnold Company account for its ratable interest therein.

d) Undistributed profits of The Penney Company since acquisition were recorded by The Arnold Company, increasing The Penney Company reciprocal account. The Arnold Company was not aware of the existence of any cash dividends when recording the undistributed subsidiary profits since acquisition, and thus made the entry on the basis of The Penney Company's reported 1971 net income.

Required:

(i)   Prepare a schedule reconciling the reciprocal accounts.
(ii) Prepare a consolidated balance sheet working paper as of December 31, 1971.

Problem 8–12

General ledger trial balances as of December 31, 1971, and 1970 for P Company and S Company follow:

	December 31, 1971		December 31, 1970	
	P Company	S Company	P Company	S Company
Cash............................	$ 21,100	$ 34,700	$ 56,700	$ 9,800
Accounts receivable.................	49,700	64,200	54,200	31,500
Inventories.......................	46,600	64,400	49,800	48,400
Other receivables—current...........	41,300	22,400	32,300	24,500
Investment in S Company...........	178,400		178,400	
Other investments.................	10,800	33,400	92,800	33,400
Land.........................	18,200	15,000	28,700	15,000
Buildings......................	135,800	87,000	106,700	65,000
Equipment......................	61,000	45,000	48,000	45,000
Total debits....................	$562,900	$366,100	$647,600	$272,600
Allowance for bad debts.............	$ 4,500	$ 3,900	$ 4,100	$ 3,700
Allowance for depreciation..........	69,500	50,600	41,300	31,200
Accounts payable..................	22,900	45,900	31,200	36,800
Notes payable....................	41,000	25,000	88,400	
Dividends payable.................		14,000		
Other accruals....................	5,900	20,800	12,700	12,600
Income taxes payable...............	19,600	19,400	36,500	12,300
Bonds payable....................			30,000	
Capital stock....................	175,000	75,000	175,000	75,000
Capital contributed in excess of par value.....................	117,000	38,200	117,000	38,200
Retained earnings.................	87,400	48,800	62,300	38,700
Net income for year...............	20,100	24,500	49,100	24,100
Total credits....................	$562,900	$366,100	$647,600	$272,600

The following information is available:

a) P Company acquired 90 percent of the outstanding stock of S Company on January 2, 1970, in exchange for:

500 shares P Company capital stock; par value $50, market value $200....	$100,000
Note payable due July 2, 1972..............................	78,400
Total..	$178,400

The above note payable due July 2, 1972, was paid on December 1, 1971.

b) In January, 1971, P Company sold some "other investments" for $101,300 that cost $85,400. In March, 1971, P Company sold a parcel of land for $18,800 that cost $10,500.

c) On June 30, 1971, P Company demolished an unneeded warehouse building that cost $18,900 and had a net book value of $5,400 on that date.

d) During 1971 P Company declared and paid cash dividends totaling $24,-000. S Company declared a cash dividend totaling $14,000 on December 1, 1971, payable on January 10, 1972, to holders of record on December 15, 1971. The dividend receivable was recorded in P Company's Other Receivables account.

e) The P Company bonds, which had a maturity date of December 1, 1973, were retired in 1971 at a total consideration of $32,500 including $600 for accrued interest and $1,900 penalty for early retirement.

f) At December 31, 1971, P Company's account, Other Receivables, includes a $25,000 noninterest-bearing note receivable from S Company. S Company's account, Accounts Receivable, included $18,500 due from P Company for merchandise purchases which amount is equal to the original cost of the merchandise to S.

g) The amounts for the net income for the year are after all deductions; no expenses or income were recorded in the retained earnings accounts.

Required:

Prepare a formal consolidated statement of source and application of funds for P Company and its subsidiary for the year ended December 31, 1971. All supporting computations, including the computation of consolidated net income, should be in good form. Any current item which changes by $15,000 or more should be disclosed separately as having a material effect on funds.

(AICPA adapted)

Problem 8–13

Control Electronics Corporation acquired a 90 percent interest in the capital stock of Gyroscope Research, Inc., on March 31, 1971, for $587,000. At this time, Gyroscope Research, Inc., had capital stock (no-par value) of $379,000 and retained earnings of $121,000. As of December 31, 1972 their trial balances were as follows:

	Control Electronics Corporation	Gyroscope Research, Inc.
Cash.	$ 147,000	$ 22,000
Accrued interest receivable.	300	
Accounts receivable.	879,000	193,000
Dividends receivable.	18,000	
Merchandise—January 1.	221,000	
Notes receivable.	50,000	10,000
Notes receivable discounted.	[35,000]	[10,000]
Other assets.	641,700	718,000
Investment in Gyroscope Research, Inc., capital stock.	587,000	
Dividends declared.	100,000	40,000
Purchases.	1,948,000	
Salaries.	400,000	650,000
Expenses.	775,000	219,200
Interest expense.		1,800
	$5,732,000	$1,844,000
Accounts payable.	$ 788,000	$ 67,400
Accrued interest payable.		600
Notes payable.		30,000
Dividends payable.	50,000	20,000
Capital stock (no-par value).	746,000	379,000
Retained earnings.	410,000	147,000
Sales.	3,700,000	
Revenues from research.		1,200,000
Interest income.	2,000	
Dividend income.	36,000	
	$5,732,000	$1,844,000
Merchandise—December 31.	$ 211,000	

Additional Information:

a)   The $30,000 notes payable of Gyroscope Research, Inc., were held by Control Electronics Corporation on January 1, 1972; subsequently, $20-000 were discounted at the Lone Star Bank. Intercompany interest expense in 1972 amounted to $800. As of December 31, 1972, one third of the accrued interest payable on the books of Gyroscope Research, Inc., was payable to Control Electronics Corporation.

b)   During 1972, Gyroscope Research, Inc., received two $5,000 notes from clients which were immediately discounted with Control Electronics Corporation. Control Electronics Corporation subsequently rediscounted one of these notes with the Lone Star Bank.

c)   Gyroscope Research, Inc., performs research work for Control Electronics Corporation, and during 1972 billed the parent $380,000, which the latter charged to "expense." As of December 31, 1972, $75,000 of these billings remain unpaid.

Required:

(i)   As of December 31, 1972, prepare a three-division consolidated statement working paper.

(ii)   Discuss the treatment of the notes in the formal consolidated balance sheet.

Problem 8–14

On April 30, 1971, Investment Company agreed to purchase the common stock of Consolidated Company for a tentative price of $180,000. The purchase price is to be reduced by the amount, if any, by which the total book value of the shares of Consolidated Company as of January 31, 1971, exceeded the total book value as of April 30, 1971.

The balance sheets of Consolidated Company were as follows:

ASSETS	April 30, 1971	Jan. 31, 1971
Current assets................................	$ 55,000	$ 56,000
Fixed assets, less accumulated depreciation........	76,000	78,000
Investment in and advances to Industries, Inc.......	20,200	14,100
	$151,200	$148,100
LIABILITIES AND OWNER'S EQUITY		
Current liabilities............................	$ 27,000	$ 30,000
Capital stock................................	17,000	17,000
Retained earnings............................	107,200	101,100
	$151,200	$148,100

The balance sheets of Industries, Inc., subsidiary of Consolidated Company, were as follows:

ASSETS	April 30, 1971	Jan. 31, 1971
Current assets.............................	$ 10,000	$ 18,100
Other assets................................	1,200	1,200
Fixed assets, less accumulated depreciation........	4,300	18,600
	$ 15,500	$ 37,900
LIABILITIES AND OWNERS' EQUITY		
Notes payable.............................	$ 5,000	$ 14,300
Accounts payable—trade.....................	5,800	8,600
Accrued liabilities..........................	2,000	2,200
	$ 12,800	$ 25,100
Long-term debt:		
Notes payable.............................	$ 18,500	$ 19,400
Advance from Consolidated Company.........	250	6,400
	$ 18,750	$ 25,800
Capital stock...............................	$ 700	$ 1,000
Paid-in capital.............................	$ 19,250	$ 10,000
Deficit......................................	$[36,000]	$[24,000]
	$ 15,500	$ 37,900

The agreement provided that the book value of Consolidated Company should be determined in accordance with generally accepted accounting principles except that the shares of Industries, Inc., should be included at their book value, if any. In the absence of a positive book value, the liabilities of Consolidated Company are to be increased by a proportionate amount of the excess of the liabilities of Industries, Inc., over its assets; the proportion shall be the percentage of outstanding stock owned. The excess of liabilities over assets shall be reduced by any loss sustained by Industries, Inc., in the transfer of certain assets to its sole minority stockholder in cancellation of its promissory note.

During the period from January 31, 1971, to April 30, 1971, accumulated advances made by Consolidated Company in the amount of $12,250 were transferred to Paid-In Capital by Industries, Inc.

On March 31, 1971, Industries, Inc., sold certain assets to its minority stockholder in consideration of the cancellation of a note payable to him. The transaction resulted in a book loss of $6,100. As part of this transaction the minority stockholder surrendered all of his stock, 30 percent of the outstanding stock, to Industries, Inc., for cancellation.

Required:

(i)   Prepare schedules showing the net book value of Consolidated Company at January 31, 1971, and April 30, 1971, computed in accordance with the terms of the sales agreement.
(ii)   Compute the adjustment, if any, to the tentative purchase price.

(AICPA adapted)

Problem 8–15

P, a holding company, owns 90 percent of the capital stock of M and 80 percent of the capital stock of O. On April 15, 1971, M sold merchandise to O for $50,000 and received from O five noninterest-bearing notes of $10,000 each, due respectively on May 15, June 15, July 15, August 15, and September 15, 1971. On April 15, M discounted the notes due May 15 and June 15, respectively, with its bank, being credited with the proceeds of $19,925. The other three notes it held. In consolidating the accounts of the three companies at the close of the fiscal year ended April 30, 1971, how should the transactions involving the notes be handled? Give reasons for your answer.

(AICPA adapted)

Chapter 9

Consolidated Financial Reports— Equity Method; Differentials

EQUITY METHOD

The analysis of Chapter 8 was based on the parent's adoption of the cost method of accounting for its investment in subsidiary stock. The principal alternative to the cost method, referred to variously as the equity method, the actual value method, or the economic basis method, requires periodic adjustments to the initial investment cost to give effect to the parent's equity in the postacquisition earnings, losses, and dividends of the subsidiary. In the following section, the equity method will be analyzed in terms of its implications on the preparation of consolidated financial statements and its significance as an alternative to the cost method.

Recording Subsidiary Earnings, Losses, and Dividends

Under the equity method, the parent company's equity in the post-acquisition earnings of a subsidiary is recorded by debiting the investment account and crediting a suitably named account, such as Undistributed Subsidiary Earnings. The reference to "undistributed" earnings emphasizes the unique *realization* criterion underlying the recognition of a subsidiary's contribution to the parent's net income. Generally, when the realization concept is applied to income on stock investments, it has been interpreted as a requirement that income not be recognized by the stockholder until declared as dividends by the issuing company. To the contrary, the equity method involves a significant relaxation of this traditional criterion. In essence, the equity method is based on the argument that the economic impact of a corporation's reported profits and losses immediately accrues to its stockholders, regardless of the timing of dividend declarations. Although an account title such as Undistributed Subsidiary Income is more descriptive of the equity method, a shortened expression, Subsidiary Income, is more frequently used.

Postacquisition losses sustained by a subsidiary affiliate are recorded in a similar manner by the parent, i.e., by a debit to Subsidiary Losses with a corresponding credit to the investment account. Such losses result from a decrease in the underlying subsidiary net assets; consequently, the parent's entry is an effort to formally recognize the unfavorable economic circumstance.

The parent company's receipt of a subsidiary cash dividend is recorded by debiting Cash and crediting the investment account. Such an entry reflects the financial realization of the parent's equity in subsidiary profits in the amount of the assets transferred; accordingly, the receipt of dividends is treated as a reduction in the reciprocal investment account balance. Since an antecedent entry has been made increasing the investment account for subsidiary profits, the parent's collection of subsidiary cash dividends is simply an act of conversion, or a partial recovery of the adjusted cost of the investment. The effect produced on the parent company's books is merely a transformation in asset form.

Entry Comparison

A comparison of the journal entries made by the parent company using both the cost and equity methods should expose some of their principal differences.

Illustration 9–1

Cost Method		Equity Method	

A 90 percent investment in subsidiary stock is acquired for $50,000.

Investment in sub-		Investment in sub-	
sidiary stock.... 50,000		sidiary stock...... 50,000	
Cash........	50,000	Cash.........	50,000

$4,000 cash dividends are paid by the subsidiary during the first year of its operations.

Cash............ 3,600		Cash.............. 3,600	
Dividend in-		Investment in	
come......	3,600	subsidiary	
		stock........	3,600

The subsidiary reports net income of $10,000 for the first year's operations.

No entry.		Investment in sub-	
		sidiary stock..... 9,000	
		Subsidiary in-	
		come........	9,000

$3,000 cash dividends are paid by the subsidiary during the second year.

Cash............ 2,700		Cash.............. 2,700	
Dividend in-		Investment in	
come......	2,700	subsidiary	
		stock........	2,700

The subsidiary reports a net loss of $2,000 for the second year.

No entry.		Subsidiary loss..... 1,800	
		Investment in	
		subsidiary	
		stock........	1,800

The reader is reminded that the entries shown in Illustration 9–1 are those recorded on the books of the parent company. They should not be confused with eliminating entries required for consolidated statement working papers.

The entries shown in Illustration 9–1 are based on the assumptions that (1) the cost of the parent's investment is equal to its equity in the subsidiary's recorded net assets; and (2) there are no transactions between the parent and the subsidiary which involve the recognition of gains or losses. In the event either, or both, of these assumptions is not valid, the parent must make special adjustments to the net income reported by the subsidiary and record its equity in the adjusted net income. Since these adjustments are also necessary in preparing consolidated statements, they will be examined in subsequent sections of the book in the context of preparing consolidated statements. The procedures for giving effect to (1) amortization of the difference between investment cost and the equity in net assets, and (2) elimination of intercompany gains and losses are described in Chapters 9, 12, and 13.

Consolidated Statement Working Paper—First Year Subsequent to Acquisition

Use of the equity method necessarily introduces changes in the financial statements of the parent company; yet, significantly, *consolidated financial statements for the affiliation remain unaffected by the parent's choice of a method of accounting for its investment.* Although there are variations in elimination details, the equity method working paper yields exactly the same consolidated statement account balances as if the cost method were employed. This will be demonstrated in the illustrative cases which follow.

Where the investment is carried on an equity basis and the consolidated income statement, statement of retained earnings, and balance sheet are prepared, it is important first to eliminate, or reverse, the effects of the parent company's entries for subsidiary profits or losses and dividends for the current year. Such an elimination, or reversal, in the consolidated statement working paper restores the investment account to that balance which prevailed at the *beginning* of the current year. A second entry is then necessary to eliminate the amount of the investment, as adjusted by the previous entry, against the stockholders' equity accounts of the subsidiary as of the *beginning* of the year. Once entries have been made to eliminate the investment in this manner, any remaining eliminations in the working paper merely duplicate those used in the cost method of accounting.

Case 1. Total (100 Percent) Ownership of Subsidiary Stock. The trial balances of X Company and Y Company on December 31, 1971, one year following X's 100 percent purchase of Y's outstanding stock for $61,000, are as follows:

	⌐—X Company—⌐		⌐—Y Company—⌐	
Cash.........................	$ 30,000		$ 8,000	
Accounts receivable.............	18,000		3,0)0	
Merchandise (1/1/71)...........	16,000		4,000	
Investment in Y Company				
stock......................	76,000			
Other assets..................	66,000		62,000	
Accounts payable..............		$ 22,000		$ 5,000
Other liabilities................		6,000		
Capital stock.................		100,000		50,000
Retained earnings (1/1/71)......		40,000		10,000
Dividends declared.............	10,000		5,000	
Sales.........................		78,000		40,000
Subsidiary income..............		20,000		
Purchases....................	42,000		20,000	
Expenses....................	8,000		3,000	
	$266,000	$266,000	$105,000	$105,000
Merchandise (12/31/71).........	$ 10,000		$ 7,000	

Based upon these data, the diagram of intercompany stock ownership and the investment elimination schedule are as follows:

Affiliation Diagram

X
100% | 1/1/71
Y

Investment Elimination Schedule

	Dr. [Cr.]
Capital stock...............	$ 50,000
Retained earnings...........	10,000
Differential.................	1,000
Investment..................	$[61,000]

The consolidated statement working paper for this case is shown in Illustration 9–2.

During 1971 the parent company made entries, the effects of which are compounded as follows:

Cash..	5,000	
Investment in Y Company stock.........................	15,000	
Subsidiary income....................................		20,000

Consequently, the first elimination in the consolidated working paper in Illustration 9–2 should reverse the effect of this entry. The account, Dividends Declared, is substituted for Cash in the original entry. The eliminating entry is then of the form:

Subsidiary income.......................................	20,000	
Dividends declared.....................................		5,000
Investment in Y Company stock......................		15,000

With the investment account restored to its beginning-of-year balance, the investment elimination entry then follows:

Capital stock...	50,000	
Retained earnings......................................	10,000	
Differential..	1,000	
Investment in Y Company stock......................		61,000

Study of the working paper for this illustration will disclose that the parent company's net income is equal to consolidated net income; also, the parent company's retained earnings are equal to the consolidated retained earnings. Necessarily this condition of equivalence will prevail where the investment account is periodically adjusted to reflect the parent's equity in subsidiary net asset changes.

Case 2. Ownership of Majority (90 Percent) of Subsidiary Stock. In this case, the data of Case 1 are modified to reflect a 90 percent acquisition.

Affiliation Diagram

$.9 \mid 1/1/71$

X

Y — .1

Investment Elimination Schedule

		Dr. [Cr.]
Capital stock.............	(1)	$ 45,000
Retained earnings.........	(2)	9,000
Differential...............		7,000
Investment..............		$[61,000]

(1) 90% of $50,000.
(2) 90% of $10,000.

The consolidated statement working paper for this case is found in Illustration 9–3.

Consolidated Statement Working Paper—Second Year Subsequent to Acquisition

In the previous illustrations, only one period of subsidiary operations separated the preparation of the consolidated statements from the date of the acquisition of subsidiary shares. In such a circumstance, the first eliminating entry for a consolidated working paper which adjusts the investment account to its beginning-of-year balance also restores the account to the original investment cost. However, where there are several intervening periods of subsidiary operations subsequent to acquisition, the regression of the first eliminating entry will extend only so far as the beginning of the current (last) year. Using the basic data of Case 2, the following example illustrates the preparation of a consolidated working paper after one additional accounting period.

Case 3. Ownership of Majority (90 Percent) of Subsidiary Stock (Second Year's Operation). The investment elimination schedule will differ from that of Case 2 only by the amounts of the retained earnings and investment elements, which indicate the effects of an additional period of subsidiary operations.

Illustration 9–2

X COMPANY AND SUBSIDIARY Y COMPANY
Consolidated Statement Working Paper
For Year Ended December 31, 1971

	X Company	Y Company	Eliminations Dr.	Eliminations Cr.	Consolidated
Income Statement:					
Sales	78,000	40,000			118,000
Subsidiary income	20,000		(1) 20,000		
Merchandise inventory (12/31/71)	10,000	7,000			17,000
Total credits	108,000	47,000			135,000
Merchandise inventory (1/1/71)	16,000	4,000			20,000
Purchases	42,000	20,000			62,000
Expenses	8,000	3,000			11,000
Total debits	66,000	27,000			93,000
Net income—carried forward	42,000	20,000	20,000	–0–	42,000
Retained Earnings Statement:					
Retained earnings, January 1, 1971:					
X Company	40,000				40,000
Y Company		10,000	(2) 10,000		
Net income—brought forward	42,000	20,000	20,000	–0–	42,000
	82,000	30,000			82,000
Dividends declared:					
X Company	10,000				10,000
Y Company		5,000		(1) 5,000	
Retained earnings, December 31, 1971—carried forward	72,000	25,000	30,000	5,000	72,000

Balance Sheet:

	X Company	Y Company	Eliminations (Dr.)	Eliminations (Cr.)	Consolidated
Cash	30,000	8,000			38,000
Accounts receivable	18,000	3,000			21,000
Merchandise inventory	10,000	7,000			17,000
Investment in Y Company stock	76,000			(1) 15,000 (2) 61,000	
Other assets	66,000	62,000			128,000
Differential			(2) 1,000		1,000
	200,000	80,000			205,000
Accounts payable	22,000	5,000			27,000
Other liabilities	6,000				6,000
Capital stock:					
X Company	100,000				100,000
Y Company		50,000	(2) 50,000		
Retained earnings—brought forward	72,000	25,000	(2) 30,000	5,000	72,000
	200,000	80,000	81,000	81,000	205,000

Explanation of eliminations:

(1) To reverse the parent company's entries during 1971 for subsidiary dividends and undistributed subsidiary net income.

(2) To eliminate the January 1, 1971, investment account balance against the corresponding stockholders' equity accounts of the subsidiary.

Illustration 9–3

X COMPANY AND SUBSIDIARY Y COMPANY

Consolidated Statement Working Paper
For Year Ended December 31, 1971

	X Company	Y Company	Eliminations Dr.	Eliminations Cr.	Minority Interest	Consolidated
Income Statement:						
Sales	78,000	40,000				118,000
Subsidiary income	18,000		(1) 18,000			
Merchandise inventory (12/31/71)	10,000	7,000				17,000
Total credits	106,000	47,000				135,000
Merchandise inventory (1/1/71)	16,000	4,000				20,000
Purchases	42,000	20,000				62,000
Expenses	8,000	3,000				11,000
Total debits	66,000	27,000				93,000
	40,000	20,000				42,000
Minority interest in net income—Y Company					2,000	2,000
Net income—carried forward	40,000	20,000	18,000	–0–	2,000	40,000
Retained Earnings Statement:						
Retained earnings, January 1, 1971:						
X Company	40,000					40,000
Y Company		10,000	(2) 9,000		1,000	
Net income—brought forward	40,000	20,000	18,000		2,000	40,000
	80,000	30,000			3,000	80,000
Dividends declared:						
X Company	10,000					10,000
Y Company		5,000		(1) 4,500	500	
Retained earnings, December 31, 1971—carried forward	70,000	25,000	27,000	4,500	2,500	70,000

Balance Sheet:

	X Company	Y Company	Eliminations Debit	Eliminations Credit	Minority Interest	Consolidated
Cash	29,500	8,000				37,500
Accounts receivable	18,000	3,000				21,000
Merchandise inventory	10,000	7,000				17,000
Investment in Y Company stock	74,500			(1) 13,500 (2) 61,000		
Other assets	66,000	62,000				128,000
Differential			(2) 7,000			7,000
	198,000	80,000				210,500
Accounts payable	22,000	5,000				27,000
Other liabilities	6,000					6,000
Capital stock:						
X Company	100,000					100,000
Y Company		50,000	(2) 45,000		5,000	
Retained earnings—brought forward	70,000	25,000	(2) 27,000	4,500	2,500	70,000
Minority interest in Y Company					7,500	7,500 M
	198,000	80,000	79,000	79,000		210,500

Explanation of eliminations:

(1) To reverse the parent company's entries during 1971 for subsidiary dividends and undistributed subsidiary earnings.

(2) To eliminate the January 1, 1971, investment account balance against 90 percent of the corresponding stockholders' equity accounts of the subsidiary.

<table>
<tr><td>**Affiliation Diagram**</td><td colspan="2">**Investment Elimination Schedule**</td></tr>
</table>

		Dr. [Cr.]
Capital stock...........	(1)	$ 45,000
Retained earnings........	(2)	22,500
Differential..............		7,000
Investment..............		$[74,500]

(1) 90% of $50,000.
(2) 90% of $25,000.

Affiliation diagram: X, .9 1/1/71, Y ←.1

This schedule demonstrates that the relevant value measures are the subsidiary's stockholders' equity account balances existing at the beginning of the current year; elimination of reciprocals accordingly relates to such balances. It is significant to note that the amounts of debit or credit differentials remain unaffected by the choice of an investment basis, i.e., whether the cost or equity method is used.

As in the previous case, it is important first to measure the effect produced on the parent company's investment account by changes in the subsidiary's residual equity during the current year. The algebraic sum of the parent's entries during the year to record the receipt of subsidiary dividends and the recognition of undistributed subsidiary earnings is:

Cash......	9,000	
Investment in Y Company stock.........	16,200	
Subsidiary income......		25,200

The necessary elimination entry on the consolidated working paper to reverse the effect of these entries takes the form:

Subsidiary income.......	25,200	
Investment in Y Company stock......		16,200
Dividends declared......		9,000

The investment elimination which follows relates, as before, to reciprocal balances of the investment account and the corresponding book value of subsidiary capital stock as of the beginning of the year. The reader will again note in Illustration 9–4 that the balances accumulated in the parent company's accounts for retained earnings, net income for the year, and dividends declared are identical in amount to their consolidated statement equivalents.

If only a consolidated balance sheet working paper is prepared, the sequence of eliminations is simplified. In this instance, Subsidiary Income and Dividends Declared for the current year will have been closed to Retained Earnings; accordingly, a working paper reversal of the type referred to earlier is unnecessary. Rather, the investment elimination schedule is prepared using the account balances at the *end* of the current year.

An Appraisal of the Cost and Equity Methods

Evaluating the cost and equity methods as alternative approaches to the parent's accounting for its interest in subsidiaries demands a consideration of each method's effects upon the reporting of (1) consolidated subsidiaries in consolidated statements, (2) unconsolidated subsidiaries in consolidated statements, and (3) all subsidiaries in the parent's separate (unconsolidated) statements.

Consolidated Subsidiaries in Consolidated Statements. Reflection on the consolidation process will disclose that the formal consolidated statements *are not affected* by the parent's choice of method of accounting for its investment. In comparing the two methods, the differences in the parent's accounts are precisely offset by differences in elimination entries utilized in the consolidation process. Whatever the balance in the parent's investment account, it is completely eliminated against the parent's equity in subsidiary ownership accounts. Likewise, all other parent company accounts relating to its investment (Dividend Income under the cost method; Subsidiary Income or Loss under the equity method) are completely eliminated in the consolidation process. Thus, the choice of cost method or equity method must be based upon considerations other than the reporting of consolidated subsidiaries in consolidated statements.

It may be argued that the equity method is somewhat more convenient in its effect on the procedures of consolidation, but this is of negligible significance. Indeed, it is more than offset by the additional effort required to make the periodic entries on the books of the parent. Subsequent analysis in this and later chapters will disclose several potentially complicated consolidation eliminations which, as previously mentioned, are also necessary adjustments to reported subsidiary net income in the event the parent chooses to record its equity in subsidiary earnings. In regard to consolidated subsidiaries, the calculations which support these eliminations are unnecessarily duplicated if the parent uses the equity method. The calculations must be made by the parent in order to make the periodic entries to record subsidiary income, and they must be made again in the process of preparing consolidated statements.

Unconsolidated Subsidiaries in Consolidated Statements. In Chapter 7, it was suggested that only the accounts of subsidiaries which are economically related and are capable of meaningful assimilation should be included in consolidated statements. Thus, for example, the accounts of banks, insurance companies, and finance companies are not generally consolidated with the accounts of industrial firms. Other subsidiaries generally excluded from consolidation include foreign subsidiaries in countries whose governments place material restrictions on the parent's ability to control the subsidiaries. These restrictions frequently raise the serious question of whether the parent can realize the profits and other benefits produced by subsidiary operations; the restrictions sometimes take the form of direct limitations on the parent's ability to repatriate subsidiary earnings (i.e., transfer funds which represent earnings out of the foreign country). It is apparent that not all affiliates adequately satisfy the requirements for inclusion in consolidated statements.

Illustration 9–4

X COMPANY AND SUBSIDIARY Y COMPANY
Consolidated Statement Working Paper
For Year Ended December 31, 1972

	X Company	Y Company	Eliminations Dr.	Eliminations Cr.	Minority Interest	Consolidated
Income Statement:						
Sales	96,000	63,000				159,000
Subsidiary income	25,200		(1) 25,200			
Merchandise inventory (12/31/72)	14,200	9,200				23,400
Total credits	135,400	72,200				182,400
Merchandise inventory (1/1/72)	10,000	7,000				17,000
Purchases	58,000	29,100				87,100
Expenses	22,500	8,100				30,600
Total debits	90,500	44,200				134,700
	44,900	28,000				47,700
Minority interest in net income—Y Company					2,800	2,800
Net income—carried forward	44,900	28,000	25,200	–0–	2,800	44,900
Retained Earnings Statement:						
Retained earnings, January 1, 1972:						
X Company	70,000					70,000
Y Company		25,000	(2) 22,500		2,500	
Net income—brought forward	44,900	28,000	25,200		2,800	44,900
	114,900	53,000			5,300	114,900
Dividends declared:						
X Company	15,000					15,000
Y Company		10,000		(1) 9,000	1,000	
Retained earnings, December 31, 1972—carried forward	99,900	43,000	47,700	9,000	4,300	99,900

Balance Sheet:

	X Company	Y Company	Eliminations Dr.	Eliminations Cr.	Minority	Consolidated
Cash	31,000	12,000				43,000
Accounts receivable	22,000	19,000				41,000
Merchandise inventory	14,200	9,200				23,400
Investment in Y Company stock	90,700			(1) 16,200 (2) 74,500		
Other assets	76,000	64,300				140,300
Differential			(2) 7,000			7,000
	233,900	104,500				254,700
Accounts payable	30,000	9,000				39,000
Other liabilities	4,000	2,500				6,500
Capital stock:						
X Company	100,000					100,000
Y Company		50,000	(2) 45,000		5,000	
Retained earnings—brought forward	99,900	43,000	(2) 47,700		4,300	99,900
Minority interest in Y Company				9,000	9,300	9,300 M
	233,900	104,500	99,700	99,700	9,300	254,700

Explanation of eliminations:
(1) To reverse the parent company's entries for subsidiary dividends and undistributed subsidiary earnings.
(2) To eliminate the January 1, 1972, investment account balance against 90 percent of the stockholders' equity account balances of the subsidiary.

In the event a subsidiary does not meet the criteria for inclusion in consolidated statements, the accountant should question whether the conditions surrounding the intercorporate investment are such as to warrant use of the equity method. If the subsidiary is excluded from consolidation only because its operations and assets are not sufficiently comparable to the parent (i.e., the financial institution-industrial firm ground), then use of the equity method would appear to be warranted. But if the subsidiary is excluded because the parent's control is suspect, the cost method may be the better method of reporting the unconsolidated subsidiary.

Subsidiaries in the Unconsolidated Statements of a Parent. In Chapter 7, it was argued that the parent company's unconsolidated statements are of limited significance. Although they have relevance to special decisions, they are often not presented in annual reports to stockholders and the public. Nonetheless, the previous analysis of unconsolidated subsidiaries in consolidated statements is equally applicable to the reporting of subsidiaries in the parent's unconsolidated statements. The equity method frequently provides the most informative presentation with respect to the evaluation of corporate investments. However, if an analysis is purposely focused on the parent corporation as a separate *legal* unit, the arguments favoring the cost method take on additional weight. The cost method is consistent with the separate legal status of the various members of the affiliation. It gives specific recognition to the legal act of declaring dividends, which is consistent with the realization concept generally applied to income recognition. Likewise, the cost method is consistent with the typical method of valuation for other assets.

Modified Equity Basis

In the event that a parent-subsidiary relationship does not warrant use of the equity method, the cost method is preferred. However, a modified equity method is sometimes proposed as a compromise between the two approaches. Using the modified equity basis, the investment account would be periodically adjusted to reflect the parent company's equity in subsidiary earnings and losses. But to the extent these earnings remain undistributed by the subsidiary, they would be identified as "unrealized" subsidiary earnings on the parent company's books, and income recognition would be deferred until receipt of cash dividends. Cash dividends would then be accounted for as in the traditional equity method by a credit to the investment account for the amount collected, with a transfer of a corresponding amount from Unrealized Subsidiary Earnings to Subsidiary Income.

The following entries relate to a 90 percent owned subsidiary whose postacquisition earnings for the first year are $30,000; cash dividends of $10,000 are assumed to have been distributed during the year by the subsidiary. Using the modified equity basis, the parent company's entries are as follows:

To record receipt of $9,000 cash dividends:

```
Cash.................................................... 9,000
    Investment in subsidiary..............................        9,000
```

To record $27,000 equity in subsidiary earnings:

```
Investment in subsidiary................................ 27,000
    Unrealized subsidiary earnings........................        27,000
```

To recognize realized subsidiary income:

```
Unrealized subsidiary earnings........................... 9,000
    Subsidiary income.....................................        9,000
```

Subsequently, as additional amounts of subsidiary earnings are distributed to the parent, amounts equal to these receipts are transferred from Unrealized Subsidiary Earnings to Subsidiary Income, not to exceed, however, the accumulated balance in the Unrealized Subsidiary Earnings account.

During the second year, if the subsidiary reported profits of $25,000 and paid cash dividends of $40,000, entries of the parent would be made as follows:

To record receipt of $36,000 cash dividends:

```
Cash.................................................... 36,000
    Investment in subsidiary..............................        36,000
```

To record $22,500 equity in subsidiary earnings:

```
Investment in subsidiary................................ 22,500
    Unrealized subsidiary earnings........................        22,500
```

To record realized subsidiary income:

```
Unrealized subsidiary earnings.......................... 36,000
    Subsidiary income.....................................        36,000
```

The amount of *unrealized* subsidiary earnings should be identified in the balance sheet of the parent company as a separate equity element.

The above sequence of entries preserves the criterion of income realization that is associated with the cost method. At the same time, it results in the same asset valuation as does the equity method. However, failing to satisfy all the arguments for either method, the compromise solution is infrequently used.

Reduction in Subsidiary Book Value below Acquisition Amount

Reduction in the book value of subsidiary stock below that existing at date of acquisition is often explained in terms of losses, dividends, or some combination of these events. The recognition of such a reduction in the accounts of the parent company, where the equity method is used, creates no special accounting difficulty. The equity method automatically provides for periodic adjustment of the investment account for *all* losses and dividends of the subsidiary, whatever their magnitude or source. However, where the cost method is in use, the treatment of this contraction in book value is not so clear-cut.

Dividends from subsidiary earnings accumulated prior to acquisition by the parent company do not have the status of income to the parent. Such receipts do not represent a return *on* a subsidiary stock investment; rather, they amount to a partial return *of* such an investment. To the extent that the subsidiary dividend distributions exceed earnings accumulations since acquisition, the excess is accounted for as a "liquidating" dividend. This is consonant with the view generally held by accountants that cash dividends are assumed to be distributed from the most recently accumulated earnings. To include dividends from preacquisition subsidiary earnings in consolidated net income is to increase affiliation net income by a portion of purchased (and eliminated) subsidiary earnings. This clearly contradicts the definition of consolidated net income as given earlier.

Consider the following example where the investment in subsidiary shares is carried by the parent at cost. If postacquisition earnings of an 80 percent owned subsidiary amount to $10,000 and if cash dividends of $15,000 are declared by the subsidiary, the parent company's entry to record the receipt of the dividends would be:

Cash... 12,000
    Dividend income....................................   8,000
    Investment in subsidiary............................   4,000

The distribution of dividends in excess of subsidiary earnings accumulated since acquisition, $5,000 in this instance, is clearly a diminution in the cost of the investment; consequently, $4,000 (80 percent of $5,000) is properly recorded as a liquidating dividend.

In the event that the reduction in subsidiary book value at acquisition is attributable to losses of the subsidiary, the parent company, using the cost method of accounting for its investment, is not obliged to recognize its equity in such losses in the investment account. However, if recovery of these losses appears unlikely and there is persuasive evidence that the investment has been permanently and materially impaired, conservative accounting would approve a reduction in the cost of the investment in the amount of the parent's equity in such losses. For example, if an 80 percent owned subsidiary suffered a loss of $10,000 which is regarded as an impairment of the investment, subsequent restoration of which is doubtful, recognition of such a loss may be journalized on the books of the parent company as follows:

Subsidiary loss.. 8,000
    Investment in subsidiary............................   8,000

Recognition of this loss requires an adjustment in the investment elimination schedule which reduces the retained earnings element and the investment element by $8,000 each. The effect produced is essentially the same as a liquidating dividend. A more complete discussion of liquidating dividends is given in Chapter 11.

DIFFERENTIALS

Identification of Differentials

Previous reference has been made to the difference which may exist between the cost of an investment in subsidiary stock and the corresponding book value of these (parent owned) shares at acquisition. It is important to identify, and reconcile where this is possible, reasons for this variance. Accountants' efforts to explain more precisely the source of this difference stem from an unwillingness to accept the arbitrary reporting of debit excesses as "goodwill from consolidation," and credit excesses as "deferred credits." Actually, differentials are usually attributable to under- or overstatement of recorded asset or liability accounts of a subsidiary, to a failure of the subsidiary to record valuable intangibles or other assets, or for other reasons, a partial enumeration of which is to be found in Chapter 7.

Effects of Subsidiary Operations on Differentials

Once identified, there remains the problem of the differential's subsequent disposition. If it is established that the differential is properly assignable to accounts the balances of which are not normally subject to systematic amortization, e.g., land, the consolidated statements will continue to report the amount of the differential as originally measured. However, where the differential relates to an account the balance of which is amortized periodically, the differential should be accorded similar treatment in consolidated financial statements. In the event a differential is allocated to the identifiable assets and liabilities of the subsidiary and there remains unallocated a residual debit differential, it is reported as "goodwill" or "excess of investment cost over fair value of subsidiary net assets." In accordance with Accounting Principles Board *Opinion No. 17,* this "goodwill" must be systematically amortized over a period not to exceed 40 years. Where there is a residual credit differential, the Accounting Principles Board, in *Opinion No. 16,* argues that it should be allocated first to the noncurrent assets of the subsidiary (excluding long-term investments in marketable securities) on the basis of their relative fair values. If noncurrent assets are thereby reduced to zero values, any remaining differential should be classified as a deferred credit and amortized into income over a period not to exceed 40 years.

Since a differential is part of the cost incurred by the parent, the amounts of minority interests in net income and retained earnings of a subsidiary remain unaffected by working paper adjustments which relate to differentials. The values of the interests of minority shareholders are calculated, as before, on the basis of accumulations recorded in the subsidiary's equity accounts.

Amortization of Differentials

The following example illustrates the disposition of differentials *where the equity method is in use.* The equity method presumes periodic adjustments of the parent's investment account for its equity in the postacquisition earnings and dividends of a subsidiary. The adjustment to reflect subsidiary earnings should be made on the basis of the parent's equity in the *reported* net income of the subsidiary, *less the current year's amortization of differential.* This refinement of the equity method accords with the Accounting Principles Board's opinion regarding the treatment of unconsolidated domestic subsidiaries in consolidated statements. In respect to the parent's reporting of its equity in the net income of such subsidiaries, the Board stated: "The amount of such earnings or losses should give effect to amortization, if appropriate, of any difference between the cost of the investment and the equity in net assets at date of acquisition and to any elimination of inter-company gains or losses that would have been made had the subsidiary been consolidated."[1]

These data are those of Cases 2 and 3, with the exception that "other assets" for companies X and Y are assumed to consist of the following:

	December 31, 1971		December 31, 1972	
	X Company	Y Company	X Company	Y Company
Land........................	$14,000	$ 5,000	$14,000	$ 5,000
Plant and equipment (net).......	52,000	57,000	62,000	59,300
	$66,000	$62,000	$76,000	$64,300

It may be further assumed that upon analyzing the transaction for the purchase of subsidiary shares, it is determined that the cost of the investment which is in excess of the parent company's equity in subsidiary book value ($7,000) may be ascribed $4,500 to plant and equipment and $2,500

---

[1] Accounting Principles Board, American Institute of Certified Public Accountants, *Opinion No. 10* (New York, 1967), p. 143. It should be observed that a parent using the equity method might elect to record its equity in the reported net income of a subsidiary *without* making the adjustments for differential amortization and intercompany profit eliminations. In this event, no special difficulty is encountered in the consolidation process; the amount of subsidiary income recorded by the parent must, in any case, be eliminated against the investment account to restore this account to its beginning-of-year balance. However, it should be noted that the reported net income of the parent does not equal consolidated net income if this abbreviated approach to the equity method is followed. The difference between the two income figures can be explained by the amount of the current amortization of differential and the parent's equity in intercompany profit items (see Chapter 12).

to land. The remaining service life of the depreciable property to which this differential payment is related is assumed to be three years.

The consolidated working paper treatment for the amortization of debit differentials in the year of acquisition of subsidiary shares is given in Illustration 9–5; a subsequent year's working paper is shown in Illustration 9–6.

Debit Differential—Period of Acquisition. In Illustration 9–5 plant and equipment is reported *net* of accumulated depreciation. Accordingly, amortization of the differential is credited to the asset account. No unusual complication would have arisen, however, if the accumulated depreciation were reported separately. In such an event, the credit for the amortization would necessarily have been made to this account.

In Case 2, X Company's recorded share of Y Company's net income was $18,000 (.9 × $20,000). In the present example, X Company's recorded share of Y Company's net income is reduced to $16,500 as a result of the additional depreciation charge of $1,500. The elimination entry to reverse the parent's recording of subsidiary income is correspondingly reduced from $18,000 to $16,500 [(.9 × 20,000) − 1,500].

Regardless of whether the equity method or cost method is utilized by the parent, the *definitions* of consolidated net income and retained earnings must be modified where a *working paper* amortization of a differential is appropriate. Consolidated net income is defined as the parent company's net income, excluding its recorded share of subsidiary dividends (or income), increased or decreased by its equity in subsidiary net profits or net losses for the period and by the current amortization of differential. Similarly, consolidated retained earnings must be restated to include the increase or decrease resulting from the cumulative amortization of differential since acquisition. However, if the subsidiary elects to adjust its accounts such that no differential emerges in the process of preparing consolidated statements, the subsequent allocation of *recorded* depreciation would preclude the need for altering the basic definitions. In the present example, the subsidiary would have had to adjust its accounts to correct for the understated assets. Importantly, the adjustment to depreciable assets would have been in the amount of $5,000, as the $4,500 differential relates to a 90 percent interest in the understated depreciable assets. This principle may be related to the total $7,000 differential as follows:

Asset	Excess of Current Value over Book Value	Purchased Interest—90 Percent Whereof
Land	$2,778	$2,500
Plant and equipment	5,000	4,500
	$7,778	$7,000

Illustration 9–5

X COMPANY AND SUBSIDIARY Y COMPANY
Consolidated Statement Working Paper
For Year Ended December 31, 1971

	X Company	Y Company	Eliminations Dr.	Eliminations Cr.	Minority Interest	Consolidated
Income Statement:						
Sales	78,000	40,000				118,000
Subsidiary income	16,500		(1) 16,500			
Merchandise inventory (12/31/71)	10,000	7,000				17,000
Total credits	104,500	47,000				135,000
Merchandise inventory (1/1/71)	16,000	4,000				20,000
Purchases	42,000	20,000				62,000
Expenses	8,000	3,000	(4) 1,500			12,500
Total debits	66,000	27,000	18,000	–0–		94,500
Minority interest in net income—Y Company					2,000	2,000
Net income—carried forward	38,500	20,000	18,000	–0–	2,000	38,500
Retained Earnings Statement:						
Retained earnings, January 1, 1971:						
X Company	40,000					40,000
Y Company		10,000	(2) 9,000		1,000	
Net income—brought forward	38,500	20,000	18,000		2,000	38,500
	78,500	30,000	27,000		3,000	78,500
Dividends declared:						
X Company	10,000					10,000
Y Company		5,000		(1) 4,500	500	
Retained earnings, December 31, 1971—carried forward	68,500	25,000	27,000	4,500	2,500	68,500

Balance Sheet:

			Eliminations		Minority Interest	Consolidated
			Dr.	Cr.		
Cash	29,500	8,000				37,500
Accounts receivable	18,000	3,000				21,000
Merchandise inventory	10,000	7,000				17,000
Investment in Y Company stock	73,000			(1) 12,000 (2) 61,000		
Land	14,000	5,000	(3) 2,500			21,500
Plant and equipment (net)	52,000	57,000	(3) 4,500	(4) 1,500		112,000
Differential			(2) 7,000	(3) 7,000		
	196,500	80,000				209,000
Accounts payable	22,000	5,000				27,000
Other liabilities	6,000					6,000
Capital stock:						
X Company	100,000					100,000
Y Company		50,000	(2) 45,000		5,000	
Retained earnings—brought forward	68,500	25,000	27,000	4,500	2,500	68,500
Minority interest in Y Company					7,500	7,500 M
	196,500	80,000	86,000	86,000	7,500	209,000

Explanation of eliminations:

(1) To record the reversal of the parent company's 1971 entries for subsidiary dividends and subsidiary earnings less the current amortization of differential.

(2) To eliminate the January 1, 1971, investment account balance against 90 percent of the corresponding stockholders' equity accounts of the subsidiary.

(3) To reclassify a $7,000 debit differential: land, $2,500, and plant and equipment (net), $4,500.

(4) To record the 1971 amortization of the differential related to plant and equipment (one third of $4,500).

Illustration 9-6

X COMPANY AND SUBSIDIARY Y COMPANY
Consolidated Statement Working Paper
For Year Ended December 31, 1972

	X Company	Y Company	Eliminations Dr.	Eliminations Cr.	Minority Interest	Consolidated
Income Statement:						
Sales	96,000	63,000				159,000
Subsidiary income	23,700		(1) 23,700			
Merchandise inventory (12/31/72)	14,200	9,200				23,400
Total credits	133,900	72,200				182,400
Merchandise inventory (1/1/72)	10,000	7,000				17,000
Purchases	58,000	29,100				87,100
Expenses	22,500	8,100	(5) 1,500			32,100
Total debits	90,500	44,200				136,200
						46,200
Minority interest in net income—Y Company					2,800	2,800
Net income—carried forward	43,400	28,000	25,200	–0–	2,800	43,400
Retained Earnings Statement:						
Retained earnings, January 1, 1972:						
X Company	68,500					68,500
Y Company		25,000	(4) 1,500 (3) 22,500	(2) 1,500	2,500	
Net income—brought forward	43,400	28,000	25,200	–0–	2,800	43,400
	111,900	53,000			5,300	111,900
Dividends declared:						
X Company	15,000					15,000
Y Company		10,000		(1) 9,000	1,000	
Retained earnings, December 31, 1972—carried forward	96,900	43,000	49,200	10,500	4,300	96,900

Balance Sheet:

Cash	31,000	12,000				43,000
Accounts receivable	22,000	19,000				41,000
Merchandise inventory	14,200	9,200				23,400
Investment in Y Company stock	87,700		(2) 1,500	(1) 14,700 (3) 74,500		
Land	14,000	5,000	(4) 2,500			21,500
Plant and equipment (net)	62,000	59,300	(3) 3,000	(5) 1,500		122,800
Differential			(3) 7,000	(4) 7,000		
	230,900	104,500				251,700
Accounts payable	30,000	9,000				39,000
Other liabilities	4,000	2,500				6,500
Capital stock:						
X Company	100,000					100,000
Y Company		50,000	(3) 45,000		5,000	
Retained earnings—brought forward	96,900	43,000	49,200	10,500	4,300	96,900
Minority interest in Y Company					9,300	9,300 M
	230,900	104,500	108,200	108,200	9,300	251,700

Explanation of eliminations:

(1) To record the reversal of the parent company's 1972 entries for subsidiary dividends and subsidiary earnings, less the current amortization of differential.

(2) To reverse the total amount of differential amortization recorded by the parent in years prior to 1972.

(3) To eliminate the January 1, 1972, investment account balance against 90 percent of the corresponding stockholders' equity accounts of the subsidiary.

(4) To allocate the differential to the appropriate understated subsidiary assets and to January 1, 1972, retained earnings (in recognition of previous years' differential amortization).

(5) To record the 1972 amortization of differential.

The $778 difference would be allocated to the minority shareholders' equity if the indicated current market values were formally recorded by the subsidiary, i.e., 10 percent of the Unrealized Appraisal Increment of $7,778.[2] It may be noted that the $778 increase in minority interest does not represent a permanent difference. After the assets (to which the $778 is allocated) are fully amortized or sold, the equity of minority interests will be the same whether or not the $778 is recognized as the differential allocated to minority interests.

In the case of a manufacturing subsidiary, the allocation of differentials has extended consequences. Where the differential is identified with depreciable property employed in the manufacturing process, the depreciation charge should relate both to cost of goods manufactured and sold *and also* to inventory. Adjustments for such items in the consolidated working paper render the reconciliation of subsidiary book net income and its consolidated basis equivalent more difficult.

Debit Differential—Period Subsequent to Acquisition.   The elimination in Illustration 9–6 are similar to those in Illustration 9–5, with the following exceptions. Since X Company's annual entry (under the equity method) to record its equity in subsidiary income reflects differential amortization of $1,500, the Investment in Y Company Stock account balance is reduced after two years by a total of $3,000 as a result of differential amortization. The elimination of subsidiary dividend declarations and the parent's recorded equity in Y Company's 1972 income restores $1,500 to the investment account. An additional elimination entry (see elimination 2 in Illustration 9–6) restores the remaining $1,500 to the investment account; in more general terms, it reverses the aggregate amount of previous years' differential amortizations. Subsequently, the normal elimination entries can be utilized to eliminate the investment account against stockholders' equity accounts of the subsidiary and to allocate the differential to appropriate accounts. In Illustration 9–6, the allocation of the $7,000 differential includes a $1,500 allocation to the retained earnings of X Company, which reflects the depreciation taken during the first postacquisition year.

It should be apparent that the additional elimination entry to reverse the aggregate amount of previous years' differential amortization booked by the parent is an optional entry that can be combined with the other elimination entries. Since the optional entry (2) restores the investment account balance (by $1,500 in Illustration 9–6), if it is omitted, the investment elimination entry (3) would disclose a differential that is smaller by $1,500. In that case, the elimination to allocate the differential (5) would not include a $1,500 debit to X Company retained earnings.

---

[2] This concept is incorporated in the consolidated statement working paper using the "entity theory," as discussed in Chapter 16.

As discussed earlier in regard to Illustration 9–5, the definitions of consolidated net income and retained earnings must be altered to incorporate these amortizations of differential. The definitional alterations are necessary whether the parent uses the cost method or the equity method.

QUESTIONS

1. In respect to subsidiary share holdings, what are the basic accounting differences between a parent company which uses the equity method and one which uses the cost method?

2. How does the realization criterion underlying the equity method differ from that underlying the cost method?

3. What differences exist in the consolidated financial statements where the equity method is used instead of the cost method?

4. For a company using the equity method, describe the relationship between the parent company's net income and the consolidated net income; and between the parent company's retained earnings balance and the consolidated retained earnings balance.

5. Is the cost or equity method to be preferred in reporting the operations of subsidiaries in consolidated statements?

6. Under what circumstances would the cost method be preferred in reporting *unconsolidated* subsidiaries in consolidated statements?

7. In reporting for subsidiaries in unconsolidated statements of a parent, what arguments can be advanced for using the cost method? The equity method?

8. What is the modified equity basis for reporting a parent-subsidiary relationship?

9. Given equivalent acquisition circumstances and the same subsequent profits and distributions of the subsidiary, which method—cost or equity—results in the largest differential in preparing consolidated statements?

10. How are the definitions of consolidated net income and retained earnings modified where it becomes necessary to amortize (on the working paper) the differential?

PROBLEMS

Problem 9–1

Kay Company has recently purchased a 90 percent interest in Hanson Industries. Having concluded that consolidated statements should be prepared, the management is debating whether to account for its interest in Hanson by the cost method or the equity method. Explain as briefly as possible the difference between the two methods that will be evidenced by an examination of the consolidated statements. You are being consulted only with respect to the consolidated reports and the way that the information provided therein might be affected by the choice of equity method or cost method.

Problem 9–2

The Parnelli Company purchased 750 shares of the capital stock of the Foyt Company on January 1, 1971, for $85,000. One year later, the following trial balances are prepared:

	Parnelli Company	Foyt Company
Cash....................................	$ 14,000	$ 23,000
Merchandise, December 31.................	45,000	30,000
Investment in Foyt Company stock..........	92,500	
Other assets (noncurrent)...................	127,500	80,000
Cost of goods sold......................	87,000	65,000
Expenses..............................	14,000	16,000
Dividends declared......................	20,000	10,000
	$400,000	$224,000
Accounts payable........................	$ 9,000	
Dividends payable.......................		$ 10,000
Other liabilities.........................	1,500	3,000
Capital stock ($100 par)...................	200,000	100,000
Retained earnings.......................	64,000	20,000
Sales.................................	118,000	91,000
Subsidiary income.......................	7,500	
	$400,000	$224,000

Required:

Prepare a consolidated statement working paper for the year ended December 31, 1971.

Problem 9–3

The Hanna Company purchased 80 percent of the capital stock of the Taylor Corporation on January 1, 1971, for $51,000, when the latter's capital stock and retained earnings were $50,000 and $10,000 respectively. Trial balances prepared on December 31, 1971, disclose the following:

	December 31, 1971	
	Hanna Company	Taylor Corporation
Cash......................................	$ 8,000	$ 5,000
Accounts receivable......................	21,000	17,000
Merchandise—January 1....................	15,000	8,000
Investment in Taylor Corporation stock.......	59,000	
Other assets.............................	54,000	48,000
Dividends declared.......................	10,000	5,000
Purchases...............................	90,000	20,000
Expenses................................	10,000	7,000
	$267,000	$110,000
Accounts payable........................	$ 5,000	$ 6,000
Advances from Hanna.....................		4,000
Other liabilities..........................	5,000	
Capital stock (par $100)...................	100,000	50,000
Retained earnings........................	40,000	10,000
Sales...................................	105,000	40,000
Subsidiary income.......................	12,000	
	$267,000	$110,000
Merchandise—December 31.................	$ 20,000	$ 10,000

Required:

On December 31, 1971, prepare a consolidated statement working paper. (Compare this working paper with that for Problem 8–2.)

Problem 9–4

Clark Motor Transit purchased in the open market 75 percent of the capital stock of Sachs and Ward, Inc., on January 1, 1971, at $14,000 more than 75 percent of its book value. During the following five years, Sachs and Ward, Inc., reported cumulative earnings of $235,000 and paid $45,000 in dividends. On January 1, 1976, minority shareholders in Sachs and Ward, Inc., have an equity of $57,500 in the net assets of the company.

Required:

If the parent company carries its investment in subsidiary stock on an equity basis—
(i)   Determine the January 1, 1971, cost of the investment, and
(ii) Calculate the investment carrying value on December 31, 1975.

Problem 9–5

On January 1, 1970, Algoe, Inc., paid $75,000 for 80 percent of Mozena Company's common stock. Mozena had $50,000 of common stock outstanding and retained earnings of $25,000. Algoe, Inc., had retained earnings of $100,000 at that date. Algoe, Inc., accounts for its interests in subsidiaries on a cost basis. Reported net incomes and dividends of each firm are as follows:

	Algoe, Inc.		Mozena Co.	
	Net Income	Dividends	Net Income	Dividends
1970............	$31,400	$15,000	$10,000	$8,000
1971............	12,000	15,000	4,000	8,000

Algoe's management concluded that the difference between the price paid for Mozena and the book value of Algoe's interest in Mozena was related to a building owned by Mozena, which had 15 years of remaining useful life, as of January 1, 1970. Management has also expressed the desire that any accounting for this difference be limited such that only the consolidated statements will be affected.

Required:

(i)   Prepare a definitional calculation of consolidated net income for 1971.
(ii) Prepare a residual calculation of consolidated retained earnings as of December 31, 1971.

Problem 9–6

X Company acquired the following investments on January 1, 1971:

90 percent of the capital stock of Y Company, cost............. $140,000
80 percent of the capital stock of Z Company, cost.............. 60,000
60 percent of the capital stock of W Company, cost............. 32,000

Additional data concerning these companies are:

	X Company	Y Company	Z Company	W Company
Capital stock (par value, $100).....................	$200,000	$100,000	$50,000	$40,000
Retained earnings, January 1, 1971......................	100,000	50,000	20,000	10,000
Net income [loss], 1971........	79,000	40,000	20,000	[5,000]
Cash dividends, 1971..........	10,000	5,000	4,000	

X Company carries its investment in subsidiaries on an equity basis; it reported a profit from its own operations in 1971 of $30,000.

Required:

(i)   Prepare journal entries for 1971 on the books of X Company reflecting its transactions with, or interest in, subsidiary companies.

(ii) Calculate the amount of consolidated net income for 1971 and the balance of consolidated retained earnings as of December 31, 1971.

(iii) Calculate the amount of minority interest in the 1971 net income [loss] and the December 31, 1971, retained earnings of subsidiary companies.

Problem 9–7

The following data relate to companies M, G, and R for the two-year period ending December 31, 1971:

	M Company	G Company	R Company
Capital stock ($100 par)....................	$200,000	$100,000	$50,000
Other contributed capital..................	20,000	3,500	1,000
Retained earnings [deficit], January 1, 1970..	250,000	40,000	[20,000]
Net income (excluding equity in subsidiary profits):			
1970..	90,000	60,000	30,000
1971..	75,000	40,000	40,000
Dividends paid:			
1970..	20,000	4,000	
1971..	20,000	10,000	5,000

In each of the following independent cases, investments in subsidiary stock are carried by the parent on an equity basis.

Case 1: M Company purchased 90 percent of the capital stock of G Company on January 1, 1970, for $130,000.

Case 2: G Company purchased 60 percent of the capital stock of R Company on January 1, 1970, for $20,000.

Case 3: M Company purchased 80 percent of the capital stock of G Company on January 1, 1971, for $164,000.

Case 4: M Company purchased 70 percent of the capital stock of R Company on January 1, 1970, for $20,000 and 60 percent of the capital stock of G Company on January 1, 1971, for $125,000.

Required:

In each of the above cases:
(i)   Calculate the balance of the investment account on December 31, 1971.
(ii) Prepare an investment elimination schedule on December 31, 1971, for a consolidated statement working paper.
(iii) Calculate the amount of consolidated net income for 1970 and 1971 and the balance of consolidated retained earnings, December 31, 1971.

Problem 9–8

The Stuchell Company purchased 80 percent of the capital stock of the Harley Corporation on January 1, 1971, for $53,600, when the latter had capital stock, $50,000, and retained earnings, $10,000. An analysis of the assets of the Harley Corporation on January 1, 1971, disclosed the existence of a patent the estimated value of which was $8,500 on January 1, 1968, the date of its issuance. The patent is important to the subsidiary in protection of specially designed and constructed sales equipment. The cost of the investment in excess of subsidiary book value at acquisition is believed to relate to the *unrecorded* patent.

Required:

(i)   Prepare an investment elimination schedule as of December 31, 1971.
(ii) Make other eliminating entries in respect to the patent for inclusion on consolidated statement working papers for the years ended December 31, 1971, and 1972.
(iii) If the subsidiary should formally record the patent in its books on January 1, 1971, previous to the purchase of its stock by Stuchell, what are the effects of this adjustment on the investment elimination schedule, the calculation of consolidated net income, and the calculation of minority interest in the net income of the subsidiary and the stockholders' equity of Harley Corporation on December 31, 1972?

Problem 9–9

On January 1, 1971, United Distributors purchased 1,200 shares of Texas Wholesalers, Inc., capital stock for $200,000 when its accumulated retained earnings were $50,000. It was determined that the excess of investment cost over the purchased equity in the book value of subsidiary stock was attributable to an undervaluation of the Land and Building accounts on the subsidiary's books. Information provided by an appraisal survey completed shortly after the investment indicated the following:

	Replacement Cost New	Sound Value
Land.....................	$ 50,000	$ 50,000
Building.................	280,000	140,000

The original estimate of service life in respect to the building remained unchanged by the appraisal, i.e., original estimate, 20 years; remaining life, 10 years.

The December 31, 1972, trial balances were as follows:

	United Distributors	Texas Wholesalers, Inc.
Merchandise, January 1	$ 50,000	$ 20,000
Land	100,000	40,000
Building	400,000	200,000
Other assets	790,000	135,000
Investment in Texas Wholesalers, Inc., capital stock	200,000	
Dividends declared	10,000	5,000
Purchases	200,000	70,000
Expenses	50,000	10,000
	$1,800,000	$480,000
Liabilities	$ 296,000	$ 20,000
Accumulated depreciation	100,000	120,000
Sales	300,000	120,000
Dividend income	4,000	
Capital stock (no par; $100 par)	742,000	150,000
Retained earnings	358,000	70,000
	$1,800,000	$480,000
Merchandise, December 31	$ 75,000	$ 10,000

Texas Wholesalers, Inc., elected not to record the value increments suggested by the appraisal.

Required:

(i) On December 31, 1972, prepare a consolidated statement working paper.

(ii) If the subsidiary had entered the appraisal increments in its books, indicate the effects produced on the eliminating entries and the amounts shown in the consolidated statements.

Problem 9–10

M Company purchased 80 percent of the capital stock of R Company on January 1, 1971, for $48,000. The balance sheets of the affiliates on this date were:

	M Company	R Company
Cash	$ 62,000	$10,000
Receivables	61,000	36,000
Merchandise	8,000	9,000
Other assets	2,000	10,000
Goodwill	2,000	5,000
	$135,000	$70,000
Liabilities	$ 10,000	$ 5,000
Capital stock (par, $100)	100,000	50,000
Retained earnings	25,000	10,000
Other contributed capital		5,000
	$135,000	$70,000

During 1971 earnings (exclusive of subsidiary profits) of each affiliate were M Company, $8,000; R Company, $5,000. Total annual profits are assumed to be reflected by increased cash balances; other account balances remain the same.

On December 31, 1971, R Company wrote off the balance of its Goodwill account to Other Contributed Capital and paid a cash dividend of $6,000.

Required:

Prepare a consolidated balance sheet working paper as of December 31, 1971. The investment in R Company stock is carried by the parent on an equity basis.

Problem 9–11

The Blair Realty Corporation purchased 90 percent of the capital stock of the Heath Company on January 1, 1971, for $31,000 when the latter had outstanding capital stock, $20,000, and retained earnings, $2,000. On this date the accounts of the Heath Company included Building, cost $30,000 (acquired January 1, 1961), and Accumulated Depreciation, $15,000. The Heath Company made $12,000 profits annually, before depreciation.

As a result of an appraisal at date of acquisition, the following is established:

Case A: The replacement cost (new) of the building is $42,000. The estimated service life remains unchanged.

Case B: Replacement cost is $30,000 (new); the revised service life of the building is determined to be 30 years.

To the extent possible, the "differential" is identified with the results of the appraisal.

Required:

Prepare a partial consolidated balance sheet working paper on December 31, 1971, for Cases A and B if—
(i)   The appraisal adjustments are recorded by the subsidiary.
(ii)   The appraisal adjustments are not recorded by the subsidiary.

Problem 9–12

The following are the balance sheets of Barton Company and Casey, Inc., as of December 31, 1970:

ASSETS	Barton Company	Casey, Inc.
Cash...............................	$ 432,576	$ 32,569
Accounts receivable....................	825,620	225,627
Inventories..........................	1,628,429	625,375
Prepaid expenses......................	36,475	5,648
Total.........................	$2,923,100	$889,219

EQUITIES		
Accounts payable......................	$ 325,647	$437,989
Federal income tax payable..............	250,000	15,000
Capital stock........................	300,000	50,000
Retained earnings.....................	2,047,453	386,230
Total.........................	$2,923,100	$889,219

As of December 31, 1970, Barton Company acquired from the stockholders all of the shares of stock of Casey, Inc., in exchange for $550,000 of Barton's 4 percent 10-year debentures. The excess cost of acquisition (excess of the purchase price over the net assets of Casey) is to be amortized on Barton's books by charges to income over a 10-year period.

For the years 1971 and 1972, operations of Casey, Inc., resulted in *losses* of $52,376 and $15,226, respectively, and operations of Barton Company resulted in *profits* of $387,465 and $420,009, respectively. Barton provided a reserve on its books by charges to income for the losses of its subsidiary. The profits shown above for Barton are *before* provision for amortization of the excess cost of acquisition and for the losses of its subsidiary, Casey. Dividends of $150,000 were paid by Barton in each of the years 1971 and 1972.

The remaining assets and liabilities of Barton and Casey at December 31, 1971, and 1972 were as shown below:

ASSETS AND LIABILITIES OF BARTON AND CASEY

	Barton		Casey	
ASSETS	1971	1972	1971	1972
Cash	$ 426,879	$ 490,327	$ 30,194	$ 31,187
Accounts receivable	897,426	940,227	200,525	203,287
Inventories	1,826,162	1,952,173	600,476	535,711
Advances to Casey, Inc.	165,000	180,000		
Prepaid expenses	32,879	34,327	5,347	4,621
LIABILITIES				
Accounts payable	357,428	298,627	287,688	226,178
Federal income taxes payable	406,000	443,500		
Advances from Barton Company			165,000	180,000

Required:

From the above information prepare a working paper for use in preparing a consolidated balance sheet as of December 31, 1972. Key and explain all entries made as adjustments or eliminations and prepare supporting schedules for major computations. (*You are to disregard any income tax effects of your entries.*)

(AICPA adapted)

Chapter 10

Interpretive Problems of Accounting for Business Combinations

The transactions which give rise to business combinations and the subsequent operations of the resultant complex economic entities have generated numerous accounting problems. Several of these issues have been analyzed in Chapters 5 through 9. In the current chapter, which concludes this unit of special focus on the varied accounting aspects of business combinations, several interpretive and reporting problems of special contemporary significance are considered.

PURCHASE VERSUS POOLING OF INTERESTS ACCOUNTING

In Chapter 5, several different bases for classifying business combinations were discussed. One of these bases, labeled the "accounting perspective," divided business combinations into "purchases" and "poolings of interests." The purpose of this classification scheme derives from the fact that there exist two uniquely different sets of accounting procedures which may be used to record business combinations. One of these sets of procedures, the "purchase method," is utilized in the event a particular business combination is classified as a *purchase* combination. Contrariwise, the "pooling of interests method" is used to account for those combinations which are classified as *pooling of interests* combinations. The process of deciding the appropriate classification of a particular combination involves a careful analysis of the conditions which surround the combination and the nature of the agreement between the combining companies.

The remainder of this section will include an examination of (1) the taxonomic criteria by which business combinations are identified as either purchases or poolings of interests; (2) the purchase method of accounting; (3) the pooling of interests method of accounting; and (4) the financial statement consequences produced by the two accounting methods. Throughout the discussion, the reader should recognize that the problem of classifying business combinations as purchases or poolings of interests exists regardless of the legal form taken by the combined entity. Thus, whether the combination results in a new corporation which replaces all of the constituents (a consolidation), or one of the constituents remains as the surviving corporation (a merger), or a parent-subsidiary relationship results (an acquisition), a combination must be classified (and accounted for) as either a purchase or a pooling of interests.

Criteria for Classifying Business Combinations

Prior to the recent issuance of Accounting Principles Board *Opinion No. 16*,[1] the distinction between a purchase and a pooling of interests was based primarily upon the question of whether the ownership interests in the *combining* companies were preserved and continued in the *combined* business entity.[2] Where the net assets of one or more of the combining companies were acquired by the payment of cash, other assets, or the issuance of debt securities, the common shareholders of the acquired companies would not maintain their ownership interests in the combined firm. Such a combination was classified necessarily as a *purchase*. In substance, the combining agreement was viewed as a purchase-sale transaction between the acquiring corporation and the stockholders of the acquired corporation. Alternatively, if the combination agreement involved an exchange of common stock for common stock, the common shareholders of the combining companies would maintain their positions as owners of the combined company. Such a combination was classified as a *pooling of interests*.

The relatively simple classification criterion described above would be satisfactory if all combination agreements involved either common stock exchanges or payment with cash, other assets, or debt. However, more complex payment methods render the classification process more difficult. The use of convertible stocks and/or bonds, stock warrants, and partial payments with cash raises the serious question of whether a combination more nearly approximates the purchase or the pooling of interests characteristics. Additionally, the issuance of stock for cash, the proceeds of which are used as payment for an acquired enterprise, raises serious doubts as to the validity of the purchase versus pooling of interests distinction. The same doubt is generated by transactions involving the purchase of treasury stock for cash and the subsequent issuance of this stock to consummate a combination.

In the attempt to clarify the classification process, the Committee on Accounting Procedure suggested several aspects or attendant circumstances

---

[1] Accounting Principles Board, American Institute of Certified Public Accountants, "Business Combinations," *Opinion No. 16* (New York, 1970).

[2] The phrases "combining companies" and "constituents or participants in the combination" are used in reference to the companies which exist prior to a combination and are combined as a result of the combination. The phrase "combined company" is used in reference to the single business entity which results from and exists after a combination, regardless of its particular legal form(s).

of a combination that should be evaluated.[3] Examples of these are the relative size of the combining firms, the extent to which assets of a combining company were abandoned, and the continuity of the combining enterprises' managements. However, since none of these circumstances were viewed as controlling or dominating influences, the ultimate classification of any specific combination became increasingly susceptible to managerial determination. Adequate planning of the transactions leading up to and finalizing a combination could frequently result in the emergence of sufficiently conflicting evidence to place the decision within the realm of management choice. Since the classification criteria did not provide a basis for a clear-cut distinction, the election between purchase or pooling of interests often reflected management's motivation to select the accounting treatment which would result in the most favorable financial reports.

A major objective of the recent Accounting Principles Board pronouncement on business combinations was to establish a more precise set of classification criteria for making the distinction between those combinations which are purchases and those which are poolings of interests. To accomplish this objective, 12 specific conditions were enumerated, *all* of which must be met if a combination is to be classified as a pooling of interests. Where these conditions are satisfied, the pooling of interests accounting method *must* be employed. In the event one (or more) of the 12 conditions is not met, the combination must be accounted for as a purchase. The 12 necessary and sufficient conditions for a pooling of interests are summarized, as follows.[4]

1. Each of the combining companies must be autonomous and must not have been a subsidiary or division of another corporation during the two-year period prior to the initiation of the combination plan. However, this does not exclude companies that were newly incorporated within the preceding two years, unless they were successors to part or all of a company which was not autonomous.

2. At the dates the plan of combination is initiated and consummated, none of the combining companies can hold as intercorporate investments more than 10 percent of the outstanding voting common stock of any combining company, unless the shares held were exchanged for shares that are issued to effect the combination plan. In other words, each of the combining companies must be independent of the other combining companies.

3. The combination must be effected by a single transaction, or in accordance with a specific plan within one year after the plan is initiated.

---

[3] Committee on Accounting Procedure, American Institute of Certified Public Accountants, "Business Combinations," *Accounting Research Bulletin No. 48* (1957), p. 24, in *Accounting Research and Terminology Bulletins,* Final Edition (New York, 1961).

[4] *Ibid.,* pp. 295–304.

4. The surviving (or resultant parent) corporation must issue *only* common stock with rights identical to those of the majority of its outstanding voting common stock, in exchange for "substantially all" of the voting common stock of the other (combining) companies outstanding at the date the plan of combination is consummated. *Opinion No. 16* specifies a detailed set of procedures for determining whether the requirement is satisfied that "substantially all" of the voting common stock be exchanged. The essence of the requirement is that 90 percent or more of the outstanding common stock of a combining company must be exchanged (between the dates the plan of combination is initiated and consummated) for the voting common stock issued by the surviving or parent (issuing) corporation.

5. Each of the combining companies must maintain substantially the same voting common stock interest; that is, none of the companies may change those interests by exchanges, retirements, or distributions to stockholders in contemplation of effecting the combination.

6. The combining companies may reacquire shares of voting common stock *only* for purposes other than business combinations, and no company may reacquire more than a normal number of shares after the date the plan of combination is initiated.

7. The ratio of the interest of an individual common stockholder to those of other common stockholders in a combining company must remain the same as a result of the exchange of stock to effect the combination.

8. The voting rights of the common stock interests in the resultant combined corporation must be exercisable by the stockholders; no mechanisms such as a voting trust can be used to deprive or restrict the common stockholders from exercising their voting rights.

9. The combination must be resolved at the date the plan is consummated, with no pending provision of the plan relating to the issue of securities or other consideration. As a consequence, the combined corporation cannot agree to contingent issuances of additional shares or other consideration to the former stockholders of a combining company.

10. The combined corporation must not agree directly or indirectly to retire or reacquire all or part of the common stock issued to effect the combination.

11. The combined corporation must not enter into other financial arrangements for the benefit of the former stockholders of a combining company, such as a guaranty of loans secured by stock issued in the combination.

12. The combined corporation must not intend to dispose of a significant part of the assets of the combining companies within two years after the combination, except to eliminate duplicate facilities or excess

capacity and those assets that would have been disposed of in the ordinary course of business of the separate company.

The Purchase Method of Accounting

A business combination which does not meet all of the 12 conditions summarized in the previous paragraphs is deemed to be a purchase. The purchase method of accounting for business combinations is but a specific application of the more general principles of accounting for purchases of all assets. Conventional accounting stipulates that purchased assets should be recorded at cost, which is established by the purchase transaction. This rule is complicated in the case of a business combination by the fact that *many* assets and liabilities are acquired rather than one asset or a single class of assets. Therefore, the total cost of the purchase must be allocated among the individual assets received and liabilities assumed. If cash is rendered in payment, the total cost of the purchased net assets is easily determinable. However, if the consideration given includes noncash items such as equity securities, the purchase price (total cost) must be determined by referring to conventional procedures for noncash acquisitions, i.e., by assessing the fair market value of the consideration given or the consideration received, whichever is most clearly evident or objectively determinable.

To provide the basis for a subsequent comparison with the pooling of interests method of accounting, three significant characteristics of the purchase method should be recognized. First, the total cost of acquiring a company typically *is not* equal to the algebraic sum of the fair market values of the company's identifiable assets and liabilities. In the context of consolidated statement preparation for parent-subsidiary relationships, appropriate methods of treating such unallocated debit or credit differentials were discussed in Chapter 9. Where the combination takes the form of a merger or consolidation, the procedures for treating differentials would be expressed in terms of entries made by the surviving corporation. Second, the fair market values of the purchased assets and liabilities (separately considered), which are recorded on the books of the combined entity, frequently differ by substantial amounts from their book values, as previously recorded by the *acquired* company. Third, the retained earnings balance of the acquired company does not carry forward to the combined entity. This is, of course, consistent with conventional practice with respect to recording purchase transactions, viz., that the purchase of an income producing asset from a previous user does not result in an increase in the acquiring firm's retained earnings. The previous *earnings* of the asset identify with the selling company and not with the transferred asset. A corollary to this proposition is that balances in the acquired company's revenue and expense accounts at the date of acquisition do not carry forward and are thus accounted for as are retained earnings of the seller.

As previously indicated, the purchase method entries to record a combination yield equivalent results whatever may be the particular legal form taken by the combination (merger, consolidation, or acquisition). If the sole surviving corporation is one of the combining companies (merger) or is a newly created corporation (consolidation), the entries to effect the combining transactions, including the valuation of purchased assets and assumed liabilities at their fair market values, are made on the books of the relevant (new or surviving) corporation. Where a parent-subsidiary relationship is created (acquisition), the investment elimination entries on the consolidated working papers provide the basis for reporting appropriate asset and equity valuations. The reader will recall that the investment elimination entries discussed in Chapters 7, 8, and 9 consistently adhered to the precepts of the purchase method of accounting. Preacquisition revenues, expenses, and retained earnings were either eliminated or were allocated to minority interests; and purchased assets and liabilities were revalued through the allocation of debit or credit differentials, with residual (unallocated) differentials recognized and treated as appropriate under the circumstances.

The Pooling of Interests Method of Accounting

In contradistinction to the accounting treatment associated with purchase combinations, the pooling of interests method is supported by the argument that some combinations are not best described by a purchase-sale transaction. Proponents of pooling of interests would argue that given the pooling conditions previously described, neither company can be said to *acquire* the other. The history of each combining company can be traced from precombination periods through the act of combining to the continued operations of the combined company. The distinct characteristics and operations of the combining firms are simply commingled in the combined company.

The accounting consequences of this view generally result in a retention and aggregation of the accounting valuations of the combining companies. Assets and liabilities are carried forward at the valuations reflected in the books of the predecessor companies; and in most instances, the stockholders' equity accounts of the transferors, excluding common stock retired, are accorded similar treatment. The retained earnings of the new enterprise may be less, but never more, than the sum of the separate retained earnings of the constituents. In the event that the stated capital of the new entity is greater than the aggregate stated capitals of the combining companies, the retained earnings of the new enterprise may be less than the sum of the amounts recorded on the books of the combining companies. In this instance, the debit difference is first applied in reduction of the amount of any other contributed capital on the books of the constituents, after which any debit residue is applied in reduction of retained earnings. Where the stated capital of the new enterprise is less than the aggregate stated capitals of its predecessors, the credit difference is reported as an addition to the contributed capital in excess of stated value of the new enterprise.

The following example illustrates accounting values assigned to the stockholders' equity accounts under each of these two pooling-of-interests conditions. Assume the following capital structures for companies X and Y:

	X Company	Y Company	Total
Contributed capital:			
Par value	$200,000	$450,000	$ 650,000
Other contributed capital*	15,000	25,000	40,000
Retained earnings	105,000	215,000	320,000
	$320,000	$690,000	$1,010,000

* The authors, for reasons of brevity, are using Other Contributed Capital as a generic term throughout this text to include the *various* elements of other contributed capital [e.g., contributed capital in excess of par (or stated) value of capital stock, contributed capital—treasury stock transactions, etc.]. Clearly, it is desirable that a more descriptive expression of each component, as discussed in *Intermediate Accounting* of this series, be used in published financial statements.

The R Corporation is organized to consolidate the resources and operations of these companies. If the R Corporation issues common stock with a total par value of $750,000 in payment for contributed resources of the constituents, the aggregate capital of the new enterprise may be classified as follows:

R Corporation

Contributed capital:	
Par value	$ 750,000
Retained earnings	260,000
Total Stockholders' Equity	$1,010,000

Thus, the $100,000 debit difference is applied first in reduction of the Other Contributed Capital, and then against Retained Earnings to the extent of $60,000. If the stated capital of the new enterprise is $600,000, the total proprietorship will consist of:

R Corporation

Contributed capital:	
Par value	$ 600,000
Other contributed capital	90,000
Retained earnings	320,000
Total Stockholders' Equity	$1,010,000

In this case, the $50,000 credit difference is added to the prior $40,000 balance in Other Contributed Capital, and the sum of the retained earnings of companies X and Y is carried forward to the R Corporation without dilution. It should be noted, however, that the total stockholders' equity remains the same in both cases, as the net assets are recorded at their prior book values.

A more complete illustration indicating the journal entries on the books of the various participants for a pooling of interests is given in Case 1.

Case 1. Consolidation Accounted for as a Pooling of Interests. The R Corporation is organized on January 1, 1971, to consolidate companies X and Y; balance sheets of the constituents on this date are:

	X Company	Y Company
Assets....................................	$310,000	$690,000
Liabilities................................	$ 10,000	$ 30,000
Capital stock (par, $100)................	200,000	500,000
Other contributed capital...............	40,000	60,000
Retained earnings......................	60,000	100,000
	$310,000	$690,000

The R Corporation issues one share of its $50 par value common stock for each $60 of net assets contributed by companies X and Y. Entries on the books of each of the combination participants are as follows:

Books of R Corporation

Assets..	1,000,000	
Liabilities..		40,000
Capital stock (16,000 shares)......................		800,000
Retained earnings................................		160,000

Distribution of R Corporation shares:
$300,000 ÷ $60 = 5,000 shares to X Company.
$660,000 ÷ $60 = 11,000 shares to Y Company.

The stated capital of R Corporation exceeds the aggregate stated capitals of X Company and Y Company; accordingly, the difference of $100,000 is applied in reduction of the total amounts of other contributed capital of these companies. The sum of the retained earnings is then carried forward without adjustment.

Books of X Company

R Corporation stock................................	300,000	
Liabilities...	10,000	
Assets...		310,000

To record the receipt of R Corporation shares and to record the transfer of net assets.

Capital stock...	200,000	
Retained earnings.....................................	60,000	
Other contributed capital.............................	40,000	
R Corporation stock.............................		300,000

To record the distribution of R Corporation shares to the shareholders of X Company.

Books of Y Company

R Corporation stock....................................	660,000	
Liabilities..	30,000	
Assets...		690,000

To record the receipt of R Corporation shares and to record the transfer of net assets.

Capital stock...	500,000	
Retained earnings.....................................	100,000	
Other contributed capital.............................	60,000	
R Corporation stock..............................		660,000

To record the distribution of R Corporation shares to the shareholders of Y Company.

The entries made by X Company and Y Company to record the receipt of R Corporation stock indicate that these shares are evaluated at the book value of the shares they are intended to replace. This valuation is preferred since recording the receipt of R Corporation shares at par value requires an adjustment to Retained Earnings and to Other Contributed Capital for "liquidation losses" which have no meaning in a pooling of interests.

If a pooling of interests takes the acquisition form in which a parent-subsidiary relationship is established between the combining companies, the investment account on the parent company's books is debited with the *par or stated value* of the parent's shares issued to consummate the combination. The *amount* of this debit represents an important difference between the pooling of interests method and the purchase method; under the purchase method, the investment account on the parent company's books is debited with the fair market value of the consideration (net assets) received (which is frequently most objectively approximated by using the total market value of the shares issued).

In the preparation of consolidated financial statements where the combination is accounted for as a pooling of interests, it is important to remember that the at-acquisition retained earnings of the subsidiary company are generally carried forward, without elimination, to augment the retained earnings accumulation of the parent company. Accordingly, consolidated retained earnings at the date of acquisition may be equal to the sum of the retained earnings of both parent and subsidiary affiliates. It will be less than this amount, however, in the event the balance of the investment account (the stated value of the parent's issued shares) is greater than the sum of the parent company's equity in the contributed capital of the subsidiary plus any Other Contributed Capital balance on the books of the parent. Where the investment account balance is less than the corresponding equity in the subsidiary's contributed capital, the credit difference is treated as an increment to consolidated Other Contributed Capital.

Consider the following examples. The stockholders' equity accounts of A Company and B Company at the date of their combination are as follows:

	A Company	B Company
Common stock (par, $100)..............	$60,000	$40,000
Other contributed capital.................		5,000
Retained earnings.......................	50,000	30,000

The stockholders of B Company exchanged 100 percent of their shares for newly issued shares of A Company common stock in the following amounts:

Assumption 1...................	400 shares
Assumption 2...................	500 shares
Assumption 3...................	300 shares

The investment elimination schedule for a consolidated statement working paper at date of acquisition is as follows:

Investment Elimination Schedule
Dr. [Cr.]

	Assumption 1	Assumption 2	Assumption 3
Common stock.................	$ 40,000	$ 40,000	$ 40,000
Retained earnings..............		5,000	
Other contributed capital.........		5,000	[10,000]
Investment....................	$[40,000]	$[50,000]	$[30,000]

It should be noted that the investment elimination schedules do not include debit or credit differentials; the differences in the stated values of the exchanged shares are entered as an adjustment to the combined other contributed capital amounts (Assumptions 2 and 3) and, where necessary, as a reduction of retained earnings (Assumption 2). With this modified investment elimination schedule, the consolidated statement working paper for a pooling of interests is then prepared in the same manner as for a purchase.

Financial Statement Differences between Purchases and Poolings of Interests

The classificational scheme that is used to distinguish between purchase combinations and pooling of interests combinations was previously discussed. The purpose of that distinction is to obviate the possibility of applying different accounting methods in situations that are essentially similar. Therefore, the purchase and pooling of interests methods *are not alternative* sets of procedures. Nevertheless, an examination of the 12 conditions which lead to the use of the pooling of interests method will disclose that two given combinations may be similar in *many* respects and yet be accounted for by different methods. Consequently, an understanding of the financial statement differences between the two methods is an important factor in the interpretation of the statements. The following discussion, which focuses on these differences, pertains to those situations where combinations are similar in important particulars but are nonetheless sufficiently different to result in the use of different methods.

Consider the difference between the two methods in respect to asset and liability valuation. In the event that an acquired company's net assets have a fair market value in excess of book value, which amount is recorded as the cost of the parent's investment, the purchase method of accounting results in a debit differential.[5] To the extent this differential is allocated to amortizable assets, future reported expenses will be increased and earnings correspondingly reduced. Further, the unallocated residual amount of differential must also be amortized (see Chapter 9), an expense that is not deductible for income tax purposes. It thereby has a magnified negative influence on future reported earnings. Should the combination be treated as a tax-free reorganization (see Chapter 5), not even the portion that is allocated to specific assets would qualify as a deductible expense. Under these circumstances, a similar business combination, although sufficiently different to require the pooling of interests method, would report smaller asset valuations and higher future earnings. Carrying forward the combined companies' assets at their book values eliminates the future expenses associated with the differential amortization (which is unrecognized). Correspondingly, future net incomes, earnings per share, and rates of return will be larger.

If the acquired firm's net assets have a fair market value (reflected in the parent's investment account) that is less than book value, the purchase method of accounting results in a credit differential. In accordance with the analysis of differentials presented in Chapter 9, this differential would be allocated to individual assets and liabilities. Thus, conversely to the debit differential illustration, the purchase method of accounting would result in smaller reported expenses and larger future net incomes, earnings per share, and rates of return.

Case 2 illustrates the effects of purchase accounting relative to pooling of interests accounting, given a situation in which the fair market value of the acquired company's net assets exceeds their total book value.

Case 2.   On January 1, 1971, the R Company issued 20,000 common shares in exchange for 100 percent of the S Company's outstanding stock. The balance sheets of R Company and S Company on January 1, 1971, immediately prior to the combination, are as follows:

---

[5] In the current discussion, it will be assumed that the combination takes the form of a parent-subsidiary relationship. Manifestly, the same arguments apply to mergers and consolidations.

	R Company	S Company
Total Assets	$2,000,000	$1,000,000
Liabilities	$ 600,000	$ 300,000
Common stock ($10 par)	400,000	200,000
Retained earnings	1,000,000	500,000
Total Equities	$2,000,000	$1,000,000

R Company's common stock had a well-established market price of $120 on January 1, 1971; because the shares were closely held, S Company's stock had no readily attainable market price. The balance sheet of R Company immediately after the common for common stock exchange will vary depending on which method of accounting is appropriate. In the illustrations of pooling of interests accounting to follow, it is assumed that the combination has met all of the 12 conditions specified earlier in this chapter. In the illustrations of purchase accounting, the assumption is made that one of the 12 conditions was not satisfied, e.g., at the date of the combination, the combined management expressly stated the intent of selling a significant portion of S Company's assets within two years after the combination and reinvesting the proceeds in a new line of operations. Immediately after the acquisition, R Company's balance sheet would appear as follows:

R COMPANY
Balance Sheet

ASSETS	Assuming Purchase Accounting	Assuming Pooling of Interests Accounting
Other assets	$2,000,000	$2,000,000
Investment in S stock	2,400,000	200,000
Total Assets	$4,400,000	$2,200,000
EQUITIES		
Liabilities	$ 600,000	$ 600,000
Common stock	600,000	600,000
Other contributed capital	2,200,000	
Retained earnings	1,000,000	1,000,000
Total Equities	$4,400,000	$2,200,000

The consolidated working papers under each of the accounting treatments are presented in Illustrations 10–1 and 10–2. The consolidated net income of R Company and its subsidiary during the years 1971–73 was $300,000, $360,000, and $420,000, excluding any deductions for the amortization of a differential. The combination was treated as a "tax-free" reorganization (see Chapter 5). Thus, none of the differential amortizations are tax deductible.

Assume that the entire differential (arising only under the purchase

Illustration 10–1

R COMPANY

Consolidated Statement Working Paper

Combination Accounted for as a Purchase

January 1, 1971

	R Company	S Company	Eliminations Dr.	Eliminations Cr.	Consolidated
Other assets.................	2,000,000	1,000,000			3,000,000
Investment in S.............	2,400,000			(1) 2,400,000	
Differential................			(1) 1,700,000		1,700,000
	4,400,000	1,000,000			4,700,000
Liabilities.................	600,000	300,000			900,000
Common stock:					
R.......................	600,000				600,000
S.......................		200,000	(1) 200,000		
Other contributed capital....	2,200,000				2,200,000
Retained earnings:					
R.......................	1,000,000				1,000,000
S.......................		500,000	(1) 500,000		
	4,400,000	1,000,000	2,400,000	2,400,000	4,700,000

Illustration 10–2

R COMPANY

Consolidated Statement Working Paper

Combination Accounted for as a Pooling of Interests

January 1, 1971

	R Company	S Company	Eliminations Dr.	Eliminations Cr.	Consolidated
Other assets.................	2,000,000	1,000,000			3,000,000
Investment in S............	200,000			(1) 200,000	
	2,200,000	1,000,000			3,000,000
Liabilities...................	600,000	300,000			900,000
Common stock:					
R..........................	600,000				600,000
S..........................		200,000	(1) 200,000		
Retained earnings:					
R..........................	1,000,000				1,000,000
S..........................		500,000			500,000
	2,200,000	1,000,000	200,000	200,000	3,000,000

method) was allocated to assets having remaining estimated useful lives of 17 years. The comparative net incomes and earnings per share under each method are as follows:

	Assuming Pooling of Interests Accounting	Less Differential Amortization	Assuming Purchase Accounting
1971: Net income	$300,000	$100,000	$200,000
Earnings per share	$5.00		$3.33
1972: Net income	360,000	100,000	260,000
Earnings per share	$6.00		$4.33
1973: Net income	420,000	100,000	320,000
Earnings per share	$7.00		$5.33

The essential facts of Case 2 are not atypical. The price paid for S Company, stated in terms of the market value of R Company's common stock, was $2,400,000, while the book value of S Company's stock was $700,000. A market value to book value ratio of 3.4 is not unusual. Furthermore, the assumed net incomes exhibit realistic relationships to total assets. Thus, the relative effect on the financial statements of the two accounting methods is easily observable.

The assumptions of Case 2 can be adapted to display the relative effect on the financial statements of the two accounting methods when the book value of S Company's net assets exceeds fair market value. For example, it may be assumed that only 5,000 shares of R Company's stock are issued in payment for S Company. The comparative consolidated financial statements in this case are left as an exercise for the reader.

HISTORICAL SUMMARIES AND FINANCIAL ANALYSES OF COMBINED BUSINESS ENTITIES

Trend Analysis

One method of evaluating the current position and future expectations of a business entity involves a careful examination of the financial trends that have been established by the firm's past history. To facilitate this type of analysis, published financial reports usually include comparative financial statements which typically extend from the past two to five years. Additionally, financial summaries (which focus upon such items as sales, earnings, earnings per share, and selected ratios) are frequently provided for as many as the past 10 or 15 years. The preparation of these comparative statements and financial summaries, as well as interpretive analysis of these data, impose unique difficulties if the period covered by the analysis includes one or more business combinations.

Participation in a business combination is usually a critical event in the history of a business entity. Managerial identity, ownership positions, legal structure, the nature of operations and resources as well as their magnitudes, and many other significant aspects of the entity may undergo dramatic change as the result of a combination. Indeed, it can be argued that many business combinations involve such sweeping changes that meaningful comparisons between the combined entity and its precombination constituents are virtually impossible. Nevertheless, there persists a compelling desire for information that may be relevant to future decisions, which has accented the importance of trend analysis extending over periods that include business combinations.

The most basic problem involved in trend analysis of combined business entities relates to the precombination operating periods; the accountant must decide what data of these periods are comparable to the postcombination financial statements. Two alternative approaches to resolving the data selection problem are utilized by accountants. One method is to select the reported precombination financial statements of the *acquiring* firm as the relevant data to compare with the postcombination financial statements of the combined entity. This approach is essentially consistent with the purchase method of accounting. If a combination is interpreted as an acquisition of assets and assumption of liabilities (which is the view implied by purchase accounting), *adjustments* of precombination statements would not appear to be warranted. Thus, historical financial summaries and comparative financial statements prepared in accordance with the purchase method do not involve retroactive combining of precombination financial data. The past financial statements of the *acquiring* firm as originally reported are the comparative base.

An alternative approach to historical trend analysis involves restatement of the precombination financial statements to retroactively reflect the combination. This method is a natural counterpart to pooling of interests accounting. Under the pooling perspective, a combined (pooled) entity involves nothing more substantive than the merging of two businesses into a single enterprise. Both continue to exist as one combined entity. Given this perspective, it is consistent to argue for the retroactive combining of precombination financial statements. Such recast statements should be comparable to postcombination statements; therefore, after a pooling of interests combination, any financial reference to precombination periods should be expressed in terms of combined data. For example, where a pooling of interests combination occurs after a balance sheet date but before statements are prepared, the subsequently prepared statements should be prepared on a combined basis.

The decision of whether or not precombination financial data are restated has a significant impact upon the trends displayed by historical comparisons. Case 3 exhibits the differences between the two methods.

Case 3. For several years, A Company and B Company have enjoyed

10 percent growth rates in their sales, earnings, and earnings per share. For 1970, these firms reported the following data:

	A Company	B Company
Sales............................	$1,000,000	$750,000
Earnings........................	100,000	75,000
Outstanding shares..............	100,000	75,000
Earnings per share..............	$1.00	$1.00

A Company acquired 100 percent of B Company's stock on January 1, 1971, in a common for common stock exchange. The exchange ratio was set at .6 to 1. During 1971, A Company and its subsidiary maintained their historical 10 percent growth rates. Financial data for 1971 were as follows:

	A Company	B Company	Consolidated
Sales......................	$1,100,000	$825,000	$1,925,000
Earnings...................	110,000	82,500	192,500
Outstanding shares...........			145,000*
Earnings per share...........			$1.33

* 100,000 + .6(75,000) = 145,000.

The historical comparisons under both alternative methods are presented in Illustration 10–3. Significantly, the restatement of precombination

Illustration 10–3

HISTORICAL COMPARISONS OF FINANCIAL DATA

	1970 Data		1971 Data	
	Absolute Amounts	As a Percentage of 1969 Amounts*	Absolute Amounts	As a Percentage of 1970 Amounts
With retroactive adjustments:				
Sales........................	$1,750,000	110	$1,925,000	110
Earnings.....................	175,000	110	192,500	110
Earnings per share............	$1.21	110	$1.33	110
Without retroactive adjustments:				
Sales........................	$1,000,000	110	$1,925,000	192.5
Earnings.....................	100,000	110	192,500	192.5
Earnings per share............	$1.00	110	$1.33	133

* The annual growth rate for sales, earnings, and earnings per share was assumed to be 10 percent for years prior to 1971.

data results in the 10 percent growth rate being maintained. Thus, if growth rates in sales, earnings, and other operating data are important variables in the decision makers' predictions of future success, restatement would seem appropriate. The large growth rates displayed by comparisons with the unadjusted base are primarily caused by the combination itself; thus, they are not likely to be maintained over several future periods. Maintaining such growth rates requires increasingly large business combinations. Indeed, the size of the firms to be acquired would have to increase at a geometrical rate.

It must be reemphasized that the restatement method is employed only when combinations are accounted for as poolings of interests. The unadjusted method is used if the purchase method is followed. Case 3 was based on the implicit assumption of unique circumstances in which the differences between the purchase and pooling of interests methods did not affect 1971 combined net income. Consequently, the difference in the reported trends was attributable entirely to the restatement or nonrestatement of the data of precombination periods.

Earnings per Share Analysis

One of the most critical items of information that is drawn from accounting reports is the earnings per share indicant. As a summary indicator of current success and future expectations of success, the absolute size, periodic variation, and growth rate of earnings per share probably have more informational significance than any other data that can be extracted from financial statements. Nonetheless, accountants frequently warn against the dangers of placing an exaggerated emphasis on earnings per share analysis. This summary indicator should always be interpreted in light of all of the other information obtainable from financial statements and other sources. Prudent accountants would acknowledge that proper analysis of all available data is superior to undue reliance on the preliminary indications of any single item such as earnings per share. Nevertheless, earnings per share continues to be of signal importance to the investing community.

The growth in number of business combinations in recent years has been accompanied by an increasing variety of financing methods. Many of these methods have an immediate or potential impact on earnings per share calculations. Even with the employment of more traditional financing methods, the act of combination often causes a sharp discontinuity in the historical trend of earnings per share. As a result, the meaning and reliability of earnings per share calculations must be viewed circumspectly. Understanding these problems and recent attempts to resolve them is a requisite part of comprehending the broader subject of accounting for business combinations.

Case 3 displayed the sharp discontinuities that can occur in historical earnings per share trends when combinations involve traditional common for common stock exchanges. This problem was also considered in Chapter 6. The critical factor which causes this phenomenon is the relative size of the combining firms' price/earnings ratios. Retroactive adjustments (used only with pooling of interests accounting) are an attempt to maintain internal growth trends. However, it must be recognized that data once reported are probably never completely overturned in the minds of investors, no matter how forcefully the retroactive adjustments may be emphasized.

Traditional Calculations. Earnings per share is a financial statistic of long standing. Traditionally, it was calculated as a quotient, the numerator of which was net income less preferred dividends declared (including current arrearages) and the denominator of which was the weighted average number of common shares outstanding. The significance of this calculation as a basic success indicator was implicitly accepted for many years. However, increasing usage of convertible securities, common stock warrants, and stock option plans has rendered this traditional calculation misleading and inadequate. As a substitute for this summary statistic, accountants have developed two calculations: primary earnings per share and fully diluted earnings per share. Sharp controversy continues to exist as to the significance and dependability of these measures as indicants of future business success. Nevertheless, they represent the only evident means of providing the information that was once supplied by the traditional earnings per share calculation.

Primary Earnings per Share. Primary earnings per share is based on a concept of "common stock equivalents" which are added to common stock presently outstanding[6] to determine the denominator in the calculation. In fact, the primary earnings per share statistic is frequently reported in financial statements as "earnings per common share and common equivalent share." The Accounting Principles Board has defined the concept of "common stock equivalent" as follows:

A common stock equivalent is a security which is not, in form, a common stock but which usually contains provisions to enable its holder to become a common stockholder and which, because of its terms and the circumstances under which it was issued, is in substance equivalent to a common stock. The holders of these securities can expect to participate in the appreciation of the value of the common stock resulting principally from the earnings and earnings potential of the issuing corporation. This participation is essentially the same as that of a common stockholder except that the security may carry a specified dividend or interest rate yielding a return different from that received by a common stockholder.[7]

The most prominent types of securities that are, or may be, common stock equivalents are (1) those which are convertible into common stock and (2) common stock options and warrants which allow the holder to purchase common shares at specified prices.

It should be apparent that the definition of common stock equivalents

---

[6] The amount to be added is the number of common shares that could be obtained through conversion or exercise of the common stock equivalents.

[7] Accounting Principles Board, American Institute of Certified Public Accountants, "Earnings per Share," *Opinion No. 15* (New York, 1969), pp. 225–26.

requires some more specific operational criteria which may be used to decide whether a specific security should be classified as a common stock equivalent or as a senior security. Without such a definitive standard, the earnings per share calculations of business firms would probably not be based on comparable classifications. With respect to all convertible securities, the Accounting Principles Board stated the following classification criterion:

. . . a convertible security should be considered as a common stock equivalent at the time of issuance if, based on its market price, it has a cash yield of less than 66⅔% of the then current bank prime interest rate. For any convertible security which has a change in its cash interest rate or cash dividend rate scheduled within the first five years after issuance, the lowest scheduled rate during such five years should be used in determining the cash yield of the security at issuance.[8]

An important implication of this criterion is that the common stock equivalent or senior status of a security is determined *only* at the time of issuance, and this status remains unchanged so long as the security remains outstanding.

With respect to common stock options, warrants, and similar obligations, the established criterion is that they be included in the common stock equivalent class at all times. This inclusion is consistent with the fact that such securities generally have no cash yield and therefore derive their value "from their right to obtain common stock at specified prices for an extended period."[9]

In respect to the calculation of primary earnings per share, it should be recognized that the assumed conversion or exercise of a common stock equivalent may be either *dilutive* or *antidilutive;* that is, the effect of the assumed conversion may be either to decrease or to increase the earnings per share figure. However, the underlying purpose of the development of the primary earnings per share statistic was to recognize that some securities (other than common stock) are likely to participate in the value increments of common stock which result from growth in earnings. If earnings are not maintained at a level which would eventually make it profitable for security holders to convert or exercise their securities, it can be assumed that such conversions may not take place. As a consequence, the calculation of primary earnings per share is based on the assumed conversion and exercise of common stock equivalents, *only if the effect of the assumed conversion or exercise is dilutive.*

Special consideration must be given to the treatment of common stock warrants (and stock options, etc.) in the calculation of primary earnings per share. So long as the number of common shares which are issuable upon the exercise of warrants is 20 percent or less of the total number of

---

[8] *Ibid.,* p. 229. If no market price is available at the time of issuance, this test is based on the fair value of the security.

[9] *Ibid.,* p. 230.

common shares outstanding at the end of the period, the treatment of warrants in this calculation is described as the "treasury stock" method. The cash proceeds from the anticipated exercise of warrants are assumed to be used to repurchase shares of common stock at the average market price during the period. If the exercise price of the warrants is less than the average market price of common stock, more common shares will have been issued than will have been repurchased; thus, the net number of common shares outstanding is increased and the warrants are *dilutive* in effect. However, if the exercise price of the warrants is greater than the average price of common stock, the cash proceeds from the assumed exercise of the warrants would provide for repurchasing more common shares than were issued when the warrants were exercised; thus, the net number of common shares outstanding is decreased and the warrants are *antidilutive*. In the latter situation, the warrants should be disregarded in calculating primary earnings per share, notwithstanding the fact that they are classified as common stock equivalents.

In the event that the number of common shares issuable upon the exercise of warrants (and stock options, etc.) exceeds 20 percent of the number of common shares outstanding at the end of the period, the previously described "treasury stock" method is rejected in the belief that it may not provide an adequate reflection of the potential dilution associated with warrants. The Accounting Principles Board described the alternative method to be utilized, as follows:

. . . all the options and warrants should be assumed to have been exercised and the aggregate proceeds therefrom to have been applied in two steps:

a.   As if the funds were first applied to the repurchase of outstanding common shares at the average market price during the period (treasury stock method) but not to exceed 20% of the outstanding shares; and then

b.   As if the balance of the funds were applied first to reduce any short-term or long-term borrowings and any remaining funds were invested in U.S. government securities or commercial paper, with appropriate recognition of any income tax effect.

The results of steps (a) and (b) of the computation (whether dilutive or antidilutive) should be aggregated and, if the net effect is dilutive, should enter into the earnings per share computation.[10]

To summarize, the denominator in primary earnings per share calculations includes the weighted average of the number of common shares outstanding plus the number of common shares that would have been issued if each dilutive common stock equivalent were converted or exercised. In general, the numerator includes (1) net income, less dividend declarations (including current arrearages) to preferred shares that are classified as senior securities; and (2) the interest charges, less tax effect, on convertible

---

[10] *Ibid.*, pp. 232–33.

bonds which are classified as dilutive common stock equivalents and on debt that would have been retired with the proceeds from the exercise of dilutive warrants.

Case 4. Primary Earnings per Share.   Western Calculations, Inc., reported net income for 1971 of $8,000,000. The firm's common stock is traded actively on the NYSE and had an average market price of $50 during the year; the December 31, 1971, price was $80. The following securities of Western Calculations were outstanding throughout 1971:

Long-term debt:
Six percent bonds, due 1980............................... $ 5,000,000
Four percent 30-year bonds, due 1990 and convertible into common stock at the rate of three shares per $100; at issuance, the prime interest rate was 7 percent; the bonds were issued at par... 10,000,000
Outstanding Shares

Stockholders' equity:
Preferred stock, issued January 1, 1971, cumulative as to dividends of $4.50, callable at $100, and convertible into common stock at the rate of two shares for each share of preferred; at issuance, the prime interest rate was 7 percent; issue price, $100........ 150,000
Preferred stock, cumulative as to dividends of $2.50, callable at $60, and convertible into common stock at the rate of one share for each share of preferred; at issuance, the prime interest rate was 4 percent; issue price was $50....................... 400,000
Common stock... 1,500,000
Warrants to purchase common stock:
100,000 shares at $20.
200,000 shares at $52.

Illustration 10–4

WESTERN CALCULATIONS, INC.

Classification of Securities
Common Stock Equivalent or Senior

Security	Cash Yield Based on Market Price at Issuance	Prime Interest Rate at Issuance	Common Stock Equivalent/Senior Classification	Criterion
Six percent bonds............			Senior	No common stock characteristics
Four percent bonds...........	4.0%	7.0%	C/S equivalent	Yield is less than ⅔ of prime rate
$4.50 preferred stock.........	4.5	7.0	C/S equivalent	Yield is less than ⅔ of prime rate
$2.50 preferred stock.........	5.0	4.0	Senior	Yield is greater than or equal to ⅔ of prime rate
Warrants at $20..............			C/S equivalent	Always C/S equivalent
Warrants at $52..............			C/S equivalent	Always C/S equivalent

Primary earnings per share calculations require a determination of which securities should be classified as common stock equivalents. Applying the rules of the Accounting Principles Board, the classification process is summarized in Illustration 10–4.

Based on the analysis of Illustration 10–4, the computation of primary earnings per share is presented in Illustration 10–5.

Fully Diluted Earnings per Share. Primary earnings per share calculations provide no indication of the potential impact upon common stockholders of possible future conversions or exercises of *senior* securities. To communicate the estimated effect of such contingencies, increasing attention is being given to fully diluted earnings per share. The fully diluted calculation "reflects the dilution of earnings per share that would have occurred

Illustration 10–5

WESTERN CALCULATIONS, INC.

Primary Earnings per Share

	Shares	Earnings
Reported net income.		$8,000,000
Common shares outstanding.	1,500,000	
Dividend requirements on $2.50 preferred stock		
($2.50 × 400,000).		−1,000,000
		$7,000,000
Effect of assumed conversion or exercise of dulutive common stock equivalents:*		
4 percent convertible bonds:		
[3(10,000,000 ÷ 100)].	300,000	
[.52(.04 × 10,000,000)].		208,000
$4.50 convertible preferred stock (2 ×		
150,000).	300,000	
Warrants for 100,000 at $20. 100,000		
(100,000 × 20) ÷ 50. . . . . −40,000	60,000	
Warrants for 200,000 at $52. 200,000		
(200,000 × 52) ÷ 50. . . . . −208,000		
	2,160,000	$7,208,000
Primary earnings per share.		$3.34

* It should be noted that each of the common stock equivalent securities for which conversion or exercise was assumed had the effect of diluting earnings per share. The warrants for 200,000 common shares at $52 were not included in the calculation since the effect of including them would have been to increase earnings per share.

if *all* contingent issuances of common stock that would individually reduce earnings per share had taken place at the beginning of the period (or time of issuance of the convertible security, etc., if later)."[11] Fully diluted earnings per share should be reported concurrently with primary earnings per share whenever present contingencies may result in future common stock

---

[11] *Ibid.*, p. 221. A reduction of less than 3 percent in primary earnings per share is not considered by the Board to be significant enough to warrant the presentation of fully diluted earnings per share.

issuances that would materially dilute primary earnings per share. It should also be reported if conversions taking place during the current period would have materially diluted primary earnings per share had they taken place at the beginning of the period (or date of issuance, if later).

The fully diluted calculation closely parallels the calculations for primary earnings per share. The principal difference between the two statistics is that fully diluted calculations include the assumed conversion and exercise of *all* potentially dilutive securities; alternatively, the primary calculations assume the conversion and exercise only of dilutive common stock equivalents. Since the essential purpose of the fully diluted statistic is to show the maximum potential dilution, "the computations of fully diluted earnings per share for each period should exclude those securities whose conversion, exercise or other contingent issuance would have the effect of increasing the earnings per share amount or decreasing the loss per share amount for such period."[12] Regarding the fully diluted calculations, one important modification in the previously described primary earnings per share calculations relates to the assumed exercise of warrants and options. In the primary calculations, it is assumed (under the treasury stock method) that the cash proceeds are used to repurchase common stock at the *average* market price during the period. In fully diluted calculations, "the market price at the close of the period reported upon should be used to determine the number of shares which would be assumed to be repurchased . . . if such market price is higher than the average price used in computing primary earnings per share."[13]

Case 5. Fully Diluted Earnings per Share. Case 5 assumes the same data as presented in Case 4. The calculation of fully diluted earnings per share requires the assumed conversion of all dilutive securities including those designated as senior securities in Illustration 10–4. The computation of fully diluted earnings per share is presented in Illustration 10–6.

Changing Conversion Rates or Exercise Prices. There are several types of corporate securities and transactions that may cause particular difficulty in earnings per share calculations. For example, a convertible security may stipulate a changing rate of conversion with the passage of time. Similarly, the price to exercise stock warrants may change. The obvious difficulty in such cases is to determine which conversion rate or exercise price should be used in computations of primary and fully diluted earnings per share. With respect to *fully diluted* earnings per share, it is reasonable to utilize the rate or price that will be most favorable to the security holders. Such a rate is consistent with the basic implication of the fully diluted statistic— the implication of portraying the maximum dilution that can occur, given current contingencies. However, conversion rates or exercise prices that are effective only in the distant future probably have little relevance to

---

[12] *Ibid.,* p. 234.
[13] *Ibid.,* p. 235.

Illustration 10–6

WESTERN CALCULATIONS, INC.

Fully Diluted Earnings per Share

	Shares	Earnings
Primary earnings per share determinants (see		
Illustration 10–5)...........................	2,160,000	$7,208,000
To reinstate the assumed exercise of $20		
warrants....................................	−60,000	
	2,100,000	$7,208,000
Effect of assumed conversion of dilutive senior		
securities:		
$2.50 convertible preferred stock:		
(1 × 400,000).............................	400,000	
(2.50 × 400,000)..........................		1,000,000
Effect of assumed exercise of dilutive stock		
warrants:		
Warrants for 100,000 at $20:		
Shares issued... 100,000		
(100,000 × 20)/80... −25,000	75,000	
Warrants for 200,000 at $52*:		
Shares issued... 200,000		
(200,000 × 52)/80... −130,000	70,000	
	2,645,000	$8,208,000
Fully diluted earnings per share.................		$3.10

* Note that the warrants for 200,000 common shares at $52 are defined as a common stock equivalent, not as a senior security. Nevertheless, they become dilutive only in the fully diluted earnings per share calculation. This was caused by the increase in the common stock market price from the $50 average price during the year to $80 at the end of the year.

current security holders. Thus, the Accounting Principles Board has concluded that the most attractive rate or price during *only* the 10 years following the latest fiscal period should be used.[14]

Selecting an appropriate conversion rate or exercise price for primary earnings per share calculations is somewhat more arbitrary. As a general rule, it seems appropriate to use the rate or price that is in effect during the period covered by the calculation. The Board provides for the following specific exceptions to this general rule:

If options, warrants or other common stock equivalents are not immediately exercisable or convertible, the earliest effective exercise price or conversion rate if any during the succeeding five years should be used. If a convertible security having an increasing conversion rate is issued in exchange for another class of security of the issuing company and is convertible back into the same or a similar security, and if a conversion rate equal to or greater than the original rate becomes effective during the period of convertibility, the conversion rate used in the computation should not result in a reduction in the

[14] *Ibid.*, p. 248.

number of common shares (or common share equivalents) existing before the original exchange took place until a greater rate becomes effective.[15]

Contingent Stock Issuances. Contingent stock issuances are an increasingly common element of the financing methods employed in business combinations. They generally involve deferred payments of an indeterminate number of common shares, with the amount to be issued depending on future earnings of the acquired firm. Additionally, the amount to be issued may depend on the market value of the stock at the future date of issuance. Both primary and fully diluted computations of earnings per share may require special refinements when such contingent stock issuances are outstanding.

In an attempt to resolve the difficulties imposed by contingent stock issuances, the Accounting Principles Board has recommended specific rules to follow. With respect to primary earnings per share, stock issuances which depend on future earnings levels should be included to the extent that shares will be issued if earnings are maintained at current levels. Further, if the number of shares to be issued depends on the future market price of the stock, the market price at the most recent balance sheet date should be used to estimate the assumed number of shares to be issued.

Fully diluted earnings per share calculations should also reflect (by inclusion in the denominator) contingent stock issuances that relate to future earnings and/or to future stock prices. But they should not be constrained by the primary calculation requirement that limits the issuance to an amount satisfied by the maintenance of current earnings. Thus, fully diluted calculations should assume the highest reasonable dilution level that can occur. Manifestly, the required increase in earnings (to attain the highest dilution level) should also be added to current earnings in the numerator of the statistic. As in the case of primary calculations, the stock price at the close of the period being reported should be used if the contingent issuances are dependent on future stock prices.[16]

Restatement of Prior Period's Earnings per Share. Several conditions may justify restating the earnings per share statistics which relate to prior periods. Such restatements would be disclosed in the presentation of comparative statements and in historical financial summaries. Among the events that would lead to restatement of prior periods' earnings per share are the following: (1) if the number of common shares outstanding changes due to stock dividends, stock splits, or reverse stock splits; (2) if prior period adjustments of net income are made; (3) if a business combination has occurred and was accounted for as a pooling of interests; (4) if the prior periods' statistics included contingent stock issuances, and at the termination of the contingency agreement the conditions have not been met; and (5) if contingent stock issuances, which were included in the statistics of

---

[15] *Ibid.*, pp. 247–48.

[16] *Ibid.*, pp. 249–50.

prior periods and remain contingently effective, are dependent on future earnings and/or stock prices, and the current (end-of-period) price and/or earnings level indicate that the assumptions which were previously used in reporting earnings per share should be modified. However, "previously reported earnings per share data should not be restated to give retroactive effect to shares subsequently issued as a result of attainment of specified increased earnings levels."[17]

Securities of Subsidiaries. The concepts "common stock equivalents" and "potential dilution associated with senior (noncommon stock equivalent) securities" are just as applicable to subsidiary corporations as they are to parent or unrelated corporations. Furthermore, it must be recognized that applying these concepts to a subsidiary company may also affect the earnings per share calculations of the parent firm if the subsidiary is consolidated or if the parent uses the equity method. In other words, earnings per share calculations for a company may be affected by the nature of the securities issued by that firm's subsidiaries.

One condition affecting primary calculations would be that in which convertible securities, stock options, or warrants of the subsidiary are common stock equivalents in relation to the subsidiary's common stock. Parent company or consolidated primary earnings per share "should include the portion of the subsidiary's income that would be applicable to the consolidated group based on its holdings and the subsidiary's primary earnings per share."[18] Although not explicitly treated in the above rule, it is necessary to decide whether a parent's "holdings" should include assumed conversions and exercises of any of the subsidiary's common stock equivalents held by the parent. An assumption of conversion or exercise would be consistent with the logic inherent in the subsidiary's primary earnings per share calculation. Thus, the authors recommend the conversions or exercises be assumed, with appropriate adjustments to the parent's earnings made for any interest or other income received by the parent as a result of owning securities which are common stock equivalents of the subsidiary.

In addition to the common stock equivalents of a subsidiary, the subsidiary may have outstanding convertible securities that are classified as senior securities. Such securities should be included in the parent or consolidated calculations of fully diluted earnings per share. Their inclusion should be handled in a similar fashion as was indicated by the above discussion of primary earnings per share.

In recent years, some subsidiaries have begun to issue securities (or warrants) that are convertible (or exercisable) into common stock of the parent. These securities should be analyzed along with those of the parent

---

[17] *Ibid.*, p. 250.

[18] *Ibid.*, pp. 251–52. Importantly, the parent's calculations for unconsolidated statements (or for an unconsolidated subsidiary in consolidated statements) are only affected if the parent uses the equity method of accounting for its investment in the subsidiary.

to determine whether they should be included in the category of common stock equivalents. If included, they will affect the parent's (and consolidated) calculations of primary earnings per share. If not, they nevertheless should be recognized in fully diluted computations.

Other Problem Areas. The previous discussion of earnings per share analysis clearly displays the variety of problems that have been encountered in recent years. A majority of these problems (and others, some of which are summarized below) have gained significance through the transactions, new financing methods, and internal structures of various combined corporate entities. Frequently, the problem conditions have arisen as a direct result of the combination transactions. Additional characteristics of the problems and recommendations regarding earnings per share analysis are outlined below.

Some of the procedures that have been developed for earnings per share calculations can be interpreted as having definite implications for other parts of the financial statements. For example, if convertible bonds are deemed to be common stock equivalents, should those bonds be classified as liabilities or as a special type of stockholders' equity? Furthermore, should the interest on those bonds be reported as an expense or as a special distribution of income? Arguments can be advanced in support on both sides of this and other similar issues arising from the earnings per share discussion. The most widely held position is that these specialized earnings per share methods should not affect the traditional methods of measurement and reporting which apply to other parts of the financial statements.[19]

Some corporations have different classes of stock outstanding which are not convertible into common stock but which participate in specified ratios with common stock as to dividends. A variety of conditions of this general nature may require an entirely different approach to earnings per share calculations. The alternative approach, referred to as the "two-class method," does not assume conversion of these securities. Instead, it recognizes the distributions made to each class of stock and computes a per share figure for the remaining amount retained. This figure is based on outstanding common shares and common stock equivalents. Finally, the retained earnings per share is added to dividends per common share to determine primary earnings per share.[20]

SEGMENTAL REPORTING

The various advantages and risks associated with diversified business operations have been subjects of discussion in the business community throughout the 20th century. The natural growth of prospering firms has often led to internally generated diversification. Complementing these

---

[19] This position is consistent with the conclusion of the Accounting Principles Board, *Ibid.*, p. 233.

[20] *Ibid.*, p. 247.

internal processes of widening product lines, expanding geographical sales coverage, and vertical assumption of supplier and seller functions, have been periodic surges of diversification by the *external* process of business combination. The recent merger movement has dramatically enhanced the diversified character of individual business firms.

It should be recognized that the unique accounting problems of reporting the operations of highly diversified businesses are not confined to combined corporate entities. Nevertheless, the processes of combining business enterprises frequently give rise to special accounting problems associated with reporting the results of diversified business activity. An obvious objective of many, perhaps most, of the recent combinations has been diversification. As a consequence, a rounded examination of accounting for combined business entities must include reference to the special problems of accounting for diversified business entities.

The Need for Segmental Reports

The basic advantages and limitations associated with consolidated statements were outlined in Chapter 7. Compared with the alternative of presenting only the parent's financial statements, consolidated statements have uniquely important informational significance. These reports clearly are a primary source of information for persons concerned with the operations and financial position of the parent's sphere of control. It should be understood that the interest in, and need for, more detailed reporting on diversified companies does not negate the need for consolidated reports. The movement toward more detailed reporting is rather an *expansion* of the basic consolidated information. Reports which cover significant subunits of a diversified firm should be perceived, therefore, as complementary to the consolidated statements. In fact, the method of reporting on subunits often involves simply expanding the consolidated statements to include more detail within these statements.

Taken alone, consolidated financial statements do not provide sufficient information regarding the various types of business activity undertaken by the consolidated entity. Revenues, expenses, and assets may be associated with vastly disparate operations; and yet they are aggregated and reported in total. It should be apparent that decisions which relate to widely diversified firms can often be facilitated by the availability of information as to the relative significance to the firm of distinct subunit operations. R. K. Mautz has defined a diversified company in a manner which emphasizes these informational needs.

A diversified company is . . . a company which either is so managerially decentralized, so lacks operational integration, or has such diversified markets that it may experience rates of profitability, degrees of risk, and opportunities for growth which vary within the company to such an extent that an investor requires information about these variations in order to make informed decisions.[21]

As is true for most informational inputs to human decision processes, it is not possible to specify clearly the precise role played by subunit reports in the decision processes of investors. Nevertheless, the need for such information on diversified firms is becoming widely recognized. This recognition is, however, of fairly recent origin. Although some firms have provided subunit data for a number of years, there presently exist no generally accepted principles of accounting in this reporting area. The discussion which follows is therefore not descriptive of established methodology. However, it does enjoy support in the reporting practices of some firms as well as in the recent research of accountants.

Identifying Significant Subunits

Several alternative classification schemes for segmenting a diversified firm may result in reports which have informational significance to investors. At least three alternatives have been given serious consideration. They are (1) geographical division, (2) product line or industrial divisions, and (3) divisions that are conformable to the internal structure of managerial control. Of course, other possible bases for segmenting a firm's operations may have significance, particularly in specific industries. For example, a division between government and private operations might provide especially relevant information for firms such as those engaged in air-frame construction.

Arguments can be marshaled in support of each of the three primary alternatives mentioned above. Casual reflection on the varying characteristics of diversified firms suggests that all three methods may be worth utilization in some cases and that no one method is logically superior in all cases. As a general rule, the necessary data can probably be accumulated most accurately and at the smallest additional cost when the basis for division conforms to the internal structure of managerial control. At least one researcher supports this basis as most appropriate.[22]

On the other hand, segmentation which meaningfully reflects differences in profitability, degrees of risk, and growth opportunities frequently follows the product lines or industrial categories in which a firm is active. Of course, for some enterprises the industrial classification would conform fairly closely to the above mentioned managerial units of control.

The geographical basis of segmentation may be highly informative for some companies, particularly in its ability to accent important distinctions between domestic and foreign operations. However, as a *comprehensive*

---

[21] R. K. Mautz, *Financial Reporting by Diversified Companies* (New York: Financial Executives Research Foundation, 1968), pp. 7–8.

[22] David Solomons, "Accounting Problems and Some Proposed Solutions," *Public Reporting by Conglomerates* in Alfred Rappaport, Peter A. Firmin and Stephen A. Zeff (eds.), (Englewood Cliffs, N.J.: Prentice-Hall, Inc., 1968), p. 96.

basis for segmentation, it appears entirely too vague. This shortcoming may be especially important with respect to asset and expense distributions, which may be geographically unrelated to corresponding revenues.

Segmentation on the basis of organizational units, which in turn reflect principal centers of profit responsibility for internal management, has more apparent potential as a primary classification scheme than do other alternatives. But, given the present stage of accounting development, this basis should not be arbitrarily imposed as a reporting requirement for all diversified firms.

A problem that relates to the selection of a basis for segmentation is the determination of how finely segmented the reports should be. An over proliferation of detail may engender sufficient confusion to outweigh the presumed informational gains. Professor Mautz argues that the selection of reporting units is essentially a management responsibility. However, he recommends that a reporting component should meet the following materiality test:

Ordinarily, a "material degree," as the term is used here, means 15% or more of a company's gross revenue. If the amounts of gross revenue are significantly disproportionate to the amounts of income from, or the assets employed in, diversified components, as compared to other components of the company, a more representative test of the materiality of the diversification should be used.[23]

Somewhat more restrictive requirements have been established by the Securities and Exchange Commission for certain reports that are filed with the SEC. These requirements are as follows:

. . . [state] the approximate amount of percentage of (i) total sales and revenues, and (ii) income (or loss) before income taxes and extraordinary items, attributable to each line of business which during either of the last two fiscal years accounted for—

(A)   10 percent or more of the total of sales and revenues.

(B)   10 percent or more of income before income taxes and extraordinary items computed without deduction of loss resulting from operations of any line of business, or

(C)   a loss which equalled or exceeded 10 percent of the amount of income specified in (B) above;

provided, that if the total sales and revenues did not exceed $50,000,000 during either of the last two years, the percentages specified in (A), (B) and (C) above shall be 15 percent, instead of 10 percent.[24]

Intersegmental Transfer Pricing

An important problem that must be resolved for the purposes of segmental reporting is the pricing of intrafirm transfers of goods and services

---

[23] Mautz, *op. cit.*, p. 158.

[24] Securities and Exchange Commission, "Adoption of Amendments to Forms S-1, S-7 and 10," *Securities Act Release No. 4988, Securities Exchange Act Release No. 8650* (Washington, D.C., July 14, 1969).

between reporting segments. Some segments exist entirely for the purpose of providing goods or services to other segments. Others are concerned with outside sales *and* intrafirm transfers. Still others deal exclusively with outsiders. To the extent that transfers are made between segments, the reported profits of both the "selling" and "purchasing" segments are directly affected by the prices at which the transfers are recorded.

An ideal basis for setting transfer prices would be the independent market prices for the same goods and services, given a perfectly competitive market. However, good approximations of these conditions rarely exist. One is much more likely to discover highly imperfect or even nonexistent markets for goods or services that are, at best, similar to those transferred between segments within an enterprise. Independent market prices for similar goods (given a sensitivity to the quantities being sold) would be an acceptable basis for recording transfer prices whenever such information is available. But a more general basis should be developed for the preponderance of intersegmental transfers.

If independent market prices are not obtainable, a strong argument can be made to eliminate from the segmental reports the supplier-servicer function of the producing (tranferor) segments. Arguing that intersegmental sales should be eliminated in *all* cases, Professor Solomons suggests the following:

. . . the best procedure seems to be to eliminate inter-divisional sales from reports to stockholders. This is really equivalent to saying that all materials or products transferred between divisions shall be transferred at cost, including a proportionate share of overhead.

.   .   .   .

As a consequence of this procedure, important divisions which work mainly or perhaps wholly for other divisions of the company . . . would disappear from the financial report, except to the extent that they had sales to outside customers. All earnings would be attributed to the divisions which market the final products. The result would be the same as if all stages of making the final product were carried on in the end-product division.[25]

Care must be taken in applying a materiality test (e.g., the SEC requirement previously cited) to divisions which have sales both to outside customers and to other divisions within the firm. If intrafirm data are to be eliminated, the test should be applied only to operations related to outside customers. Thus, the process of elimination may render immaterial the operations of a segment that first appeared to be material.

Presuming that intersegmental eliminations do not remove a segment from the roster of those for which reports will be prepared, the reports for the outside operations of such a segment may have particularly limited

---

[25] Solomons, *op. cit.*, p. 100.

significance. In many cases, the investment in assets cannot be meaningfully allocated between outside sales and intrafirm transfers. Thus, the asset investment in a segment would relate to all segmental operations including intrafirm transfers. Accordingly, return on investment calculations would not be meaningful whenever the eliminations of intrafirm sales are material. Such situations should be fully disclosed in a footnote that is referenced to both investment and operating information.

Allocation of Common Costs

Regardless of the means by which a firm is divided into subunits for reporting purposes, some expenses will be common to two or more of the reporting segments. Typical examples of such expenses would include interest, income taxes, top-management compensation, and general corporate administrative expenses. Depending on the nature of the company's operations, many of the noninventoried expenses may be at times common to more than one subunit.

The allocation of common costs to reporting segments is constrained by two conflicting objectives. On the one hand, the bases of allocation should not be arbitrary. Given this single objective, the accountant would be led to leave many common costs unallocated. Allocations that are patently arbitrary may result in the data being more misleading than informative. Contrariwise, one of the primary objectives of segmental reporting is to provide information concerning each segment's contribution to the profitability of the firm. Where common costs remain unallocated, this objective is only partially fulfilled.

Nonetheless, there exist some common expenses for which reasonable allocations between segments are virtually impossible, e.g., interest expense on corporate indebtedness. The ability to allocate most common costs depends largely upon the organization and operating procedures of each firm. Consequently, *general rules* of allocation are very difficult to prescribe. If some common costs are not allocated, the reported contribution of each division to unallocated common expenses and profits of the corporation should be clearly identified to avoid the implication that it represents net income. The words "profit" or "income" should preferably *not* be used in the description unless they carry appropriate qualifications such as "net income before interest and income taxes."

Determining Segmental Investment

Adequate evaluation of segmental performance requires that the contribution of each segment to the unallocated expenses and profits of the firm be related to the investment of resources in segmental operations. A complete balance sheet for each segment obviously cannot be prepared. Corporate equities (including liabilities) generally represent undivided interests in the entire net assets of the business, notwithstanding the fact that some may enjoy special rights in the event of insolvency. The measurement of segmental investment is therefore limited to an allocation of assets between the reporting subunits.

The difficulties of allocating a firm's assets is a problem not unlike those for common expenses. Cash, marketable securities, basic research facilities, and those assets which relate to centralized administrative and service functions are examples of assets that may be particularly difficult to identify with segments on a reasonable basis. Long-term investments usually should not be allocated to specific divisions, although the revenues associated with such assets may qualify the investments group as a reportable segment of the firm.

An Example of Divisional Reporting

Illustration 10–7 presents an example of segmental reports and related footnotes for a broadly diversified firm. Operations of the firm include activities other than those disclosed as electronics, chemicals, and machine manufacturing. However, after the allocation of common costs and elimination of intersegmental transfers, none of these activities were deemed to be individually material.

The procedures necessary to prepare such reports depend in large part on the nature of the internal accounting system employed by the firm. Segmental reports may be virtually complete as a consequence of maintaining administrative and budgetary control within the firm. A major factor necessarily is the degree of similarity between reporting segments and the internal structure of control.

ADDITIONAL PROBLEMS OF CONSOLIDATED STATEMENTS: A PREVIEW

The present chapter concludes Unit III with its special focus of attention on the varied problems of accounting for combined corporate entities. It should be recognized that many of the problem areas were given only *introductory* examination here. The analysis was particularly brief with respect to the preparation of consolidated statements—one of the most difficult and yet important aspects of current financial reporting. Unit IV builds on the introductory examination of consolidated statements contained in Chapters 7, 8, and 9. Some of the broad problem areas that are given detailed examination in Unit IV are recounted below in brief outline for the reader who plans to conclude his study with Unit III. The objective of this brief preview is merely to alert the reader to the types of consolidated statement problems which have been intentionally excluded from the previous discourse on combined corporate entities.

Chapter 11 is an examination of the problems of subsidiary liquidating dividends, realignments of subsidiary shareholders' equity and the complications of multilevel affiliations. If a subsidiary declares dividends in excess of its aggregate postacquisition net income, the parent will account for the excess as a return *of* investment. Consolidated retained earnings would therefore be reduced by the subsidiary's declaration unless the accountant makes an appropriate adjustment to prevent a dilution of this accumulation. Since consolidated retained earnings should *not* be influenced by subsidiary dividend declarations, from whatever source, a modification in the investment elimination schedule is required to counterbalance the recorded effect of the subsidiary's liquidating dividend. Similarly, if the subsidiary affiliate realigns its owners' equity accounts, for example, by issuing a stock dividend, the elimination entries for consolidated working papers must be modified to offset the effects of the realignment.

Multilevel affiliations exist where one subsidiary company is itself a parent of another company, referred to as a second level subsidiary. See the following diagram:

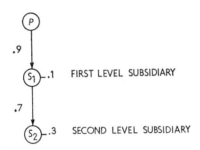

Four or more levels of subsidiaries are not unusual configurations in American business. Where there exist multilevel affiliations, the investment elimination entries and the computations of minority interests pose special problems. Obviously, each subsidiary company may have a minority interest. Additionally at each subsidiary level except the lowest, the minority shareholders may have an equity in the net income and retained earnings of lower level subsidiaries. In these kinds of affiliations, investment elimination entries must be prepared for *each* firm's equity in the next lower subsidiary's owners' equity accounts at acquisition. Significantly, since the relevant lower subsidiary may also be a parent company, the above elimination must relate to the *consolidated basis* owner's equity of the eliminated subsidiary.

Chapter 12 provides an examination of consolidated statement problems associated with profit that is recorded by one affiliate as a result of sales of assets to another affiliate. From the point of view of the consolidated entity, this *intercompany* profit constitutes nothing more than an inflation of asset value; as such, it must be treated in the consolidated statements as unrealized or unconfirmed until it is subsequently confirmed or validated by transactions with outside parties. In respect to intercompany sales (of merchandise as well as other assets), elimination entries are re-

Illustration 10–7

CONTRIBUTIONS OF MAJOR SEGMENTS TO CORPORATE EXPENSES AND PROFITS

For the Year Ended December 31, 1971

	Electronics**	Chemicals	Machine Manufacturing	Other Activities	Combined†
Operating revenues	$216,975	$354,100	$482,000	$ 67,750	$1,120,825
Other income		1,600	350	14,600	16,550
Total	$216,975	$355,700	$482,350	$ 82,350	$1,137,375
Cost of sales	$147,125	$122,150	$181,200	$ 51,000	$ 501,475
Operating expenses	56,250	149,250	187,100	20,100	412,700
Total	$203,375	$271,400	$368,300	$ 71,100	$ 914,175
Contribution to corporate expenses and profits	$ 13,600	$ 84,300	$114,050	$ 11,250	$ 223,200
Common expenses, including interest and income taxes					120,175
Net income					$ 103,025

INVESTMENT OF ASSETS IN MAJOR SEGMENTS

December 31, 1971

	Corporate*	Electronics**	Chemicals	Machine Manufacturing	Other Activities	Combined†
Fixed assets	$102,650	$688,700	$409,000	$556,350	$205,000	$1,961,700
Accumulated depreciation	36,200	361,200	195,550	131,000	71,000	794,950
Fixed Assets (Net)	$ 66,450	$327,500	$213,450	$425,350	$134,000	$1,166,750
Cash and marketable securities	$ 14,750	$ 6,100	$ 11,400	$ 24,100	$ 4,600	$ 60,950
Receivables		22,000	41,150	48,750	5,200	117,100
Inventories		47,500	43,200	72,100	9,000	171,800
Investments					109,600	109,600
Total Assets	$ 81,200	$403,100	$309,200	$570,300	$262,400	$1,626,200

* Corporate assets include all items of investment that are not capable of allocation between specific divisions.
** Approximately 30 percent of the Electronics Division's production is transferred to Machine Manufacturing. Corresponding amounts of expense have been deleted from the Electronics Division and added to the operating expenses of Machine Manufacturing. Remaining amounts shown under the Electronics Division represent sales to outside customers. Asset investment in the Electronics Division includes, however, *all* productive assets committed to that division.
† Combined operating revenues, expenses, and assets do not conform precisely with consolidated statements, since some interdivisional transfers have been included in the divisional report at market values.

quired to eliminate unconfirmed profit from consolidated reports. As appropriate events occur which validate this profit, entries also must be prepared in consolidated working papers, the effect of which is to recognize the profit in the period of its confirmation.

The recognition of gain or loss on intercompany bonds and related entries are examined in Chapter 13. If one affiliate acquires another affiliate's bonds payable, the bonds are regarded as effectively retired from the perspective of the consolidated entity. However, since this retirement is not recorded on the books of either affiliate, elimination entries must be entered in consolidated working papers which depict the constructive retirement of the bonds, recognize appropriate gain or loss, and counterbalance future amortization of premiums and discounts by the affiliates.

Chapter 13 also provides an explanation of the allocations of subsidiary net income and retained earnings that are necessary if the subsidiary has preferred shares outstanding.

The analysis of Chapter 14 relates to changes that occur in the parent company's equity in a subsidiary. If the subsidiary issues or acquires its own stock or if the parent makes more than one purchase of subsidiary stock or sells part of its investment, the equity of the parent in the subsidiary is usually changed. Special alterations in the investment elimination entries are required to reflect the effect of such changes.

Notwithstanding the usual ownership patterns of a parent-subsidiary relationship there may exist ownership arrangements in which subsidiaries own stock in each other and/or in the parent company. An example of these conditions, which are examined in Chapter 15, is depicted in the following affiliation diagram:

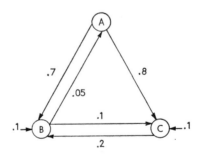

Where a consolidated entity consists of affiliates with reciprocal stockholdings, the computations of minority interests and consolidated net income and retained earnings require special procedures. Through alternative algorithms which employ successive iterations, simultaneous solution to sets of linear equations, or matrix algebra, the equity basis net income of each affiliate can be determined. Thereafter, allocations to majority and minority interests can be made by proper application of the relevant equity percentages.

QUESTIONS

1. Summarize the essential differences between business combinations which are classified as purchases and those that are deemed to be poolings of interests.

2. Contrast the purchase and pooling of interests methods of accounting with respect to (i) the valuation of net assets, (ii) the valuation of individual assets and liabilities, and (iii) the amount of retained earnings reported by the combined company.

3. In the event a business combination results in a parent-subsidiary relationship between the combining companies, what is the amount recorded in the parent's investment account—
   a) If the purchase method of accounting is employed?
   b) If the pooling of interests method is employed?

4. In postcombination periods the method of presenting financial data which relates to precombination periods is dependent upon how the combination is classified. Explain the difference between the purchase and pooling of interests methods with respect to the presentation of precombination financial information.

5. Define the concept "common stock equivalents" and suggest several reasons for including such items in calculations of primary earnings per share.

6. What is the essential distinction between *primary* earnings per share and *fully diluted* earnings per share?

7. Describe the "treasury stock" method of treating common stock warrants in earnings per share calculations.

8. In respect to the earnings per share calculations of a parent company, what is the potential significance of common stock equivalents and dilutive senior securities issued by a subsidiary?

9. Describe the type of company for which segmental financial reports would appear to have the greatest significance.

10. List three alternative bases for segmenting a diversified firm. Which of the three is preferred?

11. In respect to segmental reports, the allocation of common costs between segments is constrained by two conflicting objectives. What are they?

PROBLEMS

Problem 10–1

The stockholders and managements of Indiana Company and Wabash Corporation have agreed to combine their companies in a single transaction. According to the agreement, Indiana Company issued common stock in exchange for 100 percent of the outstanding shares of Wabash Corporation. At the date of the combination, which complies with the criteria for a pooling of interests, the stockholders' equity accounts of the companies were as follows:

	Wabash Corporation	Indiana Company
Common stock ($50 par).............	$50,000	
Common stock ($100 par).............		$80,000
Other contributed capital.............	50,000	
Retained earnings....................	30,000	100,000

Required:

Prepare the investment elimination schedule and compute consolidated retained earnings at date of combination in each of the following independent cases:

	Number of Indiana Company Shares Issued
Case I....................	1,100
Case II..................	800
Case III.................	400

Problem 10–2

Effective December 31, 1971, Wesco Corporation proposes to issue additional shares of its common stock in exchange for all of the assets and liabilities of Southco Corporation and Eastco Corporation, after which the latter two corporations will distribute the Wesco stock to their shareholders in complete liquidation and dissolution. The plan of combination has been carefully developed so as to comply with the criteria for a pooling of interests. Balance sheets of each of the corporations immediately prior to merger on December 31, 1971, are given below. The common stock exchange ratio was negotiated to be 1:1 for both Southco and Eastco.

	Wesco	Southco	Eastco
Current assets...................	$ 2,000,000	$ 500,000	$ 25,000
Fixed assets (net)...............	10,000,000	4,000,000	200,000
Total...................	$12,000,000	$4,500,000	$225,000
Current liabilities...............	$ 1,000,000	$ 300,000	$ 20,000
Long-term debt.................	3,000,000	1,000,000	105,000
Common stock ($10 par).........	3,000,000	1,000,000	50,000
Retained earnings..............	5,000,000	2,200,000	50,000
Total...................	$12,000,000	$4,500,000	$225,000

Required:

(i)   Prepare Wesco's journal entries to record the combination of Wesco, Southco, and Eastco.

(ii) Assume that the combination fails to meet the criteria for a pooling of interests because Eastco had not been an autonomous entity for two years prior to the combination. The identifiable assets and liabilities of Southco

and Eastco are all reflected in the balance sheets (above), and their recorded amounts are equal to their current fair market values. Wesco's
common stock is traded actively and has a current market price of $45.
Prepare Wesco's journal entries to record the combination.

(AICPA adapted)

Problem 10–3

On January 1, 1971, Fox, Inc., issued 100,000 common shares in exchange
for all of the outstanding common stock of Weber Company. Fox, Inc., employs
the cost method of accounting for its investment in Weber Company; Weber
Company has never declared dividends. The combination between Fox, Inc.,
and Weber Company complied with all of the criteria for a pooling of interests.
During 1971 and 1972, Weber Company sold merchandise to Fox, Inc., at
prices equal to Weber Company's cost. These sales amounted to $50,000 each
year. Selected financial data for each of the two companies are presented below:

	1969	1970	1971	1972
Sales:				
Fox.	$400,000	$440,000	$450,000	$500,000
Weber.	350,000	400,000	360,000	400,000
Net income:				
Fox.	100,000	150,000	120,000	160,000
Weber.	80,000	100,000	80,000	120,000
Earnings per share:				
Fox.	$1.00	$1.50	$.60	$.80
Weber.	.40	.50	.40	.60

Required:

(i)   Prepare a four-year financial summary of sales, net income, and earnings
      per share for Fox, Inc., and its subsidiary, to be included in the 1972
      annual report of Fox, Inc.
(ii) Assume that the combination did not comply with all of the criteria for
      a pooling of interests because some of the shares issued by Fox, Inc., to
      effect the combination were placed in a voting trust which restricted the
      voting rights of the stockholders. Fox, Inc.'s common stock is actively
      traded, and its market price at the date of combination was $40. The book
      value of Weber Company's common stock was $3,250,000 at the date of
      the combination. As a result of an analysis of Weber Company's assets
      and liabilities, the difference between the fair market value of Fox, Inc.'s
      investment and its equity in Weber Company's recorded net assets was
      allocated as follows: one half of the difference to fixed assets which have
      10 years estimated remaining useful life; and one half of the difference
      to goodwill, which management decided to amortize over 40 years. Pre-
      pare a four-year financial summary similar to that required in (i).

Problem 10–4

Sam's Pet Shops had the following securities outstanding throughout 1971:

Common stock, $10 par, average market price
during 1971 was $60, ending market price
was $60. . . . .   20,000 shares
Warrants to purchase 7,000 common shares at
$50 per share.
Bonds payable, 7 percent, issued at par, market
price throughout 1971 was approximately
par. $200,000

Sam's Pet Shops earned $40,000 net income during 1971. The effective income tax rate is 48 percent.

Required:

Calculate primary and fully diluted earnings per share for 1971.

Problem 10–5

Accounting Principles Board *Opinion No. 15* discusses the concept of common stock equivalents and prescribes methods to be used for reporting primary earnings per share and fully diluted earnings per share.

Required:

(i)   Discuss the reasons why securities other than common stock may be considered common stock equivalents for the computation of primary earnings per share.
(ii)   Define the term "senior security" and explain how senior securities which are not convertible enter into the determination of earnings per share data.
(iii) Explain how convertible securities are determined to be common stock equivalents and how those convertible (senior) securities which are not considered to be common stock equivalents enter into the determination of earnings per share data.

(AICPA adapted)

Problem 10–6

The most recently published statement of consolidated income of National Industries, Inc., a highly diversified "conglomerate" company, appears as follows:

NATIONAL INDUSTRIES, INC.

Statement of Consolidated Income
For the Year Ended July 31, 1971

Net sales.	$38,041,200
Other revenue.	407,400
Total revenue.	$38,448,600
Cost of products sold.	$27,173,300
Selling and administrative expenses.	8,687,500
Interest expense.	296,900
Total cost and expenses.	$36,157,700
Income before income taxes.	$ 2,290,900
Provision for income taxes.	1,005,200
Net income.	$ 1,285,700

Charles Norton, a representative of a firm of security analysts, visited the central headquarters of National Industries for the purpose of obtaining more information about the company's operations. In the annual report National's president stated that National was engaged in the pharmaceutical, food processing, toy manufacturing, and metal-working industries. Mr. Norton complained that the published income statement was of limited utility in his analysis of the firm's operations. He said National should have disclosed separately the profit earned in each of its component industries.

Required:

(i)   Explain what is meant by the term "conglomerate" company.
(ii) Discuss the accounting problems involved in measuring net profit by industry segments within a company.
(iii) With reference to National Industries' statement of consolidated income identify the specific items where difficulty might be encountered in measuring profit by each of its industry segments and explain the nature of the difficulty.

(AICPA adapted)

Problem 10–7

On January 1, 1971, Hawkeye, Inc., issued convertible bonds which have a total par value of $100,000 and mature on January 1, 2001. The bond indenture requires interest payments during 1971 equal to 5 percent of par; the rate of interest increases each year for 20 years by .2 percent. Thus, the rate of interest in the 21st year will be 9.0 percent; it will remain at that rate until the bonds mature. The rate at which the bonds may be converted into common stock also changes. Conversions cannot be made prior to 1974, during which year the conversion rate is one share of common stock per $100 of bond par value. Thereafter, the conversion rate increases each year for 10 years at the rate of .1 share per year. Thus, in 1984, the conversion rate will be 2.0 shares of common stock per $100 par value; after 1984, the conversion rate remains unchanged.

The bonds were issued at par (assume there are no transfer costs). The effective income tax rate is 48 percent. During 1971, Hawkeye, Inc., reported net income of $60,000, which included a deduction of $5,000 for interest expense. The company has 10,000 common shares outstanding and no other common stock equivalents or senior securities. The prime rate of interest on January 1, 1971, was 8 percent.

Required:

(i)   Determine whether Hawkeye, Inc.'s bonds payable should be classified as common stock equivalents or senior securities and explain the reasoning underlying your decision.
(ii) Calculate primary earnings per share for 1971.
(iii) Calculate fully diluted earnings per share for 1971 *or* explain why fully diluted calculations are unnecessary.

Problem 10–8

Several years ago, Walker Transportation Company purchased 80 percent of Bonanza, Inc.'s outstanding common stock; the total cost of the investment was equal to Walker's equity in Bonanza's recorded net assets. For 1971, selected financial information for the two companies is presented below. The effective income tax rate is 48 percent.

	Walker	Bonanza
Net income (excluding dividend income)...........	$ 51,000	$ 30,000
Common stock market prices during 1971:		
Average....................................	90	80
Ending.....................................	135	80
Outstanding securities:		
Bonds payable, 6 percent, due 1990,		
convertible into common stock at the		
rate of two shares per $100; bonds		
issued at par; at the date of issuance,		
prime interest rate was 8 percent...........		100,000
Preferred stock, $100 par, 5 percent,		
cumulative as to dividends.................	100,000	
Common stock, $50 par......................	500,000	300,000
Warrants to purchase common:		
1,000 Bonanza shares at $40		
1,500 Walker shares at $90		

Required:

In respect to the 1971 consolidated income statement of Walker Transportation Company and its subsidiary, calculate—
(i)   Primary earnings per share.
(ii)   Fully diluted earnings per share.

Problem 10–9

Financial statements of the Groth Corporation and Dekline Corporation are as follows:

Balance Sheets
June 30, 1971

	Groth Corporation	Dekline Corporation
ASSETS		
Cash..	$ 25,500	$ 1,500
Receivables (net)...................................	24,500	7,500
Inventories...	42,000	8,800
Due from Dekline Corporation.......................	7,600	
Fixed assets, less depreciation.......................	59,500	35,800
Other assets..	4,500	200
Total Assets.................................	$163,600	$53,800
EQUITIES		
Accounts and notes payable..........................	$ 22,600	$35,400
Due to Groth Corporation............................		7,600
Accrued expenses....................................	1,500	2,200
Federal income tax payable..........................	9,500	
Total Liabilities...............................	$ 33,600	$45,200
Capital stock, $10 par value.........................	$ 50,000	
Capital stock, $100 par value........................		$25,000
Capital contributed in excess of par value..............	30,000	32,000
Retained earnings [deficit], December 31, 1970...........	43,000	[42,300]
Net income [loss] from January 1, 1971.................	9,500	[6,100]
Dividends paid......................................	[2,500]	
Total Stockholders' Equity.......................	$130,000	$ 8,600
Total Equities................................	$163,600	$53,800

Statements of Income and Expense
For Six Months Ended June 30, 1971

	Groth Corporation	Dekline Corporation
Sales..	$150,000	$60,000
Cost of sales..................................	105,000	54,000
Gross profit...............................	$ 45,000	$ 6,000
Operating expenses...........................	31,000	8,200
Operating profit [loss]......................	$ 14,000	$ [2,200]
Other income [deductions].....................	5,000	[3,900]
Net income [loss] before taxes...............	$ 19,000	$ [6,100]
Provision for income taxes....................	9,500	
Net income after taxes......................	$ 9,500	$ [6,100]

The net incomes [losses] before income taxes for the two corporations for the last six years are as follows (net income per books and net taxable income are the same):

	Groth Corporation	Dekline Corporation
1965.........................	$18,000	$[10,000]
1966.........................	[7,500]	4,000
1967.........................	12,600	[15,000]
1968.........................	14,900	[6,000]
1969.........................	31,200	[7,000]
1970.........................	28,900	[11,100]

On July 1, 1971, the Dekline Corporation transferred to the Groth Corporation all of its assets, subject to all liabilities, in exchange for unissued Groth Corporation capital stock. Both corporations have been owned since their inception in 1965 by the same group of stockholders, although in different proportions as to individuals. The terms of the merger provided that the fair value of the stock in each case is to be its book value, except that an allowance is to be made for the value of any net operating carry-forward losses. Obtaining the benefit of the loss carry-over deduction was not the principal purpose for the merger. (Assume a 50 percent tax rate and a five-year carry-forward period.)

Required:

(i)   Compute (*a*) the number of shares of Groth Corporation to be distributed to shareholders of Dekline Corporation, and (*b*) the number of shares of Groth Corporation stock to be exchanged for each share of Dekline stock.

(ii) Prepare the journal entry on the books of Groth Corporation recording the merger with Dekline Corporation *as a pooling of interests.*

(iii) Prepare the journal entries on the books of Dekline Corporation recording the merger with Groth Corporation and the distribution of Groth Corporation stock to the stockholders of Dekline Corporation.

(AICPA adapted)

Problem 10–10

Expansions Company is a broadly diversified company whose operations involve five major divisions (A, B, C, D, and E). Consolidated sales in 1971 amounted to $61,000,000. Management has decided to include segmental reports as supplementary information to the 1971 consolidated financial statements. The identification of reporting segments is to be based on the criteria developed by the Securities and Exchange Commission.

Each division has provided income statement data, presented below, which does not reflect eliminations of sales between divisions. Further, certain common costs are accounted for by the head office and not included in the data.

(in thousands of dollars)

	A	B	C	D	E
Sales	$7,000	$22,000	$22,000	$6,000	$12,000
Cost of sales	3,400	8,800	10,000	3,000	7,600
Administrative					
expenses	1,500	3,600	3,500	300	2,000
Selling expenses	600	1,000	7,300	400	1,200
Division "profit"	$1,500	$ 8,600	$ 1,200	$2,700	$ 1,200

Additional Information:

a) Approximately 50 percent of division E's sales are to division B; the price of sales to B is equal to E's cost to manufacture the goods. Approximately

40 percent of division E's recorded administrative expenses (disregard the common costs allocable to E) can be associated with the sales to B. The remainder of division E's sales represent a totally different product line; all of the selling expenses relate to these outside sales.

b) Division D sells approximately one third of its production to division C at prices equal to D's cost of production. None of D's period expenses are related to the intercompany sales.

c) Common costs accounted for by the head office are allocated to the divisions on a variety of bases, depending on the nature of the items. In total, the common costs that are capable of reasonable allocations should be divided as follows: A, 20 percent; B, 20 percent; C, 30 percent; D, 10 percent; and E, 10 percent. The sum of these common (administrative) costs is $6,000,000.

d) All divisions utilize the LIFO method of accounting for inventories, and none of the divisions' inventory balances changed during 1971. Assume there are no income taxes.

e) Other costs incurred by the head office and not capable of reasonable allocation between divisions are administrative, $300,000; selling, $100,000.

Required:

(i) Determine which of the divisions should be reported separately in segmental reports and state the basis for your decision in each case.

(ii) Prepare a summarized income statement by segments which is reconciled with summarized consolidated data.

UNIT **IV**

CONSOLIDATED STATEMENTS: AN EXPANDED ANALYSIS

Chapter 11

Consolidated Statements—
Special Dividend Distributions;
Multilevel Affiliations

LIQUIDATING DIVIDENDS

Earlier discussion of the entries of the parent company to record the receipt of subsidiary cash dividends accented the importance of the *source* of the declarations and the *method* of accounting for the investment. Distributions which contract the subsidiary's net assets below the amount existing at acquisition call for special accounting treatment. The amount of retained earnings of the subsidiary at acquisition either identifies with the controlling stock interest, and accordingly is eliminated, or relates to the minority shareholders. It follows that only the *postacquisition* earnings of the subsidiary should be included in the calculation of consolidated net income and consolidated retained earnings. Distributions from *preacquisition* subsidiary earnings are in fact returns of capital investment and must be accounted for as liquidating dividends; upon receipt by the parent company, such receipts should be credited to the investment account.

Investment Elimination Adjustments

The accounting impact of a liquidating dividend has been briefly examined previously in terms of its effects on the separate records of the parent and subsidiary companies. It is also important, however, to measure the effects produced on consolidated statements. Consider the following illustrative case.

Case 1. Investment Carried at Cost. It is assumed that X Company acquired 90 percent of the capital stock of Y Company on January 1, 1971, at a cost of $61,000. During the first operating period thereafter, Y Company reported earnings of $6,000 and the payment of cash dividends of $8,000. Trial balances of the affiliated companies on December 31, 1971, were:

	⎯X Company⎯		⎯Y Company⎯	
Investment in Y Company stock......................	$ 59,200			
Other assets..................	114,200		$63,000	
Liabilities.....................		$ 28,000		$ 5,000
Capital stock..................		100,000		50,000
Retained earnings..............		40,000		10,000
Dividends declared.............	10,000		8,000	
Sales.........................		78,000		20,000
Dividend income...............		5,400		
Cost of goods sold.............	56,000		12,000	
Expenses......................	12,000		2,000	
	$251,400	$251,400	$85,000	$85,000

The parent company's entry to record the receipt of the cash dividend was as follows:

```
Cash....................................................... 7,200
    Dividend income......................................           5,400
    Investment in Y Company stock........................           1,800
```

The subsidiary distribution impinges upon its retained earnings at date of acquisition to the extent of $2,000; this amount is regarded as a liquidating dividend, in which the parent company's equity is $1,800. If the total amount of the dividend were recorded as Dividend Income during the period, before the amount of subsidiary earnings was determined, an adjustment for the amount of the liquidating dividend, $1,800, would be required by the parent company at the end of the period. The entry illustrated above reflects the composite effect of the dividend transaction.

The following investment elimination schedule reflects the appropriate adjustment for a liquidating dividend:

Investment Elimination Schedule
Dr. [Cr.]

	At Acquisition	Adjustment	At Consolidation
Capital stock................	$ 45,000		$ 45,000
Retained earnings...........	9,000		9,000
Dividends declared..........		$[1,800]	[1,800]
Differential.................	7,000		7,000
Investment.................	$[61,000]	$ 1,800	$[59,200]

The liquidating dividend of $1,800 is entered in the adjustment column of the schedule as a credit to Dividends Declared and a debit to the investment account. This adjustment reduces the investment account to its year-end carrying value and also completes the elimination of intercompany dividends declared during the current period (since only $5,400 are eliminated against Dividend Income).

If a consolidated balance sheet only is required, or if the consolidated statements relate to periods subsequent to the period of dividend declaration, such a credit adjustment would be applied in reduction of the retained earnings element of the elimination. The schedule would then take the following simplified form:

Investment Elimination Schedule
Dr. [Cr.]

	At Acquisition	Adjustment	At Consolidation
Capital stock................	$ 45,000		$ 45,000
Retained earnings...........	9,000	$[1,800]	7,200
Differential.................	7,000		7,000
Investment..................	$[61,000]	$ 1,800	$[59,200]

Consider the reasoning underlying the investment elimination schedule adjustment from the point of view of its effect on consolidated retained earnings. The calculation of consolidated retained earnings is essentially a summation of the retained earnings reported by the parent and the subsidiary (reduced by the parent's equity in subsidiary retained earnings at acquisition). The recording of dividends by a subsidiary reduces its reported retained earnings. However, the parent records the receipt of a liquidating dividend as a credit to its *investment* account;[1] the parent company's retained earnings are *not* increased. Consolidated retained earnings would consequently be reduced by the amount of the liquidating dividend to the parent, $1,800, *if no adjustment were made.* Yet, consolidated retained earnings should not be affected by any dividend transfers in cash from the subsidiary to the parent. The adjustment to the investment elimination schedule involves a $1,800 reduction in the elimination of subsidiary retained earnings. Thus, it cancels the effect on consolidated retained earnings of the liquidating dividend.

It is significant to note that the accountant's distinction between dividends received from preacquisition subsidiary earnings and postacquisition earnings is not recognized in the calculation of *taxable* net income. For income tax purposes, *all* subsidiary cash distributions of earnings are treated as taxable income to the investor; manifestly, this rule controverts the preferable accounting treatment.

In the accompanying working paper, Illustration 11–1, Cost of Goods Sold is used as a merchandise summary, obviating the need for purchase and inventory detail normally provided. However, no special complications are introduced by the use of this summary account.

---

[1] Or, if a credit is made to an income account, adjustment would therefore be required to reclassify the credit to the investment account.

Schedular Proof

The amount of consolidated net income may be confirmed *by definition* as follows:

Parent company's net income for 1971 (exclusive of subsidiary
dividends)... $10,000
Increased by:
Parent company's equity in subsidiary net income for 1971—
90 percent of $6,000.................................... 5,400
Consolidated net income for 1971............................ $15,400

Similarly, consolidated retained earnings as of December 31, 1971, are calculated *by definition* to be:

Parent company's retained earnings, December 31, 1971 (exclu-
sive of subsidiary dividends)............................. $40,000
Increased by:
Parent company's equity in subsidiary net income
accumulated since acquisition—90 percent of $6,000.......... 5,400
Consolidated retained earnings, December 31, 1971............... $45,400

These amounts may also be easily determined by the method of *residual calculation* illustrated in Chapter 8.

Equity Method

Where the equity method is used, liquidating dividends assume no special status, as they are accounted for as a normal consequence of the parent's entries recording the receipt of subsidiary dividends. This is demonstrated in Case 2 which follows.

Case 2. Investment on an Equity Basis. The data for Case 1 are repeated here, except for those accounting refinements required in the use of the equity method. Upon receipt of the subsidiary dividend, the following entry is made by the parent:

Cash.. 7,200
Investment in Y Company stock........................   7,200

The year-end adjustment for subsidiary net earnings would be recorded by the parent as follows:

Investment in Y Company stock............................ 5,400
Subsidiary income....................................   5,400

These entries conform to the conventional pattern of a parent company using the equity method. It is apparent that no special recognition is given to the fact that the dividend is liquidating. Under the equity method *all* subsidiary dividend declarations are treated by the parent as liquidating. The reduction in the investment account ($1,800) is merely the algebraic

X COMPANY AND SUBSIDIARY Y COMPANY
Consolidated Statement Working Paper
For Year Ended December 31, 1971

	X Company	Y Company	Eliminations Dr.	Eliminations Cr.	Minority Interest	Consolidated
Income Statement:						
Sales	78,000	20,000				98,000
Dividend income	5,400		(2) 5,400			
Total credits	83,400	20,000				98,000
Cost of goods sold	56,000	12,000				68,000
Expenses	12,000	2,000				14,000
Total debits	68,000	14,000				82,000
	15,400	6,000				16,000
Minority interest in net income—Y Company					600	600
Net income—carried forward	15,400	6,000	5,400	–0–	600	15,400
Retained Earnings Statement:						
Retained earnings, January 1, 1971:						
X Company	40,000					40,000
Y Company		10,000	(1) 9,000		1,000	
Net income—brought forward	15,400	6,000	5,400		600	15,400
	55,400	16,000			1,600	55,400
Dividends declared:						
X Company	10,000					10,000
Y Company		8,000		(1) 1,800 (2) 5,400	800	
Retained earnings, December 31, 1971—carried forward	45,400	8,000	14,400	7,200	800	45,400
Balance Sheet:						
Investment in Y Company stock	59,200			(1) 59,200		
Other assets	114,200	63,000				177,200
Differential			(1) 7,000			7,000
	173,400	63,000				184,200
Liabilities	28,000	5,000				33,000
Capital stock:						
X Company	100,000					100,000
Y Company		50,000	(1) 45,000		5,000	
Retained earnings—brought forward	45,400	8,000	14,400	7,200	800	45,400
	173,400	63,000				5,800 M
Minority interest in Y Company					5,800	
			66,400	66,400		184,200

sum of the parent's periodic entries for subsidiary dividends and earnings. Where the equity method is used, it is unnecessary to analyze subsidiary earnings appropriations in terms of the amounts which relate to the pre-acquisition or postacquisition periods.

After the effects of these entries for the current year have been reversed in the consolidated statement working paper, the investment elimination schedule indicates that the investment balance at the beginning of the year is eliminated against the corresponding January 1 elements of the sub-sidiary's net worth.

Investment Elimination Schedule

	Dr. [Cr.]
Capital stock....................	$ 45,000
Retained earnings................	9,000
Differential.....................	7,000
Investment......................	$[61,000]

Previous reference has been made to the fact that the parent company's choice of a method of accounting for subsidiary shares does not influence the form and content of consolidated reports. This equivalence of the cost and equity-basis methods in respect to consolidated financial statements is easily verified by comparing the residual, or noneliminated, balances in the working paper shown in Illustration 11–2, depicting the equity method application, with those of Illustration 11–1, where the investment was car-ried at cost.

REALIGNMENT OF SUBSIDIARY'S SHAREHOLDERS' EQUITY

Stock Dividends

From the standpoint of the issuing subsidiary, the distribution of ordi-nary stock dividends (additional shares of common stock issued to existing common stockholders) represents merely a realignment of its shareholders' equity. From the standpoint of the investor, the receipt of dividend shares of stock, whether or not the investment is controlling, is noted only by a memorandum entry. In the preparation of consolidated statements it is important to recognize that the process of capitalizing subsidiary earnings does not influence the calculation of consolidated retained earnings. The issuance of subsidiary stock dividends does not alter the basic definition of consolidated retained earnings;[2] retained earnings of the parent, related to

---

[2] It should be remembered that the definition of consolidated retained earnings assumes that the acquisition is accounted for as a purchase rather than a pooling of interests. For reasons of pedagogical simplicity, the discussion of this chapter and later chapters on consolidations assumes the purchase method of accounting, unless otherwise specifically noted. Of course, the differences between the two methods do not affect consolidation procedures that are unrelated to the investment elimination entries.

Illustration 11–2

X COMPANY AND SUBSIDIARY Y COMPANY

Consolidated Statement Working Paper

For Year Ended December 31, 1971

	X Company	Y Company	Eliminations Dr.	Eliminations Cr.	Minority Interest	Consolidated
Income Statement:						
Sales	78,000	20,000				98,000
Subsidiary income	5,400		(1) 5,400			
Total credits	83,400	20,000				98,000
Cost of goods sold	56,000	12,000				68,000
Expenses	12,000	2,000				14,000
Total debits	68,000	14,000				82,000
	15,400	6,000				16,000
Minority interest in net income—Y Company					600	600
Net income—carried forward	15,400	6,000	5,400	–0–	600	15,400
Retained Earnings Statement:						
Retained earnings, January 1, 1971:						
X Company	40,000					40,000
Y Company		10,000	(2) 9,000		1,000	
Net income—brought forward	15,400	6,000	5,400	–0–	600	15,400
	55,400	16,000			1,600	55,400
Dividends declared:						
X Company	10,000					10,000
Y Company		8,000		(1) 7,200	800	
Retained earnings, December 31, 1971—carried forward	45,400	8,000	14,400	7,200	800	45,400
Balance Sheet:						
Investment in Y Company stock	59,200		(1) 1,800	(2) 61,000		
Other assets	114,200	63,000				177,200
Differential			(2) 7,000			7,000
	173,400	63,000				184,200
Liabilities	28,000	5,000				33,000
Capital stock:						
X Company	100,000					100,000
Y Company		50,000	(2) 45,000		5,000	
Retained earnings—brought forward	45,400	8,000	14,400	7,200	800	45,400
Minority interest in Y Company					5,800	5,800 M
	173,400	63,000	68,200	68,200	5,800	184,200

its own operations (excluding subsidiary dividends received), should be increased by the parent's equity in postacquisition net income of the subsidiary.

The following cases illustrate the consolidated statement effect of a subsidiary's distribution of an ordinary stock dividend.

Case 3. Stock Dividends Less than Retained Earnings at Acquisition—Investment Carried at Cost. The data for Case 1 are repeated in the following example, with the exception that the $8,000 dividend in this instance is distributed in shares of subsidiary stock. The resulting changes are reflected in the "other assets" of the affiliates.

In the aggregation process of the consolidated working paper, consolidated retained earnings would be reduced by subsidiary stock dividends unless offsetting adjustments are made to the investment elimination entries. This would result because subsidiary reported retained earnings are reduced by the entry to record a stock dividend (together with the closing of dividends declared) and parent reported retained earnings are not correspondingly increased. To correct this deficiency, the elimination of retained earnings must be reduced (by increasing the elimination of dividends declared) by an amount equal to the parent's equity in the capitalized retained earnings. The elimination of capital stock should be increased by a corresponding amount to offset the parent's equity in the subsidiary's reported increase in capital stock.

The investment elimination schedule is as follows:

Investment Elimination Schedule
Dr. [Cr.]

	At Acquisition	Adjustment	At Consolidation
Capital stock..................	$ 45,000	$ 7,200	$ 52,200
Retained earnings............	9,000		9,000
Dividends declared...........		[7,200]	[7,200]
Differential..................	7,000		7,000
Investment..................	$[61,000]	$ –0–	$[61,000]

The adjustment of $7,200 accords with the subsidiary's entry transferring $8,000 of retained earnings to the capital stock account; 90 percent of this realignment relates to corresponding elements in the investment elimination schedule. Significantly, the investment account balance is not altered by the receipt of dividend shares, although the cost per share is necessarily reduced. Similarly, the retained earnings element (in the year of dividend distribution) and the differential also remain unaffected by the dividend adjustment.

The consolidated working paper for this case is presented in Illustration 11–3. When compared to the working paper in Illustration 11–1, it may be

Illustration 11–3

X COMPANY AND SUBSIDIARY Y COMPANY

Consolidated Statement Working Paper
For Year Ended December 31, 1971

	X Company	Y Company	Eliminations Dr.	Eliminations Cr.	Minority Interest	Consolidated
Income Statement:						
Sales	78,000	20,000				98,000
Total credits	78,000	20,000				98,000
Cost of goods sold	56,000	12,000				68,000
Expenses	12,000	2,000				14,000
Total debits	68,000	14,000				82,000
	10,000	6,000				16,000
Minority interest in net income—Y Company					600	600
Net income—carried forward	10,000	6,000	–0–	–0–	600	15,400
Retained Earnings Statement:						
Retained earnings, January 1, 1971:						
X Company	40,000					40,000
Y Company		10,000	(1) 9,000		1,000	
Net income—brought forward	10,000	6,000	–0–		600	15,400
	50,000	16,000			1,600	55,400
Dividends declared:						
X Company	10,000					10,000
Y Company		8,000		(1) 7,200	800	
Retained earnings, December 31, 1971—carried forward	40,000	8,000	9,000	7,200	800	45,400
Balance Sheet:						
Investment in Y Company stock	61,000			(1) 61,000		
Other assets	107,000	71,000				178,000
Differential			(1) 7,000			7,000
	168,000	71,000				185,000
Liabilities	28,000	5,000				33,000
Capital stock:						
X Company	100,000					100,000
Y Company		58,000	(1) 52,200		5,800	
Retained earnings—brought forward	40,000	8,000	9,000	7,200	800	45,400
Minority interest in Y Company					6,600	6,600 M
	168,000	71,000	68,200	68,200	6,600	185,000

observed that the minority interest is greater by $800, as the stock dividend merely realigns the amount of this interest between retained earnings and capital stock; in the previous case a portion of this interest ($800) was returned to the minority shareholders as a cash dividend. Consolidated net income and consolidated retained earnings are unaffected by the form, or even the fact, of a subsidiary dividend.

In respect to subsequent years' working papers, or in the event a consolidated balance sheet *only* for the current year is required, the investment elimination schedule is modified in the following respects:

Investment Elimination Schedule
Dr. [Cr.]

	At Acquisition	Adjustment	At Consolidation
Capital stock................	$ 45,000	$ 7,200	$ 52,200
Retained earnings............	9,000	[7,200]	1,800
Differential.................	7,000		7,000
Investment.................	$[61,000]	$ –0–	$[61,000]

As before, the adjustment merely reflects the effect of a value transfer among the subsidiary's shareholders' equity accounts on the relevant elements of the investment elimination schedule. A consolidated balance sheet working paper using these data is shown in Illustration 11–4.

The amount of consolidated retained earnings in Illustration 11–4, $45,400, is the sum of the parent company's retained earnings $40,000, and the *extended* balance of the subsidiary's retained earnings account, $5,400. The latter amount is the residual extension net of the elimination of purchased retained earnings and an amount allocated to minority shareholders; viewed differently, it is the parent company's equity in the undistributed earnings of the subsidiary since acquisition.

Case 4. Dividends in Excess of Retained Earnings at Date of Acquisition—Investment Carried at Cost. Here it is assumed that the stock dividend of the previous illustration is increased to $12,000; all account balances remain the same except those affected by this dividend increment.

Reference has been previously made to the accounting convention of regarding the source of cash dividends as the most recently accumulated earnings, i.e., cash distributions reduce retained earnings in the order of last-in, first-out; there is also an accounting consensus that stock dividends represent an appropriation of the earliest accumulated earnings, i.e., stock distributions reduce retained earnings in the order of first-in, first-out. If the amount of subsidiary earnings transferred to capital stock is *less* than the amount existing at date of acquisition, the amount capitalized by the subsidiary relates to eliminated retained earnings (the majority interest) plus the equity of minority interests. However, if the capitalized amount exceeds

Illustration 11–4

X COMPANY AND SUBSIDIARY Y COMPANY

Consolidated Balance Sheet Working Paper

December 31, 1971

	X Company	Y Company	Eliminations Dr.	Eliminations Cr.	Minority Interest	Consolidated
ASSETS						
Investment in Y Company stock	61,000			(1) 61,000		
Other assets	107,000	71,000				178,000
Differential			(1) 7,000			7,000
	168,000	71,000				185,000
EQUITIES						
Liabilities	28,000	5,000				33,000
Capital stock:						
X Company	100,000					100,000
Y Company		58,000	(1) 52,200		5,800	
Retained earnings:						
X Company	40,000					40,000
Y Company		8,000	(1) 1,800		* 800	5,400
Minority interest in Y Company					6,600	6,600 M
	168,000	71,000	61,000	61,000	6,600	185,000

* 10 percent of $8,000.

the at-acquisition subsidiary retained earnings, the excess ($2,000 in this case) relates to retained earnings that should be included in consolidated retained earnings ($1,800) as well as the equity of minority interests ($200). It follows from the underlying definition that consolidated retained earnings should be augmented by the parent company's equity in subsidiary earnings since acquisition, notwithstanding the fact that a portion of this amount is transferred to the subsidiary's capital stock account. The amount so transferred is clearly unavailable for dividend distribution by the parent, and this permanent limitation upon its availability may be appropriately disclosed (parenthetically or by footnote) in the consolidated statements. An argument is sometimes advanced that the restriction imposed by the capitalization of postacquisition subsidiary earnings warrants classifying this amount as Capital Surplus. In respect to this treatment, the following authoritative commentary is relevant.

Occasionally, subsidiary companies capitalize earned surplus arising since acquisition, by means of a stock dividend or otherwise. This does not require a transfer to capital surplus on consolidation, inasmuch as the retained earnings in the consolidated financial statements should reflect the accumulated earnings of the consolidated group not distributed to shareholders of, or capitalized by, the parent company.[3]

Clearly, this view is consistent with the definition of consolidated retained earnings cited earlier, and with the fact that noncapitalized undistributed earnings of the subsidiary are similarly unavailable for immediate distribution.

The investment elimination schedule is as follows:

Investment Elimination Schedule
Dr. [Cr.]

	At Acquisition	Adjustment	At Consolidation
Capital stock...............	$ 45,000	$ 10,800	$ 55,800
Retained earnings............	9,000		9,000
Dividends declared...........		[10,800]	[10,800]
Differential.................	7,000		7,000
Investment..................	$[61,000]	$ –0–	$[61,000]

Although the amount of the capitalization exceeds the retained earnings of the subsidiary at date of acquisition, special notation is not required in the investment elimination schedule. Appropriate reference, however, should be made in the consolidated statements and supporting working paper (see Illustration 11–5), indicating the extent to which subsidiary earnings

---

[3] Committee on Accounting Procedure, American Institute of Certified Public Accountants, *Accounting Research Bulletin No. 51* (1959), p. 46, in *Accounting Research and Terminology Bulletins* Final Edition (New York, 1961).

Illustration 11–5

X COMPANY AND SUBSIDIARY Y COMPANY

Consolidated Statement Working Paper
For Year Ended December 31, 1971

	X Company	Y Company	Eliminations Dr.	Eliminations Cr.	Minority Interest	Consolidated
Income Statement:						
Sales	78,000	20,000				98,000
Total credits	78,000	20,000				98,000
Cost of goods sold	56,000	12,000				68,000
Expenses	12,000	2,000				14,000
Total debits	68,000	14,000				82,000
Net income	10,000	6,000				16,000
Minority interest in net income—Y Company					600	600
Net income—carried forward	10,000	6,000	–0–	–0–	600	15,400
Retained Earnings Statement:						
Retained earnings, January 1, 1971:						
X Company	40,000					40,000
Y Company	10,000	10,000	(1) 9,000		1,000	
Net income—brought forward	10,000	6,000	–0–		600	15,400
	50,000	16,000			1,600	55,400
Dividends declared:						
X Company	10,000					10,000
Y Company		12,000		(1) 10,800	1,200	
Retained earnings, December 31 1971—carried forward	40,000	4,000	9,000	10,800	400	45,400
Balance Sheet:						
Investment in Y Company stock	61,000			(1) 61,000		
Other assets	107,000	71,000				178,000
Differential			(1) 7,000			7,000
	168,000	71,000				185,000
Liabilities	28,000	5,000				33,000
Capital stock:						
X Company	100,000					100,000
Y Company		62,000	(1) 55,800		6,200	
Retained earnings—brought forward	40,000	4,000	9,000	10,800	400	*45,400
Minority interest in Y Company					6,600	6,600 M
	168,000	71,000	71,800	71,800	6,600	185,000

* Consolidated retained earnings include $1,800 of capitalized subsidiary earnings since acquisition which are not available for distribution by the parent company.

Illustration 11–6

X COMPANY AND SUBSIDIARY Y COMPANY
Consolidated Balance Sheet Working Paper
December 31, 1971

	X Company	Y Company	Eliminations Dr.	Eliminations Cr.	Minority Interest	Consolidated
ASSETS						
Investment in Y Company stock	61,000			(1) 61,000		
Other assets	107,000	71,000				178,000
Differential			(1) 7,000			7,000
	168,000	71,000				185,000
EQUITIES						
Liabilities	28,000	5,000				33,000
Capital stock:						
X Company	100,000					100,000
Y Company		62,000	(1) 55,800		6,200	
Retained earnings:						
X Company	40,000					40,000 †5,400
Y Company		4,000		(1) 1,800	*400	
Minority interest in Y Company					6,600	6,600 M
	168,000	71,000	62,800	62,800	6,600	185,000

* 10 percent of $4,000.
† Consolidated retained earnings include $1,800 of capitalized subsidiary earnings since acquisition which are not available for distribution by the parent company.

reflected in consolidated retained earnings are permanently unavailable for dividend distribution by the parent company.

In respect to subsequent years' working papers, or in the event a consolidated balance sheet *only* for the current year is required, the investment elimination schedule may be compressed as follows:

Investment Elimination Schedule
Dr. [Cr.]

	At Acquisition	Adjustment	At Consolidation
Capital stock................	$ 45,000	$ 10,800	$ 55,800
Retained earnings............	9,000	[10,800]	[1,800]
Differential................	7,000		7,000
Investment.................	$[61,000]	$ –0–	$[61,000]

Note that the investment elimination schedule reveals clearly the capitalized portion of consolidated retained earnings, viz., the amount of the elimination credited to the subsidiary's retained earnings.

The consolidated balance sheet working paper for these data is depicted in Illustration 11–6. It is evident that consolidated retained earnings consist of the parent company's retained earnings, $40,000, adjusted for a subsidiary profit increment of $5,400. Thus, the declaration of a stock dividend, of whatever amount, is not a factor in determining consolidated retained earnings.

Case 5. Stock Dividend—Investment Carried on Equity Basis. Where the parent company uses the equity method to account for a controlling stock investment, the receipt of dividend shares from the subsidiary again introduces no new difficulty in the preparation of consolidated statements. It is unnecessary to associate the realignment in subsidiary net worth with the eliminations required for the consolidated statement working paper. The parent company, by periodic adjustment, will have recorded its equity in subsidiary earnings since acquisition; accordingly, in respect to dividend shares of the subsidiary, working paper adjustments are not required.

Using the data of Case 4, the following journal entries are recorded by the parent company in respect to subsidiary operations during 1971:

Memorandum entry to record receipt of dividend shares.

Investment in Y Company stock............................	5,400	
Subsidiary income.......................................		5,400

The first elimination for a consolidated statement working paper should restore the investment account balance to that existing at the beginning of the year:

Subsidiary income...	5,400	
Investment in Y Company stock......................		5,400

The elimination in respect to the stock dividend is as follows:

Capital stock (Y Company)............................. 10,800
    Dividends declared (Y Company).....................   10,800

The investment elimination schedule is then of the form:

Investment Elimination Schedule

	Dr. [Cr.]
Capital stock......................	$ 45,000
Retained earnings..................	9,000
Differential.......................	7,000
Investment........................	$[61,000]

In the working paper for this case, Illustration 11–7, it is important, as in the previous illustration, to call attention to the amount of consolidated retained earnings represented by capitalized subsidiary postacquisition profits. Since the investment elimination schedule under the equity method is adjusted annually to reflect the parent company's equity in the shareholders' equity accounts of the subsidiary at the start of the year, there is no explicit indication of the restriction of consolidated retained earnings in respect to dividend availability. Therefore, this amount must be calculated independently of consolidated working paper procedures (unnecessary where the cost method is used) and carried forward as supporting data. Information concerning this earnings restriction is, as before, usually provided in the formal consolidated statements by footnote appendage or parenthetical statement.

Changes in Par Value of Subsidiary Stock

If a subsidiary elects to change the legal status of its capital stock, either in the amount of the par value, from par value to no-par value, or no-par value to par value, consolidated statements are affected only to the extent of an adjustment of the investment elimination schedule. If the change occurs exclusively between Capital Stock and other elements of contributed capital, the investment elimination schedule is adjusted to reflect the realignment of the parent's equity in the contributed capital accounts of the subsidiary.

Appropriation of Retained Earnings

In the event of an appropriation of retained earnings, an adjustment is required in the investment elimination schedule comparable to that made for the distribution of dividend shares. If the amount of retained earnings transferred exceeds the amount existing at date of acquisition, appropriate footnote disclosure should be made therefor in the consolidated statements.

X COMPANY AND SUBSIDIARY Y COMPANY

Consolidated Statement Working Paper

For Year Ended December 31, 1971

	X Company	Y Company	Eliminations Dr.	Eliminations Cr.	Minority Interest	Consolidated
Income Statement:						
Sales..	78,000	20,000				98,000
Subsidiary income................................	5,400		(1) 5,400			
Total credits.......................................	83,400	20,000				98,000
Cost of goods sold...............................	56,000	12,000				68,000
Expenses...	12,000	2,000				14,000
Total debits...	68,000	14,000				82,000
	15,400	6,000				16,000
Minority interest in net income—Y Company......					600	600
Net income—carried forward....................	15,400	6,000	5,400	–0–	600	15,400
Retained Earnings Statement:						
Retained earnings, January 1, 1971:						
X Company..	40,000					40,000
Y Company..		10,000	(3) 9,000		1,000	
	15,400	6,000	(3) 5,400		600	15,400
Net income—brought forward..................	55,400	16,000	14,400		1,600	55,400
Dividends declared:						
X Company..	10,000					10,000
Y Company..		12,000		(2) 10,800	1,200	
Retained earnings, December 31, 1971—carried forward......	45,400	4,000	14,400	10,800	400	45,400
Balance Sheet:						
Investment in Y Company stock...............	66,400			(1) 5,400		
				(3) 61,000		
Other assets..	107,000	71,000				178,000
Differential...			(3) 7,000			7,000
	173,400	71,000				185,000
Liabilities...	28,000	5,000				33,000
Capital stock:						
X Company..	100,000					100,000
Y Company..		62,000	(2) 10,800		6,200	
			(3) 45,000			
Retained earnings—brought forward.........	45,400	4,000	14,400	10,800	400	*45,400
Minority interest in Y Company................					6,600	6,600 M
	173,400	71,000	77,200	77,200		185,000

* Consolidated retained earnings include $1,800 of capitalized subsidiary earnings since acquisition which are not available for distribution by the parent company.

MULTILEVEL AFFILIATIONS

Affiliation diagrams have heretofore usually been of the following basic form:

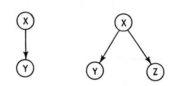

Affiliation diagrams for a parent company and three or more subsidiaries may be depicted by merely extending the second level of the diagram horizontally as necessary. In each of these cases, control is *directly* exercised by the parent company over all members of the affiliation. Yet, in many instances the intercorporate stock arrangements may indicate one subsidiary's control over other subsidiaries; in this instance, the parent's control over second-level subsidiaries is *indirect* in nature. In such cases, the associations are best described as multilevel affiliations. The following sequence of cases deals with affiliations of this form. The account balances which relate to each of these examples are:

	January 1, 1971		
	X Company	Y Company	Z Company
Capital stock..................	$200,000	$100,000	$50,000
Retained earnings..............	80,000	20,000	10,000

For reasons of simplicity, it is additionally assumed that each company reported earnings of $10,000 each year and that dividends were not declared (except in Case 9).

Case 6. Y Company purchased 80 percent of the capital stock of Z Company on January 1, 1971, for $50,000. One year later, X Company purchased 90 percent of the capital stock of Y Company for $125,000. The affiliation diagram and the investment elimination schedule follow:

Affiliation Diagram

Investment Elimination Schedule
Dr. [Cr.]

X
.9 ↓ 1/1/72
Y ← .1
.8 ↓ 1/1/71
Z ← .2

	X Company in Y Company	Y Company in Z Company	Total
Capital stock.................	$ 90,000	$ 40,000	$ 130,000
Retained earnings.............	34,200	8,000	42,200
Differential.................	800	2,000	2,800
Investment...................	$[125,000]	$[50,000]	$[175,000]

It is important to recognize that the amount of the retained earnings elimination in respect to X Company's investment in Y Company's capital stock consists of two elements: (1) X Company's purchased interest in the recorded retained earnings of Y Company at date of acquisition *and* (2) X Company's purchased interest in Y Company's equity in the *net increase* in Z Company's retained earnings since Y Company's acquisition of Z Company's capital stock. Or, described somewhat differently, the amount of the retained earnings elimination is X Company's purchased interest in the *equity basis* retained earnings of Y Company at date of acquisition.

In the investment elimination schedule above, the investment of Y Company in Z Company relates to the 80 percent purchase of subsidiary shares on January 1, 1971; the elimination of X Company in Y Company relates to the 90 percent interest acquired on January 1, 1972. In respect to the former, it is sufficient merely to eliminate 80 percent of the January 1, 1971, net worth balances of Z Company. In respect to the latter investment, however, it is important to note that on January 1, 1972, Y Company had been the controlling shareholder of Z Company for one year. As a consequence of this ownership, 80 percent of the earnings of Z Company for the year 1971 accrue to the benefit of Y Company, whether or not they have been wholly or partially distributed in dividends. Accordingly, the amount of the retained earnings elimination is 90 percent of the accumulation in Y Company's retained earnings account on January 1, 1972, *increased* by 90 percent of 80 percent of the net increase in Z Company's retained earnings (one year's profits) since Y Company acquired Z Company's capital stock. The amount of the elimination is $34,200 (90 percent of $30,000, increased by 90 percent of 80 percent of $10,000).

These data are posted to the partial consolidated statement working paper in Illustration 11–8.

The consolidated retained earnings at December 31, 1972, may be determined directly by residual calculation as follows:

	Retained Earnings December 31, 1972 [Deduction]
X Company	$100,000
Y Company	40,000
Z Company	30,000
	$170,000
Elimination: Purchased retained earnings	[42,200]
	$127,800
Minority interests:	
y in Y	$ [4,000]
z in Z	[6,000]
y in Z	*[1,600]
	$ [11,600]
Consolidated	$116,200

* (.10)(.80)($20,000).

Illustration 11-8

X COMPANY AND SUBSIDIARY COMPANIES

Partial Consolidated Statement Working Paper

For Year Ended December 31, 1972

	X Company	Y Company	Z Company	Eliminations Dr.	Eliminations Cr.	Minority Interests Y Company	Minority Interests Z Company	Consolidated
Income Statement:								
Net income................	10,000	10,000	10,000					30,000
Minority interests:								
Y Company..............						(A) 1,000 / (B) 800		[1,000]
Z Company..............							(B) 2,000	[2,800]
Net income—carried forward....	10,000	10,000	10,000	-0-	-0-	1,800	2,000	26,200
Retained Earnings Statement:								
Retained earnings, January 1, 1972:								
X Company..............	90,000							90,000
Y Company..............		30,000		(1) 34,200		(C) 3,000		[7,200]
Z Company..............			20,000	(2) 8,000			(E) 4,000	7,200
Net income—brought forward....	10,000	10,000	10,000	-0-		(D) 800 / 1,800	2,000	26,200
Retained earnings, December 31, 1972—carried forward.....	100,000	40,000	30,000	42,200	-0-	5,600	6,000	116,200
Balance Sheet:								
Investment in Y Company stock....	125,000				(1) 125,000			
Investment in Z Company stock....		50,000			(2) 50,000			
Differential—Y Company......				(1) 800				800
Differential—Z Company......				(2) 2,000				2,000
Capital stock:								
X Company..............	200,000							200,000
Y Company..............		100,000		(1) 90,000		10,000		
Z Company..............			50,000	(2) 40,000			10,000	
Retained earnings—brought forward....	100,000	40,000	30,000	42,200	-0-	5,600	6,000	116,200
Minority interest—Y Company......						15,600		15,600 M
Minority interest—Z Company......							16,000	16,000 M

(A) (.10) ($10,000) = $1,000.
(B) (.20) ($10,000) = $2,000; (.10) (.80) ($10,000) = $800.
(C) (.10) ($30,000) = $3,000.
(D) (.10) (.80) ($10,000) = $800.
(E) (.20) ($20,000) = $4,000.
[deduction]

In the above calculation, the notation introduced is a lowercase letter to denote the interest of minority shareholders in a designated subsidiary company, the latter being identified with an uppercase letter. The notation *y in Y* refers to the *direct* interest of the minority shareholders of Y Company in the recorded retained earnings of Y Company. Similarly, the expression *z in Z* indicates the *direct* interest of the minority shareholders of Z Company in the recorded retained earnings of Z Company. The notation *y in Z* refers to the *indirect* interest of the minority shareholders of Y Company in the net increase in the retained earnings of Z Company since Y Company acquired the capital stock of Z Company. Indirect interests of minority shareholders in first-level subsidiaries relate to postacquisition profits of second-level subsidiaries; direct interests, however, are calculated in terms of the total recorded accumulation of retained earnings of the subsidiary whose shares are owned.

Case 7. On January 1, 1971, X Company purchased 80 percent of the capital stock of Y Company for $100,000, and 70 percent of the capital stock of Z Company for $43,000. One year later, Y Company purchased 20 percent of the capital stock of Z Company for $15,000.

The affiliation diagram and the investment elimination schedule are as follows:

Affiliation Diagram

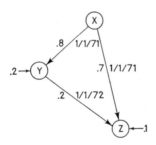

Investment Elimination Schedule
Dr. [Cr.]

	X Company in Y Company	X Company in Z Company	Y Company in Z Company	Total
Capital stock.............	$ 80,000	$ 35,000	$ 10,000	$ 125,000
Retained earnings.........	16,000	7,000	4,000	27,000
Differential...............	4,000	1,000	1,000	6,000
Investment...............	$[100,000]	$[43,000]	$[15,000]	$[158,000]

Eliminating entries for these purchases of subsidiary shares may be posted to a consolidated statement working paper in the same manner as those shown in Illustration 11–8. Other working paper details also duplicate those of this illustration.

Consolidated retained earnings on December 31, 1972, are given by the following residual calculation:

	Retained Earnings December 31, 1972 [Deduction]
X Company...	$100,000
Y Company...	40,000
Z Company...	30,000
	$170,000
Elimination: Purchased retained earnings.....................	[27,000]
	$143,000
Minority interests:	
y in Y...	$ [8,000]
z in Z...	[3,000]
y in Z...	*[400]
	$ [11,400]
Consolidated...	$131,600

* (.2)(.2)($10,000).

Case 8. On January 1, 1971, Y Company purchased 70 percent of the capital stock of Z Company for $45,000. One year later, X Company purchased 80 percent of the capital stock of Y Company for $112,000, and 20 percent of the capital stock of Z Company for $16,000. The affiliation diagram and the investment elimination schedule are:

Affiliation Diagram

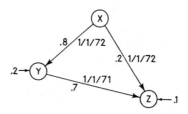

Investment Elimination Schedule
Dr. [Cr.]

	X Company in Y Company	X Company in Z Company	Y Company in Z Company	Total
Capital stock..............	$ 80,000	$ 10,000	$ 35,000	$ 125,000
Retained earnings..........	*29,600	4,000	7,000	40,600
Differential...............	2,400	2,000	3,000	7,400
Investment................	$[112,000]	$[16,000]	$[45,000]	$[173,000]

* (.8)($30,000) + (.8)(.7)($10,000).

A consolidated statement working paper is not shown, as it merely duplicates in form that of Illustration 11–8.

The residual calculation of consolidated retained earnings on December 31, 1972, follows:

	Retained Earnings December 31, 1972 [Deduction]
X Company...	$100,000
Y Company...	40,000
Z Company...	30,000
	$170,000
Elimination: Purchased retained earnings.....................	[40,600]
	$129,400
Minority interests:	
y in Y...	$ [8,000]
z in Z...	[3,000]
y in Z...	*[2,800]
	$ [13,800]
Consolidated..	$115,600

* (.2)(.7)($20,000).

Case 9. Effect of Subsidiary Dividends.   On January 1, 1971, Y Company purchased 20 percent of the capital stock of Z Company for $13,000. On January 1, 1972, X Company purchased 90 percent of the capital stock of Y Company for $120,000, and 70 percent of the capital stock of Z Company for $50,000. Cash dividend payments during 1971 were Y Company, $6,000, and Z Company, $2,000; during 1972, Z Company paid a $6,000 dividend.

The affiliation diagram and investment elimination schedule are as follows:

Affiliation Diagram

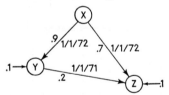

Investment Elimination Schedule
Dr.[Cr.]

	X Company in Y Company	X Company in Z Company	Y Company in Z Company	Total
Capital stock..............	$ 90,000	$ 35,000	$ 10,000	$ 135,000
Retained earnings..........	*23,040	†12,600	2,000	37,640
Differential...............	6,960	2,400	1,000	10,360
Investment................	$[120,000]	$[50,000]	$[13,000]	$[183,000]

* (.90)($30,000 − $6,000) + (.90)(.20)($10,000 − $2,000).
† (.70)($20,000 − $2,000).

Illustration 11-9

X COMPANY AND SUBSIDIARY COMPANIES

Partial Consolidated Statement Working Paper

For Year Ended December 31, 1972

	X Company	Y Company	Z Company	Eliminations Dr.	Eliminations Cr.	Minority Interests Y Company	Minority Interests Z Company	Consolidated
Income Statement:								
Net income..........	10,000	10,000	10,000	(4) 5,400				24,600
Minority interests:								
Y Company.......						(A) 1,000 (B) 80		[1,000]
Z Company.......							(B) 1,000	[1,080]
Net income—carried forward....	10,000	10,000	10,000	5,400	–0–	1,080	1,000	22,520
Retained Earnings Statement:								
Retained earnings, January 1, 1972:								
X Company.......	90,000							90,000
Y Company.......		24,000		(1) 23,040 (2) 12,600 (3) 2,000		(C) 2,400 (D) 160		[1,440]
Z Company.......			18,000	(3) 5,400			(E) 1,800	1,440
Net income—brought forward......	10,000	10,000	10,000			1,080	1,000	22,520
	100,000	34,000	28,000			3,640	2,800	112,520
Dividends declared:								
Z Company..........			6,000		(4) 5,400		600	
Retained earnings, December 31, 1972—carried forward......	100,000	34,000	22,000	43,040	5,400	3,640	2,200	112,520
Balance Sheet:								
Investment in Y Company stock....	120,000				(1) 120,000			
Investment in Z Company stock....	50,000	13,000			(2) 50,000 (3) 13,000			
Differential—X Company in Y Company....				(1) 6,960				6,960
Differential—X Company in Z Company....				(2) 2,400				2,400
Differential—Y Company in Z Company....				(3) 1,000				1,000
Capital stock:								
X Company.........	200,000							200,000
Y Company.........		100,000		(1) 90,000		10,000		
Z Company.........			50,000	(2) 35,000 (3) 10,000			5,000	
Retained earnings—brought forward....	100,000	34,000	22,000	43,040	5,400	3,640	2,200	112,520
Minority interest—Y Company....						13,640		13,640 M
Minority interest—Z Company....							7,200	7,200 M

(A) (.10) ($10,000).

(B) (.10) ($10,000) = $1,000; (.10) (.20) ($10,000 − $6,000) = $80.

(C) (.10) ($24,000).

(D) (.10) (.20) ($10,000 − $2,000).

(E) (.10) ($18,000).

In the present case, it is important to note that the receipt of subsidiary dividends is included in the annual $10,000 net incomes, and thus in the accumulated retained earnings, of the various affiliates. Accordingly, indirect minority interests relate only to the *undistributed* increase in the retained earnings of the relevant subsidiaries. Furthermore, it should be remembered that the elimination of Y Company in Z Company is made in terms of balances at date of acquisition, January 1, 1971, *not* as of the date X Company gained effective control of Z Company's capital stock, January 1, 1972. This elimination procedure is independent of the amount of the ownership interest acquired by the first-level subsidiary.

The working paper for this case is given in Illustration 11–9. It should be noted that the *total* amount of intercompany dividends is eliminated, i.e., 70 percent of $6,000 plus 20 percent of $6,000, even though a portion of these dividends is paid to another subsidiary.

The amount of consolidated retained earnings in Case 9 may be determined by residual calculation as follows:

	Retained Earnings December 31, 1972 [Deduction]
X Company	$100,000
Y Company	34,000
Z Company	22,000
	$156,000
Elimination: Purchased retained earnings	[37,640]
	$118,360
Minority interests:	
y in Y	$ [3,400]
z in Z	[2,200]
y in Z	*[240]
	$ [5,840]
Consolidated	$112,520

* (.10)(.20)($12,000).

Confirmation of consolidated retained earnings by definition takes the following form:

X Company's retained earnings, December 31, 1972 (exclusive of accumulated subsidiary dividends, $4,200)		$ 95,800
Increased by:		
Direct interest in Y Company:		
Equity in Y Company's 1972 net income (exclusive of subsidiary dividends in 1972, $1,200)—90 percent of $8,800	$7,920	
Direct interest in Z Company:		
Equity in Z Company's 1972 net income—70 percent of $10,000	7,000	
Indirect interest in Z Company:		
Equity in Z Company's 1972 net income—90 percent of 20 percent of $10,000	1,800	16,720
Consolidated retained earnings, December 31, 1972		$112,520

This definitional proof is uniquely important, as it reflects the basic phi-losophy underlying the procedural details previously outlined. Both direct and indirect interests of a parent company in various subsidiaries are measured in terms of the *total time period* since acquisition of subsidiary shares by the parent; prior holdings of subsidiary shares by first-level subsidiary affiliates either are eliminated or relate to minority shareholders. This concept is equally valid where the parent's noncontrolling interest in a second-level subsidiary precedes the establishment of effective control through a first-level connecting affiliate. Necessarily, however, consolidated statements are not warranted until the second purchase is effected, i.e., the purchase of the connecting first-level affiliate's shares. The above calcula-tions also reaffirm the argument previously made that intercompany divi-dends do not affect the amount of consolidated net income or retained earnings.

Given the special case in which a second-level subsidiary (Z) declares dividends which are *not* liquidating from the point of view of the first level subsidiary (Y) but which are in excess of Z's current year's net income, particular care must be taken in computing the y minority interest in sub-sidiary net income. Y's reported net income will exceed its equity basis net income by an amount equal to its equity in Z's current dividends from prior year's earnings. The y minority interest received credit in prior years for its share of these earnings; this was accomplished by the income state-ment calculations of y's *indirect* minority interest in Z's current retentions of net income. Thus, in the year Z's dividends exceed current net income, the calculation of y in Y (in the income statement section) must be com-puted as follows: (y percentage) (Y's reported net income − Y's equity in Z's current dividends paid from prior year's earnings).

Chain Control (Indirect) Less than 50 Percent

On occasion, intercorporate stock ownership arrangements may indicate a chain of interests, the product of which does not represent control of the lower level subsidiary, where control is defined in terms of the 50 percent stock ownership minimum. The following diagram is an example of such an affiliation:

$$
\begin{array}{c}
X \\
.7 \downarrow \\
Y \leftarrow .3 \\
.6 \downarrow \\
Z \leftarrow .4
\end{array}
$$

In this instance, the preparation of consolidated statements is warranted, notwithstanding the 42 percent indirect interest of X Company in Z Com-pany. Clearly the question of control relates to *direct* share ownership. In the illustration depicted above, control is confirmed by the percentages of stock owned independently by X Company and Y Company. Significantly, while the product of equities in the chain are important to the determination of consolidated net income and consolidated retained earnings, it is not a determinant in establishing a minimal condition for preparation of consolidated financial statements.

QUESTIONS

1. What constitutes a liquidating dividend given the perspective of the declaring corporation? To what extent is this interpretation different from a liquidating dividend viewed from the perspective of the receiving (parent) corporation?

2. If a wholly owned subsidiary declares a liquidating dividend of $5,000, explain the nature of the corresponding adjustment in the investment elimination schedule. (Assume the use of the cost method.)

3. How are liquidating dividends accounted for when the equity method is employed by the parent company?

4. Does the issuance of a stock dividend by a subsidiary alter or modify the definition of consolidated retained earnings? If so, in what manner?

5. If a subsidiary, which the parent accounts for using the cost method, declares a stock dividend, what is the effect on the investment elimination schedule for the year of declaration?

6. If a subsidiary elects to modify the legal status of its capital stock (e.g., change the par value), what is the effect of such action on the consolidated statements and the investment elimination schedule?

7. Distinguish between the nature of a direct and an indirect minority interest.

8. Assume that A Company purchases a controlling interest in B Company, which at some previous point in time had acquired a controlling interest in C Company (B Company uses the cost method). In respect to the investment elimination schedule for A Company's purchase, explain the significance of dividend income that had been previously recorded by B Company as a consequence of its investment in C Company.

9. Assume that B Company acquired 30 percent of C Company's capital stock on January 1, 1971; A Company acquired 90 percent of B Company's outstanding shares and 60 percent of C Company on January 1, 1972. If an investment elimination schedule is prepared on January 1, 1972, indicate the amount of retained earnings elimination along each line of ownership depicted in the affiliation diagram.

10. A Company is the owner of 55 percent of the outstanding stock of B Company, while B Company holds 60 percent of the shares of C Company. Are consolidated statements justified? What is the criterion to apply in making such a decision?

PROBLEMS

Problem 11–1

Bud Company purchased 80 percent of the outstanding stock of Greg, Inc., on January 1, 1970. The relevant account balances at that date are as follows:

Common stock, $100 par (Greg).....................	$ 60,000
Retained earnings (Greg)...........................	10,000
Investment in Greg, Inc............................	48,000

Greg, Inc.'s 1970 net income was $5,000. On December 31, 1970, Greg, Inc., declared a 10 percent stock dividend. At this date, the stock was selling for $200.

Required:

Prepare an investment elimination schedule covering the balance sheet dates January 1, 1970, and January 1, 1971.

Problem 11–2

On January 1, 1971, the Martin Company purchased 80 percent of the capital stock of the Louis Company for $135,000, when the latter had outstanding stock in the amount of $100,000 and retained earnings of $60,000. On December 31, 1971, the Louis Company reported net income for 1971 of $10,000 and also disclosed the payment of a December dividend of $20,000.
The investment in Louis Company stock is carried at cost.

Required:

(i)   Journalize the receipt of the dividend on December 29 by the Martin Company if payment is made in—
  (a)   Cash.
  (b)   Capital stock of the Louis Company.
(ii) Prepare an investment elimination schedule on December 31, 1971, showing the effects of each type of distribution indicated in (i).
(iii) If the Martin Company had accumulated retained earnings of $80,000, exclusive of subsidiary dividends, on December 31, 1971, calculate the amount of consolidated retained earnings on this date.

Problem 11–3

X Company purchased 90 percent of the capital stock of Y Company for $180,000. Y Company had, on this date, capital stock of $100,000 and retained earnings of $100,000. Y Company subsequently earned a profit of $10,000 and distributed a cash dividend of $30,000. X Company recorded the receipt of the dividend by a debit to Cash and a credit to Retained Earnings.

Required:

(i)   Assuming that the investment is carried at cost, give the correct entry which X Company should have made to record the receipt of the dividend.
(ii) Discuss the improper reasoning underlying the entry made by X Company.
(iii) Assume that X Company purchased only 5 percent of the stock of Y Company as a temporary investment, and that Y Company subsequently

earned $10,000 and distributed a cash dividend of $30,000. Explain how X Company should record the receipt of this dividend. If the principle applicable here is different than in (i), give the reason.

(AICPA adapted)

Problem 11–4

X Company purchased 90 percent of the capital stock of Y Company for $47,000 on January 1, 1971, when the latter had capital stock of $40,000 and retained earnings of $10,000. On this date, X Company had accumulated retained earnings of $100,000.

During 1971, X Company reported a net income of $34,500 and paid cash dividends, $20,000; Y Company earned $10,000 and declared $5,000 in dividends, payable in cash. On December 31, 1971, Y Company declared a $6,000 stock dividend.

For the year 1972, X Company had a net income of $29,000 and paid $20,000 cash dividends. Y Company earned $15,000 and paid cash dividends of $10,000. On December 31, 1972, Y Company declared a $10,000 stock dividend.

X Company carries its investment in Y Company at cost.

Required:

(i) Prepare an investment elimination schedule as of December 31, 1971, *and* compute 1971 consolidated net income and consolidated retained earnings as of December 31, 1971.

(ii) Prepare an investment elimination schedule as of December 31, 1971, *and* compute 1972 consolidated net income and consolidated retained earnings as of December 31, 1972.

(iii) Prepare those divisions of the consolidated statement working paper that can be completed with the available information on December 31, 1971, and December 31, 1972.

Problem 11–5

A summary of changes in the stockholders' equity of the Gurney and Holland companies for the two-year period ended December 31, 1971, is given following:

	Gurney Company	Holland Company
Capital stock (no-par value), January 1, 1970:		
The Gurney Company (20,000 shares issued).............	$120,000	
The Holland Company (10,000 shares issued).............		$ 80,000
Retained earnings, January 1, 1970.......................	$ 40,000	$ 38,000
Net income, 1970..	20,000	14,000
	$ 60,000	$ 52,000
Dividends paid (cash), November 15, 1970..................	5,000	8,000
Retained earnings, December 31, 1970.....................	$ 55,000	$ 44,000
Net income [loss], 1971..................................	16,000	[12,000]
	$ 71,000	$ 32,000
Dividends paid (cash), December 15, 1971..................	12,000	4,000
Retained earnings, December 31, 1971.....................	$ 59,000	$ 28,000

The Reeves Company made the following open-market purchases of capital stock:

a) Eight thousand shares of the Holland Company on January 1, 1970, cost $96,000.

b) Eighteen thousand shares of the Gurney Company on January 1, 1971, cost, $160,000.

The Reeves Company had retained earnings, excluding dividend income, of $50,000 on January 1, 1971. Its income thereafter was derived exclusively from subsidiary dividends.

Required:

(i) Prepare an investment elimination schedule for a consolidated statement working paper for the year ended December 31, 1971.

(ii) Prepare the retained earnings division of a consolidated statement working paper for the year ended December 31, 1971.

(iii) Confirm by schedular proof consolidated retained earnings, December 31, 1971, established in (ii) above.

Problem 11–6

On January 1, 1969, B Company purchased an 80 percent interest in C Company. A Company purchased a 90 percent interest in B Company on January 1, 1971. Both A and B utilize the equity method in accounting for their interests in subsidiaries. Account balances are as follows on January 1, 1971:

	A Company [Dr.] Cr.	B Company [Dr.] Cr.	C Company [Dr.] Cr.
Common stock..........................	$ 200,000	$ 100,000	$50,000
Retained earnings......................	100,000	26,000	18,000
Investment in common stock of C........		[56,400]	
Investment in common stock of B........	[120,000]		
Net income each year excluding equity in subsidiary net income..............	20,000	10,000	10,000
Dividends each year....................	10,000	5,000	6,000

Required:

(i) In general journal form, present the elimination entries to prepare a consolidated balance sheet on January 1, 1971.

(ii) Present the B Company minority interest as it should appear on the consolidated balance sheet on January 1, 1971.

(iii) Present the C Company minority interest as it should appear on the consolidated balance sheet on January 1, 1971.

Problem 11–7

Bravo Company purchased 70 percent of Charlie Company's outstanding stock on January 1, 1970. Alpha Company purchased 80 percent of Bravo Company's outstanding stock on January 1, 1971. Each of the three companies earned $10,000 from their own operations during 1970 and during 1971. Each of the three companies declared annual dividends of $6,000 during 1970 and during 1971. Each of the three firms had retained earnings of $50,000 on January 1, 1970.

Required:

(i)   Assume that Bravo and Alpha account for their interests in subsidiaries on an equity basis. In general journal form, present the entries made on the books of Alpha Company during 1971 to account for its interest in subsidiaries.

(ii) Assume that Bravo and Alpha account for their interests in subsidiaries on a cost basis. Prepare a *residual* calculation of consolidated retained income on December 31, 1971.

Problem 11–8

On January 1, 1969, X Company purchased 70 percent of the outstanding stock of Y Company. On January 1, 1970, P Company purchased 90 percent of the outstanding stock of X Company. On January 1, 1971, P Company purchased 20 percent of the outstanding stock of Y Company. P and X use the cost method of accounting for their investments in subsidiaries. The following data relate to the affiliated companies:

	P Company	X Company	Y Company
Common stock............................	$200,000	$100,000	$50,000
Retained earnings on January 1, 1969........	50,000	40,000	10,000
Reported net incomes:			
1969.................................	30,000	5,000	5,000
1970.................................	30,000	15,000	5,000
Dividends declared and paid:			
1969.................................	15,000	10,000	3,000
1970.................................	15,000	5,000	10,000

Required:

(i)   Present a *residual calculation* of consolidated retained earnings on January 1, 1970.

(ii) Present a *definitional calculation* of consolidated retained earnings on January 1, 1971.

(iii) Present a residual calculation of consolidated net income for 1970.

Problem 11–9

On January 1, 1968, the Cumley Shoe Corporation acquired an 80 percent interest in the Longhorn Leather Company upon the purchase of 1,600 shares of $100 par value stock for $200 per share. At acquisition Longhorn Leather Company had accumulated retained earnings in the amount of $150,000. During the period 1968–71, the cumulative earnings and cash dividend payments of the subsidiary were $60,000 and $40,000 respectively. For the year 1972, Longhorn Leather Company reported earnings of $5,000 and paid cash dividends of $35,000.

Required:

(i) Prepare entries on the books of the parent in respect to the investment in Longhorn Leather Company stock for the period 1968–72: (*a*) if the investment is carried at cost and (*b*) if the investment is carried on an equity basis.

(ii) As of December 31, 1972, prepare an investment elimination schedule for a consolidated statement working paper.

Problem 11–10

The Gilman Company purchased in the open market 80 shares (par, $100) of Newman, Inc., capital stock at $550 per share on January 1, 1971. The balance sheets of the affiliate companies on this date were:

	Gilman Company	Newman, Inc.
Other assets............................	$100,000	$45,000
Goodwill..............................	15,000	5,000
	$115,000	$50,000
Capital stock..........................	$100,000	$10,000
Retained earnings......................	15,000	40,000
	$115,000	$50,000

The Gilman Company made annual profits of $25,000 each year, exclusive of subsidiary dividends.

An operating summary of Newman, Inc., for the period beginning January 1, 1971, is as follows:

		Dividends Paid	
Year	Net Income	Cash	Stock
1971........................	$20,000	$15,000	
1972........................	30,000	50,000	
1973........................	25,000		$50,000
1974........................	40,000	15,000	

The investment is carried on a cost basis.

Required:

(i) Prepare an investment elimination schedule as of December 31, 1974.

(ii) Prepare a consolidated balance sheet working paper as of December 31, 1974.

Problem 11–11

On January 1, 1971, the following stockholders' equity account balances obtain:

	X Company	Y Company	Z Company
Capital stock (par, $100).......	$100,000	$50,000	$40,000
Retained earnings.............	10,000	5,000	4,000

Each company reported an annual profit of $10,000 and paid $5,000 cash dividends each year.

On January 2, 1971, Y Company purchased in the open market 80 shares of Z Company's stock for $150 per share; on January 1, 1972, X Company purchased 400 shares of Y Company's stock at $125 per share and 300 shares of Z Company's stock at $130 per share—all in the open market. The investment accounts are maintained in accordance with the cost method.

Required:

(i) Prepare an investment elimination schedule on December 31, 1972.

(ii) Prepare a schedule of majority and minority interests in retained earnings as of December 31, 1972.

Problem 11–12

The following data relate to companies P, S, G, and R:

	January 1, 1971			
	P Company	S Company	G Company	R Company
Capital stock..............	$200,000	$100,000	$50,000	$ 40,000
Retained earnings [deficit].................	100,000	80,000	20,000	[10,000]

The annual net income of each company for 1971, 1972, and 1973 is $10,000. The companies use the cost method of accounting for investments.

Required:

The following cases are assumed to be independent, except where otherwise noted. In each of the cases enumerated below—

(i) Prepare an investment elimination schedule for a consolidated statement working paper.

(ii) In Cases 1, 2, and 3, prepare a schedule of the amounts of majority and minority interests in retained earnings as of December 31, 1971, and 1972. In Case 4 make these calculations as of December 31, 1972, and 1973.

Case 1: On January 1, 1971, P Company acquired 70 percent of the capital stock of S Company for $130,000 and 80 percent of the capital stock of G Company for $58,000. On January 1, 1972, S Company acquired 10 percent of the capital stock of G Company for $10,000.

Case 2: On January 1, 1971, G Company acquired 80 percent of the capital stock of R Company for $25,000. On January 1, 1972, S Company acquired 90 percent of the capital stock of G Company for $80,000.

Case 3: On January 1, 1971, S Company acquired 70 percent of the capital stock of R Company for $23,000. On January 1, 1972, P Company acquired 90 percent of the capital stock of S Company for $180,000 and 10 percent of the capital stock of R Company for $5,000.

Case 4: The data of Case 2 are to be repeated here with the additional purchase by P Company of 90 percent of the capital stock of S Company on January 1, 1973, for $200,000.

Problem 11–13

On January 1, 1971, M Company purchased 70 percent of the capital stock of the T Company for $70,000. One year later, R Company acquired 90 percent of the capital stock of the M Company for $140,000 and 20 percent of the capital stock of the T Company for $25,000. The investments are accounted for in accordance with the cost method.

The following data relate to the affiliates for the period beginning January 1, 1971:

	R Company	M Company	T Company
Balance, January 1, 1971:			
Capital stock..............	$100,000	$100,000	$80,000
Retained earnings...........	60,000	40,000	20,000
Net income each year.........	20,000	10,000	15,000
Cash dividends each year.......	10,000	5,000	5,000

Required:
(i)   Prepare an investment elimination schedule on December 31, 1972.
(ii) Prepare retained earnings divisions of consolidated statement working papers for the years ended December 31, 1972, and December 31, 1973.
(iii) Confirm the values of consolidated retained earnings established in (ii) by schedular proof.

Problem 11–14

The following data relate to affiliated companies A, B, and C:

	A Company	B Company	C Company
January 1, 1971:			
Capital stock ($100 par)..............	$100,000	$60,000	$40,000
Retained earnings [deficit]............	20,000	6,000	[2,000]
Two-year operating summary:			
Annual profits:			
1971.........................	10,000	20,000	8,000
1972.........................	15,000	10,000	15,000
Cash dividends:			
1972.........................	5,000		4,000

Required:

In each of the following independent cases, prepare an investment elimination schedule *and* a schedule showing the calculation of majority and minority interests in retained earnings on December 31, 1971, and December 31, 1972. In all cases the investment is carried at cost.

Case 1: On January 1, 1971, A Company purchased a 90 percent interest in the capital stock of B Company for $61,000; on January 1, 1972, A Company purchased 80 percent of the capital stock of C Company for $39,000.

Case 2: On January 1, 1971, A Company purchased 80 percent of the capital stock of B Company for $55,000; on January 1, 1972, B Company purchased 90 percent of the capital stock of C Company for $45,000.

Case 3: On January 1, 1971, B Company purchased 70 percent of the capital stock of C Company for $27,000; on January 1, 1972, A Company acquired 80 percent of the capital stock of B Company for $70,000.

Case 4: On January 1, 1971, B Company purchased 70 percent of the capital stock of C Company for $27,500; on January 1, 1972, A Company acquired 80 percent of the capital stock of B Company for $70,000 and 20 percent of the capital stock of C Company for $11,000.

Problem 11–15

The following condensed balance sheets of A Company, B Company, and C Company were prepared as of December 31, 1971:

ASSETS	A Company	B Company	C Company
Current assets	$1,234,567	$ 731,282	$340,274
Investments:			
80% of B stock at cost	1,400,000		
75% of C stock at cost		540,200	
Fixed assets—net	3,030,933	1,322,607	514,987
Total	$5,665,500	$2,594,089	$855,261
LIABILITIES			
Current liabilities	$ 400,500	$ 275,389	$ 93,261
Bonds payable		750,000	
Surplus reserve for redemption of bonds		250,000	
Common stock, $100 par value	3,000,000	1,000,000	600,000
Other contributed capital	710,300		45,600
Retained earnings	1,554,700	318,700	116,400
Total	$5,665,500	$2,594,089	$855,261

The stock of C Company was acquired by B Company on January 31, 1970. Since that date C Company had total earnings of $28,400 and paid cash dividends of $40,000. B Company credited all dividends received to its income account.

A Company acquired the stock of B Company on December 31, 1971.

Required:

(i)   Prepare an investment elimination schedule on December 31, 1971.

(ii) Prepare a consolidated balance sheet working paper on December 31, 1971.

(AICPA adapted)

Problem 11–16

The following are the balance sheets of companies X, Y, and Z:

X COMPANY

Balance Sheet—December 31, 1971

ASSETS

Cash..	$ 20,000
Investment in Y Company—1,400 shares, par value $100........	210,000 (1)
Investment in Z Company—4,000 shares, par value $50..........	200,000 (2)
	$430,000

EQUITIES

Current liabilities...	$ 80,000
Collateral notes, due 1979................................	100,000
Capital stock:	
Preferred: 1,000 shares, par value $100......................	100,000
Common: 10,000 shares, no-par value......................	150,000
	$430,000

Y COMPANY

Balance Sheet—October 31, 1971

ASSETS

Cash..	$ 60,000
Receivables..................................	100,000 (3)
Inventories..................................	300,000
	$460,000

EQUITIES

Accounts payable............................		$ 16,000
Capital stock—4,000 shares, par value $100........		400,000
Retained earnings:		
Balance, November 1, 1970...................	$40,000	
Add: Profit for year.........................	14,000	
	$54,000	
Less: Dividends paid, October 31, 1971..........	10,000	44,000
		$460,000

Z COMPANY

Balance Sheet—December 31, 1971

ASSETS

Cash..	$ 10,000 (4)
Receivables..................................	40,000 (7)
Inventories..................................	100,000
Investment in Y Company—800 shares, par value $100.....................................	120,000 (5)
Investment in X Company—250 shares, preferred, par value $100.............................	25,000 (6)
Land, buildings, and equipment.................	113,000
	$408,000

EQUITIES

Accounts payable.............................		$133,000
Capital stock—4,000 shares, par value $50........		200,000
Retained earnings:		
Balance, January 1, 1971.....................	$100,000	
Deficit for year 1971........................	25,000	75,000
		$408,000

Notes:
(1) Purchased November 1, 1971 at $150 per share.
(2) Purchased January 1, 1971 at $90 per share.
(3) Includes $20,000 due from Company Z.
(4) After advancing $25,000 to X Company, which is in transit.
(5) Purchased October 31, 1971 at $150 per share.
(6) Acquired at par.
(7) Includes $25,000 advanced to X Company.

Required:

Prepare a consolidated balance sheet working paper as of December 31, 1971.

(AICPA adapted)

Chapter 12

Consolidated Statements—
Intercompany Profit

Assets are often transferred by one affiliate to another by sale or other form of conveyance; such transfers normally relate either to sales of merchandise or fixed assets. The intercompany effects of these transactions on the accounts of the affiliates must be periodically eliminated in the preparation of consolidated financial statements.

INTERCOMPANY PROFIT—MERCHANDISE

In respect to merchandise, it is necessary in the year of sale to eliminate the total amount of intercompany sales by a debit to Sales and a corresponding credit to Purchases (or Cost of Goods Sold). This procedure was previously discussed in Chapter 8. Frequently, however, the transfer price of the selling affiliate may contain elements of cost *and* profit, and vestiges of the seller's profit may remain in items of unsold merchandise of the purchasing affiliate at the end of the accounting period. In this event, the elimination of the effects of the originating transaction is incomplete to the extent of the profit residue in the inventory of the purchaser. A second elimination is required, therefore, to remove the continued presence of this evidence of the intercompany sale. The profit remnant is usually described as "unrealized intercompany inventory profit." The authors are persuaded that a more useful description should emphasize the deferral of profit until it is *confirmed* by a resale of the relevant merchandise to outside interests. Accordingly, "unconfirmed inventory profit" is preferred as a descriptive designation and is used in much of the following discussion. Clearly, profits and losses of the affiliation are ultimately validated only by transactions with nonaffiliates.

Amount of Eliminated Profit

Concerning the *amount* of intercompany profit to be eliminated, there exist two basic alternatives. One position taken is that 100 percent of the inventory profit should be eliminated, which in respect to consolidated statements results in a reduction in the inventory valuation to the selling affiliate's cost. This treatment was recommended in *Accounting Research Bulletin No. 51.*

As consolidated statements are based on the assumption that they represent the financial position and operating results of a single business enterprise, such statements should not include gain or loss on transactions among the companies in the group. Accordingly, *any* intercompany profit or loss on assets remaining in the group should be eliminated.[1]

The total elimination of intercompany inventory profit calls for a proportional adjustment of the interests of both majority and minority shareholders to the extent of the unconfirmed profit.[2]

A second position is that only the parent company's equity in the profit residue should be eliminated. The amount of the elimination is calculated in terms of the parent company's fractional interest in the profit reported by the *selling* affiliate. The effect of this treatment is to emphasize the legal equity of minority shareholders in such profit, as the dollar interest of this group remains unaffected by eliminating entries requisite to the preparation of consolidated reports. The inventory value reported in the consolidated balance sheet will accordingly include both the cost of the merchandise to the selling affiliate and the interest of the minority shareholders in the intercompany profits.

It should be noted, however, that with respect to the interest of the majority shareholders, the amounts of consolidated net income and retained earnings are equivalent for both total and fractional elimination methods.

The working paper techniques for each of these two methods are illustrated in the cases which follow.

Case 1. Total Elimination—First Year. The trial balances for companies X and Y are as follows:

| | December 31, 1971 | | | |
	X Company		Y Company	
Investment in Y Company stock.....................	$ 58,000			
Merchandise inventory (1/1/71)..................	15,000		$ 8,000	
Fixed assets.................	60,000		16,000	
Accumulated depreciation— fixed assets..............		$ 12,000		$ 4,000
Other assets................	60,000		62,000	
Liabilities..................		20,000		6,000
Capital stock...............		100,000		50,000
Retained earnings...........		40,000		10,000
Sales......................		98,000		50,000
Purchases..................	65,000		32,000	
Expenses..................	12,000		2,000	
	$270,000	$270,000	$120,000	$120,000
Merchandise inventory (12/31/71)..............	$ 19,000		$ 7,000	

[1] Committee on Accounting Procedure, American Institute of Certified Public Accountants, "Consolidated Financial Statements," *Accounting Research Bulletin No. 51* (1959), p. 43 (emphasis supplied), in *Accounting Research and Terminology Bulletins,* Final Edition (New York, 1961).

[2] Some accountants favor eliminating the total amount of inventory profit *against the interest of the majority shareholders only*. This practice, which is implicit in *Accounting Research Bulletin No. 51*, has little theoretical justification in that it violates the definition of consolidated net income cited earlier. However, the degree of distortion is not material in the event the minority in the selling affiliate is relatively small.

Illustration 12–1

X COMPANY AND SUBSIDIARY Y COMPANY
Consolidated Statement Working Paper
For Year Ended December 31, 1971

	X Company	Y Company	Eliminations Dr.	Eliminations Cr.	Minority Interest	Consolidated
Income Statement:						
Sales	98,000	50,000		(2) 20,000		128,000
Merchandise inventory (12/31/71)	19,000	7,000	(3) 600			25,400
Total credits	117,000	57,000				153,400
Merchandise inventory (1/1/71)	15,000	8,000				23,000
Purchases	65,000	32,000		(2) 20,000		77,000
Expenses	12,000	2,000				14,000
Total debits	92,000	42,000				114,000
Net income	25,000	15,000				39,400
Minority interest in net income—Y Company [10% of ($15,000 — $600)]					1,440	1,440
Net income—carried forward	25,000	15,000	20,600	20,000	1,440	37,960
Retained Earnings Statement:						
Retained earnings, January 1, 1971:						
X Company	40,000					40,000
Y Company		10,000	(1) 9,000		1,000	
Net income—brought forward	25,000	15,000	20,600	20,000	1,440	37,960
Retained earnings, December 31, 1971—carried forward	65,000	25,000	29,600	20,000	2,440	77,960
Balance Sheet:						
Investment in Y Company stock	58,000			(1) 58,000		
Merchandise inventory	19,000	7,000		(3) 600		25,400
Fixed assets	60,000	16,000				76,000
Other assets	60,000	62,000				122,000
Differential			(1) 4,000			4,000
	197,000	85,000				227,400
Accumulated depreciation—fixed assets	12,000	4,000				16,000
Liabilities	20,000	6,000				26,000
Capital stock:						
X Company	100,000					100,000
Y Company		50,000	(1) 45,000		5,000	
Retained earnings—brought forward	65,000	25,000	29,600	20,000	2,440	77,960
Minority interest in Y Company					7,440	7,440 M
	197,000	85,000	78,600	78,600	7,440	227,400

Explanation of eliminations:

It is assumed that X Company acquired 90 percent of the capital stock of Y Company on January 1, 1971, for $58,000. During 1971, Y Company sold merchandise to X Company for $20,000, on which the recorded trading profit was $4,000. On December 31, 1971, the inventory of X Company includes $3,000 of the merchandise purchased from Y Company. The investment elimination schedule is as follows:

Investment Elimination Schedule

	Dr. [Cr.]
Capital stock..........................	$ 45,000
Retained earnings.....................	9,000
Differential...........................	4,000
Investment...........................	$[58,000]

The elimination for intercompany sales, $20,000, requires a debit to Sales and a credit to Purchases. Intercompany inventory profit is eliminated by a debit to the final inventory as it appears in the income statement division of the consolidated statement working paper and a credit to the final inventory as it appears in the balance sheet division. The amount of such unconfirmed profit is $600 (20 percent of $3,000). The consolidated statement working paper for this case is presented in Illustration 12–1.

It is apparent that the inventory profit elimination reduces the interest of minority shareholders in subsidiary net income and retained earnings. To the extent that $3,000 of the sales of Y Company have not been validated by the purchasing affiliate's resale of the relevant merchandise, the intercompany profit therein of $600 creates an overstatement of subsidiary net income, *calculated on a consolidated basis.* Under the total elimination method, the rights of minority shareholders should be determined on this basis. In the present illustration, the amount of the minority interest in net income is 10 percent of the net income of Y Company *calculated on a consolidated basis,* or $1,440 [10 percent of ($15,000 − $600)].

Case 2. Total Elimination—Second Year. In continuation of Case 1, the trial balances of companies X and Y at the end of the second year of operations are as follows:

	December 31, 1972			
	X Company		Y Company	
Investment in Y Company stock..............	$ 58,000			
Merchandise inventory (1/1/72)...............	19,000		$ 7,000	
Fixed assets.................	60,000		16,000	
Accumulated depreciation— fixed assets..............		$ 15,000		$ 5,000
Other assets................	88,000		88,000	
Liabilities.................		19,000		10,000
Capital stock..............		100,000		50,000
Retained earnings...........		65,000		25,000
Sales.....................		111,000		70,000
Purchases.................	67,000		46,000	
Expenses.................	18,000		3,000	
	$310,000	$310,000	$160,000	$160,000
Merchandise inventory (12/31/72)...............	$ 23,000		$ 6,000	

During 1972 Y Company sold merchandise to X Company for $15,000, recognizing a transfer profit of $5,000; additionally, X Company sold merchandise to Y Company for $10,000, on which the profit amounted to $2,000. On December 31, 1972, the inventory of X Company contained $6,000 of merchandise purchased from Y Company, and the inventory of Y Company contained $1,000 of merchandise purchased from X Company.

The consolidated statement working paper is shown in Illustration 12–2. In this case, there exists intercompany inventory profit in both the beginning and the ending inventories of the purchasing affiliates. The elimination of profit in the beginning inventory of X Company is made by a debit to the retained earnings of Y Company (January 1, 1972, balance), as it was recognized by Y Company in 1971 and transferred to retained earnings in the accounting closing process, and a credit to the beginning inventory as it appears in the income statement division of the working paper.

Retained earnings—Y Company...............................	600	
Merchandise inventory (1/1/72)............................		600

In this instance, the total amount of inventory profit, $600, is eliminated. In respect to the final inventory, as in the previous year, it is necessary to debit the final inventory as it appears in the income statement division and credit the final inventory as it appears in the balance sheet division. The amount of elimination is $2,200 [(33⅓ percent of $6,000) + (20 percent of $1,000)].

Merchandise inventory (12/31/72)—(income statement)........	2,200	
Merchandise inventory (12/31/72)—(balance sheet)........		2,200

The interest of minority shareholders is calculated, as before, on the consolidated basis subsidiary net income. In this case, the subsidiary's reported net income of $20,000 is increased by the unconfirmed profit in the ending inventory of the previous year—confirmed during 1972—and is decreased by the unconfirmed profit in the December 31, 1972, inventory ($20,000 + $600 − $2,000). The amount of the minority interest in net income is 10 percent of this value, $18,600, or $1,860. The $200 unconfirmed profit of the parent company is not a determinant in the calculation of minority interest in the net income of Y Company, but is totally deducted from the net income of the parent company, and thus from consolidated net income. The minority interest in the subsidiary's retained earnings as of the beginning of the year is based upon the January 1 accumulation, adjusted for the elimination of intercompany profit contained in the beginning inventory which was confirmed during 1972 and accordingly is included in the subsidiary's consolidated basis net income. In that this profit element has entered the calculation of subsidiary net income in the prior period, failure to adjust *recorded* retained earnings therefor would result in a duplicate measurement of the minority interest in this amount of intercompany profit.

The previous cases have dealt with the effects on consolidated statement working papers of the elimination of 100 percent of the intercompany profit in inventories. The following cases, using the same source information, illustrate the results of eliminating *only* the parent company's fractional interest in the selling affiliate's unconfirmed profit.

Case 3. Fractional Elimination—First Year. The elimination details for the following case (see Illustration 12–3) essentially iterate those for Case 1, except that the amount of the final inventory elimination is $540 (90 percent of $600). The fractional amount to be eliminated depends upon the parent company's interest in the selling affiliate—in this case, a 90 percent equity in Y Company. Where intercompany inventory profit is thus fractionally eliminated, the interest of minority shareholders in net income is calculated on the basis of the subsidiary's *recorded* net income, without regard to eliminations required for consolidated statement purposes. Consequently, the minority interest in Y Company's net income is determined to be 10 percent of $15,000, or $1,500. Similarly, the minority interest in retained earnings is unaffected by eliminations required for consolidated statements. There is, therefore, no dilution in the legal interests of minority shareholders as a consequence of preparing consolidated financial statements.

A comparison of Illustration 12–3 with Illustration 12–1 will disclose that consolidated net income in each instance is determined to be $37,960. Similarly, consolidated retained earnings in each illustration is $77,960. Differences in the working papers may be explained in terms of the amounts of eliminated intercompany profit and the value bases for calculating minority interests. Where the intercompany inventory profit is totally elim-

Illustration 12–2

X COMPANY AND SUBSIDIARY Y COMPANY
Consolidated Statement Working Paper
For Year Ended December 31, 1972

	X Company	Y Company	Eliminations Dr.	Eliminations Cr.	Minority Interest	Consolidated
Income Statement:						
Sales	111,000	70,000	(2) 25,000			156,000
Merchandise inventory (12/31/72)	23,000	6,000	(4) 2,200			26,800
Total credits	134,000	76,000				182,800
Merchandise inventory (1/1/72)	19,000	7,000		(3) 600		25,400
Purchases	67,000	46,000		(2) 25,000		88,000
Expenses	18,000	3,000				21,000
Total debits	104,000	56,000				134,400
	30,000	20,000				48,400
Minority interest in net income—Y Company [10% of ($20,000 + $600 − $2,000)]					1,860	1,860
Net income—carried forward	30,000	20,000	27,200	25,600	1,860	46,540
Retained Earnings Statement:						
Retained earnings, January 1, 1972:						
X Company	65,000					65,000
Y Company		25,000	(1) 9,000 (3) 600		*2,440	12,960
			27,200	25,600		
Net income—brought forward	30,000	20,000	27,200	25,600	1,860	46,540
Retained earnings, December 31, 1972—carried forward	95,000	45,000	36,800	25,600	4,300	124,500

Balance Sheet:

			Eliminations			
Investment in Y Company stock.......	58,000			(1) 58,000		
Merchandise inventory......	23,000	6,000		(4) 2,200		26,800
Fixed assets......	60,000	16,000				76,000
Other assets......	88,000	88,000				176,000
Differential......			(1) 4,000			4,000
	229,000	110,000				282,800
Accumulated depreciation—fixed assets......	15,000	5,000				20,000
Liabilities......	19,000	10,000				29,000
Capital stock:						
X Company......	100,000					100,000
Y Company......		50,000	(1) 45,000		5,000	
Retained earnings—brought forward......	95,000	45,000	36,800	25,600	4,300	124,500
Minority interest in Y Company......					9,300	9,300 M
	229,000	110,000	85,800	85,800		282,800

* 10% of ($25,000 − $600).

Explanation of eliminations:
(1) Elimination of investment in subsidiary capital stock.
(2) Elimination of $25,000 intercompany sales.
(3) Elimination of $600 unconfirmed profit in the beginning inventory.
(4) Elimination of $2,200 profit in the final inventory.

Illustration 12–3

X COMPANY AND SUBSIDIARY Y COMPANY
Consolidated Statement Working Paper
For Year Ended December 31, 1971

	X Company	Y Company	Eliminations Dr.	Eliminations Cr.	Minority Interest	Consolidated
Income Statement:						
Sales	98,000	50,000	(2) 20,000			128,000
Merchandise inventory (12/31/71)	19,000	7,000	(3) 540			25,460
Total credits	117,000	57,000				153,460
Merchandise inventory (1/1/71)	15,000	8,000				23,000
Purchases	65,000	32,000		(2) 20,000		77,000
Expenses	12,000	2,000				14,000
Total debits	92,000	42,000				114,000
Net income	25,000	15,000				39,460
Minority interest in net income—Y Company [10% of $15,000]					1,500	1,500
Net income—carried forward	25,000	15,000	20,540	20,000	1,500	37,960
Retained Earnings Statement:						
Retained earnings, January 1, 1971:						
X Company	40,000					40,000
Y Company		10,000	(1) 9,000		1,000	
Net income—brought forward	25,000	15,000	20,540	20,000	1,500	37,960
Retained earnings, December 31, 1971—carried forward	65,000	25,000	29,540	20,000	2,500	77,960
Balance Sheet:						
Investment in Y Company stock	58,000			(1) 58,000		
Merchandise inventory	19,000	7,000		(3) 540		25,460
Fixed assets	60,000	16,000				76,000
Other assets	60,000	62,000				122,000
Differential			(1) 4,000			4,000
	197,000	85,000				227,460
Accumulated depreciation—fixed assets	12,000	4,000				16,000
Liabilities	20,000	6,000				26,000
Capital stock:						
X Company	100,000					100,000
Y Company		50,000	(1) 45,000		5,000	
Retained earnings—brought forward	65,000	25,000	29,540	20,000	2,500	77,960
Minority interest in Y Company					7,500	7,500 M
	197,000	85,000	78,540	78,540	7,500	227,460

Explanation of eliminations:
(1) Elimination of investment in subsidiary capital stock.
(2) Elimination of $20,000 of intercompany sales.

inated, minority interests relate to the subsidiary's net income *calculated on a consolidated basis.* Where the parent company's fractional interest in such unconfirmed profit is the amount eliminated, however, minority interests are calculated on the basis of the subsidiary's *recorded* net income, without adjustment for working paper eliminations. This latter difference is reflected in an increased inventory valuation—and a correspondingly larger measurement of minority interest—of $60 ($600 − $540).

Case 4. Fractional Elimination—Second Year. The data for Case 2 are repeated here. It is apparent that no special problems are created by the presence of *reciprocal* intercompany sales. It is sufficient to remember that the parent's equity in the selling affiliate is the determinant of the amount of profit elimination; where the selling affiliate is the parent, necessarily the amount of the elimination is 100 percent. In this instance, the intercompany profit to be eliminated from the final inventory is determined to be $2,000 [(100 percent of $200) + (90 percent of $2,000)]. The elimination in respect to the beginning inventory remains $540—the same amount eliminated at the end of the previous year. Except for the amounts of these eliminations and their effects upon the calculation of minority interest, the working paper for this case, shown in Illustration 12–4, parallels that for Case 2. In both illustrations, consolidated net income is determined to be $46,540, and consolidated retained earnings are $124,500.

100 Percent versus Fractional Elimination

The arguments which support 100 percent eliminations of intercompany inventory profit rest heavily on the single entity concept of the affiliation of companies. This view accords with pronouncements of both the American Institute of Certified Public Accountants and the American Accounting Association. Both affirm that notwithstanding the existence of legally separate business enterprises, the alliance of stock interests essentially creates an economic entity, and that consolidated financial statements should depict this extra-corporate circumstance. Apropos of inventory profit, the American Accounting Association argues:

The practice of reflecting a minority interest's share of unrealized intercompany profit as if realized, while widely accepted, conflicts with the underlying purpose of consolidated financial statements as herein contemplated, namely, to reflect the activities of a group of companies as though they constituted a single unit.[3]

The Committee on Accounting Procedure of the American Institute of Certified Public Accountants reached a similar conclusion, as follows:

The amount of intercompany profit or loss to be eliminated . . . is not affected by the existence of a minority interest. The complete elimination of the inter-

___
[3] Committee on Accounting Concepts and Standards, American Accounting Association, "Consolidated Financial Statements," Supplementary Statement No. 7, in *Accounting and Reporting Standards for Corporate Financial Statements* (Evanston, Ill., 1957), p. 45.

Illustration 12–4

X COMPANY AND SUBSIDIARY Y COMPANY

Consolidated Statement Working Paper
For Year Ended December 31, 1972

	X Company	Y Company	Eliminations Dr.	Eliminations Cr.	Minority Interest	Consolidated
Income Statement:						
Sales	111,000	70,000	(2) 25,000			156,000
Merchandise inventory (12/31/72)	23,000	6,000	(4) 2,000			27,000
Total credits	134,000	76,000				183,000
Merchandise inventory (1/1/72)	19,000	7,000		(3) 540		25,460
Purchases	67,000	46,000		(2) 25,000		88,000
Expenses	18,000	3,000				21,000
Total debits	104,000	56,000				134,460
Minority interest in net income—Y Company [10% of $20,000]					2,000	2,000
Net income—carried forward	30,000	20,000	27,000	25,540	2,000	46,540
Retained Earnings Statement:						
Retained earnings, January 1, 1972:						
X Company	65,000					65,000
Y Company		25,000	(1) 9,000 (3) 540		*2,500	12,960
Net income—brought forward	30,000	20,000	27,000	25,540	2,000	46,540
Retained earnings, December 31, 1972—carried forward	95,000	45,000	36,540	25,540	4,500	124,500
Balance Sheet:						
Investment in Y Company stock	58,000			(1) 58,000		
Merchandise inventory	23,000	6,000				27,000
Fixed assets	60,000	16,000				76,000
Other assets	88,000	88,000				176,000
Differential			(1) 4,000			4,000
	229,000	110,000				283,000
Accumulated depreciation—fixed assets	15,000	5,000				20,000
Liabilities	19,000	10,000		(4) 2,000		29,000
Capital stock:						
X Company	100,000					100,000
Y Company		50,000	(1) 45,000		5,000	
Retained earnings—brought forward	95,000	45,000	36,540	25,540	4,500	124,500
Minority interest in Y Company					9,500	9,500 M
	229,000	110,000	85,540	85,540	9,500	283,000

* 10 percent of $25,000.

Explanation of eliminations:
(1) Elimination of investment in subsidiary capital stock.
(2) Elimination of $25,000 of intercompany sales.
(3) Elimination of $540 profit in the beginning inventory.
(4) Elimination of $2,000 unconfirmed profit in the final inventory.

company profit or loss is consistent with the underlying assumption that consolidated statements represent the financial position and operating results of a single business enterprise.[4]

The arguments which support fractional elimination of intercompany profits generally emphasize the special fiduciary relationship of the majority shareholders in respect to the minority; this relationship is essentially ignored by the total elimination method. The nature of the fiduciary responsibility is described in the following quotation.

. . . a majority of the holders of stock owe to the minority the duty to exercise good faith, care, and diligence to make the property of the corporation in their charge produce the largest possible amount, to protect the interests of the holders of the minority of the stock and to secure and deliver to them their just proportion of the income and of the proceeds of the property. Any sale of the corporate property to themselves, and disposition by them of the corporation or its property to deprive the minority holders of their just share of it or to get gain for themselves at the expense of the holders of the minority of the stock, becomes a breach of duty and of trust. . . .[5]

It can be argued that the position of trust which vests in the controlling shareholders logically should extend to the preparation of consolidated financial statements, wherein profit increments due minority shareholders should not be compromised by the elimination process.

Additional support for fractional elimination relates specifically to the parent company's decision to purchase assets from subsidiary affiliates. In the parent's election to purchase from a subsidiary rather than a nonaffiliate, it is assumed that the parent anticipates a recoupment of the subsidiary's transfer profit. If operating efficiencies are comparable, this compels the parent to incur only a minimal additional cost, in the amount of the minority interest in subsidiary profit, in preference to purchasing from a nonaffiliate under its full profit margin conditions. This increment may be described as an "adjunct" cost to the majority.

Thus, the intercompany profit may be perceived as consisting of two distinct segments. Edward J. Smolinski describes these elements in the following terms:

The first, the parent's share is an item the parent will, or has already, recovered by way of the subsidiary's profit distributions—a noncost. The other, the minority's share, is likewise one which will, or has already enjoyed recovery in this manner, but by the minority—not the majority. The fact of consolidation changes nothing. Intercompany profit consists of two different and distinct elements and each is evaluated on its merits. This does not suggest that homogeneous units of inventory are valued on different bases. Nor is consolidated inventory valued on two different bases. Inventory is valued on the basis of

---

[4] *Ibid.*, p. 45.

[5] *Jones* v. *Missouri-Edison Electric Company* (1906), 114 F. 765, 771.

cost, or, the lower of cost or market, but the minority's share of intercompany profit is added as an adjunct cost.[6]

The equity of minority shareholders is clearly a unique stock interest. It relates only to the net assets of a specific subsidiary. As such, it may be realistically viewed as an "outside" interest. Consequently, proponents of fractional elimination argue that profits earned by a subsidiary which appertain to the minority interest should be protected as a cost to the majority.[7]

The authors believe that both positions are tenable and that illustrations of both alternatives will contribute to a more complete understanding of intercompany profit eliminations.

Transportation Costs on Merchandise Transfers

The sale of merchandise by one affiliate to another usually entails costs incident to the conveyance in addition to the cost of products transferred. The total cost recorded by the purchasing affiliate will accordingly include the seller's original cost, an amount of trading profit, transportation costs, and perhaps other cost supplements. Apropos of consolidated financial statements, it is important to isolate the purchasing affiliate's cost supplements in the calculation of the unconfirmed inventory profit to be eliminated. The costs of shipment are valid inventory costs to the consolidated entity; as such, they are not subject to elimination, and the amount of the seller's unconfirmed intercompany profit to be eliminated should be reduced accordingly. If fractional elimination is made, the parent company's equity is applied to this adjusted value.

Gross or Net Profit Elimination

In respect to the intercompany inventory profit, the amount of the elimination is usually determined on the basis of the selling affiliate's *gross profit rate*. It has occasionally been proposed that the *net profit rate* is the more appropriate multiplier. The use of this rate, however, would result in a smaller profit elimination, thereby enlarging the consolidated inventory by operating expense elements of the selling affiliate. Such expenses are presently inadmissible as inventoriable costs; their inclusion in inventory improperly inflates consolidated asset values. Consequently, the gross profit rate is recommended.

Inventory Market Adjustments

Where merchandise is purchased by one affiliate from another, the purchaser may adopt the pricing standard of "cost or market, whichever is lower," in respect to unsold intercompany merchandise. In this event, where market values are currently below the transfer price, the market

---

[6] Edward J. Smolinski, "The Adjunct Method in Consolidations," *Journal of Accounting Research,* Autumn, 1963, p. 168.

[7] *Ibid.,* pp. 166–69.

adjustments recorded by the purchasing affiliate should be considered in determining the amount of the unconfirmed inventory profit. The additional reduction in the inventory of the purchaser attributable to the elimination of inventory profit should be based upon cost after the adjustment for market decline. Since the market adjustment has reduced the inventory value below the original transfer price, the amount of this reduction should be used in abatement of the selling affiliate's reported trading profit in determining the unconfirmed profit to be eliminated. If the market adjustment exceeds the trading profit, no elimination is required.

INTERCOMPANY PROFIT—FIXED ASSETS

As in the case of intercompany sales of merchandise, profit elimination is also required where there are fixed asset transfers between affiliates, to the extent that the exchange price exceeds the recorded book value of the transferred asset. Upon the sale of fixed assets to an affiliate, there is, however, the additional problem of measuring and accounting for the effects of depreciation upon consolidated statements. In respect to the affiliation, profit on the sale of depreciable property remains unrealized, or unconfirmed, until the relevant property is depreciated. Confirmation or validation is accomplished through depreciation; in this sense, the process of depreciation is comparable to the transaction of resale by the purchasing affiliate in the case of intercompany inventories. The current depreciation expense measures the economic value consumed in generating revenues from nonaffiliates. Of course, if the purchasing affiliate is a manufacturer, that part of periodic depreciation which relates to the cost of finished production remains unconfirmed until sale of the manufactured product. However, a precise determination of this amount is often difficult, and is frequently ignored in the elimination process for consolidated statement preparation. The following case illustrations are based upon those account data used earlier in this chapter, except that the intercompany transfers used in subsequent cases relate to the sale of fixed assets rather than the sale of merchandise. Additionally, it is assumed that 100 percent elimination of intercompany profit is used in consolidated statement working paper preparation. This working paper is easily reconciled with that which provides for fractional elimination, as was demonstrated where there existed intercompany inventory profit.

Case 5. Total Elimination—First Year. Using the account data for Case 3, fixed assets of Y Company having a cost of $4,000, with a depreciation accumulation of $1,000, are assumed to have been sold to X Company for $5,000 on January 1, 1971. The gain of $2,000 is reported as Profit on Sale of Fixed Assets. The assets are estimated to have a remaining service life to the purchasing affiliate of five years.

The investment elimination schedule remains the same as in Case 3:

Investment Elimination Schedule

	Dr. [Cr.]
Capital stock.........................	$ 45,000
Retained earnings.....................	9,000
Differential..........................	4,000
Investment...........................	$[58,000]

The first elimination in respect to the intercompany profit is made by a debit to Profit on Sale of Fixed Assets for $2,000 and by a corresponding credit to Fixed Assets. It should be noted that this restores the book value of the selling affiliate at the date of transfer rather than the original cost less accumulated depreciation. If this latter detail is considered important to adequate disclosure, the elimination is easily revised to accommodate the additional data. In recognition of one year's depreciation subsequent to transfer, the validation of this portion of the total profit journalized by Y Company on the transfer should be recognized in the amount of $400 (one fifth of $2,000). Annual depreciation recorded by X Company (classified in the statements merely as Expense) on the basis of a five-year service life amounts to $1,000. Of this amount, $400 relates to *depreciation on profit*—an overstatement of expenses on a consolidated basis. Accordingly, the subsidiary's profit on the sale of fixed assets is confirmed, on a consolidated statement basis, in the amount of $400 (one fifth of $2,000). The second elimination reflects these objectives by a debit to Accumulated Depreciation for $400 and by a credit of the same amount to Expense (Depreciation Expense).

The consolidated statement working paper for this case is shown in Illustration 12–5.

Case 6. Total Elimination—Second Year. This is a continuation of the illustration begun in Case 5.

In a consolidated statement working paper for the second year following the intercompany sale of a depreciable fixed asset (see Illustration 12–6), that part of the original transfer profit which remains unconfirmed must be eliminated from the retained earnings of the selling affiliate, with the asset, accumulated depreciation, and expense accounts of the purchasing affiliate appropriately adjusted. This elimination is accomplished in two entries. In the present case, $1,600 should be eliminated from the retained earnings of Y Company as of the beginning of the year. This is merely the algebraic sum of the original profit elimination $2,000 and the profit confirmed by the first year's depreciation, $400. The entry for the consolidated working paper is as follows:

Retained earnings—Y Company (1/1/72).....................	1,600	
Accumulated depreciation—fixed assets.....................	400	
Fixed assets.......................................		2,000

After this elimination, the asset and related valuation accounts have been reduced to cost, on a consolidated statement basis, as of January 1, 1972.

Illustration 12–5

X COMPANY AND SUBSIDIARY Y COMPANY

Consolidated Statement Working Paper
For Year Ended December 31, 1971

	X Company	Y Company	Eliminations Dr.	Eliminations Cr.	Minority Interest	Consolidated
Income Statement:						
Sales.........................	98,000	50,000				148,000
Profit on sale of fixed assets......		2,000	(2) 2,000			26,000
Merchandise inventory (12/31/71)...	19,000	7,000				26,000
Total credits...............	117,000	59,000				174,000
Merchandise inventory (1/1/71).....	15,000	8,000				23,000
Purchases....................	65,000	32,000				97,000
Expenses (including depreciation)....	12,000	2,000		(3) 400		13,600
Total debits................	92,000	42,000				133,600
Net income...................	25,000	17,000				40,400
Minority interest in net income—Y Company [10% of (17,000 − 2,000 + 400)].....					1,540	1,540
Net income—carried forward.....	25,000	17,000	2,000	400	1,540	38,860
Retained Earnings Statement:						
Retained earnings, January 1, 1971:						
X Company.................	40,000					40,000
Y Company.................		10,000	(1) 9,000		1,000	
Net income—brought forward.....	25,000	17,000	2,000	400	1,540	38,860
Retained earnings, December 31, 1971—carried forward.........	65,000	27,000	11,000	400	2,540	78,860
Balance Sheet:						
Investment in Y Company stock.....	58,000			(1) 58,000		
Merchandise inventory...........	19,000	7,000				26,000
Fixed assets..................	65,000	12,000		(2) 2,000		75,000
Other assets..................	55,000	67,000				122,000
Differential..................			(1) 4,000			4,000
	197,000	86,000				227,000
Accumulated depreciation—fixed assets...	12,000	3,000	(3) 400			14,600
Liabilities...................	20,000	6,000				26,000
Capital stock:						
X Company.................	100,000					100,000
Y Company.................		50,000	(1) 45,000		5,000	
Retained earnings—brought forward...	65,000	27,000	11,000	400	2,540	78,860
Minority interest in Y Company.....					7,540	7,540 M
	197,000	86,000	60,400	60,400		227,000

Explanation of eliminations:

(1) Elimination of investment in subsidiary capital stock.
(2) Elimination of transfer profit on sale of fixed assets.
(3) Elimination which recognizes a partial confirmation of the transfer profit through depreciation expense for 1971.

Illustration 12-6. X COMPANY AND SUBSIDIARY Y COMPANY

Consolidated Statement Working Paper

For Year Ended December 31, 1972

	X Company	Y Company	Eliminations Dr.	Eliminations Cr.	Minority Interest	Consolidated
Income Statement:						
Sales.................................	111,000	70,000				181,000
Merchandise inventory (12/31/72).....	23,000	6,000				29,000
Total credits.......................	134,000	76,000				210,000
Merchandise inventory (1/1/72).......	19,000	7,000				26,000
Purchases............................	67,000	46,000				113,000
Expenses (including depreciation)....	19,000	3,000		(3) 400		21,600
Total debits.......................	105,000	56,000				160,600
	29,000	20,000				49,400
Minority interest in net income—Y Company [10% of ($20,000 + 400)].................					2,040	2,040
Net income—carried forward..........	29,000	20,000	–0–	400	2,040	47,360
Retained Earnings Statement:						
Retained earnings, January 1, 1972:						
X Company.........................	65,000					65,000
Y Company.........................		27,000	(1) 9,000 (2) 1,600		*2,540	13,860
Net income—brought forward..........	29,000	20,000	–0–	400	2,040	47,360
Retained earnings, December 31, 1972—carried forward....	94,000	47,000	10,600	400	4,580	126,220
Balance Sheet:						
Investment in Y Company stock........	58,000			(1) 58,000		
Merchandise inventory................	23,000	6,000				29,000
Fixed assets.........................	65,000	12,000		(2) 2,000		75,000
Other assets.........................	83,000	92,750				175,750
Differential.........................			(1) 4,000			4,000
	229,000	110,750				283,750
Accumulated depreciation—fixed assets....	16,000	3,750	(2) 400 (3) 400			18,950
Liabilities..........................	19,000	10,000				29,000
Capital stock:						
X Company.........................	100,000					100,000
Y Company.........................		50,000	(1) 45,000		5,000	
Retained earnings—brought forward....	94,000	47,000	10,600	400	4,580	126,220
Minority interest in Y Company.......					9,580	9,580 M
	229,000	110,750	60,400	60,400	9,580	283,750

* 10 percent of (27,000 – 1,600).

Explanation of eliminations:

(1) Elimination of investment in subsidiary capital stock.

(2) Elimination of January 1 unconfirmed profit on the sale of fixed assets.

(3) Elimination which recognizes a partial confirmation of the transfer profit through depreciation expense for 1972.

In respect to depreciation for the current year (the second year), an additional entry is required:

Accumulated depreciation—fixed assets......................... 400
    Depreciation expense...................................   400

As of the end of 1972, $1,200 of the original transfer profit remains unconfirmed. Upon the completion of the remaining estimated service life, all of the profit presumably will have been validated by the purchasing affiliate's annual adjustments for depreciation.

The reader is reminded that elimination of the selling company's profit recorded on the intercompany sale of merchandise or fixed assets applies equally to all types of property transfers between affiliates—whether between the parent and a subsidiary, or between two subsidiaries. Additionally, consolidated working papers make no substantive distinction between the transfer of previously employed fixed assets, or a transaction of sale of those which have been constructed by one affiliate for another. Eliminations remain essentially the same for either type of conveyance, although account designations may vary.

Transfer of Nondepreciable Fixed Assets

In the event that the transferred asset is nondepreciable, the consolidated statement elimination for intercompany profit is constant in amount each year. The profit recorded by the selling affiliate (whether the parent or subsidiary) is eliminated against the contra asset account. Assuming the profit to be eliminated is $2,000, the entry in the year of sale is:

Profit on sale of fixed assets............................. 2,000
    Fixed assets...   2,000

Significantly, when the asset is nondepreciable, the profit will remain unconfirmed, or unrealized, in all succeeding periods; however, the elimination debit in the consolidated working paper in periods following the period of acquisition will be made against the selling affiliate's retained earnings balance as of the beginning of the current period.

Retained earnings—selling affiliate (1/1).................... 2,000
    Fixed assets...   2,000

This entry will be repeated in consolidated working papers for all future periods until disposition of the asset by the purchasing affiliate. Such disposition indicates the point in time at which the transfer profit between affiliates is confirmed.

INTERCOMPANY PROFITS—RELATED TOPICS

Intercompany Profit in Multilevel Affiliations

Previous discussion of the elimination of the intercompany profit on asset transfers has focused on affiliations in which the subsidiary is one level removed from the parent company. Where there exist multilevel affiliations, however, the procedures outlined in Chapter 11 also apply.

Consider the following data and affiliation diagram in respect to companies X, Y, and Z:

Affiliation Diagram	**1971 Recorded Net Incomes**
X	X Company.................. $20,000
.9⏐1/1/70	Y Company.................. 10,000
Y ←.1	Z Company.................. 5,000
.8⏐1/1/70	The net income of Z Company is assumed to contain an element of unconfirmed intercompany profit in the amount of $2,000.
Z ←.2	

Consolidated net income may be determined by residual calculation as follows:

	Net Income—1971	
	100 Percent Elimination	Fractional Elimination
X Company....................................	$20,000	$20,000
Y Company....................................	10,000	10,000
Z Company....................................	5,000	5,000
	$35,000	$35,000
Elimination of unconfirmed intercompany profit:		
100% of $2,000.............................	2,000	
90% of 80% of $2,000.......................		1,440
	$33,000	$33,560
Minority interests:		
y in Y (10% of $10,000).....................	$ 1,000	$ 1,000
z in Z:		
20% of ($5,000 − $2,000)...................	600	
20% of $5,000.............................		1,000
y in Z:		
10% of 80% of ($5,000 − $2,000)...........	240	
10% of 80% of $5,000.....................		400
	$ 1,840	$ 2,400
Consolidated...............................	$31,160	$31,160

The calculation of consolidated net income is not fundamentally altered by the intercompany profit element existing at the second level of a multilevel affiliation. In respect to the 100 percent elimination, the minority interest in subsidiary net income—whether direct or indirect—is calculated in terms of *confirmed*, or *realized*, subsidiary net income. Where the fractional elimination is used, the amount of the minority interests is determined on the basis of the subsidiary's recorded net income. In both cases, the majority interest is augmented by the equity in confirmed subsidiary net income, yielding consolidated net income of $31,160.

Transfer Profits before Affiliation

Accountants are not agreed as to the most desirable treatment to be accorded unrealized, or unconfirmed, profits on assets transferred between companies prior to their affiliation. One position is that the profit element should *not* be eliminated from the relevant asset accounts in consolidated working papers. The argument in general runs as follows. If a newly acquired subsidiary earns a profit on the transfer of assets to the parent, or to another affiliate, prior to the acquisition of the selling subsidiary's stock by the parent, such profit is one of the factors used to determine the book value of the subsidiary's capital stock at date of acquisition, and is accordingly eliminated in the investment elimination schedule; necessarily, this profit should not again emerge as an element of consolidated net income, as the profit appropriately relates to the period in which earned.

A second position is one which supports a deduction of the preaffiliation profit existing at date of acquisition, with confirmation of such profit deferred to subsequent periods, to be recognized as a consequence of the elimination process. This treatment has been cited as a prevailing practice, based upon a study of the American Institute of Certified Public Accountants.[8] The strength of this position is to be found primarily in its appeal to conservatism with respect to asset valuation, particularly for long-lived assets, and to the fact that intercompany profit is not, or should not be, solely a function of the affiliation date. The elimination of the preaffiliation profit from the inflated asset and retained earnings of the affiliates, however, merely defers its recognition until disposition is made of the relevant assets (merchandise or fixed assets), and results in its subsequent inclusion in consolidated net income and consolidated retained earnings. Presumably the recognition of profit would follow in the next accounting period, in most instances, for items of merchandise, while its recognition in respect to fixed assets would extend over the period of remaining service life of the transferred assets. Thus, if, *in fact,* the intercompany profit relates to the period prior to acquisition of the selling affiliate, the deferment of profit recognition introduces a measure of distortion in periodic net income reporting. The distortion is short-lived, but more pronounced, in respect to merchandise; the effects are moderate, but more extended, in the case of nonmerchandise items. With respect to consolidated retained earnings, the inclusion is, of course, permanent. Where the intercompany profit arises out of transactions during the period of negotiation for an affiliate's capital stock, the argument for elimination gains additional support.

If the parent is the selling affiliate, these two positions must be interpreted merely as a question of timing of income recognition. Whether eliminated or not prior to subsequent "confirmation," the intercompany profit element will ultimately reside in consolidated retained earnings, if not

---

[8] Research Department, American Institute of Certified Public Accountants, *Survey of Consolidated Financial Statement Practices* (New York, 1956), p. 21.

consolidated net income; inclusion in the investment elimination schedule is not a relevant consideration under these circumstances.

The accounting problems in respect to the elimination of "intercompany" profit prior to stock acquisition exist also for multilevel affiliations as for the more simple intercorporate stock arrangements. The elimination decision, however, is subject to additional variables where the date of acquisition of a second-level subsidiary by a first-level subsidiary occurs earlier than the date of acquisition of the first-level affiliate by the parent company. If the profit relates to transactions between a preaffiliation subsidiary and the parent company, the above two positions are equally applicable. If, on the other hand, unconfirmed profits exist as a result of transactions between preaffiliation subsidiaries, elimination of the retained earnings of the first-level subsidiary on a consolidated basis, as described in Chapter 11, would indicate that the second position is the more tenable.

Consolidated Net Income (and Retained Earnings) Redefined

In Chapter 8, definitions were given for consolidated net income and consolidated retained earnings. These expressions did not contemplate unconfirmed, or unrealized, intercompany profit on the transfer of assets between affiliates. These concepts must therefore be redefined in terms sufficiently general to accommodate this intercompany profit element.

Consolidated net income is the parent company's net income, exclusive of subsidiary dividends, confirmed or realized in transactions with nonaffiliates, increased (or decreased) by the parent company's equity in the net income (or loss) of the subsidiary confirmed or realized on transactions with nonaffiliates.

Consolidated retained earnings are the retained earnings of the parent company, exclusive of postacquisition accumulated subsidiary dividends, confirmed or realized in transactions with nonaffiliates, increased (or decreased) by the parent company's equity in the postacquisition subsidiary net income (or loss) confirmed in transactions with nonaffiliates.

The reader will notice that these renderings are not essentially different from the earlier definitions; they simply emphasize the importance of confirmation or realization of intercompany profit before it may be included in the calculation of consolidated net income or retained earnings.

Using the data for Case 2, consolidated net income for 1972 is determined *by definition* to be:

X Company's confirmed 1972 net income ($30,000 − $200)...........	$29,800
Increased by:	
90 percent of Y Company's confirmed 1972 net income [90% of	
($20,000 + $600 − $2,000)]....................................	16,740
Consolidated net income for 1972................................	$46,540

Consolidated retained earnings as of December 31, 1972, may be similarly determined:

X Company's confirmed retained earnings, December 31, 1972
  ($95,000 − $200)... $ 94,800
Increased by:
  90 percent of Y Company's postacquisition confirmed net income
  [90% of ($15,000 + $20,000 — $2,000)]...................... 29,700
Consolidated retained earnings, December 31, 1972............... $124,500

It should be observed that the definition of consolidated net income (and retained earnings) does not depend upon the elimination method chosen, as each provides for a compensating adjustment in calculating the amount of minority interest and the valuation of the intercompany transferred asset. Inclusion of the parent company's equity in confirmed subsidiary net income is common to both methods, as explicitly revealed above, and this confirmation explains the equality of consolidated net income (and retained earnings) under both methods.

The details of consolidated net income as determined *by residual calculation* depends upon the selected elimination basis. The data for Case 2 and Case 4 emphasize this distinction.

	Case 2 *100 Percent* *Elimination*	*Case 4* *Fractional* *Elimination*
X Company's recorded 1972 net income.........	$30,000	$30,000
Y Company's recorded 1972 net income.........	20,000	20,000
	$50,000	$50,000
Elimination of intercompany profit:		
100 percent basis......................... (a)	1,600	
Fractional basis........................... (b)		1,460
	$48,400	$48,540
Minority interests:		
100 percent basis......................... (c)	1,860	
Fractional basis........................... (d)		2,000
Consolidated net income for 1972..............	$46,540	$46,540

(a) 100 percent of ($2,200 − $600).
(b) 90 percent of ($2,000 − $600) + 100 percent of $200.
(c) 10 percent of ($20,000 + $600 − $2,000).
(d) 10 percent of ($20,000).

Consolidated retained earnings at December 31, 1972, may be determined by residual calculation in a similar manner.

Intercompany Profit on Services

Affiliates of a consolidated entity may engage in intercompany sales of services which are not of a nature that allow inclusion in the inventory of the acquiring affiliate (i.e., period costs and revenues). For example, a parent company may provide certain managerial services to a subsidiary affiliate which result in revenue recorded on the books of the parent and expense recorded by the subsidiary. The confirmation of the seller's "profit" associated with such transactions is generally assumed to occur during the same period as the transfer of services. As in the case of the confirmation of fixed asset profit by depreciation, the expense of acquiring a service is presumed to generate the revenues in the same period in which the expense occurs. As a consequence, no elimination entries are required to remove such "profits" from the consolidated statements. The corresponding revenue and expense items must, of course, be eliminated, as for all other intercompany transactions.

In respect to the calculation of the minority interest in subsidiary net income (assuming 100 percent elimination of unconfirmed profit), the reader is reminded that the equity of minority interests relates to *confirmed* subsidiary net income. Thus, as an extension of the above discussion, it may be noted that the calculation of confirmed subsidiary net income does not involve adjustments to the reported subsidiary net income for such intercompany revenues and expenses transactions, since they do not generate asset valuations which require subsequent confirmation. It should also be recognized that the conventional calculation of the minority interest's equity on the basis of the subsidiary's confirmed *net* income is logically equivalent to a calculation based upon the separate elements of revenue and expense.

QUESTIONS

1. Justify the elimination of profit on interaffiliate sales of merchandise where a profit remnant remains in the ending inventory of the purchasing affiliate.

2. In the event that profit exists in the inventory of products purchased from an affiliated company, what elections exist as to the amount of elimination?

3. In regard to the impact on consolidated net income and consolidated retained earnings, what is the consequence of the decision as to the amount of intercompany profit to be eliminated?

4. In calculating the interest of minority shareholders (in net income or retained earnings) what difference is produced between the total elimination and the fractional elimination method? Why?

5. How are transportation costs incurred in transferring goods between affiliated companies accounted for in the elimination of intercompany inventory profits?

6. Indicate the profit rate—net or gross—that should be used in determining the amount of unconfirmed (intercompany) inventory profit to be eliminated, and explain the reasoning which underlies your choice.

7. Assume that two affiliates with intercompany sales of merchandise utilize the "cost or market, whichever is lower" method of pricing their inventories. What would be the effect upon the intercompany profit elimination, given a situation in which period-end market price is lower than the transfer price?

8. In what manner is intercompany profit "confirmed" or "realized"? Your answer should relate both to merchandise and fixed assets.

9. How are the definitions of consolidated net income and consolidated retained earnings modified to give effect to the new variable—intercompany profit?

10. Given interaffiliate sales of (noninventoriable) services, what eliminations should be made regarding the profit on such sales? Why?

PROBLEMS

Problem 12–1

The Hart Company owns 90 percent of the capital stock of the Lake Company. During 1971 the Hart Company sold merchandise to the Lake Company for $10,000 and purchased $5,000 of merchandise from the Lake Company. Twenty percent of all intercompany sales remains in the ending inventory of the purchasing affiliate. The beginning inventory of the Hart Company included $500 of merchandise purchased in the previous period from the Lake Company. Each company marks merchandise to sell at 25 percent above cost.

The 1971 net incomes of the Hart Company and the Lake Company were $20,000 and $10,000 respectively.

Required:

(i)   Prepare journal entries for all eliminations in respect to the intercompany sales. Assume the amount of the elimination of intercompany profit is 100 percent.

(ii) Calculate the minority interest in subsidiary net income for 1966.

(iii) Calculate 1971 consolidated net income.

Problem 12–2

Kersbergen owns 80 percent of Algoe Ltd.'s common stock. Algoe sells merchandise to Kersbergen at 50 percent over cost. During 1970 and 1971 such sales (at transfer or sales prices) amounted to $90,000 and $60,000. At the end of each year Kersbergen had in inventory one half of the amount purchased from Algoe that year. Assume that each firm reported $50,000 net income during 1971 and that Kersbergen prefers to use 100 percent elimination of intercompany profit on the consolidated statements.

Required:

(i)   Prepare a definitional calculation of consolidated net income for 1971.

(ii) Prepare a residual calculation of consolidated net income for 1971.

Problem 12–3

W Company owns 80 percent of the capital stock of Z Company. For the year ended December 31, 1971, companies W and Z reported net incomes of $24,000 and $5,000 respectively. The January 1, 1971, inventory of W Company included $1,000 of profit recorded by Z Company on 1970 sales. During 1971 companies W and Z made intercompany sales of $5,000 and $10,000 respectively, on which each recorded a markup of 25 percent on cost. The ending inventory of W Company included $1,000 of these goods, while Z Company's ending inventory included $1,500 of goods purchased from W Company.

Dividend payments during 1971 were: W Company, $10,000; and Z Company, $5,000.

Required:

Make journal entries for eliminations in respect to intercompany sales and unconfirmed inventory profit *and* compute the consolidated net income and minority interest in subsidiary net income for 1971:

(i) If the amount of the elimination is assumed to be 100 percent of intercompany inventory profit.

(ii) If the amount of the elimination is assumed to be the majority shareholders' interest in intercompany inventory profit.

Problem 12-4

On January 1, 1970, the Moyer Company purchased 90 percent of the capital stock of Bedford, Inc., when the latter had accumulated retained earnings of $30,000. Two years later, the following information is made available by the affiliate companies:

	December 31, 1971	
	Moyer Company	*Bedford, Inc.*
Sales...................................	$94,000	$43,000
Purchases..............................	50,000	26,000
Expenses...............................	4,000	2,000
Merchandise, January 1..................	18,000	8,000
Merchandise, December 31...............	24,000	12,000
Retained earnings, January 1............	92,000	43,000
Dividends declared......................	10,000	

During 1971, Bedford, Inc., sold merchandise to the Moyer Company for $20,000. Bedford, Inc., regularly marks its merchandise to sell for 20 percent above cost. Of this 1971 shipment, 30 percent remains in the inventory of the Moyer Company on December 31. At the beginning of the year (January 1, 1971) the Moyer Company's inventory contained goods purchased from Bedford, Inc., in 1970 for $3,600.

Required:

Prepare a partial consolidated statement working paper on December 31, 1971, indicating the eliminations for intercompany sales and inventory profits; also, indicate the amount of consolidated net income for 1971 and the balance of consolidated retained earnings as of December 31, 1971. It is assumed that 100 percent of intercompany inventory profit is to be eliminated.

Problem 12-5

Using the information of Problem 12-4, prepare a partial consolidated statement working paper on December 31, 1971, indicating the eliminations for intercompany sales and inventory profits; indicate also the amounts of 1971 consolidated net income and consolidated retained earnings as of December 31, 1971. *Assume that the majority interest in intercompany profits is the amount eliminated.*

Compare the 100 percent elimination (Problem 12–4) and the 90 percent elimination as they affect:

a)   Consolidated net income, 1971.
b)   Consolidated retained earnings, as of December 31, 1971.
c)   Minority interest in 1971 subsidiary net income and retained earnings as of December 31, 1971.

Problem 12–6

X Company purchased in the open market 90 percent of the capital stock of Y Company on January 1, 1971, for $2,200 less than its equity in the book value of Y Company stock. The parent uses the equity method, without adjusting for intercompany profit items. The credit differential relates to land. On December 31, 1972, the consolidated balance sheet discloses the value of the minority interest to be $8,608. Other summary information for the years 1971 and 1972 is as follows:

	1971	1972
Consolidated net income...........................	$109,200	$116,900
X Company net income (excluding interest in subsidiary profits).......................................	80,000	60,000

Additionally, an analysis of intercompany sales revealed the existence of the following unconfirmed inventory profits:

	December 31, 1971	December 31, 1972
In the inventory of—		
X Company................................	$2,000	$1,000
Y Company................................	5,000	3,000

In the preparation of consolidated financial statements, 100 percent of intercompany inventory profits is eliminated.

Y Company paid cash dividends of $20,000 in both 1971 and 1972.

Required:

(i)   Compute the cost of the investment in Y Company stock at date of acquisition.
(ii) What is the carrying value of the investment account on December 31, 1972?

Problem 12–7

On January 1, 1971, Seydel, Inc., purchased 90 percent of White Corporation's outstanding stock and concurrently White Corporation purchased 80 percent of Hanson Company's outstanding stock. Each firm had retained earnings of $40,000 at that date. On January 1, 1971, Hanson sold a truck to White for $15,000. The truck had a book value to White of $10,000 and was expected to last another five years.

Required:

(i) Following the 100 percent elimination of intercompany profits method, prepare the elimination entries relating to the truck that would be necessary on consolidated working papers for the year ended December 31, 1971.

(ii) Assume that each of the three firms reported net incomes of $10,000 during 1971 and paid dividends of $3,000. Prepare a definitional calculation of consolidated retained earnings on December 31, 1971. Both investing companies use the cost method of accounting for their subsidiary interests.

Problem 12–8

X Company has an 80 percent interest in the capital stock of Y Company. On January 1, 1971, Y Company sold a fixed asset, which cost $100,000 on January 1, 1961, to X Company for $75,000. The original estimate of service life was 20 years, and X Company decided that a remaining life of 10 years was reasonable.

Required:

(i) Prepare eliminating entries for a consolidated working paper on December 31, 1972, assuming fractional interest elimination of intercompany profits.

(ii) If the reported net income for Y Company for 1972 was $80,000, compute the minority interest therein:
   (a) Assuming fractional interest elimination of intercompany profits.
   (b) Assuming 100 percent elimination of intercompany profits.

Problem 12–9

Heath Associates, Inc., acquired 90 percent of the capital stock of the Prentice Company on January 1, 1965. On January 1, 1971, equipment originally costing the Prentice Company $60,000 on January 1, 1961, was sold to Heath Associates, Inc., for $70,000. Accumulated depreciation to the date of sale (based upon a 60-year service life) was $10,000. The 1971 net incomes of Heath Associates, Inc., and the Prentice Company were reported to be $40,000 and $38,000 respectively.

Required:

(i) Prepare eliminating entries for a consolidated statement working paper for the years ended December 31, 1971, and 1972 in respect to the equipment transfer if—
   (a) The amount of the profit elimination is 100 percent.
   (b) The amount of the profit elimination is based upon the parent company's equity in the selling affiliate.

(ii) Calculate consolidated net income for 1971 and the minority interest in the subsidiary's net income for 1971 under conditions (a) and (b) above.

Problem 12–10

The Kinley Company purchased 90 percent of the capital stock of the Hall Corporation on January 1, 1970, for $165,000, when the latter had capital stock outstanding, $100,000 and retained earnings, $80,000.

On January 1, 1971, the Hall Corporation sold land and related improvements to the Kinley Company according to the following schedule of costs and prices:

	As Recorded by Hall Corporation	Selling Price to Kinley Company
Land.......................................	$26,000	$ 30,000
Building (acquired 1/1/61).................	$94,000	
Accumulated depreciation..................	23,500	
Book value.............................	$70,500	90,000
Total.............................	$96,500	$120,000

The building was originally estimated to have a total service life of 40 years and is still being depreciated on a straight-line basis.

Operating and other data of the affiliated companies for the two-year period ended December 31, 1972, are:

	Kinley Company	Hall Corporation
Capital stock (1/1/71).....................	$200,000	$100,000
Stock dividend (9/1/72)...................		10,000
Capital stock (12/31/72)..................	$200,000	$110,000
Retained earnings (1/1/71)................	$165,000	$120,000
Net income—1971.......................	40,000	50,000
	$205,000	$170,000
Cash dividends (11/1/71).................	20,000	5,000
Retained earnings (12/31/71)..............	$185,000	$165,000
Net income—1971.......................	30,000	20,000
	$215,000	$185,000
Dividends:		
Cash (4/1/72).........................	5,000	
Stock (9/1/72)........................		10,000
Retained earnings (12/31/72)..............	$210,000	$175,000

Required:

(i) Prepare an investment elimination schedule as of December 31, 1972.

(ii) Calculate amounts of consolidated net income for 1971 and 1972.

(iii) Calculate amounts of minority interest in net income for 1971 and 1972 based upon:

(a) 100 percent elimination of unconfirmed intercompany profit.

(b) Fractional elimination of unconfirmed intercompany profit.

Problem 12–11

The Banner Corporation acquired 80 percent of the capital stock of the Ribbon Company on January 1, 1969, when the latter had capital stock of $100,000 and retained earnings of $60,000.

On January 1, 1971, the Ribbon Company sold fixed assets to the Banner Corporation for $45,000. These assets were purchased originally by the Ribbon Company for $50,000 on January 1, 1961. Accumulated depreciation to the date of sale (estimated service life 25 years) amounted to $20,000.

On December 31, 1972, the trial balances of the affiliates were:

	Banner Corporation	Ribbon Company
Merchandise, January 1	$ 12,000	$ 10,000
Fixed assets	180,000	64,000
Other assets	111,900	149,700
Investment in Ribbon Company capital stock	135,000	
Dividends declared	10,000	8,000
Purchases	80,000	60,000
Expenses	12,000	7,400
	$540,900	$299,100
Liabilities	$ 23,000	$ 8,000
Accumulated depreciation	31,200	24,000
Sales	122,000	89,000
Dividend income	6,400	
Capital stock	250,000	100,000
Retained earnings	108,300	78,100
	$540,900	$299,100
Merchandise, December 31	$ 13,500	$ 5,900

Required:

Prepare a consolidated statement working paper for the year ended December 31, 1972. The amount of the intercompany profit elimination is to be based upon the parent company's equity in the selling affiliate.

Problem 12–12

The Buckley Company purchased 80 percent of the capital stock of the Carson Company and 70 percent of the capital stock of the Diamond Company on January 1, 1970.

A summary of retained earnings changes for the two years ended December 31, 1971, follows:

	Buckley	Carson	Diamond
Retained earnings, January 1, 1970	$115,000	$ 60,000	$ 70,000
Net income, 1970	35,000	30,000	40,000
Retained earnings, January 1, 1971	$150,000	$ 90,000	$110,000
Net income, 1971	90,000	60,000	50,000
	$240,000	$150,000	$160,000
Dividends, 1971	20,000	10,000	15,000
Retained earnings, December 31, 1971	$220,000	$140,000	$145,000

Intercompany sales of merchandise during 1971 were as follows:

| | | | December 31 |
From	To	Sales	Inventory
Buckley	Carson	$20,000	$2,000
Carson	Buckley	15,000	1,000
Diamond	Carson	30,000	5,000

Intercompany sales of merchandise during 1970 include the following:

Carson	Buckley	$10,000	$2,000
Diamond	Carson	12,000	3,000

Gross profit rates (based on selling price) for 1970 and 1971 were:

Buckley.........................	20%
Carson...........................	25
Diamond.......................	30

Required:

(i)   Calculate 1971 consolidated net income.

(ii) Prepare the retained earnings division of a consolidated statement working paper for the year ended December 31, 1971. Assume fractional elimination for unconfirmed inventory profit.

(iii) Calculate the minority interest in retained earnings, December 31, 1971. Assume 100 percent elimination for unconfirmed inventory profit.

Problem 12–13

During its fiscal year ended October 31, 1971, the S Company, a wholly owned subsidiary of the P Company, sold to the latter, at a profit, materials which it used in constructing a new building for its own use. State (*a*) how the profit on the sale of these materials should be treated in preparing the consolidated financial statements of the P Company and its subsidiary as of October 31, 1971, and for the year then ended respectively, and (*b*) how it should be treated in preparing financial statements in subsequent years.

(AICPA adapted)

Problem 12–14

Item A: X Corporation manufactures at a finished cost of $20 per unit and sells to Y Corporation @ $25 per unit. Y Corporation leaves its inventory in the warehouse of X Corporation, withdrawing only as needed and pays to X Corporation storage at the rate of 50 cents per unit per month. The quantity in the inventory of Y Corporation at December 31 was purchased six months previously. Y Corporation resells at $40 F.O.B. shipping point which is the same price at which X Corporation sells to others.

Item B: X Corporation owns and operates a mine from which item B is extracted. The average cost of mining item B is $5 per ton. The cost of the mine and development thereof is subject to depletion at the rate of $2.50 per ton. The cost of loading on freight cars averages $1 per ton. Y Corporation purchases from X Corporation at cost F.O.B. the mine and transports to its plant, paying freight of $1.50 per ton. X Corporation sells approximately 75 percent of its mined product to others at a price of $15 per ton, F.O.B. the mine, and Y Corporation sells at a substantial profit after refinement.

Item C: X Corporation buys manufacturing supplies at a price of $50 per unit less trade discounts of 10/10/20. A portion of the supplies purchased by X Corporation are resold to Y Corporation at a price of $41 F.O.B. Y Corporation's plant. The freight, paid by X Corporation, amounts to 50 cents per unit. Y Corporation does not have access to the market from which X Corporation buys.

Item D: X Corporation manufactures this item at the average cost of $29 per unit and sells its total output to Y Corporation @ $35 per unit, F.O.B. X Corporation's plant under terms of a firm contract. The freight amounts to $2 per unit. The amount obtainable from X Corporation is only about 50 percent of the quantity required by Y Corporation. The balance of Y Corporation's requirements are obtained from other sources at a price of $32.50 per unit, F.O.B. Y's plant. Y resells this item at a price which yields $34 per unit after allowing for sales and handling expense.

Item E: X Corporation manufactures at a cost of $6 per unit and sells to Y Corporation and others @ $5 per unit, F.O.B. X Corporation's plant. The freight to Y's plant amounts to 75 cents per unit. Y Corporation processes this item and sells at a profit.

Required:

Consider that there were 10 units of each of the five items in the inventory of *each corporation* at the end of their concurrent fiscal years. You are to show the proper valuation at the lower of cost or market for inventory purposes in the financial statements and to explain in connection with each valuation the reason for using it. Answer for each item separately.

(i)   In the separate financial statements of X Corporation and Y Corporation.

(ii)   In the consolidated financial statements, assuming Y Corporation is a 90 percent owned subsidiary of X Corporation.

(AICPA adapted)

Problem 12–15

On January 1, 1971, X Company purchased 90 percent of the capital stock of Y Company at a cost of $85,000; concurrently Y Company purchased 10 percent of the capital stock of Z Company for $6,000. One year later, X Company acquired 70 percent of the capital stock of Z Company at a cost of $55,000. The following summary information relates to the affiliate companies:

	X Company	Y Company	Z Company
January 1, 1971:			
Capital stock............................	$100,000	$50,000	$50,000
Retained earnings.......................	100,000	40,000	20,000
Two-year operating summary:			
Reported profits:			
1971..............................	40,000	20,000	15,000
1972..............................	45,000	22,500	5,000
Cash dividends:			
1971..............................	20,000	10,000	10,000
1972..............................	20,000	15,000	5,000
Intercompany inventory profit, recognized by the selling affiliate and unconfirmed as of—			
December 31, 1971......................	4,000	3,000	
December 31, 1972......................	2,000	4,000	2,000

Required:

(i) Prepare an investment elimination schedule *and* a schedule showing the calculation of majority and minority interests in retained earnings on December 31, 1971, and December 31, 1972. (Assume 100 percent elimination in respect to unconfirmed inventory profit.)

(ii) Calculate in schedule form the amounts of consolidated net income for 1971 and 1972. (Assume 100 percent elimination in respect to unconfirmed inventory profit.)

(iii) Prepare the retained earnings division of a consolidated statement working paper for the year ended December 31, 1972.

Problem 12–16

On January 1, 1971, Y Company acquired an 80 percent interest in the capital stock of Z Company at a cost of $65,000; on January 1, 1972, X Company purchased 90 percent of the capital stock of Y Company for $150,000. The following data relate to the affiliation for the period beginning January 1, 1971:

	X Company	Y Company	Z Company
January 1, 1971:			
Capital stock..................	$200,000	$100,000	$50,000
Retained earnings..............	100,000	40,000	25,000
Two-year operating summary:			
Annual profits:			
1971.......................	20,000	10,400	55,000
1972.......................	25,600	9,200	7,000
Cash dividends:			
1971.......................	10,000	5,000	3,000
1972.......................	10,000	4,000	4,000

On January 1, 1971, Y Company purchased a building from Z Company for $100,000; the undepreciated cost to Z Company was $50,000; the remaining estimated service life was assumed to be 20 years.

Required:

(i) Prepare an investment elimination schedule *and* a schedule showing the calculation of majority and minority interests in retained earnings on December 31, 1971, and December 31, 1972. (Assume fractional elimination in respect to intercompany profit.)

(ii) Indicate by schedule calculation the amounts of consolidated net income for 1971 and 1972. (Assume fractional elimination in respect to intercompany profit.)

(iii) Prepare the retained earnings division of a consolidated statement working paper for the year ended December 31, 1972.

Problem 12–17

Padre Company, a wholesaler, purchased 80 percent of the issued and outstanding stock of Sun, Inc., a retailer, on December 31, 1967, for $120,000. At that date Sun, Inc., had one class of common stock outstanding at a stated value of $100,000 and retained earnings of $30,000. Padre Company had a $50,000 deficit balance in retained earnings.

Padre Company purchased the Sun, Inc., stock from Sun's major stockholder primarily to acquire control of signboard leases owned by Sun. The leases will expire on December 31, 1972, and Padre Company executives estimate the leases, which cannot be renewed, were worth at least $25,000 more than their book value when the stock was purchased.

The financial statements for both companies for the year ended December 31, 1971, follow:

PADRE COMPANY AND SUBSIDIARY
Financial Statements
For the Year Ended December 31, 1971
Balance Sheet

ASSETS	Padre Company	Sun Inc.
Cash.	$ 14,200	$ 19,300
Accounts receivable.	80,000	76,000
Inventories.	54,800	85,600
Other current assets.	15,000	18,200
Investment.	120,000	
Notes receivable.	8,000	
Land.	25,000	10,500
Plant and equipment.	200,000	40,000
Accumulated depreciation.	[102,000]	[7,000]
Signboard leases.		42,000
Amortization to date.		[33,600]
Total.	$415,000	$251,000

LIABILITIES AND CAPITAL

Accounts payable.	$ 35,500	$ 47,000
Dividends payable.		9,000
Other current liabilities.	24,500	12,000
Notes payable.		8,000
Capital stock.	300,000	100,000
Retained earnings.	55,000	75,000
Total.	$415,000	$251,000

Income Statement

Sales.	$420,000	$300,000
Cost of goods sold.	315,000	240,000
Gross profit.	105,000	60,000
Expenses.	65,000	35,000
Net income.	$ 40,000	$ 25,000

a) Padre Company sells merchandise to Sun, Inc., at the same prices and terms applicable to other customers. During 1971 Padre's sales to Sun totaled $100,000. Sun had $30,000 of merchandise purchased from Padre on hand on December 31, 1971, which was an increase of $10,000 over the previous year. Sun had not paid Padre for $21,000 of the merchandise in inventory and also owed Padre for a $15,000 cash advance which was in Sun's cash account on December 31, 1971.

b) On July 1, 1968, Sun purchased a parcel of land from Padre for $10,500 cash. A building on the land was also purchased the same date from Padre for $40,000; Sun paid $8,000 cash and gave a mortgage which called for four payments of $8,000 each plus interest at 6 percent to be paid annually on the anniversary of the sale. Padre credits the interest paid by Sun to Interest Expense. The land originally cost Padre $10,500, and Padre's book value of the building was $30,000 at the date of the sale. Sun estimated the building had a 20-year life and no salvage value when purchased and has computed depreciation on a monthly basis.

c) Sun declared a 9 percent cash dividend on December 20, 1971, payable on January 16, 1972, to stockholders of record on January 2, 1972. Padre carries its investment at cost and had not recorded this dividend on December 31, 1971. Neither company paid a dividend during 1971.

Required:

Prepare a three-division working paper for the preparation of consolidated financial statements for the Padre Company and its subsidiary, Sun, Inc., as of December 31, 1971.

(AICPA adapted)

Chapter 13

Consolidated Statements—
Preference Interests

INTERCOMPANY BONDS

Whenever a corporate entity issues bonds and subsequently retires some or all of these bonds at a price that is different from the book value of the bonds at the date of retirement, a gain or loss on bond retirement is realized. From the point of view of a consolidated entity, the purchase of an affiliate's bonds by another affiliate constitutes constructive retirement of the bonds. Correspondingly, where the cost to the purchasing affiliate is unequal to the carrying value of the bond liability, there exists a *consolidated basis* "gain or loss on the purchase of intercompany bonds." Significantly, this gain or loss is *not recorded* by any of the affiliates. The issuing corporation is obliged to continue the payment of interest and to record the expense as well as the amortization of any premium or discount on bonds payable. Also, the purchasing affiliate periodically records the receipt of interest and amortization of any premium or discount on bond investment with corresponding credits to interest revenue.

Eliminations at Date of Purchase

From the discussion above, it is apparent that the existence of intercompany bond holdings must be dealt with in a special manner in the preparation of consolidated statements. To remove the intercompany indebtedness, it is conventional to eliminate the *par* value of the bond investment and the *par* value of the bond liability as follows.

Bonds payable.. (par)
    Investment in bonds....................................   (par)

At the date of the bond acquisition, the above elimination would leave any premium or discount on bonds payable *and* premium or discount on bond investment as amounts yet to be eliminated. The algebraic sum of these items determines the consolidated basis gain or loss on the purchase of intercompany bonds. This is, of course, equivalent to the previous statement that the gain or loss is calculated as the difference between the carrying value of the bond liability and the acquisition cost of the bond investment. An elimination entry which removes these premium or discount balances also accomplishes the recording of the gain or loss on the consolidated income statement.

Analysis of Gain or Loss

Upon recognition of a gain or loss on the purchase of intercompany bonds, it then becomes necessary to determine an appropriate allocation of the gain or loss between the purchasing and issuing affiliates. In that one or both of the affiliates may have minority interest stockholders, the allocation of gain or loss may affect the calculations of minority interest in combined net income and resultantly, the determination of consolidated net income.

It may be argued that the total gain or loss should be allocated to the company that issued the bonds. The purchasing company would thus be perceived as simply an *agent* for the issuing affiliate; given this interpretation, the act of purchasing is deemed to be in behalf of the issuing firm which is the principal to the transaction. On the other hand, it can be argued that the gain or loss should be allocated entirely to the purchasing affiliate. In this instance, emphasis is placed on the purchase transaction, which is regarded as the critical event giving rise to the gain or loss. This event being undertaken by the purchasing affiliate, it follows that the gain or loss should be attributed to the purchaser.

The authors believe that the most reasonable analysis of gain or loss on purchase of intercompany bond recognizes that the actions of *both* affiliates are essential to the existence of a gain or loss. As such, both should participate in its effects. A recommended method of allocating the gain or loss that should be followed consistently is to assume that the constructive retirement of the bonds is effected at their par value. Thus, the gain or loss of the issuing affiliate is determined by comparing the carrying value of the bond liability (at the date the bonds are acquired by the purchasing affiliate) with the par value. Similarly, the gain or loss of the purchasing affiliate is determined by comparing its purchase price with par value. In other words, at the date of purchase, any premium on intercompany bonds payable represents gain to the issuing company; similarly, a discount on intercompany bonds payable would represent loss to the issuing company. A premium on bond investment represents a loss to the purchasing company; a discount on bond investment represents a gain. The algebraic sum of gains or losses of both affiliates constitutes the total consolidated basis gain or loss.

Eliminations after Date of Purchase

After the date of purchase, the issuing and purchasing affiliates will necessarily record cash transfers of interest. At consolidation points, such accumulations of intercompany interest expense and revenue (to the extent of cash transfers) should be eliminated against each other. Additionally, it may be necessary to eliminate contra accounts of interest receivable and interest payable. The par value of bonds payable and bond investment must also be eliminated, as previously discussed.

As an *issuing* affiliate records the amortization of premium or discount on bonds payable in periods subsequent to their "constructive retirement," the affiliate is effectively recognizing in its own records a portion of the gain or loss originally attributed to it. If not eliminated, the amount of such periodic amortizations would constitute a *double* recognition of the gain or loss in the consolidated statements. Thus, the issuing affiliate's current amortization of premium or discount (reflected as an increment or decrement to interest expense) together with the remaining premium or discount balance must be eliminated against the beginning-of-the-period retained earnings balance (or if during the same period as the purchase, against the gain or loss account).

In regard to the *purchasing* affiliate, the eliminations of amortizations of premium or discount on bond investment exactly parallel the elimination entries for the issuing affiliate. The current amortization (evidenced in the interest revenue account) and the remaining balance of premium or discount are eliminated against the beginning-of-the-period retained earnings.

The similarity between the eliminations for intercompany bond holdings and the eliminations of intercompany profit on depreciable asset transfers should now be apparent. In the case of asset transfers, an unconfirmed profit is recorded by the selling affiliate; it is deferred in the consolidated statements and is given recognition only in future periods as confirmation is accomplished through depreciation. In the case of intercompany bonds, the gain or loss is regarded as confirmed at the date of acquisition and is so recognized in the consolidated statements. The affiliates, however, record their respective elements of the gain or loss over future periods in the form of premium or discount amortizations; accordingly, *double* recognition is avoided by eliminating, in the consolidated working papers, the effects produced by these subsequent amortizations. Consequently, the result of the elimination process is to *defer* recognition of profit (or loss) on asset transfers and to *accelerate* its recognition in respect to intercompany-held bonds. In both instances, there is an evident underlying philosophy of reporting profits or losses only at the time they are confirmed by transactions with nonaffiliate interests. Obviously, this philosophy is just as applicable to the eliminations of intercompany inventory profit as it is to intercompany depreciable asset transfers and bond holdings.

As was true regarding the elimination of profit on asset transfers, accountants are not in complete agreement as to the appropriate *amount* of intercompany unamortized bond discounts or premiums to be eliminated in a consolidated working paper. Some prefer to eliminate 100 percent of these balances; others favor the elimination of amounts based upon the parent company's fractional interest in the capital stock of the relevant affiliate. Obviously, the position taken will affect the amount of gain or loss on the purchase of intercompany bonds to be recognized.

The following cases illustrate a number of different conditions of inter-company bondholdings.

Case 1. Parent Company's Bonds Acquired by Subsidiary Affiliate—100 Percent Elimination. The following data relate to X Company and its 80 percent owned subsidiary, Y Company:

	January 1, 1971, Balances	
Accounts	X Company Dr. [Cr.]	Y Company Dr. [Cr.]
4% bonds payable.	$[20,000]	
Premium on bonds payable.	[600]	
Investment in X Company bonds.		$5,000
Discount on bond investment.		[90]

The amounts of discounts and premiums on the purchase of corporate bonds are usually reflected in the balance of the bond investment account. They are given separate account identification here, and in the illustrative cases to follow, for purposes of emphasis and to expose more clearly the contra elements of the profit elimination. It is assumed that Y Company purchased $5,000 of X Company's bonds on January 1, 1971, for $4,910. The bonds mature January 1, 1974. The net incomes, excluding the effects of interest, of each company are as follows:

	1971	1972
X Company.	$30,000	$25,000
Y Company.	20,000	10,000

A schedule of eliminations in respect to these intercompany bonds is presented in Illustration 13–1. The bond elimination schedule presents a complete summarization of the elimination entries that must be made on successive consolidation dates starting with the date of acquisition and terminating on the date at which the bonds mature. In the interpretation of this schedule, the reader should take care to understand the significance of each debit or credit. The first row presents the balances (at date of acquisition) of the premium or discount accounts. The debits and credits in *all* subsequent rows represent *actions* that must be taken through periodic amortizations and eliminations.

It is evident that the consolidated basis gain (or loss) on the purchase of intercompany bonds should be recognized in the year of acquisition. In Illustration 13–1 this gain of $240 relates $150 (the premium on bonds payable) to the issuing parent company and $90 (the discount on bond investment) to the subsidiary affiliate. Since the gain is reported in the consolidated income statement in the year of bond acquisition, it is redun-

Illustration 13–1

BOND ELIMINATION SCHEDULE
Dr. [Cr.]

	Balance Sheet		Income Statement			Retained Earnings Statement	
	Premium on Bonds Payable— X Company	Discount on Bond Investment— Y Company	Gain on the Purchase of Intercompany Bonds	Interest Expense	Interest Income	Retained Earnings, January 1— X Company	Retained Earnings, January 1— Y Company
Balances on 1/1/71............	[150]	[90]					
Elimination at acquisition......	150	90	[240]				
Amortization in 1971..........	50	30					
Elimination as of 12/31/71.....	100	60	[240]	50	30		
Amortization in 1972..........	50	30					
Elimination as of 12/31/72.....	50	30		50	30	[100]	[60]
Amortization in 1973..........	50	30					
Elimination as of 12/31/73.....	-0-	-0-		50	30	[50]	[30]
Other eliminations:							
(1) Bond interest income.......			200				
Bond interest expense......		200					
(2) Bonds payable.............			5,000				
Investment in X Company bonds...	5,000						

dant to allow these same profit determinants to enter subsequent calculations of consolidated net income through amortization recorded thereafter by the separate affiliates. Accordingly, the amounts of amortization subsequently recorded in respect to these profit elements should be eliminated to avoid duplicate measurement. In consolidated statement working papers in periods following the period of intercompany bond acquisition, however, this gain should be reflected in consolidated retained earnings. In this regard, each affiliate through periodic amortization of intercompany bond premium or discount is essentially recognizing a portion of the previously recognized consolidated basis gain (or loss) on the acquisition of intercompany bonds. However, the amortization process necessarily extends the period of profit or loss recognition by the separate companies over the remaining life of these bonds. Therefore, the net elimination which must be made against the retained earnings' balances of the relevant affiliates is the original acquisition gain (or loss) adjusted for prior periods' amortization of intercompany bond discounts and/or premiums. The current period's amortization must be eliminated, as before, against the affiliates' interest income and interest expense accounts.

The eliminations as of December 31, 1971 (Illustration 13–1), in respect to the acquisition gain are made against the January 1 retained earnings of X Company in the amount of $100 ($150 − $50) and the January 1 retained earnings of Y Company in the amount of $60 ($90 − $30). The amounts of $50 and $30 represent the interest adjustments for amortization during 1971. The 1972 interest adjustments in the income statement necessarily are of the same amounts as the 1971 interest adjustments. Some accountants prefer to algebraically add the two periodic adjustments of interest income and expense, and describe the sum as the "net interest adjustment," in this case, $80 ($50 + $30). The effect produced on consolidated net income is the same, although the net adjustment obscures significant elimination details; for this reason, the authors will continue to show the interest adjustments separately.

Partial consolidated statement working papers using these data are presented in Illustration 13–2 and Illustration 13–3.

Case 2. Subsidiary Affiliate's Bonds Acquired by Parent Company— Fractional Elimination. The following data relate to X Company and its 80 percent owned subsidiary Y Company:

| | January 1, 1971, Balance | |
| | X Company | Y Company |
Accounts	Dr. [Cr.]	Dr. [Cr.]
4% bonds payable..............................		$[20,000]
Discount on bonds payable......................		600
Investment in Y Company bonds.................	$5,000	
Premium on bond investment....................	90	

Illustration 13–2

X COMPANY AND SUBSIDIARY Y COMPANY
Partial Consolidated Statement Working Paper
For Year Ended December 31, 1971

	X Company	Y Company	Eliminations Dr.	Eliminations Cr.	Minority Interest	Consolidated
Income Statement:						
Net income, before interest............	30,000	20,000				50,000
Interest income...............		230	(1) 30 (2) 200			
Gain on purchase of intercompany bonds.....				(1) 240 (2) 200		240
Interest expense................	[600]		(1) 50			[450]
Net income..............	29,400	20,230				49,790
Minority interest [20% of (20,230 + 90 − 30)].......					4,058	[4,058]
Net income—carried forward........	29,400	20,230	280	440	4,058	45,732
Balance Sheet:						
Debits:						
Investment in X Company bonds........		5,000		(3) 5,000		–0–
Credits:						
Bonds payable...........	20,000		(3) 5,000			15,000
Premium on bonds payable........	400		(1) 100			300
Discount on bond investment........		60	(1) 60			

[deduction]

Illustration 13-3

X COMPANY AND SUBSIDIARY Y COMPANY

Partial Consolidated Statement Working Paper
For Year Ended December 31, 1972

	X Company	Y Company	Eliminations Dr.	Eliminations Cr.	Minority Interest	Consolidated
Income Statement:						
Net income, before interest	25,000	10,000				35,000
Interest income		230	(1) 30 (2) 200			
Interest expense	[600]		(1) 50	(2) 200		[450]
Net income	24,400	10,230				34,550
Minority interest [20% of (10,230 − 30)]					2,040	[2,040]
Net income—carried forward	24,400	10,230	280	200	2,040	32,510
Retained Earnings Statement:						
Retained earnings, January 1, 1972:						
X Company	29,400			(1) 100	*4,058	29,500
Y Company		20,230		(1) 60	2,040	16,232
Net income—brought forward	24,400	10,230	280	200	2,040	32,510
Retained earnings, December 31, 1972—carried forward	53,800	30,460	280	360	6,098	78,242
Balance Sheet:						
Debits:						
Investment in X Company bonds		5,000		(3) 5,000		-0-
Credits:						
Bonds payable	20,000		(3) 5,000			15,000
Premium on bonds payable	200		(1) 50			150
Discount on bond investment		30	(1) 30			

[deduction]
* [20% of (20,230 + 90 − 30)]

X Company purchased $5,000 of Y Company's 4 percent bonds on January 1, 1971, for $5,090. The bonds mature January 1, 1974. Net incomes, excluding interest, of each company are as follows:

	1971	1972
X Company..............	$30,000	$25,000
Y Company..............	20,000	10,000

A schedule of eliminations in respect to these intercompany bonds is found in Illustration 13–4.

Gain or loss on the acquisition of intercompany bonds is calculated on the basis of the algebraic sum of the differences between acquisition premium and issuance discount and the par value of intercompany bondholdings. In the present case, the parent company's percentage interest in the capital stock of the relevant affiliate is controlling in respect to the amount of the elimination required for unamortized discounts and premiums. The acquisition loss relates $120 to the issuing subsidiary and $90 to the parent investor. The interest elimination in respect to amortization is treated as in the previous example. Because the relevant unamortized issuance discount and the total acquisition premium which relate to the majority shareholders as of the date of acquisition of the intercompany bonds have previously entered the calculation of the loss of $210, subsequent amortization is redundant and must be negated to avoid duplicate income recognition.

Using these data, the consolidated statement working papers for 1971 and 1972 are shown in Illustration 13–5 and Illustration 13–6. It should be observed that the minority shareholders' interest in Discount on Bonds Payable is not eliminated; it is therefore included in the consolidated balance sheet together with the discount applicable to the bonds held by nonaffiliates. In the case that all outstanding bonds payable are held by affiliates, the minority interest equity in the discount (or premium) will stand alone as a balance sheet extension; it is usually classified as a deferred charge (premium as a deferred credit). The amount of this extension identifies with the minority shareholders in respect to whom the fractional elimination does not relate. The equity of this group in the gain or loss on the acquisition of intercompany bonds is deferred for recognition through the process of amortization recorded by relevant affiliates over the remaining life of the bonds. The apparent anomaly of showing a discount or premium on intercompany bonds in the consolidated balance sheet in which the par value of the intercompany indebtedness is totally eliminated may create some confusion among statement readers. Consequently, since these balances are rarely material in amount, they may be confined with other deferred charges (credits) in the formal consolidated balance sheet.

Illustration 13-4

BOND ELIMINATION SCHEDULE

Dr. [Cr.]

	Balance Sheet		Income Statement			Retained Earnings Statement	
	Discount on Bonds Payable— Y Company	Premium on Bond Investment— X Company	Loss on the Purchase of Intercompany Bonds	Interest Expense	Interest Income	Retained Earnings, January 1— Y Company	Retained Earnings, January 1— X Company
Balances on 1/1/71............	150	90					
Parent company's equity.......	80%	100%					
Elimination at acquisition......	[120]	[90]	210				
Amortization in 1971..........	[40]	[30]					
Elimination as of 12/31/71......	[80]	[60]	210	[40]	[30]		
Amortization in 1972..........	[40]	[30]					
Elimination as of 12/31/72......	[40]	[30]		[40]	[30]	80	60
Amortization in 1973..........	[40]	[30]					
Elimination as of 12/31/73......	-0-	-0-		[40]	[30]	40	30

Other eliminations:

(1) Bond interest income.................... 200
    Bond interest expense.................. 200

(2) Bonds payable........................ 5,000
    Investment in Y Company bonds...... 5,000

Illustration 13–5

X COMPANY AND SUBSIDIARY Y COMPANY
Partial Consolidated Statement Working Paper
For Year Ended December 31, 1971

	X Company	Y Company	Eliminations Dr.	Eliminations Cr.	Minority Interest	Consolidated
Income Statement:						
Net income, before interest.........	30,000	20,000				50,000
Interest income..........	170		(1) 210	(1) 30		–0–
Loss on purchase of intercompany bonds....			(2) 200	(1) 40		[210]
Interest expense..........		[1,000]		(2) 200		[760]
Net income..........	30,170	19,000				49,030
Minority interest (20% of $19,000).....					3,800	[3,800]
Net income—carried forward.........	30,170	19,000	410	270	3,800	45,230
Balance Sheet:						
Debits:						
Discount on bonds payable........		400		(1) 80		320
Premium on bond investment......	60			(1) 60		–0–
Investment in Y Company bonds......	5,000			(3) 5,000		–0–
Credits:						
Bonds payable........		20,000	(3) 5,000			15,000

[deduction]

Illustration 13-6

X COMPANY AND SUBSIDIARY Y COMPANY

Partial Consolidated Statement Working Paper
For Year Ended December 31, 1972

	X Company	Y Company	Eliminations Dr.	Eliminations Cr.	Minority Interest	Consolidated
Income Statement:						
Net income, before interest	25,000	10,000				35,000
Interest income	170			(1) 30		-0-
Interest expense		[1,000]	(2) 200	(1) 40		[760]
				(2) 200		
Net income	25,170	9,000				34,240
Minority interest (20% of $9,000)					1,800	[1,800]
Net income—carried forward	25,170	9,000	200	270	1,800	32,440
Retained Earnings Statement:						
Retained earnings, January 1, 1972:						
X Company	30,170		(1) 60			30,110
Y Company		19,000	(1) 80		3,800	15,120
Net income—brought forward	25,170	9,000	200	270	1,800	32,440
Retained earnings, December 31, 1972—carried forward	55,340	28,000	340	270	5,600	77,670
Balance Sheet:						
Debits:						
Discount on bonds payable	30			(1) 40		160
Premium on bond investment		200		(1) 30		-0-
Investment in Y Company bonds	5,000			(3) 5,000		-0-
Credits:						
Bonds payable		20,000	(3) 5,000			15,000

[deduction]

Similar problems are presented with the minority interest's equity in Premium or Discount on Bond Investment where the *purchasing* affiliate is a subsidiary.

Case 3. Subsidiary Company's Bonds Acquired by Another Subsidiary Company—100 Percent Elimination. The following data relate to X Company and its 80 percent owned subsidiary Y Company, and its 90 percent owned subsidiary Z Company:

	January 1, 1971, Balances	
	Y Company	Z Company
Accounts	Dr. [Cr.]	Dr. [Cr.]
4% bonds payable..............................	$[20,000]	
Discount on bonds payable......................	600	
Investment in Y Company bonds..................		$5,000
Discount on bond investment....................		[90]

Z Company purchased $5,000 of Y Company's 4 percent bonds on January 1, 1971, for $4,910. The bonds mature on January 1, 1974. Net incomes earned by each company, excluding interest, were as follows:

	1971	1972
X Company................	$30,000	$25,000
Y Company................	20,000	10,000
Z Company................	10,000	5,000

The schedule of eliminations and partial consolidated statement working papers for this case are found in Illustrations 13–7, 13–8, and 13–9. It should be noted that where the intercompany bonds are confined to subsidiary members of the affiliation, elimination details are nonetheless the same as in the case of intercompany bonds which relate to a parent company and a subsidiary affiliate.

Case 4. Subsidiary Company's Bonds Acquired by Another Subsidiary —Fractional Elimination. The schedule of eliminations and partial consolidated statement working papers for this case (Illustrations 13–10, 13–11, and 13–12) are based upon the same information as in Case 3, with the exception that intercompany unamortized discounts are eliminated only to the extent of the parent's equity in the subsidiaries.

The differences in the partial consolidated statement working papers for Cases 3 and 4 can be explained in terms of the amounts of discounts eliminated and the calculation of the interests of the minority shareholders. Where the unamortized discounts are totally eliminated, both the interests of majority and minority shareholders in net income and retained earnings

Illustration 13–7

BOND ELIMINATION SCHEDULE

Dr. [Cr.]

	Balance Sheet		Income Statement			Retained Earnings Statement	
	Discount on Bonds Payable— Y Company	Discount on Bond Invest- ment— Z Company	Loss on the Purchase of Intercom- pany Bonds	Interest Expense	Interest Income	Retained Earnings, January 1— Y Company	Retained Earnings, January 1— Z Company
Balances on 1/1/71	150	[90]					
Elimination at acquisition	[150]	90	60				
Amortization in 1971	[50]	30					
Elimination as of 12/31/71	[100]	60	60	[50]	30		
Amortization in 1972	[50]	30					
Elimination as of 12/31/72	[50]	30		[50]	30	100	[60]
Amortization in 1973	[50]	30					
Elimination as of 12/31/73	–0–	–0–		[50]	30	50	[30]

Other eliminations:
(1) Bond interest income.................... 200
    Bond interest expense.................. 200
(2) Bonds payable.......................... 5,000
    Investment in Y Company bonds.... 5,000

Illustration 13–8

X COMPANY AND SUBSIDIARY COMPANIES Y AND Z
Partial Consolidated Statement Working Paper
For Year Ended December 31, 1971

	X Company	Y Company	Z Company	Eliminations Dr.	Eliminations Cr.	Minority Interests Y Company	Minority Interests Z Company	Consolidated
Income Statement:								
Net income, before interest	30,000	20,000	10,000					60,000
Interest income			230	(1) 30 (2) 200				-0-
Loss on purchase of intercompany bonds					(1) 50			[60]
Interest expense		[1,000]		(1) 60	(2) 200			[750]
Net income	30,000	19,000	10,230					59,190
Minority interests						*3,780	†1,029	[4,809]
Net income—carried forward	30,000	19,000	10,230	290	250	3,780	1,029	54,381
Balance Sheet:								
Debits:								
Investment in Y Company bonds			5,000		(3) 5,000			-0-
Discount on bonds payable		400			(1) 100			300
Credits:								
Discount on bond investment			60	(1) 60				-0-
Bonds payable		20,000		(3) 5,000				15,000

* 20 percent of ($19,000 − $150 + $50).
† 10 percent of ($10,230 + $90 − $30).
[deduction]

Illustration 13–9

X COMPANY AND SUBSIDIARY COMPANIES Y AND Z
Partial Consolidated Statement Working Paper
For Year Ended December 31, 1972

	X Company	Y Company	Z Company	Eliminations Dr.	Eliminations Cr.	Minority Interests Y Company	Minority Interests Z Company	Consolidated
Income Statement:								
Net income, before interest	25,000	10,000	5,000					40,000
Interest income			230					–0–
Interest expense		[1,000]		(1) 30 (2) 200	(1) 50 (2) 200			[750]
Net income	25,000	9,000	5,230			*1,810	†520	39,250 [2,330]
Net income—carried forward	25,000	9,000	5,230	230	250	1,810	520	36,920
Retained Earnings Statement:								
Retained earnings, January 1, 1972:								
X Company	30,000							30,000
Y Company		19,000		(1) 100	(1) 60	‡3,780		15,120
Z Company			10,230				§1,029	9,261
Net income—brought forward	25,000	9,000	5,230	230	250	1,810	520	36,920
Retained earnings, December 31, 1972—carried forward	55,000	28,000	15,460	330	310	5,590	1,549	91,301
Balance Sheet:								
Debits:								
Investment in Y Company bonds			5,000		(3) 5,000			–0–
Discount on bonds payable		200			(1) 50			150
Credits:								
Discount on bond investment			30	(1) 30				–0–
Bonds payable		20,000		(3) 5,000				15,000

* 20 percent of ($9,000 + $50).
† 10 percent of ($5,230 − $30).
‡ 20 percent of ($19,000 − $100).
§ 10 percent of ($10,230 + $60).
[deduction]

Illustration 13–10

BOND ELIMINATION SCHEDULE

Dr. [Cr.]

	Balance Sheet		Income Statement			Retained Earnings Statement	
	Discount on Bonds Payable— Y Company	Discount on Bond Investment— Z Company	Loss on the Purchase of Intercompany Bonds	Interest Expense	Interest Income	Retained Earnings, January 1— Y Company	Retained Earnings, January 1— Z Company
Balances on 1/1/71.........	150	[90]					
Parent company's equity........	80%	90%					
Elimination at acquisition........	[120]	81	39				
Amortization in 1971........	[40]	27					
Elimination as of 12/31/71......	[80]	54	39	[40]	27		
Amortization in 1972.........	[40]	27					
Elimination as of 12/31/72......	[40]	27		[40]	27	80	[54]
Amortization in 1973........	[40]	27					
Elimination as of 12/31/73......	-0-	-0-		[40]	27	40	[27]
Other eliminations:							
(1) Bond interest income........		200					
Bond interest expense........			200				
(2) Bonds payable........		5,000					
Investment in Y Company bonds........			5,000				

Illustration 13-11

X COMPANY AND SUBSIDIARY COMPANIES Y AND Z

Partial Consolidated Statement Working Paper

For Year Ended December 31, 1971

	X Company	Y Company	Z Company	Eliminations Dr.	Eliminations Cr.	Minority Interests Y Company	Minority Interests Z Company	Consolidated
Income Statement:								
Net income, before interest......	30,000	20,000	10,000					60,000
Interest income........			230	(1) 27 (2) 200				3
Loss on purchase of inter-company bonds........					(1) 40 (2) 200			[39]
Interest expense........		[1,000]		(1) 39				[760]
Net income........	30,000	19,000	10,230					59,204
Minority interests........						3,800	1,023	[4,823]
Net income—carried forward........	30,000	19,000	10,230	266	240	3,800	1,023	54,381
Balance Sheet:								
Debits:								
Investment in Y Company bonds........			5,000		(3) 5,000			-0-
Discount on bonds payable........		400			(1) 80			320
Credits:								
Discount on bond investment........			60	(1) 54				6
Bonds payable........	20,000			(3) 5,000				15,000

[deduction]

Illustration 13-12

X COMPANY AND SUBSIDIARY COMPANIES Y AND Z

Partial Consolidated Statement Working Paper
For Year Ended December 31, 1972

	X Company	Y Company	Z Company	Eliminations Dr.	Eliminations Cr.	Minority Interests Y Company	Minority Interests Z Company	Consolidated
Income Statement:								
Net income, before interest........	25,000	10,000	5,000					40,000
Interest income..................			230		(1) 40 (2) 200			3
Interest expense.................		[1,000]		(1) 27 (2) 200				[760]
Net income......................	25,000	9,000	5,230	227	240			39,243
Minority interests...............						1,800	523	[2,323]
Net income—carried forward......	25,000	9,000	5,230	227	240	1,800	523	36,920
Retained Earnings Statement:								
Retained earnings, January 1, 1972:								
X Company.....................	30,000							30,000
Y Company.....................		19,000		(1) 80		3,800		15,120
Z Company.....................			10,230		(1) 54		1,023	9,261
Net income—brought forward......	25,000	9,000	5,230	227	240	1,800	523	36,920
Retained earnings, December 31, 1972—carried forward............	55,000	28,000	15,460	307	294	5,600	1,546	91,301
Balance Sheet:								
Debits:								
Investment in Y Company bonds....			5,000		(3) 5,000			-0-
Discount on bonds payable........		200			(1) 40			160
Credits:								
Discount on bond investment......			30	(1) 27				3
Bonds payable...................		20,000		(3) 5,000				15,000

[deduction]

are proportionally adjusted; where the eliminated amounts are based upon the parent company's fractional stock interest in the relevant affiliate, only the majority shareholders' interest is influenced by the elimination. In the latter case, the interest of minority shareholders is calculated on the basis of the recorded net income and retained earnings of the subsidiary affiliate. This variation also is reflected in the working paper extensions for un-amortized discounts on the intercompany bonds.

Definitional Calculations

For Cases 3 and 4, consolidated net income may be confirmed by definition in the following manner:

	1971
X Company's confirmed net income..............................	$30,000
Increased by equity in confirmed 1971 net incomes of subsidiaries:	
Y Company—80% of ($19,000 − $150 + $50)...................	15,120
Z Company—90% of ($10,230 + $90 − $30)...................	9,261
Consolidated net income.......................................	$54,381

	1972
X Company's confirmed net income..............................	$25,000
Increased by equity in confirmed 1972 net incomes of subsidiaries:	
Y Company—80% of ($9,000 + $50)...........................	7,240
Z Company—90% of ($5,230 − $30)...........................	4,680
Consolidated net income.......................................	$36,920

The above calculations emphasize that consolidated net income is calcu-lated on the basis of the parent company's equity in the subsidiary's net income confirmed (or realized) in transactions with nonaffiliate interests. If a discount or premium on intercompany bonds is applicable to the parent company, the parent company's reported net income must be adjusted in a similar manner in calculating its confirmed net income.

Consolidated retained earnings as of December 31, 1972, may also be verified by definition:

X Company's retained earnings, December 31, 1972.................	$55,000
Increased by equity in confirmed postacquisition, cumulative net in-comes of subsidiaries:	
Y Company—80% of ($28,000 − $50).........................	22,360
Z Company—90% of ($15,460 + $30).........................	13,941
Consolidated retained earnings, December 31, 1972.................	$91,301

In this calculation, the cumulative earnings of the subsidiaries since ac-quisition are adjusted for the *net* confirmed profit (loss) that has not yet been recognized in the accounts through the amortization of discount or premium.

Interim Purchase of an Affiliate Company's Bonds

There are no conceptual differences introduced where intercompany bonds are purchased between interest dates. It is important, however, to give proper recognition to the amortization of discounts or premiums during the remaining months of the first interest period in the bond elimination schedule. Thereafter, the schedule of eliminations parallels a purchase on an interest date. For example, using the data of Case 3, assume that Z Company purchased $5,000 of Y Company's bonds on April 1, 1971, for $4,917.50 plus accrued interest of $50. This price assumes the same discount rate as before, 2¾ years before maturity.

Illustration 13–13 is a partial schedule of eliminations relating to the postacquisition period ended December 31, 1971.

PREFERRED STOCK

In the event a subsidiary affiliate has both common and preferred stock outstanding, its accumulated earnings must be apportioned between each class of stock before the preparation of consolidated financial statements can begin. It is important first to identify the amount of subsidiary retained earnings at the date of acquisition accruing to each class of stock; this allocation is used in calculating the amounts of the several elements of the investment elimination schedule. Thereafter, the postacquisition subsidiary earnings must be apportioned between the common and preferred shares in the calculation of majority and minority interests therein.

Allocation of Earnings

The process of earnings apportionment necessarily depends upon the specific preferences which attach to the preferred shares. Since these features are discussed and illustrated in detail in *Intermediate Accounting* in this series, they will be accorded only summary treatment here.

1. Where the preferred stock is nonparticipating and noncumulative, the accumulated subsidiary retained earnings relate totally to the common shares. Once dividends have been declared, the first distribution is made to preferred stockholders according to the designated preference rate; following this distribution, any residual amount is disbursed to common shareholders.

2. In the event that the preferred stock is nonparticipating but cumulative, only that portion of retained earnings which is equal to any arrearage in dividends on preferred stock is allocated to preferred shares; the remainder relates to common shares. Case 5 illustrates the preparation of consolidated statements in which the subsidiary's preferred stock is cumulative and nonparticipating.

3. Where preferred stock is noncumulative, or cumulative without arrearage in dividends, *and* fully participating, subsidiary retained earnings appertain ratably to common and preferred shares.

4. In the event that preferred stock is cumulative with dividends in arrears *and* also fully participating, the amount of retained earnings which

Illustration 13–13

BOND ELIMINATION SCHEDULE

Dr. [Cr.]

| | *Balance Sheet* | | *Income Statement* | | |
	Discount on Bonds Payable —Y Company	Discount on Bond Investment —Z Company	Loss on the Purchase of Intercompany Bonds	Interest Expense	Interest Income
Balances on 4/1/71..........	137.50	[82.50]			
Elimination at acquisition.........	[137.50]	82.50	55.00		
Amortization in 1971.........	[37.50]	22.50		[37.50]	22.50
Elimination as of 12/31/71.........	[100.00]	60.00	55.00		

Note: An extension of the above partial schedule through December 31, 1973, would duplicate the schedular details of Illustration 13–7.

are equal to any arrearage in dividends are first allocated to preferred shares, after which the remainder is ratably apportioned to common and preferred shares. Case 6 illustrates the preparation of consolidated statements where the preferred stock has these features.

Treatment in Consolidated Statements

Case 5. On January 1, 1969, X Company purchased 90 percent of the common stock of Y Company for $130,000, and 30 percent of its cumulative, nonparticipating, 6 percent preferred stock for $15,000. A summary of changes in retained earnings for each company for the two-year period ended December 31, 1970, is given as follows:

	X Company	Y Company
Retained earnings, January 1, 1969	$ 60,000	$ 40,000
Net income, 1969–70	80,000	60,000
Dividends declared, 1969–70	[30,000]	
Retained earnings, December 31, 1970	$110,000	$100,000

The December 31, 1971, trial balances of the affiliates follow:

	X Company		Y Company	
Investment in Y Company:				
Common stock	$130,000			
Preferred stock	15,000			
Other assets	203,300		$267,000	
Capital stock:				
Common stock (par, $100)		$200,000		$100,000
Preferred stock (par, $100)				50,000
Retained earnings		110,000		100,000
Dividends declared:				
Common stock			4,000	
6% preferred stock			9,000	
Sales		80,000		72,000
Dividend income—common		3,600		
Dividend income—preferred		2,700		
Costs of goods sold	42,000		31,000	
Expenses	6,000		11,000	
	$396,300	$396,300	$322,000	$322,000

There is no indication of an arrearage of dividends on preferred stock on January 1, 1969; accordingly, it is unnecessary to allocate an amount of Y Company's retained earnings to these shares. Then the investment elimination schedule takes the following form:

Investment Elimination Schedule
Dr. [Cr.]

	Common Stock	Preferred Stock	Total
Common stock..................	$ 90,000		$ 90,000
Preferred stock...................		$ 15,000	15,000
Retained earnings...............	36,000		36,000
Differential.....................	4,000		4,000
Investment.....................	$[130,000]	$[15,000]	$[145,000]

The 1971 consolidated statement working paper for this case is shown in Illustration 13–14.

If the preferred shares are cumulative and nonparticipating, it is necessary to apportion the subsidiary's net income for the current period between the common and preferred shares outstanding. The net income which relates to the preferred shares is based upon the preference rate for the year and is regarded as a deduction from the total subsidiary net income in calculating the minority interest of common shareholders. It is also necessary to calculate the minority interest in the January 1 retained earnings of the subsidiary giving appropriate effect to the arrearage in dividends then existing on the preferred shares. In the event that the preferred shares are noncumulative, it is unnecessary to make the allocation of net income except to the extent of dividends actually *paid* to preferred shareholders. Intercompany dividends are eliminated, and minority interests therein are extended both in the income statement and retained earnings statement divisions of the working paper and accordingly offset.

Case 6. On January 1, 1971, X Company acquired 90 percent of the common stock of Y Company for $62,000, and 30 percent of its 6 percent cumulative, fully participating preferred stock for $8,400. On this date preferred dividends were two years in arrears.

The trial balances of companies X and Y on December 31, 1971, are:

	⎯X Company⎯		⎯Y Company⎯	
Investment in Y Company:				
Common stock..................	$ 62,000			
Preferred stock.................	8,400			
Other assets.....................	118,350		$107,500	
Liabilities......................		$ 12,600		$ 2,000
Capital stock:				
Common stock (par, $100)........		100,000		50,000
6% preferred stock (par, $100).....				25,000
Retained earnings................		40,000		20,000
Dividends declared:				
Common stock...................			5,000	
Preferred stock.................			5,500	
Sales...........................		88,000		44,000
Cost of goods sold...............	53,000		17,000	
Expenses.......................	5,000		6,000	
Dividend income:				
Common stock...................		4,500		
Preferred stock.................		1,650		
	$246,750	$246,750	$141,000	$141,000

The investment elimination schedule follows:

Investment Elimination Schedule
Dr. [Cr.]

	Common Stock	Preferred Stock	Total
Common stock....................	$ 45,000		$ 45,000
Preferred stock.................		$ 7,500	7,500
Retained earnings...............	10,200	2,600	12,800
Differential....................	6,800	[1,700]	5,100
Investment.....................	$[62,000]	$[8,400]	$[70,400]

The consolidated working paper for Case 6 is presented in Illustration 13–15.

In Illustration 13–15, the apportionment of subsidiary retained earnings at date of acquisition is made $11,333 to common stock and $8,667 to preferred stock (arrearage for two years at 6 percent on $25,000, and one third of residual retained earnings, $17,000). Accordingly, the retained earnings elimination for common stock is $10,200 (90 percent of $11,333); the elimination of retained earnings in respect to preferred stock is $2,600 (30 percent of $8,667).

Dividends in Arrears at Acquisition—An Analysis

There is no evident consensus among accountants concerning the disposition of arrearage in dividends on preferred shares at acquisition. In Illustration 13–15, it may be noted that the receipt of dividends, which were in arrears at acquisition, are treated as income to the investing company upon receipt. This accords generally with a prevailing investment practice, which presumes that passed cumulative dividends are often heavily

Illustration 13–14

X COMPANY AND SUBSIDIARY Y COMPANY
Consolidated Statement Working Paper for Year Ended December 31, 1971

	X Company	Y Company	Eliminations Dr.	Eliminations Cr.	Minority Interest	Consolidated
Income Statement:						
Sales	80,000	72,000				152,000
Dividend income—common	3,600		(3) 3,600			
Dividend income—preferred	2,700		(4) 2,700			
Total credits	86,300	72,000				152,000
Cost of goods sold	42,000	31,000				73,000
Expenses	6,000	11,000				17,000
Total debits	48,000	42,000				90,000
	38,300	30,000				62,000
Minority interest:						
Common stock—10% of ($30,000 − $3,000)					2,700	[2,700]
Preferred stock—70% of ($3,000)					2,100	[2,100]
Net income—carried forward	38,300	30,000	6,300	–0–	4,800	57,200
Retained Earnings Statement:						
Retained earnings, January 1, 1971:						
X Company	110,000					110,000
Y Company		100,000	(1) 36,000		*9,400 †4,200	50,400
Net income—brought forward	38,300	30,000	6,300	–0–	4,800	57,200
	148,300	130,000			18,400	217,600
Dividends declared:						
Y Company—common		[4,000]		(3) 3,600	[400]	
Y Company—preferred		[9,000]		(4) 2,700	[6,300]	
Retained earnings, December 31, 1971—carried forward	148,300	117,000	42,300	6,300	11,700	217,600
Balance Sheet:						
Investment in Y Company:						
Common stock	130,000			(1) 130,000		–0–
Preferred stock	15,000			(2) 15,000		–0–
Other assets	203,300	267,000				470,300
Differential			(1) 4,000			4,000
	348,300	267,000				474,300
Capital stock:						
X Company—common stock	200,000					200,000
Y Company—common stock		100,000	(1) 90,000		10,000	
Y Company—preferred stock		50,000	(2) 15,000		35,000	
Retained earnings—brought forward	148,300	117,000	42,300	6,300	11,700	217,600
Minority interest					56,700	56,700 M
	348,300	267,000	151,300	151,300	56,700	474,300

* 10 percent of ($100,000 − $6,000).
† 70 percent of ($6,000).
[deduction]

Illustration 13-15

X COMPANY AND SUBSIDIARY Y COMPANY
Consolidated Statement Working Paper for Year Ended December 31, 1971

	X Company	Y Company	Eliminations Dr.	Eliminations Cr.	Minority Interest	Consolidated
Income Statement:						
Sales	88,000	44,000				132,000
Dividend income—common	4,500		(3) 4,500			
Dividend income—preferred	1,650		(4) 1,650			
Total credits	94,150	44,000				132,000
Cost of goods sold	53,000	17,000				70,000
Expenses	5,000	6,000				11,000
Total debits	58,000	23,000				81,000
	36,150	21,000				51,000
Minority interest:						
Common stock (10% of ⅔ of $21,000)					1,400	[1,400]
Preferred stock (70% of ⅓ of $21,000)					4,900	[4,900]
Net income—carried forward	36,150	21,000	6,150	–0–	6,300	44,700
Retained Earnings Statement:						
Retained earnings—January 1, 1971:						
X Company	40,000					40,000
Y Company		20,000	(1) 10,200 (2) 2,600		*1,133 †6,067	
Net income—brought forward	36,150	21,000	6,150		6,300	44,700
	76,150	41,000			13,500	84,700
Dividends declared—Y Company:						
Common		[5,000]		(3) 4,500	[500]	–0–
Preferred		[5,500]		(4) 1,650	[3,850]	–0–
Retained earnings, December 31, 1971—carried forward	76,150	30,500	18,950	6,150	9,150	84,700
Balance Sheet:						
Investment in Y Company:						
Common	62,000			(1) 62,000		
Preferred	8,400			(2) 8,400		
Other assets	118,350	107,500				225,850
Differential			(1) 6,800	(2) 1,700		5,100
	188,750	107,500				230,950
Liabilities	12,600	2,000				14,600
Common stock:						
X Company	100,000					100,000
Y Company		50,000	(1) 45,000		5,000	
Preferred stock:						
Y Company		25,000	(2) 7,500		17,500	
Retained earnings—brought forward	76,150	30,500	18,950	6,150	9,150	84,700
Minority interest					31,650	31,650 M
	188,750	107,500	78,250	78,250	31,650	230,950

* 10 percent of $11,333.   † 70 percent of $8,667.
‡ 10 percent of (⅔ of $30,500).   70% of (⅓ of $30,500).

discounted by corporate investors. In the event of such discounting, it is doubtful if any retained earnings of the subsidiary at date of acquisition should be allocated to preferred shares. Yet, it is evident that the cost of preferred stock anticipates this arrearage and is based thereupon, then the subsequent receipt should be treated necessarily as a liquidating dividend. In Case 6, if the evidence should support this latter position, $900 (30 percent of $3,000) of the subsidiary's preferred stock dividend payment would relate to the arrearage at acquisition; consequently, it would be recorded as a liquidating dividend, and the investment elimination schedule would be amended as follows:

Investment Elimination Schedule
Dr. [Cr.]

	Common Stock	Preferred Stock			Total
		At Acquisition	Adjustment	As Adjusted	
Common stock............	$ 45,000				$ 45,000
Preferred stock...........		$ 7,500		$ 7,500	7,500
Retained earnings.........	10,200	2,600		2,600	12,800
Dividends declared........			$[900]	[900]	[900
Differential..............	6,800	[1,700]		[1,700]	5,100]
Investment..............	$[62,000]	$[8,400]	$ 900	$[7,500]	$[69,500]

It is significant to note that the consolidated account balances remain unaffected by the choice of a method of accounting for the cumulative arrearage in dividends at acquisition. If the election is made to record the receipt as dividend income, whether or not retained earnings at acquisition are allocated, such dividends are eliminated thereafter as intercompany dividends, and do not enter the calculation of consolidated net income and consolidated retained earnings. If the receipt is regarded as a liquidating dividend, the investment account is reduced accordingly as well as the dividends declared element in the investment elimination schedule. As before, consolidated net income and consolidated retained earnings are unaffected by the dividend receipt.

Definitional Calculations

Consolidated net income in Case 6 may be confirmed by definition as follows:

X Company's 1971 net income (exclusive of subsidiary dividends)......	$30,000
Increased by:	
90 percent of Y Company's 1971 net income allocable to common stock (90% of ⅔ of $21,000)..................................	12,600
30 percent of Y Company's 1971 net income allocable to preferred stock (30% of ⅓ of $21,000)..................................	2,100
Consolidated net income for 1971..............................	$44,700

Similarly, consolidated retained earnings may be independently calculated:

X Company's retained earnings, December 31, 1971 (exclusive of post-acquisition subsidiary dividends)...............................	$70,000
Increased by:	
90 percent of Y Company's postacquisition net income allocable to common stock (90% of ⅔ of $21,000).........................	12,600
30 percent of Y Company's postacquisition net income allocable to preferred stock (30% of ⅓ of $21,000).........................	2,100
Consolidated retained earnings as of December 31, 1971..............	$84,700

QUESTIONS

1. To what extent does the purchase by one affiliate of the bonds of another affiliate parallel the acquisition and retirement by one company of all (or part) of its own outstanding bonds payable?

2. Explain the nature of the "gain or loss" on the acquisition of intercompany bonds. How is this amount determined? To what extent should it be allocated between the participating affiliates?

3. Indicate what the arguments are for assigning the total gain or loss on the purchase of intercompany bonds to the issuing company. To the purchasing company.

4. In respect to intercompany bonds the recorded amortizations of premiums and discounts on the books of the relevant affiliates are eliminated on consolidated statement working papers to avoid "double recognition." Explain this concept of double recognition and indicate why an elimination is necessary.

5. In regard to the elimination of profit on interaffiliate sales of depreciable assets, the effect of the elimination entries is to defer the profit recorded by the selling affiliate and formally recognize it over the remaining life of the relevant assets. Compare this profit *deferral* with the accounting consequence produced by elimination entries for interaffiliate bond holdings.

6. What complexity is introduced in the elimination process if an affiliate's bonds are purchased between interest dates?

7. Describe the accounting problems associated with the elimination process as a result of the subsidiary's having both common and preferred stock outstanding.

8. Assume that a subsidiary has both common and preferred stock outstanding and the preferred stock is noncumulative and nonparticipating. On what basis should the retained earnings of the subsidiary be allocated between preferred and common shares for the purpose of preparing an investment elimination schedule? How would your answer differ if the preferred stock were cumulative, in arrears, and fully participating?

9. What choices are available to the accountant concerning the disposition of dividends in arrears at the date a parent acquires the preferred and common stock of a subsidiary? What is the effect of each election upon the investment elimination schedule?

PROBLEMS

Problem 13–1

On January 1, 1965, A Company issued $100,000 of 5 percent, 10-year bonds at 105. On January 1, 1973, B Company, a 90 percent owned subsidiary, acquired $50,000 of these bonds at 102.

Required:

Prepare the eliminating entries for consolidated statement working papers on December 31, 1973, and December 31, 1974—

(i) Assuming the elimination of premium and/or discount on intercompany bonds is based upon the parent company's interest in the relevant affiliate.

(ii) Assuming 100 percent elimination of premium and/or discount.

Problem 13–2

The following data relate to the Boston Corporation and its 90 percent owned subsidiary, the Ludwig Corporation, immediately after the subsidiary acquired $2,000 of the parent company's outstanding bonds at a cost of $1,800.

	January 1, 1971	
Accounts	*Boston Corporation* Dr. [Cr.]	*Ludwig Corporation* Dr. [Cr.]
5 percent bonds payable, due on December 31, 1974....................................	$[10,000]	
Discount on bonds payable.....................	500	
Investment in Boston Corporation bonds.........		$ 2,000
Discount on bond investment..................		[200]
Net income (excluding the effects of interest) for 1971 and 1972.........................	20,000	10,000

Required:

If 100 percent of the unamortized discount on intercompany bonds is to be eliminated for consolidated statement working papers on December 31, 1971, and 1972—

(i) Journalize all eliminations in respect to the intercompany bonds.

(ii) Calculate the minority interest in subsidiary net income.

Problem 13–3

Weber Company owns 90 percent of Schwab, Inc.'s outstanding stock. On January 1, 1967, Schwab, Inc., issued 6 percent bonds, $100,000 par value, due January 1, 1977. The issue price was 103 (percent of par). Weber Company purchased $25,000 (par value) of these bonds on January 1, 1971, at 101.8 percent of par. Interest is payable twice each year on January 1 and July 1. Weber uses the 100 percent elimination method in preparing consolidated statements.

Required:

(i) Journalize all elimination entries relating to Weber's ownership of Schwab's bonds for consolidated working papers prepared on—
   (a) December 31, 1971.
   (b) December 31, 1972.
(ii) Assume that Schwab, Inc.'s 1971 net income was $20,000, excluding the deduction for interest expense. Compute the minority interest's 1971 income.

Problem 13–4

On July 1, 1970, A Company purchased $100,000 of B Company's 6 percent bonds in the open market at 111½ and accrued interest. These bonds are part of an original issue of $1,000,000 bonds sold on January 1, 1962, at 105. The bonds mature on January 1, 1982. Periodic amortization has been properly recorded by each company on December 31.

Required:

If A Company owns a 90 percent interest in the capital stock of B Company, prepare journal entries for consolidated statement working papers for the year ended December 31, 1971:

(i) If the unamortized premium on intercompany bonds is 100 percent eliminated.
(ii) If the amount of the premium elimination is based upon the parent company's equity in the subsidiary.
(iii) In (ii) above, what eliminating entries are required in respect to intercompany bonds for a consolidated balance sheet only?

Problem 13–5

On January 1, 1971, the Royal Company owns 90 percent of the capital stock of the Kopi Company and 70 percent of the capital stock of the Oslo Company. On January 1, 1965, the Kopi Company issued $100,000 of 4 percent, 10-year bonds to nonaffiliates at 96. On January 1, 1971, the Oslo Company acquired $60,000 of these bonds at 103.

The following data relate to the period January 1, 1971, through December 31, 1972:

	Royal Company	Kopi Company	Oslo Company
Retained earnings (1/1/71)........	$415,000	$283,000	$196,000
Net income (exclusive of interest on bonds):			
1971........................	100,000	50,000	60,000
1972........................	85,000	45,000	38,000

Required:

(i) Prepare eliminating entries in respect to intercompany bonds for inclusion on consolidated statement working papers for years ended December 31,

1971, 1972, 1973, and 1974; the elimination of discount/premium on intercompany bonds is based upon the parent company's fractional interest in the relevant affiliate.

(ii) Prepare partial consolidated statement working papers for the years ended December 31, 1971, and 1972.

Problem 13–6

The Burnett Company has a controlling interest in the Allison Corporation, having acquired 80 percent of its capital stock in 1965. On January 1, 1971, the Allison Corporation had outstanding an issue of $30,000 of 4 percent bonds payable, interest January 1 and July 1, the unamortized discount on which was $900, due January 1, 1974.

On May 1, 1971, the Burnett Company acquired $7,500 of these bonds at 101.6 and accrued interest. The 1971 net incomes of the affiliates, exclusive of interest, were:

Burnett Company........................ $40,000
Allison Corporation..................... 20,000

Required:

(i) Prepare a schedule of eliminating entries in respect to intercompany bonds, assuming the amounts of eliminations are based upon the parent company's equity in the subsidiary affiliate.

(ii) Prepare a consolidated income statement working paper for the year ended December 31, 1971.

Problem 13–7

On January 1, 1971, X Company acquired 800 shares of Y Company's common stock for $17,000 and 180 shares of its 5 percent cumulative, nonparticipating preferred stock for $23,000. On this date the proprietary accounts of Y Company were:

Common stock ($10 par value)................... $10,000
Preferred stock ($100 par value)................. 20,000
Retained earnings............................. 12,000

On January 1, 1971, there were two years' dividends in arrears on preferred stock.

During 1971, Y Company reported earnings of $10,000 and paid $9,000 in dividends; X Company earned $10,000, exclusive of dividend income.

Required:

(i) Prepare an investment elimination schedule on January 1, 1971.

(ii) Calculate 1971 consolidated net income and the minority interest in subsidiary net income; prepare an investment elimination schedule for December 31, 1971, consolidated statement working papers.

(iii) If the preferred stock had been cumulative and participating, calculate the consolidated net income for 1971 and the minority interest in the subsidiary's net income; prepare an investment elimination schedule for December 31, 1971, working papers.

Problem 13–8
Part A

The P Corporation bought from its wholly owned subsidiary for $16,000 certain equipment which was carried on the books of the subsidiary at a cost of $31,000 with accumulated depreciation of $17,000.

Required:

State the effect on the consolidated balance sheet of the purchase of equipment from the subsidiary. State specifically what eliminating entries, if any, should be made on the consolidated work paper used for preparation of the consolidated financial statements.

Part B

On January 1, 1967, the S Corporation issued $200,000 of 10-year 4 percent bonds. These were sold at 98, and expenses of issue were $2,400. Interest is payable January 1 and July 1.

In March, 1970, the P Corporation acquired 80 percent of the outstanding stock of S Corporation. On March 31, 1971, the P Corporation purchased on the open market $100,000 face value of S Corporation's 4 percent bonds at 90 and accrued interest.

Required:

State what eliminating entries should be made as a result of the bond transactions on the consolidated work papers used for preparation of the consolidated statements at December 31, 1971, and December 31, 1972 (assume 100 percent elimination).

(AICPA adapted)

Problem 13–9

| | Balances, December 31, 1971 | | | |
| | P Company | | S Company | |
	Debit	Credit	Debit	Credit
Cash...........................	$ 23,000		$ 30,000	
Accounts receivable..............	94,000		60,000	
Inventory, 1/1/71—cost...........	105,000		51,000	
Investment in stock of S...........	175,000			
Investment in bonds of S..........	51,800			
Other assets...................	445,000		210,000	
Current liabilities.................		$ 163,000		$ 17,100
Bonds payable—5 percent.........				200,000
Deferred bond premium...........				5,400
Sales...........................		630,000		340,000
Purchases......................	485,000		300,000	
Operating expenses..............	92,000		70,000	
Other expenses..................	22,000		15,500	
Interest and dividends.............		12,800		
Dividends paid...................	20,000		10,000	
Retained earnings, 1/1/71.........		107,000		84,000
Common stock..................		600,000		100,000
	$1,512,800	$1,512,800	$746,500	$746,500

Additional Information

a)   The investment in stock of S Company represents a 90 percent interest which was acquired January 1, 1971, for $175,000. At the same time $50,000 face amount of bonds of S were acquired for $52,000. These bonds had been issued on January 1, 1961, at 106 and are due January 1, 1981. S Company has recorded the amortization of the bond premium applicable to 1971 as an adjustment of interest expense. The stock and the bonds were purchased in the open market.

b)   Included in the Purchases account of S Company is a total of $180,000 of goods bought from P Company at 120 percent of cost to P Company. The closing inventory of S Company is estimated to include the same proportion of these purchases as of other purchases.

c)   Inventories at December 31, 1971, at cost to each company, were:

P Company....$80,000
S Company.... 45,000

Required:

Prepare the income statement section of the three division working paper for the year ended December 31, 1971. Use the 100 percent elimination method.

(AICPA adapted)

Problem 13–10

Four years ago The American Company acquired 50 percent of the preferred stock of the Banner Corporation for $55,000 and 90 percent of that corporation's common stock for $195,000. At acquisition date the Banner Corporation had retained earnings of $60,000, and dividends on the 5 percent, cumulative preferred stock were not in arrears. The investments were recorded by The American Company at the book value shown by the Banner Corporation at date of acquisition.

Consolidated statements are now being prepared as of December 31, 1972, for The American Company and its subsidiary. The financial position of the individual companies was as follows on that date:

THE AMERICAN COMPANY

Miscellaneous assets..........	$116,000	Liabilities...................	$ 50,000
Investments:		Preferred stock (4 percent).....	100,000
Banner preferred..........	50,000	Common stock.............	100,000
Banner common..........	234,000	Retained earnings...........	150,000
	$400,000		$400,000

BANNER CORPORATION

Miscellaneous assets..........	$400,000	Liabilities...................	$ 60,000
		Preferred stock (5 percent)*....	100,000
		Common stock..............	200,000
		Retained earnings...........	40,000
	$400,000		$400,000

* Preferred stock dividends are three years in arrears. No dividends have been paid on common since acquisition by The American Company. Profit in 1969 was $8,000, but losses during the past three years have totaled $23,000.

Required:

(i)   Prepare an investment elimination schedule on December 31, 1972.

(ii) Prepare a consolidated balance sheet as of December 31, 1972, in which all significant details given in the above information are fully disclosed.

(AICPA adapted)

Problem 13–11

Following are trial balances of A Company and its subsidiary, B Company, at December 31, 1971.

Debits	*A Company*	*B Company*
Cash..	$ 545,200	$ 267,300
Receivables, customers...........................	187,000	375,400
U.S. government bonds...........................	1,575,300	556,000
Inventories......................................	398,200	146,800
Investment, B Company:		
Bonds.......................................	198,000	
Capital stock.................................	300,000	
Advances....................................	226,600	
Investment, A Company bonds (at par).............		30,000
Fixed assets....................................	2,311,000	714,700
Unamortized bond discount......................		2,700
Goodwill.......................................		90,000
Cost of sales...................................	3,280,500	1,676,100
Selling and administrative expense.................	333,000	261,000
Depreciation expense............................	184,000	42,600
Interest expense................................	24,000	19,700
Bond discount amortized.........................		300
Amortization of premium on B Company bonds		
owned.......................................	2,000	
Provision for income taxes.......................	600,000	420,000
Dividends paid.................................	100,000	20,000
	$10,264,800	$4,622,600

Credits	*A Company*	*B Company*
Accounts payable...............................	$ 79,200	$ 69,500
Accrued income taxes............................	624,800	431,400
Other accrued expenses..........................	10,000	4,000
Advances from A................................		226,600
Allowance for bad debts.........................	2,500	3,200
Accumulated depreciation........................	1,420,600	302,300
Reserve for contingencies........................	1,000,000	445,000
First-mortgage 3 percent bonds...................	800,000	
First-mortgage 4 percent bonds...................		200,000
Capital stock...................................	1,000,000	200,000
Other contributed capital........................	50,200	
Retained earnings, 12/31/70......................	424,700	90,200
Sales..	4,797,300	2,644,500
Interest—U.S. government bonds...................	20,400	5,000
—intercompany bonds.....................	7,200	900
—advances to B.........................	11,700	
Dividends received..............................	16,200	
	$10,264,800	$4,622,600

A Company on January 1, 1963, purchased from security holders its 81 percent interest in the capital stock of B Company and 90 percent interest in B

Company bonds, the total consideration being $516,000 of which $216,000 was allocated to the bonds. The purpose of the purchase was to obtain additional manufacturing facilities and B Company's established markets for products similar to A Company's regular line. The retained earnings of B Company as shown by its books on December 31, 1962, was $100,000. B Company's reserve for contingencies on this date was $50,000. The 25-year first-mortgage 4 percent bonds had been originally marketed on December 31, 1955, to net 96¼.

For several years a part of the output of B Company has been an intermediate product sold to A Company at a uniform markup of 20 percent (on sales). Sales of this character recorded on B Company's books were $258,000 for 1971, of which $64,500 remained in A Company's inventory at the end of the year; the corresponding amount in A Company's inventory at the beginning of the year was $82,000.

A Company constructed a building, at a cost of $100,000, which, on January 1, 1966, was turned over to B Company for its use at a price of $120,000. Depreciation of 3 percent annually has been accrued thereon since that date.

Required:

Prepare a consolidated statement working paper for the period ended December 31, 1971. (Assume fractional elimination in respect to intercompany profit and unamortized discount on intercompany bonds.)

(AICPA adapted)

Chapter 14

Consolidated Statements—Changes in Parent Company's Equity

Interim Purchase

Attention has thus far focused on the preparation of consolidated statements where the date of acquisition of subsidiary shares and the beginning of the subsidiary's accounting period are the same. Unfortunately, the accounting convenience provided by this coincidence of dates occurs infrequently. Since an affiliate's shares are perhaps more often acquired at interim dates, it becomes important to estimate the subsidiary affiliate's net income during that portion of the current period prior to acquisition in order to establish the book value of the acquired shares.[1] The amount of the subsidiary's net income for the fractional period before acquisition of its share by a parent company is especially important to the preparation of a consolidated income statement; however, its effects must also be dealt with in the consolidated retained earnings statement and the consolidated balance sheet.

The preparation of a consolidated income statement for an affiliation normally presumes a complete accounting period for both parent and subsidiary companies. Subsidiary net income previous to acquisition is either eliminated (as a part of purchased retained earnings) or is identified with the remaining minority shareholders; the postacquisition subsidiary earnings are allocable to majority and minority shareholders on the basis of their relative equities at the end of the accounting period. Accordingly, only the parent company's equity in the postacquisition earnings of the subsidiary is a determinant in calculating consolidated net income.

Case 1. Interim Purchase of Subsidiary Shares. To illustrate the effect on the consolidated income statement of an interim purchase of subsidiary shares, assume the following revenue and expense data for companies X and Y for the year ended December 31, 1971:

---

[1] For reasons of pedagogical simplicity, the discussion of this chapter assumes that corporate acquisitions are being accounted for in accordance with the purchase method. Adaptations to conform with the pooling of interests method are left for the reader's exercise.

	X Company	Y Company
Sales....................................	$50,000	$30,000
Cost of goods sold.....................	$20,000	$10,000
Expenses..............................	10,000	8,000
Total costs and expenses................	$30,000	$18,000
Net income............................	$20,000	$12,000

It is assumed that X Company acquired 90 percent of the capital stock of Y Company on April 1, 1971, for $66,000. On January 1, 1971, Y Company had outstanding capital stock of $50,000 and retained earnings of $20,000.

The investment elimination schedule follows:

Investment Elimination Schedule

	Dr. [Cr.]
Capital stock..........................	$ 45,000
Retained earnings (1/1).................	18,000
Net income............................	* 2,700
Differential...........................	300
Investment............................	$[66,000]

* 90 percent of ¼ of $12,000.

The purchased subsidiary net income is entered in the schedule, as is the parent's purchased equity in the other stockholders' equity accounts of the subsidiary. The amount of the net income elimination presumes that the subsidiary's net income is earned uniformly throughout the year; where there is evidence of pronounced seasonality, however, appropriate emphasis should be given to periods of peak activity. Whatever the basis used, an appropriate allocation of subsidiary net income must be made to the fractional parts of the current accounting period *before* and *after* acquisition of its shares by the parent company.

In respect to consolidated statement working papers in years subsequent to the period of acquisition, the purchased net income of the subsidiary at acquisition is reflected by a corresponding increase in the amount of the retained earnings element in the investment elimination schedule. In the present example, the retained earnings elimination for the 1972 consolidated statement working paper and those for all subsequent years will be $20,700 ($18,000 + $2,700). This treatment parallels that accorded stock dividends and liquidating dividends described earlier, in which the amount of the dividends declared in the investment elimination schedule in the year of acquisition is algebraically added to the amount of the retained earnings elimination in subsequent years' schedules.

In the event that dividends are declared in the year of acquisition *prior* to the purchase of subsidiary shares, it is also appropriate to recognize this reduction in the book value of the subsidiary's capital stock as a negative element. For example, in the previous investment elimination schedule, if cash dividends of $5,000 had been paid on March 1, 1971, the schedule would have been modified as follows:

Investment Elimination Schedule

	Dr. [Cr.]
Capital stock.........................	$ 45,000
Retained earnings.....................	18,000
Net income...........................	2,700
Dividends declared....................	* [4,500]
Differential..........................	4,800
Investment...........................	$[66,000]

* 90 percent of $5,000.

It is important that the book value of subsidiary shares at acquisition be precisely determined. In the case of interim stock acquisitions by a parent corporation, the book value of undistributed earnings requires special analysis; this value is the algebraic sum of the retained earnings of the subsidiary at the beginning of the year, the estimated net income for the fractional part of the current year previous to the date of purchase, and the dividends declared during the same interval. In the investment elimination schedule for subsequent years' consolidated statement working papers, these elements will appear as one amount in the elimination of retained earnings; using the data of the previous investment elimination schedule, the retained earnings elimination would be $16,200 ($18,000 + $2,700 − $4,500).

The treatment of purchased subsidiary net income in a consolidated income statement working paper is shown in Illustration 14–1. The data are those of Case 1.

It should be observed that the working paper extension for the purchased net income of a subsidiary parallels that for minority interest in subsidiary net income. Since the preacquisition net income of the subsidiary during the period of acquisition is either eliminated or is ascribed to the remaining minority shareholders, only the subsidiary's postacquisition net income for the fractional period remaining is a determinant of consolidated net income. Also, it is apparent that the equity of minority shareholders is calculated on the basis of their year-end fractional interest. The amount of minority interest in subsidiary net income may be confirmed, however, by considering the different equities of the minority shareholders for the periods of time *before* and *after* the purchase of subsidiary shares. In Illustration 14–1, the amount of minority interest in subsidiary net income might thus be calculated:

First 3 months: 100% of ¼ of $12,000................................	$3,000
Last 9 months: 10% of ¾ of $12,000................................	900
	$3,900
Subsidiary net income purchased by majority shareholders.................	2,700
Interest in net income accruing to year-end minority shareholders..........	$1,200

Illustration 14–1

X COMPANY AND SUBSIDIARY Y COMPANY

Consolidated Income Statement Working Paper

For Year Ended December 31, 1971

	X Company	Y Company	Eliminations Dr.	Eliminations Cr.	Minority Interest	Consolidated
Sales................	50,000	30,000				80,000
Cost of goods sold.....	20,000	10,000				30,000
Expenses.............	10,000	8,000				18,000
Total expenses........	30,000	18,000				48,000
Purchased net income...	20,000	12,000				32,000
Minority interest in Y Company net income— 10% of $12,000.			2,700		1,200	[2,700] [1,200]
Net income...........	20,000	12,000	2,700	–0–	1,200	28,100

The amount of consolidated net income is confirmed *by definition* as follows:

X Company's net income............	$20,000
Increased by:	
90 percent of Y Company's net income for the period April 1, 1971, through December 31, 1971 (90% of $9,000)........	8,100
Consolidated net income............	$28,100

[deduction]

Block Purchases of Subsidiary Stock

On some occasions, the controlling interest in a subsidiary company may be established by the first purchase of its shares; on other occasions, a succession of purchases are required by the parent company to effectuate control. Where blocks of stock are acquired at different dates, it is important to examine the cost of each block and relate it to the corresponding book value of the subsidiary shares at the date these shares are acquired. Although the preparation of consolidated statements necessarily must be deferred until majority ownership of subsidiary shares exists, it remains important to analyze the cost of each block separately and in terms of the relevant acquisition book value.

Accounting Research Bulletin No. 51 supported this position:

When one company purchases two or more blocks of stock of another company at various dates and eventually obtains control of the other company, the date of acquisition (for purposes of preparing consolidated statements) depends on the circumstances. If two or more purchases are made over a period of time, the earned surplus of the subsidiary at acquisition should generally be determined on a step-by-step basis.[2]

However, the bulletin continued:

. . . if small purchases are made over a period of time and then a purchase is made which results in control, the date of the latest purchase, *as a matter of convenience,* may be considered as the date of acquisition.[3]

The latter treatment results in the exclusion from consolidated retained earnings of undistributed subsidiary profit increments which accrue to the partial holdings prior to the establishment of control. This potential exclusion of subsidiary earnings can be defended only in terms of materiality or convenience. The authors reject it on theoretical grounds in favor of the individual block analysis, the details of which are described in the paragraphs which follow.[4]

It is also important to distinguish between blocks of shares purchased in the open market and those acquired *directly* from a subsidiary affiliate. In the former case, the transaction is one relating to the parent company and one or more shareholders of the subsidiary company. Because the transaction does not directly involve the subsidiary affiliate, the purchase does not produce a change in its accounts; this type of acquisition is here-

---

[2] Committee on Accounting Procedure, American Institute of Certified Public Accountants, *Accounting Research Bulletin No. 51* (1959), p. 44, in *Accounting Research and Terminology Bulletins,* Final Edition (New York, 1961).

[3] *Ibid.* (Emphasis supplied.)

[4] This position is also consistent with the elimination procedure described in Chapter 11 for multilevel affiliations in which a second-level subsidiary affiliate's shares are acquired by a first-level affiliate after which a controlling interest in the first-level subsidiary affiliate is established by a parent company.

after referred to as an "open-market" purchase. Where shares are acquired by the parent directly from an issuing subsidiary, it is necessary to consider the effects of the transaction on the subsidiary's accounts in calculating the change in the equity interest of the parent company. Each of these types of purchases is illustrated by the following two cases.

Open-Market Purchases of Subsidiary Shares

Case 2. Block Purchases in the Open Market. X Company acquired shares of Y Company's stock according to the following schedule:

Date	Number of Shares	Cost
January 1, 1971	200	$30,000
January 1, 1972	100	17,500
January 1, 1973	100	20,000

On January 1, 1971, Y Company had $50,000 of capital stock (par, $100) outstanding and retained earnings of $20,000. Annual profits for 1971, 1972, and 1973 are assumed to be $10,000 in each year.

The investment elimination schedule is as follows:

Investment Elimination Schedule
Dr. [Cr.]

	First Block	Second Block	Third Block	Total
Capital stock..................	$ 20,000	$ 10,000	$ 10,000	$ 40,000
Retained earnings.............	(1) 8,000	(2) 6,000	(3) 8,000	22,000
Differential....................	2,000	1,500	2,000	5,500
Investment....................	$[30,000]	$[17,500]	$[20,000]	$[67,500]

(1) 40 percent of $20,000.
(2) 20 percent of $30,000.
(3) 20 percent of $40,000.

It is usual for the parent company to carry the costs of the several blocks of subsidiary shares in a single investment account. Consequently, it is sufficient to make one summary elimination for the total investment; in this case, the elimination for periods subsequent to January 1, 1973, may be expressed in journal entry form as follows:

Capital stock...	40,000	
Retained earnings...	22,000	
Differential..	5,500	
Investment in Y Company stock......................		67,500

The completion of the consolidated statement working paper (after control is established on January 1, 1972) is not further complicated by the presence of costs of separate blocks of subsidiary shares in the parent's investment account. Minority interest calculations continue to require the multiplication of the end-of-period minority interest percentage times the reported subsidiary net income for the year or retained earnings balance (or contributed capital account balances) whatever the case may be.

Acquisition of Shares Directly from Subsidiary Affiliate

As indicated earlier, where subsidiary shares are issued directly to the parent, it is important to analyze the resultant changes in the subsidiary's stockholders' equity accounts and the effect on the parent corporation's equity therein. This analysis may be accomplished by calculating the parent's equity in the subsidiary's net worth[5] immediately before and immediately after the relevant issue of its stock. By isolating the effects of this single transaction, it follows that the change in the parent's equity is identifiable with the cost of the shares purchased. Consider the following illustrative examples of new issues of subsidiary stock made directly to the parent company.

Case 3. New Shares Totally Subscribed by the Parent. On January 1, 1971, Y Company had outstanding capital stock (par, $100), $10,000, and retained earnings, $5,000. Annual profits each year are assumed to be $10,000. On January 1, 1971, X Company purchased in the open market 60 shares of Y Company's stock for $12,000. One year later, X Company totally subscribed to a new issue of 100 subsidiary shares for $15,000.

The investment elimination schedule follows:

Investment Elimination Schedule
Dr. [Cr.]

	First Block	Increase in Equity Due to Second Block	Total
Capital stock...................	$ 6,000	$ 10,000	$ 16,000
Retained earnings................	3,000	3,000	6,000
Other contributed capital...........		4,000	4,000
Differential......................	3,000	[2,000]	1,000
Investment......................	$[12,000]	$[15,000]	$[27,000]

The elements of the eliminating entry for the second block are determined in the following manner:

---

[5] For clarity of expression, the term "net worth" is periodically used in reference to the aggregate valuation of a subsidiary's stockholders' equity accounts, notwithstanding the fact that this term is preferably not used in formal financial statements.

	Y Company's Net Worth		X Company's Equity in Y Company's Net Worth		
	Before Second Block	*After Second Block*	*Before Second Block (60%)*	*After Second Block (80%)*	*Increase [Decrease]*
Capital stock............	$10,000	$20,000	$6,000	$16,000	$10,000
Retained earnings........	15,000	15,000	9,000	12,000	3,000
Other contributed capital................	–0–	5,000	–0–	4,000	4,000

In the above schedule it may be noted that the increase in X Company's equity in Y Company's net worth is explained in terms of the increases in the separate elements as indicated. These *changes* are solely a consequence of the issuance of the second block of subsidiary shares, as the effect of this transaction has been isolated by the analysis; the changes are therefore appropriately posted to the investment elimination schedule as purchased net worth.

The perceptive reader will recognize that the amounts entered in the "increase in equity due to second block" column of the investment elimination schedule do not represent a completely precise analysis of the separate elements identified with the second block. Since the purchase of new shares of subsidiary stock necessarily alters the parent's equity percentage for the first block, there should follow an adjustment of the retained earnings and other contributed capital elements of the elimination for the first block, which adjustment carries forward to the corresponding elimination elements in respect to the second block. These refinements in block analyses are unnecessary, however, unless the directly purchased shares are subsequently sold by the parent company.[6]

Case 4. New Shares Subscribed Ratably by Majority and Minority Shareholders. The data for Case 3 are repeated here with the exception that the new issue of 100 shares on January 1, 1972, is subscribed ratably by both majority and minority shareholders at $150 per share.

The investment elimination schedule follows:

---

[6] See T. H. Williams and C. H. Griffin, "The Effect of Equity Rearrangements on Consolidated Statements," *The Illinois CPA,* Summer, 1965, pp. 47–53, for a more complete discussion of this type of analysis.

Investment Elimination Schedule
Dr. [Cr.]

	First Block	Increase in Equity Due to Second Block	Total
Capital stock......................	$ 6,000	$ 6,000	$ 12,000
Retained earnings..................	3,000		3,000
Other contributed capital.............		3,000	3,000
Differential........................	3,000		3,000
Investment........................	$[12,000]	$[9,000]	$[21,000]

An analysis of the effects of the second purchase discloses the following:

	Y Company's Net Worth		X Company's Equity in Y Company's Net Worth		
	Before Second Block	After Second Block	Before Second Block (60%)	After Second Block (60%)	Increase [Decrease]
Capital stock.............	$10,000	$20,000	$6,000	$12,000	$6,000
Retained earnings.........	15,000	15,000	9,000	9,000	–0–
Other contributed capital................	–0–	5,000	–0–	3,000	3,000

In the above example, the ratable issue of subsidiary shares preserves the preexisting interests of the various shareholder groups. Where this condition obtains *and* where the new issue price is equal to the current book value of subsidiary shares, there can be neither a differential nor a retained earnings element in respect to the elimination for the second block. Where a new issue is *not* proratably subscribed by present shareholders, there will exist an elimination of retained earnings for the second block of subsidiary shares; additionally, if the issue price is other than the book value of these shares, whether subscribed proratably or not, a differential will exist.

Sale of Subsidiary Shares

Sales of subsidiary shares are accounted for by the parent corporation essentially as are other disposals of its corporate assets. In the event that the investment account is carried on an equity basis, it will reflect the parent's equity in subsidiary gains and losses as a normal consequence of periodic journal adjustments; accordingly, gains and losses on the sale of subsidiary shares are assumed to reflect market price fluctuations for reasons other than undistributed earnings or accrued losses since acquisition. Where the investment is carried at cost, however, gains and losses from the sale of subsidiary shares consist of the parent company's unrecorded interest in undistributed subsidiary earnings or accrued losses since acquisition *as well as* fluctuations in the price of the securities attributed to economic and other factors.

In the preparation of consolidated financial statements where the cost method is used, the reported gain or loss on sale of subsidiary shares must be adjusted. Part of the gain or loss reflects the undistributed subsidiary earnings or accrued losses of prior (postacquisition) periods which relate to the sold shares. These earnings or losses have already been determinants of prior years' consolidated net incomes. Thus, it would constitute double counting if they were again allowed to affect the computation of consolidated net income in the form of gain or loss on the sale of subsidiary shares. Under the *equity* basis, such earnings or losses of prior periods would have been algebraically added to the carrying value of the investment in subsidiary stock with corresponding increases (or decreases) in the parent's retained earnings. As such, they would have been excluded from the parent's reported gain or loss on sale of subsidiary shares. Therefore, given the *cost* method, the reported gain or loss must be adjusted to eliminate therefrom the amount of undistributed subsidiary earnings or accrued losses of prior (postacquisition) periods which relate to the sold shares. To complete the eliminating entry, the account to be adjusted is parent retained earnings as of the beginning of the current period. This portion of the eliminating entry has the effect of maintaining a correct determination of consolidated retained earnings, since the extension of subsidiary retained earnings related to the sold shares will now be allocated to minority interest.

Having eliminated from the reported (cost basis) gain or loss on subsidiary shares sold that element which relates to prior periods' undistributed subsidiary earnings or losses, the residual gain or loss consists of two parts: the parent company's interest in subsidiary net income, derived from these shares, for the current period prior to the date of sale, *and* the increase or decrease in value resulting from market price fluctuations attributable to other factors. That part of the residual gain or loss which relates to subsidiary earnings of the current period *prior* to the date of sale should be reported as an operating net income inclusion, with the remainder described as "gain or loss." However, accountants may, for reasons of simplicity or materiality, regard all of the residual element as "gain or loss," believing the intraperiod classificational distinction relatively unimportant. If this practical expedient is followed, the increment to be added to the parent's net income in calculating consolidated net income is then calculated on the basis of those subsidiary shares *retained* to the terminal date of the consolidated statements.

Subsidiary cash dividends during the current period are distributed to majority and minority shareholders on the basis of the relevant equity ratios which prevail at the dates of dividend declaration. Accordingly, subsidiary profits for the current period in the amount of these dividends are regarded as confirmed on a consolidated basis, and thus are not subject to reclassification between majority and minority stockholders as a consequence of the parent's partial sale of subsidiary shares. It is therefore only with respect to the *undistributed* current subsidiary earnings that the reclassification referred to above is required.

Where the equity method is used, subsidiary profits—whether or not distributed as dividends—are allocated on the basis of the effective equity ratios which relate to the presale and postsale periods; subsidiary dividends received by the parent are credited to the investment account in the conventional manner. Consequently, for an equity-basis investment, the difference between the proceeds of sale and the carrying value of the investment is wholly attributable to price fluctuation and is properly reported as "gain or loss." Necessarily, the *net* effect on the parent company's retained earnings and consolidated retained earnings will be identical with that produced by the cost method of accounting.

Upon the disposal of a partial investment of subsidiary shares, it is important to identify the shares sold. The parent company may specify the individual shares conveyed, in which case the amount of the credit to the investment account and the adjustment to the investment elimination schedule is easily determined; in the event, however, that specific identification is not indicated, it is usual to adopt the first-in, first-out rule with respect to the shares sold.

Case 5. Sale of Partial Holdings of Subsidiary Stock. Using the data of Case 2 in this example, it is assumed that on July 1, 1973, X Company sold 100 shares of Y Company's stock, representing 20 percent of the outstanding shares, to nonaffiliate interests for $18,000. It is further assumed that these shares relate to the January 1, 1971, purchase. In the absence of specific identification, this block would otherwise have been selected by applying the first-in, first-out rule.

If the investment is carried at cost, the entry for the sale is recorded by X Company as follows:

Cash.. 18,000
    Investment in Y Company stock.......................   15,000
    Gain on sale of stock...............................   3,000

The adjusted investment elimination schedule takes the following form:

Investment Elimination Schedule
Dr. [Cr.]

| | First Block | | | | | |
	At Acquisition	Adjustment	At Consolidation	Second Block	Third Block	Total
Capital stock..........	$ 20,000	$[10,000]	$ 10,000	$ 10,000	$ 10,000	$ 30,000
Retained earnings......	8,000	[4,000]	4,000	6,000	8,000	18,000
Differential...........	2,000	[1,000]	1,000	1,500	2,000	4,500
Investment............	$[30,000]	$ 15,000	$[15,000]	$[17,500]	$[20,000]	$[52,500]

The effect of the transaction of sale is to reduce each of the elements of the appropriate block in the investment elimination schedule by a percentage (50 percent) representing the ratio of the shares being conveyed (100) to the total shares in the block before the sale (200). This applies to the differential as well as to other elements, since the differential is assumed to relate proratably to *all* shares in a given block of stock. An examination of the above schedule will disclose that only those shares *retained* by the parent are determinants in subsequent calculations in respect to the investment.

As indicated earlier, where the cost method is used, the gain on sale of subsidiary shares consists of both the parent's equity in undistributed subsidiary net income since acquisition to the date of sale *and* a trading gain or loss measuring market price fluctuations of these shares. Accordingly, in the present case, $4,000 (20 percent of $20,000) of subsidiary net income which accrues to the sold shares for the years 1971 and 1972 is properly regarded as an adjustment of the parent company's January 1, 1973, retained earnings balance, and $1,000 of the subsidiary's 1973 net income (20 percent of one half of $10,000) in respect to these shares is accordingly reclassified within the income statement. As noted previously, the entry reclassifying a portion of the *cost-basis* gain between the income statement division and the retained earnings statement division of a consolidated working paper is required, while the classification distinction within the income statement division is optional.

These data are presented in Illustration 14–2 (p. 472), in which it is further assumed that there exist $80,000 of accumulated retained earnings of X Company on January 1, 1973, and $25,000 of net income in 1973, excluding the *cost-basis* gain on the sale of subsidiary shares.

Where the investment is carried on an equity basis, the entry for the sale of subsidiary shares is recorded as follows:

Cash..	18,000	
Loss on sale of stock.......................................	2,000	
Investment in Y Company stock.......................		20,000

The amount credited to the investment account is the original cost of $15,000 adjusted for 2½ years' undistributed subsidiary earnings (20 percent of $25,000), resulting in an aggregate credit of $20,000. Where the earnings for the fractional part of the current year prior to the sale have not yet been recorded by the parent company, the reported trading loss would be $1,000 and a working paper reclassification within the income statement division may be made if desired.

Case 6. Purchase and Sale of Subsidiary Shares during Current Period —Cost Basis. Following are the trial balances of companies X and Y on December 31, 1971:

Illustration 14-2

X COMPANY AND SUBSIDIARY Y COMPANY
Partial Consolidated Statement Working Paper
For Year Ended December 31, 1973

	X Company	Y Company	Eliminations Dr.	Eliminations Cr.	Minority Interest	Consolidated
Income Statement:						
Net income (excluding gain on sale of stock)	25,000	10,000				35,000
Gain on sale of stock	3,000		(2) 5,000			[2,000]
Subsidiary income				(2) 1,000		1,000
	28,000	10,000				34,000
Minority interest in Y Company net income—40% of $10,000					4,000	4,000
Net income—carried forward	28,000	10,000	5,000	1,000	4,000	30,000
Retained Earnings Statement:						
Retained earnings, January 1, 1973:						
X Company	80,000			(2) 4,000		84,000
Y Company		40,000	(1) 18,000		16,000	6,000
Net income—brought forward	28,000	10,000	5,000	1,000	4,000	30,000
Retained earnings, December 31, 1973—carried forward	108,000	50,000	23,000	5,000	20,000	120,000

[deduction]

	—X Company—		—Y Company—	
Investment in Y Company.........	$ 37,500			
Other assets.....................	138,500		$ 74,000	
Liabilities......................		$ 8,000		$ 2,000
Capital stock (par $100)..........		100,000		50,000
Retained earnings...............		40,000		10,000
Sales...........................		90,000		60,000
Cost of goods sold...............	55,000		40,000	
Gain on sale of stock.............		3,000		
Expenses.......................	10,000		8,000	
	$241,000	$241,000	$122,000	$122,000

X Company originally purchased 400 shares of Y Company's capital stock on March 1, 1971, for $50,000 and subsequently sold 100 shares on September 1, 1971, for $15,500. Since subsidiary shares are both acquired *and* sold during the current year, purchased subsidiary net income is introduced as an elimination element and subsequently adjusted in the investment elimination schedule. Subsidiary profits are assumed to have been earned uniformly throughout the year.

The investment elimination schedule is as follows:

Investment Elimination Schedule
Dr. [Cr.]

	At Acquisition	Adjustment (Sale)	At Consolidation
Capital stock..................	$ 40,000	$[10,000]	$ 30,000
Retained earnings.............	8,000	[2,000]	6,000
Net income...................	1,600	[400]	1,200
Differential...................	400	[100]	300
Investment...................	$[50,000]	$ 12,500	$[37,500]

These data are presented in Illustration 14–3.

The consolidated working paper in Illustration 14–3 indicates that consolidated net income is $34,000. A calculation by definition confirms this amount in the following manner:

X Company's 1971 net income (exclusive of "gain on sale of stock").............................		$25,000
Increased by:		
80 percent of six months' 1971 subsidiary net income (80% of $6,000)........................		4,800
60 percent of four months' 1971 subsidiary net income (60% of $4,000)........................		2,400
Gain on sale of subsidiary stock:		
Proceeds of sale.................................	$15,500	
Equity basis carrying value of shares sold...........	13,700	1,800
Consolidated net income for 1971...................		$34,000

Illustration 14–3

X COMPANY AND SUBSIDIARY Y COMPANY

Consolidated Statement Working Paper

For Year Ended December 31, 1971

	X Company	Y Company	Eliminations Dr.	Eliminations Cr.	Minority Interest	Consolidated
Income Statement:						
Sales	90,000	60,000				150,000
Gain on sale of stock	* 3,000					3,000
Total credits	93,000	60,000				153,000
Cost of goods sold	55,000	40,000				95,000
Expenses	10,000	8,000				18,000
Total debits	65,000	48,000				113,000
	28,000	12,000				40,000
Purchased net income			(1) 1,200			[1,200]
Minority interest in Y Company net income—40% of $12,000					4,800	[4,800]
Net income—carried forward	28,000	12,000	1,200	–0–	4,800	34,000
Retained Earnings Statement:						
Retained earnings, January 1, 1971:						
X Company	40,000					40,000
Y Company		10,000	(1) 6,000		4,000	
Net income—brought forward	28,000	12,000	1,200		4,800	34,000
Retained earnings, December 31, 1971—carried forward	68,000	22,000	7,200	–0–	8,800	74,000
Balance Sheet:						
Investment in Y Company	37,500			(1) 37,500		
Other assets	138,500	74,000				212,500
Differential			(1) 300			300
	176,000	74,000				212,800
Liabilities	8,000	2,000				10,000
Capital stock:						
X Company	100,000					100,000
Y Company		50,000	(1) 30,000		20,000	
Retained earnings—brought forward	68,000	22,000	7,200		8,800	74,000
Minority interest					28,800	28,800 M
	176,000	74,000	37,500	37,500		212,800

* The accountant may elect to reclassify this composite income account in the working paper in order to reflect 20 percent of the subsidiary net income for six months, $1,200, attributable to the sold shares, in which case the $3,000 reported gain would necessarily convert to a market gain of $1,800. The consolidated net income necessarily remains the same.

M [deduction]

Without reclassification of the earnings accruing to the sold shares, the calculation is based on retained shares as follows:

X Company's 1971 net income (inclusive of "gain on sale of stock")...	$28,000
Increased by:	
60 percent of subsidiary net income (60% of $10,000).............	6,000
Consolidated net income for 1971................................	$34,000

In Case 6 in respect to consolidated statement working papers prepared subsequent to 1971, the net income elimination of $1,200 will be combined with the retained earnings element yielding a total elimination in the amount of $7,200, made against the subsidiary's retained earnings as of the beginning of the relevant period.

It is important to recall that current dividends which are declared by the subsidiary during the interval between the date of the parent's purchase of its stock and the date of subsequent sale of a portion of these shareholdings are only eliminated (against Dividend Income) in the consolidated working paper to the extent of the equity percentage represented by the retained shares. The analysis of subsidiary cash dividends declared during this interval is illustrated in the following case.

Case 7. Interim Purchase and Sale of Subsidiary Shares—Effect of Cash Dividends. The data for Case 6 are repeated in this example, with the exception of changes in the accounts produced by cash dividend declarations of Y Company during 1971 as follows:

February 1.......................	$1,000
July 1..........................	3,000

Corresponding adjustments for these dividends are reflected in the "other assets" of the affiliates.

The investment elimination schedule follows, with the effect of the February 1 dividend declaration included therein:

Investment Elimination Schedule
Dr. [Cr.]

	At Acquisition	Adjustment (Sale)	At Consolidation
Capital stock.....................	$ 40,000	$[10,000]	$ 30,000
Retained earnings.................	8,000	[2,000]	6,000
Net income.......................	1,600	[400]	1,200
Dividends declared................	[800]	200	[600]
Differential......................	1,200	[300]	900
Investment.......................	$[50,000]	$ 12,500	$[37,500]

Illustration 14-4

X COMPANY AND SUBSIDIARY Y COMPANY

Consolidated Statement Working Paper
For Year Ended December 31, 1971

	X Company	Y Company	Eliminations Dr.	Eliminations Cr.	Minority Interest	Consolidated
Income Statement:						
Sales..........	90,000	60,000				150,000
Dividend income..........	2,400		(2) 1,800			600
Gain on sale of stock..........	* 3,000					3,000
Total debits..........	95,400	60,000				153,600
Cost of goods sold..........	55,000	40,000				95,000
Expenses..........	10,000	8,000				18,000
Total credits..........	65,000	48,000				113,000
	30,400	12,000				40,600
Purchased net income..........			(1) 1,200			[1,200]
Minority interest in Y Company net income—40% of $12,000..........					4,800	[4,800]
Net income—carried forward..........	30,400	12,000	3,000	-0-	4,800	34,600
Retained Earnings Statement:						
Retained earnings, January 1, 1971:						
X Company..........	40,000					40,000
Y Company..........		10,000	(1) 6,000		4,000	
Net income—brought forward..........	30,400	12,000	3,000	-0-	4,800	34,600
	70,400	22,000			8,800	74,600
Dividends declared..........		4,000		(1) 600 (2) 1,800	1,600	
Retained earnings, December 31, 1971—carried forward..........	70,400	18,000	9,000	2,400	7,200	74,600
Balance Sheet:						
Investment in Y Company..........	37,500			(1) 37,500		
Other assets..........	140,900	70,000				210,900
Differential..........			(1) 900			900
	178,400	70,000				211,800
Liabilities..........	8,000	2,000				10,000
Capital stock:						
X Company..........	100,000					100,000
Y Company..........		50,000	(1) 30,000		20,000	
Retained earnings—brought forward..........	70,400	18,000	9,000	2,400	7,200	74,600
Minority interest..........					27,200	27,200 M
	178,400	70,000	39,900	39,900		211,800

* The accountant may again elect to reclassify this composite income account in the working paper in order to reflect 20 percent of the *undistributed* subsidiary net income for six months, $600 [20 percent of ($6,000 − $3,000)] which is attributable to the sold shares; in this event the $3,000 reported gain would necessarily convert to a market gain of $2,400. The consolidated net income necessarily remains the same. [deduction]

The consolidated working paper for this case is shown in Illustration 14–4.

It should be noted that in respect to subsidiary dividends, three different conditions may exist:

1. Dividends may be declared by the subsidiary during the current period, but prior to the date of acquisition of its stock by a parent corporation. In this instance, the dividends are treated similarly to the February 1 declaration in Illustration 14–4, i.e., the amount of such dividends which relate to the purchased shares enters into the investment elimination as a reduction in the book value of these shares.

2. Dividends may be declared during the current period in the interim between the dates of purchase and partial sale of subsidiary shares. Obviously, the amount of dividend income recorded by the parent will relate to the presale equity percentage. It is appropriate, however, to eliminate only an amount of intercompany dividends based upon the percentage of ownership implicit in the *retained* shares; the amount of dividend income which relates to sold shares is regarded as having been *confirmed* on a consolidated basis. Consequently, it is reasonable to regard such income as an appropriate credit in the calculation of consolidated net income. This is the justification for not eliminating $600 of the July 1 dividend recorded by X Company in Illustration 14–4. Consolidated net income for Case 7 exceeds that for Case 6 by the amount of this confirmed subsidiary net income. In both cases the proceeds of sale remain the same, while in Case 7 the undistributed subsidiary earnings which relate to the sold shares are less by $600 than those of Case 6; in Case 7, therefore, the *market* gain is $600 higher, or $2,400. In respect to the shares sold, the sum of the parent company's equity in subsidiary earnings, confirmed by dividends, $600, and its equity in undistributed subsidiary earnings, $600 in Illustration 14–4, is equal to the parent company's equity in subsidiary net income, $1,200 none of which was confirmed through dividend payment in Illustration 14–3.

3. Dividends may be declared subsequent to both the purchase and sale of the subsidiary's shares. In this event, the parent company's year-end percentage again applies in determining the amount of the elimination, although the effect of the elimination in this instance is to eliminate completely intercompany dividend income.

Case 8. Purchase and Sale of Subsidiary Shares during the Current Period—Equity Basis. The working paper in Illustration 14–5 is an example of an interim purchase and sale of subsidiary shares where the equity method is used. The data of Case 6 are used in this illustration, with an additional assumption that subsidiary net income is recorded by the parent on the basis of the various percentages of the subsidiary's outstanding stock held by the parent company during the accounting period. This results in the classification distinction between confirmed net income and market gain that is alluded to in the note to Illustration 14–3. Should the parent company elect to record at the end of the accounting period its interest in the

Illustration 14–5

X COMPANY AND SUBSIDIARY Y COMPANY

Consolidated Statement Working Paper

For Year Ended December 31, 1971

	X Company	Y Company	Eliminations Dr.	Eliminations Cr.	Minority Interest	Consolidated
Income Statement:						
Sales	90,000	60,000				150,000
Gain on sale of stock	1,800					1,800
Subsidiary income	* 7,200		†(1) 6,000			1,200
Total credits	99,000	60,000				153,000
Cost of goods sold	55,000	40,000				95,000
Expenses	10,000	8,000				18,000
Total debits	65,000	48,000				113,000
Purchased net income	34,000	12,000				40,000 [1,200]
Minority interest in Y Company net income—40% of $12,000			(2) 1,200		4,800	[4,800]
Net income—carried forward	34,000	12,000	7,200	–0–	4,800	34,000
Retained Earnings Statement:						
Retained earnings, January 1, 1971:						
X Company	40,000					40,000
Y Company		10,000	(2) 6,000		4,000	
Net income—brought forward	34,000	12,000	7,200		4,800	34,000
Retained earnings, December 31, 1971—carried forward	74,000	22,000	13,200	–0–	8,800	74,000
Balance Sheet:						
Investment in Y Company stock	43,500			(1) 6,000 (2) 37,500		
Other assets	138,500	74,000				212,500
Differential			(2) 300			300
	182,000	74,000				212,800
Liabilities	8,000	2,000				10,000
Capital stock:						
X Company	100,000					100,000
Y Company		50,000	(2) 30,000		20,000	
Retained earnings—brought forward	74,000	22,000	13,200		8,800	74,000
Minority interest					28,800	28,800 M
	182,000	74,000	43,500	43,500	28,800	212,800

* 80 percent of $6,000 plus 60 percent of $4,000.
† This is the recorded net income on sold shares; the recorded net income on retained shares was confirmed by their sale. [deduction]

subsidiary's net income on the basis of the percentage interest implicit in the retained shares, the reported Gain on Sale of Stock for an equity-basis investment would be equivalent to the reported Gain on Sale of Stock on a cost basis, $3,000. The parent company's recorded interest in undistributed subsidiary profits of prior periods, however, is correctly classified where the equity method is used regardless of the above elections.

New Issues of Subsidiary Shares Subscribed by Minority

Changes in the equity of the parent corporation have heretofore been attributed to the purchase or sale of subsidiary shares by the parent company. However, a change in the parent company's interest may also result from the subsidiary issuance of new shares to nonaffiliates, without subscription therein by the parent company.[7] The effect of this action on the preparation of consolidated statements depends upon (1) the issue price of the new shares and (2) the parent company's method of accounting for its investment in the subsidiary. The cases which follow assume the use of the cost method, although reference will be made, as appropriate, indicating adjustments required to reconcile the cost and equity methods.

Case 9. Issuance of New Subsidiary Shares at Book Value. For purposes of this and subsequent cases, it is assumed that the following abbreviated, comparative trial balances relate to affiliate companies X and Y, except as other contributed capital must be adjusted to reflect different issue prices.

	X Company 12/31/71	X Company 12/31/72	Y Company 12/31/71	Y Company 12/31/72
Investment in Y Company stock....................	$ 50,000	$ 50,000		
Other assets................	115,000	155,000	$68,000	$93,600
	$165,000	$205,000	$68,000	$93,600
Capital stock (par $100)......	$100,000	$100,000	$50,000	$60,000
Other contributed capital.....				3,600
Retained earnings (1/1).......	40,000	65,000	10,000	18,000
Net income................	25,000	40,000	8,000	12,000
	$165,000	$205,000	$68,000	$93,600

X Company purchased 400 shares of the capital stock of Y Company on January 1, 1971, for $50,000. On January 2, 1972, Y Company issued 100 new shares to nonaffiliates for $136 per share—the existing book value of subsidiary stock. Such a transaction clearly reduces the parent company's equity percentage in the subsidiary; the analysis of the change in the parent company's monetary interest parallels the treatment described

---

[7] A similar condition obtains when there is a nonratable issue of subsidiary shares to majority and minority shareholders. Although not here illustrated, such an issue should be analyzed in the same manner as that described in the following discussion.

earlier in respect to *direct* purchases of subsidiary shares by the parent. The investment elimination schedule is as follows:

Investment Elimination Schedule
Dr. [Cr.]

	At Ac- quisition	Adjust- ment	At Con- solidation
Capital stock....................	$ 40,000		$ 40,000
Retained earnings.................	8,000	$[2,400]	5,600
Other contributed capital...........		2,400	2,400
Differential......................	2,000		2,000
Investment......................	$[50,000]	$ –0–	$[50,000]

The amount and description of the adjustments are given by the following schedular calculations:

	Y Company's Net Worth		X Company's Equity in Y Company's Net Worth		
	Before New Issue	After New Issue	Before New Issue (4/5)	After New Issue (2/3)	Increase [Decrease]
Capital stock............	$50,000	$60,000	$40,000	$40,000	$ –0–
Retained earnings........	18,000	18,000	14,400	12,000	[2,400]
Other contributed capital................	–0–	3,600	–0–	2,400	2,400

It is apparent from this analysis that the *total* monetary value of the investment in subsidiary stock remains unaffected by the new issue, although the fractional or percentage interest is diminished. This is a consequence of issuing new shares of the subsidiary at the existing book value of shares presently outstanding. It is also evident that in the preparation of a consolidated statement working paper (see Illustration 14–6), it is necessary to allocate book values on the basis of the equity percentages after the realignment in the subsidiary's net worth; this is reflected in the adjusted investment elimination schedule and in the new equity interest of the minority shareholders.

Had the equity method been used, $6,400 (80 percent of $8,000) of 1971 subsidiary earnings would have been added by adjustment to the parent company's 1971 net income and closed to its retained earnings. Thereafter, the elimination for the 1972 consolidated statement working paper would have simply recognized that $12,000, or two thirds of the subsidiary's retained earnings as of 1/1/72, should be eliminated, and the remaining $6,000 or one third of these retained earnings would be ex-

Illustration 14–6

X COMPANY AND SUBSIDIARY Y COMPANY

Consolidated Statement Working Paper

For Year Ended December 31, 1972

	X Company	Y Company	Eliminations Dr.	Eliminations Cr.	Minority Interest	Consolidated
Income Statement:						
Net income	40,000	12,000				52,000
Minority interest in Y Company net income—⅓ of $12,000					4,000	4,000
Net income—carried forward	40,000	12,000	–0–	–0–	4,000	48,000
Retained Earnings Statement:						
Retained earnings, January 1, 1972:						
X Company	65,000					65,000
Y Company		18,000	(1) 5,600		6,000	6,400
Net income—brought forward	40,000	12,000	–0–		4,000	48,000
Retained earnings, December 31, 1972—carried forward	105,000	30,000	5,600	–0–	10,000	119,400
Balance Sheet:						
Investment in Y Company stock	50,000			(1) 50,000		
Other assets	155,000	93,600				248,600
Differential			(1) 2,000			2,000
	205,000	93,600				250,600
Capital stock:						
X Company	100,000					100,000
Y Company		60,000	(1) 40,000		20,000	
Other contributed capital		3,600	(1) 2,400		1,200	
Retained earnings—brought forward	105,000	30,000	5,600		10,000	119,400
Minority interest					31,200	31,200 M
	205,000	93,600	50,000	50,000	31,200	250,600

tended to the minority interest column of the consolidated working paper. Similarly, $8,000 (two thirds of $12,000) of 1972 subsidiary net income included in the parent company's earnings would have been eliminated in the usual fashion.

Case 10. Issuance of Subsidiary Shares at More than Book Value. The data for Case 9 are repeated here, except that the new subsidiary shares are issued on January 2, 1972, at $142 per share. "Other assets" and "other contributed capital" of Y Company are adjusted accordingly.

The investment elimination schedule follows:

Investment Elimination Schedule
Dr. [Cr.]

	At Ac-quisition	Adjust-ment	At Con-solidation
Capital stock......................	$ 40,000		$ 40,000
Retained earnings..................	8,000	$[2,400]	5,600
Other contributed capital............		2,800	2,800
Differential.......................	2,000		2,000
Investment.......................	$[50,000]	$ [400]	$[50,400]

Calculations of the amounts of the above adjustments are outlined in the following schedule:

	Y Company's Net Worth		X Company's Equity in Y Company's Net Worth		
	Before New Issue	After New Issue	Before New Issue (4/5)	After New Issue (2/3)	Increase [Decrease]
Capital stock............	$50,000	$60,000	$40,000	$40,000	$ –0–
Retained earnings........	18,000	18,000	14,400	12,000	[2,400]
Other contributed capital...............	–0–	4,200	–0–	2,800	2,800

The issue of subsidiary shares at more than book value results in an increase in the parent company's monetary equity in the subsidiary in the amount of $400, although its fractional interest necessarily declined. Where the equity method is used, the adjustment for this increase in the investment value is journalized by the parent company as follows:

Investment in Y Company stock............................... 400
    Increase in equity in Y Company..........................   400

Where the cost method is used, the adjustment is entered in the consolidated statement working paper in support of the investment elimination to which it naturally relates.

The "increase (decrease) in equity in subsidiary" is usually reported as a net income (loss) adjustment to consolidated net income or as a direct credit (charge) to consolidated retained earnings. Some accountants believe, however, that this equity adjustment properly relates to contributed capital. Their argument rests on the assumption that it is improper to allow a subsidiary's trading in its own stock to be a determinant in the calculation of consolidated net income or consolidated retained earnings. Still other accountants prefer to indicate the adjusted in terms of its effect on retained earnings *and* other contributed capital, as reflected in the schedular analysis above. Should this view prevail, the change in equity adjustment for this illustration would consist of a deduction (debit) of $2,400 from consolidated retained earnings and also as an increase (credit) of $2,800 to consolidated other contributed capital.

These data are shown in Illustration 14–7, wherein the adjustment for a change in equity is reported in the income statement.

Case 11. Issuance of Subsidiary Shares at Less than Book Value. The data for Case 9 are repeated in this example, except that on January 2, 1972, the 100 shares are issued by the subsidiary at $130 per share. "Other assets" and "other contributed capital" are adjusted accordingly.

The investment elimination schedule is as follows:

Investment Elimination Schedule
Dr. [Cr.]

	At Acquisition	Adjustment	At Consolidation
Capital stock......................	$ 40,000		$ 40,000
Retained earnings..................	8,000	$[2,400]	5,600
Other contributed capital............		2,000	2,000
Differential.......................	2,000		2,000
Investment.......................	$[`0,000]	$ 400	$[49,600]

The amounts of the adjustment are calculated below:

	Y Company's Net Worth		X Company's Equity in Y Company's Net Worth		
	Before New Issue	After New Issue	Before New Issue (4/5)	After New Issue (2/3)	Increase [Decrease]
Capital stock............	$50,000	$60,000	$40,000	$40,000	$ –0–
Retained earnings........	18,000	18,000	14,400	12,000	[2,400]
Other contributed capital..............	–0–	3,000	–0–	2,000	2,000

Illustration 14–7

X COMPANY AND SUBSIDIARY Y COMPANY
Consolidated Statement Working Paper
For Year Ended December 31, 1972

	X Company	Y Company	Eliminations Dr.	Eliminations Cr.	Minority Interest	Consolidated
Income Statement:						
Net income	40,000	12,000				52,000
Increase in equity in Y Company				(1) 400		400
						52,400
Minority interest in Y Company net income—⅓ of $12,000					4,000	4,000
Net income—carried forward	40,000	12,000	—0—	400	4,000	48,400
Retained Earnings Statement:						
Retained earnings, January 1, 1972:						
X Company	65,000					65,000
Y Company		18,000	(2) 5,600		6,000	6,400
Net income—brought forward	40,000	12,000	—0—	400	4,000	48,400
Retained earnings, December 31, 1972—carried forward	105,000	30,000	5,600	400	10,000	119,800
Balance Sheet:						
Investment in Y Company stock	50,000		(1) 400	(2) 50,400		
Other assets	155,000	94,200				249,200
Differential			(2) 2,000			2,000
	205,000	94,200				251,200
Capital stock:						
X Company	100,000					100,000
Y Company		60,000	(2) 40,000		20,000	
Other contributed capital		4,200	(2) 2,800		1,400	
Retained earnings—brought forward	105,000	30,000	5,600	400	10,000	119,800
Minority interest					31,400	31,400 M
	205,000	94,200	50,800	50,800	31,400	251,200

The issue of new shares by the subsidiary at less than book value results in a decrease in the parent company's monetary equity to the extent of $400. The entry to recognize this value dilution of the investment is:

Decrease in equity in Y Company............................. 400		
Investment in Y Company stock...........................		400

The above entry is recorded by the parent company where the equity method is used; it is entered in the consolidated statement working paper where the cost method is used. A consolidated working paper is not illustrated for this case, as it merely duplicates that for Case 10, except that the decrease in equity is a negative element in respect to the calculation of consolidated net income.

Effect on Fundamental Definitions. If an "increase (decrease) in equity" results from the nonratable issue of new subsidiary shares and it is reported as an adjustment of consolidated net income and/or retained earnings, the fundamental definitions must be accordingly modified. The amount of this increase (decrease) must be added to (deducted from) the confirmed net income, or retained earnings, of the parent company in the definitional calculation. This illustrates the unique characteristic of this item, and the commitment one necessarily makes by reporting this equity change as income—viz., a restatement of the fundamental definitions of consolidated net income and retained earnings.

Treasury Stock Transactions of Subsidiary

The parent company's percentage interest and dollar equity in a subsidiary may also be increased or decreased as a consequence of the subsidiary's trading in its own shares. As in the case of new issues by the subsidiary, the effect upon the parent company's monetary equity is essentially a function of the price paid by the subsidiary for treasury shares. In the event that the treasury shares are acquired from minority stockholders at existing book value, there is no resultant change in the amount of the parent's equity. However, if the purchase price is an amount other than book value, an adjustment in the investment account is indicated. In respect to consolidated statements, the effects of treasury stock transactions with a subsidiary company's minority shareholders follow the same pattern in respect to the investment analysis as was illustrated for a subsidiary's issuance of new shares to minority stockholders.

Case 12. Purchase of Treasury Shares at Less than Book Value. Using and extending the data for Case 9, it is assumed that on January 2, 1972, Y Company acquired 50 shares of its outstanding stock from minority shareholders at $127 per share. It may be recalled that the then existing book value for these shares was $136. For purposes of consolidated statement preparation, it is both appropriate and convenient to account for the purchase of treasury stock as if these shares were retired, with due recognition being accorded purchase premiums or discounts. The balance of the account, Premium on Treasury Shares Purchased, used in the following example must necessarily be allocated subsequently between the contributed capital and retained earnings accounts of the subsidiary. In the present case, the purchase premium amounts to $1,350 (50 × $27).

The investment elimination schedule is as follows:

Investment Elimination Schedule
Dr. [Cr.]

	At Ac-quisition	Adjust-ment	At Con-solidation
Capital stock....................	$ 40,000		$ 40,000
Retained earnings................	8,000	$ 1,600	9,600
Premium on treasury shares pur-			
chased.......................		[1,200]	[1,200]
Differential......................	2,000		2,000
Investment......................	$[50,000]	$ [400]	$[50,400]

The adjustment calculations are:

	Y Company's Net Worth		X Company's Equity in Y Company's Net Worth		
	Before Pur-chase of Treasury Shares	After Pur-chase of Treasury Shares	Before Pur-chase of Treasury Shares (4/5)	After Pur-chase of Treasury Shares (8/9)	Increase [Decrease]
Capital stock...............	$50,000	$45,000	$40,000	$40,000	$ –0–
Retained earnings...........	18,000	18,000	14,400	16,000	1,600
Premium on treasury					
shares purchased.........	–0–	[1,350]	–0–	[1,200]	[1,200]

It is apparent that the subsidiary's purchase of treasury shares from minority shareholders at less than book value produces an increase in the monetary equity of the parent company. As in the case of new issues of subsidiary shares to minority stockholders, an adjustment for this change in equity must be reflected in the consolidated statements. An adjusting entry is made in the books of an equity-basis parent company as follows:

Investment in Y Company stock................................ 400
    Increase in equity in Y Company......................... 400

The above adjustment is entered only in the consolidated statement working paper in the event the cost method is used.

A working paper adjustment is also required to record the cancellation of treasury shares (recorded at cost) as follows:

Capital stock—Y Company..............................	5,000	
Premium on treasury shares purchased......................	1,350	
Treasury stock.......................................		6,350

The consolidated statement working paper is given in Illustration 14–8.

It may be noted that the premium on the purchase of treasury shares is treated in Illustration 14–8 as an adjustment to Y Company's retained earnings. However, since it either is eliminated or extended to the minority interest, this treatment has no direct effect on consolidated retained earnings. In the event that treasury shares are purchased at a discount, it is perhaps more usual to regard the amount of discount as an adjustment to other contributed capital; the consolidated working paper remains the same.

Should the subsidiary purchase treasury shares from minority shareholders at more than existing book value, there would be a corresponding decrease in the equity of the parent company. The preparation of consolidated statements in such a case would parallel in procedural detail that for Case 12.

If the decision is made by the subsidiary to resell previously acquired treasury shares, the accounting analysis of the change in the parent company's equity in the subsidiary is identical to the treatment for the issuance of subsidiary shares previously described.

With respect to the fundamental definitions, the monetary change in the parent company's equity in the subsidiary produced by treasury stock transactions affects the definitional calculations of consolidated net income and retained earnings in the same manner as the changes resulting from the sale of unissued shares.

Unconfirmed Profit on Asset Transfers

Special consideration should be given to intercompany profit eliminations where there occurs a change (either an increase or decrease) in the parent company's percentage interest in the selling affiliate during the current period. This change of equity relates importantly to the investment elimination and to the intercompany profit elimination—either 100 percent or fractional elimination.

In respect to asset transfers between affiliates, it is important that the process of profit confirmation be identified with specific time periods. The amount of cumulative confirmed profits at the start of the current year necessarily relates to that period between the originating intercompany transaction and this date; the amount of profit confirmation during the current year must identify with the relevant fractional parts of the year *before* and *after* the change of the parent company's equity in the selling subsidiary. Once these broad time intervals have been associated with the relevant confirmed profit elements, two methods of analysis are available to the accountant.

One method, which is preferred by the authors, is to calculate the amount of the investment elimination elements on the basis of the *confirmed* net income and retained earnings of the subsidiary at the date of

Illustration 14-8

X COMPANY AND SUBSIDIARY Y COMPANY
Consolidated Statement Working Paper
For Year Ended December 31, 1972

	X Company	Y Company	Eliminations Dr.	Eliminations Cr.	Minority Interest	Consolidated
Income Statement:						
Net income.........	40,000	12,000				52,000
Increase in equity in Y Company stock......				(2) 400		400
						52,400
Minority interest in Y Company net income—1/9 of $12,000......					1,333	1,333
Net income—carried forward......	40,000	12,000	–0–	400	1,333	51,067
Retained Earnings Statement:						
Retained earnings, January 1, 1972:						
X Company......	65,000					65,000
Y Company......		18,000	(3) 9,600 (1) 1,350	(3) 1,200	2,000	6,400
Premium on treasury stock purchased......					[150]	–0–
Net income—brought forward......	40,000	12,000		400	1,333	51,067
Retained earnings, December 31, 1972—carried forward......	105,000	30,000	10,950	1,600	3,183	122,467
Balance Sheet:						
Investment in Y Company stock......	50,000			(3) 50,400		–0–
Other assets......	155,000	73,650	(2) 400			228,650
Treasury stock......		6,350		(1) 6,350		–0–
Differential......			(3) 2,000			2,000
	205,000	80,000				230,650
Capital stock:						
X Company......	100,000					100,000
Y Company......		50,000	(1) 5,000 (3) 40,000		5,000	
Retained earnings—brought forward......	105,000	30,000	10,950	1,600	3,183	122,467
Minority interest......					*8,183	8,183 M
	205,000	80,000	58,350	58,350	*8,183	230,650

* 1/9 of ($50,000 + $30,000 − $6,350).

change in the parent company's equity percentage. Since an economic entity is preexistent to this transaction, it is plausible that the purchased net worth should be based upon subsidiary earnings which are then confirmed on a consolidated basis. Calculations of consolidated net income and retained earnings of subsequent periods would allocate confirmed profits of these periods on the basis of equity interests then existing. The definitional calculations of consolidated net income or retained earnings, therefore, would continue to accumulate incremental interests of confirmed subsidiary net income based upon the parent's percentage interests during the fractional periods for which the different equity interests prevail. For purposes of consolidated working paper preparation, intercompany profits are eliminated and minority interests calculated on the basis of equity percentages existing at the *end* of the accounting period. These concepts in respect to intercompany profits apply to either increases or decreases in the parent company's percentage interest in subsidiary shares and are consistent with the definitional framework constructed in the previous chapters.

A second basic elimination method calculates the amount of investment elimination elements on the basis of *reported* net income and retained earnings. This method results in an effective confirmation of that portion of the intercompany profit for those shareholders, either majority or minority, whose percentage interest in the selling affiliate is decreased. In the preparation of consolidated working papers, this method requires that the amount of the unconfirmed profit elimination be based on the percentage interest prevailing at the time of the intercompany profit transaction. In those instances where the change in equity results in a decrease in the parent company's percentage interest, some accountants advocate use of the lower percentage. This essentially is a commitment to report the lowest possible consolidated net income and is analogous to the "lower of cost or market" rule for valuation of inventories.

Since specific identification of items of inventory containing intercompany profit is often difficult to determine accurately, accountants may be justified in applying the rule of first-in, first-out with respect to the flow of inventory costs. If there is evidence to indicate that the refinement introduced by the intraperiod calculation is not materially different from an application of year-end percentages, the latter rates may be used without unusual distortion of consolidated net income.

The above commentary is equally applicable to the analysis of profit confirmation in respect to the gain (or loss) on the acquisition of intercompany bonds.

QUESTIONS

1. What is the effect upon the investment elimination schedule of an *interim* purchase of subsidiary shares? To what extent are consolidated working papers modified to reflect the presence of this new variable?

2. How is the investment elimination schedule modified if the subsidiary declares a dividend in the year of acquisition but prior to purchase by the parent company?

3. Given an interim purchase of a subsidiary's stock, how is the minority interest in subsidiary net income calculated?

4. When a parent gains control of a subsidiary by acquiring several blocks of stock at different dates, there are two alternative methods of determining the investment elimination of the subsidiary's retained earnings. What is the nature of these alternatives? Which is preferred?

5. Why is it necessary to distinguish between blocks of a subsidiary's stock purchased in the open market and stock acquired directly from the subsidiary affiliate?

6. In the event a subsidiary's shares are sold by the parent, how does the gain or loss as recorded on the books of the parent differ, depending upon whether the cost or the equity method of accounting is used?

7. The parent's recorded gain or loss (cost basis) on the sale of subsidiary shares is said to consist of three elements. What are they?

8. What criteria may be used to identify the subsidiary shares sold by a parent?

9. Assume that a parent company utilizes the cost method and the subsidiary issues to minority interests shares that previously had never been issued. What is the effect upon the investment elimination schedule if the shares were issued: (*a*) at book value; (*b*) at more than book value?

PROBLEMS

Problem 14–1

X Company purchased 40 shares of Y Company capital stock on May 1, 1971, in the open market for $8,000, and an additional 50 shares on September 1, 1971, for $11,000. A partial trial balance as of December 31, 1971, discloses the following balances:

	X Company	Y Company
Capital stock ($100 par)	$100,000	$10,000
Retained earnings (1/1)	40,000	5,000
Dividends declared	5,000	2,000
Sales	200,000	40,000
Cost of goods sold	130,000	20,000
Operating expenses	40,000	8,000
Dividend income	400	

Y Company declared a $10 dividend per share on February 1 and July 1.

It is assumed that subsidiary net income is earned uniformly throughout the year.

Required:

(i) Prepare an investment elimination schedule for consolidated working papers as of December 31, 1971, and December 31, 1972.

(ii) Prepare a consolidated income statement for the year ended December 31, 1971.

Problem 14–2

On January 1, 1971, the White Corporation acquired an 80 percent interest in the capital stock of the Blenn Company for $128,000 when the latter had capital stock outstanding, $100,000, and retained earnings, $50,000. On July 1, 1971, White purchased an additional 100 shares of Blenn stock for $17,500. Fifty shares of the original purchase (1/1/71) were sold on November 1 for $8,750.

It is assumed that the Blenn Company net income for 1971 was earned uniformly throughout the year.

The trial balances of the affiliate companies on December 31, 1971, were:

	—White Corporation—		—Blenn Company—	
Investment in Blenn Company stock....................	$137,500			
Merchandise, January 1......	21,000		$ 12,000	
Other assets................	201,250		188,000	
Liabilities..................		$ 17,250		$ 6,000
Capital stock ($100 par value)...................		200,000		100,000
Retained earnings...........		90,000		50,000
Sales......................		232,000		144,000
Purchases.................	146,000		80,000	
Expenses..................	34,250		20,000	
Gain on sale of Blenn shares...................		750		
	$540,000	$540,000	$300,000	$300,000
Merchandise, December 31...............	$ 20,250		$ 16,000	

Required:

(i) Prepare a consolidated statement working paper for the year ended December 31, 1971, together with a supporting investment elimination schedule.

(ii) Prepare a schedular proof of consolidated net income for 1971.

Problem 14–3

On January 1, 1971, the Rogers Company purchased 250 shares of the Hamilton Company common stock (par, $100) for $38,000 when the latter had capital stock outstanding in the amount of $100,000 and retained earnings of $40,000. On September 1 an additional 450 shares were acquired at a cost of $75,000. On December 1, 100 shares, purchased on January 1, were sold for $20,000.

During 1971 the earnings reported by the Rogers Company were $13,800—by the Hamilton Company, $24,000. Profits are earned uniformly throughout the year.

The Rogers Company had a $95,000 retained earnings balance on January 1, 1971.

Required:

(i)   Prepare an investment elimination schedule on December 31, 1971.
(ii) Prepare a partial consolidated statement working paper for the year ended December 31, 1971.
(iii) Calculate *by definition* the amount of consolidated net income for 1971. Identify clearly the amount of gain or loss on the sale of investment shares.

Problem 14–4

The Granville Company exhibited the following stockholders' equity balances as of January 1, 1971: capital stock ($100 par), $5,000; and retained earnings, $1,500. Granville Company reported an annual profit each year in the amount of $6,000.

Required:

Prepare an investment elimination schedule for a consolidated balance sheet as of December 31, 1973, if the Hall Company made the following block purchases of Granville stock *directly* from the issuer:

(i)   Twenty-five shares on January 2, 1971, for $2,875; 175 shares on January 1, 1972, for $21,175; and 250 shares on January 1, 1973, for $32,500.
(ii) Same data as in (i) except that Granville Company distributed cash dividends each year on December 31 in the amount of $6,300.

Problem 14–5

On January 1, 1970, balances in the stockholders' equity accounts of the Ritter Company and Webster, Inc., were as follows:

	Ritter Company	Webster, Inc.
Capital stock (par, $100)	$100,000	$50,000
Retained earnings	30,000	9,000
Earnings and dividends for the two-year period ended December 31, 1971, were:		
1970 net income	20,000	6,000
1971 net income	15,800	12,000
Cash dividends, July 1, 1971		3,000

It is assumed that the net income of each company is earned uniformly throughout the year.

The Ritter Company purchased *directly* from Webster, Inc., shares of stock in the following amounts:

January 2, 1970	250 shares	Cost, $25,000
January 1, 1971	500 shares	Cost, $60,000
October 1, 1971	750 shares	Cost, $77,000

Required:

(i)   Prepare an investment elimination schedule on December 31, 1971.
(ii) Prepare a partial consolidated statement working paper for the year ended December 31, 1971.

Problem 14–6

Allen, Inc., earned $36,000 during 1971 without significant seasonal fluctuation. The company declared and paid dividends of $3,000 on March 1 and again on August 1. On January 1, 1971, Allen's stockholders' equity appeared as follows:

Common stock ($100 par)...........	$300,000
Other contributed capital............	50,000
Retained earnings..................	100,000

On April 1, 1971, Gilpin Enterprises purchased 3,000 unissued shares from Allen, Inc., for $300,000. On September 1, 1971, Gilpin purchased 1,500 shares of Allen on the open market at $110 per share. On December 1, 1971, Gilpin sold 500 shares on the open market at $150 per share.

Required:

(i) Prepare an investment elimination schedule covering the year ended December 31, 1971. Additionally, present in journal form any other necessary elimination entries applicable to 1971, being careful to note the periods during which they would be necessary.

(ii) Prepare a residual calculation of consolidated net income for the year ended December 31, 1971, assuming that Gilpin had no income reported other than what arose from its relationship with Allen. Gilpin uses the cost basis of accounting for its interest in Allen.

Problem 14–7

Y had $100,000 capital stock (par, $100) and $54,000 retained earnings on January 1, 1970. During 1970, Y earned $36,000 uniformly throughout the year and paid a $4,500 cash dividend on May 1 and also on November 1; X reported net income of $50,000 for 1970.

X made the following purchases and sales of Y's stock: July 1, 1970—purchased 900 shares; cost, $152,100. September 1, 1970—sold 100 shares; sale proceeds, $21,000.

Additionally, on November 2, 1970, Y Company issued 200 shares to outside interests at $115 per share.

Required:

(i) Prepare an investment elimination schedule for a three-division consolidated statement working paper on December 31, 1970, and related elimination entries.

(ii) Compute consolidated net income for 1970.

Problem 14–8

On January 1, 1970, Hartley, Inc., purchased 70 percent of the capital stock of the Wyatt Company for $112,000; on July 1, 1971, an additional 10 percent of Wyatt stock was purchased by Hartley for $18,000.

On January 1, 1970, the Wyatt Company purchased 100 percent of the capital stock of the Skadden Company for $120,000. On June 30, 1971, Wyatt sold 20 percent of its holdings in Skadden stock crediting its investment account for the sale proceeds, $30,000.

An operating summary for the affiliate companies for the two years ended December 31, 1971, discloses:

	Hartley, Inc.	Wyatt Company	Skadden Company
Retained earnings (1/1/70)	$ 90,000	$ 70,000	$ 45,000
Net income—1970	20,000	64,000	15,000
Retained earnings (12/31/70)	$110,000	$134,000	$ 60,000
Net income [loss]—1971:			
January 1—June 30	40,000	[25,000]	[10,000]
July 1—December 31	42,000	58,000	40,000
	$192,000	$167,000	$ 90,000
Dividends declared, December, 1971	20,000	15,000	10,000
Retained earnings (12/31/71)	$172,000	$152,000	$ 80,000

Required:

Prepare a consolidated retained earnings statement for the year ended December 31, 1971.

Problem 14–9

On January 1, 1969, the Ries Company and Wingline, Inc., had stockholders' equity balances as follows:

	Ries Company	Wingline, Inc.
Capital stock (par, $100)	$200,000	$100,000
Other contributed capital	40,000	20,000
Retained earnings	80,000	30,000

Wingline, Inc., reported annual earnings of $10,000, $14,000, and $14,400 for each of the three years subsequent to January 1, 1969.

The following are the transactions involving Wingline, Inc., capital stock:

January 2, 1969. The Ries Company purchased 700 shares in the open market for $110,000.

January 2, 1970. Wingline, Inc., purchased 200 shares from its minority shareholders for $27,200 and recorded the treasury stock at cost.

January 2, 1971. The Ries Company purchased 800 shares of a new issue by Wingline, Inc., of 1,000 shares. The issue price to all shareholders was $206 per share.

January 2, 1972. Wingline, Inc., sold 100 of the treasury shares to minority shareholders for $15,850.

Required:

Prepare an investment elimination schedule and other related eliminating entries for each of the years 1969, 1970, 1971, and 1972.

Problem 14–10

P Corporation acquired control of S Company on June 30, 1969, by purchase in the open market of 2,800 shares of its 4,000 issued shares of $100 par value common stock. At that time S had 500 shares of its own stock held as treasury stock and carried at par.

On January 1, 1971, P acquired 200 additional shares from a minority stockholder. On December 31, 1971, by agreement with the minority stockholders, P acquired the 500 shares held in the treasury of S.

The Investment account of P, at cost, shows the following debits:

June 30, 1969, 2,800 shares of S.	$394,800
January 1, 1971, 200 shares of S purchased from outside interests—at cost.	35,000
December 31, 1971, 500 shares of S obtained from S—at cost.	90,000
Total.	$519,800

The accounts of S contained the following items:

Credits	Other Contributed Capital	Retained Earnings
June 30, 1969.	$ 74,300	$ 43,745
Earnings 6/30 to 12/31/69.		35,306
Earnings 1970.		65,754
Earnings 1971.		51,025
Premium on sale of treasury stock.	40,000	
	$114,300	$195,830
Debits		
Dividends paid 12/1/69.		$ 35,000
Dividends paid 12/5/70.		35,000
Dividends paid 12/15/71.		40,000
	–0–	$110,000
Balance 12/31/71.	$114,300	$ 85,830

Required:

(i) Prepare an investment elimination schedule as of June 30, 1969, *and* December 31, 1971.

(ii) Prepare a partial consolidated statement working paper for a consolidated balance sheet on each of the above dates.

(AICPA adapted)

Problem 14–11

The following account balances relate to the Taylor Company and the Gossett Corporation on January 1, 1968:

	Taylor Company	Gossett Corporation
Capital stock ($10 par value)...............	$50,000	$10,000
Treasury stock (at par)....................		2,000
Retained earnings.........................	20,000	8,000

Retained annual profits earned uniformly throughout each year were: Taylor Company, $10,000; and Gossett Corporation, $4,000.

On January 1, 1968, the Taylor Company purchased 500 shares of the capital stock of the Gossett Corporation for $11,000; on January 1, 1969, 200 additional shares were acquired at a cost of $6,000. On January 1, 1972, the Gossett Corporation issued its treasury shares to outsiders for $8,000. On July 1, 1972, the Gossett Corporation issued 200 shares of previously unissued stock to outsiders for $6,000.

Required:

(i) Prepare an investment elimination schedule for a consolidated statement working paper as of January 1, 1972.

(ii) Prepare a partial consolidated statement working paper for the year ended December 31, 1972, and an investment elimination schedule which relates thereto.

Problem 14–12

During 1971 the Products Company acquired a controlling interest in Designers, Inc. Trial balances of the companies at December 31, 1971, are presented below:

Debits	Products Company	Designers, Inc.
Cash.....................................	$ 100,000	$ 80,000
Notes receivable.........................	100,000	
Accounts receivable......................	200,000	100,000
Accrued interest receivable................	1,000	
Inventories..............................	924,000	125,000
Investment in Designers, Inc................	475,000	
Plant, property, and equipment..............	1,250,000	500,000
Deferred charges..........................	25,000	
Patents and licenses.......................		50,000
Cost of sales.............................	1,350,000	525,000
Administrative and selling expenses..........	251,000	174,000
Intesest expense		1,000
	$4,676,000	$1,555,000

Credits	Products Company	Designers, Inc.
Accounts payable.........................	$ 425,000	$ 80,000
Notes payable............................		75,000
Dividend payable.........................		5,000
Allowance for depreciation.................	500,000	150,000
Capital stock............................	300,000	100,000
Retained earnings........................	1,650,000	395,000
Sales and services.......................	1,800,000	750,000
Interest income..........................	1,000	
	$4,676,000	$1,555,000

The following information is available regarding the transactions and accounts of the companies:

a) An analysis of investment in Designers, Inc.:

Date	Description	Amount	Interest Acquired
January 1, 1971	Investment	$325,000	70%
September 30, 1971	Investment	105,000	20
		$430,000	90%
December 31, 1971	90% of Designers, Inc. income for 1971	45,000	
		$475,000	

The net income of Designers, Inc., for the nine months ended September 30, 1971, was $25,000.

b) An analysis of the companies' retained earnings accounts:

	Products Company	Designers, Inc.
Balance, January 1, 1971..................	$1,605,000	$400,000
December 31, 1971:		
Cash dividend declared (payable January 15, 1972).....................		[5,000]
90% of Designers, Inc. net income for 1971............................	45,000	
Balance, December 31, 1971..............	$1,650,000	$395,000

c) The patents and licenses of Designers, Inc., have a fair market value of $25,000.

d) On September 30, 1971, Products Company loaned its subsidiary $100,000 on a 4 percent note. Interest and principal are payable in quarterly installments beginning December 31, 1971.

e) Designers, Inc., sales are principally engineering services billed at cost plus 50 percent. During 1971, $40,000 was billed to Products Company of which $16,500 was treated as a deferred charge at December 31, 1971.

f)   During the year parent company sales to the subsidiary aggregated $60,000, of which $16,000 remained in the inventory of Designers, Inc., at December 31, 1971.

g)   In 1971 the parent company constructed certain tools at a cost of $15,000 which were sold to Designers, Inc., for $25,000. Designers, Inc., depreciates such tools using the straight-line method over a five-year life. One-half year's depreciation is provided in the year of acquisition.

Required:

Prepare a consolidated statement working paper for the year ended December 31, 1971. (Assume 100 percent elimination of intercompany profit.)

(AICPA adapted)

Problem 14–13

X Company purchased 800 shares of Y Company stock on January 1, 1969, for $125,000, when Y Company had capital stock ($100 par) of $100,000 and retained earnings of $50,000. X Company purchased an additional 100 shares on July 1, 1970, for $20,000. On July 1, 1971, Y Company issued 200 shares to minority shareholders for $40,000.

Intercompany profit on asset transfers by Y Company to X Company existed as follows:

a) $2,000 unconfirmed inventory profit reported in 1969, confirmed in the last six months of 1970.

b) $1,000 unconfirmed inventory profit reported in the first six months of 1970, confirmed in the first six months of 1971.

c) $10,000 unconfirmed profit on the transfer of fixed assets on July 2, 1970, the asset has an expected life of 10 years.

X Company had an annual net income of $100,000, and Y Company earned $20,000 uniformly over each year. On January 1, 1969, X Company had retained earnings of $200,000.

Required:

Prepare an investment elimination schedule, and calculate consolidated net income for 1970 and 1971 and consolidated retained earnings at December 31, 1971, both by definition and residual calculation, assuming changes in equity are based upon confirmed profits.

Chapter 15 | Consolidated Statements— Reciprocal Stockholdings

Multilevel corporate affiliations were first introduced in Chapter 11. Emphasis was there directed to unilateral ownership by one or more companies of corporate shares of other affiliated companies. Such affiliations are typically of the forms illustrated below:

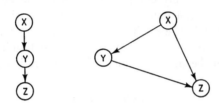

In the discussion to follow, attention will focus on bilateral stockholdings, wherein two or more of the affiliated companies are related through the reciprocal ownership of corporate stock. Necessarily the difficulty of apportioning the net incomes and accumulated earnings of the affiliates as between majority and minority shareholders is compounded by the involvements of such ownership patterns. In the ensuing discussion, the traditional method of allocating affiliation net income is considered, including the conventional solution algorithms and an introduction to the newer application of matrix algebra; thereafter, an alternative method—the treasury stock concept—is briefly outlined.

TRADITIONAL ALLOCATION METHOD

Case 1. Bilateral Stockholdings Not Involving Parent Company. Consider the following affiliation diagram:

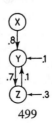

If the net incomes of companies X, Y, and Z from their own operations are $50,000, $20,000, and $10,000 respectively, one method of apportioning the total of their net incomes of $80,000 between majority and minority shareholders is by successive iteration, a variate on the trial and error method; a second method is algebraic simplification. Whatever the method chosen, it is important initially to determine the net income of each reciprocally related member of the affiliation *on a consolidated basis*. The consolidated basis net income is the net income of an affiliate reckoned in terms of its interdependency with other affiliates. In other words, the *consolidated basis* net income of a company equals the net income earned on its own operations plus its equity (accruing from its ownership of stock) in the *consolidated basis* net incomes of other affiliates. Thereafter, the consolidated basis net incomes of the several affiliates may be directly allocated to the majority and minority interests.

Successive Iteration. Where the involvements of intercompany stockholdings are not especially complex and where the number of mutually related companies is not unusually large, the successive iteration method may be easily applied. The method presumes that a consolidated basis net income in respect to a given company can be determined by a series of approximations in the manner indicated in Illustration 15–1.

Illustration 15–1

	Y Company			Z Company		
Step	Net Income from Own Operations	70% of Net Income of Z Company	Total	Net Income from Own Operations	10% of Net Income of Y Company	Total
1	$20,000	$7,000.00	$27,000.00	$10,000	$2,700.00	$12,700.00
2	20,000	8,890.00	28,890.00	10,000	2,889.00	12,889.00
3	20,000	9,022.30	29,022.30	10,000	2,902.23	12,902.23
4	20,000	9,031.56	29,031.56	10,000	2,903.16	12,903.16
5	20,000	9,032.21	29,032.21	10,000	2,903.22	12,903.22
6	20,000	9,032.25	29,032.25	10,000	2,903.23	12,903.23
7	20,000	9,032.26	29,032.26	10,000	2,903.23	12,903.23
8	20,000	9,032.26	29,032.26	10,000	2,903.23	12,903.23

Illustration 15–1 indicates that the successive iteration method proceeds with a progression of successive estimates. Each value total is based upon a sequence of approximations. The sequence of steps in the calculation continues, as illustrated, until solution value totals stabilize. In this illustration no change in the amount of total net incomes for Y Company and Z Company results after step 7. These value totals are the *consolidated basis net incomes* of companies Y and Z. Since there is no bilateral affiliation involving the parent company, X Company is not included in the iterative process in Illustration 15–1. Additionally, in general, only those subsidiary affiliates whose consolidated basis net incomes include an interest, direct or indirect, in bilaterally related affiliates must be included in this type of calculation.

Allocation of net incomes of the affiliate companies is accomplished in the following manner:

X Company's net income............................	$50,000.00	
80 percent of Y Company's consolidated basis net income (80% of $29,032.26).......................	23,225.81	
Consolidated net income............................		$73,225.81
Minority interest in Y Company:		
10 percent of Y Company's consolidated basis net income (10% of $29,032.26).......................		2,903.22
Minority interest in Z Company:		
30 percent of Z Company's consolidated basis net income (30% of $12,903.23).......................		3,870.97
Total net incomes of affiliate companies..................		$80,000.00

Although the aggregated consolidated basis net incomes exceed the aggregated reported net incomes of the bilateral affiliates, it should be observed that the allocation process results in the calculation of majority and minority interests equal in amount to the total *reported* net incomes of the three affiliates. This condition must exist, regardless of the type or complexity of the interdependency relationships. Note that Z Company's consolidated basis net income does not enter the calculation of consolidated net income; it is utilized only to determine the equity of Z Company's minority interest. This is appropriate since Y Company's consolidated basis net income includes Y's equity in Z's net income. X Company's equity in Z's net income is, therefore, included in consolidated net income as a part of the calculation which includes X's equity in Y's consolidated basis net income (80 percent of $29,032.26).

Algebraic Solution. The same interdependency structure may be more formally expressed as a system of linear equations. Where such a system is relatively simple, viz., two or three affiliates, algebraic simplification is perhaps the most easily applied solution form. Assume the following notation:

Y = Net income of Y Company on a consolidated basis.
Z = Net income of Z Company on a consolidated basis.

The problem may now be formulated and solved as follows:

$$Y = \$20,000 + .7Z,$$
$$Z = \$10,000 + .1Y.$$

$$Y = \$20,000 + .7(\$10,000 + .1Y),$$
$$Y = \$20,000 + \$7,000 + .07Y,$$
$$.93Y = \$27,000,$$
$$Y = \$29,032.26.$$

$$Z = \$10,000 + .1(\$29,032.26),$$
$$Z = \$10,000 + \$2,903.23,$$
$$Z = \$12,903.23.$$

As noted previously, X Company is not in the interdependency structure and thus is excluded from the system of equations. Given the above consolidated basis net incomes of Y Company and Z Company, the allocation of the total net incomes of the affiliates is made in the same amounts as in the illustration of the successive iteration method.

Case 2. Bilateral Stockholdings Not Involving Parent Company—A Different Affiliation.   Consider a somewhat different interdependency relationship. X Company directly controls both Y Company and Z Company, with companies Y and Z also bilaterally affiliated:

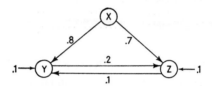

In this case, the same methods of simplification are illustrated as in the previous example.

Successive Iteration.   If the net incomes of companies X, Y, and Z earned on their own operations are $50,000, $20,000, and $10,000, the calculation of the consolidated basis net income of each reciprocally related company is reflected in Illustration 15–2.

Illustration 15–2

	Y Company			Z Company		
Step	Net Income from Own Operations	20% of Net Income of Z Company	Total	Net Income from Own Operations	10% of Net Income of Y Company	Total
1.................	$20,000	$2,000.00	$22,000.00	$10,000	$2,200.00	$12,200.00
2.................	20,000	2,440.00	22,440.00	10,000	2,244.00	12,244.00
3.................	20,000	2,448.80	22,448.80	10,000	2,244.88	12,244.88
4.................	20,000	2,448.98	22,448.98	10,000	2,244.90	12,244.90
5.................	20,000	2,448.98	22,448.98	10,000	2,244.90	12,244.90

Algebraic Solution.   The consolidated basis net incomes of companies Y and Z are calculated by algebraic solution in the following manner:

$$Y = \text{Net income of Y Company on a consolidated basis.}$$
$$Z = \text{Net income of Z Company on a consolidated basis.}$$

$$Y = \$20,000 + .2Z,$$
$$Z = \$10,000 + .1Y.$$

$$Y = \$20,000 + .2(\$10,000 + .1Y),$$
$$Y = \$20,000 + \$2,000 + .02Y,$$
$$.98Y = \$22,000,$$
$$Y = \$22,448.98 .$$

$$Z = \$10,000 + .1(\$22,448.98),$$
$$Z = \$10,000 + \$2,244.90,$$
$$Z = \$12,244.90.$$

Allocation of the net incomes of affiliate companies is as follows:

X Company's net income.....................................	$50,000.00
80 percent of Y Company's consolidated basis net income (80% of $22,448.98).......................	17,959.18
70 percent of Z Company's consolidated basis net income (70% of $12,244.90).......................	8,571.43
Consolidated net income......................................	$76,530.61
Minority interest in Y Company:	
10 percent of Y Company's consolidated basis net income (10% of $22,448.98).......................	2,244.90
Minority interest in Z Company:	
10 percent of Z Company's consolidated basis net income (10% of $12,244.90).......................	1,224.49
Total net incomes of affiliates............................	$80,000.00

Case 3. Bilateral Stockholdings Involving Parent Company. The previous illustrations have been concerned with mutually related subsidiary affiliates. The calculation of consolidated basis net incomes is not essentially different if the parent is also bilaterally related to one or more affiliates. In the example which follows it is apparent that the new interdependency structure introduces no special difficulty other than to increase the number of steps in the arithmetic simplification.

The affiliation diagram indicating the bilateral association of companies X and Z is as follows:

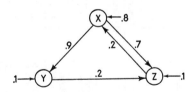

The net incomes are assumed to be the same as in the previous illustrations.

Successive Iteration. The allocation by successive iteration is given in Illustration 15–3.

Algebraic Solution.

X = Net income of X Company on a consolidated basis.
Y = Net income of Y Company on a consolidated basis.
Z = Net income of Z Company on a consolidated basis.

$$X = \$50,000 + .9Y + .7Z,$$
$$Y = \$20,000 + .2Z,$$
$$Z = \$10,000 + .2X.$$

Illustration 15–3

SUCCESSIVE ITERATION

Step	X Company				Y Company			Z Company		
	Net Income from Own Operations	70% of Net Income of Z Company	90% of Net Income of Y Company	Total	Net Income from Own Operations	20% of Net Income of Z Company	Total	Net Income from Own Operations	20% of Net Income of X Company	Total
1	$50,000	$ 7,000.00	$18,000.00	$75,000.00	$20,000	$2,000.00	$22,000.00	$10,000	$15,000.00	$25,000.00
2	50,000	17,500.00	19,800.00	87,300.00	20,000	5,000.00	25,000.00	10,000	17,460.00	27,460.00
3	50,000	19,222.00	22,500.00	91,722.00	20,000	5,492.00	25,492.00	10,000	18,344.40	28,344.40
4	50,000	19,841.08	22,942.80	92,783.88	20,000	5,668.88	25,668.88	10,000	18,556.78	28,556.78
5	50,000	19,989.75	23,101.99	93,091.74	20,000	5,711.36	25,711.36	10,000	18,618.35	28,618.35
6	50,000	20,032.85	23,140.22	93,173.07	20,000	5,723.67	25,723.67	10,000	18,634.61	28,634.61
7	50,000	20,044.23	23,151.30	93,195.53	20,000	5,726.92	25,726.92	10,000	18,639.11	28,639.11
8	50,000	20,047.38	23,154.23	93,201.61	20,000	5,727.82	25,727.82	10,000	18,640.32	28,640.32
9	50,000	20,048.22	23,155.04	93,203.26	20,000	5,728.06	25,728.06	10,000	18,640.65	28,640.65
10	50,000	20,048.46	23,155.25	93,203.71	20,000	5,728.13	25,728.13	10,000	18,640.74	28,640.74
11	50,000	20,048.52	23,155.32	93,203.84	20,000	5,728.15	25,728.15	10,000	18,640.77	28,640.77
12	50,000	20,048.54	23,155.33	93,203.87	20,000	5,728.16	25,728.16	10,000	18,640.77	28,640.77
13	50,000	20,048.54	23,155.34	93,203.88	20,000	5,728.16	25,728.16	10,000	18,640.77	28,640.77
14	50,000	20,048.54	23,155.34	93,203.88	20,000	5,728.16	25,728.16	10,000	18,640.77	28,640.77

$$X = \$50,000 + .9(\$20,000 + .2Z) + .7Z,$$
$$X = \$50,000 + \$18,000 + .18Z + .7Z,$$
$$X = \$68,000 + .88Z.$$

$$X = \$68,000 + .88(\$10,000 + .2X),$$
$$X = \$68,000 + \$8,800 + .176X,$$
$$.824X = \$76,800,$$
$$X = \$93,203.88.$$

$$Z = \$10,000 + .2(\$93,203.88),$$
$$Z = \$10,000 + \$18,640.77,$$
$$Z = \$28,640.77.$$

$$Y = \$20,000 + .2(\$28,640.77),$$
$$Y = \$20,000 + \$5,728.16,$$
$$Y = \$25,728.16.$$

Allocation of net incomes of affiliate companies:

Consolidated net income:
    80 percent of X Company's consolidated basis net income
      (80% of $93,203.88)...................................... $74,563.10
Minority interest in Y Company:
    10 percent of Y Company's consolidated basis net income
      (10% of $25,728.16)...................................... 2,572.82
Minority interest in Z Company:
    10 percent of Z Company's consolidated basis net income
      (10% of $28,640.77)...................................... 2,864.08
Total net incomes of affiliates................................ $80,000.00

In consolidated net income determination, only the nonaffiliate share-holders in the parent company constitute the majority interest. In Case 3, 20 percent of X Company's stock is held by Z Company; accordingly, the outside interest in X Company of 80 percent is the equity multiplier in calculating consolidated net income.

Intercompany Profit on Asset Transfers

For eliminations of intercompany profit on the transfer of assets between affiliate companies, the same elimination procedures control in respect to reciprocally related companies as for unilateral affiliations. The amount of the intercompany profit to be eliminated may be either 100 percent or a fractional amount based upon the parent company's equity in the selling affiliate. As was illustrated in Chapter 12, if the amount of the eliminated profit is 100 percent, the profit elimination results in a ratable diminution of the interests of both majority and minority shareholders; where the elimination relates only to the parent's equity in the selling affiliate, the amount of the elimination is absorbed totally by the majority share-holders. In the latter case, the consolidated basis net income of each subsidiary, unadjusted for intercompany profit, is the basis used in calculating the equity of minority shareholders.

Case 4. Bilateral Stockholdings Not Involving Parent. The following affiliation diagram for Case 2 is repeated here:

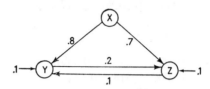

Inventory profit currently recorded by Z Company, which is unconfirmed from a consolidated standpoint, is $9,800.

Assume the following notation:

X_E = Interest of X Company in the unconfirmed inventory profit on a consolidated basis.

Y_E = Interest of Y Company in the unconfirmed inventory profit on a consolidated basis.

Z_E = Interest of Z Company in the unconfirmed inventory profit on a consolidated basis.

The various interests in the unconfirmed inventory profit are reflected as follows:

$$X_E = .8Y_E + .7Z_E ,$$
$$Y_E = .2Z_E ,$$
$$Z_E = \$9,800 + .1Y_E .$$

By substitution and simplification, solution values are determined to be:

$$X_E = \$8,600 ,$$
$$Y_E = \$2,000 ,$$
$$Z_E = \$10,000 .$$

In the consolidated working paper, the eliminating entry in respect to intercompany inventory profit is as follows:

1. If the amount of the elimination is based upon the parent company's fractional interest in the selling affiliate:

    Inventory (Income Statement division)................... 8,600
        Inventory (Balance Sheet division).................... 8,600

2. If the amount of the elimination is 100 percent of the unconfirmed profit:

    Inventory (Income Statement division)................... 9,800
        Inventory (Balance Sheet division).................... 9,800

In the latter case, minority shareholders must absorb a ratable amount of the eliminated inventory profit, calculated as follows:

Minority in Y Company (10% of $2,000)................ $ 200
Minority in Z Company (10% of $10,000)............... 1,000
                                                     $1,200

Thus the total elimination of $9,800 is allocated:

To the majority shareholders...................... $8,600
To the minority shareholders...................... 1,200
                                                   $9,800

Depending upon the method used, interests in the unconfirmed inventory profits are deducted, as appropriate, from the consolidated basis net incomes as previously calculated.

The algebraic solution may be simplified, however, in the event of a 100 percent elimination of intercompany inventory profit. Given net incomes of $50,000, $20,000, and $10,000 for companies X, Y, and Z respectively, the equation system of the mutually related subsidiaries may take the following form:

$$Y = \$20,000 + .2Z,$$
$$Z = \$200 + .1Y.$$

Z Company's net income in the second equation is reduced to $200 by deducting the $9,800 of unconfirmed inventory profit from the recorded net income of $10,000. By substitution and simplification, solution values are determined to be:

$$Y = \$20,448.98,$$
$$Z = \$ 2,244.90.$$

Allocation of the net incomes of the affiliate companies is then made as follows:

X Company's net income...................... $50,000.00
80 percent of Y Company's consolidated basis net
   income (80% of $20,448.98)................. 16,359.18
70 percent of Z Company's consolidated basis net
   income (70% of $2,244.90)................. 1,571.43
Consolidated net income...................... $67,930.61
Minority interest in Y Company:
  10 percent of Y Company's consolidated basis
   net income (10% of $20,448.98)..............   2,044.90
Minority interest in Z Company:
  10 percent of Z Company's consolidated basis
   net income (10% of $2,244.90)..............   224.49
Total confirmed net incomes of affiliates......... $70,200.00

This method implicitly deducts the majority and minority interests in the unconfirmed inventory profit, as calculated above, from the allocated shares of total net income.

Had fractional elimination been applied, the equation system would have been identical to that of Case 2 in respect to determining consolidated basis net incomes of the affiliate companies. In allocating the intercompany inventory profit element, however, $8,600 would be eliminated against the consolidated basis net income of X Company. In this instance, the allocation of net incomes of the affiliate companies is made in the following manner:

X Company's consolidated basis net income.......	$76,530.61	
Less: Unconfirmed inventory profit elimination.....	8,600.00	
Consolidated net income......................		$67,930.61
Minority interest in Y Company:		
10 percent of Y Company's consolidated basis net income (10% of $22,448.98).............		2,244.90
Minority interest in Z Company:		
10 percent of Z Company's consolidated basis net income (10% of $12,244.90).............		1,224.49
Total confirmed net incomes of affiliates..........		$71,400.00

The variation in the total of the net incomes allocated, $1,200, may be attributed to the different bases for calculating minority interests. Significantly, the amount of consolidated net income in both calculations remains the same.

Case 5. Bilateral Stockholdings Involving Parent. The following is an illustration of an affiliation involving intercompany profit in which the parent is bilaterally related to one subsidiary:

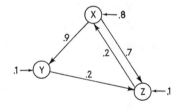

Inventory profit currently recognized by Z Company, although unconfirmed from a consolidated standpoint, is assumed to be $8,240.

Notation:

X_E = Interest of X Company in the unconfirmed inventory profit on a consolidated basis.

Y_E = Interest of Y Company in the unconfirmed inventory profit on a consolidated basis.

Z_E = Interest of Z Company in the unconfirmed inventory profit on a consolidated basis.

The interests in the unconfirmed inventory profit are:

$$X_E = .9Y_E + .7Z_E,$$
$$Y_E = .2Z_E',$$
$$Z_E = \$8,240 + .2X_E.$$

By substitution and simplification, solution values are determined to be:

$$X_E = \$8,800,$$
$$Y_E = \$2,000,$$
$$Z_E = \$10,000.$$

Since consolidated net income is but 80 percent of the parent company's consolidated basis net income (recall that only the parent company's shares held by nonaffiliate interests are determinants of consolidated net income), the effect of the above unconfirmed profit elimination is a reduction of consolidated net income by $7,040 (80 percent of $8,800).

The eliminating entry for consolidated working papers is:

1. If the amount of the elimination is based upon the parent company's equity in the selling affiliate:

    Inventory (Income Statement division).................. 7,040
        Inventory (Balance Sheet division)................   7,040

2. If the amount of the elimination is 100 percent of the unconfirmed profit:

    Inventory (Income Statement division).................. 8,240
        Inventory (Balance Sheet division)................   8,240

In this instance, the amounts of minority interests in the unconfirmed profit on a consolidated basis are calculated as follows:

Minority interest in Y Company (10% of $2,000)............. $ 200
Minority interest in Z Company (10% of $10,000)...........   1,000
                                              $1,200

Thus, the total elimination of $8,240 is allocated:

To the majority shareholders...................... $7,040
To the minority shareholders......................   1,200
                                             $8,240

Case 6. Comprehensive Problem. On January 1, 1971, X Company purchased 90 percent of the capital stock of Y Company and 70 percent of the capital stock of Z Company for $185,000 and $95,000 respectively. On the same date, Y Company acquired 20 percent of the capital stock of Z Company for $27,500 and Z Company purchased 20 percent of the capital stock of X Company for $75,000. January 1, 1971, stockholders' equity balances of the affiliate companies were:

	X Company	Y Company	Z Company
Capital stock (par, $100)...........	$200,000	$100,000	$80,000
Retained earnings.................	150,000	100,000	50,000

The affiliation diagram, which is identical to that in Case 5, is repeated following:

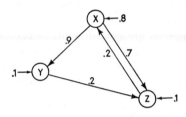

The investment elimination schedule for this affiliation is:

Investment Elimination Schedule
Dr. [Cr.]

	X Company in Y Company	X Company in Z Company	Y Company in Z Company	Z Company in X Company
Capital stock.................	90,000	56,000	16,000	40,000
Retained earnings.............	90,000	35,000	10,000	30,000
Differential..................	5,000	4,000	1,500	5,000
Investment...................	[185,000]	[95,000]	[27,500]	[75,000]

Trial balances of the affiliates after two years' operations are:

	X Company		Y Company		Z Company	
			December 31, 1972			
Investment in Y Co...............	$185,000					
Investment in Z Co...............	95,000		$ 27,500			
Investment in X Co...............					$ 75,000	
Merchandise, Jan. 1..............	24,000		16,000		15,000	
Other assets....................	125,000		231,500		88,000	
Liabilities.....................		$ 20,000		$ 29,000		$ 7,000
Capital stock...................		200,000		100,000		80,000
Retained earnings...............		180,000		126,000		65,000
Sales..........................		200,000		145,000		98,000
Purchases......................	150,000		115,000		60,000	
Expenses.......................	21,000		10,000		12,000	
	$600,000	$600,000	$400,000	$400,000	$250,000	$250,000
Merchandise, December 31........	$ 45,000		$ 26,000		$ 14,000	

X Company's inventory on January 1, 1972, contained goods sold during the previous year by Z Company on which the latter recorded a profit of

$2,472. Z Company sold merchandise during 1972 to Y Company for $40,000. On December 31, 1972, the inventory of Y Company contained a quantity of these goods on which the profit recorded by Z Company was $8,240.

The 1972 net incomes of the various affiliates are allocated on a consolidated basis as follows:

X = Net income of X Company on a consolidated basis.
Y = Net income of Y Company on a consolidated basis.
Z = Net income of Z Company on a consolidated basis.

$$X = \$50,000 + .9Y + .7Z,$$
$$Y = \$30,000 + .2Z,$$
$$Z = \$25,000 + .2X.$$

By substitution and simplification, solution values are determined to be:

$$X = \$120,145,$$
$$Y = \$39,806,$$
$$Z = \$49,029.$$

The unconfirmed profit in the *beginning* inventory is allocated on a consolidated basis among the affiliates in the following manner:

X_B = Interest of X Company in the unconfirmed beginning inventory profit on a consolidated basis.
Y_B = Interest of Y Company in the unconfirmed beginning inventory profit on a consolidated basis.
Z_B = Interest of Z Company in the unconfirmed beginning inventory profit on a consolidated basis.

$$X_B = .9Y_B + .7Z_B,$$
$$Y_B = .2Z_B,$$
$$Z_B = \$2,472 + .2X_B.$$

By substitution and simplification, solution values are determined to be:

$$X_B = \$2,640,$$
$$Y_B = \$600,$$
$$Z_B = \$3,000.$$

The various affiliates' interests in the $8,240 unconfirmed profit in the *ending* inventory, on a consolidated basis, were calculated in Case 5. The amounts of such interests were:

$$X_E = \$8,800,$$
$$Y_E = \$2,000,$$
$$Z_E = \$10,000.$$

In respect to both beginning and ending inventories, the amount of the elimination (see Illustration 15–4) is based upon the fractional elimination method, viz., 80 percent of $2,640, or $2,112, and 80 percent of $8,800, or $7,040.

Since consolidated statements are being prepared a year subsequent to the year of acquisition, the recorded retained earnings as of the beginning of the year must be adjusted to reflect the net increases in prior years on a consolidated basis. The 1971 net increase in the retained earnings of each affiliate company calculated on a consolidated basis is determined as follows:

X_R = Net increase in retained earnings of X Company as of January 1, 1972, on a consolidated basis.

Y_R = Net increase in retained earnings of Y Company as of January 1, 1972, on a consolidated basis.

Z_R = Net increase in retained earnings of Z Company as of January 1, 1972, on a consolidated basis.

$$X_R = \$30,000 + .9Y_R + .7Z_R ,$$
$$Y_R = \$26,000 + .2Z_R ,$$
$$Z_R = \$15,000 + .2X_R .$$

By substitution and simplification, solution values are determined to be:

$$X_R = \$80,826 ,$$
$$Y_R = \$32,233 ,$$
$$Z_R = \$31,165 .$$

The amounts of minority interests in the retained earnings of companies Y and Z on January 1, 1972, are based upon the recorded retained earnings balances of each subsidiary on January 1, 1971, increased (or decreased) by the percentage interests of minority shareholders in the consolidated basis *net* increases (or decreases) in the retained earnings of each subsidiary since January 1, 1971.

Minority interest in Y Company:

10 percent of retained earnings on January 1, 1971 (10% of $100,000)	$10,000	
10 percent of Y Company's consolidated basis net increase in retained earnings for 1971 (10% of $32,233)	3,223	$13,223

Minority interest in Z Company:

10 percent of retained earnings on January 1, 1971 (10% of $50,000)	$ 5,000	
10 percent of Z Company's consolidated basis net increase in retained earnings for 1971 (10% of $31,165)	3,116	$ 8,116

The consolidated statement working paper for this case is given in Illustration 15–4. As previously mentioned, the fractional elimination method is used for intercompany inventory profits.

Consolidated Net Income—Alternative Calculation. The amount of consolidated net income in Case 6 may be confirmed by adapting the equation system on page 511 to directly include the effects of unconfirmed intercompany profit recorded by the selling affiliate (100 percent elimination method). The amounts of intercompany profit in the beginning and ending inventories of the purchasing affiliate were reported to be $2,472 and $8,240, respectively. Accordingly, the *adjusted* net income of Z Company (the selling affiliate) is reduced to $19,232 ($25,000 + $2,472 − $8,240).

The equation system may then be rewritten as follows:

$$X = \$50,000 + .9Y + .7Z,$$
$$Y = \$30,000 + .2Z,$$
$$Z = \$19,232 + .2X.$$

By substitution and simplification, solution values are determined to be:

$$X = \$113,985,$$
$$Y = \$38,406,$$
$$Z = \$42,029.$$

Consolidated net income is now determined to be $91,188 (80 percent of $113,985), and since consolidated net income is unaffected by the elimination method, this confirms the amount reported in Illustration 15–4.

Dividends and the Allocation of Affiliation Net Income

In the event that there exists dividend income on the books of an affiliate, it is important to exclude such income in the allocation of net income as previously described. It is redundant and inaccurate to apportion both the dividend income received from an affiliate as well as the gross amount of the net income of such affiliate. Consequently, only the net incomes of the various bilaterally associated companies *exclusive of dividends received* should be taken into account in formulating the equation system of interdependency. In calculating the net increase in retained earnings on a consolidated basis, however, the *recorded* retained earnings of each affiliate as of the start of the year, adjusted for unconfirmed profits as of that date, are compared with the retained earnings at acquisition, as the dividends merely confirm the previously calculated interests in the affiliates' net incomes which exclude intercompany dividend income.

Purchase of Shares in a Mutually Related Subsidiary

Reference has been repeatedly made to the necessity for eliminating the parent company's purchased equity in the accumulated retained earnings of a subsidiary at date of acquisition, assuming the purchase method of accounting for the acquisition is employed. In the event the subsidiary is a preexisting member of a reciprocally related corporate affiliation, it is important that the consolidated basis retained earnings of the subsidiary on

Illustration 15–4

X COMPANY AND SUBSIDIARY COMPANIES Y AND Z

Consolidated Statement Working Paper
For Year Ended December 31, 1972

	X Company	Y Company	Z Company	Eliminations Dr.	Eliminations Cr.	Minority Interests Y Company	Minority Interests Z Company	Consolidated
Income Statement:								
Sales	200,000	145,000	98,000	(5) 40,000				403,000
Merchandise, 12/31	45,000	26,000	14,000	(7) 7,040				77,960
Total credits	245,000	171,000	112,000					480,960
Merchandise, 1/1	24,000	16,000	15,000		(6) 2,112			52,888
Purchases	150,000	115,000	60,000		(5) 40,000			285,000
Expenses	21,000	10,000	12,000					43,000
Total debits	195,000	141,000	87,000					380,888
Net income	50,000	30,000	25,000					100,072
Minority interest in:								
Y Company (10% of $39,806)				3,981		3,981		[3,981]
Z Company (10% of $49,029)				4,903			4,903	[4,903]
Net income—carried forward	50,000	30,000	25,000	47,040	42,112	3,981	4,903	*91,188
Retained Earnings Statement:								
Retained earnings, January 1:								
X Company	180,000			(4) 30,000				150,000
Y Company		126,000		(1) 90,000		13,223		22,777
Z Company			65,000	(2) 35,000			8,116	9,772
				(3) 10,000				
				(6) 2,112				
				47,040				
Net income—brought forward	50,000	30,000	25,000		42,112	3,981	4,903	91,188
Retained earnings, December 31—carried forward	230,000	156,000	90,000	214,152	42,112	17,204	13,019	273,737

Balance Sheet:

	X Company	Y Company	Z Company	Eliminations Dr.	Eliminations Cr.	Minority Y	Minority Z	Consolidated
Investment in Y Company	185,000				(1) 185,000			-0-
Investment in Z Company	95,000	27,500			(2) 95,000 / (3) 27,500			-0-
Investment in X Company					(4) 75,000 / (7) 7,040			-0-
Merchandise	45,000	26,000	75,000	(1) 5,000				77,960
Other assets	125,000	231,500	14,000					444,500
Differential			88,000	(2) 4,000 / (3) 1,500 / (4) 5,000				15,500
	450,000	285,000	177,000					537,960
Liabilities	20,000	29,000	7,000					56,000
Capital stock:								
X Company	200,000			(4) 40,000				160,000
Y Company		100,000		(1) 90,000		10,000		
Z Company			80,000	(2) 56,000 / (3) 16,000			8,000	
Retained earnings—brought forward	230,000	156,000	90,000	214,152	42,112	17,204	13,019	273,737
Minority interest in Y Company						27,204		27,204 M
Minority interest in Z Company							21,019	21,019 M
	450,000	285,000	177,000	431,652	431,652	27,204	21,019	537,960

* Using the data previously calculated, consolidated net income may be verified; it is 80 percent of ($120,145 + $2,640 − $8,800), or $91,188.
[deduction]

this date be used as a basis for determining the amount of the retained earnings elimination. Similarly, where the parent is a controlling shareholder in a subsidiary prior to the latter's purchase of the parent's stock, it is also important that the parent's consolidated basis retained earnings be used in calculating the amount of the retained earnings elimination; necessarily, this amount is the at-acquisition equity-basis retained earnings of the parent.

Matrix Applications for Complex Affiliations

The benefits to be derived from a matrix formulation of "complex" intercorporate stockholdings are especially significant and are illustrated in the paragraphs which follow.[1]

Assume the following affiliation diagram and supporting data for the year 1971 are given:

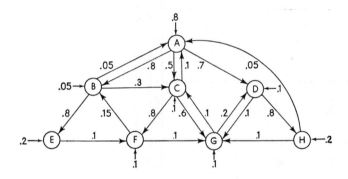

Reported net incomes for 1971 are:

A Company	$ 40,000
B Company	30,000
C Company	30,000
D Company	40,000
E Company	10,000
F Company	20,000
G Company	10,000
H Company	20,000
	$200,000

No dividends were paid by any of the companies during the year. As illustrated previously, the consolidated basis net incomes of the individual companies may be defined in algebraic form. Letting $A, B, \ldots, H$ denote net incomes of the respective companies on a consolidated basis, there results:

---

[1] See Appendix 1 for a review of certain basic characteristics of matrices.

$$A = \$40,000 + .80B + .50C + .70D ,$$
$$B = \$30,000 + .80E + .30C + .05A ,$$
$$C = \$30,000 + .80F + .60G + .10A ,$$
$$D = \$40,000 + .80H + .10G ,$$
$$E = \$10,000 + .10F ,$$
$$F = \$20,000 + .15B + .10G ,$$
$$G = \$10,000 + .10C + .20D ,$$
$$H = \$20,000 + .05A + .10G .$$

These equations may be rearranged in a form exhibiting the underlying matrix structure as follows:

$$
\begin{array}{lllllll}
+ \quad A \; -.80B \; -.50C \; -.70D & & & & = \$40,000 \\
-.05A + \quad B \; -.30C & \quad -.80E & & & = \$30,000 \\
-.10A \qquad + \quad C & \quad -.80F \; -.60G & & = \$30,000 \\
\qquad\qquad\qquad + \quad D & \quad -.10G \; -.80H & = \$40,000 \\
\qquad\qquad\qquad\qquad + \quad E \; -.10F & & = \$10,000 \\
-.15B & \quad + \quad F \; -.10G & & = \$20,000 \\
\qquad -.10C \; -.20D & \quad + \quad G & & = \$10,000 \\
-.05A & \quad -.10G \; + \quad H & = \$20,000 .
\end{array}
$$

Based upon this equation system, the problem may be easily expressed in matrix form:

$$
\begin{bmatrix}
1 & -.80 & -.50 & -.70 & 0 & 0 & 0 & 0 \\
-.05 & 1 & -.30 & 0 & -.80 & 0 & 0 & 0 \\
-.10 & 0 & 1 & 0 & 0 & -.80 & -.60 & 0 \\
0 & 0 & 0 & 1 & 0 & 0 & -.10 & -.80 \\
0 & 0 & 0 & 0 & 1 & -.10 & 0 & 0 \\
0 & -.15 & 0 & 0 & 0 & 1 & -.10 & 0 \\
0 & 0 & -.10 & -.20 & 0 & 0 & 1 & 0 \\
-.05 & 0 & 0 & 0 & 0 & 0 & -.10 & 1
\end{bmatrix}
\begin{bmatrix}
A \\ B \\ C \\ D \\ E \\ F \\ G \\ H
\end{bmatrix}
=
\begin{bmatrix}
\$40,000 \\ \$30,000 \\ \$30,000 \\ \$40,000 \\ \$10,000 \\ \$20,000 \\ \$10,000 \\ \$20,000
\end{bmatrix}.
$$

There now remains the arithmetical problem of calculating the inverse of this 8 × 8 coefficient matrix.[2] After this inverse is computed, the matrix formulation assumes the form shown in Illustration 15–5.

By the simple process of matrix multiplication, the values for the consolidated basis net incomes of the eight companies are easily determined:

$$
\begin{bmatrix}
A \\ B \\ C \\ D \\ E \\ F \\ G \\ H
\end{bmatrix}
=
\begin{bmatrix}
\$203,322 \\ \$ 80,741 \\ \$ 99,114 \\ \$ 70,245 \\ \$ 13,550 \\ \$ 35,507 \\ \$ 33,961 \\ \$ 33,562
\end{bmatrix}.
$$

---

[2] See Appendix 1 for the iterative procedure to calculate the inverse of a matrix.

Illustration 15–5

$$
\begin{bmatrix} A \\ B \\ C \\ D \\ E \\ F \\ G \\ H \end{bmatrix}
=
\begin{bmatrix}
1.19654 & 1.09201 & 1.01394 & 1.01372 & .87361 & .89852 & .88069 & .81097 \\
.10622 & 1.15050 & .43101 & .13985 & .92040 & .43685 & .32746 & .11188 \\
.14971 & .27266 & 1.24678 & .28506 & .21813 & 1.01924 & .90131 & .22805 \\
.05244 & .05040 & .06535 & 1.08473 & .04032 & .05631 & .24009 & .86778 \\
.00185 & .01763 & .00784 & .00455 & 1.01410 & .10768 & .01629 & .00364 \\
.01848 & .17631 & .07843 & .04552 & .14105 & 1.07685 & .16293 & .03642 \\
.02546 & .03735 & .13775 & .24545 & .02988 & .11319 & 1.13815 & .19636 \\
.06237 & .05834 & .06447 & .07523 & .04667 & .05624 & .15785 & 1.06018
\end{bmatrix}
\begin{bmatrix} \$40{,}000 \\ \$30{,}000 \\ \$30{,}000 \\ \$40{,}000 \\ \$10{,}000 \\ \$20{,}000 \\ \$10{,}000 \\ \$20{,}000 \end{bmatrix}
$$

Consolidated net income for 1971 and the minority interests in subsidiary net incomes are now calculated as before:

Allocation of net incomes:		
Consolidated net income (.80 × $203,322)............		$162,658
Minority interests:		
B Company (.05 × $80,741).....................	$4,037	
C Company (.10 × $99,114).....................	9,911	
D Company (.10 × $70,245).....................	7,025	
E Company (.20 × $13,550).....................	2,710	
F Company (.10 × $35,507).....................	3,551	
G Company (.10 × $33,961).....................	3,396	
H Company (.20 × $33,562).....................	6,712	37,342
Total net incomes of affiliates.....................		$200,000

The increased number of affiliates and the additional involvements of the intercorporate stockholdings obviously introduce a number of complications in the arithmetic calculations of the consolidated basis net incomes. However, once these values are determined, the allocation of net incomes is only slightly more tedious than less complex affiliation structures.

A problem such as this may be solved using the iterative (trial and error) method. However, the practical value of the matrix method derives from the *permanence* of the inverse of the coefficient matrix. If there are no changes in the intercorporate shareholdings, the consolidated basis net incomes are easily determined each period (month, quarter, etc.) with one matrix multiplication. This characteristic of the matrix representation greatly alleviates the arithmetic complexities, as a single calculation of the inverse of the coefficient matrix provides a continuing basis for the relatively simple calculation of the desired solutions in subsequent periods.

TREASURY STOCK SOLUTION

Some accountants take the position that the purchase of a parent company's stock by a subsidiary affiliate is not essentially unlike the parent's acquisition of "treasury shares." Where such stockholdings are thus accorded the status of treasury shares, it is appropriate to deduct the cost of these shares from the amounts of contributed capital and retained earnings of the parent company in the preparation of consolidated financial statements. In this accounting treatment, the calculation of minority interests (unlike the conventional algebraic solution) is based upon the recorded amounts of a subsidiary's retained earnings arising from its own operations —*calculated without regard to the effects of bilateral share ownership.*

While the treasury stock method of accounting for a parent company's shares held by a subsidiary affiliate has not yet achieved a substantial following, it has received the approval of some accountants. The Committee on Concepts and Standards of the American Accounting Association in 1954 recommended that—

Shares of the controlling company's capital stock owned by a subsidiary before the date of acquisition of control should be treated in consolidation as treasury stock. Any subsequent acquisition or sale by a subsidiary should likewise be treated in the consolidated statements as though it had been the act of the controlling company.[3]

If consolidated statements are prepared on the date reciprocal ownership of shares is established, the conventional and treasury stock methods produce similar results (varying only in the amount of the differential in this transaction). Also, if the *total* amount of the subsidiaries' outstanding shares are held either by the parent or other subsidiaries, the effects produced on consolidated statements are again essentially the same. However, where neither condition prevails, the allocated amounts from applying the two methods will usually continue to diverge, in some instances materially.

In the following example, consolidated balance sheets are prepared both on the date of bilateral affiliation and on a subsequent date.

Case 7.   On January 1, 1971, X Company purchased 80 percent of the capital stock (par, $100) of Y Company concurrent with the latter's purchase of 20 percent of the capital stock (par, $100) of X Company. On this date, the balance sheet of each company is as follows:

	X Company	Y Company
Investments in corporate stock:		
X Company		$ 50,000
Y Company	$120,000	
Other assets	170,000	95,000
	$290,000	$145,000
Liabilities	$ 10,000	$ 5,000
Capital stock	200,000	100,000
Retained earnings	80,000	40,000
	$290,000	$145,000

A consolidated balance sheet on this date is given following:

X COMPANY AND SUBSIDIARY
Consolidated Balance Sheet
January 1, 1971

ASSETS

Other assets	$265,000
Cost of investment in excess of corresponding book value of subsidiary stock	8,000
	$273,000

---

[3] Committee on Accounting Concepts and Standards, American Accounting Association, "Consolidated Financial Statements," in *Accounting and Reporting Standards for Corporate Financial Statements* (*Supplementary Statement No. 7*) (Evanston, Ill., 1957), p. 44.

EQUITIES

Liabilities...		$ 15,000
Minority interest:		
Capital stock, Y Company......................	$ 20,000	
Retained earnings, Y Company..................	8,000	28,000
Owners' equity:		
Capital stock, X Company:		
Issued......................................	$200,000	
Held by Y Company.........................	40,000	
Held by nonaffiliates.........................		160,000
Retained earnings:		
Consolidated retained earnings.................	$ 80,000	
Premium on treasury stock purchased...........	10,000	70,000
		$273,000

The reader will note that the conventional solution, incorporating the investment elimination of Y Company in X Company (see p. 522), would add to the consolidated balance sheet a $6,000 credit differential (contra to the $8,000 differential), and accordingly reduce consolidated retained earnings to $64,000 ($80,000 − 20 percent of $80,000).

Case 8. In this example, the data of Case 7 are repeated, adjusted for 1971 earnings. It is assumed that the net income of each affiliate for 1971 is $30,000, with a corresponding increase in the amount of "other assets."

A consolidated balance sheet on December 31, 1971, is presented as follows:

X COMPANY AND SUBSIDIARY
Consolidated Balance Sheet
December 31, 1971

ASSETS

Other assets......................................		$325,000
Cost of investment in excess of corresponding book value of subsidiary stock.....................		8,000
		$333,000

EQUITIES

Liabilities.......................................		$ 15,000
Minority interest:		
Capital stock, Y Company......................	$ 20,000	
Retained earnings, Y Company..................	14,000	34,000
Owners' equity:		
Capital stock, X Company:		
Issued......................................	$200,000	
Held by Y Company.........................	40,000	
Held by nonaffiliates.........................		160,000
Retained earnings:		
Consolidated retained earnings.................	*$134,000	
Premium on treasury stock purchased..........	10,000	124,000
		$333,000

* $100,000 + 80% of $30,000 = $134,000.

Use of the conventional solution format in this instance will yield different allocations of retained earnings as between majority and minority shareholders. At acquisition, the following investment elimination would be made:

Investment Elimination Schedule
Dr. [Cr.]

	X Company in Y Company	Y Company in X Company
Capital stock..........................	$ 80,000	$ 40,000
Retained earnings......................	32,000	16,000
Differential...........................	8,000	[6,000]
Investment............................	$[120,000]	$[50,000]

The conventional solution provides for the elimination of the "investment" of Y Company in X Company, in addition to the principal investment elimination of X Company in Y Company. The interdependency structure may be represented by an equation system as follows:

X_R = Net increase in retained earnings of X Company since January 1, 1971, on a consolidated basis.

Y_R = Net increase in retained earnings of Y Company since January 1, 1971, on a consolidated basis.

$$X_R = \$30,000 + .8Y_R,$$
$$Y_R = \$30,000 + .2X_R.$$

By substitution and simplification, solution values are found to be:

$$X_R = \$64,285.71; 80\% \text{ whereof} = \$51,428.57,$$
$$Y_R = \$42,857.14; 20\% \text{ whereof} = \$8,571.43.$$

It follows that the allocation of $132,000 of retained earnings of companies X and Y (the combined retained earnings, $180,000, less the sum of the retained earnings eliminations, $48,000) is made:

Consolidated retained earnings ($64,000 + $51,428.57)............	$115,428.57
Minority interest ($8,000 + $8,571.43)........................	16,571.43
Total..	$132,000.00

In the illustrated treasury stock treatment, the allocation was made:

Consolidated retained earnings (net of premium on treasury stock purchased)..	$124,000.00
Minority interest..	14,000.00
Total..	$138,000.00

The difference of $6,000 ($138,000 − $132,000) is attributable to the aforementioned alternative of either eliminating 20 percent of the retained earnings of the parent company ($16,000), or charging the premium on the treasury stock ($10,000) against consolidated retained earnings. However, the important difference exhibited in the postacquisition consolidated balance sheets is the disparity in the relative shares of the remaining retained earnings; this difference is a function of the different allocation ratios inherent in each method.

The allocation differences are magnified as the nonaffiliate shareholder interests in the mutually related affiliates increase; additionally, these differences continue to increase in succeeding consolidated financial statements.

QUESTIONS

1. Define a "bilateral stockholding" and illustrate by example (diagram) such an affiliation.
2. What is meant by "consolidated basis net incomes" of reciprocally related members of an affiliation?
3. Briefly describe the successive iteration method in the context of a consolidation process involving reciprocal stockholdings.
4. Given a situation in which the affiliates of a consolidated entity have reciprocal stockholdings, explain why the sum of the consolidated basis net incomes exceeds the sum of the reported net incomes, notwithstanding the fact that the ultimate determination of majority and minority interests are equal in total to the summed reported net incomes.
5. Explain any additional complications in the calculation of consolidated net income that result from a situation in which the bilateral stockholdings involve the parent.
6. How is the elimination of intercompany profits on the transfer of assets complicated by the existence of reciprocal stockholdings?
7. What effect does the presence of dividend income on the books of an affiliate have upon the allocation of net income in a bilateral association?
8. What do you see as the principal advantage of the matrix method over the iterative (trial-and-error) method in calculating the consolidated basis net incomes of the reciprocally related affiliates?
9. How does the determination of minority interests differ as between the treasury stock method and the conventional algebraic solution?
10. Under what conditions do the treasury stock and conventional methods yield essentially equivalent results in calculating the consolidated basis net incomes of the several affiliates?

PROBLEMS

Problem 15–1

For the year 1971, companies X, Y, and Z report net incomes of $30,000, $20,000, and $9,500 respectively.

Required:

Compute consolidated net income and the minority interest in subsidiary net income for the year 1971 in each of the following independent cases:

Case 1:   X Company has an 80 percent interest in Y Company, and Y Company has a 10 percent interest in X Company.

Case 2:   X Company owns 80 percent of the stock of Y Company, Y Company owns 80 percent of the stock of Z Company, and Z Company has a 10 percent interest in Y Company.

Case 3:   X Company has a 90 percent interest in Y Company, Y Company has a 60 percent interest in Z Company, and Z Company has a 10 percent interest in X Company.

Problem 15–2

A Company owns 90 percent of the capital stock of B Company, 80 percent of the capital stock of C Company, and 80 percent of the capital stock of D Company. Additionally, C Company owns 80 percent of the capital stock of E Company, and E Company holds 5 percent of the outstanding stock of C Company.

Net incomes for the year 1971, exclusive of dividends, were:

A Company	$50,000
B Company	30,000
C Company	32,000
D Company	30,000
E Company	20,000

Required:

Compute consolidated net income for 1971 and the minority interests in subsidiary net income. (Solution hint: Draw the affiliation diagram.)

Problem 15–3

A Company owns 80 percent of the capital stock of B Company, 70 percent of the capital stock of C Company, 60 percent of the capital stock of D Company, and 70 percent of the capital stock of E Company. Additionally, B company owns 20 percent of the capital stock of C Company, D Company owns 30 percent of the capital stock of E Company, C Company owns 10 percent of the capital stock of B Company, and E Company owns 20 percent of the capital stock of D Company.

Net incomes and dividends paid for the year 1971 were:

	Reported Net Income	Dividends Paid
A Company	$84,000	$40,000
B Company	32,000	5,000
C Company	26,900	10,000
D Company	43,000	20,000
E Company	43,000	10,000

Required:

Compute consolidated net income for 1971, and the minority interests in subsidiary net income. (Solution hint: Draw the affiliation diagram.)

Problem 15–4

The financial facts shown below pertain to corporations R and S which had mutual holdings of capital stock during and at the end of the fiscal year 1971.

There has been no change in the mutual holdings during the year. Each corporation carries its investment account at cost.

	Corporation R	Corporation S
Of the issued capital stock:		
R owns.................................	10 percent	50 percent
S owns.................................	20 percent	10 percent
Net assets (exclusive of investment accounts), December 31, 1971....................	$540,000	$590,000
Dividends declared during 1971.............	?	18,000
1971 net income (after taxes), exclusive of dividends............................	53,000	60,000

Required:

(i) Compute the dollar equity of outside shareholders in the total net assets of R and S, respectively.

(ii) Compute the dollar amount of dividends declared in 1971 to which the outside shareholders of R are entitled, assuming that R declared as dividends its total 1971 net income after taxes.

(AICPA adapted)

Problem 15–5

On January 1, 1969, A Company purchased 80 percent of the capital stock of B Company, and B Company concurrently purchased 10 percent of the capital stock of A Company.

A three-year summary of retained earnings changes is given as follows:

	A Company	B Company
Balance, January 1, 1969....................	$ 50,000	$20,000
Net income, 1969–70.......................	40,000	25,000
	$ 90,000	$45,000
Dividends declared, 1969–70.................	10,000	5,000
Balance, January 1, 1971....................	$ 80,000	$40,000
Net income, 1971..........................	24,000	16,000
	$104,000	$56,000
Dividends declared, 1971....................	10,000	5,000
Balance, December 31, 1971.................	$ 94,000	$51,000

Required:

Prepare partial consolidated income and retained earnings working papers for the year ended December 31, 1971.

Problem 15–6

On January 1, 1970, the Gregory Company purchased 80 percent of the capital stock of the Morris Company and 60 percent of the capital stock of the Adams Company. On January 1, 1971, the Morris Company purchased 30 percent of the capital stock of the Adams Company. Also on January 1, 1971, the Adams Company purchased 20 percent of the capital stock of the Gregory Company.

During 1971 the net income reported by each affiliate was:

Gregory Company	$42,800
Morris Company	40,000
Adams Company	10,000

Required:

(i) Calculate consolidated net income for 1971.

(ii) Calculate consolidated net income for 1971, assuming unconfirmed inventory profit is included in the selling affiliate's accounts as follows:

Morris Company	$3,000
Adams Company	2,000

(Assume fractional elimination in respect to intercompany profit.)

Problem 15–7

A diagram depicting the intercompany stock ownership of companies X, Y, and Z on January 1, 1971, is given following:

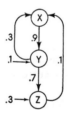

Operating data for the affiliates for 1971 are:

	X Company	Y Company	Z Company
Recorded net income	$80,000	$45,000	$36,000
Cash dividends paid	6,000	10,000	8,000

Y Company's net income includes $3,000 of unconfirmed profit in the ending inventory of X Company; the originating sale was made during 1971.

Required:

Prepare the eliminating entry for unconfirmed inventory profit and calculate majority and minority interests in 1971 net income assuming:

(i)   One hundred percent elimination of unconfirmed inventory profit.
(ii) Fractional elimination of unconfirmed inventory profit.

Problem 15–8

On January 1, 1971, A Company purchased 80 percent of the capital stock of B Company and 60 percent of the capital stock of C Company. On the same date, B Company acquired 20 percent of the capital stock of C Company and C Company acquired 30 percent of the capital stock of A Company.

The trial balances of the affiliate companies on December 31, 1971, were as follows:

	A Company		B Company		C Company	
Investment in B Company	$ 67,000					
Investment in C Company	35,000		$ 12,000			
Investment in A Company					$ 45,000	
Merchandise, January 1	15,000		15,000		13,000	
Other assets	73,000		84,000		31,000	
Liabilities		$ 5,000		$ 10,000		$ 4,000
Capital stock		100,000		50,000		40,000
Retained earnings, January 1		50,000		30,000		10,000
Sales		80,000		50,000		60,000
Purchases	40,000		25,000		20,000	
Expenses	5,000		4,000		5,000	
	$235,000	$235,000	$140,000	$140,000	$114,000	$114,000
Merchandise, December 31	$ 10,000		$ 14,000		$ 8,000	

Merchandise sold by C Company to B Company during 1971 amounted to $20,000. On December 31, 1971, a quantity of these goods, on which C Company recorded a profit of $2,316, remained in the inventory of B Company. It is assumed that the amount of the inventory profit elimination is based upon the parent company's equity in the selling affiliate.

Prepare a consolidated statement working paper for the year ended December 31, 1971.

Problem 15–9

The P Corporation has made substantial advances of cash to S Corporation, its wholly owned subsidiary. S uses some of the cash to purchase a block of P Corporation stock in the open market. S also issues some of its own stock, which it sells to P, using the cash received to repay the advances received from P.

Required:

Give your opinion of each of the following practices:

(i)   The stock of P owned by S is shown as an "Investment" on the consolidated balance sheet of P and S.
(ii) Dividends on the stock of S are shown as nonoperating income on the income statement of P.

(iii)   The total of dividends declared but not paid on the stock of P are shown as a current liability on the consolidated balance sheet of P and S.

(AICPA adapted)

Problem 15–10

From the following data, prepare a consolidation of the balance sheets of the Top Holding Company and its subsidiaries:

	Top Holding Company	R Company	S Company
ASSETS			
Current assets..........................	$150,000	$30,000	$118,110
Property, less accumulated depreciation......	47,000	5,500	130,000
Investment R Company stock:			
90 percent...........................	18,000		
10 percent...........................			2,500
Investment S Company stock:			
75 percent...........................	45,000		
15 percent...........................		9,000	
Investment S Company bonds.............	41,500		
	$301,00	$44,500	$250,610
EQUITIES			
Current liabilities.......................	$ 80,000	$23,000	$ 70,000
Bonds payable.........................			100,000
Capital stock..........................	200,000	30,000	50,000
Retained earnings at acquisition...........		1,500	5,000
Retained earnings [deficit]................	21,500	[10,000]	25,610
	$301,500	$44,500	$250,610

The investments in R Company stock are carried at cost less subsequent net losses; the investments in S Company stock are carried at cost. The bonds were acquired at a $1,500 discount and are held for cancellation.

(AICPA adapted)

Chapter 16

Consolidated Statements—Miscellaneous; Branch Accounting

THE ENTITY THEORY

The preparation of consolidated financial statements has heretofore emphasized the unique importance of the controlling shareholders—i.e., those individuals (excluding affiliates) owning voting shares of the parent company. This is essentially a *proprietary theory* approach—similar in concept to most of the accounting conventions for single enterprises. Notwithstanding this emphasis, special effort has been made to disclose the value of the rights of minority claimants. The separateness of this shareholder interest group is indicated by its classification between the liabilities and stockholders' equity divisions in the consolidated balance sheet.

Theorists have sometimes taken the position, however, that the total resources of an enterprise have a unity or entity status in which the various owner and creditor claimants have an undivided and indistinguishable interest. An extension of this concept to the preparation of consolidated financial statements was made in 1944 by Professor Maurice Moonitz in a monograph, *The Entity Theory of Consolidated Statements*. This monograph gives expression, in perhaps its most refined form, to the relevance of the entity concept to the reports of corporate affiliations. In respect to equity interests, the entity theory, literally interpreted, denies the primacy of the controlling shareholder group; rather, its interest is fused with those of minority shareholders and is accorded no preferential accounting treatment, either in measurement or classification.

Prevailing practices of consolidated statement preparation cannot be neatly summarized as being wholly consistent with either the proprietary theory or the entity theory. Of course, these theories do not provide contradictory arguments for all aspects of consolidated statement preparation. Nevertheless, the entity theory has definite implications regarding several computations and forms of presentation in consolidated statements. Specific areas influenced by the principal thrust of the entity theory argument include the treatment of differentials resulting from the investment elimination, the amount of the unconfirmed (or unrealized) profit elimination on

529

asset transfers among affiliates, the elimination of unamortized discounts or premiums on intercompany bondholdings, and the calculations and disclosure of the equity of minority shareholders.

Debit and Credit Differentials

Where less than 100 percent of a subsidiary company's stock is purchased by a parent company, it is usual to recognize the variation between the acquisition cost and the corresponding equity in the subsidiary's stockholders' equity accounts as a debit or credit differential in the consolidated statements. The entity theorist would insist that the *total* differential implicit in the purchase cost (not merely the excess amount attributable to the majority interest payment) be formally recognized. For example, if 90 percent of a subsidiary's capital stock is acquired at a cost of $8,100 more than the equity in the corresponding book value of the subsidiary's shares, a differential would be recognized in the amount of $9,000 ($8,100 ÷ 90%), appropriate credit therein being given to minority shareholders for $900. Thus, the $8,100 reflects the cost to acquire a 90 percent interest in the undervalued or unrecorded assets—tangible or intangible.

The differential may be introduced as a result of the investment elimination entry made on consolidated working papers; in this case the differential is disclosed *only* on the consolidated financial statements. Alternatively, the subsidiary company's accounts may be formally adjusted by the differential increment or decrement implicit in the investment elimination; in this case, the differential is recognized in the subsidiary company's financial statements as well as the consolidated statements. The argument is made that formal adjustment of a subsidiary's accounts is more appropriate where there exists virtually 100 percent ownership of a subsidiary's shares than where there is a significantly large group of minority stockholders. If one accepts the implications of the entity theory, however, the recognition of the *total* differential implicit in the purchase cost eliminates the need for concern over the size of minority interest holdings. Consolidated statements would remain the same, whether or not the subsidiary records the differential.

Intercompany Profit on Asset Transfers

Reference has been made previously to the necessity for eliminating unconfirmed intercompany profit on sales of merchandise or other assets between corporate affiliates. The previous discussion of this matter recognized two alternative procedures: eliminating 100 percent of such profit or the parent company's fractional interest therein. The entity theorist would argue for a total elimination of the intercompany profit element, proportionally applied to majority and minority shareholders. This view harmonizes with the concept of an integrated proprietary equity; a partial elimination (a controlling interest is unconfirmed intercompany profit) preserves the separate identities of majority and minority shareholders.

Defense of the latter treatment rests heavily on the argument that such intercompany profit is confirmed, or realized, *from the viewpoint of minority shareholders.* The entity theorist would answer that consolidated statements are not presumed to be based upon any distinction, legal or otherwise, between shareholder classes. The reader is encouraged to refer again to Chapter 12 to review the consolidated statement working papers which distinguish between the fractional elimination and the 100 percent elimination of unconfirmed profit on intercompany asset transfers. It is sufficient to note here that neither consolidated net income nor consolidated retained earnings is a function of the amount of the eliminated profit. Reconciliation of the two views in respect to the intercompany profit elimination is explained in terms of the calculation of the amount of minority interests.

Unamortized Discounts/Premiums on Intercompany Bondholdings

It is appropriate to eliminate unamortized discounts or premiums on intercompany-held bonds *as if* such bonds were retired at par value. From the standpoint of the entity, the purchase transaction is not essentially unlike that of a company's purchase of its own bonds, i.e., the acquisition of treasury bonds. For an affiliation of companies, the purchase of intercompany bonds—essentially a constructive bond retirement—may produce "gain" or "loss" to the extent of intercompany unamortized discounts or premiums on the books of the relevant affiliates. The amount of gain or loss given recognition in consolidated statements may be either total or fractional. The 100 percent recognition of the amount of such gain or loss accords with the entity theory; recognition of a partial amount ignores the bond retirement effect in respect to the minority shareholders. In either case, it remains important to eliminate the effects of subsequent amortization of discounts or premiums in order to neutralize any duplicate recognition of gain or loss on acquisition. In regard to intercompany bondholdings, the arguments which were offered in respect to the amount of the confirmed profit recognition are equally valid, whether in defense of, or in rejection of, the entity theory.

Minority Shareholder Interests

The acceptance of the entity notion for consolidated statements carries with it the obligation to regard all shareholders as equal per share claimants to the combined resources of the affiliated companies. The presentation of shareholders' interests should be made in such manner as to clearly indicate the values attributable to controlling and noncontrolling interests, *but without reference to legal preference or implications as to hierarchical status.* Clearly, according to this view, an identification of minority interests as liabilities in consolidated statements is inappropriate; it may also be questioned whether the compromise consolidated balance sheet position between the liabilities and the controlling stockholders' equity divisions does not also violate the spirit of the entity theory. Additionally, the measurement of consolidated net income is necessarily independent of assignments of interests therein to the shareholder groups. Thus, consolidated net income must be redefined under the entity theory as the confirmed profits of the parent company, exclusive of subsidiary dividends, plus the confirmed profits of the subsidiary company. In contrast to the conventional calculational technique, this revised definition focuses upon the income aggregates after eliminations but before deduction of "minority interest." The consolidated net income is then allocated between the two shareholder groups in the normal manner. Calculation of consolidated retained earnings, and relative interests therein, proceeds in an analogous fashion.

Illustrative Problem—Entity Theory

X Company purchased 90 percent of the capital stock of Y Company on January 1, 1971, for $64,800. Trial balances of the affiliates on December 31, 1971, are as follows:

	X Company	Y Company
Investment in capital stock of Y Company.........	$ 64,800	
Merchandise, January 1........................	30,000	$ 20,000
Other assets.................................	127,200	89,000
Purchases...................................	90,000	70,000
Expenses....................................	10,000	8,000
	$322,000	$187,000
Liabilities....................................	$ 2,000	$ 7,000
Capital stock (par, $100)......................	100,000	50,000
Retained earnings............................	60,000	20,000
Sales.......................................	160,000	110,000
	$322,000	$187,000
Merchandise, December 31.....................	$ 20,000	$ 15,000

Sales of merchandise by Y Company to X Company during 1971 amounted to $40,000; the cost of these goods to Y Company was $32,000; $5,000 of this merchandise remained in the inventory of X Company on December 31, 1971.

Based upon the entity theory, the investment elimination schedule for a 1971 consolidated statement working paper would take the following form:

Investment Elimination Schedule
Dr. [Cr.]

Capital stock.....................................	$ 45,000
Retained earnings................................	18,000
Differential......................................	* 2,000
Differential—minority interest therein................	[200]
Investment......................................	$[64,800]

* 90x = $1,800,
  x = $2,000.

The consolidated statement working paper for this example is presented in Illustration 16–1.

Accounting for the amortization of differentials parallels the treatment used in the conventional consolidated statement working paper. In respect

Illustration 16–1

X COMPANY AND SUBSIDIARY Y COMPANY

Consolidated Statement Working Paper
For Year Ended December 31, 1971

	X Company	Y Company	Eliminations Dr.	Eliminations Cr.	Consolidated	Minority	Majority
Income Statement:							
Sales	160,000	110,000	(2) 40,000		230,000		
Merchandise, December 31	20,000	15,000	(3) *1,000		34,000		
Total credits	180,000	125,000			264,000		
Merchandise, January 1	30,000	20,000			50,000		
Purchases	90,000	70,000		(2) 40,000	120,000		
Expenses	10,000	8,000			18,000		
Total debits	130,000	98,000			188,000		
Net income	50,000	27,000			76,000		
Assignable to minority shareholders—10% of ($27,000–*$1,000)						2,600	
Assignable to majority shareholders							73,400
Net income—carried forward	50,000	27,000	41,000	40,000	76,000	2,600	73,400
Retained Earnings Statement:							
Retained earnings, January 1:							
X Company	60,000				60,000		60,000
Y Company		20,000	(1) 18,000		2,000	2,000	
Net income—brought forward	50,000	27,000	41,000	40,000	76,000	2,600	73,400
Retained earnings, December 31—carried forward	110,000	47,000	59,000	40,000	138,000	4,600	133,400
Balance Sheet:							
Investment in capital stock of Y Company	64,800			(1) 64,800			
Merchandise, December 31	20,000	15,000			34,000		
Other assets	127,200	89,000			216,200		
Differential			(1) 2,000	(3) 1,000	2,000		
	212,000	104,000			252,200		
Liabilities	2,000	7,000			9,000		
Capital stock:							
X Company	100,000				100,000		100,000
Y Company		50,000	(1) 45,000		5,000	5,000	
Differential—minority interest therein				(1) 200	200	200	
Retained earnings—brought forward	110,000	47,000	59,000	40,000	138,000	4,600	133,400
	212,000	104,000	106,000	106,000	252,200	9,800	233,400

* Gross profit percentage: $\dfrac{\$8,000}{\$40,000} \times 100\% = 20\%$.

Unconfirmed inventory profit: 20% of $5,000 = $1,000.

to the entity theory, however, the amortization would necessarily relate both to the majority and the minority shareholder interests. Elimination of unconfirmed profit on asset transfers other than merchandise would also duplicate the procedural detail described for inventories. Similar treatment would also be accorded the elimination of unamortized discounts or premiums on intercompany-held bonds. Apropos of consolidated net income and retained earnings, this working paper reflects the revised definitions discussed above.

The formal financial statements are as follows:

X COMPANY AND SUBSIDIARY Y COMPANY
Consolidated Income Statement
For Year Ended December 31, 1971

Sales..		$230,000
Cost of sales:		
Merchandise, January 1......................	$ 50,000	
Purchases.................................	120,000	
	$170,000	
Merchandise, December 31...................	34,000	136,000
Operating margin............................		$ 94,000
Expenses....................................		18,000
Consolidated net income.....................		$ 76,000
Assignable to minority shareholders.............		$ 2,600
Assignable to majority shareholders.............		73,400

X COMPANY AND SUBSIDIARY Y COMPANY
Consolidated Balance Sheet
December 31, 1971

ASSETS		EQUITIES	
Merchandise.................	$ 34,000	Liabilities...................	$ 9,000
Other assets................	216,200	Stockholders' equity:	
Unrecorded asset value implicit		Majority shareholders.......	233,400
in the purchase cost which is		Minority shareholders.......	9,800
in excess of corresponding			
book value of subsidiary			
stock....................	2,000		
	$252,200		$252,200

While the entity theory has not yet developed a substantial following among accountants, several of its recommendations have been ratified by action of authoritative accounting organizations. Responsible committees of both the American Institute of Certified Public Accountants and the American Accounting Association have published statements which support the 100 percent elimination of unrealized intercompany profit on asset transfers among corporate affiliates. The position of the American Accounting Association is as follows:

The object of consolidated statements is to describe the fianancial activities and position of a group of companies as if they were a single entity. All reciprocal accounts and any gain or loss on intercompany transactions unrealized at the balance sheet date from the point of view of the affiliated group as an entity should therefore be eliminated.[1]

ALTERNATIVE WORKING PAPER FORMS

The three-division *horizontal* form of consolidated statement working paper has been consistently used throughout the previous chapters. Consistency of usage has obvious advantages for instructional purposes. There are, however, a wide variety of working paper forms that can be used in the preparation of consolidated statements. Regardless of the particular form used, the fundamental principles of consolidated statement preparation remain the same. Specific forms may have special advantages in differing situations, but the resultant consolidated statements are not dependent on the form selected. As examples of alternative working paper forms that can be used in consolidated statement preparation, brief consideration will be given to the trial balance working paper and the vertical working paper.

The Trial Balance Working Paper

As an alternative to the three-division working paper that utilizes the financial statements of each affiliate as input data, consolidated statements may be prepared by using the trial balances of the constituent companies. Where the account data are summarized in this form, a different working paper construction may be used which obviates the necessity of preclassifying the accounts in financial statement terms. One appropriate format provides vertical columns for the individual statements, arranged in sequence, to which the account balances *net of eliminations* are extended. The alert reader will recognize that the differences introduced by such a working paper are primarily subtleties of form. For example, the three-division horizontal working paper provides for the collection and summation of account information in respect to a given statement in vertically arranged subdivisions, while the trial balance form simply calls for a series of vertical columns as the organizing framework for statement classification and summation.

For illustrative purposes, assume that X Company acquired 90 percent of the capital stock of Y Company on January 1, 1971, at a cost of $61,000. The December 31, 1971, trial balances of companies X and Y are as follows:

---

[1] Committee on Accounting Concepts and Standards, American Accounting Association, *Accounting and Reporting Standards for Corporate Financial Statements* (Evanston, Ill., 1957), p. 9.

	┌─── X Company ───┐		┌─── Y Company ───┐	
Cash....................................	$ 29,500		$ 8,000	
Accounts receivable...................	18,000		3,000	
Merchandise (1/1/71).................	16,000		4,000	
Investment in Y Company stock........	61,000			
Other assets..........................	66,000		62,000	
Accounts payable.....................		$ 22,000		$ 5,000
Other liabilities......................		6,000		
Capital stock.........................		100,000		50,000
Retained earnings (1/1/71)............		40,000		10,000
Dividends declared...................	10,000		5,000	
Sales.................................		78,000		40,000
Dividend income......................		4,500		
Purchases............................	42,000		20,000	
Expenses.............................	8,000		3,000	
	$250,500	$250,500	$105,000	$105,000
Merchandise (12/31/71)	$ 10,000		$ 7,000	

Based on the data provided above, a trial balance working paper is presented in Illustration 16–2.

The Vertical Working Paper

In addition to the working papers referred to previously, other forms have been recommended, some of which have special practical significance. One of these is the *vertical* working paper. Its arrangement consists of a vertical enumeration of the constituent companies, with the financial statement account descriptions extended horizontally in columns. Separate divisions of the working paper may be provided, as in the case of the three-division *horizontal* form. Eliminations are entered in lines provided beneath the relevant account columns. Where the number of affiliates is large, the compactness of this form makes it particularly useful. It may easily accommodate small affiliation groups of several companies, or corporate families consisting of as many as a hundred or more companies. Other working paper constructions become more difficult to use with the increase in number of affiliates.

For purposes of comparison, the vertical working paper in Illustration 16–3 makes use of the same data that was previously used to illustrate the trial balance working paper.

Even a cursory examination of this working paper will reveal that while the summation of affiliate account balances—net of eliminations—is clearly evident, there is no indication of the value of the separate equities of the majority and minority shareholders. Calculation of these interests must be provided by a supporting schedule. Such a schedule should disclose the majority and minority interests in net income, capital stock, retained earnings, and the other stockholders' equity accumulations of the affiliate companies. In the present case, such a schedule might well assume the form depicted in Illustration 16–4.

OTHER TOPICS

Equally Divided Ownership among Shareholder Groups

On occasions there may exist two unique and separately identifiable shareholder groups, each owning 50 percent of the voting stock of a single corporation. Necessarily this joint ownership confers the right of joint management of the subsidiary's operations. A question may arise in such a circumstance as to the status of each shareholder group in respect to the jointly owned subsidiary in the preparation of consolidated financial statements. Although control, defined in terms of an absolute majority of voting shares, is not evident, manifestly there does exist a jointly shared financial control. In this instance, it may be argued that both shareholder groups are co-participants in the management of a commonly owned subsidiary and accordingly each may include the accounts of the subsidiary in a consolidated financial statement, with the contra ownership reported as a minority interest.

At the present time, however, subsidiaries whose shares are equally divided between two shareholder groups are frequently not included in the consolidated statements of either "parent." Exactly the same problem exists in more acute form where there are more than two shareholder groups, each having an equal equity in the subsidiary's outstanding shares. If the total number of shareholder groups is small, the subsidiary may not even *publish* financial statements which are available to the public. Further, if the "parent" ownership groups account for their investments on a cost basis and the subsidiary does not declare dividends, it is possible for stockholders of the "parents" to be completely uninformed as to the impact of subsidiary operations.

In the event that consolidated statements are not prepared so as to include the operations of jointly owned subsidiaries, as described above, the investor corporations should report their proportionate interests in the subsidiary operations by the equity method in the manner advocated for unconsolidated subsidiaries. Additionally, the annual reports of the investor corporations should include summarized descriptive information concerning the operations and financial position of such nonreporting companies in which they have material investments.

Consolidated Income Tax Returns

Technical rules respecting the preparation of consolidated income tax returns are usually complex and are clearly beyond the scope of this text. Yet, a few summary comments seem appropriate.

An election to file either a separate or consolidated tax return is available to member corporations of an "affiliated group." To qualify as an "affiliated group," there must exist a corporate ownership chain in which a major parent corporation owns at least 80 percent of the voting power of all classes of stock of the several affiliates; additionally, at least 80 percent

Illustration 16–2

X COMPANY AND SUBSIDIARY Y COMPANY

Trial Balance Consolidated Statement Working Paper
For Year Ended December 31, 1971

Debits	X Company	Y Company	Eliminations Dr.	Eliminations Cr.	Income Statement	Retained Earnings Statement	Minority Interest	Balance Sheet
Cash	29,500	8,000						37,500
Accounts receivable	18,000	3,000						21,000
Merchandise inventory (1/1/71)	16,000	4,000			20,000			
Investment in Y Company stock	61,000			(1) 61,000				
Other assets	66,000	62,000						128,000
Dividends declared	10,000	5,000		(2) 4,500		10,000	500	
Purchases	42,000	20,000			62,000			
Expenses	8,000	3,000			11,000			
Differential			(1) 7,000					7,000
	250,500	105,000						
Merchandise inventory (12/31/71)	10,000	7,000						
Income statement debits—Y Company— deducted contra		27,000						
Total debits—deducted contra					93,000	10,000	500	210,500

Credits	Credits	Eliminations				
Accounts payable	22,000					27,000
Other liabilities	6,000					6,000
Capital stock:						
X Company	100,000					100,000
Y Company	50,000	(1) 45,000			5,000	
Retained earnings, January 1, 1971:						
X Company	40,000					40,000
Y Company	10,000	(1) 9,000		40,000	1,000	
Sales	78,000		118,000			
	40,000					
Dividend income	4,500	(2) 4,500				
	250,500					
Merchandise inventory (12/31/71)	10,000		17,000			
	7,000					
Total credits	47,000		135,000	40,000	6,000	
Total debits	27,000		[93,000]	[10,000]	[500]	
Combined net income			42,000			
Income statement credits—Y Company	20,000					
Income statement debits—Y Company	2,000					
Net income—Y Company			[2,000]		2,000	
Minority interest—10% whereof			40,000	40,000		
Consolidated net income				70,000		70,000
Consolidated retained earnings					7,500	7,500 M
Minority interest in Y Company	65,500	65,500	65,500			210,500

[deduction]

Illustration 16–3

X COMPANY AND SUBSIDIARY Y COMPANY
Vertical Consolidated Statement Working Paper
For Year Ended December 31, 1971

Income Statement:

	Sales	Dividend Income	Merchandise, December 31	Total Credits	Merchandise, January 1	Purchases	Expenses	Total Debits	Net Income
X Company	78,000	4,500	10,000	92,500	16,000	42,000	8,000	66,000	26,500
Y Company	40,000		7,000	47,000	4,000	20,000	3,000	27,000	20,000
Total	118,000		17,000	139,500	20,000	62,000	11,000	93,000	46,500
Eliminations:									
(2)		4,500		4,500					4,500
Net	118,000	–0–	17,000	135,000	20,000	62,000	11,000	93,000	42,000

Retained Earnings Statement:

	Balance, January 1	Net Income	Total	Dividends Declared	Balance, December 31
X Company	40,000	26,500	66,500	10,000	56,500
Y Company	10,000	20,000	30,000	5,000	25,000
Total	50,000	46,500	96,500	15,000	81,500
Eliminations:					
(1)	9,000		9,000		
(2)		4,500	4,500	[4,500]	
Net	41,000	42,000	83,000	10,500	72,500

Balance Sheet:

	Cash	Accounts Receivable	Merchandise, December 31	Investment in Company Y	Other Assets	Differential	Total	Accounts Payable	Other Liabilities	Capital Stock	Retained Earnings	Total
X Company	29,500	18,000	10,000	61,000	66,000		184,500	22,000	6,000	100,000	56,500	184,500
Y Company	8,000	3,000	7,000		62,000		80,000	5,000		50,000	25,000	80,000
Total	37,500	21,000	17,000	61,000	128,000		264,500	27,000	6,000	150,000	81,500	264,500
Eliminations:												
(1)				[61,000]		7,000	[54,000]			45,000	9,000	[54,000]
Net	37,500	21,000	17,000	–0–	128,000	7,000	210,500	27,000	6,000	105,000	72,500	210,500

Notation for eliminations: Dr. [Cr.].

Illustration 16–4

EQUITY ALLOCATION SCHEDULE

	Total	Elimination	Amount to Be Allocated	Minority Interest	Majority Interest
Capital stock:					
X Company........	100,000		100,000		100,000
Y Company........	50,000	45,000	5,000	5,000	
	150,000	45,000	105,000	5,000	100,000
Net income:					
X Company........	26,500	4,500	22,000		22,000
Y Company........	20,000		20,000	2,000	18,000
	46,500	4,500	42,000	2,000	40,000
Retained earnings:					
X Company........	56,500	4,500	52,000		52,000
Y Company........	25,000	9,000 [4,500]	20,500	*2,500	†18,000
	81,500	9,000	72,500	2,500	70,000

* 10 percent of $25,000.
† $20,500 −$2,500.

of each class of nonvoting stock of at least one affiliate must also be held by the major parent company. The election to file a consolidated return relates to all domestic affiliates; foreign corporations are not normally includible.

Among the advantages of filing consolidated income tax returns are the following: (1) intercompany dividends are not includible in consolidated taxable income; (2) gains on the sale or exchange of property between members of the affiliated group are usually not recognized; and (3) current year's losses of one affiliate may be offset against the current year's net income of another.

The following disadvantages should also be noted: (1) an election to file a consolidated return applies to all future years unless specified qualifying conditions are met; (2) each affiliate is required to use the same taxable year and to adopt a generally uniform method of accounting; and (3) losses in transactions with affiliate members are not recognized in determining consolidated taxable income.

Listing on the New York Stock Exchange

Reference was made in Chapter 7 to the requirements of the Securities and Exchange Commission in respect to form and content of consolidated financial statements. The New York Stock Exchange has also indicated the importance of an informative disclosure in the published reports for corporate affiliations. Accordingly, the following provisions are made a part of its listing requirements:

The current form of the listing agreements requires that there be published and submitted to stockholders annually a consolidated balance sheet as of the end of the previous fiscal year, and a consolidated income statement and consolidated surplus [retained earnings] statement for such previous fiscal year, including the listed company and its subsidiaries, i.e., companies, a majority of whose equity stock is owned by the listed company.

If such consolidated statements excluded any company, a majority of whose equity stock is owned, directly or indirectly, by the listed company: (*a*) the caption of, or a note to, such statements shall show the degree of consolidation; (*b*) the consolidated income account shall reflect, in a footnote or otherwise, the listed company's portion of the undistributed earnings, or of the losses, of such unconsolidated, majority-owned companies for the period covered by the consolidated income statements; and (*c*) the consolidated balance sheet shall reflect, in a footnote or otherwise, the extent to which the equity of the listed company in such unconsolidated, majority-owned companies has increased, or diminished, since the date of acquisition as a result of profits, losses, and distributions.

Under unusual circumstances making consolidated statements inappropriate, there may be published and submitted to stockholders annually, in lieu of such consolidated statements, the statements of the listed company as a separate entity, and the statements of each company in which it owns, directly or indirectly, a majority of the equity stock.

In accordance with good accounting practice, appropriate reserves shall be made against profits arising out of all transactions with unconsolidated subsidiaries in either parent company statements or consolidated statements.

Such statements shall reflect the existence of any default in interest, cumulative dividends, sinking fund or redemption fund provisions of the company and of any majority-owned company, whether consolidated or unconsolidated.[2]

Combined Statements

Where the criteria used in the preparation of consolidated financial statements for an affiliation of commonly controlled companies are not fully met, it may nonetheless be desirable and meaningful to prepare *combined* statements. Such statements are often to be preferred to the separate statements of the several affiliates. They may be especially informative when an individual exercises financial or managerial control over a number of operationally related companies, or when several companies are under common management; additionally, they are sometimes used to disclose the financial status of a group of unconsolidated subsidiaries. In preparing combined statements, the effects of intercompany transactions (including unconfirmed profit remnants) should be eliminated as in the preparation of consolidated financial statements.

CONSOLIDATED STATEMENTS—A REVIEW

Consolidated financial statements are the summary reports of an affiliation of companies, prepared without regard to the separate legal status of

---

[2] New York Stock Exchange, *Company Manual* (Section A4), 1957, pp. A–64–65.

member affiliates. Among the criteria for determining the propriety of including the accounts of a subsidiary in consolidated statements are the parent company's ownership of more than 50 percent of its voting shares, the present exercise and anticipated continuity of effective managerial and financial control by the parent company, a general homogeneity of assets and operations of the affiliates, and a general coincidence of accounting periods. Consolidated statements purport to reflect the results of transactions of the affiliation with nonaffiliate interests; accordingly, to the extent that there are intercompany transactions among the affiliates, their effects must be excluded from the accounts of the consolidated statements. Among the more important types of such eliminations are the following:

1. *Investment elimination.* Of first importance in the sequence of eliminations is the elimination of the investment account of the parent company against the parent's equity in the corresponding book value of the subsidiary's capital stock. Essentially, this elimination results in a substitution of the subsidiary's net assets for the parent company's investment account. The substitution is made in terms of total subsidiary net assets, and the minority shareholders' equity therein is given appropriate recognition in the financial statements. In the event that there exist several classes of subsidiary stock, it is important that an appropriate allocation of the subsidiary's total stockholders' equity be made as between the different classes. If the subsidiary's shares are purchased in blocks at different dates, it is also important to analyze the book value appertaining to each block separately at the relevant acquisition date. Although control may be deferred until a subsequent purchase, the elimination in respect to the first purchase should relate to the at-acquisition book values of subsidiary stock. Where shares are purchased directly from a subsidiary affiliate, it is important to determine the changes produced in the accounts of the subsidiary as a result of the new issue. For this reason, it is desirable to compare the parent's equity in the stockholders' equity accounts of the subsidiary immediately before the new issue with the equity immediately after the issuance. The variation in dollar equity is identified as the increase (decrease) attributable to the new issue.

2. *Asset-liability eliminations.* All assets which arise out of intercompany transactions for which there exist offsetting liabilities on the books of an affiliate must be eliminated. The amount of the elimination is 100 percent, notwithstanding the parent company's less-than-100-percent share ownership in the relevant affiliate.

3. *Revenue-expense eliminations.* Revenues and expenses produced by intercompany transactions must also be totally eliminated. As in the case of asset-liability eliminations, the amount of the elimination is not a function of the parent company's equity in the participating affiliates.

4. *Intercompany profit eliminations.* To the extent that asset transfers between affiliates result in profit recognition by the selling affiliate, a residue of which remains in the assets of the purchasing affiliate, such profit should be eliminated. The amount of the profit, unconfirmed or unrealized

from the point of view of the consolidated entity, may be either totally or partially eliminated. Some accountants prefer the fractional elimination, believing that the legal interests of minority shareholders should not be diminished, or otherwise compromised, by the elimination process. There is authoritative support, however, for the 100 percent elimination, the results of which are that the eliminated profit is absorbed ratably by both majority and minority shareholders of the selling affiliate.

5. *Intercompany bond eliminations.* As in the case of other intercompany transactions, it is important to eliminate the effects of intercompany-held bonds. No special difficulty is encountered where the carrying value of the bond investment and the book value of the bond liability are both equal to the par value of the bonds. However, where this equivalence does not exist, due to unamortized issuance discount or premium and/or purchase discount or premium, there exists a consolidated basis "gain or loss" on the acquisition (constructive retirement) of these bonds. The amount of such gain or loss to be reported in the consolidated income statement may be either 100 percent, or the majority shareholders' interest therein. This choice of elimination method essentially parallels that for unconfirmed intercompany profit on asset transfers.

It is important to recognize that the accountant's election to eliminate all, or a fractional interest in, these profit elements will affect the reported interests of minority shareholders. The majority interest elimination requires that the amount of minority interests be calculated on the basis of a subsidiary's recorded book net income. The 100 percent elimination requires that the amount of minority interests be calculated on the basis of the subsidiary's *confirmed* net income.

BRANCH ACCOUNTING

Business expansion is achieved by carefully conceived programs for new investment in productive assets or by plans to improve and optimize the use of present facilities. Any substantive enlargement in the scale of business operations, however, entails significant organizational changes. Expansion may take the form of an integration of allied business interests by merger agreements, or by an investment in the corporate stock of affiliate companies. On other occasions, expansion may be accomplished by the creation of new sales—and perhaps production—outlets to exploit heretofore undeveloped geographic areas or to more intensively cultivate existing markets. In the latter instance, agencies or branch offices are often the optimal organizational forms.

Agencies and Branches

While both the agency and the branch office are vehicles for enlarging sales volume, they exhibit a number of significant operational differences. An agency usually carries sample or display merchandise and accepts orders for delivery by the home office only. The credit status of prospective buyers is appraised, and judgments in respect thereto are rendered by the home office; customers' remittances are normally made to the home office. On the other hand, a branch normally carries a full complement of merchandise, makes the usual warranties respecting quality, makes collections of accounts receivable, and functions in many respects as an autonomous and formally structured business unit.

While these characteristics are descriptive in general terms of the typical agency and branch, it is not unusual to find compromise forms of business subdivisions. On occasions, the agency may carry a full line of merchandise, make collections of accounts receivable, or otherwise accept responsibilities normally reserved to the branch. Similarly, a branch may sometimes be denied some of the autonomy of operation previously noted.

The extent of branch self-management is a function of corporate policy in regard to decentralized operating and administrative control. While different branches within the same company may be accorded different degrees of administrative authority, the status of each branch as an operating subdivision will usually be established by general standards which extend company-wide.

The data accumulation process for the operations of agencies does not introduce any new accounting problems, as an agency is essentially little more than an extension of existing sales territories; consequently, the discussion which follows will be confined to accounting for branches.

Branch Accounts

Branch accounting is essentially an application of the controlling account principle in which the subsidiary records are those of a reasonably independent operating unit. In respect to transactions with the branch, it is conventional for the home office to adopt an account terminology which clearly identifies and describes branch operations. The accounts are selected on the basis of expected frequency of use, their relevance to branch operations, and their contribution to overall accounting control. The general ledger controlling account is variously referred to as Branch Current, Branch Account, or Investment in Branch.

Equivalence of debit and credit balances is preserved in the branch ledger by the use of a Home Office Current account, which is reciprocal to the Branch Current account. The Home Office Current account has a number of properties which traditionally characterize a proprietorship account, particularly in respect to the branch closing process; branch profits and losses are periodically closed thereinto. However, viewed more precisely, the account has no special identity, and its balance is perhaps best described as merely the algebraic sum of all other account balances in the branch ledger.

The Branch Current account is normally charged with the cost of assets or services contributed to the branch by the home office and is credited with remittances from the branch. Periodically, the account is adjusted to give effect to branch net income or loss. Where there are numerous branches, the use of separate current accounts for each branch is often desirable. Although there is no evident consensus as to the specific accounts most appropriate for inclusion in the branch records, it is usual to find only those accounts most closely allied with branch operations, such as those which relate to sales, accounts receivables, inventories, expenses incurred by the branch, etc. It is not uncommon to find the accounts of the branch fixed assets in the home office records; yet, depreciation expense in respect thereto may be recorded by the branch making use of the property. In some instances, other expenses incurred by the home office which are in support of branch operations may also be allocated to the benefiting branch. Notice of such expense assignment should be given the relevant branch for purposes of entry in the branch records. Such an identification of expenses with specific branches makes it possible to measure more accurately the operating efficiency of each branch as an independent entity. Those expenses incurred by the home office for the benefit of several branches which do not accommodate to convenient allocation, however, are best reflected in aggregates in combined financial statements of the branches and the home office. If expenses applicable to one or more branches are not formally assigned to, and recorded by, the branches, they are usually charged against the branch net income or loss recorded by the home office in the closing process.

Illustrative Entries

The following transactions relate to the establishment of a branch and its first month's operations:

(1) Cash is transferred to the branch, $1,000.
(2) Merchandise costing $5,000 is shipped to the branch. Billing of home office shipment is made at cost.
(3) Expenses are incurred and paid by the branch, $200.
(4) Additional merchandise, costing $2,500, is acquired by the branch from outside wholesalers.
(5) Branch credit sales are $8,000.
(6) Branch collections on account amount to $4,700.
(7) Cash remitted by the branch to the home office is $1,000.
(8) Closing entries are prepared by the branch; a monthly operating summary is submitted to the home office. The month-end branch inventory is $1,800.

Journal entries for these transactions are recorded on the books of the home office and branch in Illustration 16–5. Additional entries by the home office are necessary to close the revenue and expense accounts from its own operations. It should be noted that the Shipments to Branch account (on the home office books) is a contra account to Purchases or Cost of Goods

Illustration 16–5

Home Office Books

(1) Branch current.... 1,000
    Cash.... 1,000

(2) Branch current.... 5,000
    Shipments to branch.... 5,000

(7) Cash.... 1,000
    Branch current.... 1,000

(9) Branch current.... 2,100
    Branch net income.... 2,100

Branch Books

(1) Cash.... 1,000
    Home office current.... 1,000

(2) Shipments from home office.... 5,000
    Home office current.... 5,000

(3) Expenses.... 200
    Cash.... 200

(4) Purchases.... 2,500
    Accounts payable.... 2,500

(5) Accounts receivable.... 8,000
    Sales.... 8,000

(6) Cash.... 4,700
    Accounts receivable.... 4,700

(7) Home office current.... 1,000
    Cash.... 1,000

(8) Sales.... 8,000
    Merchandise inventory.... 1,800
    Purchases.... 2,500
    Shipments from home office.... 5,000
    Expenses.... 200
    Income summary.... 2,100

(9) Income summary.... 2,100
    Home office current.... 2,100

Manufactured on the books of the home office; consequently, it necessarily *always* reflects the *cost* of goods shipped and is closed at the end of the accounting period. Contrariwise, the Shipments from Home Office account (on the branch books) is equivalent to a Purchases account and accordingly reflects the intracompany billing price; it also is closed at the end of the accounting period. These reciprocal accounts are used for the purpose of maintaining accounting control of intracompany merchandise shipments.

At completion of a period of branch operations, it is customary for the branch to render operating and position statements to the home office, supported in most instances by transaction details in respect to branch inventories and the Home Office Current account. The latter information may be especially useful where there exist foreign branches and where there are numerous cash remittances to and from the home office. Once these data are compiled, it is frequently desirable to prepare combined financial statements of the home office and branch.

Combined Financial Statements

While the separate statements of the branch and home office disclose much useful information in respect to the operations of each division, they do not adequately convey important analytical data about the composite business unit. To merely include in the home office operating statement a single figure for branch net income or loss is not fully informative. Summary disclosures concerning total sales, cost of sales, and operating expenses of the business unit as a whole are often more meaningful than data revealed in the separate statements of the affiliate divisions; indeed, they are required in company-wide policy decisions.

Combined statements of the home office and branch are needed to reflect the effects of transactions of the total business entity with outside interests. Accordingly, the effects of transactions between the home office and branches (or between branches) must be eliminated to avoid value overstatement or duplicate measurement in the accounts. Combined statements make use of the *principle of substitution*—the branch's asset, liability, and operating accounts are substituted for the Branch Current account. This is accomplished in a combined statement working paper by *eliminating* the Branch Current account against the Home Office Current account. To the extent that there are evidences in other accounts of intracompany transactions, their effects must also be eliminated. For example, balances found in the reciprocal Shipments to Branch–Shipments from Home Office accounts, and Remittances to Home Office–Remittances from Branch accounts (the latter accounts reflecting periodic cash transfers) must also be eliminated, as they represent only the internal movements of company resources. *The eliminating entries are working paper entries only;* accordingly, they are not entered on the books of either the home office or the branch.

One familiar form of combined statement working paper is given in

Illustration 16–6

X COMPANY

Combined Statement Working Paper for Year Ended December 31, 1971

	Home Office	Branch	Eliminations Dr.	Eliminations Cr.	Combined
Income Statement:					
Sales	100,000	31,000			131,000
Merchandise, December 31	10,000	4,000			14,000
Shipments to branch	12,000		(2) 12,000		
Total credits	122,000	35,000			145,000
Merchandise, January 1	15,000				15,000
Purchases	65,000	9,000			74,000
Shipments from home office		12,000		(2) 12,000	
Expenses	7,000	4,000			11,000
Total debits	87,000	25,000	12,000	12,000	100,000
Net income—carried forward	35,000	10,000	12,000	12,000	45,000
Retained Earnings Statement:					
Retained earnings, January 1	10,000				10,000
Net income—brought forward	35,000	10,000	12,000	12,000	45,000
Retained earnings, December 31—carried forward	45,000	10,000	12,000	12,000	55,000
Balance Sheet:					
Cash	40,000	15,000			55,000
Accounts receivable	22,000	20,000			42,000
Merchandise, December 31	10,000	4,000			14,000
Branch current	17,000			(1) 17,000	
Other assets	14,000				14,000
	103,000	39,000			125,000
Liabilities	8,000	12,000			20,000
Capital stock	50,000				50,000
Retained earnings—brought forward	45,000	*10,000	12,000	12,000	55,000
Home office current		17,000	(1) 17,000		
	103,000	39,000	29,000	29,000	125,000

* Increment to Home Office Current due to periodic branch net income.

Illustration 16–6. As a basis for this illustration, the trial balance information for the home office and branch on December 31, 1971, is provided:

	Home Office	Branch
Cash.	$ 40,000	$15,000
Accounts receivable.	22,000	20,000
Merchandise, January 1.	15,000	
Branch current.	17,000	
Other assets.	14,000	
Purchases.	65,000	9,000
Shipments from home office.		12,000
Expenses.	7,000	4,000
	$180,000	$60,000
Liabilities.	$ 8,000	$12,000
Capital stock.	50,000	
Retained earnings.	10,000	
Home office current.		17,000
Sales.	100,000	31,000
Shipments to branch.	12,000	
	$180,000	$60,000
Merchandise, December 31.	$ 10,000	$ 4,000

The working paper (Illustration 16–6) is divided into three divisions to
accommodate the preparation of the income statement, the retained earnings statement, and the balance sheet. The balances in the reciprocal accounts are eliminated as noted. The reader will observe that the working
paper in Illustration 16–6 refers to retained earnings balances in respect to
both the home office and the branch. As noted earlier, the branch does not
ordinarily accumulate branch profits and losses in a retained earnings
account; rather, it records such profits and losses as adjustments in the
Home Office Current account, and the beginning balance of "retained
earnings" of the branch will always necessarily be zero. Accordingly, variation in the balances of the Home Office Current account as found in the
combined statement working paper and as reported in the branch's period-
end balance sheet may be explained in terms of the branch's periodic profit
or loss. However, the working paper format does indicate the total retained
earnings for the composite entity at the end of the period, i.e., the accumulated earnings of the home office increased or decreased by the branch net
profit or loss for the period.

The formal combined statements are easily prepared using the data
found in the "combined" column of the working paper. The combined
statements for the affiliate divisions of X Company are presented in Illustration 16–7.

Branch Billing in Excess of Cost

The home office may elect to bill the branch at a value in excess of
cost—either at retail price or at an arbitrary amount above cost. Where
either of these conditions obtains, the branch manager frequently is not
given complete information concerning the cost of branch shipments; there-

Illustration 16–7

X COMPANY

Income Statement
For Year Ended December 31, 1971

Sales..		$131,000
Cost of sales:		
Merchandise, January 1........................	$15,000	
Purchases....................................	74,000	
	$89,000	
Merchandise, December 31......................	14,000	75,000
Gross margin.....................................		$ 56,000
Expenses...		11,000
Net Income.......................................		$ 45,000

X COMPANY

Retained Earnings Statement
For Year Ended December 31, 1971

Retained earnings, January 1.......................................	$10,000
Net income, 1971...	45,000
Retained earnings, December 31...................................	$55,000

X COMPANY

Balance Sheet
December 31, 1971

ASSETS		EQUITIES	
Cash....................	$ 55,000	Liabilities...............	$ 20,000
Accounts receivable......	42,000	Capital stock............	50,000
Merchandise.............	14,000	Retained earnings........	55,000
Other assets.............	14,000		
Total Assets.........	$125,000	Total Equities.......	$125,000

fore, net profit as reckoned by the branch will necessarily require adjustment by the home office to the extent of realized intracompany profit, i.e., only the intracompany profit in the unsold branch merchandise is deferred. Consider the following transactions which illustrate the accounting consequence of this type of billing:

(1) Merchandise costing the home office $4,000 is billed to the branch at $5,000.
(2) One half of the above shipment is sold by the branch for $3,000.
(3) The branch closes its books and reports its net income to the home office.

The journal entries for these transactions, or events, are recorded on the books of the home office and branch in Illustration 16–8.

Clearly the net income calculation of the branch is based upon fragmentary data in respect to merchandise costs; these are the only data, however, which are available to the branch accountant. The home office,

Illustration 16-8

Home Office Books

		Dr.	Cr.
(1)	Branch current	5,000	
	Shipments to branch (at cost)		4,000
	Intracompany inventory profit		1,000
(3)	Branch current	500	
	Branch net income		500
	Intracompany inventory profit	500	
	Branch net income		500

Branch Books

		Dr.	Cr.
(1)	Shipments from home office	5,000	
	Home office current		5,000
(2)	Accounts receivable	3,000	
	Sales		3,000
(3)	Merchandise inventory	2,500	
	Sales	3,000	
	Shipments from home office		5,000
	Income summary		500

possessed of complete information in respect to intracompany billing, is able to make appropriate adjustment for the intracompany inventory profit. That amount of the profit on the original shipment subsequently *confirmed* by branch sales is appropriately transferred in the home office closing process to branch net income; the amount of profit identified with unsold branch merchandise is reserved as a credit in the Intracompany Inventory Profit account until the relevant units are sold. The balance in the Intracompany Inventory Profit account should be reported as a deduction from the balance in the Branch Current account in the balance sheet of the home office. In combined statements prepared before closing, the Intracompany Inventory Profit account is eliminated as a part of the Shipments to Branch–Shipments from Home Office elimination and accordingly does not appear as an extended value in the combined statement working paper. Additionally, the unconfirmed profit in the ending inventory of the branch is eliminated. To the extent that the accountant may favor disclosing the amount of inventory profit, it may be retained in the combined balance sheet as a deduction from the profit-inflated inventory, reducing the latter to cost.

Illustrative Problem

The following illustrative problem introduces a combined statement working paper involving residual intracompany inventory profit. The following are the trial balances of the home office and branch on December 31, 1971:

	Home Office	Branch
Cash.	$ 40,000	$ 15,000
Accounts receivable.	22,000	20,000
Merchandise, January 1.	15,000	12,000
Branch current.	53,000	
Other assets.	14,000	50,000
Purchases.	65,000	9,000
Shipments from home office.		36,000
Expenses.	7,000	4,000
	$216,000	$146,000
Liabilities.	$ 18,000	$ 12,000
Capital stock.	50,000	
Retained earnings.	10,000	
Home office current.		53,000
Sales.	100,000	81,000
Shipments to branch.	30,000	
Intracompany inventory profit.	8,000	
	$216,000	$146,000
Merchandise, December 31.	$ 10,000	$ 4,800

The home office bills all shipments to the branch at 20 percent above cost. The branch's beginning and ending inventories consist exclusively of merchandise purchased from the home office.

The combined statement working paper for this problem is shown in Illustration 16–9. It may be observed that the beginning inventory of the branch, $12,000, is profit inflated to the extent of $2,000. This amount

Illustration 16–9

X COMPANY

Combined Statement Working Paper for Year Ended December 31, 1971

	Home Office	Branch	Eliminations Dr.	Eliminations Cr.	Combined
Income Statement:					
Sales	100,000	81,000			181,000
Merchandise, December 31	10,000	4,800	(4) 800		14,000
Shipments to branch	30,000		(3) 30,000		
Total credits	140,000	85,800			195,000
Merchandise, January 1	15,000	12,000		(2) 2,000	25,000
Purchases	65,000	9,000			74,000
Shipments from home office		36,000		(3) 36,000	
Expenses	7,000	4,000			11,000
Total debits	87,000	61,000			110,000
Net income—carried forward	53,000	24,800	30,800	38,000	85,000
Retained Earnings Statement:					
Retained earnings, January 1	10,000				10,000
Net income—brought forward	53,000	24,800	30,800	38,000	85,000
Retained earnings, December 31—carried forward	63,000	24,800	30,800	38,000	95,000
Balance Sheet:					
Cash	40,000	15,000			55,000
Accounts receivable	22,000	20,000			42,000
Merchandise, December 31	10,000	4,800		(4) 800	14,000
Branch current	53,000			(1) 53,000	
Other assets	14,000	50,000			64,000
	139,000	89,800			175,000
Liabilities	18,000	12,000			30,000
Capital stock	50,000				50,000
Retained earnings—brought forward	63,000	*24,800	30,800	38,000	95,000
Home office current		53,000	(1) 53,000		
Intracompany inventory profit	8,000		(2) 2,000 (3) 6,000		
	139,000	89,800	91,800	91,800	175,000

* Increment to Home Office Current due to periodic branch net income.

must be eliminated from both the Merchandise, January 1 and Intracompany Inventory Profit accounts. Similarly, Shipments from Home Office, $36,000, contains a profit factor of $6,000, which reconciles the contra shipment accounts. It is important that the reciprocal shipment accounts be eliminated, together with the residual $6,000 of intracompany inventory profit. Finally, there remains an elimination in respect to the profit element in the final inventory of the branch. The branch inventory, $4,800, contains $800 of intracompany profit. It is sufficient to make this elimination by merely reducing the inventory value as it appears in the income statement division and also as it appears in the balance sheet division of the combined statement working paper.

The home office may prefer to bill the branch at retail price. Such a billing often serves to improve merchandise control in respect to branch operations. Where the billing is made at an established sales price, necessarily the difference between the value of goods available for sale and the value of goods sold is the retail value of unsold merchandise. Comparison of this amount with a physical inventory permits easy detection of inventory discrepancies. By the simple expedient of applying the relevant gross profit rate, the inventory at retail may be translated to cost. The use of this method obviously results in the calculation of a branch net loss in amount equal to the branch's operating expenses. Combined statements are prepared in the same manner as illustrated previously for billings at arbitrary values in excess of cost.

Where the branch is billed at an arbitrary value in excess of cost, the billing may nonetheless be competitive with quotations from outside suppliers. To this extent, the branch profit and loss statement remains a fairly reliable index of operating efficiency in respect to competitive enterprises. Where the billing is at retail price, the branch's operating statement can hardly be more than a statistical summary of revenues and expenses. In this instance, an index of the branch management's efficiency must necessarily relate to the minimization of operating expenses, or more precisely, maximization of sales volume and minimization of the ratio of operating expenses to sales.

Reconciling Adjustments

Attention has been heretofore directed to the necessity for eliminating all intracompany reciprocal account balances in the preparation of a combined financial statement for the branch and home office. Frequently these accounts will not carry equivalent balances on specified statement dates. These variations can often be explained in terms of inventory shipments or cash remittances in transit. It is accordingly necessary to give effect to these, and other adjustments, in order to establish reciprocity prior to the making of eliminating entries. It is preferable that adjustments be made on the books of the affected division before the preparation of a combined statement working paper is begun; however, they may be entered on the working paper in the same manner as eliminating entries.

Transshipments of Merchandise

On occasions, it may be necessary for one branch to ship merchandise to a second branch. In such a circumstance, it is important that each branch record the transaction so as to give appropriate recognition to the effect produced *on the home office books*. For example, the receiving branch should debit the accounts of the assets received and credit the Home Office Current account; contrariwise, the shipping branch should reduce by appropriate entries both its Home Office Current account and the accounts for the assets transferred. It is unusual for branches to carry current accounts with other branches; rather, intrabranch transactions are ordinarily analyzed in terms of accountability to the home office.

Freight on assets transferred by the home office to a branch is properly included as an element of asset cost to the receiving branch. However, where assets are transshipped from one branch to another, it is appropriate to include in the cost of the asset only that amount of freight as would have been paid had the shipment been directed originally from the home office to the ultimate branch recipient. Payments in excess of this amount are normally charged to expense by the home office, the assumption being that the home office is at least nominally responsible for the excess charge resulting from indirect routing.

Freight on branch transshipments is illustrated below. It is assumed that merchandise costing the home office $1,000 is shipped to Branch A. Freight on this shipment, $80, is paid by the home office. Subsequently, these goods are transshipped to Branch B, with the payment of additional freight of $40 by Branch A. It is determined that direct routing from the home office to Branch B would have resulted in an aggregate freight cost of $100. Entries for these transactions are as follows:

Home Office

Branch A current..	1,080	
Shipments to Branch A..............................		1,000
Cash...		80
Shipments to Branch A...................................	1,000	
Shipments to Branch B..............................		1,000
Branch B current..	1,100	
Excess freight on branch transshipment....................	20	
Branch A current......................................		1,120

Branch A

Shipments from home office..............................	1,000	
Freight-in...	80	
Home office current..................................		1,080
Home office current..	1,120	
Shipments from home office..........................		1,000
Freight-in...		80
Cash..		40

Branch B

Shipments from home office.............................1,000	
Freight-in... 100	
Home office current....................................	1,100

Other Accounting Systems

On occasions, the home office may elect to centralize the accounting for all branch operations within the structure of home office records. This may result in the creation of a separate set of accounts to identify the details of branch operations, or these operations may be subsumed in the same system of accounts as are used in nonbranch transactions. In either circumstance, the documentary evidences of all branch transactions must be regularly submitted to the home office for entry. Such a system is not essentially unlike that used for agencies.

On other occasions, the accounting system may take the form of a complete record-keeping by *both* branch and home office in respect to all branch transactions. Necessarily this duplication has disadvantages. Yet, the more complete dissemination of accounting information may, in fact, promote greater operating efficiencies in the administrative decentralization than the added cost of maintaining duplicate records would appear to indicate.

QUESTIONS

1. Describe the calculations of debit and credit differentials where the entity theory of consolidated statements is accepted.
2. What is the entity theorist's position regarding the amount of elimination of intercompany profits on asset transfers?
3. If the stock of a corporation is owned in equal amounts by a small number of corporate shareholders, what procedures should be followed in preparing financial statements for each investor corporation to reflect its investment in the stock?
4. Enumerate several advantages and disadvantages of filing consolidated tax returns.
5. What criteria are often cited for determining the propriety of including the accounts of a specific subsidiary in consolidated statements?
6. What is the relationship between and the function of the accounts "Branch Current" and "Home Office Current"?
7. What is meant by the "principle of substitution" as applied to branch accounting?
8. If the home office elects to bill the branch for merchandise at a price in excess of cost, why would it be preferable to use a price above cost but less than retail?
9. What are "reconciling adjustments" in branch accounting?

PROBLEMS (Consolidated Statements)

Problem 16–1

The Tucker Company acquired an 80 percent interest in the capital stock of the Taylor Corporation on January 1, 1971, for $90,000. On December 31, 1971, the trial balances of the affiliated companies are:

	Tucker Company	Taylor Corporation
Cash...	$ 40,000	$ 32,000
Receivables.................................	20,000	16,000
Merchandise, January 1......................	12,000	8,000
Investment in Taylor Corporation common stock.......................................	90,000	
Long-lived assets............................	93,000	41,000
Other assets.................................	17,000	35,000
Dividends declared...........................		10,000
Purchases...................................	50,000	43,000
Expenses....................................	18,000	15,000
	$340,000	$200,000
Payables....................................	$ 12,000	$ 10,000
Capital stock:		
Tucker Company............................	100,000	
Taylor Corporation.........................		60,000
Retained earnings:		
Tucker Company............................	120,000	
Taylor Corporation.........................		40,000
Sales.......................................	100,000	90,000
Dividend income............................	8,000	
	$340,000	$200,000
Merchandise, December 31....................	$ 10,000	$ 16,000

Required:

Using the "entity theory," prepare:

(i)   A consolidated statement working paper for the year ended December 31, 1971.

(ii) A consolidated balance sheet as of December 31, 1971, and a consolidated income statement for the year then ended.

Problem 16–2

On January 1, 1971, the Irwin Corporation acquired 90 percent of the capital stock of the Prentice Company for $84,000 and 80 percent of the capital stock of Simons, Inc., for $70,000. Accumulated retained earnings of the Prentice Company and Simons, Inc., at acquisition were $40,000 and $20,000 respectively.

Trial balances of the affiliate companies on December 31, 1972, are given following:

	Irwin Corp.	Prentice Co.	Simons, Inc.
Cash...........................	$ 19,000	$ 23,000	$ 7,000
Receivables....................	41,000	27,000	12,000
Merchandise, January 1...........	11,000	8,000	7,000
Investment in Prentice Com-			
Company......................	84,000		
Investment in Simons, Inc..........	70,000		
Other assets.....................	8,000	74,000	86,000
Dividends declared...............		6,000	4,000
Purchases.......................	57,000	64,000	33,000
Expenses.......................	10,600	5,000	10,000
	$300,600	$207,000	$159,000
Payables.........................	$ 18,000	$ 5,000	$ 12,000
Capital stock (par $100)...........	100,000	50,000	60,000
Retained earnings................	80,000	70,000	35,000
Sales...........................	94,000	82,000	52,000
Dividend income.................	8,600		
	$300,600	$207,000	$159,000
Merchandise, December 31........	$ 6,000	$ 10,000	$ 8,000

During 1972 Simons, Inc., made sales to the Irwin Corporation in the amount of $12,000. In respect to these sales $4,000 remain in the December 31 inventory of Irwin. Simons, Inc., regularly marks up goods 25 percent on selling price on sales to both affiliates and nonaffiliates.

Required:

Using the "entity theory," prepare a consolidated statement working paper for the year ended December 31, 1972.

Problem 16–3

The Cruse Company purchased 80 percent of the capital stock of Summers, Inc., on January 1, 1971, for $51,000. One year thereafter, trial balances of the respective companies were:

	December 31, 1971	
	Cruse Company	Summers, Inc.
Cash.......................................	$ 22,000	$ 12,500
Notes receivable............................	5,000	2,000
Merchandise, January 1......................	28,000	11,000
Investment in Summers, Inc..................	51,000	
Other assets................................	58,000	80,500
Dividends declared..........................	8,500	5,000
Purchases..................................	161,000	83,000
Freight-in..................................	1,000	200
Selling expenses............................	18,000	11,100
Administrative expenses.....................	9,300	5,700
	$361,800	$211,000

	—December 31, 1971— Cruse Company	Summers, Inc.
Accounts payable..........................	$ 18,000	$ 12,000
Other liabilities...........................	3,000	16,000
Capital stock (par, $100).................	100,000	50,000
Retained earnings.........................	31,000	12,000
Sales......................................	205,000	121,000
Dividend income...........................	4,000	
Interest income............................	800	
	$361,800	$211,000
Merchandise, December 31................	$ 41,000	$ 18,000

"Other liabilities" of Summers, Inc., include a $3,000 noninterest-bearing note payable to the Cruse Company.

Required:

Prepare a *trial balance* consolidated statement working paper for the year ended December 31, 1971.

Problem 16–4

On January 1, 1967, A Company acquired 80 percent of the capital stock of B Company and 90 percent of the capital stock of C Company.

The following operating summary relates to the affiliation for the year ended December 31, 1971:

	—Companies—		
	A	B	C
Recorded net income, 1971...........	$65,000	$40,000	$26,000
Dividends paid:			
Cash.........................	10,000	5,000	–0–
Stock........................	2,000	5,000	4,000
Recognized intercompany inventory profit, unconfirmed on:			
January 1.......................		6,000	
December 31....................	4,000	1,000	2,000

A Company acquired on January 1, 1971, machinery and equipment from B Company on which the latter recorded a profit of $10,000. On January 1, 1971, it was estimated that the equipment had a remaining service life of 10 years.

C Company acquired on January 1, 1971, $20,000 of 5 percent bonds of A Company for $23,000. The bonds with 20 years' maturity were issued by A Company on January 1, 1961, at 90.

Required:

Calculate *by definition* consolidated net income for 1971.

Problem 16–5

You are to select from the alternatives presented *all* of those which correctly complete each of the following numbered statements. Note that some of the questions may contain more than one correct statement.

1. Consolidated statements are used to present the result of operations and the financial position of—
   a) A company and its branches.
   b) A company and its subcontractors.
   c) A company and its subsidiaries.
   d) Any group of companies with related interests.
   e) None of the above.
2. Consolidated statements are intended primarily for the benefit of—
   a) Stockholders of the parent company.
   b) Taxing authorities.
   c) Management of the parent company.
   d) Creditors of the parent company.
   e) None of the above.
3. A consolidated statement for X, Y, and Z is proper if—
   a) X owns 100 percent of the outstanding common stock of Y and 49 percent of Z; Q owns 51 percent of Z.
   b) X owns 100 percent of the outstanding common stock of Y; Y owns 75 percent of Z.
   c) X owns 100 percent of the outstanding common stock of Y and 75 percent of Z. X bought the stock of Z one month before the statement date, and sold it six weeks later.
   d) There is no interrelation of financial control among X, Y, and Z. However, they are contemplating the joint purchase of 100 percent of the outstanding common stock of W.
   e) X owns 100 percent of the outstanding common stock of Y and Z. Z is in bankruptcy.
4. H is the parent company and would probably treat K as an investment and not a consolidated subsidiary in the proposed consolidated statement of H, J and K if—
   a) H and J manufacture electronic equipment; K manufactures ball bearings.
   b) H and J manufacture ball-point pens; K is a bank.
   c) K has assets of $1,000,000 and an outstanding bond issue of $750,-000. H holds the bonds.
   d) Same as (c), except that outsiders hold the bonds.
   e) None of the above.
5. Parent company P has a fiscal year ending June 30, 1971. Subsidiary S's fiscal year ends May 31, 1971. Therefore:
   a) A consolidated statement cannot properly be prepared for P and S.
   b) S's May 31, 1971, statement can be used for consolidation with P's June 30, 1971, statement, provided disclosure (or some recognition) is made of any June event which materially affected S.
   c) If the consolidated statement is permissible, it will be dated June 30, 1971.
   d) If the consolidated statement is permissible, it will be dated May 31, 1971.
   e) None of the above.
6. In preparing consolidated statements, elimination is necessary for—
   a) Net (intercompany) profit or loss on assets remaining within the group.

b) Gross (intercompany) profit or loss on assets remaining within the group.

c) Net (intercompany) profit or loss on transactions with subsidiaries not consolidated; the investment being carried at cost.

d) Gross (intercompany) profit or loss on transactions with subsidiaries not consolidated; the investment being carried at cost.

e) None of the above.

7. P owns 90 percent of the stock of S. W owns 10 percent of S's stock. In relation to P, W is considered as—

 a) An affiliate.

 b) A subsidiary not to be consolidated.

 c) A minority interest.

 d) A holding company.

 e) None of the above.

8. The cost of a parent company's investment in a subsidiary exceeded its equity in the book value of the subsidiary's net assets at the acquisition date. The parent company made the investment because of the subsidiary's ownership of valuable patents which were carried on its books at net cost, $1,000. In the consolidated statements, the excess of the parent's cost over its equity in the book value of the subsidiary's net assets should be shown as:

 a) An increase in patents.

 b) Goodwill.

 c) Excess of book value over purchase price.

 d) Surplus from consolidation.

 e) None of the above.

9. P's cost of investment in M exceeded its equity in the book value of M's net assets at the acquisition date. The excess is not attributable to specific assets. In the consolidated statements, this excess should be:

 a) Eliminated.

 b) Allocated proportionately to the subsidiary's fixed assets.

 c) Shown on the balance sheet as surplus from consolidation.

 d) Shown on the balance sheet as excess of cost of stock of subsidiary over book value.

 e) None of the above.

10. P's cost of investment in J was less than its equity in the book value of J's net assets at the acquisition date. The difference is related to the decline in value of J's machinery. In the consolidated statements, this difference should be shown on the balance sheet as—

 a) A reduction in machinery.

 b) Capital surplus.

 c) Surplus from consolidation.

 d) Excess of book value over purchase price.

 e) None of the above.

11. P Company purchased the outstanding common stock of S as follows:

> 10 percent, January 2, 1971.
>
> 25 percent, June 1, 1971.
>
> 25 percent, August 1, 1971.
>
> 40 percent, September 30, 1971.

The fiscal year of each of the companies ends on September 30. S's stock was acquired by P at book value. Consolidated net income for the fiscal year ended September 30, 1971, would include the following earnings of the subsidiary:

a)   10 percent of earnings, January–May, 1971.

b)   35 percent of earnings, June–July, 1971.

c)   60 percent of earnings, August–September, 1971.

d)   60 percent of earnings, January–September, 1971.

e)   None of the above.

12.   P Company had 300,000 shares of stock outstanding. It owned 75 percent of the outstanding stock of T. T owned 20,000 shares of P's stock. In the consolidated balance sheet, P Company's outstanding stock may be shown as:

a)   280,000 shares.

b)   300,000 shares less 20,000 shares of treasury stock.

c)   300,000 shares.

d)   300,000 shares footnoted to indicate that T holds 20,000 shares.

e)   None of the above.

13.   P Company and its subsidiary S filed separate income tax returns. P's tax included $70,000 attributable to unconfirmed profits on sales to S. In preparing consolidated financial statements:

a)   The entire intercompany profit should be eliminated; taxes need not be adjusted.

b)   Taxes of $70,000 should be deferred.

c)   The intercompany profit should be reduced by $70,000 before elimination, *and* taxes of $70,000 should be deferred.

d)   Income taxes should be recomputed, and a revised return should be filed.

e)   None of the above.

14.   Combined financial statements are justified for the following:

a)   A group of subsidiaries not consolidated.

b)   Corporations engaged in similar or related operations, owned by the same (individual) stockholder.

c)   A group of companies under common management.

d)   Any group of companies with related interests.

e)   None of the above.

15.   The preferable method of presenting subsidiaries not consolidated in financial statements is:

a)   At market value, adjusted through income.

b)   At market value, adjusted through retained earnings.

c)   At cost, plus the parent's share of the subsidiaries' undistributed net income (or minus the net loss), since acquisition, adjusted annually through income.

d)   At cost, plus the parent's share of the subsidiaries' undistributed net income (or minus the net loss), adjusted annually through retained earnings.

e)   At consolidated group's equity in net realizable value of assets of subsidiaries not consolidated.

16.   It is an acceptable accounting treatment to carry investments in subsidiaries not consolidated at cost:

a)   Under no circumstances.

b)   With dividends included in income as received.

c)   Less provision for any permanent material impairment of the investment.

d)   If there is disclosure, by footnote or otherwise, of the equity of the consolidated group in the net assets of subsidiaries not consolidated.

e)   None of the above.

17. "Negative goodwill" is:

a)   Not acceptable terminology for statement purposes.

b)   Subtracted from goodwill, if any, for statement purposes.

c)   Synonymous with surplus from consolidation.

d)   Also known as excess of book value over purchase price.

e)   None of the above.

18. P Company owns 75 percent of the outstanding common stock of S. During 1971, P's unconfirmed profits on its transactions with S amounted to $50,000. The elimination for intercompany profit is:

a)   Not necessary.

b) $50,000.

c) $37,500.

d)   Allocated between P Company and the minority stockholders.

e)   None of the above.

19. P and its subsidiaries, T and V, have issued combined statements for a number of years. In connection with a proposed bank loan, P has been requested to present a statement to the bank which will indicate P's financial position at December 31, 1971. The following will supply the desired information:

a)   A copy of the consolidated statement at December 31, 1971.

b)   A copy of P's financial statement at December 31, 1971, on which the investments in T and V are reported at the current carrying value.

c)   A copy of the consolidated statement and of the separate parent company (P) statement, both at December 31, 1971.

d)   A copy of the consolidated statement at December 31, 1971, modified so that one column is used for P and other columns for T and V.

e)   A copy of separate financial statements of P, T, and V as of December 31, 1971.

20. The stockholders of S sold all of its common stock, 1,000 shares, to P Company, receiving in return 5,000 shares of P Company stock. On the day prior to the sale, P stock sold for $40 per share; S stock sold for $195 per share. P stock has a par value of $20 per share. S stock has a par value of $50 per share. This is not a pooling of interests.

The investment by P may be recorded on its books at:

a) $200,000, only.

b) $195,000, only.

c) $100,000.

d) $50,000.

e)   Either $200,000 or $195,000.

(AICPA adapted)

Problem 16–6

The individual and consolidated statements of companies X and Y for the year ending December 31, 1972, are as follows:

	X Company	Y Company	Consolidated
Cash and receivables...................	$ 35,000	$108,000	$ 97,400
Inventories...........................	40,000	90,000	122,000
Plant (net)...........................	460,000	140,000	600,000
Appraisal increase in plant (net)...........			50,000
Investment in Y.......................	245,000		
X bonds owned........................		103,000	
	$780,000	$441,000	$869,400
Current payables......................	$ 70,000	$ 23,000	$ 53,000
Dividends payable.....................	10,000	8,000	12,400
Mortgage bonds.......................	200,000	50,000	150,000
Capital stock.........................	300,000	200,000	300,000
Retained earnings.....................	200,000	160,000	231,000
Minority interest.....................			123,000
	$780,000	$441,000	$869,400
Sales................................	$600,000	$400,000	$760,000
Cost of sales.........................	360,000	280,000	403,000
Gross profit..........................	$240,000	$120,000	$357,000
Operating expenses....................	130,000	54,000	184,000
Operating profit......................	$110,000	$ 66,000	$173,000
Interest income.......................	1,800	5,000	1,800
Dividend income......................	11,200	–0–	–0–
Total............................	$123,000	$ 71,000	$174,800
Interest expense......................	$ 10,000	$ 3,000	$ 8,000
Provision for income taxes..............	56,000	34,000	90,000
Nonrecurring loss.....................			3,000
Minority share.......................			5,400
Net income..........................	$ 57,000	$ 34,000	$ 68,400
Dividends...........................	20,000	16,000	24,800
Transfer to retained earnings............	$ 37,000	$ 18,000	$ 43,600

X Company purchased its 70 percent interest in Y Company several years ago. X Company sells its product in part to Y Company for further processing, and in part to other firms. The inventories of Y Company included an inter-company markup at both the beginning and end of the year. Cash transfers are made between the companies according to working capital needs.

Early in 1972, Y Company purchased $100,000 face value of the bonds of X Company as a temporary investment. These are carried on Y's books at cost.

Required:

On the basis of the information you can develop from an analysis of the individual and consolidated statements, answer the six questions below.

Show clearly all computations necessary to support your answers.

1. Does X Company carry its *Investment in Y* on the cost or equity (accrual) basis? State the reason for your conclusion.
2. The *Appraisal Increase* represents a revaluation of the *total* of Y Company's assets on the basis of the price paid by X Company for its interest in Y. What was the balance of *Y's Retained Earnings* at date of acquisition?
3. Prepare a reconciliation schedule which will explain clearly the difference between X Company's *Retained Earnings* at December 31, 1972, $200,000,

and the *Consolidated Retained Earnings* at December 31, 1972, $231,000.
4. What is the nature of the *Nonrecurring Loss* on the consolidated income statement? Show the consolidating elimination entry from which it originated.
5. Show the amounts of intercompany debts, excluding the bonds, and show which company is the debtor and which is the creditor in each instance.
6. Prepare a schedule reconciling the sum of the *Cost of Sales* of X and Y individually with the *Consolidated Cost of Sales*. Show clearly the intercompany markup in the beginning and ending inventories of Y Company and how you determined the amounts.

(AICPA adapted)

Problem 16–7

On January 1, 1971, Prent Company purchased a controlling interest in Alec Company. The general ledger trial balances for Prent Company and Alec Company at December 31, 1971, are as follows:

Prent Company and Subsidiary

GENERAL LEDGER TRIAL BALANCES

December 31, 1971

Debits	Prent Company	Alec Company
Cash.....................................	$ 37,900	$ 29,050
Marketable securities......................	33,000	18,000
Trade accounts receivable..................	210,000	88,000
Intercompany receivables...................	24,000	
Inventories...............................	275,000	135,000
Machinery and equipment...................	518,000	279,000
Investment in Alec Company at cost..........	96,000	
Patents...................................	35,000	
Cost of sales.............................	510,000	374,000
Depreciation expense.......................	65,600	11,200
Administrative and selling expenses..........	130,000	110,500
Dividends declared........................	7,500	10,000
Total Debits........................	$1,942,000	$1,054,750

Credits		
Dividends payable..........................	$ 7,500	
Trade accounts payable....................	103,900	$ 96,050
Accrued expenses..........................	91,600	78,000
Intercompany payables......................	8,000	
Allowance for bad debts....................	6,800	2,300
Accumulated depreciation...................	298,200	196,700
Capital stock, par value $10.................	150,000	
Capital stock, par value $5.................		22,000
Paid-in capital in excess of par value..........	36,000	
Paid-in capital in excess of par value..........		14,000
Retained earnings.........................	378,000	
Retained earnings.........................		112,000
Sales and services.........................	850,000	530,000
Dividend income..........................	4,800	
Other income.............................	7,200	3,700
Total Credits......................	$1,942,000	$1,054,750

The following information is also available:

a) Prent Company purchased 1,600 shares of Alec Company's outstanding stock on January 1, 1970, for $50,000 and on January 1, 1971, purchased an additional 1,400 shares for $46,000.

b) An analysis of the stockholders' equity accounts at December 31, 1970, and 1969 follows:

	Prent Company		Alec Company	
	December 31, 1970	December 31, 1969	December 31, 1970	December 31, 1969
Capital stock, par $10............	$150,000	$150,000		
Capital stock, par $5.............			$ 20,000	$ 20,000
Paid-in capital in excess of par value...............	36,000	36,000	10,000	10,000
Retained earnings...............	378,000	285,000	112,000	82,000
Total.........	$564,000	$471,000	$142,000	$112,000

c) Alec Company's marketable securities consist of 1,500 shares of Prent Company stock purchased on June 15, 1971, in the open market for $18,000. The securities were purchased as a temporary investment and were sold on January 15, 1972, for $25,000. Prent utilizes the treasury stock method to eliminate reciprocal stockholdings which represent temporary investments and records treasury stock at cost.

d) On December 10, 1971, Prent Company declared a cash dividend of $.50 per share payable January 10, 1972, to stockholders of record on December 20, 1971. Alec Company paid a cash dividend of $1 per share on June 30, 1971, and distributed a 10 percent stock dividend on September 30, 1971. The stock was selling for $15 per share ex-dividend on September 30, 1971. Alec Company paid no dividends in 1970.

e) Alec Company sold machinery with a book value of $4,000 and a remaining life of five years to Prent Company for $4,800 on December 31, 1971. The gain on the sale was credited to the Other Income account.

f) Alec Company includes all intercompany receivable and payable accounts in its Trade Accounts Receivable and Trade Accounts Payable accounts.

g) During 1971 the following intercompany sales were made:

	Net Sales	Included in Purchaser's Inventory at December 31, 1971
Prent Company to Alec Company........	$ 78,000	$24,300
Alec Company to Prent Company........	104,000	18,000
Total........................	$182,000	$42,300

Prent Company sells merchandise to Alec Company at cost. Alec Company sells merchandise to Prent Company at regular selling price to make a normal profit margin of 30 percent. The market value of all inventory was in excess of cost at December 31, 1971. There were no intercompany sales in prior years.

Required:

(i)   Prepare an investment elimination schedule for the three division consolidated working paper on December 31, 1971.

(ii) In general journal form, present all additional elimination entries that would be entered on the December 31, 1971, consolidated working paper. Prent eliminates 100 percent of unconfirmed intercompany profits.

(AICPA adapted)

Problem 16–8

After completing the audit of P Company and its subsidiaries for the year ended December 31, 1971, you have prepared the following trial balances and your working papers disclose the following:

a)   P Company acquired 4,000 shares of X Company common stock for $310,000 on January 1, 1970, and an additional 500 shares for $40,000 on January 1, 1971.

b)   P Company acquired all of Y Company's 8,000 outstanding shares on January 1, 1970, for $650,000. On January 1, 1971, Y Company issued 2,000 additional shares to the public at $85 per share. P Company has no investments other than the stock of companies X and Y.

c)   On January 1, 1964, Y Company issued $200,000 of 10-year, 4 percent first-mortgage bonds at 98. On January 1, 1971, X Company purchased $150,000 (face value) of these bonds in the open market at 98. Interest is paid on the bonds on June 30 and December 31.

d)   Condensed balance sheets for X Company and Y Company at the start of business on January 1, 1970, and January 1, 1971, are presented below:

	X Company 1/1/71	X Company 1/1/70	Y Company 1/1/71	Y Company 1/1/70
Current assets............	$225,000	$195,000	$205,000	$280,400
Plant and equipment.....	350,000	305,000	623,800	613,000
Unamortized bond discount..............			1,200	1,600
Total............	$575,000	$500,000	$830,000	$895,000
Current liabilities........	$125,000	$100,000	$105,000	$ 95,000
Bonds payable..........			200,000	200,000
Capital stock— par $50..............	250,000	250,000	400,000	400,000
Retained earnings........	200,000	150,000	125,000	200,000
Total............	$575,000	$500,000	$830,000	$895,000

e)   Total dividends paid during 1971 were as follows:

P Company................ $24,000
X Company................ 25,000
Y Company................ 10,000

In addition to the dividend payments, P Company and X Company each declared dividends of $1 per share payable in January, 1972.

f) On June 30, 1971, P Company sold equipment with a book value of $8,000 to X Company for $10,000. X Company depreciates equipment by the straight-line method based on a 10-year life. P Company credited the gain on the sale of equipment to Retained Earnings.

g) P Company consistently sells to its subsidiaries at a price which results in a gross profit of 25 percent on sales. Companies X and Y sell to each other and to P Company at cost. Prior to 1971 intercompany sales were negligible, but during 1971, the following intercompany sales were made:

	Total Sales	Included in Purchaser's Inventory, 12/31/71
P Company to X Company.............	$172,000	$20,000
P Company to Y Company.............	160,000	40,000
X Company to Y Company.............	25,000	5,000
X Company to P Company.............	28,000	8,000
	$385,000	$73,000

h) At December 31, 1971:

P Company owed X Company....................	$24,000
X Company owed Y Company...................	16,000
Y Company owed P Company...................	12,000
	$52,000

i) Trial balances at December 31, 1971, were as follows:

	P Company	X Company	Y Company
Cash........................	$ 33,000	$ 41,500	$ 175,200
Accounts receivable............	85,000	97,500	105,000
Inventories....................	137,500	163,000	150,000
Investment in X Company.......	350,000		
Investment in Y Company.......	650,000		
Bonds of Y Company..........		147,000	
Plant and equipment...........	700,000	525,000	834,000
Unamortized bond discount......			800
Cost of sales.................	2,500,000	1,200,000	1,400,000
Operating expenses............	405,000	280,000	290,500
Interest expense...............	16,200	2,500	9,500
	$4,876,700	$2,456,500	$2,965,000

	P Company	X Company	Y Company
Accounts payable..............	$ 202,000	$ 150,500	$ 90,000
Dividends payable.............	12,000	5,000	
Bonds payable.................	400,000		200,000
Accumulated depreciation.......	402,000	325,000	240,000
Sales.........................	2,950,000	1,550,000	1,750,000
Interest income on bonds.......		6,000	
Dividend income...............	30,500		
Capital stock, par $50..........	600,000		
Capital stock, par $50..........		250,000	
Capital stock, par $50..........			500,000
Capital in excess of par.........			70,000
Retained earnings, P Company................	280,200		
Retained earnings, X Company................		170,000	
Retained earnings, Y Company................			115,000
	$4,876,700	$2,456,500	$2,965,000

Required:

Prepare a consolidated statement working paper, with supporting computations, for the year ended December 31, 1971. Assume 100 percent elimination in respect to intercompany profit.

(AICPA adapted)

PROBLEMS (Branches)

Problem 16–9

The Cincinnati home office of The Geis Company regularly acquires merchandise at a cost of $4 a unit, which is subsequently marked to sell at $6 a unit by both the home office and its Athens branch. During 1970 the home office purchased 4,000 units, sold 3,000 units, and shipped 500 units to the branch. During 1971 the home office purchased an additional 4,500 units, sold 3,200 units, and made a second shipment of 1,000 units to the Athens branch.

Branch sales of units acquired from the home office were: 400 units in 1970 and 900 units in 1971.

Required:

(i) Journalize all transactions on the books of The Geis Company and its Athens branch (including closing entries) for the years 1970 and 1971 *if* the home office bills merchandise shipped to the branch at $4 a unit.

(ii) Same conditions as in (i) except that the home office bills merchandise shipped to the branch at $5 a unit.

Problem 16–10

Using the data of Problem 16–9, prepare working papers for a *combined* income statement for The Geis Company and its Athens branch for the years 1970 and 1971 if—

(i) The home office bills merchandise shipped to the branch at $4 a unit.

(ii) The home office bills merchandise shipped to the branch at $5 a unit.

Problem 16–11

Edwards Company opened a Dallas branch in January, 1971. During 1971, Edwards recorded merchandise transfers to the branch and merchandise returns from the branch with the following entries.

Branch current....................................	156,000	
Sales...		156,000
Sales returns.....................................	3,900	
Branch current...................................		3,900

Transfers to and from the branch were recorded by Edwards at 130 percent of Edwards' cost.

The Dallas branch reported to the home office a net loss of $12,000 for 1971. In addition, the branch reported a closing inventory of $65,000, all of which was acquired from the home office.

Required:

Assume that the home office books have not been closed for 1971. Prepare the journal entries on the books of the home office that are necessary at the end of 1971 to (1) correct the accounts of the home office and (2) recognize the results of branch activities during 1971.

Problem 16–12

The Longley Company of Indianapolis regularly distributes its products through branch retail sales outlets. Shipments to its Frankfort branch are billed as follows: Case A, at cost; Case B, 25 percent above cost; Case C, retail price at date of shipment.

During the year the Frankfort branch received merchandise from the home office, cost, $60,000. Additionally, the branch recorded credit sales of $81,000; made collections on account, $64,000; paid expenses, $14,000; and remitted cash to the Indianapolis home office, $61,200. The December 31 final inventory of the branch was: Case A, $6,000; Case B, $7,500; and Case C, $9,000.

The trial balance of the Indianapolis home office on December 31 was:

	Case A	Case B	Case C
Cash.......................	$ 39,000	$ 39,000	$ 39,000
Accounts receivable..........	45,000	45,000	45,000
Branch current..............	[1,200]	13,800	28,800
Purchases...................	150,000	150,000	150,000
Expenses...................	17,200	17,200	17,200
	$250,000	$265,000	$280,000
Accounts payable............	$ 20,000	$ 20,000	$ 20,000
Shipments to branch.........	60,000	60,000	60,000
Intracompany inventory			
profit....................		15,000	30,000
Capital stock...............	40,000	40,000	40,000
Sales......................	130,000	130,000	130,000
	$250,000	$265,000	$280,000
Merchandise, Decem-			
ber 31....................	$ 8,000	$ 8,000	$ 8,000

Required:

(i)   Journalize the transactions of the branch for the year, as recorded by the Indianapolis home office and the Frankfort branch.
(ii) Prepare closing entries for the branch and home office.
(iii) Prepare a combined statement working paper (Case C only).

Problem 16–13

The Koufax Sporting Goods Company of Los Angeles decided on July 1, 1971, to establish sales branches in Chicago and New York as a means of expanding and improving its services to customers in these areas. Transactions with these branches for the month of July are as follows:

July 1   The home office transferred $75,000 cash to the Chicago branch and $100,000 to the New York branch to be used as working funds.
      2   Merchandise costing $310,000 was shipped to the New York branch and was billed at 140 percent of cost. Freight charges, paid by the home office, amounted to $1,400.
      3   Merchandise costing $225,000 was shipped to the Chicago branch and was billed at a 25 percent markup on the invoice price. Freight charges of $888 were paid by the Chicago branch.
      10   Fixed assets costing $400,000 were purchased for the use of the Chicago branch and $500,000 were purchased for the New York branch. General ledger control over fixed assets is maintained by the home office.
      15   Timely reporting is facilitated by the use of electronic data processing equipment; as a consequence, the first semimonthly summary of operating data was received on July 15 and disclosed the following:

	Branches	
	Chicago	*New York*
Credit sales....................	$42,000	$57,000
Collections on account..........	34,000	41,000
Expenses......................	8,000	12,000
Payments on account...........	6,400	9,700

      17   Merchandise previously shipped to Chicago was transshipped to New York. These goods, on which freight charges amounted to $147, had been billed to Chicago at $20,000. Additional freight paid by the New York branch for the transshipment amounted to $68. Had the shipment been initially directed to New York, transportation costs would have totaled $175.
      20   The home office shipped additional merchandise to branches as follows: Chicago, $150,000 cost; New York, $200,000 cost. The terms of branch billing remain unchanged. Freight charges, paid by the home office, were $700 on the Chicago shipment and $1,150 on the New York shipment.
July 31   The semimonthly operating summary is as follows:

	Branches	
	Chicago	*New York*
Credit sales.................	$122,100	$150,800
Collections on account........	97,700	128,100
Expenses....................	19,000	27,000
Payments on account........	19,600	26,300

31   Cash remittances to the home office were:

New York branch..............$125,000
Chicago branch............... 100,000

Required:

(i)   Prepare journal entries for July for each branch and the home office. (In the home office books, use separate accounts in respect to the transactions of each branch.)

(ii) Prepare closing entries, given the following additional information:

(*a*)   Inventories, July 31:

New York branch................... $560,000
Chicago branch.................... 360,000

Inventories are determined by physical count; freight charges on merchandise shipments are not allocated to inventory.

(*b*)   Depreciation on fixed assets is regularly recorded by the home office. Depreciation expense for the month of July is:

Property at New York branch........... $500
Property at Chicago branch............. 400

Problem 16–14

On July 1, 1971, the Demaris Company, central distributor for Arlo Metal Castings, Inc., organized a southwest sales outlet in El Paso. Following are the home office–branch transactions for the month of July:

July 1   The Demaris Company transferred $2,500 to its El Paso branch for operating fund purposes.

2   Merchandise costing the home office $3 per unit was shipped to the branch at an invoice price of $5 per unit. One thousand units were shipped on July 2; a second order was to be filled by local suppliers.

2   Shipping costs on the above were paid:

By the home office............................$150
By the branch................................ 50

5   Additional merchandise was acquired by the El Paso branch from regional distributors, 500 units @ $3.10.

7   Display equipment was purchased by the home office, cost $3,600, and delivered to El Paso branch. Fixed asset accounts are kept by the home office.

10   Branch sales for the period July 3–10: On account, 800 units @ $5.

18 Branch collections on account, $3,200.
25 Branch sales for the period July 11–24: On account, 500 units @ $5.
29 Cash remittance by branch to home office, $1,000.
30 Monthly summary of branch cash expenses:

Advertising..............	$ 40
Sales commissions.........	650
Miscellaneous............	10

31 Depreciation recorded by the Demaris Company for July included $150 which related to the display equipment used by the El Paso branch. Insurance on this equipment was amortized by the home office in the amount of $25.
31 Inventories of merchandise at El Paso on July 31 included:

From the home office.............	150 units @ $5.00
From local suppliers..............	50 units @ $3.10

Required:

Journalize the above transactions on the books of the Demaris Company and the El Paso branch office and prepare closing entries for July month-end statements.

Problem 16–15

Sales distribution of the Electronic Transistor Company is principally conducted by its home office and one centrally located branch. Units of merchandise shipped to the branch are uniformly priced at 120 percent of cost. The trial balances of the home office and branch at December 31, 1971, are as follows:

	‌December 31, 1971‌	
	Home Office	Branch
Cash.....................................	$ 125,200	$ 17,600
Marketable securities......................	229,000	
Accounts receivable (net)...................	172,700	84,300
Inventory—January 1, 1971.................	341,000	133,200
Branch current...........................	122,300	
Fixed assets (net).........................	1,172,600	
Purchases................................	2,450,000	
Expenses.................................	381,000	78,100
Shipments from home office................		811,200
	$4,993,800	$1,124,400
Accounts payable..........................	$ 397,000	$ 12,400
Accrued expenses.........................	14,100	1,700
Capital stock.............................	1,000,000	
Retained earnings.........................	172,300	
Home office current.......................		72,300
Sales....................................	2,547,000	1,038,000
Shipments to branch......................	701,000	
Intracompany inventory profit..............	162,400	
	$4,993,800	$1,124,400
Inventory—December 31, 1971..............	$ 284,000	$ 120,000

An examination of duplicate deposit tickets on January 3, 1971, discloses that the branch made a $20,000 deposit to the credit of the home office on December 31, 1971.

Required:

(i)   Prepare a working paper for a combined statement for the home office and branch for the year ended December 31, 1971.

(ii) Journalize adjusting and closing entries for the branch and home office.

Problem 16–16

You are the accountant for the Johnson Export Company. The trial balance at December 31, 1971, follows:

	Home Office	Branch
Cash.	$ 15,000	$ 2,000
Accounts receivable.	20,000	17,000
Inventory—December 31, 1971.	30,000	8,000
Fixed assets—net.	150,000	
Branch office current.	44,000	
Cost of sales.	220,000	93,000
Expenses.	70,000	41,000
Total.	$549,000	$161,000
Accounts payable.	$ 23,000	
Mortgage payable.	50,000	
Capital stock.	100,000	
Retained earnings—January 1, 1971.	26,000	
Sales.	350,000	$150,000
Accrued expenses.		2,000
Home office current.		9,000
Total.	$549,000	$161,000

The following additional information is also brought to your attention:

a)   The branch receives all of its merchandise from the home office. The home office bills goods to the branch at 125 percent of cost. During 1971 the branch was billed for $105,000 on shipments from the home office.

b)   The home office credits Sales for the invoice price of goods shipped to the branch.

c)   On January 1, 1971, the inventory of the home office was $25,000. The branch books showed a $6,000 inventory.

d)   The home office billed the branch for $12,000 on December 31, 1971, representing the branch's share of expenses paid at the home office. The branch has not recorded this billing.

e)   All cash collections made by the branch are deposited in a local bank to the account of the home office. Deposits of this nature included the following:

Amount	Date Deposited by Branch	Date Recorded by Home Office
$5,000.	December 28, 1971	December 31, 1971
3,000.	December 30, 1971	January 2, 1972
7,000.	December 31, 1971	January 3, 1972
2,000.	January 2, 1972	January 5, 1972

f) Expenses incurred locally by the branch are paid from an imprest bank account which is reimbursed periodically by the home office. Just prior to the end of the year the home office forwarded a reimbursement check in the amount of $3,000 which was not received by the branch office until January, 1972.

g) It is not necessary to make provisions for federal income tax.

Required:

(i) Prepare a working paper for a combined statement for the home office and branch for the year ended December 31, 1971.

(ii) Prepare a reconciliation of the Branch Current and Home Office Current accounts showing the correct book balance.

(AICPA adapted)

Chapter 17

Accounting for International Operations

The essentially uninterrupted expansion of American business activity since World War II has included a significant increase in what may be broadly classified as international operations. For many companies, these operations consist merely of trading activity (imports or exports) with suppliers or customers that are domiciled in other countries. On a larger scale, this growing involvement in foreign operations may take the form of investment in foreign firms, and/or the establishment of foreign branches or subsidiaries, either to carry on productive operations or to serve as sales outlets or both.

Although there are business enterprises whose foreign investments are so extensive and diverse that they might be characterized as international in scope, having no particular identification with a specific country, each firm must necessarily select one country within which its parent corporation has legal recognition and sanctuary. Additionally, the necessity of accumulating financial information about the entire business enterprise compels that one country's currency be identified as the unit of account by which financial information will be aggregated. Yet, the basic financial records of each segment of the firm are generally expressed in terms of the currency of the particular country within which the segment conducts its operations. Thus, a major problem of accounting for foreign operations relates to the translation of each segment's financial data into a common currency unit. Also, transactions between parties that are located in different countries generally require one party to *purchase* the currency of another country. Such actions interject a new variable into the determination of profit; the fluctuations in the value of one country's currency may result in gains or losses to a firm of another country which utilizes the currency of the first country.

This chapter provides an overview of the principal accounting issues related to transactions involving foreign currencies and to the translation (conversion) of monetary expressions stated in terms of one country's currency into that of another country. However, attention will also focus on several other important factors that are only indirectly related to the difference between currencies.

577

Currency Exchange Rates

From the perspective of any given country, foreign currencies may be viewed as commodities that have specifiable *prices* in terms of the domestic currency. These prices, or rates of exchange, express the relative values of the two currencies. Historically, these rates purported to equate the gold content of the different currencies. However, this is no longer a significant relationship. Presently, two principal types of exchange rates are important: (1) *free* rates, which reflect the fluctuating market prices of the currency as an economic good (a function of supply and demand); and (2) *official* rates, which are established by each government. A given country may have several official rates, each of which pertains to a designated type of economic and financial activity and which reflects governmental policies in respect to desired economic development. The existence of multiple exchange rates normally creates no special difficulty in recording *transactions* with a foreign enterprise, as the recording process accepts the status of the exchange transaction as a *fait accompli,* i.e., the relevant rate is specified by the nature of the transaction to be recorded.

The difference between free and official exchange rates tends to be more significant in the translation of account *balances* than it is in recording specific transactions. This can be attributed to the fact that several transactions, completed at different points in time, produce an account balance for which a *single* exchange rate is not obviously applicable. However, the differences between free and official exchange rates are often small for many free world countries. All countries belonging to the International Monetary Fund, which comprises a majority of those free world countries that are significantly engaged in foreign trade, are required to maintain their "free" exchange rates within 1 percent (plus or minus) of their official rates.[1]

Since the currency exchange rate between two countries is merely a ratio, it may be stated in terms of either country's currency. If one unit of foreign currency is expressed in terms of its domestic monetary equivalent, the exchange rate is said to be quoted *directly*. On the other hand, if one unit of domestic currency is set equal to its equivalent in foreign units, the quotation is said to be *indirect*. In the United States at the present time, foreign exchange rates are quoted directly. Thus, for example, exchange quotations are stated as follows:

Country, Currency, and Official Rate	Dollar Equivalent of One Foreign Unit (Free Rate)
Britain (pound, $2.40)	$2.3900
France (franc, $.20255)	.20205
Mexico (peso, $.08)	.0801

---

[1] Governments satisfy this requirement by actively buying or selling their own currencies as it becomes necessary to support or depress the market price and maintain it within the required percent of the established official rate.

To facilitate hedging against fluctuations in the exchange rate, a futures market in foreign currencies also exists. Futures quotations, also expressed directly, represent the current cost of purchasing (or selling) foreign currency units for delivery at a specified future date.

Transactions with Foreign Companies

One of the important accounting problems of foreign operations relates to transactions between enterprises that are located in two different countries having different currencies. In such instances, one of the parties to the transaction must accept its obligation (or receive its payment) in terms of a foreign currency. The party that undertakes this rather unique function frequently incurs an *exchange gain or loss,* depending upon the direction and amount of the fluctuation in exchange rates between the date of billing and the date of payment. For example, if a domestic importer who purchases merchandise abroad is billed *in a foreign currency,* the invoice amount may be translated into domestic currency through the current rate of exchange (free or official) at the billing date. To extinguish the created debt, however, the domestic importer must, within the time interval between the billing date and the due date, acquire foreign currency. In the event that exchange rates have fluctuated in the period between the date of purchase and the subsequent acquisition of foreign currency, gain or loss clearly results and identifies with the domestic importer. Had the billing been expressed in domestic monetary units, the exchange gain or loss would have been that of the foreign exporter. A parallel may be easily drawn for a domestic exporter and a foreign importer. To guard against the hazards of loss from exchange rate fluctuations, a domestic importer, concurrent with the purchase of merchandise abroad, may also purchase foreign currency for future delivery. Billing and settlement are thereby made in terms of the same rate of exchange. A similar precaution may be taken in respect to a domestic exporter, who may elect to sell foreign currency for future delivery where the settlement of the account receivable is to be made in foreign monetary units.

In order to illustrate the accounting for import-export operations, consider the following transactions for the Leader Corporation (alternative billing terms will be considered separately):

1. The Leader Corporation (domiciled in the United States) sold merchandise to the East Indies Company of London when the rate of exchange was $2.40. The billing is expressed in dollars/pounds as follows: (*a*) $24,000, (*b*) £10,000.
2. The Leader Corporation purchased merchandise from the Villa Company of Mexico City when the rate of exchange was $.08. The billing is expressed in dollars/pesos as follows: (*a*) $10,000, (*b*) 125,000 pesos.
3. Payment of the East Indies Company account with the Leader Corporation was received when the exchange rate was $2.42.

4. Remittance was made to the Villa Company by the Leader Corporation when the exchange rate was $.0808.
5. The Leader Corporation sold merchandise to the Acapulco Company of Mexico for 100,000 pesos when the exchange rate was $.0807 (equivalent to $8,070 at this time). Concurrent with the sale of merchandise, the Leader Corporation also sold 100,000 pesos for future delivery at $.0807.
6. The Leader Corporation received payment from the Acapulco Company when the exchange rate was $.0793; thereupon, delivery of future exchange was made to the exchange broker.

Ignoring the effects of commissions and other service charges, the entries on the books of the Leader Corporation for these transactions are as follows:

		(a) Where Billing Is in Domestic Currency (Dollars)		(b) Where Billing Is in Foreign Currency (Pounds Sterling or Pesos)	
(1)	Accounts receivable..........	24,000		24,000	
	Sales...................		24,000		24,000
(2)	Purchases..................	10,000		10,000	
	Accounts payable.........		10,000		10,000
(3)	Cash......................	24,000		24,200	
	Exchange gain or loss.....				200
	Accounts receivable.......		24,000		24,000
(4)	Accounts payable.............	10,000		10,000	
	Exchange gain or loss.........			100	
	Cash....................		10,000		10,100
(5)	Accounts receivable...........			8,070	
	Sales...................				8,070
	Due from exchange broker.....			8,070	
	Liability for currency sold.................				8,070
(6)	Liability for currency sold......			8,070	
	Cash......................			8,070	
	Due from exchange broker...............				8,070
	Accounts receivable.......				8,070

It should be observed that an exchange gain or loss exists only when the contract or billing price is expressed in terms of a foreign currency. The above exchange gains or losses clearly emerge as a consequence of the settlement transactions. Two alternatives are possible with respect to disclosing these gains and losses in the operating statement:

1. Offset the exchange gains and/or losses against the related Sales and Purchases accounts of the originating transactions. This method recognizes

the revenue or cost of foreign transactions as the consideration required to settle an indebtedness to a foreign enterprise at the *time of payment*.

2. Recognize the exchange gains and/or losses with separate disclosure as a "financial" item. The validity of this classification is best illustrated by reexamining the sale transaction which was accompanied by a concurrent transaction in exchange futures. By selling pesos for future delivery, the exporter was able to hedge against possible future reductions in the value of the peso. Had no such collateral transaction been effected, an exchange loss of $140 would have been sustained, as the exchange rate declined from $.0807 at the date of sale to $.0793 at the date of settlement. Conversely, an importer may *purchase* foreign exchange for future delivery, thereby obviating the possibility of loss should rates of exchange increase. If the billing is thus expressed in foreign currency units, and if it is assumed to accurately reflect a freely negotiated exchange price in equivalent dollars, based upon prevailing rates of exchange at the date of purchase or sale, the originating entry correctly measures the operating cost or revenue. Any resulting exchange gain or loss represents a financial decision to speculate in exchange rates, and accordingly should be disclosed in the operating statement as a financial item.[2]

In the event transactions in currency futures are not engaged in, the accountant must make additional elections in respect to transactions (for which settlement is to be made in foreign currency units) which are initiated before, and consummated after, the preparation of financial statements. In regard to these elections, one question is: Should the created receivable or payable be valued at the original exchange value or at its current exchange value? An assignment of current exchange value would follow from the adoption of a consistent "value" approach to the measurement of monetary items (which the authors believe to be preferable). In many respects, the problem is similar to the valuation of marketable securities. Correspondingly, the conventional treatment would seem to indicate the need for either a parenthetical disclosure or a "lower ('higher' for liabilities) of cost or market" analysis.

Translation of Account Balances

A recurring problem of accounting for foreign operations is the translation or restatement of account balances expressed in a foreign currency to monetary equivalents expressed in domestic currency. Obviously, this is an essential step if one is to prepare combined or consolidated financial statements for a domestic firm with one or more foreign branches or subsidiaries. *The primary objective of the translation process is to obtain valuations (in domestic terms) that are essentially consistent with domestic account-*

---

[2] A similar analysis was advanced in *Willard Helburn, Inc.* v. *Commissioner,* 214 F.2d 815 (C.A. 1st, 1954), wherein an exchange gain—which was largely due to a devaluation of the pound sterling between the purchase and settlement dates—was held to constitute taxable income.

ing principles which control the valuations of the specific accounts being translated. For example, if an account balance refers to fixed tangible assets, generally accepted accounting principles require that the account reflect the unexpired original cost of the asset. Therefore, the procedures for translation should accomplish the conversion of the cost balance expressed in foreign currency to a domestic monetary expression which also reflects unexpired original cost.

The critical choice in translating foreign account balances is selecting the exchange rate(s) to be employed in the calculations. Recognizing that foreign exchange rates vary over time, sometimes with large fluctuations, it is clear that many alternative exchange rates *could* be used in the translation process. Some of the possible rates are (1) the prevailing rate at the balance sheet date; (2) the average rate in existence during the reporting period; and (3) other historical rates effective at past points in time.

Historical Exchange Rates. Historical exchange rates are generally utilized in the monetary conversion process when accounting principles require that the account balance in question be stated in terms of unexpired original cost. The specific rate to be used is the rate that was in effect at the date of the investment. Regardless of how exchange rates may fluctuate after the date of investment, use of the historical rate (at the investment date) will accomplish the conversion of original cost stated in foreign currency to original cost stated in domestic currency. One must be circumspect in identifying the relevant investment date. In general, the date of the investment should be interpreted to mean the date on which the relevant assets were purchased. However, if a domestic company acquires a preexisting foreign enterprise already engaged in operations, the historical cost items previously purchased by the foreign operation should be translated using the exchange rate in effect when the domestic firm established control.

Case 1. Domestic Industries, Inc., acquired machinery for use in its manufacturing operation in England at a cost of £5,000 when the exchange rate was $2.40. Domestic purchased the £5,000 from its local bank for $12,000, then remitted the £5,000 to the machinery supplier. Accounting records are being maintained in England. Assuming a five-year life, no salvage value, and straight-line depreciation, the related account balances after three years would be translated as follows:

	Pounds	Historical Exchange Rate	Dollars
Machinery, at cost...............	5,000	$2.40	12,000
Accumulated depreciation........	3,000	2.40	7,200

The $12,000 original cost to Domestic is preserved in the accounts by continuing to use the $2.40 historical exchange rate, notwithstanding the possibility that the current exchange rate may have changed since the original investment.

Current Exchange Rates. The current exchange rate, i.e., the rate in effect at the balance sheet date, is generally used in the translation process when the weight of accounting principles suggests that the specific account balances in question should reflect *current monetary equivalents.* For example, cash balances in foreign currencies are only significant in terms of their current (and future) ability to satisfy obligations of the enterprise. The historical cost of establishing cash balances is not relevant to current financial position; accordingly, the historical exchange rate would be inappropriate. Since cash balances in foreign currencies represent the rights to a determinate number of foreign currency units, the current exchange rate will translate that data into domestic equivalents without altering the essential meaning of cash.

Average Exchange Rates. As a practical expedient and compromise, the average exchange rate during a reporting period is often applied to revenue and expense account balances since the transactions underlying these balances generally occur periodically throughout a reporting period. A rigid compliance with the basic translation objectives would call for translating each revenue and expense transaction at the rate in existence at the transaction date. However, averages are usually employed because the accounting system frequently does not accommodate such procedural refinements. Of course, some operating statement items, such as depreciation expense, represent historical cost allocations (not current transactions) and are, therefore, translated by using historical rates.

Foreign operations is one significant area of accounting in which many contemporary practices have developed without adequate support and guidance by the American Institute of Certified Public Accountants. The latest pronouncement of significance to the international operations area was published almost 20 years ago by the Committee on Accounting Procedures.[3] The authors of that pronouncement recommended, in essence, that current exchange rates be utilized to translate current assets and current liabilities and that historical exchange rates be used with respect to other balance sheet categories. Average exchange rates were recommended for converting income statement accounts which reflect current-period transactions.[4]

The research of more recent studies has generally recognized that the "current" and "noncurrent" balance sheet categories are not appropriate classifications for deciding whether current or historical exchange rates

---

[3] Committee on Accounting Procedure, American Institute of Certified Public Accountants, *Accounting Research Bulletin No. 43* (1953) in *Restatement and Revision of Accounting Research Bulletins,* Final Edition (New York, 1961), chap. xii. Slight modification of the "Foreign Operations and Foreign Exchange" chapter of this bulletin was made in 1965 by the Accounting Principles Board in its *Opinion No. 6.*

[4] *Ibid.,* pp. 113–15.

should be used.[5] A more reasonable basis is to classify balance sheet items as monetary or nonmonetary. Monetary items are rights to, or obligations for, a fixed or determinable number of currency units. In a balance sheet context, monetary items usually include cash, receivables (short and long term, which includes notes and bonds), and all liabilities other than those that are to be liquidated by expending nonmonetary resources. Since the economic significance of monetary items on financial position is current, realizable (or obligatory) value, the exchange rate that is currently effective at the balance sheet date would appear to be the appropriate basis for translating monetary items.

Nonmonetary balance sheet items are most often accounted for in terms of original cost accumulations and expirations. Contrary to the methods of accounting for monetary items, the valuations of these items do not purport to bear a close relationship to current monetary equivalents. As indicated in Case 1, historical exchange rates provide translations that maintain historical costs and are accordingly consistent with the generally accepted cost principle, which controls the valuation of most nonmonetary items.

An alternative argument can be advanced that all real account balances should be translated at the current exchange rate on the balance sheet date. A tenable position is that the equivalent domestic values of *all* foreign investments and obligations, whether monetary or nonmonetary, are directly related to the current exchange rate. This argument, however, enjoys little support at the present time.

It should be recognized that the previous discussion of the general methods of translating account balances does not provide a comprehensive elaboration of the many special problems that may arise in converting specific accounts which have rather unique characteristics. For example, special care should be taken in translating inventory values that are accounted for in terms of the "cost or market, whichever is lower" rule.

For purpose of the cost or market test, it seems preferable to determine cost as local [foreign] currency cost translated into dollars at rates prevailing at the dates of purchase or manufacture. For the same purpose, market is local [foreign] currency selling price less selling and other local [foreign] expenses, translated into dollars at the end-of-period rate of exchange.[6]

Foreign Currency Devaluations.   More often than not in recent years, the major changes in foreign exchange rates have come in the form of sudden governmental actions which restate the legal exchange rate to which the government commits its support. The preponderance of such actions in recent years has involved *devaluations* of a specific foreign currency. For

---

[5] See, for example, the National Association of Accountants' "Management Accounting Problems in Foreign Operations," *N.A.A. Research Report 36* (New York, 1960).

[6] *Ibid.*, p. 29.

example, the British government recently devalued the pound from $2.80 to $2.40. An act of devaluation raises a serious problem in the account translation process where historical exchange rates are employed. The immediate effect of a devaluation is to make the foreign currency, as well as the value of past investments in the foreign country, worth *less* in terms of the domestic currency. As a general rule, it would, therefore, seem appropriate to utilize postdevaluation exchange rates to translate all monetary and *nonmonetary* balance sheet items.[7] The exchange rate following a devaluation should be consistently applied thereafter to translate nonmonetary items which were purchased prior to the date of the devaluation. Note that this decision involves a significant modification of the previously discussed rule for converting nonmonetary items. Current revenue and expense items during the year of the devaluation should be translated by applying the exchange rate in effect at the date of the revenue and expense transactions.

Foreign Exchange Gains and Losses

The exchange gains and losses that result from credit transactions with foreign buyers or sellers were discussed earlier in this chapter. Unless such transactions are hedged with concurrent purchases or sales in the foreign currency futures market, gains or losses will arise as a result of variations in the exchange rate during the time interval between the transaction date and the date of settlement. Of course, the gain or loss only accrues to the party that accepts its receipt or is obliged to make payment in terms of another country's currency.

Exchange gains or losses also emerge in the process of translating the account balances of foreign branches and subsidiaries. To the extent that the current exchange rate on the balance sheet date is used in the translation process, rate changes from one date to the next will result in exchange adjustment gains or losses. If the current rate is applied to all monetary items, as recommended by the authors, the exchange adjustment gain or loss will represent ". . . the gains or losses caused by [the] changing dollar value of foreign assets and liabilities which represent contractual rights to cash, or to the receipt of cash, or contractual obligations for the disbursement of cash. Only if this is the case does the exchange adjustment have real significance in terms of managerial action and responsibility assignment."[8]

As previously stated, the exchange gains or losses arising from completed transactions with foreign buyers and sellers should be reported in the income statement which pertains to the period of their occurrence. However, accountants are not agreed as to the appropriate treatment of ex-

---

[7] This argument is consistent with the conclusions drawn by Professor Samuel R. Hepworth in *Reporting Foreign Operations* (Ann Arbor: Bureau of Business Research, University of Michigan, 1956), chap. v.

[8] *Ibid.,* p. 11.

change adjustment gains or losses arising from the translation of account balances. Some subscribe to the recognition of losses currently in the operating statement and to the deferral of gains in the balance sheet. Consistent with this position, if the exchange adjustment is a credit, the gain is deferred and may be described as a Reserve for Unrealized Profit in Foreign Exchange. Once created, this reserve is available thereafter to absorb exchange losses of subsequent periods. Exchange losses, i.e., debit exchange adjustments, which exceed the amount of accumulated reserve balances are reported as losses of the current period. This is the position taken—although it is not a compelling advocacy—in *Accounting Research Bulletin No. 43.*

Realized losses or gains on foreign exchange should be charged against or credited to operations. Provision should be made, ordinarily by a charge against operations, for declines in translation value of foreign net current and working assets (unrealized losses). Unrealized gains should preferably be carried to a suspense account, except to the extent that they offset prior provisions for unrealized losses, in which case they may be credited to the account previously charged.[9]

In addition to this view advocating a different treatment for gains and losses, a second argument is made that *both* gains and losses should be given recognition in the current period's operating statement. Finally there is also some support for deferring *both* gains and losses. The authors believe that the realization principle is adequately satisfied by the change in exchange rates, and consequently support the recognition of both gains and losses in the income statement of the current period.

Exchange adjustment gains and losses were previously defined in terms of foreign investments and obligations of a *monetary* nature; however, this definition is subject to an important exception. If, as recommended earlier, postdevaluation exchange rates are used to translate *all* asset and liability accounts following a devaluation of foreign currency, the calculation of the exchange adjustment gain or loss must include the reduction in domestic value of the *nonmonetary* items.

Foreign Branches

The following two sections of this chapter give special attention to the problems associated with accounting for foreign branches and foreign subsidiaries. In this discussion, it should be apparent that many of the accounting problems of foreign operations are common to both *branches*

---

[9] Committee on Accounting Procedure, *Accounting Research Bulletin No. 43,* p. 113. Note that the statement by the Committee on Accounting Procedure refers to the translation values of net current and working assets, which is contrary to the authors' position that exchange adjustment gains or losses should relate to all monetary items. However, this difference in measuring the *amount* of the exchange adjustment does not affect the additional question of how gains or losses should be reported.

and *subsidiaries*. Accordingly, the reader should remain alert to the frequent applicability of the discussion to either type of investment.

Accounting for foreign branches is not essentially unlike that for domestic branches; most of the new accounting problems introduced relate to the translation of foreign currencies to domestic monetary units. Necessarily, the accounts of foreign business subdivisions are expressed in units of the local currency and accordingly must be translated to equivalent domestic units before they are meaningful in the preparation of combined financial statements. Most of the procedures needed for this translation process have been described in the previous discussion. There remains only the special case of branch accounts that have reciprocal balances in home office accounts, and these are translated simply by restating them in domestic currency amounts equal to the balances in the contra home office accounts. This conversion accomplishes the same results that would be obtained if each transaction accumulated in the reciprocal accounts were translated using the historical exchange rate effective at the transaction date.

The journalizing of transactions for a domestic home office and a foreign branch involve few differences from those recorded in the case of a domestic branch. Transactions of the branch are, of course, recorded in foreign monetary units. Additionally, it may be desirable to maintain a separate record of currency movements between the home office and branch. Special "remittance" accounts, which facilitate this objective, are utilized to record the intracompany currency transfers of each period; at the end of the period, the remittance accounts are closed to the relevant Branch Current or Home Office Current accounts.

Consider the following transactions, which are journalized in Illustration 17–1:

(1)   A Houston home office opened a Mexico City branch, forwarding to it a draft for 24,000 pesos, purchased at $.080, to be used for working fund purposes.

(2)   Merchandise costing the home office $4,131 was shipped to the branch when the current rate of exchange was $.081.

(3)   The branch acquired from regional distributors additional merchandise on account for 18,000 pesos.

(4)   The branch purchased fixed assets locally for 90,000 pesos, giving a 60-day noninterest-bearing note in payment. The accounts in respect to these assets are customarily carried on the books of the branch. The rate of exchange at date of purchase was $.079.

(5)   Sales on account recorded by the branch were 62.500 pesos.

(6)   Collections on account amounted to 31,000 pesos.

(7)   Cash expenses paid by the branch were 7,600 pesos.

(8)   A remittance of 32,000 pesos was made by the branch to the home office; the rate of exchange was $.084.

(9)   Month-end adjustments were recorded by the branch for:

Illustration 17–1

HOUSTON HOME OFFICE BOOKS
(In Dollars)

(1) Remittance to branch............ 1,920
    Cash................................. 1,920

(2) Branch current.................... 4,131
    Shipments to branch............ 4,131

(8) Cash................................ 2,688
    Remittance from branch........ 2,688

MEXICO CITY BRANCH BOOKS
(In Pesos)

(1) Cash................................. 24,000
    Remittance from home office.... 24,000

(2) Shipments from home office..... 51,000
    Home office current............. 51,000

(3) Purchases......................... 18,000
    Accounts payable............... 18,000

(4) Fixed assets...................... 90,000
    Notes payable.................. 90,000

(5) Accounts receivable.............. 62,500
    Sales............................ 62,500

(6) Cash................................ 31,000
    Accounts receivable............ 31,000

(7) Expenses........................... 7,600
    Cash............................. 7,600

(8) Remittance to home office...... 32,000
    Cash............................. 32,000

(9) Depreciation expense............ 850
    Provision for doubtful accounts. 525
    Accumulated depreciation....... 850
    Allowance for doubtful accounts. 525

Depreciation.................................. 850 pesos
Provision for doubtful accounts................. 525 pesos

The final inventory of the branch consisted of 24,000 pesos of merchandise received on shipment from the home office; unsold merchandise purchased locally amounted to 5,475 pesos.

The average rate of exchange during the period was $.075, while the current rate of exchange at the end of the month was $.085.

The adjusted trial balance of the Mexico City branch at the end of the first month's operations is as follows:

	⸻(In Pesos)⸻	
Cash...	15,400	
Accounts receivable..........................	31,500	
Allowance for doubtful accounts..................		525
Fixed assets..................................	90,000	
Accumulated depreciation.......................		850
Accounts payable.............................		18,000
Notes payable................................		90,000
Remittance from home office...................		24,000
Remittance to home office......................	32,000	
Home office current...........................		51,000
Sales..		62,500
Shipments from home office....................	51,000	
Purchases....................................	18,000	
Expenses (cash)..............................	7,600	
Depreciation.................................	850	
Provision for doubtful accounts..................	525	
	246,875	246,875

The branch closing entries take the following form:

	⸻(In Pesos)⸻	
Inventory......................................	29,475	
Sales...	62,500	
Purchases.................................		18,000
Shipments from home office.................		51,000
Expenses..................................		7,600
Depreciation...............................		850
Bad debts.................................		525
Income summary...........................		14,000
Income summary...............................	14,000	
Home office current........................		14,000
Remittance from home office...................	24,000	
Home office current...........................	8,000	
Remittance to home office......................		32,000

At the end of each period, the branch will provide the home office with copies of its adjusted trial balance, closing entries, financial statements, and a summary of the transaction details of its Home Office Current account. These data, before they are useful to the home office, must be converted into domestic currency. The working paper in Illustration 17–2 provides a convenient vehicle for summarizing these data and translating

Illustration 17–2

MEXICO CITY BRANCH
Translation Working Paper
(Date)

	Adjusted Trial Balance (Pesos)	Exchange Rates Code	Exchange Rates Rate	Adjusted Trial Balance (Dollars)	Income Statement (Dollars)	Balance Sheet (Dollars)
Debits						
Cash.	15,400	C	.085	1,309.00		1,309.00
Accounts receivable.	31,500	C	.085	2,677.50		2,677.50
Fixed assets.	90,000	O	.079	7,110.00		7,110.00
Remittance to home office.	32,000	R		2,688.00		2,688.00
Shipments from home office.	51,000	R		4,131.00	4,131.00	
Purchases.	18,000	A	.075	1,350.00	1,350.00	
Expenses.	7,600	A	.075	570.00	570.00	
Depreciation.	850	O	.079	67.15	67.15	
Bad debts.	525	C	.085	44.63	44.63	
	246,875					
Inventory:						
From home office.	24,000	O	.081			1,944.00
From foreign suppliers.	5,475	A	.075			410.63
Exchange adjustment loss.				83.00	83.00	
Net income—branch.					796.35	
				20,030.28	7,042.13	16,139.13
					7,042.13	

Credits						
Allowance for doubtful accounts	525	C	.085	44.63		44.63
Accumulated depreciation	850	O	.079	67.15		67.15
Accounts payable	18,000	C	.085	1,530.00		1,530.00
Notes payable	90,000	C	.085	7,650.00		7,650.00
Remittance from home office	24,000	R		1,920.00		1,920.00
Home office current	51,000	R		4,131.00		4,131.00
Sales	62,500	A	.075	4,687.50	4,687.50	4,131.00
	246,875					
Inventory:						
From home office	24,000	O	.081		1,944.00	
From foreign suppliers	5,475	A	.075		410.63	
Net income—branch						796.35
				20,030.28	7,042.13	16,139.13

CODE:
C = current rate of exchange, end of month, $.085.
O = original rate of exchange, date of purchase.
R = balance of reciprocal account, home office books.
A = average rate of exchange for the month, $.075.

them into equivalent domestic monetary units. The combined statement working paper may be easily prepared beginning with the final columns of the translation working paper.

When the adjusted trial balance of a foreign branch is translated into equivalent domestic currency units, only infrequently are the sum of the debit and the sum of the credit account balances equal, as may be noted in the working paper in Illustration 17–2. The amount necessary to reconcile these sums is the *exchange adjustment gain or loss*. The gain or loss is stated in terms of domestic currency units and must be recorded by the home office in the closing entry sequence. Referring to the example, the entry to record this loss would be as follows.

Exchange adjustment loss	83.00	
Branch current		83.00

In subsequent accounting periods, double counting of the exchange adjustment loss is prevented by translating (in the working paper) the Home Office Current account into an amount in domestic currency equal to the new balance in Branch Current.

It should be noted that this process of translating the Home Office Current account precludes the possibility of observing equivalent (domestic) balances in the two reciprocal accounts as a test or confirmation that *all* reciprocal transactions have been recorded in both accounts. Such a test was suggested in Chapter 16 as a means of determining whether any reciprocal adjustments should be recorded on the books of a domestic branch and/or home office. Since the test cannot be applied to a foreign branch, the possible need for reconciling adjustments must be determined by a comparative audit of the entries recorded in each reciprocal account.

Foreign Subsidiaries

In the event that international operations take the form of an investment in foreign subsidiaries, the accounts of the foreign subsidiaries should be included in consolidated statements if the parent exercises sufficient control over the subsidiary. In determining the presence of effective parent control, the same criteria should apply for both foreign and domestic affiliates. Yet, the accountant should be especially alert to the limitations of consolidated financial statements which include foreign subsidiaries. "In view of the uncertain values and availability of the assets and net income of foreign subsidiaries subject to controls and exchange restrictions and the consequent unrealistic statements of income that may result from the translation of many foreign currencies into dollars, careful consideration should be given to the fundamental question of whether it is proper to consolidate the statements of foreign subsidiaries with the statements of United States companies."[10]

---

[10] *Ibid.,* p. 112. The reader should note that the problem of assessing the sufficiency of parental control over a foreign subsidiary may also be relevant to the preparation

The American Institute of Certified Public Accountants indicates that there are at least four methods of disclosing in financial statements information respecting foreign subsidiaries:

(a)   To exclude foreign subsidiaries from consolidation and to furnish (1) statements in which only domestic subsidiaries are consolidated and (2) as to foreign subsidiaries, a summary in suitable form of their assets and liabilities, their income and losses for the year, and the parent company's equity therein. The total amount of investments in foreign subsidiaries should be shown separately, and the basis on which the amount was arrived at should be stated. If these investments include any surplus [retained earnings] of foreign subsidiaries and such surplus had previously been included in consolidated surplus, the amount should be separately shown or earmarked in stating the consolidated surplus in the statements here suggested. The exclusion of foreign subsidiaries from consolidation does not make it acceptable practice to include intercompany profits which would be eliminated if such subsidiaries were consolidated.

(b)   To consolidate domestic and foreign subsidiaries and to furnish in addition the summary described in (a) (2) above.

(c)   To furnish (1) complete consolidated statements and also (2) consolidated statements for domestic companies only.

(d)   To consolidate domestic and foreign subsidiaries and to furnish in addition parent company statements showing the investment in and income from foreign subsidiaries separately from those of domestic subsidiaries.[11]

Although information on foreign subsidiaries may be presented in several ways, increasingly they are included in the consolidated statements. While careful consideration must be given to the limitations on parent control that may be imposed by foreign governments, through exchange restrictions and other means, "the burden of proof would seem to fall on those favoring exclusion of a foreign subsidiary's accounts from consolidation. . . ."[12]

Upon the acquisition of foreign shares, the parent company should record the investment at cost, expressed in domestic currency. If the parent elects to carry the investment thereafter on an equity basis, periodic adjustment is necessarily required to record the parent's equity in the postacquisition increases and decreases in the subsidiary's stockholders' equity—again expressed in domestic currency. A principal accounting problem in the preparation of consolidated statements involving foreign subsidiaries, as in the case of foreign branches, relates to the translation of foreign currency. Once the accounts of the foreign subsidiary are translated into their

---

of combined statements for a domestic home office and a foreign branch. It may occur that foreign governmental restrictions, or similar factors, so inhibit the home office's operational and financial control over a foreign branch that the preparation of combined financial statements should be avoided.

[11] *Ibid.,* pp. 112–13.

[12] Hepworth, *op. cit.,* p. 171.

domestic monetary equivalents, the procedural details for completing consolidated statement working papers merely duplicate those outlined earlier for corporate affiliations involving domestic subsidiaries. The bases for translating the accounts of a foreign subsidiary remain the same as for foreign branches. The only new elements relate to the capital accounts of the subsidiary. The subsidiary's capital stock is normally translated at the rate of exchange existing at the date of its acquisition. Contributed capital in excess of par value of capital stock is likewise translated at the rate of exchange at date of acquisition.[13] Finally, the retained earnings of the subsidiary at the beginning of the statement period is converted on the basis of the contra *dollar* balance at the end of the previous period, and any increment or decrement is calculated from the translated effects of the income statement and dividend declarations.

Exchange Gains and Losses.   Typically, the exchange adjustment that derives from translating a foreign subsidiary's accounts to domestic currency is treated (in consolidated working papers) as an adjustment to the reported subsidiary net income of the current period. As a consequence, it is carried forward in the working papers to subsidiary retained earnings. In subsequent periods, the translation of subsidiary retained earnings at the beginning of the period is effected by using the last end-of-period domestic amount; thus, the exchange adjustment gains or losses of prior periods are prevented from being double counted.

Transactions between a domestic parent and a foreign subsidiary should be recorded in the same manner as transactions between unrelated firms. Thus, exchange gains or losses may be realized as a result of exchange rate changes between the billing and payment dates. All foreign subsidiary account balances which represent transactions between consolidated affiliates should be translated into domestic amounts equivalent to the reciprocal account balances of the parent. Given this translation rule, the exchange gains or losses resulting from transactions between affiliates will not be recognized in the process of converting account balances; they will be booked only as a result of completed transactions. The possibility of double counting will thereby be avoided.

Additional Problem Areas

It should be clear that a listing of potential problem areas associated with accounting for international operations would be virtually limitless. Since accounting reports depend on a wide variety of social, economic,

---

[13] Following a devaluation, the parent *may* record a loss and correspondingly reduce its investment account; if so, the postdevaluation exchange rate should be used to translate the elements of contributed capital. If the parent does not record the loss, the exchange rate at the date of acquisition should be used. In the latter event, the loss associated with the devaluation will be disclosed entirely in the exchange adjustment gain or loss, which is calculated in the translation working paper. The reader will recall that following a devaluation, all monetary and nonmonetary assets and liabilities are translated by the use of the postdevaluation exchange rate.

legal, and even political relationships, the potential problem areas of international accounting may emerge from the differences between any of these relationships in the various countries. Previous discussion has already indicated instances in which the legal framework and institutions of each country, as well as the political relations between countries, can have a significant impact on the accounting procedures selected to characterize operations in foreign countries.

Perhaps the most important problem area the international accountant must face is the wide variation in countries' "generally accepted" accounting principles. For example, many countries accept periodic revaluation of properties—in either direction—as an appropriate accounting procedure. Similarly, depreciation policies may diverge from the typical methods followed in the United States to the extreme of allowing periodic depreciation to be arbitrarily determined by management. Still another variation relates to general price-level adjustments, which are not acceptable in many countries but are widely employed in others.

Because of the diversity in such problems, it is not practicable to examine here the special "corrections" that must be made in specific instances. Manifestly, the accountant is bound by the objective of reporting in comparable terms all of the data included in the financial statements. Additionally, he usually must select methods that are generally accepted in the country where the statements will be used. At the present time these objectives can be only partially attained.

QUESTIONS

1. What are some of the important factors that affect the accounting procedures for a company engaging in foreign operations?
2. Explain why the existence of several exchange rates is perhaps a more significant factor in translating account balances than it is in translating particular business transactions.
3. Distinguish between quoting an exchange rate for a given currency "directly" or "indirectly."
4. What is an "exchange gain or loss" and under what conditions does it exist?
5. In translating foreign account balances to their domestic currency equivalents, what catalog of exchange rates can be used? When would each be appropriate?
6. How does the classification of balance sheet items as "monetary" or "nonmonetary" affect the selection of an exchange rate?
7. Subsequent to a foreign currency devaluation, what exchange rates should be used for items on the balance sheet and income statement?
8. How is the exchange adjustment gain or loss recorded when accounting for foreign branches?
9. What limiting factors affect the decision as to whether or not a foreign subsidiary should be consolidated with a domestic parent?

PROBLEMS

Problem 17–1

John Weber is planning a trip through several foreign countries, during which he expects to purchase and inspect the products sold in each country that compete with those of his employer. In anticipation of the trip, Weber purchases $300 worth of each country's currency. He received the following amounts:

Country	Currency	Amount Received
Belgium	Franc	14,925
Denmark	Krone	2,256
France	Franc	1,667
Italy	Lira	187,500

Required:

State the exchange rate between U.S. dollars and each foreign currency purchased by Weber. Express each rate:

(i)   Directly.
(ii) Indirectly.

Problem 17–2

Prepare the journal entries to record the following transactions on the books of Schwab Corporation.

a) The Schwab Corporation purchased merchandise from the Z Company of France for 50,000 francs when the exchange rate for the franc was $.02. Concurrently, the Schwab Corporation purchased 25,000 francs for future delivery at $.02.

b) The Schwab Corporation paid the Z Company for transaction (a) when the exchange rate for the franc was $.018. The futures purchased in (a) were received from the exchange broker.

c) The Schwab Corporation sold merchandise to the D Company of West Germany for 10,000 Deutschemarks when the exchange rate for the Deutschemark was $.25. Concurrently, the Schwab Corporation sold 5,000 Deutschemarks for future delivery at $.25.

d) The Schwab Corporation received payment from the D Company for transaction (c) when the exchange rate for the Deutschemark was $.22. The futures sold in (c) were delivered to the exchange broker.

Problem 17–3

The X Corporation engaged in the following international transactions during December, 1971 (all purchase and sales invoices are expressed in foreign currency):

a) The X Corporation sold merchandise to the Y Company of Italy for 1,000,000 lire when the exchange rate for the lira was $.0016. Concurrently, the X Corporation sold 500,000 lire for future delivery at $.0016.

b)   The X Corporation received payment from the Y Company in respect
to transaction (a) when the exchange rate for the lira was $.0017. The
futures sold in (a) were delivered to the exchange broker.
c)   The X Corporation purchased merchandise from the A Company of
Great Britain for 1,000 pounds when the exchange rate for the pound
was $2.40. Concurrently, the X Corporation purchased 500 pounds for
future delivery at $2.40.
d)   The X Corporation paid the A Company for the merchandise purchased
in transaction (c) when the exchange rate for the pound was $2.45. The
futures purchased in (c) were received from the exchange broker.
e)   The X Corporation purchased merchandise from the B Company of
Mexico for 20,000 pesos when the exchange rate for the peso was $.08.
f)   The X Corporation sold merchandise to the C Company of Mexico for
10,000 pesos when the exchange rate for the peso was $.08.

Required:
(i)   Prepare the journal entries to record the above transactions on the books
of the X Corporation.
(ii)   If the debts created by the last two transactions remain unpaid on December 31, 1971, discuss their valuation if the exchange rate is (a)
$.10, or (b) $.06. Would your answer be different if the X Corporation
had purchased, or sold, foreign exchange (pesos) for future delivery?

Problem 17–4

Journalize the following transactions of the Black and White Company (a
New York corporation) arising from its foreign operations:

June 1   Purchased merchandise from an Edinburgh, Scotland, manufacturer
at an invoice cost of £1,000. On this date the exchange rate for
pounds was $2.40.
5   Purchased merchandise from a Glasgow, Scotland, manufacturer.
The billing is rendered for $2,000. The exchange rate for pounds
is $2.42.
7   Sold merchandise to a Toronto wholesaler. Billing price is $4,000
(Canadian dollars), and the exchange rate for Canadian dollars is
$1.02.
15   Paid £500 on account to the Edinburgh manufacturer. The exchange
rate is $2.35.
20   Paid the amount due the Glasgow manufacturer.
25   Returned merchandise to the Edinburgh manufacturer and received
credit for £100. The exchange rate is $2.35.
28   Received full payment on account from the Toronto wholesaler.
The exchange rate is $.98.
30   Remitted final payment to the Edinburgh manufacturer. The exchange rate is $2.36.

Problem 17–5

The following accounts are taken from the December 31, 1971, trial balance
of a foreign subsidiary. The parent company acquired a controlling interest in

the subsidiary on January 1, 1965. In order to prepare consolidated statements on December 31, 1971, the balances of these (and other) accounts expressed in foreign currency units must be converted to their domestic monetary equivalents.

Indicate the basis for converting each of the following accounts by placing the relevant letter of the *Table of Exchange Rates and Other Values* in the blank provided.

(1) Capital stock _____
(2) Dividends declared _____
(3) Depreciation expense _____
(4) Fixed assets (acquired 1/1/63) _____
(5) Contributed capital in excess of par _____
(6) Retained earnings _____
(7) Administrative salaries _____
(8) Accounts receivable _____
(9) Inventory (1/1/71) _____
(10) Advances from parent _____
(11) Fixed assets (acquired 1/1/69) _____
(12) Purchases _____
(13) 5% bonds payable (dated 1/1/69, maturity 1/1/89) _____
(14) Inventory (12/31/71) _____
(15) Sales _____
(16) Purchases returns _____
(17) Cash _____
(18) Accumulated depreciation _____
(19) Prepaid expenses _____
(20) Allowance for doubtful accounts _____

Table of Exchange Rates and Other Values

A Exchange rate, 12/31/71
B Exchange rate, 1/1/71
C Average exchange rate for the year 1971
D Exchange rate, 1/1/69
E Exchange rate, 1/1/65
F Exchange rate, 1/1/63
G Balance in "contra" account in the parent company's books
H Dollar balance on the 12/31/70 consolidated working paper
I Percentage basis of related account
J Calculated from related accounts

Problem 17–6

The Overseas Trading Company, a U.S. corporation with several foreign subsidiaries, appended the following footnote to its December 31, 1971, financial statements:

" 'Marketable securities' includes $15,100 of freely transferable import certificates issued by the government of a foreign country. The certificates entitle the bearer to import into the foreign country certain restricted luxury items (costing up to 40% of the invoice prices of the exports on which the certificates were issued) that cannot otherwise be imported. They were issued by the foreign government as an incentive to export goods from the foreign country and were valued at market on the dates received (current market, $15,250). Our foreign subsidiary received the certificates as a consequence of its sales transactions which were exports from the foreign country. The subsidiary does not import luxury items and expects to sell all certificates during the next operating period. The foreign government's policy is expected to continue indefinitely."

Required:

(i) Discuss the propriety of valuing the certificates at market on the dates they are received.

(ii) Discuss the propriety of treating the credit arising from the receipt of the certificates as—
  (*a*) A reduction of cost of goods sold.
  (*b*) An addition to stockholders' equity.
  (*c*) An addition to other or special income.
  (*d*) An addition to gross sales.

(AICPA adapted)

Problem 17–7

Trial balances as of December 31, 1972, of the Parent Company and its two subsidiaries were:

	Parent Company Dr.	Parent Company Cr.	Domestic Subsidiary Dr.	Domestic Subsidiary Cr.	Mexican Subsidiary (Pesos) Dr.	Mexican Subsidiary (Pesos) Cr.
Cash....................	$ 10,000		$ 1,500		10,000	
Accounts receivable—trade.	30,000		8,000		35,000	
Accounts receivable—merchandise in transit to domestic subsidiary....	4,000					
Inventories..............	20,000				83,000	
Investments at cost:						
Domestic subsidiary 900 shares acquired 12/31/71.............	9,000					
Foreign subsidiary 1,000 shares acquired 12/31/71.............	12,000					
Fixed assets.............	45,000		3,500		175,000	
Goodwill...............			2,000			
Cost of sales............	300,000		15,000		300,000	
Depreciation............	3,000		200		7,000	
Taxes..................	15,000		400		15,000	
Selling expenses..........	42,000		2,400		27,000	
Administrative and general expenses.............	35,000		2,000		18,000	
Dividends declared.......			1,000			
Sales—trade.............		$400,000		$21,000		381,000
Sales—domestic subsidiary.		10,000				
Accounts payable—trade..		25,000				
Dividend payable........				1,000		
Long-term debt, due 1/1/75.						100,000
Accumulated depreciation..		15,000		2,000		75,000
Capital stock............		50,000		*10,000		*100,000
Retained earnings, 1/1/72..		25,000		2,000		7,000
	$525,000	$525,000	$36,000	$36,000	670,000	670,000

* 1,000 shares issued and outstanding.

In April, 1972, the Mexican peso was devalued from U.S. $.12, the prevailing rate of exchange on December 31, 1971, to $.08, which was also the prevailing rate of exchange on December 31, 1972. The Parent Company did not change the valuation of its investment in the Mexican Subsidiary following the devaluation. On the consolidation working papers for December 31, 1971, the retained earnings balance of the Mexican Subsidiary at the end of the year was calculated to be U.S. $840.

Required:

(i)   Prepare working trial balance in U.S. dollars for the Mexican subsidiary.
(ii) Prepare working papers for consolidated statements.

(AICPA adapted)

Problem 17–8

The adjusted trial balances of the Dallas Company and its Holland branch on December 31, 1971, were:

	Dollars		Guilders	
Cash.	$ 27,800		18,300	
Accounts receivable.	32,000		30,000	
Allowance for doubtful accounts.		$ 400		300
Merchandise inventory (1/1).	24,000		9,000	
Plant and equipment.	140,000		68,000	
Accumulated depreciation.		25,000		12,000
Accounts payable.		20,000		7,000
Remittance to home office.			20,000	
Remittance from branch.		4,200		
Shipments from home office.			42,000	
Shipments to branch.		7,000		
Branch current.	21,560			
Home office current.				108,000
Sales.		100,000		78,000
Purchases.	76,360		10,000	
Expenses.	12,000		8,000	
Capital stock.		150,000		
Retained earnings.		27,120		
	$333,720	$333,720	205,300	205,300
Merchandise inventory (12/31).	$ 18,000		12,000	

The plant and equipment carried on the books of the branch were acquired in foreign markets in 1963 when the exchange rate was $.26.

The Holland branch inventory on January 1 included 7,000 guilders of merchandise received from the home office, which cost the latter $1,470; the remainder was acquired from local suppliers in Holland.

The December 31 branch inventory consisted of 7,500 guilders of merchandise acquired by current shipment from the home office; all other merchandise was purchased locally. Annual adjustments for depreciation (5 percent annual rate) and doubtful accounts (1 percent of receivable balance) have been made.

Exchange rates:

January 1, 1971.	$.23
December 31, 1971.	.20
Average for 1971.	.24

Required:

(i) Prepare a working paper to convert the branch trial balance to dollars, indicating operating statement and balance sheet extensions.

(ii) Journalize closing entries for the home office.

Problem 17–9

The following are the account balances and the amounts at which they were converted into dollars by the home office as of January 1, 1971:

JOHNSON COMPANY

MANCHESTER BRANCH

	Sterling	Sterling	Dollars	Dollars
Cash.	£3,300		$13,530	
Accounts receivable.	2,000		8,200	
Allowance for bad debts.		£ 50		$ 205
Inventory.	2,500		10,250	
Fixed assets.	1,000		4,200	
Accumulated depreciation.		100		420
Accounts payable.		1,300		6,530
Current account.		7,350		29,025
	£8,800	£8,800	$36,180	$36,180

The following transactions were completed by the branch during 1971.

a) Home office shipped merchandise costing $48,600 to branch, exchange rate being $4.05.

b) For use at branch, home office shipped equipment costing $8,120; exchange rate, $4.06.

c) Sales made by branch on account £6,000.

d) Remittance by branch to home office, £3,000 draft, sold in New York at $4.08.

e) Purchases by branch, £3,500, on account.

f) Collections by branch on account, £5,200.

g) Branch paid expenses, £1,100.

h) Payments of account payable by branch, £1,300.

i) Cash sales, £3,200.

j) Remittance by branch, £1,000; sold in New York for $4,120.

k) Adjustments for the period ended December 31, 1971, were as follows:

Estimated depreciation, £300; estimated bad debts, £60; accounts receivable written off as uncollectible, £48; final inventory of merchandise, £12,000, which is made up partially of current purchases by the branch and partially of shipments from the home office. Analysis of the final inventory discloses that a translation on the basis of historical exchange rates results in a U.S. equivalent of $49,000; the current rate of exchange at the end of the period, $4.10; the average rate of exchange was computed to be $4.09.

Required:

(i) Journal entries on the books of the home office and of the branch to record these transactions.

(ii) Branch working paper in dollars.

(iii) Closing entries on the branch books.

(iv)   Entries on the home office books to take up branch profit and record the exchange adjustment (assume exchange adjustment losses are currently recognized, and profits deferred).

Problem 17–10

a)   The Wagner Manufacturing Corporation during the current year opened a manufacturing and selling branch in X country. At the year-end the official rate of currency exchange with country X was 12 to $1 and the unofficial free market rate was 15 to $1. In combining the statements of the branch with those of the parent at year-end, at what value would the following branch accounts be reflected in the combined balance sheet?
  (1)   Accounts receivable.
  (2)   Fixed assets.
  (3)   Inventories.
  (4)   Short-term debt.
  (5)   Long-term debt.
b)   How is the gain or loss resulting from the translation of the foreign currency into U.S. currency reflected in the balance sheet of Wagner Corporation at year-end?
c)   On June 30, 1971, Wagner sold merchandise costing $75,000 to Jones located in Y country, taking a note payable in Y currency, which at the official rate of exchange on the date of sale had a fair market value of $100,000. On December 31, 1971, the note was worth $75,000 due to a change in the rate of exchange. On March 15, 1972, the note was paid in full; and when immediately converted to U.S. dollars, Wagner received $125,000. What journal entries are required at June 30, 1971, December 31, 1971, and March 15, 1972? *Explain.*

(AICPA adapted)

Problem 17–11

Copra Trading Company established a foreign branch office on Arpoc Cay in 1964 to purchase local products for resale by the home office and to sell company products.

You were engaged to examine the company's financial statements for the year ended December 31, 1971, and engaged a chartered professional accountant in Arpoc to examine the branch office accounts. He reported that the branch accounts were fairly stated in pesos, the local currency, except a franchise fee and any possible adjustments required by home office accounting procedures were not recorded.

Your examination disclosed the following information:

a)   The peso was devalued July 1, 1967, from four pesos per $1 to eight pesos per $1. The former rate of exchange had been in effect since 1959. On January 1, 1971, the exchange rate was eight pesos per $1. During 1971, the exchange rate gradually changed until on December 31, it was 10 pesos per $1.
b)   A billing of $4,000 was included in the Branch Current account covering a shipment of merchandise made on December 29, 1971, which was not

received or recorded by the branch in 1971. Sales to the branch are marked up 33⅓ percent on cost and shipped F.O.B. home office. Branch sales to home office are made at branch cost.

c) The branch had a beginning and ending inventory on hand valued at 80,000 pesos of which one half at each date had been purchased from the home office. The home office had an inventory at December 31, 1971, valued at $520,000. Appropriate rates for translating inventories are .125 for the beginning inventory and .1125 for the ending inventory.

d) The Investment in Branch is the unamortized portion of a $7,500 fee paid in January, 1970, to a U.S. firm for marketing research for the Branch. Currency restrictions prevented the branch from paying the fee, which was paid by the home office. The home office agreed to take merchandise in repayment over a five-year period during which the fee is to be amortized.

COPRA TRADING COMPANY AND BRANCH OFFICE
Trial Balances
At December 31, 1971

Debits	Branch Office Trial Balance (in Pesos)	Home Office Trial Balance (in Dollars)
Cash....................................	210,000	$ 90,000
Trade accounts receivable...................	240,000	160,000
Branch current account....................		20,250
Inventory...............................	80,000*	510,000*
Prepaid expenses.........................	10,000	24,000
Fixed assets.............................	800,000	750,000
Investment in branch......................		6,000
Purchases...............................	1,180,000	3,010,000
Purchases from branch.....................		140,000
Operating and general expenses.............	190,000	680,000
Depreciation expense......................	100,000	50,000
Total debits......................	2,810,000	$5,440,250

Credits		
Allowance for depreciation...................	650,000	350,000
Current liabilities........................	220,000	240,000
Home office current account................	130,000	
Long-term indebtedness....................	130,000	200,000
Capital stock.............................		300,000
Retained earnings.........................		155,250
Sales....................................	1,680,000	4,115,000
Sales to Branch..........................		80,000
Total credits......................	2,810,000	$5,440,250

* At January 1, 1971.

e) The branch incurred its long-term indebtedness in 1966 to finance its most recent purchase of fixed assets.

f) The government of Arpoc imposes a franchise fee of 10 pesos per 100 pesos of net income of the branch in exchange for certain exclusive trading rights granted. The fee is payable each May 1 for the preceding calendar year's trading rights and had not been recorded by the Branch at December 31.

Required:

Prepare a working paper to present the combined income statement and combined balance sheet of Copra Trading Company and its foreign branch office with all amounts stated in U.S. dollars.

(AICPA adapted)

UNIT V | FIDUCIARY ACCOUNTING

Chapter 18

Corporate Liquidation and Reorganization

Accounting problems relating to the expansion of corporate business through mergers and acquisitions were considered in Unit III. Based on an assumption of continuity with respect to the operations of a corporate affiliation, Unit IV comprised an extended analysis of consolidated statements. A set of circumstances may exist, however, which calls for a contraction in the scale of business activity, or disinvestment. Financial distress, which is a significant factor in corporate disinvestment, may result from managerial miscalculation, operation malfunction, unfavorable economic influences, competitive market encroachments, and for numerous other reasons. Consequently, it may be useful at this time to examine some of the accounting problems which relate to corporate liquidation and reorganization.

LIQUIDATION

A corporation's existence may be terminated either by *voluntary* or *involuntary* petition. Voluntary dissolution may be initiated by the incorporators in the event that the corporation has not commenced business or issued shares of stock; subsequently, a corporation may be voluntarily dissolved with consent of the shareholders. Involuntary dissolution may be initiated by the corporate shareholders (or directors), by the state, or by creditors.

In respect to action taken by the state, the Business Corporation Act of Texas, for example, provides that a corporation may be involuntarily dissolved as a consequence of any of the following:

(1) The corporation or its incorporators have failed to comply with a condition precedent to incorporation; or

(2) The original articles of incorporation or any amendments thereof were procured through fraud; or

(3) The corporation has continued to transact business beyond the scope of the purpose or purposes of the corporation as expressed in its articles of incorporation; or

(4) A misrepresentation has been made of any material matter in any application, report, affidavit, or other document submitted by such corporation pursuant to this Act.

(5)   The corporation has failed to file any report within the time required by law, or has failed to pay any fees, franchise taxes or penalties prescribed by law when the same have become due and payable; or

(6)   The corporation has failed to maintain a registered agent in this state as required by law [Texas Business Corporation Act, Art. 701].

In regard to involuntary dissolution initiated by creditors, the National Bankruptcy Act provides that three or more persons who have provable claims fixed as to liability and liquidated (certain) as to amount, aggregating in total $500 or more, may file a petition in bankruptcy against any qualified debtor, or if the total number of creditors is less than 12, then one such creditor, whose claim is $500 or more, may file [Section 59(b)].

A debtor's financial distress may be produced by, or result in, a condition of *insolvency*. It is important to distinguish between insolvency in the equity sense and its bankruptcy meaning. *Equity insolvency* exists when a debtor is unable to pay his debts as they mature. *Bankruptcy insolvency* is interpreted by the National Bankruptcy Act as a condition where the aggregate of a debtor's property at fair valuation is less than the amount of his existing liabilities [Section 1(19)]. It is apparent that insolvency in the bankruptcy sense may exist without a condition of equity insolvency, e.g., where there has been a value shrinkage in noncurrent assets without a parallel reduction in the amount of long-term debt. It is perhaps more usual to find the converse—an insolvent debtor in the equity sense who is solvent by the bankruptcy definition.

Early in the history of the United States, the Congress was given constitutional authority to enact uniform bankruptcy laws. The first act was passed in 1800. Other laws were enacted in 1841 and 1867, after the repeal of predecessor statutes. The fourth and final National Bankruptcy Act was passed in 1898. Although the 1898 Act has been frequently amended, it remains currently effective in all states. Perhaps the most significant amendment thereto was the Chandler Act of 1938 which revised and enlarged many provisions of the 1898 statute. The amended federal law currently contains 15 chapters, 7 relating to bankruptcy, 6 pertaining to debtor relief, and 2 which refer to Maritime Commission liens and railroad adjustments.[1]

It is important that state *insolvency* legislation and jurisdiction be clearly distinguished from federal *bankruptcy* legislation and jurisdiction. Insolvency laws are the enactments of the several states relating to the equitable distribution of the resources of a distressed debtor, while the National Bankruptcy Act is the controlling federal statute in such proceedings. The federal law is accorded superior constitutional status, and the

---

[1] Hereafter, provisions of the National Bankruptcy Act will be cited by section number, enclosed in brackets, following the relevant provisions. The cited sections of the Act may be found under Title 11 of the United States Code Annotated by observing the cross referencing table provided in the U.S.C.A. The reader is referred to the U.S.C.A. for complete statements of the cited sections as well as related interpretations by the courts.

insolvency laws of the several states must necessarily be consistent therewith. The state statutes remain operative to the extent they do not controvert the federal Act.

Bankruptcy (National Bankruptcy Act)

A business enterprise confronted with financial failure may undertake reorganization or dissolution voluntarily or involuntarily under the aegis of federal or state law. However, an insolvent debtor's action taken under state laws resulting in voluntary or involuntary receivership automatically constitutes an "act of bankruptcy," thereby providing the basis for legal action under the National Bankruptcy Act.

It is the purpose of the National Bankruptcy Act to provide for an orderly and equitable distribution of a bankrupt debtor's property among his creditors; once the bankruptcy proceedings are terminated, the debtor is discharged of most of his unpaid debts (some are not dischargeable), after which he may initiate steps for financial rehabilitation and renew business operations.

Who May Become a Bankrupt.   Any person, except a municipal, railroad, insurance, or banking corporation or a building and loan association, is entitled to the benefits of the Act as a voluntary bankrupt.

Any natural person, except a wage earner or farmer, and any moneyed, business, or commercial corporation, except a building and loan association, a municipal, railroad, insurance, or banking corporation, owing debts in the amount of $1,000 or over, may be adjudged an involuntary bankrupt upon default or an impartial trial and shall be subject to the provisions and entitled to the benefits of the Act. The status of an alleged bankrupt as a wage earner or farmer shall be determined as of the time of the commission of the act of bankruptcy [Section 4].

Acts of Bankruptcy.   Before creditors can proceed to have a debtor adjudged bankrupt, the debtor must have committed an act of bankruptcy. A debtor has committed an act of bankruptcy if he has:

(1)   concealed, removed, or permitted to be concealed or removed any parts of his property, with intent to hinder, delay, or defraud his creditors or any of them; or

(2)   transferred, while insolvent, any portion of his property to one or more of his creditors with intent to prefer such creditors over his other creditors; or

(3)   suffered or permitted, while insolvent, any creditor to obtain a lien upon any of his property through legal proceedings and not having vacated or discharged such lien within thirty days from the date thereof or at least five days before the date set for any sale or other disposition of such property; or

(4)   made a general assignment for the benefit of his creditors; or

(5)   while insolvent or unable to pay his debts as they mature, procured, permitted, or suffered voluntarily or involuntarily the appointment of a receiver or trustee to take charge of his property; or

(6)   admitted in writing his inability to pay his debts and his willingness to be adjudged a bankrupt [Section 3].

Courts of Bankruptcy.   The District Courts of the United States are bankruptcy courts having exclusive original jurisdiction over bankruptcy matters. These courts conduct equity proceedings and may be referred to as courts of equity. Court officials include the District Judge, an appointed referee, and often a designated trustee (or trustees). A referee is appointed by the judge of the bankruptcy court for a six-year term and is normally authorized to conduct all necessary bankruptcy proceedings. The actions of the referee remain subject to review by the judge, and the referee must render reports periodically to the court in respect to his findings of fact and conclusions of law.

The National Bankruptcy Act also creates the office of trustee. At the first meeting of the creditors of the bankrupt, a trustee is appointed. If the creditors fail to select a trustee, the court will make the appointment. Among other duties, trustees will:

(1)   collect and reduce to money the property of the bankrupt estates, under the direction of the court, and close up the estates as expeditiously as is compatible with the best interests of the parties in interest;

(2)   deposit all money received by them in designated depositories;

(3)   account for and pay over to the estates under their control all interest received by them upon funds belonging to such estates;

(4)   keep records and accounts showing all amounts and items of property received and from what sources, all amounts expended and for what purposes, and all items of property disposed of;

(5)   examine all proofs of claims and object to the allowance of such claims as may be improper;

(6)   furnish such information concerning the estates of which they are trustees and their administration as may be requested by parties in interest;

(7)   report to the courts in writing the condition of the estates, the amounts of money on hand, and such other details as may be required by the courts, within the first month after their appointment and every two months thereafter, unless otherwise ordered by the court;

(8)   make final reports and file final accounts with the courts fifteen days before the days fixed for the final meetings of the creditors; and

(9)   lay before the final meetings of the creditors detailed statements of the administration of the estates [Section 47(a)].

When a petition in bankruptcy has been filed in a court of equity, a receiver often is selected to take possession of the debtor's property. His role is essentially that of a custodian. He serves until such time as the petition is either dismissed or a trustee is appointed and qualified. In some instances, the receiver may be continued as trustee.

Liquidation Sequence.   Once a distressed debtor has been judicially determined a bankrupt, the progress of dissolution consists of four additional steps: (1) marshaling and protection of the debtor's property, (2) conversion of the noncash assets, (3) equitable distribution of the proceeds from conversion to those creditors having provable claims and in the order of their priority, and (4) formal discharge of the bankrupt debtor.

The trustee or receiver accepts custodial responsibility for the debtor's property for the purpose of preserving and protecting the interests of the several creditors. Legal title to the property vests in the trustee when it is surrendered to his custody. Upon being adjudged a bankrupt, the debtor has the duty to prepare a schedule showing the amount and kind of his property, the location thereof and its money value, and a list of all his creditors, including all persons asserting contingent, unliquidated, or disputed claims, showing their residence, if known, and the amount due to or claimed by each of them [Section 7(a)].

A creditor having a claim against a bankrupt estate must present a *proof of claim* within six months after the first creditors' meeting. A proof of claim consists of a statement under oath, in writing and signed by a creditor, setting forth the following: the claim; the consideration therefor; whether any, and if so, what securities are held therefor; whether any, and if so, what payments have been made thereon; and that the claim is justly owing from the bankrupt to the creditor [Section 57(a)].

Liabilities Proved and Allowed. Debts of the bankrupt which may be proved and allowed against his estate include, among others, those which are founded upon:

(1) a fixed liability, as evidenced by a judgment, or an instrument in writing, absolutely owing at the time of the filing of the petition, whether then payable or not;

(2) an open account, or a contract express or implied;

(3) provable debts reduced to judgments after the filing of the petition and before the consideration of the bankrupt's application for discharge;

(4) the right to recover damages in any action for negligence instituted prior to and pending at the time of the filing of the petition in bankruptcy; and

(5) claims for anticipatory breach of contracts, executory in whole or in part, including unexpired leases of real or personal property [Section 63(a)].

Liabilities Having Priority. Certain classes of a distressed debtor's obligations must be fully satisfied before settlement is made with other creditors. A priority status attaches to the following debts, and distribution is made in the indicated order:

(1) the actual and necessary costs and expenses of preserving the estate of the bankrupt subsequent to filing the petition, and the filing fees paid by creditors in involuntary cases;

(2) wages, not to exceed $600 to each claimant, which have been earned within three months before the date of the commencement of the proceeding, due to workmen, servants, clerks, or traveling or city salesmen on salary or commission basis, whole or part time, whether or not selling exclusively for the bankrupt;

(3)   taxes legally due and owing by the bankrupt to the United States or any State or any subdivision thereof; and

(4)   debts owing to any person, including the United States, who by the laws of the United States is entitled to priority, and rent owing to a landlord who is entitled to priority by applicable state law, *provided,* however, that such priority for rent to a landlord shall be restricted to the rent which is legally due and owing for the actual use and occupancy of the premises affected, and which accrued within three months before the date of bankruptcy [Section 64(a)].

Setoff or Counterclaim.   In all cases of mutual debts or mutual credits between the estate of a bankrupt and a creditor, one debt is set off against the other, and only the balance is allowed or paid [Section 68].

Discharge of Debtor.   Following the conversion of a debtor's assets and an equitable distribution of the proceeds among his several creditors, the debtor is released from all of his debts provable in bankruptcy. A discharge in bankruptcy provides an effective release in respect to these debts, *except* such as:

(1)   are due as a tax levied by the United States, or any State, county, district, or municipality;

(2)   are liabilities for obtaining money or property by false pretenses or false representations, or for willful and malicious injuries to the person or property of another;

(3)   have not been duly scheduled in time for proof and allowance;

(4)   are for wages which have been earned within three months before the commencement of the proceedings in bankruptcy due to workmen, servants, clerks, or traveling or city salesmen, on salary or commission basis, whole or part time, whether or not selling exclusively for the bankrupt; or

(5)   are due for moneys of an employee received or retained by his employer to secure the faithful performance by such employee of the terms of a contract of employment [Section 17].

Assignment for Benefit of Creditors

Liquidation proceedings normally are carried out through formal bankruptcy *or* an informal assignment for the benefit of creditors. The latter proceeding is merely an arrangement whereby the corporate property is transferred to designated assignees (the assignees frequently are also creditors). The assignee compares to a trustee in bankruptcy proceedings. He takes possession of the debtor's assets, converts the noncash assets, makes distributions to creditors with due regard to the priority of their claims, and renders a final accounting upon a closing of the estate. Assignment may be preferred to bankruptcy proceedings in that the debtor has the authority to designate the liquidator (assignee), often enjoys reduced legal expenses, and has fewer constraints as to time in respect to conversion and ultimate distribution. Unlike bankruptcy proceedings, there is no formal discharge of the distressed debtor in an assignment for the benefit of creditors.

Many states have enacted statutes which provide for assignments. An assignment for the benefit of creditors constitutes an act of bankruptcy, however, and the assignee is compelled to surrender custody of the debtor's property should a petition in bankruptcy be filed.

The Statement of Affairs

Previous reference has been made to the importance of filing schedules of assets, liabilities, and exempt property by the bankrupt. Failure to file such reports may result in the debtor's loss of discharge or his suffering of other penalties. Among the reports of special importance is the *statement of affairs*, which must be filed five days prior to the first meeting of the creditors [Section 7(a)(9)]. This statement, which details the realization proceeds expected from the conversion of the debtor's assets juxtaposed against the claims of secured and unsecured creditors, may be especially useful in aiding the debtor in determining the extent of his financial deficiency.

The statement of affairs exhibits some of the properties of the familiar corporate balance sheet; yet, there are significant differences. Most importantly, the underlying assumption of business continuity is rejected in favor of a liquidation emphasis; manifestly, this has implications for the valuation of corporate assets. In general, expected realizable values are substituted for unamortized costs. In order to assign these values to individual assets, however, the "liquidation concept" must be more definitively formulated. For example, anticipated liquidation within 30 days often produces a different estimate of realizable value than a liquidation period of six months. Thus, if the ultimate liquidation period is indefinite, adequate disclosure may be better served by preparing more than one statement under different time assumptions. The classificational format of the balance sheet is essentially an ordered enumeration of assets in relative liquidity sequence, with liabilities grouped in two broad time-oriented classes. In the statement of affairs, however, the assets are classified according to their availability to creditors, viz., those pledged with fully secured creditors, those pledged with partially secured creditors, and those which are free or unencumbered. Similarly, liabilities are classed in terms of their legal preferences, viz., priority claims, obligations which are fully secured, obligations which are partially secured, and unsecured claims. It is evident that the statement of affairs is primarily oriented toward the legal status of claims against the enterprise rather than the cost of future service potentials. As an obvious corollary of this new emphasis, stockholders' equity accounts lose their significance in the statement of affairs. In fact, they are only included in a supporting statement, primarily as an explanation of the current insolvency condition.

Illustrative Problem. Preliminary to the preparation of a statement of affairs, a conventional balance sheet should be prepared, supported by additional supplementary data, including estimates of realization proceeds from noncash assets. Other relevant information should also be accumulated in respect to pledged assets and liabilities which are expected to emerge during the course of the liquidation proceedings.

The balance sheet of the Roman Company on March 31, 1971, is as follows:

THE ROMAN COMPANY

Balance Sheet

March 31, 1971

ASSETS

Cash...	$ 1,850
Accounts receivable......................................	21,200
Notes receivable...	15,000
Merchandise..	41,000
Arco common stock (60 shares at cost).................	5,800
Land..	6,500
Building (net of depreciation)...........................	92,000
Machinery and equipment (net of depreciation)..........	43,000
	$226,350

EQUITIES

Bank loan—First State Bank............................	$ 10,000
Notes payable..	70,000
Accounts payable..	90,625
Accrued wages...	3,775
Accrued interest:	
Bank loan...	375
Notes payable.......................................	600
Retained earnings [deficit]...............................	[99,025]
Capital stock...	150,000
	$226,350

Based upon an estimated interval of time for liquidation, the land is appraised at $7,800 and the building is estimated to have a current market value of $85,000. The machinery and equipment are valueless except as salvage, $8,000. Merchandise has a current salable value of $20,000. On March 31, the Arco common stock is quoted on the security exchange at 110. Receivables are estimated to be collectible according to the following schedule:

Notes receivable....................	100 percent
Accounts receivable:	
$10,000.........................	100 percent
10,000.........................	70 percent
1,200.........................	Uncollectible

The First State Bank loan is secured by the Arco common stock, and the notes payable are secured by a first mortgage on the land and building.

The statement of affairs of the Roman Company is shown in Illustration 18–1.

A *deficiency account* (Illustration 18–2) frequently is appended to the statement of affairs and provides supporting detail in respect to estimated gains and losses on realization, the algebraic sum of which, when added to

Illustration 18–1

THE ROMAN COMPANY
Statement of Affairs
March 31, 1971

Assets

Book Value			Realizable Value
	Assets pledged with fully secured creditors:		
$ 6,500	Land		$ 7,800
92,000	Building		85,000
			$92,800
	Notes payable	$70,000	
	Accrued interest	600	70,600
			$22,200
	Assets pledged with partially secured creditors:		
5,800	Arco common stock		$ 6,600
	Bank loan—First State Bank	$10,000	
	Accrued interest	375	10,375
	Free assets:		
1,850	Cash		1,850
15,000	Notes receivable		15,000
21,200	Accounts receivable		17,000
41,000	Merchandise		20,000
43,000	Machinery and equipment		8,000
	Realizable value of uncommitted assets		$84,050
	Liabilities having priority		3,775
	Net free assets		$80,275
	Estimated deficiency to unsecured creditors		14,125
$226,350			$94,400

Liabilities and Stockholders' Equity

Book Value			Unsecured
	Liabilities having priority:		
$ 3,775	Accrued wages		$ 3,775
	Fully secured creditors:		
70,000	Notes payable	$70,000	
600	Accrued interest	600	
	Partially secured creditors:		
	Bank loan—First State Bank:		
10,000	Principal	$10,000	
375	Accrued interest	375	
		$10,375	
	Arco common stock	6,600	$ 3,775
	Unsecured creditors:		
90,625	Accounts payable		90,625
	Stockholders' equity:		
150,000	Capital stock		
[99,025]	Retained earnings [deficit]		
$226,350			$94,400

the total stockholders' equity reflected in the balance sheet, explains the impairment of capital—the estimated deficiency to unsecured creditors.

Illustration 18–2

THE ROMAN COMPANY

Deficiency Account

March 31, 1971

Estimated losses:	Estimated gains:	
Accounts receivable........... $ 4,200	Land...................... $ 1,300
Merchandise................. 21,000	Arco common stock......... 800
Machinery and equipment..... 35,000	Capital stock................ 150,000
Building.................... 7,000	Retained earnings [deficit]...... [99,025]
	Estimated deficiency to un-	
	secured creditors.......... 14,125
$67,200	$ 67,200

Statement Annotations

Assets Pledged with Fully Secured Creditors. In this category are listed those assets having a fair valuation equal to, or in excess of, the debts for which they have been pledged as collateral.

Assets Pledged with Partially Secured Creditors. Under this heading are listed those assets having a fair valuation less than the amount of the debts for which they have been pledged to secure.

Free (or Uncommitted) Assets. These assets are unencumbered and are not otherwise identified with a specific liability. This includes that portion of assets pledged with fully secured creditors in excess of the amount of the related liability.

Liabilities Having Priority. These are debts which, by statute— Section 64(a)—must be liquidated before uncommitted assets are available for the payment of unsecured debts.

Fully Secured Liabilities. These are liabilities which are protected by the pledge of specific assets which are expected to realize at least as much as the amount of the related obligations.

Partially Secured Liabilities. These liabilities represent obligations of the debtor for which specific assets have been pledged, the estimated value of which is less than the related obligation. The amount of these liabilities not covered by secured assets reverts to the status of unsecured claims.

Unsecured Liabilities. These debts have no designated legal priority, and no specific property is available as collateral to insure their payment.

Stockholders' Equity. The balances of capital stock and retained earnings are entered only in the "book value" column in the statement of affairs. However, they are included in the deficiency account, indicating thereby the extent to which estimated gains and losses on realization can be absorbed by the existing stockholders' equity.

Special Problems

Reserves. Accountants are encouraged to limit use of the word "reserve" and to adopt more descriptive and more meaningful terminology. Notwithstanding the fact of poor terminological identification, these items must nonetheless be properly classified in the statement of affairs. When the term is used to describe a valuation account, the balance should be deducted from the related asset, with the "net" value of the asset extended to the book value column in the statement of affairs. In the case of liability "reserves," credit balances should be classified in a manner consistent with the priority and security provisions cited earlier. Indeed, such items in the liability category frequently have a priority status, such as "Reserve for Federal Income Taxes." Appropriations of retained earnings, or "surplus reserves," are elements of the stockholders' equity and should be so reported.

Contingent Liabilities. Since contingent liabilities, as such, have no place in the statement of affairs, their probable status by the end of the liquidation period must be ascertained and correctly described. For example, notes receivable which have been discounted, for which there is little likelihood of dishonor, should be omitted from the statement of affairs. In respect to those notes for which dishonor is likely, however, the face amount of the notes should be reported as a liability on the credit side of the statement and extended to the "unsecured" column.

Other "contingent" liabilities should be similarly reported in the statement of affairs as unsecured claims to the extent there is a reasonable probability that such an obligation will, in fact, exist within the period during which a claim may be filed.

Accrued Interest. Accrued interest receivable or payable should be added to the obligation to which it relates. In the event a note receivable is pledged to secure a debt, the interest accrued thereon is usually considered as additional security and is reported as a complement of the note. Similarly, accrued interest on notes payable should be associated with the related notes.

Prepaid Insurance. The appropriate treatment in the statement of affairs of unexpired premiums on insurance depends upon the circumstances of each case. Although there may be a determinable cash surrender value of an insurance policy, it is not available except upon cancellation of the policy; further, the cash surrender value may expire before the expected date at which liquidation will be completed. Accordingly, unless such cancellation is expected, it is usual to report unexpired premiums only in terms of book value, without an anticipation of any realizable value.

Discount on Capital Stock. In the event capital stock is sold at a discount, creditors often have a claim against the shareholders in the amount of the unpaid discount. If it is probable that the discount is recoverable from existing shareholders, i.e., it has a cash realizable value, then it is appropriate to report this value as an unencumbered asset, but only to the extent of the creditors' deficiency. However, because there may exist reasonable doubt as to the accuracy of other realizable values, it may be expedient to evaluate the discount at its total collectible amount—whether or not necessary to cover a creditor deficiency.

Extended Usefulness of the Statement of Affairs

The statement of affairs presently occupies a relatively unimportant position in the catalogue of accounting reports. Its status is at least partially related to the essentially ex post facto nature of the statement. It may, in fact, be categorized as a financial autopsy, as it reflects the undesirable financial circumstance which then exists, with an analysis of the individual value losses generating the impairment of capital.

It is not inconceivable, however, that the concepts embodied in the statement of affairs might be usefully employed in the forward planning of management. For example, in preparing financial statements for short-term credit purposes, the concept of value is often more significant than that of unexpired costs. Rather than modify or provide interpretive elaboration of the conventional balance sheet to reflect such value adjustments, such as lower of cost or market in respect to inventories—an essentially inconsistent position when related to the going-concern assumption—the accountant might profitably extend the use of the statement of affairs. With an accepted emphasis on realizable asset values and the legal status of debts, this statement may be a valuable tool for financial analysis and interpretation. By recognizing the need for unique financial statements for various special purposes, balance sheet concepts may be more easily integrated with the income determination objective without undesirable exceptions.

REORGANIZATION

As an alternative to liquidation, a distressed debtor may attempt to rehabilitate a financially floundering business through reorganization. Usually, the value of business resources to a going concern is greater than the realization proceeds which derive from forced liquidation. A debtor contemplating some form of continuity of corporate life, instead of immediate dissolution, has recourse to both judicial and nonjudicial remedies. Among the latter are agreements executed by the creditors to extend the settlement period, composition agreements, voluntary assignments for the benefit of creditors, and creditor management committees. Judicial remedies usually involve the creation of an equity receivership or formal reorganization under Chapter X of the National Bankruptcy Act.

Nonjudicial Remedies

Extending the Settlement Period. Where the debtor's distress is clearly temporary in nature, it may be expedient—and advantageous—for his creditors to merely extend the period for the payment of outstanding obligations. This arrangement allows the debtor to continue management of the business, wherein he may be expected to convert such assets, without pain of forced liquidation, as will produce realization proceeds sufficient to liquidate existing debts. Such an agreement is often effective where the scale of business is small and there are relatively few creditors.

Composition Settlement.   A settlement by composition refers to an arrangement, contractually entered into by the debtor and his creditors *and* between the several creditors, in which the creditors agree to accept less than original contract amounts in full payment of their claims. These settlements, which originate with the debtor, provide for ratable distribution of the debtor's assets in full discharge of his obligations. Usually, in circumstances where composition settlements are employed, the debtor is insolvent within the bankruptcy meaning of this expression.

If there is a small number of dissenting creditors, a composition may nonetheless be executed if the assenting creditors allow full, or some preferred, payment of the obligations of the dissenting group. Throughout the proceedings, the debtor must remain completely candid in respect to disclosing his total assets; he must demonstrate no unauthorized preference for any creditor. The means of payment are usually cash and/or notes. Such an arrangement frequently is favored by the creditors in that it often prevents costly delays in final debt retirement.

Voluntary Assignment for the Benefit of Creditors.   An insolvent debtor may elect to convey his property by assignment to a trustee or assignee for the benefit of his creditors. The purpose of such assignment is to enable the debtor's representative to convert the property, as may be necessary, and to distribute the proceeds ratably among the creditors. If contractually agreed to by the several creditors, the assignment may result in the debtor's discharge from his debts. Should there remain any undistributed assets, they are returned by the trustee to the debtor. A voluntary assignment for the creditors' benefit constitutes an act of bankruptcy.

Creditor Management Committee.   The creditor management committee is a form of debtor-creditor alliance which provides for creditor committee management of the debtor's business for the purposes of rehabilitation, reorganization, or eventual liquidation. The control of the business rests with the committee, which may elect to contribute new capital if it appears financially and operationally feasible. Frequently, it is necessary to make use of an extension of the settlement period as a vehicle of financial revival. Properties are normally returned to the debtor when obligations have been discharged or otherwise provided for.

Judicial Remedies

Should the debtor prefer to employ legal remedies instead of the non-judicial remedies outlined above, he may elect to enter a petition for equity receivership, or he may initiate reorganization proceedings under the debtor relief provisions of the National Bankruptcy Act.

Equity Receivership. Receivership for insolvent debtors may be a consequence of voluntary or involuntary petition. A court of equity having jurisdiction over such proceedings may be either a federal or state tribunal. A receiver is appointed by the court to receive custody of the debtor's property in order to prevent unwarranted attachments of the assets to the detriment of the creditors and the business. Normally the receiver operates the business with a view to rehabilitation, or failing that, an orderly liquidation. The receiver continues as the administrative and operating head of the business pending adoption of a plan of reorganization. If the terms of the proposed reorganization are not agreeable to dissenting creditors, it may become necessary to either "buy them off" or proceed with a judicial sale. In the event of sale, the proceeds of realization are equitably distributed to the recalcitrant creditors. Because the judicial sale is often costly and dilatory, and in order to safeguard minority interests, the court may establish an "upset" price below which bids are not accepted.

Equity receiverships which relate to large corporations are normally within the jurisdiction of the federal courts. However, because this type of litigation has generally proven to be unusually long and expensive, federal equity receiverships are not utilized as often as in the past; rather, distressed debtors are more frequently electing the debtor relief provisions of the National Bankruptcy Act.

Chapter X (National Bankruptcy Act). A petition for reorganization under Chapter X of the National Bankruptcy Act is filed in a United States District Court. The petition may be voluntarily initiated by the debtor corporation, or involuntarily filed by three or more creditors, or an indenture trustee acting in their behalf, whose liquidated (certain) claims aggregate $500 or more. This petition may be filed either before or after an adjudication in bankruptcy. Upon approval of the petition, the judge will either appoint a disinterested trustee, or continue the debtor in possession of the business assets. In the event that the debtor's liabilities exceed $250,000, a trustee *must* be appointed.

Upon appointment, the trustee will take title to the debtor's assets and endeavor to continue without interruption the normal operations of the business. Frequently, he will retain the operating personnel of the debtor. Upon appointment and qualification, the trustee, together with his other responsibilities:

(1)   shall, if the judge shall so direct, investigate the acts, conduct, property, liabilities, and financial condition of the debtor, the operation of its business and the desirability of the continuance thereof, and any other matter relevant to the proceeding or to the formulation of a plan, and report thereon to the judge;

(2)   shall report to the judge any facts ascertained by him pertaining to fraud, misconduct, mismanagement and irregularities, and to any causes of action available to the estate;

(3)   shall, at the earliest date practicable, prepare and submit a brief state-

ment of his investigation of the property, liabilities, and financial condition of the debtor, the operation of its business and the desirability of the continuance thereof, in such form and manner as the judge may direct, to the creditors, stockholders, indenture trustees, the Securities and Exchange Commissions, and such other persons as the judge may designate; and

(4)   shall give notice to the creditors and stockholders that they may submit to him suggestions for the formulation of a plan, or proposals in the form of plans, within a time therein named [Section 167].

Once a plan of reorganization has been prepared and filed with the court, all interested parties—including creditors and shareholders—are heard concerning any objections they may choose to interpose. The plan must in all respects be fair and equitable, preserving the previous priorities of the various interested parties. Additionally, the plan must be feasible. The debtor corporation to be reorganized must demonstrate the existence of sufficient working capital, sound credit potential, earnings of sufficient amount to meet fixed charges, and financially sound capitalization. Necessarily, there must be additional evidence of good management. The fairness and feasibility of the plan is clearly a function of the financial adjustments included therein. These may include capital restructuring, debt abatement or elimination, and a modification of interest rates. With respect to the valuation of assets of the debtor corporation in the reorganization process, the significant values are those which are expected to be realized on the basis of a going concern. These values often, although not inevitably, coincide with current market values.

Once the plan has been approved, it is presented to the creditors and shareholders for ratification. Before final confirmation, the plan must be formally agreed to in writing by those creditors holding two thirds of claims filed and allowed. The reorganized debtor corporation continues thereafter with a new corporate life, subject only to such obligations as are imposed by the plan.

RECEIVERS' ACCOUNTS

In the event that a fiduciary assumes responsibility for the management of a distressed business, the appropriate scope of the system of accounts to be maintained must be established. Where a receiver is appointed by a court of equity, legal title to the assets of the debtor is usually conveyed to the receiver, who is then accountable to the court of his appointment, to the creditors, and to other interested parties. The receiver may elect to open new books of account, or he may continue the old books. The books of the distressed debtor are occasionally continued primarily for reasons of simplicity in record-keeping. Frequently, however, it may be desirable in an equity receivership to open new books to facilitate distinguishing between those obligations of the debtor which existed prior to the appointment of the receiver and those created after his appointment.

In the event that a separate set of accounts is maintained by the receiver, it is important to determine specifically which of the debtor's assets are to be conveyed to the receiver. His accountability necessarily relates only to those assets designated by the order of his appointment. The debts preexistent to the receivership usually remain in the debtor's books, although their liquidation frequently is the responsibility of the receiver. For this reason, the receiver should clearly identify "new" and "old" debts; similarly, a distinction should be made between the "old" assets, and those newly acquired during receivership. This is particularly important in respect to receivables. Receivable balances existing previous to the appointment of a receiver are the responsibility of the fiduciary only in respect to collection; accountability in respect to balances created subsequent to the receiver's appointment extends both to the prudence of granting credit and also to the effectiveness in account collection. Procedural details in accounting for an equity receivership are described in the illustrative example to follow.

Illustrative Problem.   The account balances of the Insolvo Company on March 31, 1971, are:

Cash.	$ 600
Accounts receivable.	4,000
Notes receivable.	5,800
Merchandise.	18,000
Long-lived assets.	24,000
Other assets.	2,600
	$55,000
Allowance for doubtful accounts.	$ 400
Accumulated depreciation.	2,000
Accounts payable.	21,000
Capital stock.	40,000
Retained earnings [deficit].	[8,400]
	$55,000

A petition for equity receivership was filed by the Insolvo Company, and Charles Louis was appointed receiver to assume management responsibility on April 1. For the period April 1 through August 31, the following transactions were completed:

(1)   All corporate assets were transferred to the receiver; existing debts of the Insolvo Company were continued in the corporate books of account; new accounts were opened by the receiver in respect to the transferred assets.

(2)   Credit purchases of merchandise were $40,000.

(3)   Credit sales amounted to $69,000; cash sales were $4,000.

(4)   Collections of cash were made on:

Notes receivable.	$ 4,800
Accounts receivable (old).	2,100
Accounts receivable (new).	51,000

(5)   Payments were made by the receiver as follows:

Accounts payable (old)	$16,000
Accounts payable (new)	34,000
Operating expenses	2,500
Receiver's expenses	1,000

(6) Adjustments recorded on August 31 by the receiver were:

Depreciation (5 months)	$1,200
Estimated doubtful accounts:	
Accounts receivable (old)	950
Accounts receivable (new)	1,600
Accounts written off:	
Accounts receivable (old)	400
Notes receivable	1,000

(7) Closing entries were made by both the receiver and the Insolvo Company on August 31; unsold merchandise on this date was $16,000.

Entries for these transactions are journalized in Illustration 18–3 (pp. 624–625).

A working paper which combines the accounts of the corporation and the receiver (before giving effect to closing entries) for the purpose of preparing conventional financial statements is shown in Illustration 18–4. The formal statements may be easily extracted therefrom.

In the event that the receivership is terminated on August 31, a return of the corporate management to Insolvo officials by Charles Louis would be recorded by an entry in the books of the receiver as follows:

The Insolvo Company—in receivership	59,350	
Allowance for doubtful accounts (old)	950	
Allowance for doubtful accounts (new)	1,600	
Accumulated depreciation	3,200	
Accounts payable (new)	6,000	
Cash		9,000
Accounts receivable (old)		1,500
Accounts receivable (new)		18,000
Merchandise		16,000
Long-lived assets		24,000
Other assets		2,600

The contra entry in the Insolvo Company books is:

Cash	9,000	
Accounts receivable	19,500	
Merchandise	16,000	
Long-lived assets	24,000	
Other assets	2,600	
Allowance for doubtful accounts		2,550
Accumulated depreciation		3,200
Accounts payable		6,000
Charles Louis, receiver		59,350

REALIZATION AND LIQUIDATION ACCOUNT

Conventional financial statements often reflect only an ancillary objective of a fiduciary; it may be more important to summarize periodically the

Illustration 18–3

Receiver's Books

(1)
Cash	600	
Accounts receivable (old)	4,000	
Notes receivable	5,800	
Merchandise, April 1	18,000	
Long-lived assets	24,000	
Other assets	2,600	
Allowance for doubtful accounts (old)		400
Accumulated depreciation		2,000
Insolvo Company—in receivership		52,600

(2)
Purchases	40,000	
Accounts payable (new)		40,000

(3)
Cash	4,000	
Accounts receivable (new)	69,000	
Sales		73,000

(4)
Cash	57,900	
Notes receivable		4,800
Accounts receivable (old)		2,100
Accounts receivable (new)		51,000

(5)
Accounts payable (new)	34,000	
Insolvo Company—in receivership	16,000	
Operating expenses	2,500	
Receiver's expenses	1,000	
Cash		53,500

Corporation's Books

(1)
Charles Louis, receiver	52,600	
Allowance for doubtful accounts	400	
Accumulated depreciation	2,000	
Cash		600
Accounts receivable		4,000
Notes receivable		5,800
Merchandise		18,000
Long-lived assets		24,000
Other assets		2,600

(2) No entry.

(3) No entry.

(4) No entry.

(5)
Accounts payable	16,000	
Charles Louis, receiver		16,000

(6)

	Debit	Credit
Depreciation expense	1,200	
Bad debts expense	2,550	
Accumulated depreciation		1,200
Allowance for doubtful accounts (old)		950
Allowance for doubtful accounts (new)		1,600
Bad debts expense	1,000	
Allowance for doubtful accounts (old)	400	
Notes receivable		1,000
Accounts receivable (old)		400

(7)

	Debit	Credit
Sales	73,000	
Merchandise, August 31	16,000	
Merchandise, April 1		18,000
Purchases		40,000
Operating expenses		2,500
Receiver's expenses		1,000
Bad debts expense		3,550
Depreciation expense		1,200
Income summary		22,750
Income summary	22,750	
Insolvo Company—in receivership		22,750

(6) No entry.

(7)

	Debit	Credit
Charles Louis, receiver	22,750	
Income summary		22,750
Income summary	22,750	
Retained earnings		22,750

Illustration 18–4

THE INSOLVO COMPANY—IN RECEIVERSHIP

Combined Account Working Paper
For Five Months Ended August 31, 1971

	Receiver's Accounts	Insolvo Accounts	Eliminations Dr.	Eliminations Cr.	Income Statement	Balance Sheet
Cash	9,000					9,000
Accounts receivable (old)	1,500					1,500
Accounts receivable (new)	18,000					18,000
Merchandise, April 1	18,000				18,000	
Long-lived assets	24,000					24,000
Other assets	2,600					2,600
Purchases	40,000				40,000	
Operating expenses	2,500				2,500	
Receiver's expenses	1,000				1,000	
Depreciation expense	1,200				1,200	
Bad debts expense	3,550				3,550	
Charles Louis, receiver		36,600		(1) 36,600		
	121,350	36,600				
Merchandise, August 31	16,000				22,750	16,000
Net income					89,000	71,100
Allowance for doubtful accounts (old)	950					950
Allowance for doubtful accounts (new)	1,600					1,600
Accumulated depreciation	3,200					3,200
Accounts payable (old)		5,000				5,000
Accounts payable (new)	6,000					6,000
Capital stock		40,000				40,000
Retained earnings [deficit]		40,000 [8,400]				40,000 [8,400]
Sales	73,000				73,000	
Insolvo Company—in receivership	36,600		(1) 36,600			
	121,350	36,600	36,600	36,600		
Merchandise, August 31	16,000					
Net income	16,000				16,000	22,750
					89,000	71,100

liquidation and distribution activities of the fiduciary. A special report which accommodates this objective is the *realization and liquidation account*. The reference to *account* in the title of the report accents the traditional format of the statement. Other arrangements of the account information have been suggested and are referred to subsequently in this chapter.

The realization and liquidation account is essentially a statement of accountability, reflecting the activities of the fiduciary—either a receiver or a trustee—in converting the debtor's noncash assets and proceeding with the orderly distribution of the proceeds in settlement of the debtor's several liabilities. To this report is normally appended the fiduciary's cash account. The orthodox report form consists essentially of three principal divisions. These basic segments are outlined as follows:

Assets

Assets to be realized	xxx	Assets realized (conversion proceeds)	xxx
Assets acquired (or discovered)	xxx	Assets not realized	xxx

Liabilities

Liabilities liquidated	xxx	Liabilities to be liquidated	xxx
Liabilities not liquidated	xxx	Liabilities incurred	xxx

Revenues and Expenses; Gains and Losses

Supplementary charges	xxx	Supplementary credits	xxx

A summation of the debits in the three statement categories juxtaposed against the summation of credits will disclose an imbalance, which may be described as the net gain or loss for the liquidation period.

Using the data for the receivership previously discussed, the conventional realization and liquidation account takes the form shown in Illustration 18–5. The receiver's Cash account is given following:

Cash

(1) Balance, March 31	600	(5) Accounts payable (old)	16,000
(3) Sales	4,000	(5) Accounts payable (new)	34,000
(4) Accounts receivable (old)	2,100	(5) Operating expenses	2,500
(4) Accounts receivable (new)	51,000	(5) Receiver's expenses	1,000
(4) Notes receivable	4,800	Balance, August 31	9,000
	62,500		62,500
Balance, August 31	9,000		

The Insolvo Company's stockholders' equity accounts are:

Capital Stock

		(1) Balance, March 31	40,000

Retained Earnings

(1) Balance, March 31	8,400	Net income (April 1 to August 31) 22,750

The use of the numeric codes to identify contra elements in the realization and liquidation account indicates that the statement may be easily prepared by entering the transactions of the fiduciary directly into the relevant statement categories. This connective notation would not, however, appear in the formal report.

Statement Annotations

Assets to Be Realized.   Included in this category are the *carrying values* of all assets of the debtor at the date of the fiduciary's appointment (or at the beginning of the current period if the statement is not a cumulative record of fiduciary activities).

Assets Acquired.   These are additional assets which are acquired (or discovered) during the period of fiduciary accountability.

Assets Realized.   This description reflects the extent of conversion of noncash assets, with the *realization proceeds* therefrom the appropriate value measure.

Assets Not Realized.   This summarizes the assets on hand at the date of the preparation of the statement, usually valued at the same amount indicated in the original accountability (assets to be realized or assets acquired).

Liabilities to Be Liquidated.   These obligations of the debtor are those existing at the date of appointment of the fiduciary (or the beginning of the current period if the statement is not a cumulative record of fiduciary activities).

Liabilities Incurred.   These liabilities are the additional obligations assumed by the fiduciary during the period of his accountability.

Liabilities Liquidated.   These are the debt cancellations during the period, identified by creditor class.

Liabilities Not Liquidated.   These are the unpaid claims existing at the end of the period to which the statement refers.

Supplementary Charges.   For the most part these are the expenses incurred during the period of receivership, although they do not include asset expirations or specific losses on the conversion of noncash assets.

Supplementary Credits.   These credits include revenues earned during the period, other than amortization of deferred income items; specific gains on the conversion of noncash assets are not included.

Special Problems

The reader will observe that the net income (or loss) for the period is the algebraic sum of the debit and credit balances in the above 10 categories. Additionally, it is important to note that because asset credits are

Illustration 18–5

THE INSOLVO COMPANY
CHARLES LOUIS—RECEIVER
Realization and Liquidation Account
April 1, 1971 to August 31, 1971

Assets to be realized:			**Liabilities to be liquidated:**		
(1) Accounts receivable (old).....	4,000		(1) Accounts payable (old).....		21,000
Less: Allowance for doubtful			**Liabilities incurred:**		
accounts (old).....	400	3,600	(2) Accounts payable (new).....		40,000
(1) Notes receivable.....		5,800	**Supplementary credits:**		
(1) Merchandise.....		18,000	(2) Sales.....		73,000
(1) Long-lived assets.....	24,000		**Assets realized:**		
Less: Accumulated depreciation.....	2,000	22,000	(4) Accounts receivable (old).....		2,100
(1) Other assets.....		2,600	(4) Accounts receivable (new).....		51,000
Assets acquired:			(4) Notes receivable.....		4,800
(3) Accounts receivable (new).....		69,000	**Assets not realized:**		
Supplementary charges:			Accounts receivable (old).....	1,500	
(2) Purchases.....		40,000	Less: Allowance for doubtful accounts (old).....	950	550
(5) Operating expenses.....		2,500	Accounts receivable (new).....	18,000	
(5) Receiver's expenses.....		1,000	Less: Allowance for doubtful accounts (new).....	1,600	16,400
Liabilities liquidated:			Merchandise.....		16,000
(5) Accounts payable (old).....		16,000	Long-lived assets.....	24,000	
(5) Accounts payable (new).....		34,000	Less: Accumulated depreciation.....	3,200	20,800
Liabilities not liquidated:			Other assets.....		2,600
Accounts payable (old).....		5,000			
Accounts payable (new).....		6,000			
Net income.....		22,750			
		248,250			248,250

expressed in terms of realization proceeds, net income (or loss) is partially explained in terms of the changes in asset categories as well as by the supplementary charges and credits for the period.

Sales and Purchases.   The fiduciary may record merchandise purchased as either "assets acquired," or as "supplementary charges." Similarly, sales may be recorded as either "assets realized," or as "supplementary credits." If operating transactions are relatively numerous, the supplementary charge-credit categories are preferred.

Cash Discounts.   The fiduciary may choose between one of two alternative methods in recording cash discounts in respect to receivables and payables. For accounts payable, the amount of the obligation net of discounts and allowances may be debited to "liabilities liquidated" when payment is made. Although the discount and allowance variance between "liabilities to be liquidated" and "liabilities liquidated" is not specifically identified by this treatment, the variance nonetheless enters the calculation of realization gain or loss, as there will be no remaining balance in "liabilities not liquidated."

If the fiduciary should elect to debit "liabilities liquidated" with the invoice billing (gross) when payment is made, then a contra credit equal to the amount of discounts and allowances will appear as a "supplementary credit." This purchase discount and allowance credit is again a factor in the calculation of realization gain or loss, although in this instance it is separately identified.

A parallel accounting treatment may be applied to receivable balances and related sales discounts and allowances.

Depreciation and Uncollectibles.   Depreciation expense and estimated bad debts usually are not separately identified in the realization and liquidation account. They are reflected, however, in the estimated period-end balances in the accumulated depreciation and allowance for uncollectibles accounts, which are reported contra in "assets not realized." The expenses are thus factors in the calculation of net income or loss for the period.

Accruals.   Where the amounts of accrued income items in the "assets to be realized" category are subsequently realized at larger amounts, two alternative accounting treatments are available. The accountant may credit "assets realized" with the amount accrued at the start of the period, crediting the additional amount collected to "supplementary credits." Or, the increase in the amount of the accrual since the start of the period may be entered as accrued interest in "assets acquired," with a contra credit to "supplementary credits." The subsequent collection may then be recorded by a credit to "assets realized." Comparable treatment may be accorded accrued expenses.

Favorable or Unfavorable Settlement of Liabilities.   In the event that the creditors agree to accept less than face value for their obligations, the settlement discount should be preferably reported as a "supplementary credit," with the total amount of the canceled obligation reported as "liabilities liquidated." In the event a premium payment is required in order to liquidate an overdue indebtedness, accounting treatment would parallel that for a discount settlement; accordingly, the amount of the premium should be entered as a "supplementary charge."

Illustrative Problem—Alternative Statement Form

When continuing the business operations is a significant part of the trustee's responsibilities, the conventional account form of the realization and liquidation statement is often restructured in a columnar format with emphasis on both operating results and liquidation activities. This is illustrated below.

Account balances of the Crescent Company on May 1, 1971, were as follows:

Cash...........................	$ 900	Allowance for doubtful accounts.....	$ 700
Notes receivable.................	8,000	Accumulated depreciation..........	1,400
Accounts receivable..............	14,000	Accounts payable................	26,000
Merchandise....................	26,000	Capital stock....................	40,000
Equipment.....................	8,600	Retained earnings [deficit].........	[10,600]
	$57,500		$57,500

The creditors of the Crescent Company selected a trustee, Paul Martin, to operate the business until conditions warranted its return to the corporate management. Transactions from May 1 through November 1, 1971, were:

(1) Additional equipment was discovered, value $1,100.
(2) Merchandise was purchased on account, $50,000.
(3) Sales were: credit, $84,000; cash, $10,500.
(4) Collections were made as follows: notes receivable, $7,000; accounts receivable (old), $9,200; accounts receivable (new), $74,000.
(5) Payments made by the fiduciary were: accounts payable (old), $21,000; accounts payable (new), $16,000; operating expenses, $9,000; ABC 5 percent bonds, $1,600; trustee's expenses, $5,000. Discounts taken on accounts payable (old) were $400; on accounts payable (new), $360.
(6) Accounts receivable (old) written off were $550; the remaining balance of notes receivable was considered uncollectible.
(7) November 1, 1971, adjustments are required in respect to—

Taxes accrued since May 1.................................	$800
Depreciation, May 1 to November 1.........................	940
Estimated uncollectible accounts (required balances in allowance accounts):	
Old accounts...	600
New accounts..	780

(8) Merchandise inventory on November 1 was $24,000. Management of the business was returned to officers of the Crescent Company on November 1.

The statement of realization, liquidation, and operations is shown in Illustration 18–6 (pp. 632–633). Although the inclusion of the corporation

Illustration 18-6

THE CRESCENT COMPANY—IN RECEIVERSHIP
PAUL MARTIN, TRUSTEE

Realization, Liquidation, and Operations
For Six Months Ended November 1, 1971

Debits	Balances, May 1	Transactions and Adjustments Debit	Transactions and Adjustments Credit	Profit and Loss and Realization and Liquidation Dr. [Cr.]	Trading Dr. [Cr.]	Balances, November 1
Cash	900	(3) 10,500 (4) 90,200	(5) 52,600			49,000
Assets to be realized:						
Notes receivable	8,000		(4) 7,000	1,000		–0–
Accounts receivable (old)	14,000		(4) 9,200 (6) 550			4,250
Allowance for doubtful accounts (old)	[700]		(7) 450			[600]
Merchandise, May 1	26,000	(6) 550	(8) 26,000			–0–
Equipment	8,600					8,600
Accumulated depreciation	[1,400]		(7) 940			[2,340]
Assets discovered:						
Equipment		(1) 1,100				1,100
Assets acquired:						
Accounts receivable (new)		(3) 84,000	(4) 74,000			10,000
Allowance for doubtful accounts (new)			(7) 780			[780]
ABC bonds		(5) 1,600				1,600
Merchandise, November 1		(8) 24,000				24,000
	55,400					94,830

Account						
Liabilities to be liquidated:						
Accounts payable (old)	26,000	(5) 21,400				4,600
Liabilities incurred:						
Accounts payable (new)		(5) 16,360	(2) 50,000			33,640
Accrued taxes			(7) 800			800
Stockholders' equity:						
Capital stock	40,000					40,000
Deficit	[10,600]		(1) 1,100			[9,500]
Supplementary charges:						
Purchases of merchandise		(2) 50,000			50,000	
Trustee's expenses		(5) 5,000		5,000		
Operating expenses		(5) 9,000			9,000	
Taxes		(7) 800			800	
Depreciation		(7) 940			940	
Bad debts expense		(7) 780			780	
Loss on realization of accounts receivable (old)		(7) 450		450		
Merchandise, May 1		(8) 26,000			26,000	
Supplementary credits:						
Merchandise, November 1			(8) 24,000		[24,000]	
Sales of merchandise			(3) 94,500		[94,500]	
Discount on purchases			(5) 760		[760]	
Loss on realization				6,450		[6,450]
Profit on trading					[31,740]	31,740
	55,400	342,680	342,680			94,830

equity accounts implies that the receiver is using the "old" books, only minor modifications are required to reflect the accounts in a "new" set of books established by the receiver. Additionally, more formal summaries of results of operations and realization and liquidation proceedings may be prepared from this detailed statement of the trustee's activities.

QUESTIONS

1. Who may initiate a petition for the *voluntary* dissolution of a corporation? The *involuntary* dissolution of a corporation?
2. List three "acts of bankruptcy." Why is the committing of such an act significant?
3. What is the liquidation sequence once a debtor has been judicially determined a bankrupt?
4. Certain classes of a distressed debtor's liabilities must be fully satisfied before other creditors can receive a settlement. What are they?
5. What is a "statement of affairs"? What distinguishes this statement from the conventional balance sheet?
6. How should contingent liabilities be reported in the statement of affairs?
7. Can you project an extension in the usefulness of a statement of affairs for financially prospering enterprises—the going concerns?
8. Briefly describe what is meant by an "equity receivership."
9. What unique classification and descriptive distinctions should be made in the set of accounts that are prepared to record the actions of the receiver in a reorganization?
10. What purpose is served by the preparation of the realization and liquidation account? In outline, cite the several categories found in the realization and liquidation account.

PROBLEMS

Problem 18–1

For several years Martin supplied raw materials to Western, Inc., who processed the goods into a finished product for sale to retail customers.

Martin supplied goods to Western on credit terms, and to secure his claim for unpaid goods, Martin obtained and properly perfected a "floating lien" on all of the goods sold to Western.

Six months ago Martin heard that Western, Inc., was in financial difficulty and stopped selling goods to the firm. Martin was not paid by Western for several shipments of goods and heard that recently Western made a general assignment for the benefit of its creditors. Also Martin heard that a group of Western's creditors may attempt to place Western into bankruptcy.

Required:
(i) Has Western committed an "act of bankruptcy"? Explain.
(ii) Is the commission of an "act of bankruptcy" necessary to become a voluntary bankrupt? Explain.

(iii)   Under what circumstances may Western's creditors proceed to have Western adjudicated an involuntary bankrupt?

(iv)   Assume that Western's creditors may proceed to have it adjudicated an involuntary bankrupt. What action would they have to take in order to commence a bankruptcy proceeding?

(v)   Will the number of creditors required to commence an involuntary bankruptcy proceeding vary depending upon the number of Western's creditors? Explain.

(vi)   How will Martin be treated in the bankruptcy proceedings if Western is adjudicated a bankrupt? Explain.

(AICPA adapted)

Problem 18–2

You are to determine whether each of the legal conclusions is true or false according to the general principles of bankruptcy law.

(i)   In order for a person to be adjudged a bankrupt under the Bankruptcy Act—

    (1)   He must owe debts totaling more than $2,000.

    (2)   There must be at least three creditors.

    (3)   A petition in bankruptcy must be filed by a majority of creditors.

    (4)   The creditor must agree to the commencement of bankruptcy proceedings.

    (5)   A petition in bankruptcy must be filed.

(ii)   Acts of bankruptcy include a debtor—

    (6)   Making a fraudulent conveyance.

    (7)   Intentionally making a preference.

    (8)   Making a general assignment for the benefit of creditors.

    (9)   Orally admitting his willingness to be adjudged a bankrupt.

    (10) Requesting the appointment of a receiver immediately before becoming insolvent.

(iii)   Bankruptcy proceedings may be instituted against any person or corporation, including—

    (11) A married woman.

    (12) A municipal corporation.

    (13) A banking corporation.

    (14) A building and loan corporation.

    (15) A partnership.

(iv)   Classes of claims which have priority under the provisions of the Bankruptcy Act include—

    (16) Expenses of bankruptcy administration.

    (17) Wages earned within one year before the date of bankruptcy.

    (18) Debts of less than $50.

    (19) Taxes.

    (20) Claims of creditors which are outstanding for more than three years.

(v)   Debts discharged by completion of bankruptcy proceedings and discharge of the debtor include—

    (21) Contract obligations which are not due until three years following the act of bankruptcy.

(22) Trade accounts payable.
(23) Taxes.
(24) Debts incurred within one month after the bankrupt's discharge.
(25) A debt arising from the commission of a willful injury.

(AICPA adapted)

Problem 18–3

C. A. Mautz, toy manufacturer, on October 31, 1971, prepared the following enumeration of resources and creditor claims:

Resources:
Petty cash, $250, including expense vouchers for $119.
Cash, $2,579.
Accounts receivable, $3,460, of which $3,230, are believed to be collectible.
Toy materials and supplies, $12,000; estimated market value, $8,400.
Toys in process, $8,100; estimated market value, $2,000.
Building, $20,000; estimated market value, $8,000.
Display equipment, $11,800; estimated market value, $9,400.
Claims:
Accounts payable:

Gem Supply Company	$ 2,800
Ornamental Trinkets, Inc.	6,300
R. M. Brown	14,100
A. K. Moyer	1,700

Notes payable:
American State Bank, $20,000. The display equipment is pledged as collateral.
Texas Finance Company, $15,000. Unsecured notes receivable, $10,000, and warehouse receipts for finished goods are pledged as collateral. The finished goods (manufactured toys) have a book value of $8,000 and an estimated current value of $7,500. The notes receivable are estimated to be fully collectible.
Accrued wages, $1,625.

Required:

(i)   Prepare a statement of affairs as of October 31, 1971.
(ii) Prepare a schedule of payments to creditors on this date, indicating whether the amount of the settlement is a full or partial liquidation.

Problem 18–4

A receiver was appointed on September 30, 1971, for Harkins, Inc. On this date, the following balance sheet accounts are available:

ASSETS

Petty cash			$ 60
Cash in bank			2,800
Accounts receivable	$32,000		
Notes receivable	20,000	$52,000	
Allowance for bad debts		340	51,660
Accrued interest, notes receivable			600
Merchandise			28,000
Prepaid insurance			240
Prepaid advertising			190
Building	$80,000		
Accumulated depreciation	21,000	59,000	
Furniture and fixtures	$ 7,200		
Accumulated depreciation	1,600	5,600	
Organization costs			1,650
Goodwill			4,000
			$153,800

EQUITIES

Accrued wages..	$ 2,500	
Accrued property taxes.............................	1,810	
Accounts payable....................................	79,000	
Notes payable.......................................	15,000	
Accrued interest payable............................	150	$ 98,460
Contributed capital:		
Common stock...................................	$70,000	
Premium...	2,000	
	$72,000	
Retained earnings:		
Deficit...	16,660	55,340
		$153,800

It is estimated that conversion of assets will realize cash in the following amounts:

Notes receivable (with accrued interest).............	$19,100
Accounts receivable...............................	25,000
Merchandise......................................	18,500
Building..	22,000
Furniture and fixtures.............................	2,000

Notes payable of $10,000 are secured by merchandise, the book value of which is $20,000. Notes payable of $5,000 are secured by the furniture and equipment. Interest expense is allocable ratably to all outstanding notes payable.

Required:

(i)   Prepare a statement of affairs as of September 30.

(ii) Prepare a supporting deficiency account or report on this date.

Problem 18–5

The Machine Manufacturing Company has been forced into bankruptcy as of April 30, 1971. The following list of account balances was prepared by the company bookkeeper as of April 30, 1971:

Cash...	$ 2,700
Accounts receivable...............................	39,350
Notes receivable..................................	18,500
Inventories:	
Raw materials.................................	19,600
Work in process...............................	35,100
Finished machines.............................	12,000
Supplies......................................	6,450
Tools...	14,700
Prepaid expenses..................................	950
Plant and property:	
Land..	20,000
Buildings......................................	75,000
Machinery.....................................	80,900
	$325,250

Note payable to the First Bank...................	$ 15,000
Notes payable to suppliers......................	51,250
Accounts payable..............................	52,000
Accrued salaries and wages.....................	8,850
Accrued property taxes.........................	2,900
Employees' taxes withheld......................	1,150
Accrued wage taxes............................	600
Accrued interest on bonds......................	1,800
First-mortgage bonds payable...................	90,000
Accumulated depreciation—buildings.............	33,750
Accumulated depreciation—machinery...........	32,100
Common stock ($100 par value).................	75,000
Deficit.......................................	[39,150]
	$325,250

Additional Information:

a) Of the total accounts receivable $10,300 are believed to be good. The other accounts are doubtful, but it seems probable that 20 percent finally can be collected.

b) A total of $15,000 of the notes receivable have been pledged to secure the note payable to the First Bank. All except $2,500 of these appear to be good. Interest of $800 is accrued on the $12,500 of good notes pledged and $300 is accrued on the $15,000 payable to the bank. The remaining notes are not considered collectible.

c) The finished machines are expected to be sold for one-third above their cost, but expenses in disposing of them will equal 20 percent of their sales price. Work in process can be completed at an additional cost of $15,400, of which $3,700 would be material used from the raw material inventory. The work in process, when completed, will probably sell for $40,000, and costs of sale will be 20 percent of sales price. The raw material not used will realize $8,000. Most of the value of tools consists of special items. After completion of work in process, the tools should sell for $3,000. The supply inventory which will not be needed to complete work should sell for $1,000.

d) Land and buildings are mortgaged as security for bonds. They have an appraised value of $95,000. The company recently purchased $20,000 of machinery on a conditional sales contract. It still owes $12,000 principal on this contract which is included in the notes payable. These machines, having a current used value of $10,000, are repossessed. The Machine Manufacturing Company remains liable for the unpaid obligation. Depreciation taken on these machines amounts to $1,800. The remaining machinery is believed to be salable at $10,000, but costs of selling it may be $1,000.

Required:

(i) Prepare a statement showing the estimated deficiency to unsecured creditors, indicating clearly the causes of the deficiency. You need not consider any expenses of liquidation which are not stated in the information given.

(ii) Compute the percentage of probable payments to unsecured creditors.

(AICPA adapted)

Problem 18–6

The financial condition of the Rawley Manufacturing Corporation was very unstable, although it had unimpaired contributed capital in the amount of $60,000 and accumulated earnings of $8,522. This condition was attributable to a deficiency of quick assets: cash, $265, and trade receivables, $4,062. Its current obligations to trade creditors amounted to $25,289. Other assets were raw materials, $16,000; work in process, $34,400; finished goods, $5,700; machinery and dies, $33,384. In order to continue operations, it was necessary to obtain sufficient cash to meet current payrolls and to pay miscellaneous expenses.

At a meeting of the principal creditors, it was decided to advance $6,000 to the Rawley Manufacturing Corporation to enable it to meet obligations presently due; additionally, it was decided to permit continuance of operations until the present in-process stock could be completed and sold. These operations were to be conducted by a trustee appointed by the creditors.

Transactions completed during the trusteeship were cash disbursements for labor, $16,625; for expenses, $4,530; and for additional dies, $750; raw materials purchased on account, $6,300; sales on account, $72,300; loss on collection of old accounts, $380; expenses incurred, on account, $15,000. Unliquidated account balances at the termination of the trusteeship period were as follows: accounts receivable (new), $3,382; accounts payable (new), $89; raw materials, $2,000; finished goods, $30,000; and machinery and dies, $34,134.

Required:

Prepare in orthodox form a statement of realization and liquidation with supporting schedules. Ignore the effects of depreciation in the determination of operating profit.

Problem 18–7

Using the data of Problem 18–6, prepare *in columnar form* a realization and liquidation statement. Ignore the effects of depreciation in the determination of operating profit.

Problem 18–8

The Hardhyt Corporation is in financial difficulty because of a deficiency in sales volume. Its stockholders and principal creditors want an estimate of the financial results of the liquidation of the assets and liabilities and the dissolution of the corporation. The corporation's trial balance follows:

HARDHYT CORPORATION

Postclosing Trial Balance
December 31, 1971

Cash...	$ 1,000	
Accounts receivable............................	20,500	
Allowance for bad debts........................		$ 350
Inventories.....................................	40,000	
Supplies inventory..............................	3,000	
Downhill Railroad 5 percent bonds.............	5,000	
Accrued bond interest receivable...............	750	
Advertising....................................	6,000	
Land...	4,000	
Building.......................................	30,000	
Accumulated depreciation—building.............		5,000
Machinery and equipment......................	46,000	
Accumulated depreciation—machinery and equipment.....................................		8,000
Accounts payable..............................		26,000
Notes payable—bank...........................		25,000
Notes payable—officers........................		20,000
Payroll taxes payable..........................		800
Wages payable.................................		1,500
Mortgage payable..............................		42,000
Mortgage interest payable......................		500
Capital stock..................................		50,000
Retained earnings.............................	29,100	
Reserve for product guarantees................		6,200
	$185,350	$185,350

The following information has been collected in anticipation of a meeting of the stockholders and principal creditors to be held on January 2, 1972.

a) Cash includes a $300 protested check from a customer. The customer stated that he would have funds to honor the check in about two weeks.

b) Accounts receivable include accounts totaling $10,000 that are fully collectible and have been assigned to the bank in connection with the notes payable. Included in the unassigned receivables in an uncollectible account of $150. The Allowance for Bad Debts account of $350 now on the books will adequately provide for other doubtful accounts.

c) Purchase orders totaling $9,000 are on hand for the corporation's products. Inventory with a book value of $6,000 can be processed at an additional cost of $400 to fill these orders. The balance of the inventory, which includes obsolete materials with a book value of $1,200, can be sold for $10,500.

d) In transit at December 31 but not recorded on the books was a shipment of defective merchandise being returned by a customer. Mr. Hardhyt, president of the corporation, had authorized the return and the refund of the purchase price of $250 after the merchandise had been inspected. Other than this return Mr. Hardhyt knows of no other defective merchandise that would bear upon the appropriated Reserve for Product Guarantees account. The merchandise being returned has no salvage value.

e) The Supplies Inventory is comprised of advertising literature, brochures, and other sales aids. These could not be replaced for less than $3,700.

f) The Downhill Railroad bonds are recorded at face value. They were purchased in 1968 for $600, and the adjustment to face value was credited to Retained Earnings. At December 31, 1971, the bonds were quoted at 18.

g) The Advertising account represents the future benefits of a 1971 advertising campaign. Ten percent of certain advertising expenditures were placed in the account. Mr. Hardhyt stated that this was too conservative and that 20 percent would result in a more realistic measure of the market that was created.

h) The land and building are in a downtown area. A firm offer of $50,000 has been received for the land which would be used as a parking lot; the building would be razed at a cost of $12,000 to the buyer. Another offer of $40,000 was received for the real estate which the bidder stated would be used for manufacturing that would probably employ some Hardhyt employees.

i) The highest of the offers received from used machinery dealers was $18,000 for all of the machinery and equipment.

j) One creditor, whose account for $1,000 is included in the accounts payable, confirmed in writing that he would accept 90 cents on the dollar if the corporation paid him by January 10.

k) Wages payable include year-end adjustments of $325 payable to certain factory employees for their overtime during the busy season.

l) The mortgage payable is secured by the land and building. The last two monthly principal payments of $200 each were not made.

m) Estimated liquidation expenses amount to $3,200.

n) For income tax purposes the corporation has the following net operating loss carry-overs (the tax rate is 50 percent):

1969	$10,000
1970	12,000
1971	8,000

Required:

(i) Prepare a statement of affairs. Assets should be classified according to their availability for secured and unsecured creditors, and liabilities should be classified according to their legal priority and secured status. The statement should have the following column headings:

For Assets:
  Book Value
  Assets
  Appraised Value
  Estimated Amount Available
  Loss or Gain on Realization

For Liabilities and Capital:
  Book Value
  Liabilities and Capital
  Amount Unsecured

(ii) Prepare a schedule indicating the estimated settlement per dollar of unsecured liabilities.

(AICPA adapted)

Problem 18–9

The Specialty Shops Company was unable to meet its obligations. As a result, John Mann was appointed receiver on February 5, 1971. The following accounts were taken from the books as of that date:

Cash.....................................	$ 764
Accounts receivable.....................	5,928
Merchandise............................	16,536
Prepayment of expenses.................	704
Fixtures...............................	12,342
	$36,274

Accounts payable.......................	$15,987
Notes payable..........................	3,500
Accrued wages, taxes, etc...............	1,275
Accrued rent...........................	600
Accumulated depreciation...............	3,803
Capital stock..........................	10,000
Retained earnings......................	1,109
	$36,274

In the period from February 5, to April 30, 1971, the receiver's actions resulted in the following:

a) An audit of the accounts receivable disclosed that there were an additional $423 of accounts receivable which had not been brought on the books.

b) Merchandise costing $8,310 was sold for cash.

c) A portion of the fixtures, which cost $5,376 and had accumulated depreciation of $942, was sold.

d) Accounts receivable totaling $1,882 were collected. Other accounts amounting to $741 have been determined to be worthless.

e) Claims have been approved and paid for $903 of the wages and taxes which were accrued at February 5. Wage claims for $125 which were unrecorded on February 5 have also been approved and paid. Other claims have not yet been paid.

f) Expenses for wages and supplies used in liquidating the business to April 30 amounted to $1,245. Fees for the receiver need not be considered.

g) Rent under leases has continued to accrue in the amount of $900. Interest of $70 has accrued on notes payable.

h) Cash receipts and cash disbursements show the following:

Cash receipts:

Collection of accounts..................	$1,882
Sales of merchandise...................	9,108
Sale of fixtures.......................	1,000

Cash disbursements:

Accrued wages and taxes...............	1,028
Expenses of the receivership...........	1,245

Required:

Prepare a formal statement of realization and liquidation and related gain and loss account for the period ended April 30, 1971.

(AICPA adapted)

Problem 18–10

JONES, INC.

Balance Sheet, as of March 31, 1971

(Prepared by the Company's Bookkeeper)

ASSETS

Current Assets:			
Cash			$ 2,000
Notes receivable	$ 4,640		
Less: Notes receivable discounted	4,640		
Accounts receivable			4,000
U.S. Treasury bonds			10,000
Inventories:			
Finished goods	$15,000		
Work in process	4,500		
Raw materials	6,000	25,500	
Total Current Assets			$ 41,500
Other Assets:			
Subscriptions to capital stock			12,500
Investments			2,300
Property and equipment:			
Real estate	$45,000		
Factory equipment	24,000		
	$69,000		
Less: Accumulated depreciation	20,000		49,000
Total Assets			$105,300

LIABILITIES

Current Liabilities:			
Notes payable:			
To Manufacturers' Trust Co.	$10,000		
To Alex Smith	25,000	$35,000	
Accounts payable		24,000	
Accrued liabilities:			
Salaries and wages	$ 992		
Property taxes	460	1,452	
Total Current Liabilities			$ 60,452
Long-Term Liabilities:			
First mortgage on real estate	$15,000		
Second mortgage on real estate	20,000		35,000
Total Liabilities			$ 95,452

CAPITAL

Capital stock—authorized, subscribed and issued, 500			
shares, par $100 per share		$50,000	
Less: Deficit		[40,152]	9,848
Total Liabilities and Capital			$105,300

An analysis of the company's accounts disclosed the following:

a)   Jones, Inc., started business April 1, 1966, with authorized capital of $50,000, represented by shares of $100 par value each. Of the 500 authorized shares, 375 were fully paid at par and 125 were subscribed at par, payment to be made on call.

b)   The Manufacturers' Trust Company holds $10,000 of U.S. Treasury bonds as security for its $10,000 loan; it also holds the first mortgage of $15,000 on the company's real estate, interest on which is paid through March 31, 1971.

c)   The real estate includes land, which cost $5,000, and a building erected thereon at a cost of $40,000. Of the accumulated depreciation, $5,000 is applicable to the building and $15,000 to the factory equipment. The realizable value of the real estate is estimated to be $30,000.

d)   The note payable to Alex Smith is secured by a chattel mortgage on factory equipment and the inventories. Interest on the note has been paid through March 31, 1971.

e)   Alex Smith holds the second mortgage on the real estate.

f)   The notes receivable, $4,640, which were discounted, though not yet due, are deemed uncollectible.

g)   Of the $4,000 of accounts receivable, $2,000 are considered good; of the remaining $2,000 it is expected that one half will be uncollectible.

h)   Inventories are valued at cost; finished goods are expected to yield 110 percent of cost. Goods in process cost $4,500 and have a realizable value, if scrapped, of $900. It is estimated, however, that the work in process can be completed into finished goods by the use of $1,200 of raw material and an expenditure of $1,400 for labor and other costs. The raw material deteriorates rapidly, and is estimated to realize only 25 percent of cost.

i)   The factory equipment, which cost $24,000 on April 1, 1966, is considered to have a realizable value of $5,000 at March 31, 1971.

j)   The subscription to the capital stock for 125 shares at par, is due from Wyman Jones, president of the company, and is fully collectible.

k)   Investments include 15 shares (a 1 percent interest) of the common stock of the Bourbon Company, acquired at a cost of $1,500, but with a market value of $3,390 at March 31, 1971; and 20 shares of treasury stock for which the company paid $800.

l)   No expenses of liquidation nor accruals not specifically mentioned need be considered.

The committee has called for payment of the capital stock subscription and has decided to have the goods in process converted into finished goods, which are expected to realize 110 percent of cost. Completion of goods in process can be done so quickly that no further expenses than those mentioned above will be incurred.

Required:

(i)   Prepare a statement of affairs on March 31, 1971.

(ii) Prepare a supporting deficiency account detailing estimated gains and losses.

(iii) Calculate amounts and settlement percentages for each class of creditors.

(AICPA adapted)

Problem 18–11

The Neversink Corporation advises you that it is facing bankruptcy proceedings. As the company's CPA you are aware of its condition.

The balance sheet of the Neversink Corporation at June 30, 1971, and supplementary data are presented below:

ASSETS

Cash...	$ 2,000
Accounts receivable, less allowance for bad debts.......	70,000
Inventory, raw material............................	40,000
Inventory, finished goods...........................	60,000
Marketable securities..............................	20,000
Land..	13,000
Buildings, less allowance for depreciation.............	90,000
Machinery, less allowance for depreciation............	120,000
Goodwill..	20,000
Prepaid expenses..................................	5,000
Total Assets...............................	$440,000

LIABILITIES AND CAPITAL

Accounts payable..................................	$ 80,000
Notes payable.....................................	135,000
Accrued wages....................................	15,000
Mortgages payable................................	130,000
Common stock....................................	100,000
Retained earnings [deficit].........................	[20,000]
Total Liabilities and Capital....................	$440,000

Supplementary Data:

a) Cash includes a $500 travel advance which has been expended.
b) Accounts receivable of $40,000 have been pledged in support of bank loans of $30,000. Credit balances of $5,000 are netted in the accounts receivable total.
c) Marketable securities consisted of government bonds costing $10,000 and 500 shares Bartlett Company stock. The market value of the bonds is $10,000 and the stock is quoted at $18 per share. The bonds have accrued interest due of $200. The securities are collateral for a $20,000 bank loan.
d) Appraised value of raw materials is $30,000 and finished goods is $50,000. For an additional cost of $10,000, the raw materials would realize $70,000 as finished goods.
e) The appraised value of fixed assets is: land, $25,000; buildings, $110,000; machinery, $75,000.
f) Prepaid expenses will be exhausted during the liquidation period.
g) Accounts payable include $15,000 of withheld payroll taxes and $6,000 of obligations to creditors who had been assured by the president they would be paid. There are unrecorded employer's payroll taxes in the amount of $500.
h) Wages payable are not subject to any limitations under bankruptcy laws.
i) Mortgages payable consist of $100,000 on land and buildings, and a

$30,000 chattel mortgage on machinery. Total unrecorded accrued interest on these mortgages amounted to $2,400.

j) Estimated legal fees and expenses in connection with the liquidation are $10,000.

k) Probable judgment on a pending damage suit is $50,000.

l) You have not rendered an invoice for $5,000 for last year's audit, and you estimate a $1,000 fee for liquidation work.

Required:

(i) Prepare a statement of affairs.

(ii) Compute the estimated settlement per dollar of unsecured liabilities.

(AICPA adapted)

Problem 18–12

The Martin Manufacturing Company cannot meet its obligations, and a receiver is appointed on April 28, 1971. The books are closed on that date and the following trial balance drawn off:

Cash		$ 800
Receivables		1,400
Finished goods		100,000
Materials and supplies		15,000
Goods on consignment (out)		220,000
Employees' bonds		4,700
Unexpired insurance		800
Machinery and equipment		507,300
		$850,000

Accounts payable		$110,000
Bank overdraft		1,000
Bank loans		105,000
Smith and Company		250,000
Acceptances		23,000
Collateral notes payable		4,700
Lease—machinery		30,000
Accrued interest on lease		2,000
City taxes accrued		4,000
Mortgage on machinery		100,000
Accrued interest on mortgage		3,000
Accumulated depreciation		7,300
Capital stock—preferred		100,000
Capital stock—common		100,000
Retained earnings		10,000
		$850,000

On November 20, 1971, the receiver, having disposed of all assets except $400 accounts receivable which he considers doubtful calls upon you to prepare an interim statement for the information of shareholders and creditors. An examination of the company's and the receiver's books and records discloses the following:

a) Cash receipts:

Collection of accounts receivable............................	$ 1,000
Rebate upon cancellation of all insurance....................	100
Proceeds from surrender of insurance policy on life of manager...	1,000
Sales of finished goods during receivership..................	75,000
Rent of sublet portion of building.........................	1,000
Unclaimed wages......................................	500
Interest on bank account................................	200
Sale of all goods and supplies on hand after operations were discontinued......................................	25,000
Sale of all machinery and equipment owned..................	200,000
	$303,800

b) Cash disbursements:

City taxes...	$ 4,000
Interest on city taxes....................................	400
Mortgage...	100,000
Interest on mortgage....................................	5,000
Labor, materials, and other operating and general expenses during receivership......................................	61,000
	$170,400

c)   Of the stocks on hand on April 28, finished goods costing $60,000 were sold during the receivership operations and $9,000 materials and supplies were used.

d)   The accounts payable are understated by $10,000 and include an item of $5,000 which is in dispute.

e)   The merchandise on consignment was pledged as collateral for the advances by Smith & Company and was accepted by them in part payment of these advances at full book value.

f)   The collateral notes payable were for accommodation of employees and were secured by deposit of bonds. The notes were paid by the employees and the bonds returned to them.

g)   The lease covered machinery worth $30,000 used by the company under a lease agreement. It was returned by the receiver and was accepted in full satisfaction of this agreement and all interest accrued.

h)   Claims were filed for all liabilities except an item of $7,000 accounts payable.

i)   Receiver's fees need not be considered.

Required:

Prepare a columnar statement showing the realization of assets, liquidation of liabilities, and operations during the receivership; also indicate amounts of unsecured creditors' claims and available assets on November 20, 1971.

(AICPA adapted)

Problem 18–13

The stockholders of the Agriculture Equipment Company, vendors of horse-drawn machinery, resolved at their meeting of June 13, 1971, to liquidate as of

August 31, 1971. The May 31, 1971, financial statement on which the stock-holders predicated their decision to liquidate follows:

AGRICULTURE EQUIPMENT COMPANY
Balance Sheet
As at May 31, 1971

ASSETS

Cash...	$ 36,750
Accounts receivable.............................	33,500
Inventory.......................................	120,250
Total Current Assets.........................	$190,500
Furniture, fixtures, trucks, etc., less accumulated depreciation..................................	20,500
Land and building less accumulated depreciation.......	30,000
Total Assets...............................	$241,000

EQUITIES

Accounts payable, including taxes....................		$ 15,600
Interest accrued on mortgage.......................		250
Accrued payroll.................................		450
Total Current Liabilities.......................		$ 16,300
6% mortgage due January 1, 1973..................		10,000
Capital stock, 4,200 shares, par value $50...........		210,000
Retained earnings—balance at January 1, 1971........	$24,050	
Less loss for 5 mos. to May 31, 1971..............	19,350	
Balance.......................................		4,700
Total Equities..............................		$241,000

According to the stockholders' resolution of June 13, the liquidation is to be effected by the directors (who, being principal stockholders, serve without compensation) as follows:

"The $15,000 cash bid of a local real estate operator for the equity in the land and building is to be accepted immediately, the purchaser to assume the outstanding mortgage of $10,000 and to pay all expenses of title search, closing, etc. Title is to pass as of June 30, 1971, and Agriculture Equipment Company is to pay mortgage interest accrued to that date. Insurance and taxes prepaid prior to June 30, 1971, are to be absorbed by vendor.

"All merchandise on hand is to be offered for sale at 80 percent of regular sales prices, such special sale to be conducted from June 17 to June 26 (both dates inclusive). These sales are to be on a strictly cash basis and to be final—no returns permitted.

"An auction is to be conducted on June 29 on the company's premises and is to include all merchandise not disposed of during the previous 10-day sale. All furniture, fixtures, and trucks and other equipment are also to be auctioned at this time. All sales made at such auction are to be strictly cash and final.

"Any merchandise still remaining unsold after the auction is to be advertised daily in newspapers of neighboring communities and disposed of at best prices obtainable.

"All employees, except the manager-bookkeeper, are to be given immediate notice of their release, at the close of business on June 30, and to be paid up to July 31. The manager-bookkeeper is to be given immediate notice of his release effective August 31, 1971, on which date he will be paid his salary for the four months ending December 31.

"A liquidating dividend (final) is to be paid on September 2, 1971, to all stockholders of record as of August 31, 1971."

Sales of merchandise to regular customers on credit for the period from June 1 to 16 inclusive amounted to $9,500 and were merged with the liquidation sales. All merchandise unsold after the auction was finally disposed of in August.

Depreciation subsequent to May 31, 1971, may be ignored.

Following is a summary of the cash transactions for the three months ended August 31, 1971:

Cash Transactions

		Dr.	Cr.
June	Cash sales—regular	$ 5,850	
	Accounts receivable collections	23,500	
	Cash sales (special 20% discount)	47,350	
	Cash received from auction sales:		
	Merchandise	31,500	
	Furniture, fixtures, and trucks	8,250	
	Auctioneer's commission and expenses		$ 2,850
	Interest on mortgage paid to May 31		300
	Proceeds from sale of land and building	15,000	
	Officers and office salaries (including separation		
	payments and $450 accrued payroll)		5,550
	Accounts payable		15,600
July	Accounts receivable collections	1,250	
	Postauction sales:		
	Merchandise	3,500	
	Furniture, fixtures, and trucks	2,300	
	Salary of manager-bookkeeper for July		400
Aug.	Accounts receivable collections (final)	3,700	
	Collection agency fees		375
	Salary of manager-bookkeeper (including separation		
	payment)		2,000
	Legal fees and expenses re liquidation		675
		$142,200	$27,750

Required:

Prepare from the foregoing information:

(i) A columnar working sheet showing the postings of cash transactions, the adjustments, losses of realization and expenses of liquidation, and the cash available for final distribution.

(ii) A statement showing the amount of cash to be distributed as a liquidating dividend to each of the following stockholders:

A	1,600 shares
B	1,200 shares
C	900 shares
D	360 shares
E	140 shares
Total	4,200 shares

(AICPA adapted)

Chapter 19

Accounting for Estates and Trusts

ADMINISTRATION BY A FIDUCIARY

Introduction

A *fiduciary* is a person to whom is entrusted the property of another for safekeeping, management, and/or distribution, and who is accountable therefor to various interested parties. Either an individual or a corporation may serve in this capacity. The importance of the fiduciary relationship has been indicated previously in references to receivers and trustees for financially distressed businesses. The fiduciary occupies an equally important role in respect to the administration of estates and trusts.

Upon the death of an individual (the *decedent*), it is necessary that a personal representative of the deceased assume custody and control of his estate. In the event that the decedent has executed a valid will in which is indicated his choice of a representative, his wishes will normally control. In such a circumstance, the decedent is said to have died *testate,* he is referred to as the *testator,* and when confirmed by court appointment, his representative is known as the *executor.* Should the decedent fail to execute a valid will, he is said to have died *intestate,* and his representative selected by the court is known as an *administrator.* If there exists a will, the last expressions of the decedent contained therein usually will govern the distribution of his estate; if no will exists, or if the will is determined to be invalid, the various state *laws of descent and distribution* will control the disposition of the decedent's estate. The laws of descent control the disposition of real property; the laws of distribution regulate the disposition of personal property.

The administration of estates normally comes within the purview of courts referred to as *probate, surrogate, orphan's,* or *county* courts. Before a will can become an effective instrument of fiduciary authority, it must be *admitted to probate.* To probate a will is to prove its validity, i.e., to prove that it was executed by a competent decedent without duress or other improper influence, and that it represents the last expressions of the decedent concerning the disposition of his property. Witnesses to the signing of the will may be called upon to testify as to these and other

650

matters and the genuineness of the various signatures. Once the will is admitted to probate, the court may then proceed to the appointment of an executor. If the person named in the will is able and willing to serve, he is usually confirmed by the court and is issued *letters testamentary,* which are the evidence of his formal authority to assume the role of fiduciary. If an administrator is appointed, he is similarly issued *letters of administration* empowering him to act as fiduciary.

Role of the Fiduciary in Estate Administration

While one is not bound to accept appointment as a fiduciary, once it has been accepted there is a commitment to faithfully discharge the obligations of that trust. The fiduciary must first seek out and take possession of the property of the deceased; he is then charged with exercising reasonable prudence in respect to the care and management of the property. Consequently, he is required to keep estate resources invested to the extent that investments may profitably be made; to liquidate all just debts of the decedent, including estate and inheritance taxes; and to distribute the decedent's property according to the provisions of the will or in the manner prescribed by law.

Real property of the testator usually passes directly by *devise* to *devisees* identified in the will, legal title vesting in the latter at the date of the decedent's death. However, since the fiduciary is frequently called upon to include both real and personal property in various reports required by governmental agencies, including those submitted for federal estate and state inheritance tax purposes, it may be desirable to include real property in the inventory of the decedent's assets. While the fiduciary has no accountability with respect thereto, he may petition the court to allow the sale of such property in order to meet the obligations of the decedent when personal property is clearly inadequate for this purpose.

Inventory of Assets

The fiduciary is required to submit a complete inventory of the properties of the decedent to the court of his appointment. This inventory should contain a full and complete description of all assets which are entrusted to the care and management of the fiduciary. Some of the assets may have no apparent value; yet, for reasons of completeness in the enumeration, such items should be detailed, with an indication of no value. Among the assets often included in an estate inventory are bank balances, valuables in locked depositories, corporate and government securities, advances to legatees, accrued interest, dividends receivable, accounts and other receivables, judgments payable to the estate, and interests in jointly owned property. The proceeds from a life insurance policy for which the estate is the indicated beneficiary are properly included as an estate asset; in the event that other beneficiaries are specified, payment is made directly to those named, and the relevant insurance contracts are excluded from the estate inventory. Where the estate includes a partnership interest, this property right must be disclosed and evaluated. Valuation may require liquidation of the partnership, unless continuity is provided for and assured by the decedent's will or the partnership agreement.

The assignment of value to estate assets is the primary responsibility of the fiduciary, although he may be aided by court-appointed appraisers. For example, the Texas Probate Code provides:

Within ninety days after his qualification, unless a longer time shall be granted by the court, the representative shall file with the clerk of court a verified, full and detailed inventory, in one written instrument, of all the property of such estate which has come to his possession or knowledge, which inventory shall include:

(a) all real property of the estate situated in the State of Texas;

(b) all personal property of the estate wherever situated. The representative shall set out in the inventory his appraisement of the fair market value of each item thereof as of the date of death in the case of grant of letters testamentary or of administration or as of the date of grant of letters of guardianship, as the case may be; provided that if the court shall appoint an appraiser or appraisers of the estate, the representative shall determine the fair market value of each item of the inventory with the assistance of such appraiser or appraisers and shall set out in the inventory such appraisement. The inventory shall specify what portion of the property, if any, is separate property and what portion, if any, is community property. If any property is owned in common with others, the interest owned by the estate shall be shown, together with the names and relationship, if known, of co-owners. Such inventory, when approved by the court and duly filed with the clerk of court, shall constitute for all purposes the inventory and appraisement of the estate referred to in this Code. The court for good cause shown may require the filing of the inventory and appraisement at a time prior to ninety days after the qualification of the representative [Section 250].

The statutes of the various states often provide that in addition to real property, specific items of personalty pass directly to the distributees. These items may include specified household effects, clothing of the decedent, and other personal effects which are considered of special value to the surviving spouse and/or minor children. Legal title to all personal property not so exempted vests in the fiduciary. Only those items of personalty for which the fiduciary assumes legal responsibility are included in the inventory of assets.

When assets are discovered subsequent to the filing of the inventory, it is appropriate that the fiduciary file a supplemental report, enumerating these additions. The sum of the original and supplemental listings comprises the *corpus,* or the *principal,* of the estate at date of the decedent's death.

Claims against the Estate

The fiduciary is obliged in most states to give public notice to those having claims against the estate of the decedent requesting them to make a presentment of these claims within a specified period of time. Presentment may be made either to the fiduciary or to the court. The fiduciary must necessarily determine the validity of the claims, rejecting those considered to be invalid; in this connection, he is required to exhaust all appropriate legal defenses, including the statute of limitations and the statute of frauds. The length of time allowed for creditors to file a claim against the estate varies among the several states; a period frequently prescribed is one year from the date of the publication of the first notice. In many states this period has been shortened to six months or less.

Once the validity of claims has been confirmed, the fiduciary must establish the *sequence of paying* the various obligations and proceed with their settlement. In the event the estate is solvent, the order of settlement may not be especially important. However, for insolvent estates, the statutes provide the priority sequence which the fiduciary must follow if he is to avoid personal liability for improper distribution. The following order of payment is fairly typical:

1. Funeral and administration expenses.
2. Debts which are secured by a lien on the decedent's property.
3. Taxes, including estate and inheritance taxes.
4. Judgments in force which are a lien against property of the decedent at time of death.
5. Provable debts against the estate.
6. Wages due domestics or other employees.
7. Sustenance payments to the widow for a specified period of time.

The Texas Probate Code provides for the following priorities in respect to the claims against the estates of decedents:

Class 1. Funeral expenses and expenses of last sickness for a reasonable amount to be approved by the court, not to exceed one thousand dollars, any excess to be classified and paid as other unsecured claims.

Class 2. Expenses of administration and expenses incurred in the preservation, safe-keeping, and management of the estate.

Class 3. Claims secured by mortgage or other liens so far as the same can be paid out of the proceeds of the property subject to such mortgage or other lien, and when more than one mortgage or lien shall exist upon the same property, the oldest shall be first paid; but no preference shall be given to such mortgage or other lien.

Class 4. All other claims legally exhibited within one year after the original grant of letters testamentary or of administration.

Class 5. All claims legally exhibited after the lapse of one year from the original grant of letters testamentary or of administration [Section 322].

Where the decedent's estate is small, the involvements of estate administration may be reduced somewhat. The Model Small Estates Act provides for the following simplified procedure:

Summary Administration of Small Estates. If it shall appear at the time of the appointment of a personal representative or at any time subsequent thereto by an allegation in the petition for the appointment of the personal representative, by a separate affidavit or otherwise, that the value of the entire estate, less liens and encumbrances, does not exceed $10,000, the court in its discretion may authorize a summary administration of the estate in any one or more of the following respects:

(1) By ordering that notice be given to creditors to present their claims within [three (3) months] after the first publication of such notice or be barred as in other cases;

(2) By dispensing with notice by publication in any or all subsequent portions of such proceedings and ordering that notice be given by posting or mailing in lieu of publication;

(3) By appointing but one appraiser for valuing the assets of the estate;

(4) By dispensing entirely with the appointment of an appraiser, if the value of the estate is readily determinable, and by authorizing the personal representative alone to appraise the estate;

(5) By exercising its discretion in fixing the amount of the bond of the personal representative, or dispensing with such bond, but in the absence of special circumstances, the bond shall be fixed in the amount of the value of any part of the estate which the court can determine from examination that the personal representative could easily convert during the period of administration plus the value of the gross annual income of the estate;

(6) By conferring upon the personal representative full power to sell, lease for periods not exceeding one year, mortgage, assign, transfer or convey any property of the estate upon such terms and conditions and for such considerations as he may determine, without any other order or confirmation of the court; or

(7) By ordering final distribution of the estate at any time after the expiration of such [three (3) months'] period after the first publication of notice to creditors.

In any such case creditors not presenting their claims within the time stated in the notice to creditors shall be barred as in other cases. No error in the statement of the value of the estate or the subsequent discovery of additional assets shall affect the validity of any order directing the summary administration of the estate or any order or proceeding in connection with the administration of the estate. Any person dealing with a personal representative upon whom powers have been conferred as herein prescribed shall be entitled to rely fully upon the powers so conferred upon him, but such personal representative in exercising any such powers shall be held accountable to the estate and shall make a final report and account of his administration to be settled by the court as in other cases [Model Small Estates Act, Section 11, 9C, U.L.A.].

Bequests of Personal Property

A testator's bequest of personal property is referred to as a *legacy;* the recipient is called a *legatee.* Legacies are classified as specific, demonstrative, general, and residual.

1. A *specific* legacy is a bequest of personal property which is specifically identified in the will; it normally consists of such items as clothing, ornaments, furniture, securities, and other personal effects.
2. A *demonstrative* legacy is a testamentary bequest payable out of a designated fund or specified asset accumulation. Gifts of cash payable out of a designated bank account and the bequest of a quantity of grain from a specified granary are examples of demonstrative legacies.
3. A *general* legacy, unlike a demonstrative legacy, is a bequest of money or other property without special designation as to source.
4. A *residual* legacy is the terminal distribution of personal property after all debts have been paid and all other legacies distributed or otherwise provided for. A residual legatee receives the residue of the estate.

Legacies are distributed in the priority outlined above; in the event there is insufficient property to satisfy all legacies, they will be abated or scaled down in the reverse of this order. A legacy may not always be paid, even though there exists a solvent estate; in such an instance, the default is termed a "failure" of a legacy. Failure may exist where the legatee has died previous to the testator's death, the property has undergone deterioration or has suffered destruction, or there exist provisions in the will which controvert public policy.

The statutes of many states provide for bequests by *advancement* where the decedent dies intestate. Should the decedent during his lifetime make a gift of property to individuals (usually children or lineal descendents) who would otherwise be entitled to inherit a part of the estate of the donor upon his death, the bequest may be regarded as an advancement in anticipation of the advancee's intestate share. However, all gratuitous *inter vivos* transfers before death are regarded as absolute gifts, not advancements, unless contrary intent can be demonstrated.

Role of the Fiduciary in Trust Administration

Provision may be made by a testate decedent that property comprising his estate, or a part thereof, shall be placed in trust. A *trust* is an arrangement whereby title to property is transferred to a *trustee,* either an individual or corporation, who holds or manages the property for the benefit of others. While there are various types of trusts, two classes predominate—living trusts and testamentary trusts. *Living trusts, or trusts inter vivos,* are created and become operative during the lifetime of the creator. A *testamentary trust* is created by provision in the will of the testator. In the event the trustee is also specified in the will, he becomes a *testamentary trustee.*

A trust is created or established by a *donor, trustor,* or *founder;* those expected to derive benefit therefrom are *beneficiaries.* The trust agreement may provide that the principal of the trust shall eventually be distributed to one beneficiary while income is to be currently awarded another. However, the principal and income beneficiary may be the same person; for example, the income only of a trust may be distributed to a beneficiary until he attains his majority, after which the principal is conveyed to him. The income beneficiary is called a *cestui que trust*. If he receives income for life, he is referred to as a *life tenant*. The recipient of the principal of the trust is termed a *remainderman*.

A trustee normally has only such authority as is conveyed to him by the trust instrument. This authority usually includes:

1.   The incurrence of those costs and expenses necessary to the preservation of the trust principal.
2.   The sale, exchange, or improvements in respect to existing realty.
3.   The settlement, totally or by compromise, of claims against the trust estate.
4.   The making of new investments and disposition of existing investments.
5.   The distribution of property to distributees as provided in the trust agreement.
6.   The making of advances to beneficiaries.
7.   The payment to or expending of income for the benefit of minors.

A testamentary trustee does not accept an accountability as a fiduciary until trust property is conveyed to him. Legal title to real property customarily vests in the trustee upon the decedent's death; title to personal property, however, passes to the trustee with the transfer of property. The trustee is charged with exercising that degree of care in respect to trust property as he would exercise as a reasonably prudent businessman acting in his own self-interest. The creator of a trust may, by provision in the trust instrument, reserve unto himself the right to relieve the trustee from duties and liabilities otherwise imposed upon him; similarly, by express provision in the trust instrument, the creator of the trust may add to or impose new duties, restrictions, privileges, and powers upon the trustee. The trustee may also be relieved of his duties by a court of competent jurisdiction. The Uniform Trusts Act specifically provides that such a court may, for cause shown and upon notice to the beneficiaries, relieve a trustee from any or all of the duties and restrictions which would otherwise be imposed upon him [Uniform Trusts Act, Section 19, 9C, U.L.A.].

The trustee should weigh carefully the desirability of investing uncommitted cash accumulations in income-producing assets, subject to existing statutory constraints. Where there is reasonable doubt as to the propriety of a proposed course of action in respect to investments, the trustee should seek the opinion of legal counsel; he is usually allowed a reasonable period of time in which to make such investments without penalty for uninvested funds. He is under a special duty to keep separate the trust assets from his own property, unless a contrary provision exists in the trust instrument. In the event of loss which may arise from commingling of trust and other properties, courts have held the trustee guilty of a breach of trust.

DUAL BASES OF ACCOUNTABILITY

Principal (Corpus) and Income Distinguished

It is especially important that the fiduciary carefully identify those elements which comprise the principal of an estate or trust and those which make up its income. A testator's direction that the principal and income from an estate shall be distributed to different beneficiaries accents the importance of this distinction. The fiduciary is also required in many instances to calculate and pay taxes upon income and principal separately. The principal-income distinction is difficult to make, and often subtle, because of the diverse provisions of state statutes and the special characteristics of the elements themselves. The decedent may expressly indicate, either in the will or in the trust indenture, the criteria to be used in making the identification; where no such provision exists, the courts must necessarily look to the statutes for distinguishing characteristics. It is important that accounting records be established and maintained by the fiduciary in such manner as to preserve this distinction.

The principal of an estate normally consists of the aggregate of the decedent's property at the date of his death, including items of accrued income which then attach thereto. Necessarily, assets existing at date of death, although discovered subsequent to the filing of the inventory, are properly includible in the principal of an estate. Gains recognized on the conversion of principal assets are treated as increments to principal. Reductions in principal are usually a result of the fiduciary's expenditures for debts of the decedent, funeral expenses and expenses of last illness, expenses incurred in administering the estate as contrasted with those incurred to generate estate income, losses from the sale or conversion of principal assets, and distributions to legatees.

The income of an estate is the increase or growth in estate properties subsequent to the decedent's death which is not attributable to the conversion of principal assets. Usually this increase can be ascribed to the earnings which derive from the profitable employment of principal assets. The income of an estate is decreased by those expense items which are associated with the earning of estate income and by distributions to income beneficiaries.

In respect to charges against and credits to income and principal, the Revised Uniform Principal and Income Act contains the following general provisions:

(a) Unless the will otherwise provides and subject to subsection (b), all expenses incurred in connection with the settlement of a decedent's estate, including debts, funeral expenses, estate taxes, interest and penalties concerning taxes, family allowances, fees of attorneys and personal representatives, and court costs shall be charged against the principal of the estate.

(b) Unless the will otherwise provides, income from the assets of a decedent's estate after the death of the testator and before distribution, including income from property used to discharge liabilities, shall be determined in accordance with the rules applicable to a trustee under this Act and distributed as follows:

> (1) to specific legatees and devises, the income from the property bequeathed or devised to them respectively, less taxes, ordinary repairs, and other expenses of management and operation of the property, and an appropriate portion of the interest accrued since the death of the testator and of taxes imposed on income (excluding taxes on capital gains) which accrue during the period of administration;

> (2) to all other legatees and devisees, except legatees of pecuniary bequests not in trusts, the balance of the income, less the balance of taxes, ordinary repairs, and other expenses of management and operation of all property from which the estate is entitled to income, interest accrued since the death of the testator, and taxes imposed on income (excluding taxes on capital gains) which accrue during the period of administration, in proportion to their respective interests in the undistributed assets of the estate computed at times of distribution on the basis of inventory value.

(c) Income received by a trustee under subsection (b) shall be treated as income of the trust [Revised Uniform Principal and Income Act, Section 5, 9B, U.L.A.].

There are a number of circumstances for which the above generalizations are not completely descriptive. They are discussed in the following section.

Special Problems

Accrued Items. Accruals of income at the date of the decedent's death are normally regarded as components of estate principal; such accruals often consist of interest on receivable or investment balances. Interest on these assets earned during tenancy is regarded as income of the estate. In respect to savings accounts and time deposits, accrued interest is regarded as either principal or income depending upon when the interest credit is made available to the depositor. Accrued interest payable normally follows the same classification rules with respect to income or principal as does interest receivable, i.e., interest accrued to the date of the testator's death is a debt of the estate and accordingly chargeable to principal when disbursed; interest paid or incurred subsequently is ordinarily chargeable to income.

In most states, rents receivable at the date of the decedent's death are includible in the principal of the estate; the amount of rent earned during tenancy is regarded as income. Similarly, rent expense payable at date of death is a charge against the estate principal, while accruals thereafter are charges against income.

It is assumed that taxes on real property of the testator customarily do not accrue. The tax expense rather is regarded as relating to the period when the tax becomes a lien on the assessed property. Where the lien becomes effective before the decedent's death, the tax expense is chargeable to the principal of the estate; where the lien becomes effective subsequent to the decedent's death, the expense is a charge against income. As indicated earlier, estate taxes are levied against and payable out of the principal assets of the estate. Income taxes, however, must be identified with the elements making up the taxable base. The amount of income tax which relates to gains or losses on the conversion of principal assets is chargeable to principal; the amount levied on normal operating net income during the administration of the estate is chargeable against income. Income taxes for a fractional period prior to the decedent's death are payable out of the principal of the estate.

Dividends Received.   Corporate dividends are not generally accounted for on an accrual basis. Ordinary cash dividends declared prior to the decedent's death are a part of the principal of the estate; declarations subsequent to death usually represent income of the estate. In some states, the significant identifying date is the date of record. In respect to dividends which are declared and received during tenancy, the statutes of the several states are not wholly agreed as to the most appropriate accounting classification. Some follow the Massachusetts rule, which generally provides that all cash dividends, whatever their magnitude and from whatever source, are to be regarded as income accruing to the income beneficiary; stock dividends, however, are regarded as additions to principal. In application of this rule, the *form* of the dividend controls. Other states follow the Pennsylvania rule which emphasizes the *source* of the declaration. If it is determined that the dividend is payable out of earnings accumulated prior to the creation of the trust estate, all dividends— whether in cash or shares of stock—are regarded as belonging to principal. However, if it is established that only those earnings accumulated subsequent to the formation of the trust estate are declared as dividends, the receipt (including the market value of stock dividends) is accorded the status of income. The distinction is frequently implemented in terms of whether the dividend is ordinary or extraordinary. Where dividends relate partially to earnings accumulated prior to the creation of the trust estate and partially subsequent thereto, the fiduciary may apportion the receipt as between income and principal. In this allocation, reliance is usually placed on the relative book values of the corporate stock at the date of the decedent's death and at the date of dividend payment. If the book value after the dividend payment is less than the book value at date of the decedent's death, an amount equivalent to the reduction in value shall be credited to principal with the residual amount of the receipt regarded as income. Stock dividends are accorded parallel treatment, although the allocation is made in terms of shares of stock.

Stock rights which are a part of the decedent's estate at death, or which are acquired subsequently in respect to corporate securities belonging to the deceased at date of death, are elements of principal; accordingly, proceeds from the sale of such rights, reflecting conversion gains and losses, are also regarded as principal.

In respect to corporate distributions, the underlying emphasis of the Massachusetts rule is clearly reflected in the Revised Uniform Principal and Income Act:

(a) Corporate distributions of shares of the distributing corporation, including distributions in the form of a stock split or stock dividend, are principal. A right to subscribe to shares or other securities issued by the distributing corporation accruing to stockholders on account of their stock ownership and the proceeds of any sale of the right are principal.

(b) Except to the extent that the corporation indicates that some part of a corporate distribution is a settlement of preferred or guaranteed dividends accrued since the trustee became a stockholder or is in lieu of an ordinary cash dividend, a corporate distribution is principal if the distribution is pursuant to

(1) a call of shares;

(2) a merger, consolidation, reorganization, or other plan by which assets of the corporation are acquired by another corporation; or

(3) a total or partial liquidation of the corporation, including any distribution which the corporation indicates is a distribution of assets, other than cash, pursuant to a court decree or final administrative order by a government agency ordering distribution of the particular assets.

(c) Distributions made from ordinary income by a regulated investment company or by a trust qualifying and electing to be taxed under federal law as a real estate investment trust are income. All other distributions made by the company or trust, including distributions from capital gains, depreciation, or depletion, whether in the form of cash or an option to take new stock or cash or an option to purchase additional shares, are principal.

(d) Except as provided in subsections (a), (b), and (c), all corporate distributions are income, including cash dividends, distributions of, or rights to subscribe to, shares or securities or obligations of corporations other than the distributing corporation, and the proceeds of the rights or property distributions. Except as provided in subsections (b) and (c), if the distributing corporation gives a stockholder an option to receive a distribution either in cash or in its own shares, the distribution chosen is income.

(e) The trustee may rely upon any statement of the distributing corporation as to any fact relevant under any provision of this Act concerning the source or character of dividends or distributions of corporate assets [Revised Uniform Principal and Income Act, Section 6, 9B, U.L.A.].

These provisions, particularly subsection (e), extend the "form" test of the Massachusetts rule to include a "source" test in certain instances. However, this latter criterion logically does not include ordinary stock dividends, as in the Pennsylvania rule.

In most states, the courts have held that dividends payable from sources other than earnings relate to principal. Script and property dividends are accorded treatment equivalent to cash dividends. Liquidating dividends are accounted for by the fiduciary as in a commercial enterprise, i.e., they are regarded as a return of capital and are accordingly classified as adjustments of principal.

Partnership Earnings. It is normally assumed that partnership profits do not accrue. Partnership net income is determined as a consequence of, and concurrent with, a formal closing of the partnership books. Where the partnership books are closed upon the death of a partner, the calculated share of profits assigned to the deceased partner for the fractional period previous to the date of death is normally regarded as principal of his estate. In the event the partners, pursuant to provisions of the partnership agreement, elect not to close the partnership books until a date subsequent to the testator's death, there is no evident consensus among accountants as to the disposition of partnership earnings for the interval between the last closing date prior to the decedents' death and the subsequent closing date. Should the partnership agreement provide for interest on partners' capitals, such interest prior to the decedent's death is includible in principal; that which accrues during the subsequent period is income.

Depreciation and Maintenance. Depreciation (or value exhaustion) may or may not be chargeable against the income of an estate or trust during a period of tenancy. This question depends upon the testator's intentions, as indicated in the will or trust instrument, in respect to preserving the principal of the estate intact.

Expenditures for repairs, and other maintenance outlays, the effect of which is to materially improve or enhance the value of estate or trust properties follow traditional rules of capitalization, i.e., they are normally chargeable to principal. However, those expenditures the benefits of which merely preserve the normal operating efficiency of the depreciable assets are regarded as income charges. Where the benefits relate partially to principal and partially to income, an apportionment of the expenditure should be made, based upon estimates of measurable benefit.

In the event that trust estate properties consist of wasting assets, i.e., mineral deposits, timber, etc., the wishes of the testator will also control in respect to charges for depletion. If there is persuasive evidence that the testator intended to preserve for the remainderman the undiminished value of the original property, the fiduciary should withhold for the remainderman income in an amount equal to the value exhaustion for depletion. However, if the evidence indicates that income, without reduction in amount for depletion, should accrue to the benefit of the income beneficiary, the principal should be reduced accordingly by the amount of cumulative depletion allowances.

Discount/Premium on Bond Investments. Corporate bonds held by the decedent are usually evaluated in terms of prices established by exchange quotations or over-the-counter trading at the date of the decedent's death. To the extent that premiums or discounts are reflected in these quotations, a question exists as to subsequent amortization by the fiduciary. A position often taken is that no provision should be made for the amortization of premium or the accumulation of discount. According to this view, principal is not regarded as having been affected so long as the estate consists of the specific assets inventoried, and the periodic interest receipts are classified as estate income. Consequently, the act of disposing of the bonds becomes the critical point for recognizing the increase or impairment in the value of estate corpus.

In respect to bonds *acquired by the fiduciary during tenancy,* however, premiums are customarily amortized while discounts are not amortized. This convention in respect to amortization is manifestly inconsistent with the treatment of premiums or discounts on bond investments included in the original estate inventory. Of course, the wishes of the testator will prevail should they indicate otherwise. In recording amortization, it is important to recognize that brokerage expenses and transfer fees are elements of investment cost. As in the case of securities existing at date of death, gains and losses on the conversion of subsequently acquired investments are regarded as principal.

Expenses.   Those expenses which are clearly identifiable with the conservation, management, and distribution of the principal of the trust-estate are appropriate charges against principal; however, income of the trust-estate must bear the charges for expenses which pertain to the earning of income during a period of tenancy. The Revised Uniform Principal and Income Act enumerates various expense items to be charged either against income or against principal.

(a) The following charges shall be made against income:

(1) ordinary expenses incurred in connection with the administration, management, or preservation of the trust property, including regularly recurring taxes assessed against any portion of the principal, water rates, premiums or insurance taken upon the interests of the income beneficiary, remainderman, or trustee, interest paid by the trustee, and ordinary repairs;

(2) a reasonable allowance for depreciation on property subject to depreciation under generally accepted accounting principles, but no allowance shall be made for depreciation of that portion of any real property used by a beneficiary as a residence or for depreciation of any property held by the trustee on the effective date of this Act for which the trustee is not then making an allowance for depreciation;

(3) one-half of court costs, attorney's fees, and other fees on periodic judicial accounting, unless the court directs otherwise;

(4) court costs, attorney's fees, and other fees on other accountings or judicial proceedings if the matter primarily concerns the income interest, unless the court directs otherwise;

(5) one-half of the trustee's regular compensation, whether based on a percentage of principal or income, and all expenses reasonably incurred for current management of principal and application of income;

(6) any tax levied upon receipts defined as income under this Act or the trust instrument and payable by the trustee.

(b) If charges against income are of unusual amount, the trustee may by means of reserves or other reasonable means charge them over a reasonable period of time and withhold from distribution sufficient sums to regularize distributions.

(c) The following charges shall be made against principal:

(1) trustee's compensation not chargeable to income under subsections (a) (4) and (a) (5) above, special compensation of trustees, expenses reasonably incurred in connection with principal, court costs and attorney's fees primarily concerning matters of principal, and trustee's compensation computed on principal as an acceptance, distribution, or termination fee;

(2) charges not provided for in subsection (a), including the cost of investing and reinvesting principal, the payments on principal of an indebtedness (including a mortgage amortized by periodic payments of principal), expenses for preparation of property for rental or sale, and, unless the court directs otherwise, expenses incurred in maintaining or defending any action to construe the trust or protect it or the property or assure the title of any trust property;

(3) extraordinary repairs or expenses incurred in making a capital improvement to principal, including special assessments, but, a trustee may establish an allowance for depreciation out of income to the extent permitted by subsection (a) (2);

(4) any tax levied upon profit, gain, or other receipts allocated to principal notwithstanding denomination of the tax as an income tax by the taxing authority;

(5) if an estate or inheritance tax is levied in respect of a trust in which both an income beneficiary and a remainderman have an interest, any amount apportioned to the trust, including interest and penalties, even though the income beneficiary also has rights in the principal [Revised Uniform Principal and Income Act, Section 13, 9B, U.L.A.].

Where this Act has not been adopted, and in the absence of contrary statutory requirements, the general criteria cited earlier in respect to charges against principal and income normally apply.

FIDUCIARY ACCOUNTS AND REPORTS

Fiduciary accounting accents the importance of delegated authority. The accounts of the fiduciary should clearly disclose the measure of his accountability and the extent to which it has been discharged. This emphasis on accountability compels a change in the fundamental accounting equation, which is modified as follows:

$$\text{Estate (Trust) Assets} = \text{Accountability}$$

It is evident that this accountability is stated in terms of total assets, without deducting the amount of existing claims against the estate or trust. A fiduciary is responsible for all of the assets entrusted to him; payment of existing claims is one way that a fiduciary discharges that responsibility.

The accounts and reports of the fiduciary should be kept in such form and detail as to sharply focus upon the *dual* responsibility of the fiduciary —in respect to income *and* in respect to principal. While the statutes of the various states provide important criteria for making this distinction, in many instances they do not prescribe the exact form and content of the fiduciary's accounts and reports.

Accounting Procedures and Entry Sequence for an Estate

Once the inventory of the decedent's assets has been filed, books of the estate should be opened in which are debited the accounts for assets enumerated in the inventory with a contra credit to Estate Principal, or Estate Corpus. Separate accounts should be provided for cash which is includable in the principal of the estate and cash which accumulates during tenancy and otherwise qualifies as estate income. The valuations assigned the various noncash assets are those indicated in the inventory. The Estate Principal, or Estate Corpus, account is credited with the gross amount of the inventory and represents the *initial* accountability of the fiduciary. In the event that other assets are discovered subsequent to the filing of the inventory, accounts should be opened for such assets with appropriate credits to Assets Subsequently Discovered. This account is a suspended credit to Estate Principal, to which it is closed at the end of the fiduciary accounting period.

Liabilities of the decedent are not recorded by the fiduciary until paid. Upon payment, an account—Debts of the Decedent Paid—is debited for the liquidation settlement. This transaction represents a reduction in the accountability of the fiduciary; accordingly, Debts of the Decedent Paid is essentially a suspended debit to Estate Principal. In respect to both assets and liabilities, the amount of account detail (and the necessity for subsidiary records) will be governed by the magnitude and diversity of assets in, and the number of claimants against, estate properties.

Gains or losses on the conversion of principal assets increase or decrease the accountability of the fiduciary in respect to the principal of the estate. Gain on Realization should be credited for conversion gains, and Loss on Realization should be debited for conversion losses; both accounts are closed to Estate Principal at the end of the accounting period. The increased (decreased) accountability of the fiduciary as a consequence of his profitable (unprofitable) employment of estate assets is not an attempt to measure net income; rather, it reflects a dominant stewardship orientation, the historical prototype of which is found in the master-slave relationship of Roman times. In this era, the slave was charged with funds entrusted to him by his master and with the increase attributable to fortunate investments; subsequently, he was discharged of his accountability to the extent of his repayment of resources advanced or accumulated or by other disposition as directed by the master. Most economic theories of income and asset valuation manifestly are not relevant to this type of fiduciary relationship. Correspondingly, the objectives of income determination and of stewardship reporting are essentially contradictory and are not accommodated by a single theoretical framework.

In addition to paying the debts of the decedent, the accountability of the fiduciary is further decreased by disbursements for funeral and administration expenses. A single Funeral and Administration Expenses account may be used for these outlays, or it may be desirable to identify the various expenses separately. Where a single account is used, its inclusions usually consist of expenses of last illness, funeral expenses, payments to the executor or trustee for administrative services to conserve the estate principal, accountant's, attorney's, and appraiser's fees, and court costs. The fiduciary's accountability in respect to principal is also decreased by the payment of estate taxes and the distribution of legacies. If a legacy involves the distribution of specific assets, the valuation assigned the distributed assets is the carrying value (accountability basis) of each asset, regardless of its current market value. This procedure is consistent with a stewardship, or accountability, objective. Where there are relatively few legatees, a single account—Legacies—may be sufficient; however, if the number of legatees is large, it may be desirable to use a separate account for each legatee. Where state inheritance taxes are to be charged against the legatees' accounts, or where it is necessary to reduce the legacies, it is especially important that separate accounts be maintained.

In respect to the fiduciary's accountability as to income, it is conventional to open an Income account to which are credited the various items of income for the estate. One account may be used for this purpose, or where there are numerous sources of income, several accounts which are descriptive as to source may be appropriate. Similarly, expenses incurred which are chargeable to such income should be debited to an Expenses–Income account or to several expense accounts detailing the nature of the expense. It is important that account designations clearly indicate an identification with either income or principal, where the conventional terminology does not convey the fact of this association. Distributions to income beneficiaries are usually charged to a Distribution to Income Beneficiary account, with the name of the indicated donee often appended.

Illustrative Problem

The following is a simplified case illustration of estate-trust accounting. William Archer died on June 1, 1971. His will, admitted to probate on June 10, 1971, provided that Andrew Archer, Sr., son of the decedent, be appointed executor. The will also provided that specific legacies of $2,500 cash be awarded to Andrew Jr. and Mark, grandsons of the decedent; $12,000 and the decedent's personal automobile to Andrew Sr.; personal effects and estate income to the widow, Alice; and the remainder of the estate property, after payment of debts and expenses and distribution of legacies, to be placed in trust. The income from the trust is to be paid to the widow during her lifetime, with the principal to be distributed equally to Andrew Jr. and Mark upon the widow's death.

Andrew Archer, Sr., filed the following inventory with the probate court on June 25:

Cash in bank..	$ 28,000
Personal effects...	750
Life insurance policies payable to the estate......................	30,000
1,000 shares of Edens Company $50 par value common stock—at market...	49,000
500 shares of Cincy, Inc., 6 percent, $30 par value preferred stock— at market..	15,000
20 Burnett Corporation 5 percent 30-year $1,000 bonds (interest payable March 1 and September 1).............................	19,600
Automobile...	2,600
Dividend receivable (declared May 15, payable July 15, Edens Company common)...	1,500
Interest receivable (Burnett Corporation bonds)..................	250
	$146,700

On the same date, the fiduciary opened accounts for the estate of William Archer and recorded the inventory as follows:

June 25	Cash—principal............................. 28,000	
	Personal effects.............................. 750	
	Life insurance................................ 30,000	
	Edens Company common stock................. 49,000	
	Cincy, Inc. preferred stock.................... 15,000	
	Burnett Corporation bonds.................... 19,600	
	Automobile................................. 2,600	
	Dividend receivable.......................... 1,500	
	Interest receivable........................... 250	
	Estate principal............................	146,700

Transactions and entries of the fiduciary in the period following were:

June 28   Public notice was given that creditors of the estate of the decedent should make a presentment of their claims.

July 15   Paid funeral expenses, $1,400.

	Funeral and administration expenses........... 1,400	
	Cash—principal.......................	1,400

July 16   Collected dividends on Edens stock.

	Cash—principal............................ 1,500	
	Dividend receivable....................	1,500

July 20   Undeposited cash, $1,200, discovered among the decedent's personal belongings.

		Cash—principal..............................	1,200	
		Assets subsequently discovered...........		1,200

July 31 Received payment on insurance policies.

		Cash—principal...........................	30,000	
		Life insurance..........................		30,000

Aug. 15 Sold 100 shares of Cincy, Inc., stock for $4,000.

		Cash—principal...........................	4,000	
		Cincy, Inc., preferred stock..............		3,000
		Gain on realization.....................		1,000

Sept. 1 Collected interest on Burnett Corporation bonds.

		Cash—principal...........................	250	
		Cash—income............................	250	
		Interest receivable......................		250
		Income................................		250

Sept. 15 Paid debts of the decedent, $2,950.

		Debts of the decedent paid..................	2,950	
		Cash—principal........................		2,950

Oct. 1 Paid cash legacies provided for in the will.

		Legacy—Andrew Archer, Sr..................	12,000	
		Legacy—Andrew Archer, Jr..................	2,500	
		Legacy—Mark Archer......................	2,500	
		Cash—principal........................		17,000

Oct. 3 Delivered automobile (current market value, $1,800) to Andrew Archer, Sr.

		Legacy—Andrew Archer, Sr..................	2,600	
		Automobile.............................		2,600

Oct. 3 Delivered decedent's personal effects to widow.

		Legacy—Alice Archer.......................	750	
		Personal effects........................		750

Oct. 10 Collected cash dividend of $1,000 on Edens Company common stock.

		Cash—income.............................	1,000	
		Income................................		1,000

Oct. 15 Paid attorney's fees, $1,000, and other administrative expenses, $2,500. Of the latter, $200 relates to income.

		Funeral and administration expenses...........	3,300	
		Expenses—income........................	200	
		Cash—principal......................		3,300
		Cash—income........................		200

Oct. 30 Three percent semiannual dividend declared on Cincy, Inc., preferred stock.

Dividend receivable..........................	360	
Income..............................		360

Nov. 1   Income of the estate in the amount of $500 is distributed to the widow.

Distribution to income beneficiary—Alice Archer	500	
Cash—income..........................		500

Nov. 5   Two hundred shares of Edens Company common stock were sold for $9,000.

Cash—principal...........................	9,000	
Loss on realization........................	800	
Edens Company common stock...........		9,800

Dec. 1 $250 interst accrued on Burnett Corporation bonds to December 1.

Interest receivable..........................	250	
Income..............................		250

Dec. 1   The executor rendered an accountability report to the probate court.

Charge and Discharge Statement

A report detailing the particulars of estate administration should be prepared and submitted periodically to the court of appropriate jurisdiction. Such a report is the charge and discharge statement. It may be regarded as an interim or a final statement of the fiduciary's accountability, depending upon the period of time normal to the completion of the settlement of the estate. The general form of the statement is normally prescribed by the statutes of the various states; however, there is no apparent consensus as to a single most desirable form. The two-division statement to be illustrated in the following pages is generally descriptive of many of the reports presently in use.

The charge and discharge statement is a classified enumeration of the estate resources for which the fiduciary is accountable, and a description of the manner in which he has discharged his accountability during the period of his administration. His responsibilities for principal and income are separately reported. In respect to *principal,* the report indicates those asset categories for which the fiduciary *charges* himself, or has accepted a custodial responsibility. They include:

1. Assets enumerated in the inventory.
2. Assets subsequently discovered.
3. Gains recognized on the conversion or other disposition of principal assets.

There follows the discharge of the fiduciary's accountability, i.e., the offered justification for which the fiduciary *credits* himself. These credits include:

1. Payment of funeral and administration expenses.
2. Debts of the decedent paid.
3. Estate and inheritance taxes paid.
4. Payment or distribution of legacies.
5. Losses realized on conversion or other disposition of principal assets.

To the extent that there remains an undistributed asset accumulation, as would exist in respect to an interim report, or in a final report preceding the transfer of assets to a testementary trust, these accounts should be enumerated with assigned valuations.

In respect to income, the fiduciary *charges* himself for income earned since the date of the decedent's death. Items of income, if significant, should be identified as to source. Dispositions of income for which the fiduciary customarily *credits* himself include:

1. Expenses which are chargeable to such income.
2. Payments or other distributions to income beneficiaries.

Some accountants prefer to prepare separate reports for income and principal; their contents would necessarily be the same as the categories described above for a two-division statement.

Using the data of the estate of William Archer, a charge and discharge statement as of December 1 would assume the form shown in Illustration 19–1.

This statement (page 670) is a summary report and where necessary should be supported by schedules providing informative details with respect to each of the major categories. If subsequent reports are necessary, they are prepared on a cumulative basis and will continue to disclose fully the fiduciary's activities during the period of his accountability.

Closing Entries

When activities of estate administration are concluded, a final report is rendered, after which the fiduciary closes the accounts of the estate. In respect to principal, this involves closing to Estate Principal those relevant accounts created during the administration representing increases or decreases in the fiduciary's accountability. Accordingly, Assets Subsequently Discovered, Gains and Losses on Realization, Debts of the Decedent Paid, Legacies Paid or Distributed, and Funeral and Administration Expenses are closed to Estate Principal. Similarly, the accounts which are chargeable to Income should be closed thereunto. They include Expenses—Income and Distributions to Income Beneficiary. Unless assets remain for some ultimate disposition, these entries should reduce all accounts to zero balances.

Properties Transferred to Trustee

In the illustration begun earlier in this chapter, provision was made for the transfer of estate properties to a trustee, *after* the fiduciary's payment of

Illustration 19–1

ESTATE OF WILLIAM ARCHER
ANDREW ARCHER, SR., EXECUTOR

Charge and Discharge Statement
June 1, 1971, to December 1, 1971

AS TO PRINCIPAL

I charge myself with:

Assets per inventory..............................		$146,700
Assets subsequently discovered....................		1,200
Gain on realization.............................		1,000
Total.......................................		$148,900

I credit myself with:

Funeral and administration expenses...............	$ 4,700	
Debts of decedent paid..........................	2,950	
Legacies paid or distributed:		
Andrew Archer, Sr............................	14,600	
Andrew Archer, Jr............................	2,500	
Mark Archer................................	2,500	
Alice Archer................................	750	
Loss on realization.............................	800	28,800
Balance as to principal...........................		$120,100

Which includes:

Cash..		$ 49,300
Edens Company common stock.....................		39,200
Cincy, Inc., preferred stock.......................		12,000
Burnett Corporation bonds.......................		19,600
Total.......................................		$120,100

AS TO INCOME

I charge myself with:

Income collected or accrued.......................		$ 1,860

I credit myself with:

Expenses chargeable to income....................	$ 200	
Distribution to income beneficiary.................	500	700
Balance as to income.............................		$ 1,160

Which includes:

Cash..		$ 550
Dividend receivable.............................		360
Interest receivable..............................		250
Total.......................................		$ 1,160

debts of the decedent and expenses of administration and the payment and/or delivery of legacies. If it is assumed that the transfer of properties is made concurrent with the rendering of the charge and discharge statement on December 1, 1971, the following entries are required to close the books of the estate and to open the trust accounts:

Executor's Books

Dec. 1	Assets subsequently discovered................	1,200	
	Gain on realization.........................	1,000	
	Estate principal........................		2,200

Dec. 1	Estate principal............................	28,800	
	Debts of the decedent paid...............		2,950
	Funeral and administration expenses........		4,700
	Legacy—Andrew Archer, Sr...............		14,600
	Legacy—Andrew Archer, Jr...............		2,500
	Legacy—Mark Archer...................		2,500
	Legacy—Alice Archer...................		750
	Loss on realization.....................		800
Dec. 1	Income..................................	700	
	Expenses—income......................		200
	Distributions to income beneficiary........		500
Dec. 1	Estate principal............................	120,100	
	Income.................................	1,160	
	K. L. Mantle, trustee...................		121,260
Dec. 1	K. L. Mantle, trustee.......................	120,100	
	Cash—principal.......................		49,300
	Edens Company common stock...........		39,200
	Cincy, Inc., preferred stock..............		12,000
	Burnett Corporation bonds..............		19,600
Dec. 1	K. L. Mantle, trustee......................	1,160	
	Cash—income........................		550
	Dividend receivable.....................		360
	Interest receivable.....................		250

Trustee's Books

Dec. 1	Cash—principal............................	49,300	
	Edens Company common stock..............	39,200	
	Cincy, Inc., preferred stock.................	12,000	
	Burnett Corporation bonds.................	19,600	
	Trust principal.......................		120,100
Dec. 1	Cash—income............................	550	
	Dividend receivable......................	360	
	Interest receivable.......................	250	
	Income................................		1,160

The trustee normally accepts fiduciary responsibility concurrent with the transfer of trust property to him. All accrued income prior to the creation of a living trust is includable as trust principal; income earned thereafter is distributable to income beneficiaries. In respect to testamentary trusts, however, the trust usually becomes effective at date of death and income earned thereafter is trust income, nothwithstanding a delay in the transfer of trust properties to the trustee.

The trustee's accounting essentially parallels that of the executor. The Trust Principal and Income accounts are the summary accounts of the trustee, indicating his separate accountability as to both principal and income.

The trustee should render periodic reports of his stewardship to the court recounting the activities of his trust administration. As in the case of estates, the content of such statements depends upon the statutory provisions of the relevant state. The Uniform Trustees Accounting Act suggests that interim reports contain:

(a) the period which the account covers;

(b) the names and addresses of the living beneficiaries known to the trustee, with a statement as to those known to be minors or under legally declared disability; and a description of any possible unborn or unascertained beneficiaries; and the name of the surety or sureties on the trustee's bond with the amount of such bond;

(c) in a separate schedule the trust principal on hand at the beginning of the accounting period and the then status of its investment; the investments received from the settlor and still held; additions to trust principal during the accounting period with the dates and sources of acquisition; investments collected, sold or charged off during the accounting period, with the date and purpose of each; and trust principal on hand at the end of the accounting period, how invested, and the estimated market value of each investment;

(d) in a separate schedule the trust income on hand at the beginning of the accounting period, and in what form held; trust income received during the accounting period, when, and from what source; trust income paid out during the accounting period, when, to whom, and for what purpose; trust income on hand at the end of the accounting period, and how invested;

(e) that neither any seller of, nor buyer from, the trustee of trust property during the accounting period was at the time of such sale or purchase (1) in the case of a corporate trustee, an affiliate, or any officer, employee, or nominee of the trustee or of an affiliate; or was (2) in the case of a non-corporate trustee a relative, partner, employer, employee, or business associate; but none of the provisions of this subsection shall apply to purchases and sales made by brokers for the trustee or to stock exchanges;

(f) a statement of unpaid claims with the reason for failure to pay them, including a statement as to whether any estate or inheritance taxes have become due with regard to the trust property, and if due, whether paid;

(g) a brief summary of the account;

(h) such other facts as the court may by rule or court order require.

Within thirty days after the end of each yearly period thereafter during the life of the trust the testamentary trustee then in office shall file with the same court an intermediate account under oath showing corresponding facts regarding the current accounting period [Section 3, Uniform Trustees Accounting Act, 9C, U.L.A.].

As to the final accounting, the Act provides:

Within [   ] days after the termination of every testamentary trust the trustee, and in the case of the transfer of the trusteeship due to the death, resignation, removal, dissolution, merger or consolidation of a sole trustee, the successor in interest of the old trustee, shall file with the [probate court of the county where the will was admitted to probate] a final account under oath, showing for the period since the filing of the last account the facts required by Section 3 regarding intermediate accountings and in case of termination of the trust the distribution of the trust property which the accountant proposes to make [Section 4, Uniform Trustees Accounting Act, 9C, U.L.A.].

QUESTIONS

1. Briefly describe the responsibilities of a fiduciary (executor, administrator) in the administration of an estate.
2. What types of assets are frequently excluded from the fiduciary's inventory of assets?
3. What is a typical *sequence of payment* for the various estate obligations?
4. The fiduciary must distinguish in his records between the principal (corpus) and the income of an estate or trust. Why?
5. As a general rule, how are accruals of income and expense identified with the principal and with the income of an estate?
6. Should depreciation be charged against the principal or income of an estate?
7. What is the fundamental equation for fiduciary accounting? For what reason is this expression stated in terms of claims against the estate or trust?
8. Once an inventory of the decedent's assets has been filed, what accounts should be opened by the executor (administrator) in which to record the transactions for the estate?
9. What is the *charge and discharge statement?* What information does it provide?

PROBLEMS

Problem 19–1

Lloyd Carlisle died on January 18, 1971. His will was admitted to probate on February 5, and Arthur Waddell was appointed executor of the estate. The following transactions relate to the executorial period, February 6 through July 1, 1971:

a) Waddell filed the following inventory of Carlisle's assets with the court:

Cash on deposit, Second National Bank.	$ 5,690
Undeposited currency.	220
Common stock, Stuchell Corporation:	
1,000 shares (par, $10) @ $27.	27,000
6%, 20-year Harley Company debentures:	
10 bonds @ $200.	2,000
Automobile.	4,300
Household furnishings.	1,950
Life insurance, payable to the estate.	10,000
Dividends receivable, Stuchell stock:	
Dividend declared January 15, 1971.	800
Interest receivable:	
Harley Company bonds (January 1 and July 1)	
January 1 to January 18.	6

b) Funeral expenses of $934 were paid by Waddell.
c) Six $1,200 Arnheim, Inc., bonds, 5 percent November 1 and May 1, were discovered upon search of the decedent's personal belongings.
d) The life insurance policy was collected.
e) Notice was published for the presentment of claims against the estate,

after which debts of the decedent amounting to $1,450, were validated and paid.

f) The dividend on Stuchell stock was collected.

g) Common stock of the Stuchell Corporation was sold for cash, $24,600.

h) Executorial fees were paid Waddell in the amount of $2,100.

i) The May 1 interest collection was made on Arnheim, Inc., bonds.

j) The automobile was sold for $3,100 cash.

k) According to the conditions of the will, a cash legacy was paid to Mary Carlisle, the widow, in amount of $10,000.

l) The July 1 interest collection was made on Harley Company debentures.

m) All income earned to July 1 was distributed to the widow; all other assets remaining in the estate were distributed equally to Tom and Larry Carlisle, sons of the decedent.

Required:

(i) Journalize the above transactions on the books of Arthur Waddell, executor.

(ii) Make closing entries on July 1 to close the executor's books.

Problem 19–2

Arnold Simon, attorney-at-law, died on July 1, 1971. His partner, Herbert Canby was appointed executor of his estate and filed with the probate court on July 18 the following inventory of assets of the deceased:

Deposit balance, First State Bank..............................	$ 3,000
4% RX bonds, interest payable April 1 and October 1 (par, $40,000)...	34,600
Accrued interest on RX bonds................................	400
6% cumulative Cleburne, Inc., preferred stock, 200 shares (par, $35,000)..	18,900
100 shares of Bancroft-Benson no-par common stock..............	4,200
Value of properties established by court-appointed appraisers:	
Office building of the law partnership (separately owned by Simon)..	48,000
Automobile..	2,200
	$111,300

An additional 200 shares of Bancroft-Benson were discovered by the executor on September 1.

The office building was sold on September 14 to Bruegman and Sons, realtors, for $41,000; the 300 shares of Bancroft-Benson were sold on September 21 for $13,100. On October 1 interest was collected on the RX bonds.

During the three months ended October 1, 1971, the executor made the following payments:

Funeral expenses.......................	$ 2,500
Administrative expenses.................	1,900
Debts of the decedent..................	16,100

The will of the deceased provides that legacies and income be distributed as follows:

To widow, Mary:
Cash, $34,000.
Cleburne stock.
Income of estate.
To son, Arnold, Junior:
Cash, $20,000.
Automobile.
To son, Charles:
Cash, $20,000.
RX bonds.

Required:

(i) Prepare the executor's journal entries for estate transactions for the quarter ended October 1, 1971.

(ii) Journalize the distribution of income and the distribution of legacies on October 2; make closing entries for the estate.

Problem 19–3

William Fess was named executor of the estate of Parker Allen, who died on March 13, 1971. On December 31, 1971, the executor prepared the following trial balance:

ESTATE OF PARKER ALLEN
Trial Balance
December 31, 1971

Investments:		
Stocks....................................	$17,500	
Bonds.....................................	42,000	
Accrued interest receivable.....................	75	
Cash—principal.............................	10,850	
Cash—income..............................	1,925	
Household effects.............................	2,375	
Loss on realization...........................	650	
Gain on realization...........................		$ 1,200
Assets subsequently discovered..................		4,200
Debts of decedent paid........................	5,600	
Funeral expenses..............................	950	
Administration expenses........................	2,250	
Estate corpus.................................		79,275
Income.......................................		3,175
Expenses—income............................	180	
Distribution to income beneficiary...............	995	
Legacy—Arnold Allen........................	2,500	
	$87,850	$87,850

Required:

Prepare a charge and discharge statement for the estate of Parker Allen.

Problem 19–4

Alex Dunn, Jr., died on January 15, 1971; his records disclose the following estate:

Cash in bank..	$ 3,750
6% note receivable, including $50 accrued interest.............	5,050
Stocks...	50,000
Dividends declared on stocks......................................	600
6% mortgage receivable, including $100 accrued interest........	20,100
Real estate—apartment house.....................................	35,000
Household effects..	8,250
Dividend receivable from Alex Dunn, Sr., trust fund...........	250,000
Total...	$372,750

On July 1, 1953, the late Alex Dunn, Sr., created a trust fund, with his son, Alex Dunn, Jr., as life tenant, and his grandson as remainderman. The assets in the fund consist solely of the outstanding capital stock of Dunn, Inc., namely, 2,000 shares of $100 par each. At the creation of the trust, the book—as well as the market—value of these shares was $400,000 and at December 31, 1970, was $500,000. On January 2, 1971, Dunn, Inc., declared a 125 percent cash dividend payable February 2, 1971, to shareholders of record January 12, 1971.

The executor's transactions from January 15, to 31, 1971, were as follows:

Cash receipts:

Jan. 20	Dividends......................................		$ 1,500.00
	25	6% notes receivable...........................	5,000.00
		Interest accrued on note.......................	58.33
		Stocks sold, inventoried at $22,500...............	20,000.00
		6% mortgage sold............................	20,100.00
		Interest accrued on mortgage...................	133.33
	28	Sale of assets not inventoried....................	250.00
	29	Real estate sold...............................	30,000.00
			$77,041.66

Cash disbursements:

Jan. 20	Funeral expenses.............................		$ 750.00
	23	Decedent's debts...............................	8,000.00
	25	Decedent's bequests............................	10,000.00
	31	Distribution of income to widow.................	500.00
			$19,250.00

Required:

Prepare a charge and discharge statement for the executor for the period from January 15 to January 31, 1971.

(AICPA adapted)

Problem 19–5

Andrew Baker, partner in Baker-Barton Farm Implements, died on March 31, 1970. Thad Barton was named executor of his partner's estate which consisted of the following:

Cash..	$ 22,100
Livestock..	48,000
Ranch land and improvements including farm buildings, fencing, etc.—at appraised valuation..............................	25,500
4% Gantry Company debentures, interest January 1 and July 1 (par, $60,000)..	62,500
Interest receivable—Gantry Company debentures..............	600
150 shares Collegaire common stock (par, $30,000).............	26,000
One-half interest in Baker-Barton partnership—at appraised valuation..	84,000
	$268,700

Legacies are to be distributed as follows:

a) Livestock and ranch properties to the widow, Shirley, together with the deceased's partnership interest in Baker-Barton Farm Implements.
b) $30,000 par value of Gantry Company debentures to son, Richard.
c) Collegaire common stock to Fabens Military Academy.
d) Residual estate, after payments of funeral and administrative expenses, debts of decedent and other specific bequests, to the widow. Income of the estate, excluding partnership net income, is to be distributed as collected to the son, Richard Baker. The interest of the deceased in partnership net income was 50 percent and is bequeathed to the widow.

Transactions of the executor were:

Apr. 2 Filed the March 31 inventory of the deceased.
15 Paid funeral and administrative expenses, $3,100.
30 Sold $30,000 par value of Gantry Company debentures for $28,750 and accrued interest.
30 Distributed estate income.
May 1 Paid debts of decedent, $9,400.
10 Paid federal estate and state inheritance taxes, $31,300.
20 Dividends declared on Collegaire stock on April 14 were received, $600.
21 Distributed estate income.
July 1 Collected interest on Gantry Company debentures.
1 Partnership profits for the second quarter of 1970 are reported to be $6,200.
1 Distributed estate income, legacies, and residual estate properties as provided in the will.

Required:

(i) Prepare entries on the books of the executor through July 1, 1970.
(ii) Journalize entries to close the books of the estate.

Problem 19–6

Arthur Taine died in an accident on May 31, 1971. His will, dated February 28, 1965, provided that all just debts and expenses be paid and that his property be disposed of as follows:

Personal residence—devised to Bertha Taine, widow.

United States Treasury bonds and Puritan Company stock— to be placed in trust. All income to go to Bertha Taine during her lifetime, with right of appointment upon her death.

Seneca Company mortgage notes—bequeathed to Elaine Taine Langer, daughter.

Cash—a bequest of $10,000 to David Taine, son.

Remainder of estate—to be divided equally between the two children, Elaine Taine Langer and David Taine.

The will further provided that during the administration period Bertha Taine was to be paid $300 a month out of estate income, calculated and reported on a cash basis. David Taine was named as executor and trustee.

An inventory of the decedent's property was prepared. The fair market value of all items as of the date of death was determined. The preliminary inventory, before the computation of any appropriate income accruals on inventory items, follows:

Personal residence property.....................................	$ 45,000
Jewelry—diamond ring...	9,600
York Life Insurance Company—term life insurance policy on life of Arthur Taine:	
Beneficiary—Bertha Taine, widow.............................	120,000
Granite Trust Company—3% savings bank account, Arthur Taine, in trust for Phillip Langer (grandchild), interest credited January 1 and July 1; balance May 31, 1971...........................	400
Fidelity National Bank—checking account; balance May 31, 1971.....	143,000
$100,000 United States Treasury bonds, 3%, 2004, interest payable March 1 and September 1.................................	100,000
800 shares Puritan Company common stock......................	64,000
700 shares Meta Mfg. Company common stock....................	70,000
$9,700 Seneca Company first-mortgage notes, 6%, 1975, interest payable May 31 and November 30.............................	9,900

The executor opened an estate bank account to which he transferred the decedent's checking account balance. Other deposits, through July 1, 1972, were as follows:

Interest collected on bonds:	
$100,000 United States Treasury:	
September 1, 1971...	$ 1,500
March 1, 1972..	1,500
Dividends received on stock:	
800 shares Puritan Company:	
June 15, 1971, declared May 7, 1971, payable to holders of record as of May 27, 1971..	800
September 15, 1971..	800
December 15, 1971..	1,200
March 15, 1972...	800
June 15, 1972..	800
Net proceeds of June 19, 1971, sale of 700 shares of Meta Mfg. Company..	68,810

Payments were made from the estate's checking account through July 1, 1972, for the following:

Funeral expenses..	$ 2,000
Assessments for additional 1969 federal and state income taxes ($1,700) plus interest ($110) to May 31, 1971............................	1,810
1971 income taxes of Arthur Taine for the period January 1, 1971, through May 31, 1972, in excess of amounts paid by the decedent on declarations of estimated tax..................................	9,100
Federal and state fiduciary income taxes, fiscal years ending June 30, 1971 ($75), and June 30, 1972 ($1,400).........................	$ 1,475
Federal and state estate taxes......................................	58,000
Monthly payments to Bertha Taine: 13 payments of $300............	3,900
Attorney's and accountant's fees...................................	25,000

The executor waived his commission. However, he desired to receive his father's diamond ring in lieu of the $10,000 specific legacy. All parties agreed to this in writing, and the court's approval was secured. All other specific legacies were delivered by July 15, 1971.

Required:

Prepare a charge and discharge statement as to principal and income, and its supporting schedules, to accompany the attorney's formal court accounting on behalf of the executor of the estate of Arthur Taine for the period from May 31, 1971, through July 1, 1972. The following supporting schedules should be included:

1. Original Capital of Estate.
2. Gain on Disposal of Estate Assets.
3. Loss on Disposal of Estate Assets.
4. Funeral, Administration, and Other Expenses.
5. Debts of Decedent Paid.
6. Legacies Paid or Delivered.
7. Assets (Corpus) on Hand, July 1, 1972.
8. Proposed Plan of Distribution of Estate Assets.
9. Income Collected.
10. Distribution of Income.

(AICPA adapted)

Problem 19–7

Using the data of Problem 18–6, prepare a charge and discharge statement for the trustee for the interim period of operations and partial liquidation of the Rawley Manufacturing Corporation.

Problem 19–8

The will of E. M. Dodd, who died on December 31, 1968, provided cash bequests of $40,000 to Mrs. Dodd and $15,000 each to two children, the residuary estate to be divided equally among the three beneficiaries. Mrs. Dodd was appointed executrix and trustee without fees or other emoluments.

By court order Mrs. Dodd was to receive a family allowance of $4,000 a month, commencing January 1, 1969, payable from income or from any cash principal available if the income should be inadequate. The estate never had enough cash available to pay the full allowance nor could any part of the cash bequests be paid. Accordingly a considerable liability to Mrs. Dodd had accumulated toward the end of 1974 for the unpaid portion of the family allowance, as shown by the following trial balance of the estate ledger at December 31 of that year:

Cash...	$ 200	
Securities......................................	20,000	
Building A.....................................	200,000	
Accumulated depreciation.........................		$ 36,000
Building B.....................................	160,000	
Accumulated depreciation.........................		38,400
Mortgage—building B............................		32,000
Revolving fund—building A.......................	1,800	
Revolving fund—building B.......................	2,400	
Mrs. E. M. Dodd—family allowance................		288,000
Mrs. E. M. Dodd—paid on account.................	178,000	
Estate corpus....................................		168,000
	$562,400	$562,400

The balance in the estate corpus account was made up as follows:

Appraisal of assets...	$365,000
Deduct—funeral expenses, etc.................................	15,000
	$350,000
Add—income:	
Dividends received..	6,000
Rentals, after deducting expenses and mortgage interest to date.....	100,000
	$456,000
Deduct—family allowance....................................	288,000
Balance...	$168,000

For want of cash the beneficiaries decided to settle all liabilities by transfer of property, and they requested their attorney to petition the court for approval of the following agreement to take effect as of December 31, 1974:

> The building B and its revolving fund are to be conveyed to Mrs. Dodd subject to the mortgage. In turn she agrees to waive all her claims against the estate for expenditures not refunded to her, including one of $5,000 for estate income taxes paid by her and not collected from the estate, and in addition to pay attorney's fees of $6,000 for the estate. Furthermore, all beneficiaries agree to have the family allowance discontinued after December 31, 1974, and also to waive their claims to the cash bequests.

The court gave its approval to the agreement and ordered an intermediary accounting by the trustee as of December 31, 1974.

Required:

Based upon the above information, prepare:

(i) Columnar work sheet showing the trial balance before and after adjustment.

(ii) Statement of Mrs. Dodd's account.

(iii)   Trustee's intermediary accounting in the form of a charge and discharge statement.

(AICPA adapted)

Problem 19–9

James Roe died on December 31, 1971, and left an estate that was to be divided equally among his four children, all legally of age:

> Mary Roe Powell
> Albert Roe
> Edward Roe
> Ethel Roe

All funeral expenses, doctor's bills, and other liabilities, including all death duties and estate taxes, were to be paid by the Cohasset Trust Company from a fund that had been provided by the deceased during his lifetime and was on deposit with the trust company. Any balance remaining in this fund, after all payments had been made, was to be retained by the trust company in payment for its services. The trust company agreed to accept that balance in full settlement.

Two trusts will ultimately be set up—one for Mary and the other for Ethel. The eldest son, Albert, was appointed sole executor and trustee of the estate and of the trusts to be created. The principal of each trust was to remain intact during the beneficiary's lifetime, but each beneficiary had the right of appointment (by this right each daughter could direct to whom the principal of her trust should be paid at her death). The two sons, Albert and Edward, were each to receive their one-quarter share without any restrictions. The net income from the estate was to be distributed semiannually.

The inventory of the estate consisted of—

Cash in bank..	$ 100,000
$400,000, 3⅜% municipal bonds at market value............	400,000
20,000 shares of no-par value stock of Roe Manufacturing Company, appraised at..............................	5,400,000
1,000 shares Cohasset Trust Company stock of $100 par, market value $300 per share...........................	300,000
Waterfront property at Cohasset Bay, appraised at...........	800,000
	$7,000,000

The heirs decided to leave the estate undivided for the present under the trusteeship of Albert Roe who, with his brother Edward and his brother-in-law John Powell, continued the management of the Roe Manufacturing Company.

The coupons of the municipal bonds were payable on June 30 and December 31. The Roe Manufacturing Company continued to pay each month a dividend of 50 cents per share and the Cohasset Trust Company paid a dividend of $12.50 per share, both on June 1 and December 1. No income was received from the Cohasset Bay property.

On July 1, 1972, Ethel Roe was killed in an automobile accident. By the terms of her will, appointing Albert Roe executor, she left $500,000 in specific bequests, the balance of her estate to be equally divided among her brothers and sister. The estate of Ethel Roe consisted solely of her interest in the estate of her father, with the exception of cash in bank which was just enough to pay burial costs, death duties, and all other liabilities.

The executor of the estate of James Roe, with the consent of the court and of the other heirs, decided to advance to the estate of Ethel Roe the $500,000 required to pay the specific bequests and to charge the amount against her share in the estate of James Roe. It was likewise decided to grant the requests of Albert Roe for an advance of $200,000 and of Edward Roe for an advance of $100,000 against their shares in the latter estate. Both agreed to interest charges on these advances from July 1, 1972, at a reasonable rate that would also be fair to the Mary Roe Powell trust, but no interest would be charged on the $500,000 advanced to the estate of Ethel Roe.

In order to provide the necessary cash funds on July 1, 1972, the $400,000 municipal bonds and the 1,000 shares Cohasset Trust Company stock were sold respectively for $420,000 and $320,000 net after broker's commissions, taxes, and other selling expenses, and on that date the above advances were made.

No change in the executorship and trusteeship of Albert Roe was to take place on account of Ethel Roe's death, but with the consent of the court and of the heirs, her remaining interest in her father's estate was to be divided as of the date of her death in accordance with the terms of her will.

The trustee paid the following expenses in 1972:

Incidental expenses for the year applicable in equal amounts to the
    six months before and after the death of Ethel Roe............ $ 1,290
Taxes on real estate, payable in June and December.............. 18,000

Trustee's commissions at the legal rates for "receiving and paying out" as follows:

        5% on the first........................ $ 2,000
        2½% on the next....................... 20,000
        1½% on the next....................... 28,000
        2% on the balance.

One half of these rates is for receiving and one half for paying. The same rates apply to principal and to income cash. These commissions are paid June 30 and December 31.

Required:

(i)   Prepare a columnar work sheet to which the transactions in the six months before and after division of the Ethel Roe estate are posted so as to produce the balance sheets of the estate of James Roe immediately after the division of the estate of Ethel Roe on July 1, 1972, and on December 31, 1972. Show the calculation of the rate of interest charged to Albert and Edward Roe and give the reason why the use of that rate should be considered fair to the Mary Roe Powell trust.

(ii)   Prepare the trustee's intermediary accounting as at December 31, 1972, in the form of a charge and discharge statement, showing the payments to each beneficiary.

                                              (AICPA adapted)

UNIT VI

INSTITUTIONAL AND SOCIAL ACCOUNTING

Chapter 20

Principles of Governmental Accounting

The principal orientation of current accounting research is the development of an internally consistent and articulated accounting theory for profit-oriented commercial enterprises. There is, however, a parallel need —equally compelling—for analysis and methodological refinement in other accounting domains. In this chapter, the underlying concepts of governmental accounting will be outlined briefly; an introduction to national income accounting will follow in Chapters 21 and 22. Each of these subjects is dealt with primarily in terms of underlying characteristics and basic accounting concepts; accordingly, procedural detail is presented only in digest or summary form. For a more complete discussion, the reader is referred to texts devoted exclusively to these matters.

BASIC CONCEPTS OF GOVERNMENTAL ACCOUNTING

Several fundamental propositions which relate to governmental accounting *generally* will be discussed before attention is directed to more specific accounting relationships. Following an exploratory treatment of the fundamental notion of funds, the reader is introduced briefly to the related concepts of expendable and nonexpendable funds, budgeting and budgetary acounting, encumbrances and obligations, appropriations, and apportionments and allotments.

The Nature of Funds

Every accounting system must incorporate some type of *unit* concept which provides a basis for deciding fundamental questions such as: What economic events should be recorded by the system and what events should be disregarded? In regard to accounting for profit-oriented businesses, the accounting unit is generally described as an *entity*. Thus, partnerships, corporations, and corporate affiliations are typical examples of accounting entities. In governmental accounting, the primary accounting unit is referred to as a *fund*. The National Committee on Governmental Accounting defined a *fund* and pointed out its significance in the following terms:

Governmental accounting systems should be organized and operated on a fund basis. A fund is defined as an independent fiscal and accounting entity with a self-balancing set of accounts recording cash and/or other resources to-gether with all related liabilities, obligations, reserves, and equities which are segregated for the purpose of carrying on specific activities or attaining certain objectives in accordance with special regulations, restrictions, or limitations.[1]

This definition emphasizes the separate and distinct character of a fund. *Specific* activities or objectives are attributable to a fund; the fiscal and accounting unit is *independent;* the set of accounts is *self-balancing;* the resources and related liabilities are segregated. However, this should not be misinterpreted as an implication that one governmental organization represents one fund. Many governmental organizations, e.g., a city, in-clude many separately identifiable activities, each of which may justify the creation of a separate fund. Obviously, the number of funds which may be identified will depend, in part, upon the size and operational spectrum of the governmental entity.

Although the concept of separate funds in governmental accounting essentially reflects the impact of inherent legal restrictions, Professor William J. Vatter foresees a much broader application and has accordingly generalized the fund concept.[2] Professor Vatter observes that some eco-nomic unit must always serve as an accounting frame of reference. Choice of the optimum unit is, therefore, an especially important first step in the accounting process. In the fund theory of accounting, it is proposed that such a unit should be devoid of personal implications, as are alleged to exist in the proprietary and entity theories; at the same time, the unit must be adequately defined with a clear specification of its boundaries. The principal emphasis of the fund theory is that it focuses on a specified area of operations, a center of interest, which significantly does not depend upon legal or other forms of personality. The fund configuration is that of a unit of activity to which a collection of assets relates. Since the operations of the fund entail acquisition and disposition of various kinds of assets, the fund accounts must include a record of the restrictions or limitations on the use of these assets, i.e., a unique form of equity. Some types of asset re-ceipts carry no special restrictions other than those implicit in the definition of the fund. Such an asset inflow should be recorded in special accounts as revenue. Since the operations of the fund also involve the release of services in order to achieve the objectives of the fund, expense accounts must be provided. This collection (or system) of accounts reflects the essence of the fund, encompassing the operational concepts of assets, specific restrictions on assets, revenue and expense, and fund surplus (balance of unrestricted assets). The use of funds in governmental accounting conforms closely with this theoretical structure. Additionally, while the business entity is

---

[1] National Committee on Governmental Accounting, Municipal Finance Officers Association of the United States and Canada, *Governmental Accounting, Auditing, and Financial Reporting* (Chicago, 1968), pp. 6–7.

[2] William J. Vatter, *The Fund Theory of Accounting and Its Implications for Financial Reports* (Chicago: The University of Chicago Press, 1947), p. 12.

presently conceived to be the nucleus for commercial accounting, Vatter argues that the fund may be a more appropriate and efficient unit of account.

Expendable and Nonexpendable Funds

An expendable fund is an aggregation of resources which are totally available for expenditure in achieving the objectives of the fund. Revenues for such a fund may derive from taxes, fees, special assessments, proceeds of bond issues, or interfund transfers. Fund *expenses* include those expenditures required for services, supplies, *and equipment*. Since existing fixed assets represent prior expenditures of a fund, they are, perforce, *excluded* from an enumeration of resources of an expendable fund. The appropriateness of this approach to the concept of fund resources will be examined subsequently in more detail.

A nonexpendable fund requires that the principal or capital balance of the fund be preserved intact. A revolving fund which is expected to generate revenues sufficient in amount to cover operating expenses of the fund, without dilution of principal, is an example of a nonexpendable fund. Additionally, a trust fund which permits the expenditure of income only is a nonexpendable fund. The expendable fund will be emphasized in this chapter, with only brief mention made of nonexpendable funds.

The Budget and Budgetary Accounting

The operations of expendable revenue funds, which encompass the principal recurring activities of a governmental body, are normally controlled by a system of budgets and budgetary accounting. The objectives of a governmental budget for an expendable fund are usually a combination of both planning and control. Initially, the governmental budget is an estimate of anticipated expenditures during a given period or for a specified purpose, with proposed methods of financing the budget objectives—i.e., a planning budget. Once approved, however, the estimated expenditures are translated into expenditure authorizations, which represent specific legislative or higher administrative approved amounts. Thus, the budget (as modified) becomes a relatively inflexible control device which operationally prohibits unfavorable variances from budgetary estimates. Consequently, rather than serving as a useful guide or standard by which to measure efficient performance, the governmental budget is often a rigid instrument of control, expressed in the form of legal ceilings for the amount of expenditures.

Although budgets are widely used in commercial accounting to facilitate planning and control, they generally are not recorded in the accounts. In governmental accounting, on the other hand, the authorized budget is formally recognized in special *budgetary* accounts. In effect, each fund has a self-balancing, independent set of budgetary accounts which are used to accumulate and preserve budgetary information, i.e., estimated revenues and authorized expenditures. These accounts constitute a formal record of the financial plan. In contrast to the budgetary accounts, different accounts are used to record actual transactions; these are generally referred to as *proprietary* accounts. Significantly, the balance in a given proprietary account, e.g., Revenues, can be compared with its corresponding budgetary account, Estimated Revenues, to evaluate how closely actual operations have conformed to what was budgeted. Indeed, subsequent analysis will show how corresponding budgetary and proprietary accounts are closed in one entry, thereby leaving a permanent record of the difference between budgeted and actual data.

Even though expenditures are initially restricted by the creation of different funds, a formal budget is necessary to indicate amounts to be spent for each activity financed by the individual funds. In the absence of economic competition and the discipline of the profit motive, the government must place greater reliance on budgets and budgetary control as an effective means of controlling expenditures. It is obvious, however, that budgetary control limits only the amount of the total expenditures for each program; without further analyses and additional controls, this technique fails to measure the type of efficiency indicated by a comparison of "standard costs" of program accomplishments with actual costs.

Encumbrances and Obligations

A system of *encumbrances* is a means of restricting or reserving available spending authority pending the recording of actual liabilities and/or expenditures. As purchase orders and other commitments for expenditures are approved, the authority to make expenditures is restricted so as to ensure the future availability of assets to pay for the approved expenditures. Until the actual expenditure has been determined and charged against the spending authority of the fund, the encumbered portion of available funds may not be used for purposes other than those contemplated at the time resources are thus restricted. If it is then determined that an excessive amount of resources has been encumbered, the difference between the amount of the original encumbrance and the amount of the actual liability may be re-encumbered for other purposes. Budgetary control is accordingly exercised by application of the encumbrance concept concurrent with the execution of bilateral agreements, i.e., at the time of commitment (executory contract stage), rather than at the time of the receipt of goods or the rendering of services.

In federal governmental accounting, a system of *obligations* is used to accomplish essentially the same objectives as encumbrances in state and local governmental accounting. The Unliquidated Obligations account is a budgetary account which refers to a reservation of available funds to meet specific commitments. Thus, the term "obligation" in federal governmental accounting is operationally equivalent to the term "encumbrance" in state and local governmental accounting.

Appropriations

An appropriation is a formal authorization to a governmental unit or agency to commit not more than a stated amount of fund resources for specified entity purposes, usually within a given period of time. The appropriation is the source of available spending authority, or available funds, referred to above. The authorization has two principal objectives: (1) to provide an upper limit on amounts that may be encumbered, or obligated, and (2) to authorize payments to be made to liquidate obligations when the amounts are confirmed and actual liabilities are established, either during the appropriation period or in a subsequent period. An appropriation normally expires at the end of the budget period, and an unobligated (unencumbered) balance is usually withdrawn or canceled. Most of the activities of federal governmental agencies are financed through direct appropriations by the Congress to draw on the General Fund of the United States Treasury, whereas agencies of state or local governments receive their spending authority primarily from state legislatures or municipal councils.

Professor Vatter argues that the concepts of appropriations and encumbrances have special implications for the "equities" concept in accounting. He states:

The treatment of encumbrances and appropriations in fund accounting suggests that "equities"—or whatever the items on the right-hand side of the balance sheet may be called—are not mere legal liabilities. Rather, these items seem to be viewed clearly as restrictions against the fund of assets, and they serve to earmark portions of the aggregate assets in the fund for specific purposes or to state just what specific provisions must be borne in mind in the management of the assets of the fund.[3]

Allotments and Apportionments

Allotments (state and local) and apportionments (federal) are methods of allocating appropriations over the budget period. They represent a partial release of a unit's appropriation for a given subinterval of time by the legislative or administrative body, and operate as a form of expenditure control. This type of control is designed to prevent overexpenditure in the early part of the budget period; the hope is to eliminate the need for deficiency appropriations that might otherwise develop at the end of the period.

Where the number of administrative levels within a governmental entity is large, both of these terms may be used to indicate the allocation process at different levels. For example, in the federal government, the Congress *appropriates* a certain amount of spending authority; the Budget Director thereafter *apportions* elements of this authority over the budget period to

---

[3] *Ibid.,* p. 41.

various agencies, e.g., the Department of Defense; finally, the Department of the Army receives period *allocations* from the Defense Department, which it then *allots* for the same time period to lower command (administrative) units for ultimate use in program implementation. Notwithstanding this seeming confusion of terms, the basic objective of apportionments and/or allotments remains invariant, viz., partial periodic releases of spending authority over the budgetary period.

STATE AND LOCAL GOVERNMENTAL UNITS

The financial management of both state and local governmental units requires essentially the same type of information and reports; each is subject to comparable legal constraints. Consequently, the basic account structure described following generally applies to either type of entity.

The accounting principles which relate to state and local governments, and derivative procedures and systems, were effectively summarized in 1968 by the National Committee on Governmental Accounting (see Appendix 2).[4] These principles reflect the basic objectives of governmental accounting, viz., (1) assistance in, and validation of, compliance with appropriate statutory provisions, and (2) disclosure of the financial condition and operations of the governmental unit. The principal differences in accounting for profit-oriented enterprises and institutional entities are largely attributable to the overriding importance of legal requirements in respect to the latter type of entity.

The number and the type of separate funds included in an efficient accounting system depend upon relevant statutory provisions and the amount of effective control exercised through the financial management of resources. It is important to note, however, that an excessive number of funds frequently introduces an undesirable inflexibility into the financial system. In the discussion to follow, the basic characteristics of the principal funds of a conventional governmental unit or subdivision will be emphasized; minimal attention is given to procedural detail. Skill in manual record-keeping for the various funds, a facility which frequently accents their inherent interrelationships, may be gained by the reader in working the problems provided at the end of the chapter.

Although the nature of the accounting entities for "general fixed assets" and "general long-term debt" is not, in fact, consonant with the concept of a fund, these separate, self-balancing sets of accounts are conventional inclusions in a governmental accounting system, and thus are discussed with the traditional funds.

---

[4] National Committee on Governmental Accounting, *op. cit.* This analysis of applicable principles and procedures is a revised edition of two earlier documents: *Municipal Accounting and Auditing,* originally published in 1951; and *A Standard Classification of Municipal Accounts,* published in 1953.

General Fund

The General Fund, or General Revenue Fund, is used to account for all revenues, and the activities financed by these revenues, which are not reflected in a special fund. In terms of scope, most of the current operations of the governmental unit are financed by the General Fund. Accordingly, a variety of sources provide revenue for, and a wide range of activities are financed by, this omnibus fund.

The principal revenue sources of the General Fund of a municipality include such items as property taxes, licenses, fines, penalties, and other fees. Conventional expenditure classifications include the functions provided by the fire, police, and sanitation departments, and administrative or clerical activities. Some capital outlays also are directly financed by the General Fund. An additional classification indicating the purpose of the outlay, e.g., wages, supplies, etc., will often support these primary (functional) expenditure summaries.

In accounting for the General Fund, account recognition should be given to the approval of the budget. This is effected by formally journalizing the budgetary accounts, viz., the Estimated Revenues for the period, the Appropriations (authorized expenditures) which operate as a control on actual expenditures for the period, and the increment (decrement) to Fund Balance[5] for the budgeted surplus (deficit). Such an entry may take the following form:

Estimated revenues..................................	200,000	
Appropriations.....................................		198,000
Fund balance......................................		2,000

These data reflect a budget which anticipates a $2,000 surplus, i.e., an excess of estimated revenues over authorized expenditures. Although it may not be immediately clear why estimated revenues are entered as debits and appropriations (the authority to incur expenses) are entered as credits, subsequent analysis of the closing entries will clarify the appropriateness of this entry. Additionally, this summary entry for the budgetary accounts anticipates the use of subsidiary ledgers in which are accumulated relevant data indicating the sources of estimated revenues, and the functional allocations of authorized expenditures. Other data may also be provided in these subsidiary accounts as necessary.

The recording of receivables generated by earned revenues and their subsequent collection is not significantly different from commercial accounting procedures. Property taxes—the principal source of General Fund revenue—are recorded at the time of assessment (essentially an accrual accounting basis). Concurrently, an allowance for estimated uncollectible accounts is established. This entry is of the following form:

---

[5] A frequently used, alternative title for the Fund Balance account is Unappropriated Surplus. Fund Balance, however, is the terminology recommended by the National Committee on Governmental Accounting.

Taxes receivable...	150,000	
Allowance for uncollectible accounts................		10,000
Revenues...		140,000

At the time any portion of the tax levy becomes delinquent, it is transferred to Taxes Receivable—Delinquent, and the related allowance account is reclassified accordingly. If the receivable balance is ultimately collected, the allowance is closed to the Fund Balance account. Other reveneus, such as licenses and fees, are conventionally recorded, on a cash basis, in the same Revenues account. This proprietary account for revenues actually earned is usually supported by detailed source data in the same subsidiary ledger which is used for estimated revenues. Thus, both estimated and actual revenues, classified by source, are juxtaposed in the same subsidiary revenue ledger. Certain unrestricted receipts which are not budgeted, such as the proceeds from the sale of fixed assets, frequently accrue to the benefit of the General Fund. However, these receipts are normally entered in a separate acount, Surplus Receipts, to distinguish them from currently budgeted revenues.

In governmental accounting, proper budgetary control requires the use of an encumbrance system in which a record of future commitments is established as soon as orders are placed or contracts are issued. When the actual liability is determined, the entry for the encumbrance is reversed and the actual liability is recorded. On this date, an authorized expenditure of an appropriated fund is assumed to have occurred, although actual cash disbursements may be deferred. Appropriations for salaries and wages, bond interest, and other recurring expenditures often are not encumbered but are recorded concurrent with the liquidating payment. Typical entries to record an encumbrance and to record the subsequent reversal and related expenditure are as follows:

Encumbrances...	11,000	
Reserve for encumbrances...........................		11,000
Appropriation expenditures.............................	10,500	
Vouchers (accounts) payable.........................		10,500
Reserve for encumbrances..............................	11,000	
Encumbrances......................................		11,000

It should be noted in the above entries that the actual expenditure of authorized funds is less than the amount previously encumbered. Although precautions may be taken to insure that encumbrances are sufficient in amount to cover related subsequent expenditures, it is not unlikely that the appropriation expenditure may exceed the encumbrance. In any event, the amount encumbered is merely reversed, and the actual liability and expenditure recorded.

If an expenditure does not represent a claim against an individual, an organizational entity, or some other fund, it is recorded merely as an Appropriation Expenditure, or as a direct charge against Fund Balance if it were not previously budgeted. Accordingly, the purchase of a fixed asset with General Fund resources is accounted for not unlike a current "expense."

As in the case of Revenues, Encumbrances and Appropriation Expenditures are summary accounts. Consequently, these planned and actual expenditures, classified according to function, are also entered in an appropriation subsidiary ledger. This accumulation of detailed operating expenditures, by functions, is particularly important, since comparison of these totals (past and future expenditures) with the amounts appropriated discloses the degree of compliance with budgetary restrictions. Within each functional category, more refined classifications may be indicated, or coded, as is additionally required by legislative or administrative bodies.

At the end of the fiscal period, the budgetary and operating accounts are closed, and residual balances are transferred to Fund Balance. Given a circumstance where estimated revenues exceed actual revenues and where appropriations exceed expenditures and encumbrances, the following closing entries are illustrative:

Revenues..	199,000	
Fund balance...	1,000	
Estimated revenues..............................		200,000
Appropriations...	198,000	
Appropriation expenditures........................		180,000
Encumbrances....................................		15,000
Fund balance....................................		3,000

The closing entry sequence, with each corresponding set of budgetary and proprietary accounts being closed in a separate entry, results in separate debits and/or credits to the Fund Balance, each of which indicates the difference between budgeted and actual data. A $4,000 credit balance remains in the Fund Balance account:

Budgeted surplus...	$2,000
Excess of appropriations over appropriation expenditures and	
encumbrances...	3,000
	$5,000
Less: Excess of estimated revenues over actual revenues...........	1,000
Fund balance...	$4,000

The balance in this budgetary account (Fund Balance) approximates the "actual" surplus from the operations of the current period, calculated as follows:

Actual revenues...	$199,000
Actual expenditures.....................................	180,000
	$ 19,000
Encumbrances (estimated amount of future expenditures)........	15,000
Surplus from current operations..........................	$ 4,000

It is well to note, however, that the possible difference between the amounts encumbered and the subsequent actual liabilities is essentially analogous to errors in estimated expense accruals in respect to profit-motivated commercial enterprises.

The Reserve for Encumbrances account is not closed at the end of the fiscal period, since it represents commitments made which are not as yet firmly established as determinable liabilities. In the following period, this reserve is often reclassified as Reserve for Encumbrances—Prior Year. Thereafter, a distinction is made between those expenditures which relate to current year's encumbrances and those which relate to prior years' encumbrances; expenditures associated with prior years' appropriations are charged directly against the Reserve for Encumbrances—Prior Year, or recorded in Appropriation Expenditures—Prior Year, which is closed against the corresponding reserve at the end of the period. It is this "real account" property that makes the Reserve for Encumbrances especially useful. Within a given period, it serves no special purpose, as the "nominal" budgetary accounts, Encumbrances and Appropriation Expenditures, effectively measure the use of available funds. However, since the unexpended and unencumbered portion of a current appropriation usually lapses at the end of the fiscal period, as indicated by the illustrative closing entry, the authority to expend funds from prior years' appropriations is reflected in the Reserve for Encumbrances account balance. Significantly, however, since a liability does not then exist, this account is normally included with Fund Balance (unappropriated surplus) in the enumeration of fund equities to indicate the amount of the total surplus of the governmental entity at the end of the fiscal period.

Where fund assets are segregated for a specified purpose or usage, it is often desirable to adjust the Fund Balance account by creating a reserve account balance equal in amount to the asset. If, for example, a $1,000 debit balance exists in Petty Cash, a reserve could be set up as follows:

Fund balance. 1,000
    Reserve for petty cash.   1,000

As a consequence of such an entry, the Fund Balance account would indicate only the unappropriated resources (or deficit) available for subsequent appropriations. If the asset cost were originally recorded as a debit to Appropriation Expenditures, such as occurs with the purchase of supplies, the entry above would be modified to record the asset, i.e., substitute the asset account for Fund Balance. The closure of Appropriation Expenditures will then accomplish the desired reduction in Fund Balance.

The General Fund frequently engages in transactions with other funds of the governmental unit. For example, Debt Service Fund contributions are frequently financed by the General Fund; additionally, the General Fund may contribute the initial capital necessary to create an Intragovernmental

Service Fund; also, unappropriated surpluses of other funds are frequently transferred to the General Fund by the legislative body. As indicated by the nature of the transaction, either a debtor-creditor relationship should be recorded, or the Fund Balance account should be adjusted for the receipt or expenditure.

The catalog of financial statements for the General Fund usually includes (1) a balance sheet, (2) a statement analyzing the changes in Fund Balance, (3) a statement comparing actual revenues with estimated revenues, and (4) a statement comparing appropriations with expenditures and encumbrances. The balance sheet is relatively conventional; however, the equity section normally carries the descriptive caption, "Reserves and Fund Balance," or alternatively, "Reserves and Surplus." Also, as previously noted, fixed assets are usually excluded from the enumeration of fund assets. The analysis of changes in Fund Balance relates to both the budgetary and proprietary operations of the General Fund, and thus reflects the overall results of the governmental unit's operations of the period. The statement of appropriations, expenditures, and encumbrances reflects the extent to which departments have complied with legal constraints in respect to amounts authorized.

Special Revenue Funds

Special Revenue Funds are sometimes established to account for revenues from specific tax assessments or other special sources which are to be used to finance specified activities. They are usually provided for by statute or charter. Typical activities include the operations of public parks and schools which are administered by special boards or commissions. The number of special revenue funds utilized should be kept to a minimum, however, since the usual activities of these funds often may be satisfactorily financed and managed through the General Fund, thereby eliminating unnecessary confusion in the financial reports and minimizing rigidities in the financial structure which hinder planning.

Once created, however, each Special Revenue Fund should be accounted for as a separate entity. Resources are restricted to the activities anticipated by the creating authority and should not be diverted to other uses. The operation of a Special Revenue Fund is usually controlled by the general budget of the governmental unit, and thus requires both budgetary and proprietary accounts. The accounting sequence for such a fund and the periodic financial statements are essentially the same as those prepared for the General Fund.

Intragovernmental Service Funds

Intragovernmental Service Funds, sometimes referred to as revolving funds or working capital funds, are established to finance activities of a manufacturing or service nature—e.g., shops and garages, central purchases, and stores departments. These functional unit subdivisions provide services primarily for the benefit of other departments of the governmental unit and are to be distinguished from activities financed primarily from the sale of products or services to the public; the latter are typically accounted for by Enterprise Funds.

An Intragovernmental Service Fund may be initially established and financed by advances from the General Fund, by the sale of bonds, or by resources contributed by two or more funds. This initial contribution may be reported as Capital, or Contributions from the X Fund. The fund operates, and is accounted for, in much the same manner as a commercial business enterprise, except that its objective is to earn sufficient revenues to absorb operating costs rather than to maximize profits.

Cost accounting records aid in establishing prices for services performed by Intragovernmental Service Funds for other departments. Necessarily, the total expenditures of such a fund are limited to the amounts which various departments are authorized to spend for its services. Consequently, it is unnecessary for a legislative body to restrict its expenditures through appropriations. A formal plan or legal budget is not required, and budgetary accounts such as those typically used in other funds to indicate compliance with statutory provisions are unnecessary.

Fixed assets which are acquired by an Intragovernmental Service Fund are recorded as assets of the fund, as depreciation thereon must be provided for and included in the pricing base if the fund is to be kept intact.

The financial statements required for adequate reporting of an Intragovernmental Service Fund include a balance sheet and a statement of operations. The forms of these statements essentially parallel those of conventional statements for a commercial enterprise engaged in a similar activity.

Special Assessment Funds

Special Assessment Funds are used primarily to finance permanent improvements or services, such as sidewalks or road construction, which are to be paid for wholly, or in part, from special tax levies against the benefited properties. Improvements or services of this type are to be distinguished from those which benefit the entire community and are paid for from general revenues or through the issuance of general obligation bonds. For each special assessment project, a new fund is created. If the improvements are initially to be financed by bond issues (pending receipt of assessments), the bond proceeds are accounted for by this fund, as well as the assessments ultimately collected, which are then used to pay the bond interest and principal.

The legislative authorization for a Special Assessment Fund, unlike the fiscal period appropriations in respect to the General Fund, relates specifically to a single project, whatever may be the time required for its completion. Each project, and thus each fund, requires separate accounting and reporting. Both budgetary and proprietary accounts are used, as well as appropriation and encumbrance procedures. Initially, upon creation of the fund, Improvements Authorized is debited and Appropriations credited; when the assessments are levied, an appropriate receivables account is debited, and Improvements Authorized is credited. Since the costs of improvements constructed are recorded as expenditures of the fund and thereafter closed to the Appropriations account, no record is made in the fund of the investment in fixed assets. However, upon the completion of the project, an entry is made in the General Fixed Assets group of accounts (to be discussed later) in which the total cost of the improvements constructed is debited to relevant asset accounts; contra credits are made to an investment account. Fund Balance is credited for interest on the assessments and is debited for interest payments on outstanding bonds.

The recommended financial statements for a Special Assessment Fund include a balance sheet, a statement of cash receipts and disbursements, and a statement comparing expenditures and encumbrances with appropriations.

Capital Projects Funds

In 1968 the National Committee on Governmental Accounting recommended that Capital Projects Funds be established as a replacement and expansion of the more traditional Bond Funds. Bond Funds are used to account for the proceeds of general bond issuances, except for those which relate to and are accounted for by Special Assessment Funds and Enterprise Funds. Capital Projects Funds, on the other hand, give recognition to the fact that many major capital projects are now financed by a variety of sources in addition to bond issuances. Excluding the capital additions of Special Assessment and Enterprise Funds, Capital Projects Funds are designed to account for the *receipt* and *expenditure* of all resources used for the acquisition of major, long-term capital additions and improvements.

Following a memorandum recording of a capital project authorization, assets are generally recorded with debits to descriptive receivable accounts or cash and corresponding credits to Appropriations, if desired, or Fund Balance. Normal encumbrance procedures and accounts are employed in regard to fund disbursements. Once the acquisition or construction is completed, the capital outlays are recorded in the General Fixed Assets group of accounts and the Capital Projects Fund is closed. If a bond issuance were the means of financing, provision is usually made to retire these bonds either from the Debt Service Fund or from the General Fund. The bonds are not typically recorded as a liability of the Capital Projects Fund. After the closing of the Appropriation and Expenditure accounts, as well as premiums and/or discounts on any bonds issued, any remaining Fund Balance in the Capital Projects Fund is transferred to an appropriate fund. If bonds were issued to finance the capital project, the balance should be transferred to the fund from which resources are to be provided for bond retirement, i.e., the Debt Service Fund. Otherwise, the transfer generally is to the General Fund.

Statements which disclose the financial condition and operations of a Capital Projects Fund include a balance sheet, an analysis of changes in the fund balance, and a statement of estimated and actual revenue.

Debt Service Funds

If long-term debt is to be repaid from the resources of Special Assessments Funds or is issued to support the activities of Enterprise Funds, those designated funds generally account for the servicing of the debt. Regarding other long-term, governmental debt, Debt Service Funds are established to account for payments of interest, principal, and other related charges.

Budgetary accounts are employed to record contributions and earnings necessary to service the debt. Similarly, the Appropriations account is credited for the debt-servicing payments that must be made during the period. Contributions to the fund are credited to revenues, and cash payments for interest, debt retirements, and fiscal agent service costs are debited to Expenditures. In the case of term bonds, the Debt Service Fund accumulates investments until the maturity date of the bonds, at which time its aggregate resources should be at least equal in amount to the maturity value of the bonds. The bonds are not recorded as liabilities of the Debt Service Fund until they mature, at which time the bond liability is credited and Expenditures is debited. Expenditures is closed, as is also Appropriations, to Fund Balance; and the bond liability is paid for with the cash realized from investments of the Debt Service Fund.

The financial statements that must be prepared to adequately disclose the financial position and operations of a Debt Service Fund include a balance sheet and a statement of revenues, expenditures and Fund Balances. Interim financial statements which facilitate the management of the fund include comparisons between budgeted and actual revenues, and between budgeted and actual expenditures.

Trust and Agency Funds

Trust and Agency Funds are created to account for money and property received and held by a governmental unit as trustee, or agent, for individuals or other governmental units. Separate accounts should be established and maintained for the transactions and balances of each Trust or Agency Fund. With the exception of Pension Funds, budgetary accounts are not required in accounting for this type of fund. The accounting procedures significantly parallel those found in nongovernmental fiduciary accounting. Where the trust fund is nonexpendable, a distinction between principal and income should be carefully preserved.

Financial statements for Trust and Agency Funds normally include a balance sheet, a statement of cash receipts and disbursements, and a statement showing changes in fund reserves or balances.

Enterprise Funds

Enterprise Funds exist primarily to finance services rendered to the public. They are typically self-supporting and include such activities as electric, gas, or water utilities, air terminal service, and public housing. The accounting for such funds follows the basic pattern of accounting for a commercial business enterprise. Budgets are frequently prepared, and expenditures are not controlled by means of restrictive appropriations.

Fixed assets acquired and used by Enterprise Funds should be capitalized and carried in the enumeration of fund assets; their costs should be systematically allocated (charged to expense) over their estimated lives.

Financial statements of Enterprise Funds are analogous to those prepared for private enterprises. In the case of an Enterprise Fund balance sheet, fixed assets are typically listed first in the enumeration of assets, and bonds payable rank first in the order of fund liabilities. This variant from the conventional balance sheet classification sequence is adopted to accent the dominant long-term character of the fund.

General Fixed Assets—A Self-Balancing Group of Accounts

The accounts for Enterprise Funds, Intragovernmental Service Funds, and Trust Funds include fixed assets which are the property of these funds. Other fixed assets of the governmental unit, however, are grouped in a general category—General Fixed Assets. These assets are frequently acquired using the proceeds of general obligation bonds, i.e., they are financed from Capital Projects Funds; they may also be purchased out of general revenues, financed from special assessments, or acquired by gift. Since they are not properly regarded as assets of the acquiring fund, the cost is recorded as an Appropriation Expenditure. Accordingly, this class of fixed assets is carried in a separate, self-balancing set of accounts.

Fixed assets should be valued at original cost, or, if acquired by gift, at appraised valuation at date of receipt; the contra credit(s) is made to one or more investment accounts. The investment accounts are designed to disclose the sources of the resources used to acquire the fixed assets, e.g., general fund revenues, general obligation bonds, federal grants, etc. Since general fixed assets are assumed to be nonproductive of taxes or other general revenues, depreciation is not generally recorded in the general accounting records. This failure to record cost expiration is a significant point of departure from profit-oriented enterprise accounting, wherein depreciation is an important factor in net income determination. Any disposition of fixed assets is recorded by reversing the entry of acquisition.

The balance sheet of the General Fixed Asset group should disclose both the amount of fixed assets, classified by type, and the corresponding investment accounts indicating the source of the asset acquisitions. In addition, a statement of the changes in general fixed assets for the period, classified by source, function, and activity, may be useful.

General Long-Term Debt—A Self-Balancing Group of Accounts

The amount of unmatured bonds which are payable from general revenues should be carried in a separate and independent self-balancing group of accounts. The General Long-Term Debt accounts should reflect the present value of principal and interest payable in the future; this present value is often represented as the principal amount of the bonds. Prior to 1968, the National Committee on Governmental Accounting recommended that the *total* amount of principal *and* interest to be paid in future years should be shown in the Long-Term Debt accounts. This practice continues to be employed in many systems. Contra accounts (debit) indicate the amount of resources currently available as well as the amounts yet to be provided for the retirement of these unmatured bonds.

This collection of accounts is neither used to account for the proceeds from the sale of bonds, nor for the payment of principal and interest thereon. Rather, it is merely used to record the amount of outstanding bonded debt of the governmental unit at a specific point in time. There is, however, a relationship between this group of accounts and other funds. At the time bonds are issued (the proceeds of which are generally accounted for through a Capital Projects Fund), a credit entry is made in the General Long-Term Debt account group to record the liability created by the issue. The offsetting debit is to an account entitled Amount to Be Provided for Payment of Principal. Annual increases in the balance of Debt Service Funds should be reflected in this group of accounts to the extent that these investment amounts are specifically designated for payment of the liabilities. If the Debt Service Fund accumulation relates only to bond principal, Amount in Debt Service Fund is debited and Amount to Be Provided for Payment of Principal is credited. As liquidating payments are applied in reduction of bond principal out of the Debt Service Fund resources, the originating entry to record the liability is reversed to the extent of debt abatement and the appropriate contra accounts are credited. As observed earlier, a bond liability may also be accounted for in a Special Assessment Fund or in an Enterprise Fund; in such instances, these bonds may not be included in the General Long-Term Debt group of accounts, as they refer to specific commitments of other funds. However, if the bonds are general obligation bonds, thereby affecting the general credit of the governmental unit, the bonds should be included in the General Long-Term Debt group of accounts as well as the accounts of the specific fund to which they relate.

For reporting purposes, a statement of general long-term debt should be prepared indicating the amount of bonds payable in future years and the amount presently available and to be provided for their retirement.

Summary

This description of funds and the related two groups of self-balancing accounts has necessarily been abbreviated. The authors have sought merely to accent the outstanding characteristics of each fund, with emphasis on the General Fund in respect to procedural detail. Although some mention was made of the use of subsidiary ledgers in reference to the operation of the General Fund, it should be recognized that these data provide basic information for all of the funds. Hopefully, the most prominent characteristics of local and state accounting have been exposed, even though in broad outline.

FEDERAL GOVERNMENT

Introduction

Accounting in the federal government began with an Act of Congress in 1789 which established the United States Treasury. For 130 years, the Treasury maintained the government's accounts. During this period, however, the federal government's accounting methods remained essentially unchanged, with a predominant emphasis upon compiling evidence to determine whether or not a specific governmental agency's transactions compiled with its appropriations and other Congressional directives.

The first substantial effort directed toward accounting reform was the enactment of the Budget and Accounting Act of 1921. This Act was the first law to give expression to the concept of the Presidential Budget; in this regard, provision was made for the creation of the administrative office of the Bureau of the Budget. Additionally, the General Accounting Office, a legislative agency, was established with a Comptroller General as its principal officer. Various proposals have been made during the past two decades for improving accounting in the federal government, including the recommendations of the first and second Hoover Commission reports (1949 and 1955). Particularly significant legislative responses were the Budget and Accounting Procedures Act of 1950 and Public Law 863 (1956); the latter Act contains many of the proposals of the second Hoover Report, including the provision for accrual accounting in agency systems.

Currently, the executive branch of the federal government is charged with the development of accounting systems and procedures, limited only by the outline of basic principles and standards established by the Comptroller General. The governmental agency is regarded as the fundamental accounting entity, and its executive head assumes responsibility for agency activities, including accounting. It is therefore inappropriate to speak of *the* accounting system of the federal government. Federal governmental accounting is essentially a collection of the separate accounting systems of its many agencies and the Treasury Department. The accounts of each agency are ordinarily maintained on a decentralized basis; the Treasury Department, as the central fiscal agent of the federal government, is responsible for integrating, or consolidating, the separate accounts of the various agencies.

Basic Objectives

The objectives of accounting in the federal government, as set out in Section 111 of the Budget and Accounting Procedures Act of 1950, may be briefly summarized as follows:

Accounting in the Federal government must provide (1) full disclosure of the results of financial operations, (2) adequate financial information needed in the management of operations and the formulation and execution of the budget, (3) effective control over income, expenditures, funds, property, and other assets, and (4) evidence that financial transactions have been consummated in accordance with laws, regulations, or other legal requirements.[6]

These objectives are comparable to those of commercial enterprise accounting, with two significant exceptions. The strong, even dominating, emphasis that there must be accumulated evidence indicating that financial transactions of a governmental agency accord with legal requirements is one basic difference; the other exception relates to the relative lack of emphasis in governmental accounting on measuring the economic progress of the accounting entity over a period of time. Progress is not measured in governmental entities in terms of monetary or economic increments which are beneficial to owners or investors; rather, the financial activities of such entities accent the importance of administering and expending resources in the most appropriate manner for the attainment of service objectives. Where the "results of operations" are expressed primarily in terms of the degree of attainment of social or service goals, the primary function of accounting becomes one of reporting effectively on how resources are acquired, administered, and used in attainment of these goals.

As a general rule, the governmental accounting process has not included attempts to measure "outputs" or the degree of attainment of social or service goals. However, considerable effort has been concentrated in recent years on the development and implementation of budgeting systems which incorporate such measurements. These Planning-Programming-Budgeting Systems require a careful analysis of "program structures," which involves the identification of general objectives, the refinement of general objectives into a detailed outline of subobjectives, and the classification of governmental expenditures in terms of specific programs that are planned to accomplish specific subobjectives. Following the analysis of program structures, special emphasis is placed upon cost-effectiveness analyses which utilize "benefit" measures to the extent possible; the ultimate goal of these

---

[6] Adapted from Sec. 111, P. L. 864, 81st Congress, 64 Stat. 832.

studies is to provide decision makers with significant information as to the comparative effectiveness of alternative governmental programs.

Basic Accounting Procedures

In 1948, the Accounting Systems Division of the General Accounting Office was established. The objective of this division, later subsumed under the office of the Comptroller General, was to establish accounting principles and standards of general applicability to governmental units and to assist agencies in the structuring of accounting systems. These objectives have been aided in their implementation by the issuance of three types of memoranda having general application:

1. GAO General Regulations. These are mandatory for all agencies of the government, and are generally procedural in nature.
2. Accounting Systems Memoranda. Less formal devices than the Regulations, these memoranda make interim changes in the former and are usually concerned with individual problems.
3. Accounting Principles Memoranda. These are general statements having broad application which purport to establish the underlying foundation on which federal government accounting is to be based.

In accounting for federal governmental agencies and their subunits, the use of budgetary accounts essentially parallels their use by state and local governments. In other respects, the accounting process more closely resembles commercial enterprise accounting. The basic reporting entity in federal governmental accounting is the executive agency, which is an independent reporting unit. Periodically the Treasury Department consolidates the reports of the various agencies. Prior to 1968, the overall financial plans and reports for the federal government were summarized in three partially complementary and partially competing budgets: (1) the administrative budget; (2) the consolidated cash budget; and (3) the national income accounts budget. In 1967, the President's Commission on Budget Concepts recommended "that a unified summary budget statement be used to replace the present three or more competing concepts. . . ."[7] As a consequence, the unified budget is now the primary summary statement of the federal government, supported, of course, by a variety of more detailed statements and analyses. The unified budget is comprised of four basic sections: budget appropriations; budget receipts, expenditures, and lending; means of financing; and outstanding federal securities and federal loans at the end of the year.

Most operations of the federal government are financed and controlled by a General Fund of the Treasury Department; however, there exist a number of trust funds, for which the beneficiaries are individuals or foreign governments. The General Fund accommodates within its accounts struc-

---

[7] *Report of the President's Commission on Budget Concepts* (Washington, D.C.: U.S. Government Printing Office, 1967), p. 6.

ture a large number of agency funds which are created by Congress by appropriation for administrative purposes. Each of these funds identifies with an agency or department of the federal government. An outline of these fund relationships is:

General Fund of the Treasury
    Expendable funds of the agencies
        General appropriated funds
        Special appropriated funds
    Revolving funds of the agencies
        Government corporations
        Non-incorporated activities
Trust and Deposit Funds[8]

An expendable fund is one which is available for making expenditures for designated purposes; necessarily, it does not include fixed assets. A revolving fund is a self-sustaining fund which in the long run is expected to generate revenues equivalent in amount to its operating expenses. A separate set of budgetary accounts for each fund is desirable, but this need not imply a physical separation of resources or the keeping of separate accounting records for each fund.

The proprietary accounts of some governmental agencies are currently maintained on a cash basis, notwithstanding the passage, in 1956, of Public Law 863, which made the conversion to accrual accounting mandatory for all agencies. The conversion to an accrual basis is being carried out to a significant degree, however, following the 1967 recommendations of the President's Commission on Budget Concepts.

Property accounting in the federal government is the responsibility of that executive agency which acquires, uses, and disposes of expendable materials, supplies, and fixed assets. Accounting Principles Memorandum No. 1 provides that the accountable value of acquired property is its original cost, or, if cost is not available, the appraised valuation at date of acquisition. In respect to depreciation of fixed assets, the criterion of "usefulness" is recommended. The Memorandum recommends the recording of depreciation for those agencies, and in respect to those projects, in which fixed assets represent a significant portion of the resources employed, such as transportation facilities, public utilities, and construction agencies. Depreciation should also be provided where costs are important determinants of price, and in those circumstances where the activity of the agency involves program use (as contrasted with administrative use) of fixed assets. Depreciation is not ordinarily recorded where fixed assets are relatively unimportant in discharging the routine functions of the agency.

---

[8] Howard W. Bordner, "Appropriations and Funds," *The Federal Accountant,* December, 1957, p. 12.

Federal Agency Accounting—An Illustrative Example

The basic concepts which underlie the accounting system of an agency of the federal government will be briefly illustrated in the following paragraphs, although an explanation of many of the administrative details and methodological subtleties are omitted.

The agency is assumed to be financed initially, and primarily, by appropriations of the federal government. Once the appropriation is established by an enactment of the Congress, the agency records this fact as follows:

Fund balances with U.S. Treasury...................... 225,000
    Unapportioned appropriations......................   225,000

This entry reflects the availability of funds on the books of the Treasury for discharging agency functions during the current period.

Although funds have been appropriated to the agency, final authority to use these funds depends upon action by the Bureau of the Budget. Although this apportionment may be scheduled for release periodically over the fiscal period, it will be here assumed that $210,000 is apportioned for immediate use. The agency records this event in the following manner:

Unapportioned appropriations........................ 210,000
    Unallotted apportionments........................   210,000

This reflects the extent to which Treasury funds may be expended through an authorized disbursing agent. The $15,000 reservation of appropriated funds by the Bureau of the Budget may be subsequently apportioned to the agency, or it may be used for other authorized purposes—including a planned saving by the executive branch of the federal government.

If the agency head subsequently allots $200,000 to agency divisions and subdivisions, against which they may make commitments during the year, the following entry is made:

Unallotted apportionments.......................... 200,000
    Unobligated allotments..........................   200,000

The effect of this entry is to reserve $10,000 of the total spending authority of the agency for unexpected requirements—an internal administrative control through financial management. Actually only a portion of the agency's spending authority is usually made available to operating units periodically (quarterly) during the year in order to prevent a unit's overspending during the first months of the fiscal year. The Unobligated Allotments account is, of course, supported by a collection of detailed, subsidiary allotment accounts.

Orders are placed for equipment in the amount of $50,000 and supplies in the amount of $40,000:

Unobligated allotments................................ 90,000
    Unliquidated obligations..........................   90,000

This entry essentially parallels the encumbrance process for local and state governmental units, with the term "obligations" substituted for "encumbrances."

The equipment, cost $51,000, and supplies, cost $38,000, are received by the agency:

Unliquidated obligations.............................. 90,000		
Unobligated allotments............................		90,000

Fixed assets.. 51,000		
Inventories... 38,000		
Accounts payable..................................		89,000

Unobligated allotments.............................. 89,000		
Expended appropriations...........................		89,000

In this entry sequence, the obligation entry is reversed, and the assets and liabilities are recorded. Additionally, the Unobligated Allotments is reduced by the amount of confirmed expenditures. Thus, the Unobligated Allotments account continues to reflect the available obligational authority.

Salaries of $100,000 are approved for payment without prior obligation:

Salaries.. 100,000		
Accounts payable..................................		100,000

Unobligated allotments.............................. 100,000		
Expended appropriations...........................		100,000

The recorded liabilities are certified for payment by a disbursing agent of the Treasury:

Accounts payable.................................... 189,000		
Fund balances with U.S. Treasury..................		189,000

An additional allotment of $5,000 is made to one of the agency divisions; supplies in the amount of $4,900 are ordered by the division:

Unallotted apportionments........................... 5,000		
Unobligated allotments............................		5,000

Unobligated allotments.............................. 4,900		
Unliquidated obligations..........................		4,900

At the end of the fiscal period, there exist accrued salaries of $7,000; additionally, it is determined that supplies in the amount of $30,000 have been consumed during the period.

Salaries.. 7,000		
Accrued salaries..................................		7,000

Unobligated allotments.............................. 7,000		
Expended appropriations...........................		7,000

Operating expenses.................................. 30,000		
Inventories.......................................		30,000

No adjustment of the budgetary accounts is required in respect to the consumption of supplies, as obligational authority was expended at the time the supplies were received. (The assumption is made that depreciation on fixed assets is not to be recorded; if depreciation were recorded, the entry would parallel that for the recognition of expense for materials consumed.) At the end of the fiscal year, the agency trial balance is as follows:

Fund balances with		Accrued salaries.	$ 7,000
U.S. Treasury.	$ 36,000	Unobligated allotments.	4,100
Inventories.	8,000	Unallotted apportionments.	5,000
Fixed assets.	51,000	Unapportioned appropriations.	15,000
Salaries.	107,000	Unliquidated obligations.	4,900
Operating expenses.	30,000	Expended appropriations.	196,000
	$232,000		$232,000

The period-end closing entries for the agency are:

Unobligated allotments.	4,100	
Unallotted apportionments.	5,000	
Unapportioned appropriations.	15,000	
Fund balances with U.S. Treasury.		24,100

Expended appropriations.	196,000	
Salaries.		107,000
Operating expenses.		30,000
Invested capital.		59,000

The first entry above reflects the expiration of obligational authority at the end of the fiscal year, leaving a Fund Balance with the U.S. Treasury of $11,900—equal in amount to the accrued liability of $7,000 and the unliquidated obligation (comparable to a Reserve for Encumbrances) of $4,900. The second entry closes current expenses and expended appropriations, with the difference of $59,000 representing the increase in net assets during the period (inventory of $8,000 and fixed assets of $51,000). This increment in Invested Capital is, of course, distorted to the extent of unrecorded depreciation on the fixed assets.

An unclassified statement of financial position at the end of the period would assume the following form:

AN AGENCY FINANCED FROM APPROPRIATIONS
Statement of Financial Position
June 30, 1971

ASSETS

Fund balances with U.S. Treasury.	$11,900
Inventories.	8,000
Fixed assets.	51,000
	$70,900

LIABILITIES, UNLIQUIDATED
OBLIGATIONS, AND INVESTED CAPITAL

Accrued salaries.	$ 7,000
Unliquidated obligations.	4,900
Invested capital.	59,000
	$70,900

In addition to the statement of financial position, other statements often prepared by an agency include analyses of changes in invested capital, the status of appropriations, and reconciliation of program costs with obligations.

In this illustrative example, many types of recurring transactions have been omitted. Rather, emphasis has focused on the summary effect of transactions and the complementary nature of budgetary (control) and proprietary accounts of a federal governmental agency.

REGULATORY ACCOUNTING

Frequently, because of a condition of limited competition (or no competition) in a given industry, regulatory agencies are established to protect the public from unwarranted abuses and discrimination, while concurrently assuring the regulated industry of receiving a fair return on its investment. In respect to public utilities, the regulating agency operates primarily as a guardian of the public in its role as consumer. Other commissions and agencies emphasize the public as an investor. For example, the Securities and Exchange Commission is especially concerned with the form and content of published financial statements, in order that there may be a full and complete disclosure to investors of all material facts concerning securities publicly offered for sale. Manifestly, regulatory accounting relates principally to the accumulation of those data, and in such form, as will enable the regulating agency to accomplish its service function to the public.

Five regulatory agencies (Interstate Commerce Commission, Federal Power Commission, Federal Communications Commission, Federal Maritime Commission, Civil Aeronautics Board) are presently authorized to prescribe uniform systems of accounts for industries subject to their jurisdiction. Others, such as the Federal Trade Commission and the Rural Electrification Administration, prescribe reporting rules but not complete accounting systems. The authority of the Securities and Exchange Commission over accounting practice is expressed in very general terms; however, it is implemented by regulations which often specify the form and content of financial statements.

Prescribed Accounts and Reports

The uniform systems of accounts, cited above, are typically described in terms of charts of accounts, accompanied by detailed explanations of the composition of the individual accounts. While the installation of the accounting system remains the primary responsibility of the regulated company, the latter must usually file a copy of its manual or chart of accounts with the relevant commission, and report any subsequent changes thereto. Periodic financial reports are also required of the regulated company, and its accounts are usually subject to a periodic audit by the staff of the regulatory commission.

Among the activities often performed by a regulatory commission in respect to accounting and reporting systems are the following:[9]

1. Prescribe a uniform system of accounts with which regulated companies must comply.
2. Issue rulings and interpretative elaborations periodically in respect to various procedures outlined in the system.
3. Give notice of approval before specified types of accounting transactions are completed.
4. Review the financial statements of regulated companies on a continuing basis.

It is evident that the authority of the regulatory commission in recording and reporting requirements often extends beyond the prescription of uniform accounts. In addition to the activities cited above, the commission will often formulate rules for the valuation of plant and other properties, establish regulations as to the retention of records, engage in analyses to develop the cost of performing specific services, and set depreciation rates.

Theoretical Framework

Regulatory accounting has developed largely through trial and error. The proliferation of independent agencies, the desire for autonomy, and the resulting lack of communication between agencies have all impeded the development of a common underlying theoretical framework in regulatory accounting.

Because of the importance of rate regulation, public utility accounting manifestly emphasizes the rate base and operating income. Rate making consists of compiling the various cost elements to provide the relevant service, which include operating expenses, depreciation, depletion and amortization, taxes, and the allowable return on the rate base. This summation of costs should be equivalent to the revenues required by the utility; accordingly, it is used in establishing the rate for consumers. The rate base includes the cost of plant devoted to the particular service, reduced by accrued depreciation, and increased by an allowance for working capital.

The emphasis on operating income has generated the concept of "above- or below-the-line" revenues and expenses. "Above-the-line" items consist of all revenues and expenses that relate directly to regulated services, and thus enter into the computation of operating income, while other items not so defined are accounted for "below-the-line." In this context, net operating income is the amount returned on the rate base. It is therefore evident that the problems of regulatory accounting relate primarily to a determination of the proper inclusions in operating income and the appropriate components of the rate base.

[9] "Federal Communications Accounting Explained" (Government and Industry Section) *The Federal Accountant,* June, 1963.

In spite of the heterogeneity implicit in the various agency systems, there are nonetheless some fundamental propositions to which all generally subscribe. They include the *standard of reasonableness* and the concept of *original cost*. The *standard of reasonableness* is defined as the right of a commission or agency to pass upon the justice and fairness of charges to the accounts of the regulated enterprise; additionally, it provides a rationale for determining the amount of operating expenses to be charged to consumers (by inclusion in the rate base).[10] Consequently, the level of costs incurred, or allowed, in providing the service should not exceed that level which would prevail were the enterprise not protected by monopolistic privilege. The *original cost* concept relates to fixed assets acquired by a regulated company, and in general, accents the importance of cost to the owner who first dedicated the properties to public service. For newly created assets, this measurement is comparable to cost valuation in conventional accounting. Any excess of acquisition cost over original cost is recorded in a separate account by the regulated company, to be disposed of subsequently as directed by the regulatory commission. Depreciation is normally computed on original cost, on the basis that charges to expense in a regulated company should relate to actual costs first incurred, without inflation by amounts added by subsequent transfers. Regulatory systems of accounts usually reject "goodwill" and "going value" as amortizable parts of the cost of acquisition.

GOVERNMENTAL ACCOUNTING SYSTEMS RECONSIDERED

Federal and Nonfederal Systems Compared

Federal governmental accounting exists in an environmental setting, and is sustained by a type of authority which is substantially different from that of state and local governmental accounting. The federal government carries on a wide variety of activities, all of which are subject, in respect to accounting principles and standards, to supervision and control by the Comptroller General. Accounting functions are accordingly closely coordinated. At the state and local levels, on the other hand, the accounting function is carried on within autonomous units or subdivisions, each of which is relatively free to elect its own system of accounts. Improvement and consistency at the state and local level depend upon the ability of an organization, without significant formal authority, to provoke wide acceptance and use of what it believes to be sound accounting principles.

Although each federal appropriation is assumed to create a fund, the operations of which must accommodate to legal constraints, the reporting entity remains the agency. In state and local governmental accounting,

---

[10] Hussein A. Sharaf, "An Evaluation of the Regulative Aspects of Accounting Requirements for Public Utilities in the United States" (Ph.D. dissertation, The University of Illinois, 1959), p. 7.

however, each fund is a separate entity having its own set of accounts. Individual appropriations do not establish funds; rather, they represent authorizations and limitations on expenditures for a specific purpose in respect to an existing fund. In both instances, however, the fund concept operates as an instrument of control.

In respect to fixed assets, state and local governments frequently use a single group of self-balancing accounts for all fixed assets, with the exception of those included in revolving-type funds such as Enterprise Funds. In the federal government, each agency is regarded as a separate operating entity which controls and accounts for specific fixed assets. For this reason, the recording of depreciation is perhaps more widely accepted within the federal system than in state and local governments.

Governmental and Commercial Accounting Compared

Because governmental accounting is not a homogeneous function, it is difficult to contrast in any meaningful manner governmental accounting taken as a whole with accounting for commercial enterprises. Yet, there are certain fundamental differences. Governmental accounting emphasizes the fund as a nucleus of accounting activity, as compared to the operating entity in commercial accounting. The related technique of recording outstanding purchase orders or contractual commitments by the use of an encumbrance or obligation system significantly departs from accounting for commercial business enterprises. This practice, which accents the equity side of the balance sheet, emphasizes restrictions upon assets, rather than the reporting of legal liabilities only. With respect to operations, governmental activity is in most instances nonprofit oriented, while the motivation to maximize wealth is an overriding business objective which underlies commercial accounting. Nonetheless, concepts of revenue are similar in both systems, and concepts of expense differ materially only in respect to depreciation and amortization.

QUESTIONS

1. What is a "fund" in a governmental accounting context?
2. Distinguish between *expendable* and *nonexpendable* funds.
3. What are the primary objectives of a governmental budget for an expendable fund?
4. Distinguish between *budgetary* and *proprietary* accounts.
5. What is the purpose of a system of encumbrances? How does it differ from a system of obligations?
6. Describe the function of the General Fund or General Revenue Fund.
7. What kinds of statements are used to report the activities of the General Fund?
8. Characterize and distinguish between an agency *expendable* fund and an agency *revolving* fund.

9. Describe the principal differences between federal governmental and state or local governmental accounting.

PROBLEMS

Problem 20–1

(i)   Reference is frequently made in governmental accounting to "budgetary" and "proprietary" accounts. Define these expressions as they relate to the governmental entity. Do budgetary accounts have a parallel in commercial enterprise accounting? Does the budget occupy the same role in both accounting systems?

(ii) The concept of a "fund" is inherent in governmental accounting systems. Discuss the nature of this concept, and distinguish the unique characteristics of the various equities which are implicit therein.

Problem 20–2

The following account balances were included in the January 1, 1971, trial balance of the General Fund of the City of Towersburg:

Reserve for encumbrances—prior year	$20,000
Unappropriated surplus	42,000

During the 1971 fiscal year, the General Fund engaged in the following transactions:

a)   The budget for the 1971 fiscal year was adopted, with estimated revenues of $300,000 and appropriations of $295,000.

b)   The general tax levy for the year was $250,000; estimated uncollectible accounts amount to $10,000.

c)   Wages and salaries in the amount of $90,000 were approved for payment. (These expenditures were processed without prior encumbrance.)

d)   Supplies ordered in 1970 were received at a cost of $21,000. This closes all purchase orders from the prior year.

e)   Negotiations for the purchase of a building were completed, the construction cost of which was estimated to be $150,000.

f)   Payment was made for the approved vouchers in (c) and (d) above.

g)   Revenue from licenses and fees in the amount of $50,000 was collected.

h)   Collections of current taxes in the amount of $200,000 were received.

i)   The purchase of the building in (e) above was approved for payment, the settlement price being $140,000.

j) $10,000 was received from the sale of fixed assets.

k)   An invoice of $20,000 was received for gas and electricity from the appropriate municipal subdivision.

l)   Orders were placed for supplies in the amount of $60,000.

Required:

(i)   Prepare journal entries to record these 1971 transactions of the General Fund, and indicate what other funds, if any, are affected.

(ii) Prepare closing entries for the General Fund.

(iii) Prepare an analysis of Fund Balance for 1971.

Problem 20–3

The Sleepy Haven Township's adjusted trial balance for the General Fund at the close of its fiscal year ending June 30, 1971, is shown following:

SLEEPY HAVEN TOWNSHIP

General Fund Trial Balance

June 30, 1971

Cash..	$ 1,100	
Taxes receivable—current (Note 1).................	8,200	
Allowance for uncollectible taxes—current..........		$ 150
Taxes receivable—delinquent.....................	2,500	
Allowance for uncollectible taxes—delinquent.......		1,650
Miscellaneous accounts receivable.................	4,000	
Allowance for uncollectible accounts...............		400
Due from Intragovernmental Service Fund..........	5,000	
Appropriation expenditures (Note 2)...............	75,500	
Encumbrances.................................	3,700	
Revenues (Note 3).............................		6,000
Due to Enterprise Fund.........................		1,000
Vouchers payable..............................		2,000
Reserve for encumbrances—prior year..............		4,400
Reserve for encumbrances.......................		3,700
Surplus receipts (Note 4).......................		700
Appropriations................................		72,000
Fund balance..................................		8,000
	$100,000	$100,000

Note 1: The current tax roll and miscellaneous accounts receivable, recorded on the accrual basis as sources of revenue, amounted to $50,000 and $20,000 respectively. These items have been recorded on the books subject to a 2 percent provision for uncollectible accounts.

Note 2: Includes $4,250 paid during the fiscal year in settlement of all purchase orders outstanding at the beginning of the fiscal year.

Note 3: Represents the difference between the budgeted (estimated) revenues of $70,000 and the actual revenues realized during the fiscal year.

Note 4: Represents the proceeds from the sale of equipment damaged by fire.

Required:

(i) Prepare in columnar form an Analysis of Changes in Fund Balance for the year ending June 30, 1971, with column headings: "Estimated," "Actual," and "Excess or Deficiency of Actual Compared with Estimated."

(ii) Prepare a General Fund balance sheet at June 30, 1971.

(AICPA adapted)

Problem 20–4

The following balances relate to the General Fund of the City of Vandalia on July 1, 1971:

Cash........................	$28,500	Vouchers payable..............	$12,000
Taxes receivable—delinquent.....	31.200	Reserve for encumbrances.......	14,000
Allowance for uncollectible taxes		Reserve for materials and	
receivable—delinquent........	[2,800]	supplies....................	5,300
Materials and supplies...........	5,300	Fund balance.................	30,900
	$62,200		$62,200

During the fiscal year ended June 30, 1972, the following transactions were completed:

a) The annual budget was adopted by the City Council; it provided for estimated revenues of $325,000 and appropriations of $328,000.

b) The current year's tax bill was levied in the amount of $300,000, of which $14,000 of receivable balances were estimated to be uncollectible.

c) Vouchers were approved in respect to all encumbrances of July 1, 1971. Orders for new equipment were placed in the amount of $28,000.

d) Receivables for delinquent taxes were collected, $23,000, with interest and penalties of $460.

e) Cash of $20,000 was advanced to the General Fund by the Debt Service Fund.

f) The equipment ordered in (c) was vouchered for $30,000.

g) Vouchers were approved for wages and salaries, $225,000.

h) Vouchers were approved for the purchase of materials and supplies, $65,000.

i) Collections of $274,000 were made in respect to current year tax assessments; unpaid receivable balances were transferred to the Taxes Receivable—Delinquent account.

j) Additional collections for the issuance of licenses and permits amounted to $30,000.

k) Vouchers were paid, $330,000.

l) Orders were placed for additional materials and supplies in the amount of $20,000. Supplies on hand on June 30, 1972, were $12,000.

Required:

(i)   Prepare journal entries for the General Fund for the transactions enumerated above.

(ii) Journalize closing entries for the General Fund for the fiscal year ended June 30, 1972.

(iii) Prepare a balance sheet for the General Fund as of June 30, 1972.

Problem 20–5

The Town of Sargentville uses budgetary accounts and maintains accounts for each of the following types of funds:

Symbol	Fund
A	Capital Projects Fund
B	General Long-Term Debt
C	General Fund
D	Property Accounts (General Fixed Assets)
E	Debt Service Fund
F	Special Assessment Fund
G	Special Revenue Fund
H	Trust and Agency Fund
S	Enterprise Fund
T	Intragovernmental Service Fund

The chart of accounts of the *General Fund* follows:

Symbol	Account
1	Appropriations
2	Cash
3	Due from other funds
4	Due to other funds
5	Encumbrances
6	Expenditures
7	Reserve for encumbrances
8	Revenues
9	Revenues (estimated)
10	Surplus receipts
11	Fund balance
12	1971 taxes receivable
13	Vouchers payable

The following transactions were among those occurring during 1971:

a) The 1971 budget was approved. It provided for $520,000 of General Fund revenue and $205,000 of school fund revenue.

b) The budgeted appropriations for the General Fund amounted to $516,000.

c) An advance of $10,000 was made from the General Fund to a fund for the operation of a central printing service used by all departments of the municipal government. (This had not been budgeted and is not expected to be repaid.)

d) Taxes for General Fund revenues were levied, totaling $490,000.

e) Contractors were paid $200,000 for the construction of an office building. The payment was from proceeds of a general bond issue of 1970.

f) Bonds of a general issue, previously authorized, were sold at par for $60,000 cash.

g) Orders were placed for supplies to be used by the Health Department—estimated cost, $7,500.

h) Vouchers were approved for payment of salaries of town officers in the amount of $11,200. (No encumbrances are recorded for wages and salaries.)

i) The supplies ordered in (*g*) were received and vouchers were approved for the invoice price of $7,480.

j) Fire equipment was purchased for $12,500 and the voucher approved.

k) A payment of $5,000 was made by the General Fund to a fund for eventual redemption of general obligation bonds.

l) Of the taxes levied in (*d*), $210,000 were collected.

m) Taxes amounting to $1,240, written off as uncollectible in 1968, were collected. No amount was in the budget for such collections.

n) $1,000 of the advance made in (*c*) was returned because it was not needed.

o) Supplies for general administrative use were requisitioned from the store's fund. A charge of $1,220 is made for the supplies.

p) The General Fund advanced $30,000 cash to provide temporary working capital for a fund out of which payment will be made for a new sewerage installation. Eventual financing will be by means of assessments on property holders on the basis of benefits received.

q) Equipment from the Highway Department was sold for $7,000 cash. This sale was not included in the budget and depreciation is not funded.

r) The town received a cash bequest of $75,000 for the establishment of a Scholarship Fund.

s) Previously approved and entered vouchers for payment of Police Department salaries of $6,200 and for the transfer of $500 to the Police Pension Fund were paid.

t) Receipts from licenses and fees amounted to $16,000.

Required:

Prepare a table indicating for each transaction, by means of the appropriate numerals, the account debited and the account credited in the General Fund. If a transaction requires an entry in any fund(s) other than the General Fund, indicate the fund(s) affected by appropriate notation.

(AICPA adapted)

Problem 20–6

The following information pertains to the operations of the General Fund of the X County. Functions of this county government include operating the county jail and caring for the county courts.

Funds to finance the operations are provided from a levy of county taxes against the various towns of the county, from the state distribution of unincorporated business taxes, from board of jail prisoners assessed against the towns and against the state, and from interest on savings accounts.

The balances in the accounts of the fund on January 1, 1971, were as follows:

Cash in savings accounts.	$ 60,650
Cash in checking accounts.	41,380
Cash on hand (undeposited prisoners' board receipts).	320
Inventory of jail supplies.	3,070
Due from towns and state for board of prisoners.	3,550
General Fund balance.	108,970

The budget for the year 1971 as adopted by the county commissioners provided for the following items of revenue and expenditure:

(1)	Town and county taxes.	$20,000
(2)	Jail operating costs.	55,500
(3)	Court operating costs.	7,500
(4)	Unincorporated business tax.	18,000
(5)	Board of prisoners (revenue).	5,000
(6)	Commissioners' salaries and expenses.	8,000
(7)	Interest on savings.	1,000
(8)	Miscellaneous expenses.	1,000

General Fund balance was appropriated in sufficient amount to balance the budget. At December 31, 1971, the jail supply inventory amounted to $5,120, cash of $380 was on hand, and $1,325 of prisoners' board bills were unpaid. The following items represent all of the transactions which occurred during the year, with all current bills vouchered and paid by December 31, 1971:

Item (1) was transacted exactly as budgeted.

Item (2) cash expenditures amounted to	$55,230
Item (3) amounted to	7,110
Item (4) amounted to	18,070
Item (5) billings amounted to	4,550
Item (6) amounted to	6,670
Item (7) amounted to	1,050
Item (8) amounted to	2,310

During the year, $25,000 was transferred from the savings accounts to the checking accounts.

Required:

From the above information, prepare a work sheet providing columns to show:

(i)   The transactions for the year.

(ii) Variances between budgeted and actual revenues and expenditures for the year.

(iii) Balance sheet of the General Fund, December 31, 1971.

(AICPA adapted)

Problem 20–7

The City of Bergen entered into the following transactions during the year 1971:

a) A bond issue was authorized by vote to provide funds for the construction of a new municipal building which it was estimated would cost $500,000. The bonds were to be paid in 10 equal installments from a Debt Service Fund, payments being due March 1 of each year. Any balance of the Capital Projects Fund is to be transferred directly to the Debt Service Fund.

b) An advance of $40,000 was received from the General Fund to underwrite a deposit on the land contract of $60,000. The deposit was made.

c) Bonds of $450,000 were sold for cash at 102. It was decided not to sell all of the bonds because the cost of the land was less than was expected.

d) Contracts amounting to $390,000 were let to Michela and Company, the lowest bidder, for the construction of the municipal building.

e) The temporary advance from the General Fund was repaid and the balance on the land contract was paid.

f) Based on the architect's certificate, warrants were issued for $320,000 for the work completed to date.

g) Warrants paid in cash by the treasurer amounted to $310,000.

h) Due to changes in the plans the contract with Michela and Company was revised to $440,000; the remainder of the bonds were sold at 101.

i) Before the end of the year the building had been completed and additional warrants amounting to $115,000 were issued to the contractor in final payment for the work. All warrants were paid by the treasurer.

Required:

(i)   Record the above transactions in Capital Projects Fund T-accounts. Designate the entries in the T-accounts by the numbers which identify the data.

(ii) Prepare applicable fund balance sheets as of December 31, 1971, considering only the proceeds and expenditures from capital projects fund transactions.

(AICPA adapted)

Problem 20–8

The City of Larkspur provides electric energy for its citizens through an operating department. All transactions of the Electric Department are recorded in a self-sustaining fund supported by revenue from the sales of energy. Plant expansion is financed by the issuance of bonds which are repaid out of revenues.

All cash of the Electric Department is held by the City Treasurer. Receipts from customers and others are deposited in the Treasurer's account. Disbursements are made by drawing warrants on the Treasurer.

The following is the postclosing trial balance of the department as of June 30, 1971:

Cash on deposit with City Treasurer	$ 2,250,000	
Due from customers	2,120,000	
Other current assets	130,000	
Construction in progress	500,000	
Land	5,000,000	
Electric plant	*50,000,000	
Accumulated depreciation—electric plant		$10,000,000
Accounts payable and accrued liabilities		3,270,000
5% electric revenue bonds		20,000,000
Accumulated earnings		26,730,000
	$60,000,000	$60,000,000

* The plant is being depreciated on the basis of a 50-year composite life.

During the year ended June 30, 1972, the department had the following transactions:

a) Sales of electric energy—$10,700,000.
b) Purchases of fuel and operating supplies (on account)—$2,950,000.
c) Construction of miscellaneous system improvements (financed from operations)—$750,000.
d) Fuel consumed—$2,790,000.
e) Miscellaneous plant additions and improvements placed in service— $1,000,000 (depreciate ½ year).
f) Wages and salaries paid—$4,280,000.
g) Sale on December 31, 1971, of 20-year 5 percent electric revenue bonds, with interest payable semiannually—$5,000,000.
h) Expenditures out of bond proceeds for construction of Larkspur Steam Plant Unit No. 1 and control house—$2,800,000.
i) Operating materials and supplies consumed—$150,000.
j) Payments received from customers—$10,500,000.
k) Expenditures out of bond proceeds for construction of Larkspur Steam Plant Unit No. 2—$2,200,000.
l) Warrants drawn on City Treasurer in settlement of accounts payable— $3,045,000.
m) Larkspur Steam Plant placed in service June 30, 1972.

Required:

A work sheet for the Revenue Fund of the Electric Department showing:

(i)   The balance sheet amounts at June 30, 1971.
(ii) The transactions for the year.
(iii) The balance sheet amounts at June 30, 1972.
(iv) The sources and applications of funds during the year.

(AICPA adapted)

Problem 20–9

You were engaged to examine the financial statements of the Mayfair School District for the year ended June 30, 1971, and were furnished the General Fund trial balance which appears on page 720.

Your examination disclosed the following information:

a) The recorded estimate of losses for the current year taxes receivable was considered to be sufficient.

b) The local government unit gave the school district 20 acres of land to be used for a new grade school and a community playground. The unrecorded estimated value of the land donated was $50,000. In addition a state grant of $300,000 was received and the full amount was used in payment of contracts pertaining to the construction of the grade school. Purchases of classroom and playground equipment costing $22,000 were paid from general funds.

c) Five years ago a 4 percent, 10-year, sinking fund bond issue in the amount of $1,000,000 for constructing school buildings was made and is outstanding. Interest on the issue is payable at maturity. Budgetary requirements of an annual contribution of $130,000 ($90,000 principal and $40,000 interest) and accumulated earnings to date aggregating $15,000 were accounted for in separate Debt Service Fund accounts.

d) Outstanding purchase orders for operating expenses not recorded in the accounts at year-end were as follows:

Administration	$1,000
Instruction	1,200
Other	600
Total	$2,800

e) The school district operated a central machine shop. Billings amounting to $950 were properly recorded in the accounts of the General Fund but not in the Intragovernmental Service Fund.

Required:

(i)   Prepare the formal adjusting and closing entries for the General Fund.
(ii) The foregoing information disclosed by your examination was recorded only in the General Fund. Prepare the formal adjusting journal entries for the (1) General Fixed Asset Group, (2) General Long-Term Debt, and (3) Intragovernmental Service Fund, to correct the failure to record the relevant transactions of 1971 and previous years.

(AICPA adapted)

MAYFAIR SCHOOL DISTRICT
General Fund Trial Balance
June 30, 1971

	Debit	Credit
Cash...	$ 47,250	
Taxes receivable—current year....................	31,800	
Estimated losses—current year taxes..............		$ 1,800
Temporary investments..........................	11,300	
Inventory of supplies...........................	11,450	
Buildings.....................................	1,300,000	
Estimated revenues.............................	1,007,000	
Appropriations—operating expenses..............		850,000
Appropriations—other expenditures..............		150,000
State grant revenue.............................		300,000
Bonds payable.................................		1,000,000
Vouchers payable..............................		10,200
Due to Intragovernmental Service Fund...........		950
Operating expenses:		
Administration.............................	24,950	
Instruction................................	601,800	
Other.....................................	221,450	
Transfer to Debt Service Fund (principal and		
interest).................................	130,000	
Capital outlays (equipment).....................	22,000	
Revenues from tax levy, licenses, and fines........		1,008,200
General fund balance...........................		87,850
Total.................................	$3,409,000	$3,409,000

Problem 20–10

The accounting systems of federal and nonfederal governmental units and commercial enterprises converge in a number of important respects. Yet, there remain significant differences.

Required:

(i) Contrast federal and nonfederal governmental accounting systems, accenting the salient features of each.

(ii) Characterize and compare governmental and commercial enterprise accounting.

Problem 20–11

The Intergalaxy Division, an agency of the federal government, was established on July 1, 1972. The activities of the agency will be financed by annual appropriations.

During the fiscal year ended June 30, 1973, the following transactions, in sequence, were completed:

a) An appropriation of $500,000 was approved by Congress for the Intergalaxy Division.

b) The Bureau of the Budget apportioned $450,000 to the agency.

c) The agency director allotted $440,000 to operating units for carrying out assigned projects.

d)   An order was placed in the amount of $200,000 for equipment to monitor planned space flights.

e)   Salaries of $125,000 were approved for payment without prior obligation.

f)   Supplies of $80,000 were ordered.

g)   The equipment, cost $200,000, and supplies, cost $78,000, were received.

h)   The recorded liabilities were certified for payment by a disbursing agent of the Treasury.

i)   Upon request by the Intergalaxy Division, the Bureau of the Budget apportioned an additional $45,000 to the agency. Concurrently, the agency director allotted an additional $54,000 to operating unit subdivisions.

j)   A research contract for $85,000 was granted to Space University.

k)   Services of $25,000 were received under the research contract; the remaining services are to be received in the next fiscal period.

l)   On June 30, 1973, accrued salaries of $4,000 and depreciation of $20,-000 were recorded; additionally, it was determined that the inventory of supplies amounted to $10,000.

Required:

(i)   Prepare journal entries to record the above transactions.

(ii) Prepare a preclosing trial balance for the agency.

(iii) Prepare closing entries.

(iv) Prepare a statement of financial position at June 30, 1973.

Problem 20–12

Regulatory accounting underlies the delicate process of harmonizing the sometimes divergent interests of government, private enterprise, and the public. In view of its manifest importance, the theoretical framework for regulatory accounting should consistently and completely facilitate the objectives of the regulating agencies.

Required:

(i)   What are the primary objectives of regulatory bodies?

(ii) What basic accounting criteria, or standards, are relevant to the regulation of public utilities?

(iii) Among the propositions applicable to the valuation of fixed assets, it is usually pointed out that public utilities have traditionally capitalized the interest charges on funds borrowed to finance the construction of plant and equipment. Explain the significance of this position, and relate it, if possible, to the basic accounting standards in (ii) above.

Chapter 21

National Income Accounting—I

INTRODUCTION

The principles which underlie the measurement of financial position and results of operations for profit-motivated business enterprises have had a relatively long evolutionary development. Progress is also evident, albeit slow, in the theory of accounting for nonprofit institutions. However, the historical emphasis on individual economic units, or microanalysis, perhaps has unduly constrained the potential growth of the accounting discipline. The accounting function of measuring economic status and accomplishment is relevant to all well-defined economic entities. One such entity which has heretofore attracted comparatively little attention and interest of many accountants is the national economy and its major subdivisions, an examination of which is called macroanalysis. The accumulation of statistical information concerning the economic activities of the national economy, however, grows increasingly important. Economists are continuing to refine their methods of classifying and summarizing this macroeconomic information; accordingly, its use by government, business, and individual consumers is noticeably expanding. Governmental subdivisions use these statistics as a basis for major policy decisions; businessmen rely on them to gauge future movements of demand and requirements for capital investment; and individual consumers rely on these data as a harbinger of the future course of business activity and therefore use them as indexes for personal investment. Consequently, accountants' improvement of the measurement processes, through reclassifications of basic source data and by suggested methodological refinements, should contribute to the validity of economic decisions at all levels of authority.

Accounting for the activity of the national economy is closely related to traditional accounting for the business unit. The major statements currently being prepared, as well as those which are proposed as being useful for the national accounting entity, are enumerated below:

1. *National income and product account.* This statement[1] provides an important index of the economic *output* of the national economy for a

---

[1] Reference is often to an "account" rather than a statement, because the traditional format of the statement is analogous to a T-account. In this regard, the underlying concepts of the realization and liquidation account (referred to in Chapter 18) may be useful in interpreting the national income and product account.

specified period of time. The basic criterion used to test whether or not an activity constitutes economic production is its identification with the market economy, i.e., is it reflected in a market transaction? This criterion, however, is subject to exception; it is modified to include imputed values for certain fundamental, nonmarket activities, and to exclude certain market transactions which are not regarded as socially useful. The report is similar to the conventional income statement for a profit-motivated business enterprise, although a single residual amount is not prominently displayed in the measurement process or classification format. One segment of the account displays the total value of the nation's output, classified so as to indicate how this total output was distributed among the four major sectors of the national economy; necessarily, this analysis of national output excludes transactions which are merely intrasector transfers. This segment of the account, which essentially parallels the credit side of an orthodox ledger account, measures the nation's total output by summing the market values of the final product flows. The contra, or debit, portion of the account details the charges against (the costs incurred to produce) aggregate national output, and accordingly includes the income accruing to the various factors of production (wages, rent, interest, and profits). It also includes other nonincome-producing charges. Since the contra totals merely represent different ways of classifying the same total output—in the same sense that the sales of a business are equal to the sum of its costs, expenses, and operating (or trading) profit—they are necesarily equal.

2. *National balance sheet.* Although a national balance sheet is not currently included in the catalog of macroaccounting statements, it has often been proposed as a valuable addition to the present complement of financial statements for the national economy. Such a report would, of course, reflect a consolidation of the assets and liabilities of all the residents of the United States, with a derivative measurement of the current "net worth" of the national economy.

3. *Balance of payments statement.* This statement is a consolidated account of the transactions between resident and foreign interests. It includes economic intercourse of both financial and nonfinancial types.

4. *Flow-of-funds statement.* This statement, modeled after the balance of payments statement, traces the movement of financial resources through the various productive and trading activities within the domestic national economy. The economic analysts of the Federal Reserve System are particularly interested in the flow-of-funds statement. They take primary responsibility for its preparation. Conceptually, this report parallels the source and application of funds statement prepared for an individual profit-motivated business enterprise.

5. *Input-output tables.* Originally developed by Professor Wassily Leontief, these tables provide extensive detailed information concerning an important segment of the national product accounts. Based upon a division of the economy into industrial categories, the report uses a matrix format to indicate the sources of each industry's inputs and the consumers of each

industry's outputs. The interindustry relationships which are revealed by this type of analysis quantitatively describe the basic *structure* of the national economy.

Essentially, each of these statements relates to a consolidation of the economic activities of the various producing units within the national economy. If the source information available to the "social" accountant were comparable to and in the form of that of the typical business enterprise, standard consolidation techniques might well be applied in preparing summary statements. Unfortunately, however, the several government subdivisions that prepare and publish these statements must rely upon unintegrated statistical data from many diverse sources, which in many instances virtually defy summation. The underlying consolidation concept, nonetheless, should aid in the comprehension of the various techniques and procedures which are now employed in the preparation of these statements.

The remaining analysis of Chapters 21 and 22 is focused on the development of the national income and product account and the underlying accounts pertaining to each sector of the economy. The perceptive reader will recognize that many of the issues to be examined are relevant to the other statements previously described, e.g., the national balance sheet. Nevertheless, the discussion will be limited to the national income and product account and the related sector accounts.

BASIC OBJECTIVE

The national income and product statement measures in current dollar units the socially useful output of the economy for a specified period of time—conventionally one year. The statement reflects, as its underlying philosophy, the traditional economic definition of national income, i.e., the amount of goods or services that could be consumed during a specified time interval, without a dilution in the productive capacity of the national economy to generate the same quantity of goods or services in the succeeding period. Instead of calculating a single index, however, several related, but individually important, indexes are cited and identified in the statement.

The basic structure of the national income accounting system is based upon a division of the United States economy into four distinct *sectors* or major economic groups: (1) business, (2) consumers (or households), (3) government, and (4) foreign interests (or rest of the world). Each of the four sectors may be characterized as displaying unique and individually significant economic behavior and motivations. As a consequence, it is important to measure the contribution of each sector to the total output of the economy and to disclose the effects of transactions between the sectors. Accounts for each sector, which are essentially subordinate or subsidiary in relation to the national income and product account, can be designed to report both the output originating in the sector and the transactions indicating interdependence with other sectors.[2] The data relating to each of the four sectors may be consolidated in order to provide the data included in the national income and product account. As the principal summary account of the system, the national income and product account measures the total output of the national economy.

The business sector account is essentially a consolidated income statement for the entire business system: the accounts for the remaining three sectors report current receipts and expenditures in respect to "nonprofit" activities. Except for saving and investment, the duality of transaction effects is evident in that the current transactions of one sector are reflected contra in one or more of the other sector accounts, in the tradition of debits and credits. For example, wage payments to employees in the business sector (debits) are reported as income (credits) in the personal (or household) sector account. In order to achieve a completely integrated accounting system, an additional account, gross saving and investment, is introduced with saving reported as credits therein and investment as debits. As a consequence of the structure of the system, gross saving must necessarily be equivalent to gross investment.[3] These sectoral interrelationships are graphically depicted on page 729 in conjunction with a more precise rendering of several definitions of important elements of the national income and product account. The Business sector account is not typically included in the publicly reported statistical summaries because of its close similarity to the national income and product account and the rather detailed analyses which are usually available as supplementary data. Nevertheless, the authors prefer to include it in this series of statements in the belief that it promotes understanding of the underlying structure of the national accounting system. The important accounting relationship between the national income and product account and the reported sector accounts cannot be adequately analyzed without giving careful attention to the account of the business sector.

From the previous comments, certain fundamental conclusions in respect to national income accounting can readily be drawn.

1. Emphasis is placed on the production or output of an activity, as contrasted with the enterprise accountant's conventional focus of attention on the completed sale.

2. Attention is directed primarily toward acts generating *economic goods,* excluding certain personal activities (such as the activities of a

---

[2] It should be noted that the format of the summary account relating to each sector, as published in the *Survey of Current Business,* Department of Commerce, does not provide sufficient detail to indicate the contribution of each sector to national income and product. More detailed information is, however, available in the form of supporting tables. Readers may also find national income and product account data in the monthly *Economic Indicators,* prepared for the Joint Economic Committee by the President's Council of Economic Advisors, and in the *Federal Reserve Bulletins.*

[3] This relationship is developed in greater detail in studies in economic theory.

housewife). Consequently, a *market transaction* is regarded as fundamentally important as a basic measure of economic activity. It should be noted, however, that this emphasis on market value confirmation is for reasons of convenience and practicality, rather than for theoretical reasons, as the measurement problems in respect to a number of personal activities are manifold and especially difficult. However, some exceptions to the market transaction criterion are made. Three general types of market transactions are specifically excluded from the national product total: (*a*) illegal activities; (*b*) sales of goods that were produced and recognized in previous periods, e.g., capital gains and losses; and (*c*) transfer payments. Illegal activities are excluded because they do not qualify as being *socially useful,* as defined by the generally accepted social mores of the time. Capital gains or losses, such as result from the sale of an existing asset (previously included in the national product measurement at the time it was produced), are excluded because they do not constitute additional economic output. Also, such gains or losses as result from changes in the general level of prices or exogenous shifts in demand are excluded as unpredictable and outside the sphere of productive economic activity. Finally, transfer payments, which are essentially redistributions of income and thus do not result from current economically productive activity, are also excluded. Government payments for such items as social security benefits, relief and unemployment benefits, and interest on the public debt are a principal source of transfer payments. Personal transfer payments to foreigners and interest paid by consumers are similarly excluded.[4] Business transfer payments, such as losses on bad debts and charitable contributions, are excluded from factor costs in the computation of national income but are subsequently included in accumulating charges against gross output. In contrast to the excluded market transactions, certain nonmarket activities are considered sufficiently important and measurable to deserve the assignment of an *imputed* value. The value of output consumed by the producer (principally agricultural), perquisites for employees, and the rental value of residential housing are three important items to which imputed values are estimated and assigned in the national product total.

3. In the measurement of the value of output for a specified period, it is important to distinguish between *final* and *intermediate* products. If the value of the output of each producing unit were merely summed without adjustment, the resultant total would necessarily include duplicate measurement of those goods that are transferred from one producing unit to another. For example, the value of a manufactured automobile is measured

---

[4] Due to the wartime origin of a substantial portion of the public debt, interest on the debt is excluded because it is not considered to be closely related to the value of the government's physical assets and thus not a valid determinant of economic output. The exclusion of consumer interest payments is also argued to be essentially unproductive of economic services. This exclusion policy is the subject of considerable controversy; nevertheless, it is consistent with the recommendations of the United Nations.

by its selling price, which value is properly included in the national product total. However, if the total output of steel companies—measured in sales adjusted for variations in inventory—were added to the total sales of automobiles, the value of steel used in automobile manufacturing would be double-counted in computing the value of current output. Thus, a working distinction may be drawn: *intermediate products* are those products which are purchased for resale, with or without further physical transformation or processing, and *final products* are those purchases which are not resold during the current period; viewed differently, intermediate products are regarded, in total, as expense charges of the purchasing company. The total value of final products is the significant index which constitutes the current output for the period.

4. As suggested above, *current market prices* are used in measuring the value of economic output. Manifestly, this objective creates a need for price adjustment if traditional accounting evaluations of inventory changes are used as source data.

BASIC DEFINITIONS

It has been previously observed that the value of the output of the national economy may be calculated by summing either the values of final products, *or* by summing payments to the various factors of production plus certain nonincome charges. This principle of dualism is implicit in the following definitions of the various elements that compose the aggregative process.

Gross national product (GNP) is defined as the total national production of goods and services for a specified period of time (usually one year), valued at current market prices. One method of measuring GNP is to sum the value of final products, excluding therefrom the values of intermediate products, goods produced in prior periods although not then sold, and financial transfers unrelated to current production. In this *final products approach,* an increase in inventories is considered to have been purchased by the producer for investment and is included in the final products valuation along with other capital investments in the year of acquisition. This method may be symbolically represented:

$$GNP = C + P + G + E,$$

where C denotes sales of goods and services to consumers; P denotes *gross* sales of products to business for final use as producers' (capital) goods, including inventory changes; G denotes sales of goods and services to government; and E denotes net sales to the rest of the world, i.e., net exports. An equivalent amount would result from aggregating each economic unit's contribution to the total product and thereafter subtracting the value of intermediate goods. Since the sales and purchases of intermediate goods (intrasector transactions)[5] are thus eliminated, only the value of final product remains. For an individual business enterprise, the difference between the value of its finished production and the value of its purchases of intermediate goods is the value added by the economic unit; accordingly, this method of measuring gross national product is called the *value added method*.

The latter measurement process may be further enlarged to yield a dual approach formulation for GNP. For each firm, the value added (sales plus inventory increase, less intermediate purchases) either accrues as income (wages, rent, interest, and profits) to the factors of production or relates to other "nonincome" charges such as indirect business taxes (sales, excise, and property taxes), business transfer payments, and capital consumption (depreciation and other capital costs). Therefore, gross national product (or gross national income) may be *defined* in still another manner as the sum of incomes accruing to the various factors of production plus nonincome charges against production. In symbolic notation, the *factor payments approach* may be represented:

$$GNP = W + R + I + P + T + X + D,$$

where W denotes wages, R denotes rental income of persons, I denotes net interest paid to households, P denotes profits, T denotes indirect business taxes, X denotes business transfer payments, and D denotes depreciation or capital consumption. This specification of the factors of production (and other charges) is based upon the economic theorist's traditional classification of fundamental economic inputs.

By appropriate recombinations of the aggregates contained in the factor payments approach, several additional important measurements may be derived. While the gross national product quantifies the gross value of the output of the economy, it may also be useful to define an index of output which recognizes the value of existing goods consumed in current production. This amount, gross national product minus capital consumption, is defined as *net national product* (NNP). This index of productivity in many respects is theoretically superior to GNP, which includes in the measure of current output the gross sales of capital goods. To the extent of current capital consumption on the existing capital stock, gross capital formation includes production designed solely for capital replacement, which purchases become, in fact, intermediate products. That is, depreciation of capital is conceptually equivalent to any raw material input.

That GNP clearly does not measure net capital formation may be simply illustrated. If during an accounting period, one machine tool were used to produce one additional machine tool, and if at the end of the accounting period, the producing tool proved to be valueless, i.e., completely con-

---

[5] If the eliminations were not intrasector, i.e., if the basic consolidating unit were the national economy, *all* sales and purchases would be self-canceling.

sumed, gross investment (product) would be calculated as the value of one machine tool at current prices, and net investment (product), or the addition to the productive capacity of the economy, would be zero. If, however, five new machine tools were produced, gross investment would be equal to the value of five machine tools at current prices, and net investment would be equal to the value of four machine tools at current prices. Thus, gross investment is necessarily nonnegative, whereas net investment may be either positive, negative, or zero. Unfortunately, the estimate of NNP suffers from the practical impossibility of obtaining a reliable measure of *net* capital formation, since an estimate of the capital consumption allowance based upon current prices is not available. Use of existing enterprise accounting data for depreciation does not affect the calculation of GNP (except to the extent of the conceptual question of inconsistency introduced by including only the net flow of goods and services to consumers, while reporting the gross flow of capital production), as counterbalancing "errors" exist in both profits and capital consumption.

Another measurement total of signal importance in the interpretation of economic data is *national income*. National income is defined as the sum of all income payments accruing to the factors of production during a specified

Illustration 21–1

THE FLOW OF MONEY INCOME IN A GIVEN TIME PERIOD

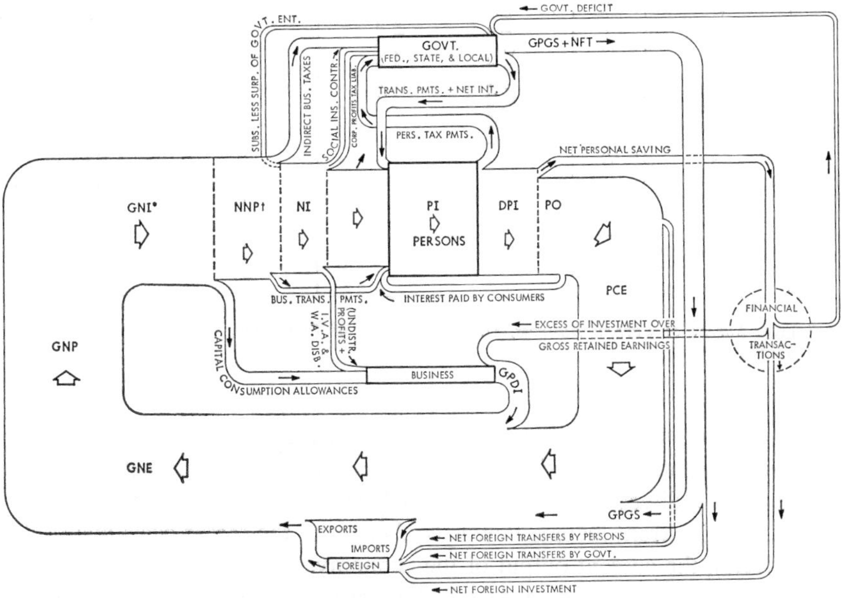

* The term "Gross National Income" is not used in the national income accounts; the more precise term is "Charges against GNP."
† The more precise term is "Charges against NNP," though it is usually shown simply as "NNP" in the national income accounts.
Source: Robert C. Turner, Indiana University.

Illustration 21–2

THE NATIONAL INCOME AND PRODUCT ACCOUNTS—1969

**Relation of the Four Major Measures of Production and Income Flows
(in billions of dollars)**

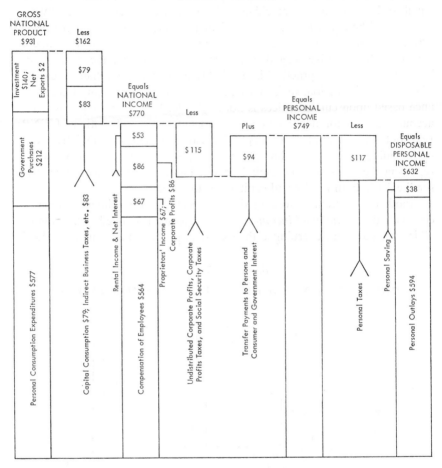

Source: *Survey of Current Business,* U.S. Department of Commerce, Office of Business Economics, July, 1970, p. 16.

period of time, usually a year. Calculated as a residual, in terms of statement components discussed to this point, national income is net national product less indirect business taxes and business transfer payments. This expression of current income flow is equivalent to the factor costs incurred in producing the current output of the economy.

In addition to these three principal indexes of economic activity, reference is frequently made to two other important aggregates. *Personal income* is defined as the current receipts of income by individuals from whatever source. Thus personal income, as contrasted with national income, includes transfer payments received by individuals and interest payments paid by government and consumers; it excludes undistributed earnings of corporations, corportate income tax liabilities, and social security contributions. Manifestly, personal income is not an index of national production. *Disposable personal income* is defined as personal income reduced by personal tax payments. This measurement indicates in a very general way the amount of consumer purchasing power generated during the current period.

Disposable personal income may also be analyzed in terms of its primary components: (1) personal outlays and (2) personal saving. Personal outlays consist of personal consumption expenditures, net personal transfer payments to foreigners, and consumer interest payments.

These concepts are summarized in graphic form in Illustrations 21–1 and 21–2. Illustration 21–1 indicates the *flow* of income and expenditures in relation to the various aggregates included in the national income and product account. Illustration 21–2 exhibits the magnitudes of the several aggregates (except net national product) for the year 1969.

THE BUSINESS SECTOR—A SINGLE FIRM ILLUSTRATION

A significant part of the output of the national economy originates in the business sector. For this reason, and because the business environment is familiar to most accountants, an individual business unit and the business sector will be used as representative models to outline the underlying concepts and to further illustrate the accumulation and summation (consolidation) of the source information.

The "duality principle" previously alluded to in the definition of gross national product is easily illustrated by considering a hypothetical income statement for an individual business enterprise. An assumed income statement for such an entity is given in Illustration 21–3. If this statement were recast using the basic format of the national income and product account, it would assume the form shown in Illustration 21–4.

This special rendering of the income statement for an individual business unit emphasizes several important attributes. First, it demonstrates that the form of the report is similar to the income summary account conventionally used by the single enterprise in closing revenues and expenses at the end of a given accounting period. Second, the total of the right (or credit) side of the account indicates the gross value of business output, $210,000, for the elapsed time period, i.e., the value of sales increased by the value of the addition to inventory.[6] For the economy as a whole, a consolidation of sales and inventory changes is a measurement of gross national product. It

---

[6] The question of an appropriate inventory valuation will be considered later in the chapter.

Illustration 21–3

BUSINESS X

Income Statement

For Year Ended December 31, 1971

Sales...............................		$200,000
Cost of goods sold:		
Inventory, January 1................	$ 30,000	
Purchases.........................	130,000	
	$160,000	
Inventory, December 31.............	40,000	
Cost of goods sold.................		120,000
Gross profit.........................		$ 80,000
Operating expenses:		
Salaries...........................	$ 40,000	
Interest...........................	5,000	
Rent..............................	5,000	
Depreciation......................	10,000	60,000
Net Income........................		$ 20,000

should be noted that the variations in inventory value *must* be disclosed on the right side of the account, either positively (inventory increase) or negatively (inventory decrease), if the inventory change and sales total is to reflect the value of gross output. Third, the contra, or left (debit), side of the income and product account generates the same total, $210,000, by summing the period's expenses and the residual profits of the business. Although only the factor costs, indirect business taxes and depreciation are elements used in consolidating business sector subaccounts, these data illustrate the dualism implicit in the calculation of gross national product. Finally, in respect to consolidating all the units in the business sector, and the subsequent consolidation of the business and other sectors into the national income and product account, it is evident that Business X did not, in fact, add $210,000 value to the output of the national economy during this specified period. Since the materials purchased from other business units already had a value of $130,000, the *value added by Business X*

Illustration 21–4

BUSINESS X

Income and Product Account

For Year Ended December 31, 1971

Purchases	130,000	Sales	200,000
Salaries	40,000	Inventory increase	10,000
Interest	5,000		
Rent	5,000		
Depreciation	10,000		
Profits	20,000		
	210,000		210,000

amounted to only $80,000 ($210,000 − $130,000). Note that the value added is equal to the sum of the factor costs and depreciation [($40,000 + $5,000 + $5,000 + $20,000) + $10,000]. However, if the sales of Business X were the only sales of final product (to business on capital account, consumers, government, or rest of the world), the amount of the value added to output *by the business sector* would be $210,000, excluding changes in inventories in other business enterprises. It is apparent that one or more other businesses partially fabricated the units purchased by Business X and incurred total factor costs plus other nonincome charges of $130,000, since the value of output necessarily must equal the sum of the values of these inputs. This interdependency will be revealed more completely in the following description of the consolidation of all firms in the business sector.

CONSOLIDATION OF THE BUSINESS SECTOR

The value of the business sector output is, in principal, essentially a summation of the individual income and product accounts of all the entities in the sector. The United States Department of Commerce delimits the scope of this sector as follows:

The business sector is defined broadly to include all organizations which produce goods and services for sale at a price intended at least to approximate costs of production. In the main, it covers all private enterprises organized for profit, both corporate and noncorporate, including farm operators, independent professional practitioners, and lessors of real property. Mutual financial institutions, cooperatives, and nonprofit organizations serving business are also included, as well as government enterprises. Owner-occupied houses and buildings used by nonprofit institutions serving individuals are considered to be business establishments selling their current services to their owners.[7]

The income and product account for the business sector consists of data collected from various sources, including federal and state governmental agencies, the manufacturing census data, and numerous others; patently, the actual account is *not* a summation of the operating statements of the individual enterprises in the business sector. A centralized information system by means of which these data may be collected is not yet available. However, it may be useful in the discussion to follow to adopt the fiction of consolidation, as this type of summation is especially revealing in respect to the details of sector transactions. The following example, which illustrates the consolidation of four business units, will focus attention on the underlying concepts and the nature of the individual items included in the consolidated business sector account.

For illustrative purposes, the business sector is assumed to consist of

---

[7] Office of Business Economics, United States Department of Commerce, *National Income, 1954 Edition* (Washington, D.C.: U.S. Government Printing Office, 1954), p. 40.

four economic units: W Steel Company, X Electronics Company, Y Machine Tool, Inc., and Z Department Store, Inc. With the exception of the Z Department Store, Inc., all are manufacturers.[8] The income statement and a supporting schedule for the W Steel Company (Illustrations 21–5 and 21–6) are given detailed consideration for purposes of emphasizing the rearrangement and translation of these data into a form reflecting the essential concepts of the national income and product account.

The calculation of 1971 output of the W Steel Company is analogous to the explanation of the income and product account of Business X discussed previously. The gross value of the output of the W Steel Company may be computed in summary form as follows:

Sales...............................		$38,000
Increase [decrease] in inventories:		
Raw materials........................	$[2,000]	
Goods in process....................	[4,000]	
Finished goods......................	1,000	[5,000]
1971 output of W Steel Company........		$33,000

As noted earlier, however, the $33,000 gross output of W does not represent the value added by W to the gross output of the business sector. The income and product accounts of all business firms must be consoli-

Illustration 21–5

W STEEL COMPANY

Income Statement
For Year Ended December 31, 1971

Sales...		$38,000
Cost of goods sold:		
Finished goods inventory, January 1, 1971...........	$ 1,000	
Cost of goods manufactured (see supporting schedule		
—Illustration 21–6)............................	25,000	
	$26,000	
Finished goods inventory, December 31, 1971........	2,000	24,000
Gross profit..		$14,000
Operating expenses:		
Wages and wage supplements.......................	$ 4,000	
Interest...	1,000	
Rent...	2,000	
Property taxes....................................	1,000	8,000
Net income before federal income taxes...............		$ 6,000
Federal income taxes.............................		2,500
Net income.......................................		$ 3,500
Gain on sale of fixed assets.........................		1,500
Net income plus nonrecurring gain...................		$ 5,000

Note: Cash dividends of $1,000 were paid during 1971 to nonbusiness shareholders. The remainder of net income, $2,500, and the gain on sale of fixed assets, $1,500, are transferred to W's undistributed profits.

---

[8] These particular hypothetical companies have been selected as reasonably representative of a cross section of the activities of profit-oriented companies in the national economy.

Illustration 21–6

W STEEL COMPANY

Schedule of Cost of Goods Manufactured
For Year Ended December 31, 1971

Raw materials:

Raw materials inventory, January 1, 1971............	$ 3,000	
Purchases.......................................	9,000	
	$12,000	
Raw materials inventory, December 31, 1971.........	1,000	$11,000
Direct labor and wage supplements....................		6,000
Overhead costs:		
Indirect labor and wage supplements................	$ 1,000	
Depreciation.....................................	2,000	
Supplies (nonfactor costs).........................	1,000	4,000
Total manufacturing costs............................		$21,000
Add: Goods in process inventory, January 1, 1971......		6,000
Total goods in process during 1971....................		$27,000
Deduct: Goods in process inventory, December 31, 1971...		2,000
Cost of goods manufactured..........................		$25,000

dated, with intrasector transactions eliminated, to derive the total output of the sector. For reasons of simplicity, it is here assumed that each company classifies its sales according to consumer class. For W, the following analysis is available:

Sales of final product:		
To households.......................	$ 1,000	
To government......................	1,000	
To foreigners.......................	2,000	$ 4,000
Change in inventory..................		[5,000]
Sales of intermediate product:		
To X Electronics Company............	$ 9,000	
To Y Machine Tool, Inc..............	23,000	
To Z Department Store, Inc...........	2,000	34,000
Output during 1971...................		$33,000

It is additionally assumed that rent and interest payments are made to individuals rather than to other entities in the business sector; if not, they would accordingly be eliminated, as the underlying factor costs would thus originate in other enterprises within the business sector. W's purchases of intermediate products consist of $9,000 materials and $1,000 supplies.

The above data are translated in the consolidated business sector working paper in Illustration 21–7. The detailed reclassification of the disposition of W's product is sufficiently general to allow the use of summary information for the remaining three companies without providing their separate income statements and supporting schedules.

The consolidated business income and product account for the year

Illustration 21-7

BUSINESS SECTOR
Consolidated Working Paper
For Year Ended December 31, 1971

	W Steel Company	X Electronics Company	Y Machine Tool, Inc.	Z Dept. Store, Inc.	Eliminations Dr.	Eliminations Cr.	Consolidated
Outputs							
Sales of final product:							
To households........	1,000	5,000		20,000			26,000
To government........	1,000	10,000		5,000			16,000
To foreigners........	2,000	2,000					4,000
To business firms (capital goods)...			60,000				60,000
	4,000	17,000	60,000	25,000			106,000
Change in inventory...	[5,000]	8,000	10,000	[2,000]			11,000
Sales of intermediate product:							
To W Steel Company...		3,000		7,000	(1) 10,000		
To X Electronics Company...	9,000			5,000	(1) 14,000		
To Y Machine Tool, Inc....	23,000	10,000		1,000	(1) 34,000		
To Z Department Store, Inc....	2,000	5,000			(1) 7,000		
	34,000	18,000		13,000			—0—
Capital gain...	1,500				(2) 1,500		—0—
	34,500	43,000	70,000	36,000			117,000
Inputs							
Factor costs:							
Wages and wage supplements...	11,000	10,000	18,000	12,000			51,000
Rent...	2,000	2,000	1,000	6,000			11,000
Interest...	1,000	2,000	1,000	3,000			7,000
Profits:							
Corporate profits tax liability...	2,500	4,000	2,000	2,000			10,500
Corporate profits after taxes:							
Dividends...	1,000	1,000	2,000	1,000			5,000
Undistributed profits...	4,000	4,000	3,000	2,000		(2) 1,500	11,500
	21,500	23,000	27,000	26,000			96,000
Nonincome charges:							
Indirect business taxes*...	1,000	2,000	1,000	1,000			5,000
Purchases of intermediate products:							
From W Steel Company...		9,000	23,000	2,000		(1) 34,000	
From X Electronics Company...	3,000		10,000	5,000		(1) 18,000	
From Z Department Store...	7,000	5,000	1,000			(1) 13,000	
	10,000	14,000	34,000	7,000			—0—
Capital consumption (depreciation)...	2,000	4,000	8,000	2,000			16,000
	34,500	43,000	70,000	36,000	66,500	66,500	117,000

Explanation of eliminations:

(1) To eliminate intrasector sales and purchases.

(2) To eliminate capital gain against undistributed profits.

* Indirect business taxes include all tax payments by businesses that are not based upon profits. An additional nonincome charge, not displayed above, is business transfer payments (bad debts, gifts, etc.).

Illustration 21–8

BUSINESS SECTOR

Consolidated Income and Product Account

For Year Ended December 31, 1971

Factor payments:		Consolidated sales:	
Wages and wage supplements	51,000	To households	26,000
Rent	11,000	To government	16,000
Interest	7,000	To business on capital account	60,000
Corporate profits before income		To foreigners	4,000
taxes:		Change in inventories	11,000
Corporate profits tax liability	10,500		
Dividends	5,000		
Undistributed profits	11,500		
INCOME ORIGINATING IN BUSINESS			
SECTOR	96,000		
Indirect business taxes	5,000		
CHARGES AGAINST NET PRODUCT	101,000		
Capital consumption allowance	16,000		
CHARGES AGAINST BUSINESS GROSS			
PRODUCT	117,000	BUSINESS GROSS PRODUCT	117,000

ended December 31, 1971, constructed from the consolidated working paper takes the form shown in Illustration 21–8.

The consolidation accomplished, the following conclusions may be drawn:

1. The basic elimination in the consolidation of the economic units in the business sector relates to the intrasector sales and purchases. It should be noted, however, that a detailed classification of intrasector transactions is unnecessary, as all purchases of noncapital goods are, *by definition,* intermediate product acquisitions; therefore, in consolidating the business sector accounts, the usual account classifications (Purchases, Supplies, Repairs and Maintenance, etc.) should provide sufficient information.

2. As noted earlier, profits derived from the transfer of existing assets are excluded from the income and product account of the sector because they do not provide value increment to the *output* of the current period. Accordingly, in this example, W's capital gain from the sale of fixed assets was eliminated against W's reported undistributed profits, excluding thereby this element from the aggregative process.

3. In the detailed analysis of W's output, the algebraic sum of sales of final product ($4,000) and change in inventories ([$5,000]) resulted in a negative balance of $1,000, thereby creating the deception of a negative contribution to business gross product. That this is patently illusory is demonstrated by noting the $23,000 total of W's noneliminated inputs, viz., factor costs of $20,000 ($21,500 − $1,500), nonincome charges of $1,000, and depreciation of $2,000. This sum represents the value added by W during the current period. To the extent that W's intermediate prod-

uct sales have passed through the business sector to the ultimate consumer, these costs are implicitly contained in the current business income and product account in the "consolidated sales." To the extent that W's intermediate sales are included in the year-end inventory of another enterprise in the business sector, the costs are implicitly contained in the "change in inventories," which, as previously noted, is accounted for by the purchaser as an investment. Herein exists a basic difference in consolidating the business sector accounts as contrasted with the preparation of consolidated statements for individual business units. Profits which are included in the value of goods purchased by another firm in the business sector and which remain in the purchasing company's inventory at the end of the accounting period are not eliminated, because these profits are valid factor costs of the current period; consequently, they are determinants in the measurement of current output of the sector.

4. It may be noted that corporate profits before dividends and income taxes are included as a factor cost; yet, they are separately identified with the three ultimate recipients (government, personal stockholders, and the corporation) in the income and product account. This treatment is consistent with the inclusion of net income of unincorporated business before taxes (not here illustrated) as a factor cost. The analysis of the profits by recipient also provides important information which is useful in reconciling reported totals for national income, personal income, and disposable personal income. The reader, by referring again to Illustration 21–1, will note the graphic representation of these relationships.

5. In addition to intrasector purchases of "raw materials," all other intrasector purchases of goods and services must be eliminated. In the previous example, the elimination of W's supplies acquisitions with other intermediate purchases is a case in point. Additionally, rent or interest paid to another business enterprise is not a factor cost of the sector and must be eliminated; intrasector dividends are similarly eliminated. Only sales of final product are extended to the consolidated column of the working paper; however, significantly, those factor costs which originate in enterprises which sell supplies or services are not eliminated as they constitute a portion of the total factor cost of the products ultimately sold as final products.

While these brief comments are intended to clarify some of the rather elusive items cited in the previous illustrative example, several significant inclusions in the business sector account warrant additional explanation and are discussed in the following section.

SPECIAL PROBLEMS IN THE BUSINESS SECTOR

Inventory Valuation Adjustment

The business income and product account seeks to measure current output in terms of *current market prices*. The important effect of inventory changes on this computation has been previously demonstrated. Since the social accountant relies strongly upon the financial statements of the business unit for his basic source data *in respect to these inventory changes,* the effect of the enterprise accountant's use of the cost principle in inventory valuation must be tested in terms of its appropriateness for national income accounting.

The effects of price fluctuation on the inventory valuation adjustment will be illustrated by the following two hypothetical cases with both FIFO and LIFO cost flows considered.

Case 1. This case will assume an *increase* in the quantity of inventory during the accounting period. The following data are given:

	Units	Price/Unit
Inventory, January 1, 1971.............	5,000	
FIFO...........................		$4.00
LIFO...........................		3.00
1971 purchases (production)...........	20,000	5.00
1971 sales......................	15,000	8.00

Based upon these data, the following partial income statements may be prepared:

	FIFO	LIFO
Sales......................	$120,000	$120,000
Cost of sales:		
Inventory, January 1.............	$ 20,000	$ 15,000
Purchases....................	100,000	100,000
	$120,000	$115,000
Inventory, December 31..........	50,000	40,000
	$ 70,000	$ 75,000
Gross profit................	$ 50,000	$ 45,000

The accountant may elect other inventory pricing methods which would result in different measurements of inventory and profit. Necessarily, the dollar value of the *change in inventory* will vary depending upon the pricing method chosen: $30,000 under FIFO, and $25,000 under LIFO. Since the change in inventory is a significant factor in the calculation of current output for the business sector, this valuation takes on special importance. In determining sector output, the increase of 5,000 units in inventory should be valued at the current market (replacement) price, and the cost of goods sold should be based similarly upon this price. The following calculations reflect these current price data:

Sales......................................	$120,000
Cost of sales (15,000 @ $5).................	75,000
Gross profit...............................	$ 45,000
Inventory increase (5,000 @ $5).............	$ 25,000

Clearly, the LIFO method produces the appropriate value for both profits and change in inventory where there has been an *increase* in the quantity of inventory during the period.[9] On the other hand, the FIFO method over-states the change in inventory and profits by $5,000. If this overstatement may be likened to a "gain," it would appear to be attributable to the sale of the prior period's production (beginning inventory), the accounting cost of which ($4) is below current replacement cost ($5); so conceived, it is essentially a "capital gain," i.e., it is an exogenous shift in prices not re-lated to *current output,* and thus is not a proper inclusion in the output calculation of the current period. This "book profit" produced by the FIFO method is eliminated by means of an *inventory valuation adjustment,* which in the present case would assume the following journal entry form:

Change in inventories...................................... 5,000
    Inventory valuation adjustment........................   5,000

The inventory valuation is an adjustment of reported profits; thus, since profits are included as a debit with the other factor costs, this particular adjustment effectively reduces reported profits in the income and product account. Similarly, the change in inventories reported on the credit side of the account is also reduced.

Case 2.   In order to illustrate a *decrease* in the quantity of inventory during the accounting period, the previous data are repeated with the exception that sales are assumed to be 22,000 units. Partial income state-ments under the different pricing methods are as follows:

	FIFO	LIFO
Sales................................	$176,000	$176,000
Cost of sales:		
Inventory, January 1................	$ 20,000	$ 15,000
Purchases.........................	100,000	100,000
	$120,000	$115,000
Inventory, December 31.............	15,000	9,000
	$105,000	$106,000
Gross profit........................	$ 71,000	$ 70,000

In this case, the appropriate values for profits and change in inventories in respect to sector output are:

Sales... $176,000
Cost of sales (22,000 @ $5)......................... 110,000
Gross profit.. $ 66,000
Inventory decrease (2,000 @ $5)..................... $ 10,000

It is apparent that both the FIFO and LIFO pricing methods fail to produce appropriate measurements of "real" output and profits where there is an inventory quantity decrease; the required adjustment would be $5,000 if FIFO were used, and $4,000 if LIFO were used. In both instances, the

---

[9] Since a national "balance sheet" is not currently being prepared, the fact that the ending inventory is not valued at current replacement prices is not especially significant.

inventory decrease, as adjusted, is larger than the inventory decrease as measured by the pricing methods cited, viz.,

	(FIFO)	(LIFO)
Change in inventories..............	5,000	4,000
Inventory valuation adjustment.................	5,000	4,000

In both of these cases, the assumption was made that the price level was increasing. If the price level were decreasing, the two inventory pricing methods would produce analogous results, although reported profits would be increased, or debited, in the income and product account, and the change in inventories would be correspondingly credited.

The previous examples have outlined the basic concepts underlying the inventory valuation adjustment. Since the measure of GNP assumes an evaluation of current output at current market prices, i.e., a dollar measure of "real" output, inventory valuations taken from enterprise accounting records frequently must be adjusted to achieve this result. Similarly, where the reported profits reflect an excess of replacement cost over recorded cost (a condition existing under FIFO pricing and a rising price level), the excess margin is viewed essentially as a capital gain realized on the sale of existing assets, and thus is excluded from the current period's output. It should be noted, however, that the previous illustrations have assumed a discontinuous shift in prices, i.e., the prices were uniform *during* the period but were different from those of the prior period. This assumption is frequently unrealistic, and the adjustment actually should be made on the basis of *average prices* during the current period. Using FIFO pricing, the required adjustment (estimated as a fraction of the total reported inventories) may be computed by using composite price indexes to convert reported inventories for the two years to constant dollars, after which the indicated changes in constant dollar valuations are converted to current dollars (in a manner similar to the dollar value LIFO method); for LIFO inventory pricing, the reported change as reckoned in enterprise accounting is accepted without adjustment for quantity increases; however, in the event of a quantity decrease, a conversion adjustment to current prices is necessary. Manifestly, a deficiency in information concerning the base layers of LIFO inventories would create a potentially significant error; yet, considered in relation to *total* inventories, without distinction as to layers, the magnitude of the possible error appears less important.

Imputed Values

Four major value imputations are injected into the income and product account for the business sector: (1) the value of providing occupancy in respect to owner-occupied residences, (2) the value of farm output consumed by the producer, (3) salaries paid in kind, and (4) nonmonetary product flows of financial intermediaries. As previously noted, these represent significant contributions to the income and product flows of the economy which are not reflected in market transactions and for which values must be assigned or imputed.

In order that comparable treatment may be accorded owner-occupied and rental housing, it is assumed that home ownership implies that the owner (regarded as a business) sells occupancy to the owner (regarded as a tenant). Thus, the gross value of providing occupancy is entered in the business account as sales to households, and the net rental income, after due recognition is given to maintenance, repairs, and other relevant business expenses, is recorded as a factor cost—"rental income of persons." The expenses which relate to such income are treated in a manner analogous to that of a single enterprise, i.e., an interest payment on a mortgage is entered as a factor cost originating in the business sector, indirect business taxes and depreciation are reflected as previously indicated, and other expenses, such as maintenance and repairs, are treated as intermediate sector purchases, to be eliminated against the corresponding revenue of other businesses in the consolidation process.

The value of food and fuel produced on farms for personal consumption is accorded similar treatment. The gross value of this consumption is recorded as sales to households. Manifestly, this inclusion obviates the necessity of allocating farm expenses between market output and personally consumed output. Rather, the total farm expenses are treated in the same manner as other business expenses. The net income of farms (gross imputed and actual sales to households less expenses) is then included in the "income of unincorporated enterprises"—a factor cost.

The value of perquisites, such as food and lodging, to employees in industries in which this amount is material represents a third major value imputation. It is treated as an additional factor cost on the debt side of the income and product account of the business sector, and as sales to households on the credit side of this account. Since the cost to the employer is the measure of this factor cost, this imputation has the effect of transforming an intermediate purchase into a factor cost (wages and salaries).

The final imputed item, the income and product flows of commercial banks, investment trusts, and insurance companies, is a complex and, as yet, an unresolved problem. Essentially, it involves recognition of services provided without explicit charges to customers, e.g., services related to demand deposits in a commercial bank.

Governmental Operating Enterprises and Subsidies to Business

In the definition of the business sector, it was indicated that specific governmental enterprises or subdivisions whose costs are recovered, or substantially recovered, from operating revenues from the sale of goods or services are included in the business sector. In a sense, these are the "profit-oriented" agencies of the government. Principal examples are the postal service and public utilities. However, there are other governmental entities or operations in which only a nominal part of the total operating costs relate to revenues derived from the business sector, such as a state university; these are excluded from the business sector.

The revenues of those governmental enterprises which qualify as business sector members are additive elements in calculating the gross product originating in the sector, and with certain significant exceptions, the expenses of such agencies are treated as factor costs or intermediate purchases, depending on their nature. The exceptions relate to profits, interest, depreciation, and capital formation. In the income and product account, profits of such enterprises (described as "current surplus of governmental enterprises")—before depreciation and interest—are included as a nonincome *charge* against the net product of the sector. Interest expense, for reasons given earlier, is included with the net interest payments of nonprofit oriented governmental divisions. Depreciation is neither a profit determinant of the government enterprise nor an inclusion in the capital consumption allowance; furthermore, purchases of capital goods by these governmental units are not included with gross private domestic investment, but rather with government purchases, reported as "sales to government" in the income and product account. Clearly, none of these exceptions affect the equality of debits and credits in the account, and it is assumed that the resulting classifications reflect more clearly the underlying economic motivations.

Unlike revenues of profit motivated governmental agencies, direct subsidies to business enterprises are not considered additions to current output. Rather, these intersector payments are presumably made to generate factor incomes within the particular business enterprise. Therefore, the value of the output of the subsidized industry is measured by current market prices, and the subsidies are *deducted* from other nonincome charges. Since the subsidy represents revenue to the recipient business, it effectively increases profits, and thus total factor cost; subsequently, it is deducted (credit balance) in computing charges against net and gross product of the sector.

These two economic measures are reported as a single item in the income and product account due to the potential complexity involved in attempting to segregate implicit subsidies paid through governmental enterprises from other expenditures of these entities.

Classification of Taxes

Although the classification of the various taxes has been previously alluded to, the following additional comments are appropriate. Employment taxes are included with wages and salaries, a factor cost, because they are additive elements in the cost of acquiring labor. Corporate profits taxes are also included among the factor costs on the assumption that they are not transferred or passed along to other taxpayers; contrariwise, indirect business taxes (property, excise, etc.) are included with nonincome charges, as it is assumed they are ultimately borne by the consumer and are transferred to him. Although the theory of tax transference and incidence is controversial, the above rationale underlies the current treatment of taxes in the computation of income and output totals.

A COMPREHENSIVE EXAMPLE

Although it has been previously noted that the business sector account is omitted currently from published statistical summaries, it nonetheless provides a meaningful framework to support the accountant's study of national income accounting. For this reason, discussion of this sector will be concluded with a more detailed illustration of the business income and product account—an account that includes most of the taxonomic divisions found in the *national* income and product account. These data are presented in Illustration 21–9. Since, unfortunately, an integrated social accounting system does not now exist, the aggregation of independent data for the contra sides of the account will yield a difference which carries the de-

Illustration 21–9

BUSINESS SECTOR

Consolidated Income and Product Account
For Year Ended December 31, 1971

Compensation of employees:		Consolidated sales:	
Wages and salaries	240,000	To households	372,000
Supplements:		To government	35,000
Employer contributions for		To business on capital account	85,000
social insurance	6,000	To foreigners	3,000
Other labor incomes	7,000	Change in inventories	15,000
Rental income of persons	17,000		
Net interest	7,000		
Income of unincorporated enter-			
prises and inventory valuation			
adjustment	75,000		
Corporate income and inventory			
valuation adjustment:			
Corporate income before taxes:			
Corporate income tax liability	35,000		
Corporate income after taxes:			
Dividends	18,000		
Undistributed profits	25,000		
Inventory valuation adjustment	[10,000]		
INCOME ORIGINATING IN BUSINESS			
SECTOR	420,000		
Indirect business taxes	50,000		
Business transfer payments	2,000		
Statistical discrepancy	1,000		
Subsidies minus current surplus of			
governmental enterprises	*[1,000]		
CHARGES AGAINST NET PRODUCT	472,000		
Capital consumption allowances	38,000		
CHARGES AGAINST BUSINESS GROSS			
PRODUCT	510,000	BUSINESS GROSS PRODUCT	510,000

* This *deduction* implies that subsidies exceed the current surplus of governmental enterprises in the amount of $1,000.

scription, "statistical discrepancy."[10] Although the source of these data is hypothetical, the illustrative examples in the following chapter will be integrated with this business sector account.

QUESTIONS

1. What properties of the national economy are portrayed in the national income and product account?
2. As a general rule, the basic measure of economic activity reported in the national income and product account is the market transaction. Some market transactions, however, are not provided for in this general rule. What are they? What *nonmarket* activities represent exceptions to this rule?
3. Describe three methods which can be used to measure GNP.
4. Explain why net national product, as compared to gross national product, may be a theoretically superior index of national productivity.
5. What is "national income" and how is it calculated?
6. Define and distinguish between "personal income" and "disposable personal income."
7. How is "value added" determined for an individual business or for the entire business sector?
8. If the algebraic sum of a company's sales of final product and change in inventories resulted in a negative balance, would this necessarily indicate a negative contribution to business gross product? Why?
9. Contrast the disposition of intercompany inventory profits in both national income accounting and financial accounting.
10. What is the impact of subsidies from government to business upon the income and product account for the business sector?

PROBLEMS

Problem 21–1

The social accountant in establishing value measurements of economic activity emphasizes the importance of "market transactions."

Required:
(i) Enumerate and discuss three principal classes of market transactions which are excluded from national income and product calculations.
(ii) Describe four major classes of nonmarket transactions which are included by imputation in the measurement of national product.

Problem 21–2

For each numbered statement listed, select the lettered statements which correctly finish the sentence.
    i) Current surplus of governmental enterprises is—
        (a) Excluded from national income.

---

[10] This value is normally reflected on the debit side of the account, as the estimates of output values are considered more reliable than the independent measurements of factor inputs and other debits.

    (*b*)   Treated in the business sector account in the same manner as are business transfer payments.

    (*c*)   Essentially like corporate profits and is therefore accorded similar status in the determination of income originating in the business sector.

    (*d*)   Essentially equivalent to government subsidies to business.

    (*e*)   Defined, with slight modifications, as the excess of tax receipts over governmental purchases of goods and services and governmental transfer payments.

ii)   Income originating in the business sector includes—

    (*a*)   Compensation of employees.

    (*b*)   Capital consumption allowances.

    (*c*)   Rental income of persons.

    (*d*)   Inventory valuation adjustment (plus or minus).

    (*e*)   Indirect business taxes.

iii)   Personal income—

    (*a*)   Is one of four major indicators of national production.

    (*b*)   Consists of personal outlays and personal saving.

    (*c*)   Is a major component of national income.

    (*d*)   Is a factor of production that is displayed on the debit side of the business sector account.

    (*e*)   May be defined as current receipts by individuals from whatever source.

iv)   Gross national product—

    (*a*)   Was negative during the worst year of the Great Depression (1932).

    (*b*)   Could be calculated by summing the value added by each economic unit in the economy.

    (*c*)   Is larger than net national product by an amount equal to capital consumption allowances and national defense expenditures.

    (*d*)   Is the total contribution of the business sector to the economy.

    (*e*)   Is defined, according to the final products approach, as sales to consumers, sales to government, sales of capital goods (including inventory changes) to business, and net export sales to foreigners.

v)   Net interest, one of the factor incomes—

    (*a*)   Excludes the interest paid by consumers on loans to finance consumption expenditures.

    (*b*)   Excludes interest payments by one business firm to another business firm.

    (*c*)   Excludes interest payments by the federal government.

    (*d*)   Excludes interest payments by business firms to individuals.

    (*e*)   Is a positive element in the calculation of national income.

vi)   Intermediate products—

    (*a*)   Are sold by one business unit to another business unit and implicitly included in the sales reported by the purchaser.

    (*b*)   Are the result of a kind of business activity that does not have an impact on gross national product.

    (*c*)   Represent an important element in the factor payments approach to the calculation of gross national product.

    (*d*)   Are exemplified by lumber sales to furniture manufacturers.

(e)   Are implicitly included in gross national product but are excluded from net national product.

vii)   A comparison of corporate financial accounting and national income accounting would suggest that—

(a)   Gross national product is more comparable with sales than with net income.

(b)   In general, they both require the same basis of revenue realization.

(c)   The elimination of intercompany transactions in the preparation of consolidated statements are similar to the eliminations necessary to prepare the business sector account.

(d)   The expense versus profit distinction that is apparent in corporate accounting is not applicable to the national income and product account.

(e)   The "nonincome charges" identified with the business sector account would generally be treated as expenses in corporate accounting.

viii)   In regard to the function of accounting for national economic activity—

(a)   The national balance sheet is widely used as an indicator of the nation's wealth.

(b)   Input-output tables provide detailed information on the flows of resources between industries.

(c)   The flow-of-funds statement is a consolidated account of the transactions between resident and foreign interests.

(d)   The national income and product account is a highly summarized report in comparison with input-output tables.

(e)   The balance-of-payments statement is a summarized version of the flow-of-funds statement.

Problem 21–3

The income statement of the Apple Company for the year 1971 is as follows:

APPLE COMPANY

Income Statement
For Year Ended December 31, 1971

Sales.		$300,000
Cost of goods sold:		
Inventory, January 1.	$ 60,000	
Purchases.	190,000	
	$250,000	
Inventory, December 31.	40,000	
Cost of goods sold.		210,000
Gross profit.		$ 90,000
Operating expenses:		
Salaries.	$ 30,000	
Interest.	8,000	
Rent.	10,000	
Payroll taxes.	1,000	
Property taxes.	6,000	
Supplies.	5,000	
Depreciation.	10,000	70,000
Net Income.		$ 20,000

The following information is also available:

a) Interest of $1,000 was paid to households; the remainder was paid to other businesses.

b) Rent of $5,000 was paid to households; the other $5,000 was paid to Jones Realty Company.

Required:

(i) Recast the income statement of the Apple Company in a form to reflect the underlying concepts of national income accounting, i.e., in income and product account form.

(ii) Calculate the income originating in the Apple Company during 1971.

(iii) Calculate the "value added" to current output by the Apple Company during 1971 using:
   a) Measures of output.
   b) Measures of input.

(iv) Prepare the eliminating entry required to "consolidate" the Apple Company accounts with the accounts of other businesses in the income and product account of the business sector.

Problem 21–4

The operating results of the Constant Manufacturing Corporation for 1971 are as follows:

CONSTANT MANUFACTURING CORPORATION
Income Statement
For Year Ended December 31, 1971

Sales.		$200,000
Cost of sales:		
Finished goods inventory, January 1, 1971.	$ 30,000	
Cost of goods manufactured (see supporting		
schedule).	120,000	
	$150,000	
Finished goods inventory, December 31, 1971.	20,000	130,000
Gross profit.		$ 70,000
Operating expenses:		
Wages and wage supplements.	$ 10,000	
Interest.	5,000	
Rent.	5,000	
Property taxes.	5,000	
Depreciation.	10,000	
Bad debts.	1,000	36,000
Net income before federal income taxes.		$ 34,000
Federal income taxes.		15,000
Net income.		$ 19,000
Gain on sale of securities.		1,000
Net income and nonrecurring gain.		$ 20,000

CONSTANT MANUFACTURING CORPORATION

Schedule of Cost of Goods Manufactured
For Year Ended December 31, 1971

Raw materials:

Raw materials inventory, January 1, 1971	$10,000	
Purchases	70,000	
	$80,000	
Raw materials inventory, December 31, 1971	20,000	$ 60,000
Direct labor and wage supplements		40,000
Overhead costs:		
Indirect labor and wage supplements	$10,000	
Supplies	5,000	
Rent	10,000	
Depreciation	15,000	40,000
Total manufacturing costs		$140,000
Add: Goods in process inventory, January 1, 1971		20,000
Total goods in process during 1971		$160,000
Deduct: Goods in process inventory, December 31, 1971		40,000
Cost of goods manufactured		$120,000

Additional Data:

a) Cash dividends of $10,000 were paid during 1971—$8,000 to a parent corporation and $2,000 to nonbusiness shareholders.

b) Interest payments are to households.

c) Rent on the plant is paid to the parent corporation; rent on the sales office is paid to an individual household.

Required:

(i) Recast the income statement of the Constant Manufacturing Corporation in a form to reflect the underlying concepts of national income accounting, i.e., in income and product account form.

(ii) Calculate the income originating in the Constant Manufacturing Corporation during 1971.

(iii) Calculate the "value added" to current output by the Constant Manufacturing Corporation during 1971 using:

a) Measures of output.

b) Measures of input.

(iv) Prepare the eliminating entry which would be required for the intrasector transactions of the Constant Manufacturing Corporation during 1971 if a consolidated income and product account working paper were prepared for the business sector.

Problem 21–5

The following data for the year 1971 have been accumulated from various sources:

a) Sales:
　　Capital goods:
　　　　To business... $100,000
　　　　To government....................................... 10,000
　　Other goods and services:
　　　　To business... 300,000
　　　　To households...................................... 400,000
　　　　To government....................................... 30,000
　　　　To foreigners (net).................................. 10,000

b) Reported change (increase) in inventories:
　　Corporate enterprises.................................... 25,000
　　Unincorporated businesses............................... 10,000
　　Inventory valuation adjustment (debit):
　　　　Corporate enterprises.................................. 10,000
　　　　Unincorporated businesses.............................. 5,000

c) Reported net income after income taxes:
　　Corporate enterprises.................................... 100,000
　　Unincorporated businesses............................... 25,000

d) Income tax liabilities:
　　Corporate enterprises.................................... 80,000
　　Unincorporated businesses............................... 10,000

e) Other business taxes:
　　Property taxes.. 42,000
　　Excise taxes.. 9,000

f) Dividend payments to households........................... 40,000
g) Government subsidies to business........................... 20,000
h) Losses on bad debts...................................... 5,000
i) Current surplus of governmental enterprises (after
　　depreciation of $10,000).............................. 15,000
j) Rental income of persons.................................. 5,000
k) Net interest... 10,000
l) Capital consumption allowance............................. 40,000
m) Compensation of employees:
　　Wages and salaries...................................... 240,000
　　Supplements:
　　　　Employer contributions for social insurance................ 5,000
　　　　Other labor incomes................................... 10,000
　　Employees' contributions for social insurance................. 5,000

Required:

Prepare a consolidated income and product account for the business sector for the year ended December 31, 1971.

Problem 21–6

The business sector of the national economy is assumed to consist of two companies, Alpha and Omega. Their operating statements for the year ended December 31, 1971, are as follows:

	Alpha Company	*Omega Company*
Sales.....................................	$725,000	$840,000
Cost of sales:		
Inventory, January 1....................	$120,000	$140,000
Purchases.............................	290,000	325,000
	$410,000	$465,000
Inventory, December 31.................	80,000	150,000
	$330,000	$315,000
Gross profit............................	$395,000	$525,000
Wages.................................	$ 90,000	$115,000
Rent...................................	10,000	18,000
Interest................................	5,000	7,000
Depreciation...........................	5,000	10,000
	$110,000	$150,000
Net income before taxes, dividends, and		
capital gains.........................	$285,000	$375,000
Gain on sale of capital assets..............	$ [10,000]	
Federal income taxes....................	110,000	$150,000
Dividends paid.........................	35,000	45,000
	$135,000	$195,000
Undistributed net income..................	$150,000	$180,000

An analysis of sector sales follows:

	Alpha	*Omega*
Sales of final products:		
To households.......................	$300,000	$475,000
To government.......................	75,000	45,000
To foreigners.......................	25,000	30,000
Sales of intermediate products:		
To Alpha.............................		290,000
To Omega.............................	325,000	
	$725,000	$840,000

Required:

Prepare a 1971 consolidated income and product account for the business sector, supported by a consolidated working paper.

Problem 21–7

The business sector of the national economy of W consists of three enterprises: companies X, Y, and Z. Their individual operating statements for 1971 follow:

	X Company	Y Company	Z Company
Sales..............................	$1,315,000	$1,900,000	$1,650,000
Cost of sales:			
Inventory, January 1.................	$ 125,000	$ 450,000	$ 350,000
Purchases.........................	475,000	1,300,000	475,000
	$ 600,000	$1,750,000	$ 825,000
Inventory, December 31..............	100,000	375,000	425,000
Total........................	$ 500,000	$1,375,000	$ 400,000
Gross profit.........................	$ 815,000	$ 525,000	$1,250,000
Operating expenses:			
Wages............................	$ 115,000	$ 90,000	$ 140,000
Rent..............................	40,000	50,000	100,000
Interest...........................	10,000	5,000	
Supplies..........................		15,000	
Depreciation......................	70,000	105,000	165,000
	$ 235,000	$ 265,000	$ 405,000
Net operating profit...................	$ 580,000	$ 260,000	$ 845,000
Gain on sale of securities..............	5,000		
Loss on disposal of fixed assets.........		15,000	
Net profit...........................	$ 585,000	$ 245,000	$ 845,000

An analysis of the sales of each company is as follows:

X Company:			
To Y Company....................	$1,315,000		
Y Company:			
To households....................		$ 950,000	
To X Company....................		475,000	
To Z Company....................		475,000	
Z Company:			
To government....................			$ 825,000
To X Company (on capital			
account).........................			825,000
	$1,315,000	$1,900,000	$1,650,000

Required:

(i)   Prepare a consolidated statement working paper for the business sector of W for the year ended December 31, 1971.

(ii) Prepare an income and product account for the business sector for the year ended December 31, 1971.

(iii) It is evident that all of X Company's sales were intrasector. Does this imply that value to sector output was not added by X Company during the current period? If value was added, what is its amount?

Problem 21–8

An examination of the operating data of the Richardson Corporation for 1971 reveals the following:

	Units	Price/Unit
Inventory, January 1, 1971.................	20,000	
FIFO......................................		$ 8.00
LIFO......................................		10.00
Purchases.................................	100,000	7.00
Sales:		
Case I.....................................	90,000	12.00
Case II....................................	100,000	12.00
Case III...................................	110,000	12.00

Required:

(i) For each of the three cases, prepare an analysis of the reported gross profits and inventory changes under both FIFO and LIFO pricing, *and* calculate *real* gross profits and inventory changes.

(ii) Using both FIFO and LIFO pricing methods for each case, prepare journal entries which reflect the adjustment to the reported data which would be required in the preparation of an income and product account.

Problem 21–9

The following "account" balances are assumed to reflect the relevant data for the 1971 operations of the several classes of unincorporated businesses in the River Economy:

	Owner-Occupied Housing	Farms	Governmental Operating Enterprises	Subsidized Businesses	Other Businesses
Credits					
Sales:					
To households...........		$15,000	$10,000	$ 6,000	$29,000
To government..........		5,000	1,000		16,000
To business (noncapital)...			3,000		6,000
Changes in inventories.......		[1,000]	3,000	1,000	6,000
Gross rental value..........	$20,000				
Gross value of product consumed................		3,000			
Gross value of perquisites.....		1,000			2,000
Subsidy income............				6,000	
	$20,000	$23,000	$17,000	$13,000	$59,000
Debits					
Wages paid...............		$ 5,000	$ 7,000	$ 4,000	$20,000
Imputed wages............		1,000			2,000
Indirect business taxes.......	$ 2,000	2,000	1,000	1,000	6,000
Repairs and maintenance.....	1,000	2,000	1,000	1,000	1,000
Interest on debt (to households)................	3,000	4,000	2,000	1,000	4,000
Supplies..................		1,000			2,000
Depreciation..............	4,000	2,000	5,000	2,000	8,000
	$10,000	$17,000	$16,000	$ 9,000	$43,000
Net income or current surplus.	$10,000	$ 6,000	$ 1,000	$ 4,000	$16,000

Required:

(i) Prepare a consolidated business sector working paper for the River Economy for 1971.

(ii) Prepare a consolidated income and product account for the River Economy for 1971.

Chapter 22

National Income Accounting—II

OTHER SECTOR ACCOUNTS

The income and product account for the busines sector is, in respect to underlying concepts, essentially a prototype of the national income and product account. However, in order to complete an analysis of the national income accounting system, the remaining sector accounts and the gross saving and investment account will be defined and the significant characteristics of each will be discussed briefly.

Household (Personal) Sector

This sector is defined as follows:

The personal sector of the economy covers essentially the consuming public. It consists chiefly of individuals in their capacity as income receivers and consumers, but it includes also nonprofit institutions, private trust funds, and private pension, health, and welfare funds.[1]

Although this description emphasizes the general consuming public, the reader will recall that certain output-producing functions of individuals, such as home ownership, were included in the consolidated business sector. Therefore, any production, or output, which originates exclusively *in the household sector* must be defined independently of these quasi-business, quasi-personal activities.

The household sector account is essentially a consolidated statement of *receipts* and *expenditures* of individuals; many of the transactions are intrasector and must accordingly be eliminated; yet, significantly, *some* intrasector transactions are not eliminated. On the receipts, or credit, side of the account are enumerated the various types of incomes *received* during the current period. As noted in Illustrations 21–1 and 21–2 of the previous chapter, this enumeration includes not only factor income but also transfer payments from the business and government sectors. Although transfer payments do not augment national income, from the viewpoint of individuals and households they do constitute revenue receipts. On the expendi-

---

[1] Office of Business Economics, United States Department of Commerce, *National Income, 1954 Edition* (Washington, D.C.: U.S. Government Printing Office, 1954), p. 49.

tures, or debit, side of the account, payments to other sectors are detailed, with the net increment, or the residual balance, denoted as personal saving of individuals. *Income originating in the household sector* consists of compensation of employees (primarily wage payments of nonprofit institutions and compensation of domestic servants). It should be observed that the *net* salary payments to sector wage earners after deduction of payroll taxes are not eliminated, although they also appear as a credit in the household sector account. Should these contra amounts be eliminated, as most intrasector transactions are eliminated in the consolidated income and product account for the business sector, gross national product would be reduced accordingly. Prior to 1965, consumer interest payments were included in national income. Although they are now excluded from national income, they continue to be shown on both sides of the personal income and outlay account without elimination.

The income and outlay account of the personal (or household) sector is shown in Illustration 22–1.

It is evident that in Illustration 22–1 the wages and salaries of $12,000

Illustration 22–1

PERSONAL SECTOR

Income and Outlay Account
For Year Ended December 31, 1971

Personal tax payments		40,000	Wage and salary disbursements:			293,000
Personal consumption expendi-			From business	240,000		
tures:		387,000	From government	40,000		
Wages and sala-			From households	12,000		
ries	12,000		From foreigners	1,000		
Wage supple-			Other labor income:			10,000
ments	2,000		From business	7,000		
INCOME ORIGINAT-			From government	2,000		
ING IN PER-			From households	1,000		
SONAL SECTOR	14,000		Less: Personal contributions for			
Purchases from			social insurance			[6,000]
business	372,000		Proprietor's income:			75,000
Net imports	1,000		Farm	20,000		
Interest paid by consumers		4,000	Business and pro-			
Personal transfer payments to for-			fessional	55,000		
eigners (net)		1,000	Rental income of persons			17,000
Personal saving		27,000	Dividend income			19,000
			Personal interest income:			21,000
			Net interest	8,000		
			Paid by govern-			
			ment	9,000		
			Paid by consum-			
			ers	4,000		
			Transfer payments:			30,000
			Business	2,000		
			Government	28,000		
PERSONAL TAXES, OUTLAY, SAVING		459,000	PERSONAL INCOME			459,000

are included in both factor costs and wage and salary receipts; the wage supplements of $2,000 in the factor cost enumeration are included to the extent of $1,000 on the receipts side of the account. The $1,000 difference represents employer contributions for social insurance—a receipt in the government sector. Additionally, the $6,000 amount for social insurance withheld by both business and individuals is included in the receipts enumeration as a negative quantity. Certain intersector transactions are easily identifiable in the relevant accounts, e.g., consolidated sales to households, $372,000, reported in the business sector as output, are equal to net purchases from business, $372,000, reported in the household sector as personal consumption expenditures. These, and other, interrelationships between the sector accounts will be examined more completely in the discussion of the consolidation of the various sector accounts.

The data displayed in Illustration 22–1 may, of course, be further summarized. Alternatively, the underlying data can be reclassified to emphasize

Illustration 22–2

CLASSIFICATIONS OF PERSONAL CONSUMPTION EXPENDITURE

| | | Type of Items Purchased | | |
Supplying Sector	*Total Expenditures*	*Durable Goods*	*Nondurable Goods*	*Services*
Purchases from business	372,000	60,000	179,000	133,000
Purchases from foreigners	1,000		1,000	
Purchases from persons:				
Wages and salaries	12,000			12,000
Wage supplements	2,000			2,000
Total	387,000	60,000	180,000	147,000

other important aspects of economic activity. For example, personal consumption expenditure can be classified to indicate the types of goods purchased rather than the sector which supplied the goods. Illustration 22–2 displays this reclassification. It should be apparent that alternative classification schemes can be developed in regard to most of the information included in the sector accounts. The data published by the Department of Commerce include several detailed classificational analyses, as well as highly summarized accounts. The pattern of classification utilized in Illustration 22–1 is particularly important in determining national income by sector. Other purposes may lead the statement user to select tables that are structured in terms of another format.

Government Sector

The delimitation of the government sector is indicated as follows:

The government sector includes Federal and State and local general governments and the social insurance funds administered by them. These funds comprise those set up under the Social Security and Railroad Retirement programs, State health insurance funds, the retirement funds established for government employees, and military life insurance funds.[2]

The inclusion of government enterprises in the business sector has been previously discussed, and the underlying characteristics of the two basic types of governmental activity should therefore be familiar to the reader.

As in the case of the personal account, the account for the government sector is essentially a consolidated statement of *receipts* and *expenditures*. The receipts, or credits to the account, reflect the different types of tax revenue earned during the current period, with the exception of personal tax receipts which are accounted for on a *cash* basis. In respect to debits, the *income originating in the government sector* is measured by the amounts of salaries and wage supplements, including imputations, earned during the period, i.e., the value of output is measured by the factor costs incurred. As mentioned before, interest is excluded from this sum because, ostensibly, it correlates very little with current output. Unlike owner-occupied residences, an imputation of occupancy value for government property is not made because of the conceptual and practical impediments of obtaining valid statistical bases. It should be noted that this measurement of the government's contribution to national income and

Illustration 22–3

GOVERNMENT SECTOR

Receipts and Expenditures Account

For Year Ended December 31, 1971

Purchases of goods and services		84,000	Personal tax receipts:		40,000
Purchases of direct services:			Federal	36,000	
Wages and salaries	40,000		State and local	4,000	
Wage supplements	5,000		Corporate income tax accruals		35,000
INCOME ORIGINATING IN GOVERNMENT SECTOR	45,000		Indirect business tax accruals		50,000
			Contributions for social insurance:		
			Personal contribution		6,000
Net purchases from business	35,000		Employer contribution:		
			Business		6,000
Net purchases from foreigners	4,000		Households and institutions		1,000
Transfer payments:		32,000	Government		3,000
To persons	28,000				
To foreigners (net)	4,000				
Net interest paid		9,000			
Subsidies less current surplus of governmental enterprises		1,000			
Surplus on income and product account		15,000			
GOVERNMENT EXPENDITURES AND SURPLUS		141,000	GOVERNMENT RECEIPTS		141,000

---

[2] *Ibid.*, p. 53.

product requires a sharp distinction in respect to those disbursements made to individuals for compensation and those which are merely transfer payments.

The government receipts and expenditures account is shown in Illustration 22–3. It may be observed that the residual balancing value for the government sector is described as "Surplus on Income and Product Account." As previously discussed with respect to the household sector account, alternative classification schemes can be developed for the receipts and expenditures of government. For example, governmental purchases of goods and services are classified in Illustration 22–3 in terms of the sectors of the economy from which the purchases were made; they may also be classified in terms such as the following:

Purchased by federal government:		$50,000
National defense..................................	$44,000	
Other...	6,000	
Purchases by state and local governments..............		34,000
Total purchases of goods and services................		$84,000

Rest of World Sector—Foreign Transactions Account

It is necessary for reasons of completeness to include this sector in the system of national income accounts to accommodate those transactions, engaged in by economic units composing the national economy, which are not otherwise accounted for in other sectors. The "foreign" sector is defined as follows:

The rest of the world covers foreign countries, territories and possessions of the United States, international organizations, and the United States monetary gold stock. The gold stock is included in this sector because net acquisitions of gold by the monetary authorities from domestic sources are considered foreign investment.[3]

Prior to an examination of the foreign transactions account, it may be beneficial to review the nature of the other sector accounts previously discussed. In respect to each of the sectors (business, households, and government), the related sector account reflects the viewpoint of the sector. For example, the account related to the government sector depicts the expenditures and receipts *of government*. In a consistent fashion, it would be possible to prepare an account related to the rest of world sector which would take the point of view of the rest of the world. Given this perspective, business sector sales to foreigners would, for example, be disclosed as *purchases* from business; similarly, wages and salaries earned by U.S. residents as employees of foreign corporations would be labeled as purchases of factor costs (services). As a matter of fact, the foreign sector account was prepared in these terms prior to 1958.

---

[3] *Ibid.,* p. 56.

It should be apparent that transactions between the United States and the rest of the world can also be described from the vantage point of the United States. From this view, business sales to foreigners and wages earned by U.S. residents as employees of foreign corporations are described as *exports* of goods and services. Since 1958, the account which relates to the foreign sector has been constructed from the point of view of the United States. Consistent with this view, the account is titled the Foreign Transactions Account.

The data which underlie the preparation of the foreign transactions account are presented in Illustration 22–4. These data essentially represent

Illustration 22–4

REST OF WORLD SECTOR—TRANSACTIONS DATA

For Year Ended December 31, 1971

	Debit	Credit
Consolidated business sales to foreigners	$13,000	$10,000
Income originating in the foreign sector:		
Wages received from foreigners	1,000	
Interest received from foreigners	1,000	
Foreign branch profits	2,000	
Dividends	1,000	
Purchases from foreigners:		
By government	2,000	6,000
By households		1,000
Transfer payments to foreigners:		
By government		4,000
By persons		1,000
Net foreign investment		[2,000]
	$20,000	$20,000

a consolidated statement of transactions involving receipts and expenditures between the foreign sector and the various domestic sectors. The *factor costs* (income originating in the foreign sector) enumerated in Illustration 22–4 represent net payments (inflow of factor incomes) made by foreigners to factors of production residing in the United States. This reckoning contrasts with the alternative of defining national income and product as the *output* which actually originates within the United States. Thus, when a foreign branch located in the United States pays wages and salaries to residents of the United States, the amounts paid are included appropriately in the aggregative process; profits of the branch, however, accrue to nonresidents and are excluded. Accordingly, only a portion of the factor costs identified with domestic output is included in national output, as some profit elements are excluded. Contrariwise, wages and salaries paid by a foreign branch of a domestic company are excluded from domestic output, while branch profits are included in the domestic output. Consequently, output originating in the United States but accruing to foreign persons is a negative contribution, while output originating in the rest of the world but accruing to United States residents is a positive or additive element; the values of these outputs are reflected "net" in the purchases of factor cost, viz., the net international flow of factor incomes. Since the other sector accounts overstate factor costs by the amount of payments to nonresidents, this methodology both reflects the net change in the international asset position and accomplishes a correcting adjustment to factor costs accruing to residents.

In addition to factor costs, the transactions data in Illustration 22–4 include purchases (and sales) of goods and services by various domestic sectors. Government transfer payments to foreigners reflect all nonmilitary grants to foreigners (military grants are treated as United States government expenditures for goods and services). Personal transfer payments to foreigners represent personal remittances which are not payments for imported goods and services.

Illustration 22–5 presents the foreign transactions account, which is

Illustration 22–5

REST OF WORLD SECTOR

Foreign Transactions Account
For Year Ended December 31, 1971

Exports of goods and services	20,000	Imports of goods and services	17,000
		Government transfer payments to foreigners !	4,000
		Personal transfer payments to foreigners	1,000
		Net foreign investment	[2,000]
RECEIPTS FROM FOREIGNERS	20,000	PAYMENTS TO FOREIGNERS	20,000

essentially a summarization of the data included in Illustration 22–4. The format of the foreign transactions account emphasizes the domestic output consumed by the rest of the world (a positive component of gross national product), and foreign output purchased by domestic sectors (a reduction of gross national product, either as an intermediate purchase by business, or as a personal or government expenditure not related to domestic output). To the extent that exports exceed imports and transfer payments to foreigners, domestic residents have made investments in foreign countries. This is described as net foreign investment. In Illustration 22–5, exports are smaller than imports and transfer payments to foreigners; as a consequence, net foreign investment is negative.

Gross Saving and Investment Account

Most transactions affecting units of the national economy are recorded in conventional contra debit-credit form in two or more sector accounts; manifestly, *intersectoral* transactions exhibit this basic accounting dualism. Additionally, there exists an amount in each sector account, essentially a residual balance (undistributed profits, personal saving, government surplus, and net foreign investment), which indicates the increase or decrease in sector equity generated during the current period. In order to complete, or to effectively close, the accounting system, such that it demonstrates both intrasector and intersector equality of debits and credits, it is necessary to add one additional account, *the gross saving and investment account*. Basically, this account includes all those items which are not completely reported in one or more of the other sector accounts. For example, consider a transaction such as business sales to government. The amount of these sales is included in the business sector account as a credit and in the government sector account as a debit. On the other hand, undistributed corporate profits are recorded only as a debit in the business

Illustration 22–6

"CAPITAL SECTOR"

Gross Saving and Investment Account
For Year Ended December 31, 1971

Business purchases on capital account	85,000	Corporate income:	
		Undistributed corporate income	25,000
Change in inventories	15,000	Corporate inventory valuation	
Net foreign investment	[2,000]	adjustment	[10,000]
		Foreign branch profits	2,000
		Capital consumption	38,000
		Personal saving	27,000
		Government surplus on income and	
		product account	15,000
		Statistical discrepancy	1,000
		GROSS SAVING AND STATISTICAL DIS-	
GROSS INVESTMENT	98,000	CREPANCY	98,000

sector account. A contra credit for this amount is not to be found in any other sector account. If a sector balance sheet were prepared, a corresponding credit would appear. Unfortunately, however, the catalog of sector accounts does not now include the balance sheet. The inclusion of these contra transaction elements in a gross saving and investment account for which there is no appropriate sector account is an implicit expression of the increases (decreases) which would appear in the investment and equity sections of a comparative balance sheet.

The gross saving and investment account is shown in Illustration 22–6. Note that the statistical discrepancy, entered in the business sector account for illustrative purposes only, carries forward to the "capital sector" account. This extension completes the integration, in a debit-credit sense, of all data in the illustrative accounts.

The classificational schema adopted for the gross saving and investment account in Illustration 22–6 reflects important economic data which underlie many basic economic decisions. On the debit side of the account, gross investment in assets is indicated; on the credit side, sources of financing these additions to the assets of the United States are enumerated.

Since the *gross* value of investments is reported on the debit side of this account, capital consumption must therefore be reflected on the credit or gross saving side of the account. If *net* investments were considered more significant, the capital consumption allowance would be reported as a negative element on the debit side of the account.

It should be apparent that alternative classification schemes can be developed for the data in Illustration 22–6 so that additional information is available. For example, the debit side of the account may be restated as follows:

Gross private domestic investment			100,000
New construction:		50,000	
Residential nonfarm	23,000		
Other	27,000		
Producers of durable equipment		35,000	
Change in inventories:		15,000	
Farm	5,000		
Nonfarm	10,000		
Net foreign investment			[2,000]
GROSS INVESTMENT			98,000

INTEGRATION OF ACCOUNTS

The accounting integration of the four sector accounts and the gross saving and investment account will now be illustrated using a schedular presentation similar to that which will be later used to consolidate the sector accounts into a national income and product account. The data contained in the sequence of sector accounts illustrated earlier are recast in Illustration 22–7.

With the data of the sectors juxtaposed as in Illustration 22–7, certain important accounting system properties are evident. First, each sector reflects intrasector equality of debits and credits (columnar equality). Second, each line item description indicates intersector equality of debits and credits (row equality). For example, consolidated business sales appear as credits in the business sector and debits (purchases) in the other sector accounts; net business sales to the rest of the world are expanded in the rest of the world columns so as to indicate exports and imports by business. This property is clearly revealed by the tabular arrangement of data. It is consequently evident that national income accounting possesses both vertical and horizontal equality of debits and credits—a four-dimensional equality property.

Illustration 22–7

X ECONOMY

Enumeration of Economic Data by Sector

For Year Ended December 31, 1971

	Business Dr.	Business Cr.	Households Dr.	Households Cr.	Government Dr.	Government Cr.	Rest of World Dr.	Rest of World Cr.	Saving and Investment Dr.	Saving and Investment Cr.
Consolidated business sales:										
To households.........		372,000	372,000							
To government.........		35,000			35,000					
To foreigners.........		3,000								
To business on capital account...		85,000							85,000	
Change in inventories.........		15,000							15,000	
Wages and salaries.........	240,000		12,000	287,000	40,000	6,000	13,000	10,000		
Wage supplements.........	13,000		2,000	10,000	5,000	10,000				
Interest.........	7,000		4,000	21,000	9,000		1,000	1,000		
Rent.........	17,000			17,000						
Profits:										
Unincorporated enterprises and inventory valuation adjustment.........	75,000			75,000						
Foreign branches.........							2,000	6,000		7,000
Foreign dividends.........				1,000			1,000			
Corporate income:										
Tax liability.........	35,000					35,000				
Dividends.........	18,000			18,000						
Undistributed profits.........	25,000									25,000
Inventory valuation adjustment.........	[10,000]									[10,000]
Indirect business taxes.........	50,000					50,000				
Personal taxes.........			40,000			40,000				
Purchases from rest of world:										
By government.........					4,000			4,000		
By households.........	2,000		1,000	2,000				1,000		
Business transfer payments.........				28,000	32,000					
Government transfer payments to foreigners.........										
Personal transfer payments to foreigners (net).........			1,000		1,000		1,000			
Subsidies minus current surplus of governmental enterprises.........	[1,000]									
Capital consumption allowances.........	38,000									38,000
Statistical discrepancy.........	1,000									1,000
Personal saving.........			27,000							27,000
Government surplus on income and product transactions.........					15,000					15,000
Net foreign investment.........							2,000	[2,000]	[2,000]	
	510,000	510,000	459,000	459,000	141,000	141,000	20,000	20,000	98,000	98,000

THE NATIONAL INCOME AND PRODUCT ACCOUNT

It is now appropriate to combine the four sector accounts into the national income and product account for the period. Since each of the sector accounts represents, to a large extent, a "consolidated" statement of current transactions with other sectors, the national income and product account is essentially the result of a summation process. If the national economy were literally conceived to be one entity, all intra- and intersector transactions would necessarily be subject to elimination in a consolidating working paper; there would be no value remnants to be extended to the "consolidation" column. Consequently, the contributions of each of the sectors to national income and product, once they are accurately defined and precisely measured, are algebraically summed *without* elimination. These sector contributions have been outlined in the previous discussion, and accordingly only the contributions to national income and product will be separately disclosed in each of the sector accounts in the national income and product account working paper as indicated in Illustration 22–8.

Illustration 22–8 reflects certain elections, previously discussed, either to include or to exclude the results of specific types of transactions. For example, government and consumer interest payments are excluded from factor costs. Had the amount of these interest payments been considered as a factor cost, i.e., related to current output, they would have been included in the "income originating" in the government and household sector accounts; accordingly they would have been enumerated in this working paper as an increase in interest (increase in national income) and also as increases in government and household expenditures (increase in gross national product). Government and consumer interest payments do, in fact, represent expenditures within the framework of their respective sectors; yet in the national income and product aggregation, they are excluded, together with the corresponding interest income of individual recipients, as they represent merely a transfer payment. Thus, in one sense, the classification within the sector accounts indicates, implicitly, the eliminations made in the final summation. On the other hand, net purchases of government from abroad are included with other government purchases. The inclusion of this item in net purchases of government (a credit in this case) *and* in imports (a debit), both of which are included on the credit side of the account, effectively eliminates it as a contributor to gross output. Finally, this working paper introduces minor terminological changes in the output (credit) side of the national income and product account. For example, sales to persons are in fact personal consumption expenditures. Thus, sales to persons by business ($372,000), by other persons—factor services ($14,000), and by the rest of the world—net imports ($1,000) comprise total personal consumption expenditures ($387,000). Since currently the national income and product account is actually prepared by a measurement of expenditures, this terminology—indicating sales by consumer classes—is chosen to indicate the underlying source data.

Illustration 22–8

X ECONOMY

National Income and Product Working Paper
For Year Ended December 31, 1971

	Business	Households	Government	Rest of World	National Income and Product Debit	National Income and Product Credit
Sector contributions to gross product:						
Sales of goods and services for:						
Personal consumption	372,000	14,000	45,000	1,000		387,000
Government expenditures	35,000			4,000		84,000
Business capital purchases	85,000					85,000
Net exports	3,000					3,000
Change in inventories	15,000			5,000		15,000
GROSS PRODUCT OF SECTOR	510,000	14,000	45,000	5,000		574,000
Income originating in sectors:						
Compensation of employees:						
Wages and salaries	240,000	12,000	40,000	1,000	293,000	
Wage supplements	13,000	2,000	5,000		20,000	
Interest	7,000			1,000	8,000	
Rent	17,000				17,000	
Income of unincorporated enterprises and inventory valuation adjustment	75,000				75,000	
Corporate profits and inventory valuation adjustment:						
Corporate income tax liability	35,000				35,000	
Corporate income after taxes:						
Dividends	18,000			1,000	19,000	
Undistributed profits	25,000			2,000	27,000	
Inventory valuation adjustment	[10,000]				[10,000]	
INCOME ORIGINATING IN SECTOR	420,000	14,000	45,000	5,000	484,000	
Nonincome charges:						
Indirect business taxes	50,000				50,000	
Business transfer payments	2,000				2,000	
Statistical discrepancy	1,000				1,000	
Subsidies minus current surplus of governmental enterprises	[1,000]				[1,000]	
CHARGES AGAINST NET PRODUCT OF SECTOR	472,000	14,000	45,000	5,000	536,000	
Capital consumption allowance	38,000				38,000	
CHARGES AGAINST GROSS PRODUCT OF SECTOR	510,000	14,000	45,000	5,000	574,000	

Illustration 22–9

X ECONOMY

National Income and Product Account
For Year Ended December 31, 1971

Compensation of employees:	313,000	Personal consumption expendi-	
Wages and salaries 293,000		tures	387,000
Supplements:		Gross private domestic investment	100,000
Employer contri-		Net exports of goods and services:	3,000
bution for so-		Exports 20,000	
cial insurance 10,000		Imports 17,000	
Other labor in-		Government purchases of goods	
come 10,000		and services	84,000
Net interest	8,000		
Rental income of persons	17,000		
Proprietors' income	75,000		
Corporate net income and inven-			
tory valuation adjustment:			
Net income before income tax:	81,000		
Corporate in-			
come tax lia-			
bility 35,000			
Corporate in-			
come after			
taxes:			
Dividends 19,000			
Undistributed			
profits 27,000			
Inventory valuation adjustment	[10,000]		
NATIONAL INCOME	484,000		
Indirect business taxes	50,000		
Business transfer payments	2,000		
Current surplus of governmental			
enterprises less subsidies	[1,000]		
Capital consumption allowances	38,000		
Statistical discrepancy	1,000		
CHARGES AGAINST GROSS			
NATIONAL PRODUCT	574,000	GROSS NATIONAL PRODUCT	574,000

The formal national income and product account prepared from the working paper is shown above in Illustration 22–9.

RESTATEMENT OF GUIDING CONCEPTS

In earlier discussion, the underlying definitions and motivating concepts for the basic account structure used to measure the national income created and output produced during a given period have been briefly described. There follows a review of these various elements and their interrelationships as summarized in 1954 by the United States Department of Commerce and revised in the intervening years. Although minor changes are to be found in subsequent descriptions, this enumeration of definitions and explanations accents the basic philosophy of the actual data-accumulation agency.

I. NATIONAL INCOME AND PRODUCT AGGREGATES

National Income is the aggregate earnings of labor and property which arise from the current production of goods and services by the Nation's economy. Thus, it measures the total factor costs of the goods and services produced by the economy. The Nation's economy in this context refers to the labor and property supplied by the residents of the Nation. Earnings are recorded in the forms in which they accrue to residents of the Nation, inclusive of taxes on those earnings. As such, they consist of the compensation of employees, the profits of corporate and unincorporated enterprises, net interest, and the rental income flowing to persons.

Gross National Product or Expenditure is the market value of the output of goods and services produced by the Nation's economy, before deduction of depreciation charges and other allowances for business and institutional consumption of durable capital goods. Other business products used up by business in the accounting period are excluded. The Nation's economy in this context refers to the labor and property supplied by residents of the Nation. Gross national product comprises the purchases of goods and services by consumers and government, gross private domestic investment (including the change in business inventories), and net exports.

Net National Product or Expenditure is the market value of the net output of goods and services produced by the Nation's economy. All business products used up by business in the accounting period are excluded. The Nation's economy in this context refers to the labor and property supplied by residents of the Nation. Net national product comprises the purchases of goods and services by consumers and government, net private domestic investment (including the change in business inventories), and net exports.

Personal Income is the current income received by persons from all sources, inclusive of government and business transfer payments and government and consumer interest payments but exclusive of transfers among persons. Not only individuals (including owners of unincorporated enterprises), but nonprofit institutions, private trust funds, and private pension, health, and welfare funds are classified as "persons." Personal income is measured on a before-tax basis, as the sum of wage and salary disbursements, other labor income, proprietors' and rental income, interest and dividends, and transfer payments, minus personal contributions for social insurance.

Disposable Income is the income remaining to persons after deduction of personal tax and nontax payments to general government.

II. COMPONENTS OF NATIONAL INCOME AND PRODUCT AGGREGATES

A. *National Income*

Compensation of Employees is the income accruing to persons in an employee status as remuneration for their work. From the employer's standpoint, it is the direct cost of employing labor. It is the sum of *wages and salaries* and *supplements to wages and salaries.*

Wages and Salaries consists of the monetary remuneration of employees commonly regarded as wages and salaries, inclusive of executives' compensation, commissions, tips, and bonuses, and of payments in kind which represent income to the recipients.

Supplements to Wages and Salaries is the monetary compensation of employees not commonly regarded as wages and salaries. It consists of employer contributions for social insurance; employer contributions to private pension, health, and welfare funds; compensation for injuries; directors' fees; pay of the military reserve; and a few other minor items of labor income.

Income of Unincorporated Enterprises measures the monetary earnings and income in kind of sole proprietorships, partnerships, and producers' cooperatives from their current business operations—other than the supplementary income of individuals derived from renting property. As with *corporate profits,* capital gains and losses are excluded and no deduction is made for depletion.

Inventory Valuation Adjustment measures the excess of the value of the change in the volume of nonfarm business inventories, valued at average prices during the period, over the change in the book value of nonfarm inventories. This adjustment is required because corporate profits and income of unincorporated enterprises are taken inclusive of inventory profit or loss, as is customary in business accounting, whereas only the value of the real change in inventories is counted as current output in the national product. No valuation adjustment is required for farm inventories because farm income is measured exclusive of inventory profits.

Rental Income of Persons consists of the monetary earnings of persons from the rental of real property, except those of persons primarily engaged in the real estate business; the imputed net rental returns to owner-occupants of nonfarm dwellings; and the royalties received by persons from patents, copyrights, and rights to natural resources.

Corporate Profits Before Tax is the earnings of corporations organized for profit which accrue to residents of the Nation, measured before Federal and State profit taxes, without deduction of depletion charges and exclusive of capital gains and losses. Profits accruing to residents are measured by eliminating intercorporate dividends from profits of domestic corporations and by adding the net receipts of dividends and branch profits from abroad. In other major respects, the definition of profits is in accordance with Federal income tax regulations.

Corporate Profits Tax Liability comprises Federal and State taxes levied on corporate earnings. Disbursements of tax refunds are deducted from tax liability in the year in which the tax liability was incurred.

Net Interest measures total interest (monetary and imputed, private and government) accruing to United States persons and governments minus total interest paid by United States governments and by consumers. Interest paid by consumers and by government (Federal and State and local) is deducted because it is not considered income arising in current production. It is necessary not only to exclude the portion of it paid directly to persons and governments, but also to deduct the portion of it paid to business, because the latter is reflected in the incomes paid out or retained by the business system. The *imputed interest* component of net interest is measured in general as the excess of property income received by financial intermediaries from funds entrusted to them by persons over property income actually returned in monetary form by these intermediaries to persons. A portion of imputed interest is numerically equal to the value of financial services received by persons without explicit payment; the remainder represents property income withheld by life insurance companies and mutual financial intermediaries on the account of persons.

B. *Gross National Product*

Personal Consumption Expenditures consists of the market value of purchases of goods and services by individuals and nonprofit institutions and the value of food, clothing, housing, and financial services received by them as income in kind. It includes the rental value of owner-occupied houses but does not include purchases of dwellings, which are classified as capital goods.

Gross Private Domestic Investment consists of acquisitions of newly produced capital goods by private business and nonprofit institutions and of the value of the change in the volume of inventories held by business. It covers all private new dwellings, including those acquired by owner-occupants.

Net Exports consists of (1) domestic output sold abroad over purchases of foreign output, and (2) production abroad credited to United States-owned resources over production at home credited to foreign-owned resources.

Government Purchases of Goods and Services measures purchases of goods and services by government bodies, exclusive of acquisitions of land and used depreciable assets and of current outlays of government enterprises. It consists of general government expenditures for compensation of employees, purchases from business (net of sales by government of consumption goods and materials), net government purchases from abroad excluding international contributions, and the gross investment of government enterprises. Therefore, *government purchases of goods and services* excludes transfer payments, government interest, and subsidies, as well as loans and other financial transfers outside the scope of income and product transactions.

C. *Personal Income and Disposition of Income*

Wage and Salary Disbursements is equal to *wages and salaries,* except that retroactive wages are counted when paid rather than when earned.

Other Labor Income is the same as *supplements to wages and salaries* exclusive of employer contributions for social insurance in national income.

Proprietors' and Rental Income is the sum of *income of unincorporated enterprises and inventory valuation adjustment* and *rental income of persons* as given in the components of national income.

Dividends measures cash dividend disbursements by corporations organized for profit to stockholders who are United States persons.

Personal Interest Income measures total interest (monetary and imputed, private and government) accruing to United States persons. The *imputed interest* component of personal interest income is the same as in national income.

Transfer Payments to Persons consists of monetary income receipts of individuals from government and business (other than government interest) for which no services are rendered currently, of government payments and corporate gifts to nonprofit institutions, and of individuals' bad debts to business.

Personal Contributions for Social Insurance consists of payments by both employees and self-employed. Contributions of the self-employed, which relate to old-age and survivors insurance, were first made in 1952.

Personal Tax and Nontax Payments consists of the taxes levied against individuals, their income, and their property that are not deductible as expenses of business operations, and of other general government revenues from individuals in their personal capacity. It includes payments for such specific services as are provided within the framework of general government activity. It excludes, however, purchases from government enterprises. Tax refunds are deducted from payments as of the time of refund.

Personal Outlays include personal consumption expenditures, interest paid by consumers, and personal transfer payments to foreigners (net). Personal consumption expenditures is the same as in gross national product. Personal transfer payments to foreigners (net) consist of remittances to foreigners that are not in payment for imports and are therefore excluded from personal consumption expenditure.

Personal Saving is the excess of personal income over personal consumption expenditures, personal tax and nontax payments, interest paid by consumers, and personal transfer payments to foreigners (net). It consists of the current saving of individuals (including owners of unincorporated businesses), nonprofit institutions, and private pension, health, welfare, and trust funds. Personal saving may be in such forms as changes in cash and deposits, security holdings, indebtedness, and reserves of life insurance companies and mutual savings institutions, the net investment of unincorporated enterprises, and the acquisition of real property net of depreciation.

D. *Reconciliation Items Between National Income and Gross National Product*

Depreciation Charges represents the charges made by private businesses against receipts for the current consumption of durable capital goods and comparable allowances for nonprofit institutions. It includes depreciation charges against owner-occupied houses. Depreciation reported by business is not adjusted for changes in the replacement value of capital goods, except for farm enterprises [capital consumption].

Accidental Damage to Fixed Capital measures the value of the physical losses by fire, natural events, and other accidents to fixed capital of private business, not covered by depreciation charges [capital consumption].

Capital Outlays Charged to Current Expense represents new construction and purchases of new durable capital goods included in *gross private domestic investment* that are charged as current expense by business rather than entered on capital account [capital consumption].

Indirect Business Tax and Nontax Liability consists of tax liabilities incurred by businesses, except corporate income taxes, and other general government revenues from business. It includes all sales taxes. It includes payments for such specific services as are provided within the framework of general government activity. It excludes, however, purchases from government enterprises. Government receipts from the sale of surplus property are not included in this item. Tax liabilities are net of refunds.

Business Transfer Payments represent transfers from business to persons which are charges against business product for which no return in the form of factor services is received. Major items included are corporate gifts and allowances for consumer bad debts.

Subsidies Minus Current Surplus of Governmental Enterprises:

Subsidies are the monetary grants provided by government to private business.

Current surplus of government enterprises represents the excess of sales receipts over current operating costs of government enterprises. In the calculation of the current surplus, no deduction is made for charges to depreciation or other reserves and interest is not counted in either receipts or costs.

Subsidies and current surplus are shown as a single item because of the difficulties involved in segregating subsidies paid through Federal Government enterprises from other expenditures of these enterprises.

Statistical Discrepancy is the excess of the value of the estimated gross national product computed by the final products method over its independently estimated value computed by adding necessary conceptual adjustments to the national income.

SUMMARY

The account structure described in this and the previous chapter illustrates the basic concepts underlying the system of national income accounting. Yet these details necessarily reflect only a portion of the principles and procedural subtleties that are involved in the actual compilation and presentation of the data by the United States Department of Commerce. Indeed, over one hundred pages of supplementary tables are presented annually to complement and enlarge upon the summary accounts, including analyses of income distribution, industrial patterns, expenditure shifts, etc. One inclusion of interest to many accountants is the adjustment of some items in the accounts for fluctuations in the value of the monetary unit. Several subdivisions in each major segment of the supplementary tables are devoted to disclosing comparative figures in constant dollars. This price-index deflation of dollar output to real output illustrates an approach to the vexing price-level problem which parallels several current recommendations of prominent accountants in respect to financial statements for profit-motivated enterprises.

Since there does not now exist a centralized information collection system to accumulate the basic data important to national income accounting, various sources must be used. These include most of the departments of the federal government, state unemployment agencies, manufacturing census data, and others. The difficulty of assimilating these data explains partially the previously mentioned statistical discrepancy. Continuing efforts are being made to improve the statistical reliability of the data estimates. Success in these efforts, rather than in basic changes in the underlying concepts, offers the greater immediate promise of progress in national income and product reporting.

QUESTIONS

1. Define the household (personal) sector.
2. Of what does "income originating in the household sector" consist?
3. How is the government sector defined?
4. From what accounting perspective is the foreign transactions account prepared?
5. How are wage payments and profits of foreign branches located in the

United States and U.S. branches located in foreign countries included in the definition of national income?

6. What is the gross saving and investment account? What is its purpose?

7. If the national economy were conceived to be one entity rather than a collection of sectors, what eliminations would be necessary in order to prepare a "consolidated" report?

8. Why are government and consumer interest payments excluded from factor costs in computing GNP?

9. List those items which are necessary to reconcile national income and gross national product.

10. Explain the source of the "statistical discrepancy" reported in the national income and product account.

PROBLEMS

Problem 22–1

Given the information in Table 1 (p. 773) concerning the several sector accounts of Unitex, prepare a national income and product account (supported by a working paper) for the year 1971.

Problem 22–2

The consolidated income and product account for the business sector of X Country is given for the year ended December 31, 1971:

BUSINESS SECTOR—X COUNTRY

Consolidated Income and Product Account

For Year Ended December 31, 1971

Compensation of employees	80,000	Consolidated sales:	
Rental income of persons	8,000	To households	100,000
Net interest	7,000	To government	20,000
Income of unincorporated enter-		To business on capital account	40,000
prises and inventory valuation		To foreigners	5,000
adjustment	10,000	Change in inventories	[15,000]
Corporate income and inventory			
valuation adjustment:			
Corporate income before taxes:			
Corporate income tax liability	10,000		
Corporate income after taxes:			
Dividends	8,000		
Undistributed profits	5,000		
Inventory valuation adjustment	2,000		
INCOME ORIGINATING IN BUSINESS			
SECTOR	130,000		
Indirect business taxes	8,000		
Business transfer payments	3,000		
Subsidies minus current surplus of			
governmental enterprises	[1,000]		
CHARGES AGAINST NET PRODUCT	140,000		
Capital consumption allowance	10,000		
CHARGES AGAINST BUSINESS GROSS			
PRODUCT	150,000	BUSINESS GROSS PRODUCT	150,000

Table 1

	Business Sector Dr.	Business Sector Cr.	Household Sector Dr.	Household Sector Cr.	Government Sector Dr.	Government Sector Cr.	Rest of World Sector Dr.	Rest of World Sector Cr.	Saving and Investment Dr.	Saving and Investment Cr.
Consolidated business sales:										
To households		236,000	236,000							
To government		19,000			19,000					
To foreigners		14,000					14,000			
To business on capital account		81,000							81,000	
Change in inventories		[10,000]							[10,000]	
Wages and salaries	190,000		8,000	221,000	25,000	3,000	1,000			
Wage supplements	9,000		1,000	8,000	2,000	4,000				
Interest	4,000		2,000	10,000	3,000		1,000			
Rent	14,000			14,000						
Profits:										
Unincorporated entities:										
As recorded	40,000			40,000						
Inventory valuation adjustment	[5,000]			[5,000]						
Corporate entities:										
Undistributed	20,000									20,000
Inventory valuation adjustment	[10,000]									[10,000]
Tax liability	2,000					2,000				
Dividends	7,000			7,000						
Foreign branches							1,000			1,000
Foreign dividends				500			500			
Indirect business taxes	38,000					38,000				
Personal taxes			25,000			25,000				
Purchases from rest of world:										
By governments					2,500			2,500		
By households			1,000					1,000		
Transfer payments:										
Business	1,000			1,000						
Government				14,000	15,500			1,500		
Subsidies minus current surplus of governmental enterprises	[2,000]				2,000					
Capital consumption allowance	30,000									30,000
Statistical discrepancy	2,000									2,000
Personal saving			37,500							37,500
Government surplus on income and product transactions					3,000					3,000
Net foreign investment								12,500	12,500	
	340,000	340,000	310,500	310,500	72,000	72,000	17,500	17,500	83,500	83,500

Problem 22–2—Continued

The following information for 1971 is also available:

(1)	Income taxes paid by persons............................	$30,000
(2)	Salaries to household servants...........................	5,000
(3)	Salaries paid by X Country businesses to foreign residents.....	2,000
(4)	Salaries paid by foreign businesses and governments to X Country residents.......................................	3,000
(5)	Dividends received by persons from abroad................	5,000
(6)	Interest paid by households on loans from other households...	4,000
(7)	Salary payments by X Country government to civil servants (residents).......................................	20,000
(8)	Government aid to foreign countries (nonmilitary)...........	3,000
(9)	Social security payments by government to residents.........	10,000
(10)	Imports by households................................	1,000
(11)	Government interest payments to residents................	5,000
(12)	Of the $7,000 net interest reported in the consolidated income and product account of the business sector, $1,000 was paid to foreign residents.	

Required:

Prepare an enumeration of sector accounts for the year ended December 31, 1971, in a form which reveals the basic account properties of each sector.

Problem 22–3

Refer to the facts presented in Problem 22–2.

Required:

(i)   Prepare a consolidated national income and product working paper for the year ended December 31, 1971.

(ii) Compute gross national product, net national product, national income, personal income, and disposable personal income.

Problem 22–4

The following 1971 sector accounts are available for the national economy of Bulmania:

PERSONAL SECTOR

Income and Expenditure Account
For Year Ended December 31, 1971

Personal consumption expendi- tures:		Wage and salary receipts:	
Purchases of direct services:		From business	300,000
Compensation of employees:		From government	50,000
Wages and salaries paid	20,000	From households and institu- tions	20,000
Wage supplements:		From foreigners	10,000
Employer contributions		Other labor incomes:	
for social insurance	3,000	From business	10,000
Other labor incomes	2,000	From government	8,000
INCOME ORIGINATING IN, AND NET		From households and institu- tions	2,000
AND GROSS PRODUCT OF,		Less: Personal contributions for	
PERSONAL SECTOR	25,000	social insurance	[16,000]
Net purchases from business	465,000	Income of unincorporated enter-	
Net imports from rest of world	5,000	prises and inventory valuation	
Personal interest payments	5,000	adjustment	80,000
Personal tax payments	50,000	Personal interest income	30,000
Personal saving	70,000	Rental income of persons	20,000
		Dividend income	70,000
		Transfer payments	36,000
PERSONAL TAXES, OUTLAY AND			
SAVING	620,000	PERSONAL INCOME	620,000

GOVERNMENT SECTOR

Receipts and Expenditures Account
For Year Ended December 31, 1971

Purchases of goods and services:		Personal tax receipts	50,000
Purchases of direct services:		Corporate income tax accruals	100,000
Wages and salaries	50,000	Indirect business tax accruals	40,000
Wage supplements:		Contributions for social insurance:	
Employer contributions for		Personal contributions	16,000
social insurance	4,000	Employer contributions:	
Other labor incomes	8,000	Business	10,000
INCOME ORIGINATING IN, AND		Households and institutions	3,000
NET AND GROSS PRODUCT		Government	4,000
OF, GOVERNMENT SECTOR	62,000		
Net purchases from business	100,000		
Net purchases from rest of world	10,000		
Net interest	20,000		
Transfer payments to persons	31,000		
Subsidies less current surplus of			
governmental enterprises	5,000		
Surplus on income and product			
transactions	[5,000]		
GOVERNMENT EXPENDITURES AND			
SURPLUS	223,000	GOVERNMENT RECEIPTS	223,000

"CAPITAL SECTOR"

Gross Saving and Investment Account

For Year Ended December 31, 1971

Business purchases on capital		Personal saving	70,000
account	150,000	Undistributed corporate profits	30,000
Change in inventories	[50,000]	Corporate inventory valuation	
Net foreign investment	25,000	adjustment	[10,000]
		Capital consumption allowance	40,000
		Government surplus on income	
		and product transactions	[5,000]
GROSS INVESTMENT	125,000	GROSS SAVING	125,000

Required:

Prepare a consolidated income and product account of the business sector of Bulmania for the year ended December 31, 1971.

Problem 22–5

PERSONAL SECTOR

Income and Expenditure Account

For Year Ended December 31, 1971

Personal consumption ex-		Wage and salary receipts:	
penditures:		From business	232,000
Purchases of direct		From government	30,000
services:		From households	20,000
Compensation of em-		Other labor income:	
ployees:		From business	10,000
Wages and salaries		From government	2,000
paid	20,000	From households	2,000
Wage supplements	4,000	Less: Personal contributions	
INCOME ORIGINATING		for social insurance	
IN, AND NET AND		(withheld)	[5,000]
GROSS PRODUCT OF,		Income of unincorporated	
PERSONAL SECTOR	24,000	enterprises and inven-	
Net purchases from		tory valuation adjust-	
business	260,000	ment	20,000
Interest paid	6,000	Personal interest income	18,000
Personal tax payments	30,000	Rental income of persons	21,000
Personal saving	60,000	Dividend income	25,000
		Transfer payments	5,000
PERSONAL TAXES, OUTLAY			
AND SAVING	380,000	PERSONAL INCOME	380,000

GOVERNMENT SECTOR

Receipts and Expenditure Account
For Year Ended December 31, 1971

Purchases of goods and services:		Personal tax receipts	30,000
Purchases of direct services:		Corporate income tax accruals	60,000
Wages and salaries paid	30,000	Indirect business tax accruals	20,000
Wage supplements	5,000	Contributions for social insurance:	
INCOME ORIGINATING IN, AND NET AND GROSS PRODUCT OF, GOVERNMENT SECTOR	35,000	Personal contributions	5,000
		Employer contributions:	
Net purchases from business	80,000	Business	9,000
Net interest	7,000	Households	2,000
Transfer payments	4,000	Government	3,000
Subsidies less current surplus of governmental enterprises	2,000		
Surplus on income and product transactions	1,000		
GOVERNMENT EXPENDITURES AND SURPLUS	129,000	GOVERNMENT RECEIPTS	129,000

Additional Information:

a)   Change in inventories, $30,000 (increase).
b)   Capital consumption allowance, $60,000.
c)   Business sales on capital account, $85,000.
d)   There were no transactions during 1971 with foreigners.

Required:

Calculate the following:

  (i)   Business gross product.
 (ii)   Gross national product.
(iii)   Net national product.
 (iv)   Business transfer payments.
  (v)   Net interest paid by business.
 (vi)   Business contributions to social insurance.
(vii)   Income originating in the business sector.
(viii)   Undistributed corporate profits and inventory valuation adjustment.
 (ix)   Gross investment (calculate by using debit components).
  (x)   Gross saving (calculate by using credit components).

Problem 22–6

The accounts for the business sector and the personal sector for the year 1971 are as follows:

BUSINESS SECTOR

Consolidated Income and Product Account
For Year Ended December 31, 1971

Compensation of em-		Consolidated sales:	
ployees:		To households	470,000
Wages and salaries	300,000	To government	100,000
Supplements:		To business on capital	
Employer contributions		account	150,000
for social insurance	10,000	To foreigners	30,000
Other labor incomes	10,000	Change in inventories	[50,000]
Rental income of persons	20,000		
Net interest	10,000		
Income of unincorporated			
enterprises and inven-			
tory valuation adjust-			
ment	80,000		
Corporate income and in-			
ventory valuation			
adjustment:			
Corporate income before			
taxes:			
Corporate income tax			
liability	100,000		
Corporate income after			
taxes:			
Dividends	70,000		
Undistributed profits	30,000		
Inventory valuation ad-			
justment	[10,000]		
INCOME ORIGINATING IN			
BUSINESS SECTOR	620,000		
Indirect business taxes	40,000		
Business transfer payments	5,000		
Subsidies minus current			
surplus of govern-			
mental enterprises	[5,000]		
CHARGES AGAINST NET			
PRODUCT	660,000		
Capital consumption			
allowance	40,000		
CHARGES AGAINST BUSINESS			
GROSS PRODUCT	700,000	BUSINESS GROSS PRODUCT	700,000

PERSONAL SECTOR

Income and Expenditure Account
For the Year Ended December 31, 1971

Personal consumption		Wage and salary receipts:	
expenditures:		From business	300,000
Purchases of direct		From government	50,000
services:		From households and	
Compensation of em-		institutions	10,000
ployees:		From rest of world	10,000
Wages and salaries		Other labor incomes:	
paid	10,000	From business	10,000
Wage supplements:		From government	8,000
Employer contribu-		From households and	
tions for social		institutions	2,000
insurance	3,000	Less: Personal contributions	
Other labor in-		for social insurance	
comes	2,000	(withheld)	[16,000]
INCOME ORIGINATING		Income of unincorporated	
IN, AND NET AND		enterprises and inven-	
GROSS PRODUCT OF,		tory valuation adjust-	
PERSONAL SECTOR	15,000	ment	80,000
Net purchases from		Personal interest income	40,000
business	470,000	Rental income of persons	20,000
Personal interest pay-		Dividend income	70,000
ments	10,000	Transfer payments	36,000
Net imports from rest			
of world	5,000		
Personal tax payments	50,000		
Personal saving	70,000		
PERSONAL TAXES, OUTLAY			
AND SAVING	620,000	PERSONAL INCOME	620,000

Additional data for 1971 are:

a) Government contributions for social insurance, as an employer, amounted to $4,000.

b) International aid during 1971 amounted to $10,000; no other government transactions with the foreign sector occurred during 1971.

Required:

(i) Prepare the government sector account for 1971.

(ii) Based upon the data given above, calculate gross national product, net national product, national income, personal income, and disposable personal income.

Problem 22–7

The following sector accounts relate to the Ameritex economy for the year ended December 31, 1971:

BUSINESS SECTOR

Income and Product Account
For Year Ended December 31, 1971

Factor payments:		Sales:	
Wages and wage supple-		To households	325,000
ments	256,000	To government	29,000
Rent	20,000	To foreigners	21,000
Interest	5,000	To business on capital	
Profits:		account	121,000
Unincorporated		Change in inventories	20,000
entities:			
Undistributed	60,000		
Inventory valuation			
adjustment	5,000		
Corporate entities:			
Undistributed	80,000		
Inventory valuation			
adjustment	20,000		
Tax liability	16,000		
Dividends	4,000		
INCOME ORIGINATING IN			
THE BUSINESS SECTOR	466,000		
Indirect business taxes	25,000		
Subsidies less current sur-			
plus of governmental			
enterprises	[5,000]		
Statistical discrepancy	1,000		
CHARGES AGAINST NET			
PRODUCT	487,000		
Capital consumption			
allowance	29,000		
CHARGES AGAINST BUSINESS			
GROSS PRODUCT	516,000	BUSINESS GROSS PRODUCT	516,000

HOUSEHOLD SECTOR

Income and Outlay Account
For Year Ended December 31, 1971

Personal consumption expenditures:		Wage and salary receipts:		
Purchases of direct services:		From business		244,000
Compensation of employees:		From government		55,000
Wages and salaries paid	13,000	From households		13,000
Wage supplements	6,000	From foreigners		4,000
		Other labor income:		
INCOME ORIGINATING IN HOUSEHOLD SECTOR	19,000	From business		6,000
Net purchases from business	325,000	From government		2,000
Interest paid	3,000	From households		3,000
Net imports	1,000	Less: Personal contributions for social insurance (withheld)		[6,000]
Personal tax payments	48,000	Income of unincorporated entities and inventory valuation adjustment		65,000
Personal transfer payments to foreigners (net)	1,000	Personal interest income		12,000
Personal saving	25,000	Rental income of persons		20,000
		Dividend income		4,000
PERSONAL TAXES, OUTLAY AND SAVING	422,000	PERSONAL INCOME		422,000

GOVERNMENT SECTOR

Receipts and Expenditures Account
For Year Ended December 31, 1971

Purchases of goods and services:		Personal tax receipts	48,000
Purchases of direct services:		Corporate income tax accruals	16,000
Wages and salaries	55,000	Indirect business tax accruals	25,000
Wage supplements	5,000	Contributions for social insurance:	
INCOME ORIGINATING IN GOVERNMENT SECTOR	60,000	Personal contributions	6,000
Net purchases from business	29,000	Employer contributions:	
Net purchases from rest of world	1,000	Business	6,000
Net interest	3,000	Households	3,000
Transfer payments to foreigners	4,000	Government	3,000
Subsidies less current surplus of governmental enterprises	5,000		
Surplus on income and product transactions	5,000		
GOVERNMENT EXPENDITURES AND SURPLUS	107,000	GOVERNMENT RECEIPTS	107,000

Required:

(i)   Prepare a foreign transactions account and the saving and investment account for 1971. Hint: It may be helpful to prepare an enumeration of sector accounts working paper.

(ii)   Prepare a national income and product account working paper for 1971.

Problem 22–8

The sector accounts of the Z Economy for the year 1971 are as follows:

PERSONAL SECTOR

Income and Outlay Account
For Year Ended December 31, 1971

Personal tax payments		80,000	Wage and salary disbursements:		370,000
Personal consumption expenditures:		495,000	Manufacturing	250,000	
Durable goods	100,000		Other private	50,000	
Nondurable goods	250,000		Government	70,000	
Services	145,000		Other labor income		10,000
Interest paid by consumers		5,000	Less: Personal contributions for social insurance		[15,000]
Personal saving		60,000	Proprietors' income:		85,000
			Farm	25,000	
			Business and professional	60,000	
			Rental income of persons		25,000
			Dividends		60,000
			Personal interest income:		65,000
			Net interest	10,000	
			Interest paid by consumers	5,000	
			Net interest paid by government	50,000	
			Transfer payments:		40,000
			Business	5,000	
			Government	35,000	
PERSONAL TAXES, OUTLAYS, AND SAVING		640,000	PERSONAL INCOME		640,000

GOVERNMENT SECTOR

Receipts and Expenditures Account
For Year Ended December 31, 1971

Purchases of goods and services:		130,000	Personal tax receipts:			80,000
Federal:	90,000		Federal	70,000		
National			State and local	10,000		
defense	50,000		Corporate income tax accruals			100,000
Other	40,000		Indirect business tax accruals			60,000
State		40,000	Contributions for social			
Transfer payments:		60,000	insurance:			35,000
To persons	35,000		Employer	20,000		
Foreign (financial aid)	25,000		Personal	15,000		
Net interest paid		50,000				
Subsidies less current surplus of						
governmental enterprises		5,000				
Surplus on income and product						
account		30,000				
GOVERNMENT EXPENDITURES AND SURPLUS		275,000	GOVERNMENT REVENUE			275,000

REST OF WORLD SECTOR

Foreign Transactions Account
For Year Ended December 31, 1971

Exports of goods and services	80,000	Imports of goods and services	60,000
		Transfer payments from Z	
		government	25,000
		Net foreign investment	[5,000]
RECEIPTS FROM FOREIGNERS	80,000	PAYMENTS TO FOREIGNERS	80,000

"CAPITAL SECTOR"

Gross Saving and Investment Account
For Year Ended December 31, 1971

Gross private domestic investment:		200,000	Personal saving	60,000
New construction:	120,000		Undistributed corporate profits	80,000
Residential non-			Corporate inventory valuation	
farm	50,000		adjustment	[25,000]
Other	70,000		Capital consumption allowance	50,000
Producers' durable			Government surplus on income	
equipment	90,000		and product account	30,000
Change in inventories:	[10,000]			
Farm	10,000			
Nonfarm	[20,000]			
Net foreign investment		[5,000]		
GROSS INVESTMENT		195,000	GROSS SAVING	195,000

Required:

Prepare the national income and product account for the Z Economy for 1971.

UNIT VII

SPECIAL SALES CONTRACTS

Chapter 23

Accounting for Consignments

Nature of Consignments

A consignment is a conveyance of the custody of goods from the owner, designated the *consignor,* to one who acts as his agent, designated the *consignee.* The agent, who is often locationally more accessible to available markets than is the consignor, undertakes to sell the consigned merchandise for the owner under a commission arrangement. Viewed legally, the transfer of the custody of goods is a bailment; accordingly, the laws of agency control in respect to determining the rights and responsibilities of each party (the consignor as principal, the consignee as agent). In respect to the consignor, the transaction for the transfer of goods is often described as a *consignment out;* to the consignee, the receipt of these goods is frequently termed a *consignment in.*

The basic distinction between a sale and a consignment relates to the passage of legal title. In a transaction of sale, legal title vests in the buyer concurrent with the delivery of goods—either to the buyer or to a common carrier. Notwithstanding the fact that there is also a change in the custody of goods in a consignment transaction, legal title continues to identify with the consignor until the relevant goods are sold by the consignee to a third party. Legal title thus passes directly from the consignor to the ultimate transferee, the buyer, when the sale is completed.

In recognition of the unique characteristics of consignment transactions, the following fundamental criteria are appropriate guidelines for accounting procedures:

1. Since title to consigned goods continues to vest in the consignor, such goods should be reported in the inventory of the consignor and excluded from the inventory of the consignee.
2. Goods on consignment do not create revenue, or satisfy the revenue realization criterion, for either the consignor or consignee until they are sold to a third party.
3. The consignor is accountable as owner for all costs incurred which directly relate to the goods from date of shipment to the date of sale by the consignee, except as may otherwise be provided by specific contractual agreement between the parties.

4.   The consignee, in his capacity as a bailee, is charged with the exercise of due care with respect to the goods held on consignment; accordingly, it may be appropriate to maintain a notational or memorandum record of consigned goods awaiting sale.

Several reasons why a consignment arrangement may be advantageous to both the consignor and the consignee are recounted as follows: *First,* it may be an appropriate vehicle for enlarging channels of distribution for new products, particularly where the demand for these products is uncertain. Additionally, if the goods are high unit-cost items and if the risks of obsolescence and price change are great, retailers may hesitate to purchase such goods; yet, they may be willing to display and to sell them on the condition that the consignor carry the burden of inventory investment and risk. *Second,* there is an obvious investment advantage to the consignee, since he is not compelled to make a commitment of funds in advance of ultimate sale. *Third,* in respect to the consignor, the retention of legal title should serve to reduce his credit risk. In the event of the legal dissolution of the consignee enterprise, creditors of the consignee may not attach these goods as would be possible if the good were *sold* on credit. *Fourth,* the consignor establishes and continues to retain control over the selling price of consigned merchandise; the exercise of this authority is seldom possible when the goods are sold to the retailer. Notwithstanding these apparent advantages to the consignor and consignee, there has been a noticeable decrease in the use of consignments in recent years, primarily due, no doubt, to improvements in the distribution function generally and to more liberal return privileges on sales contracts.

Rights and Responsibilities Relating to Consignments

Consignment provisions should be outlined clearly in a written contract executed by the consignor and the consignee, dealing with such matters as commissions, allowable terms of sale, responsibility for the collection of accounts receivable and losses from uncollectible accounts, expenses of the consignee in respect to the receipt, maintenance, and sale of consigned merchandise, remittances to the consignor, care and protection of the consigned goods, and the nature and time schedule for reports to be rendered by the consignee. In respect to other matters not specifically referred to in the consignment agreement, the laws of bailment and agency establish the rights and responsibilities of the parties. Since these rights and responsibilities are reciprocally related, i.e., a right of the consignee translates as a responsibility of the consignor, the primary provisions relating to the consignee only are enumerated as follows:

1.   *Rights of the consignee:*
      a)   The right to compensation for selling the consigned goods and reimbursement for necessary expenses connected therewith. The commission (or other form of reimbursement) to be allowed the

consignee is normally a negotiated value between the parties. Reimbursement for necessary expenses often covers such expenditures as freight, insurance, storage, and the usual warranty costs.

b) The right to make the usual, but not extraordinary, warranties in respect to the quality of merchandise; the consignor is then bound by such warranties.

c) The right to extend credit for the sale of consigned merchandise in terms consistent with those which are conventional in business enterprises selling similar goods; the consignor may limit this right by express agreement. The receivables from the sale of consigned merchandise (and any related bad debt losses) are those of the consignor. If the consignee, by contractual agreement, assumes responsibility for the collection of these receivables, he is called a *del credere agent,* and is normally allowed extra compensation for the additional risk assumed.

2. *Responsibilities of the consignee:*

a) To care for and protect the goods held on consignment in a prudent and responsible manner.

b) To exert reasonable efforts to sell the goods in compliance with the terms of the consignment contract. In granting credit (if this is not denied by the contract), the consignee must exercise a degree of prudence consonant with the credit standards of similar types of business enterprises. The goods should be sold at prices specified by the consignor and in the absence of specification, at a price that appears to represent the best interests of the consignor. Similarly, the consignee should exercise reasonable diligence in the collection of receivables.

c) To keep the consignor's goods separate and apart from other goods in order to assure their easy identification. This requirement normally presumes physical separation; however, in the event this proves to be impractical, the consignee should maintain accounting records in sufficient detail to permit identification of consigned goods. A collateral obligation, although related to the separation of consigned merchandise, is the responsibility to preserve the separateness of consignment transactions in the accounting records; sales, reimbursable expenses, inventory, and accounts receivable from consignments all must be clearly designated in order that the interests of the consignor may be distinguished and protected.

d) To render periodic reports and to make liquidating settlements in respect to consignment transactions (goods received, sold, and on hand) as specified in the consignment contract. The contract may require monthly, weekly, or even daily reports to the consignor. The periodic report is typically referred to as an *account sales.* It should specify the goods received on consignment, those sold, relevant expenses, the amount due the consignor, and the amount remitted. A representative form of an account sales is shown in Illustration 23–1.

Illustration 23–1

ACCOUNT SALES

Matthewson Retailers
Houston, Texas
(Consignee)

			No. J-4
			March 31, 1971
			Date

Sold for Account and Risk of (consignor):
    Jackson Manufacturing Company
    231 Makin Street
    Moline, Illinois

Account sales of:

    Color Television Sets (Model AK-320)

Date	Explanation	Quantity		Amount
March 1	Balance on hand (carried forward)	–0–		$ –0–
March 1–31	Received	15		
	TOTAL	15		$ –0–
March 1–31	Sales:			
	TV Sets (AK-320) @ $400 each	10		4,000
	GROSS			$4,000
	Charges:			
	Warranty adjustments (on sets sold)		$ 20	
	Local freight (on 15 sets)		15	
	Commissions (20%)		800	835
	NET			$3,165
March 31	Remittance enclosed			$3,165
March 31	Balances	5		$ –0–

ACCOUNTING BY THE CONSIGNEE

Since legal title to consigned goods does not vest in the consignee, formal inclusion of these units in the inventory of the consignee is unwarranted and incorrect. However, as previously noted, the consignee will usually find it desirable to use various memoranda to record merchandise held on consignment, detailing both the kind and quantity of consigned units.

In respect to transactions involving the sale of consigned merchandise and related expenses, it is customary to record the relevant data in a special summary Consignment In account. This account is credited with the proceeds from the sale of consigned merchandise and is debited for reimbursable expenses incurred in connection therewith and for commissions earned by the consignee. Consequently, the Consignment In account is essentially a reflection of a bilateral debtor-creditor relationship. If the account indicates a residual credit balance, it is evident that an indebtedness flows from the consignee to the consignor; alternatively, should a debit balance exist, the receivable indicates an indebtedness payable to the consignee.

The Consignment In account may be supported by subsidiary records, depending upon the need for additional account detail. The data usually contained in the summary account and the related subsidiary records are the basic source information for the *account sales,* which is fundamentally a classified enumeration of all transactions between the consignor and the consignee, concluding with the calculation of their reciprocal debtor-creditor status. Where transactions are executed with several consignors, it is appropriate that an account sales should be submitted to each; accordingly, it may also be desirable to establish a separate Consignment In account for each consignor. In the event the number of consignors is unusually large, these separate accounts logically comprise the subsidiary records.

Illustrative Entries

Following are the entries made by a consignee (Matthewson Retailers) for certain typical consignment transactions (the data used are the March transactions reported in the account sales in Illustration 23–1):

1. To record the receipt of 15 color TV sets from the Jackson Manufacturing Company.

   Prepare a memorandum entering thereon the fact of the receipt of the consigned goods, the name of the consignor, the quantity of units ordered and received, and the storage or display location.

2. To record drayage (local transportation) on the 15 TV sets delivered to Matthewson Retailers.

Consignment in—Jackson Manufacturing Company.......	15	
Cash..		15

3. To record the sale of 10 TV sets @ $400 each.

Cash (or Accounts receivable—consignment sales)........	4,000	
Consignment in—Jackson Manufacturing Company.......................................		4,000

4. To record the outlay for warranty adjustments on TV sets sold during March.

Consignment in—Jackson Manufacturing Company.......	20	
Cash..		20

5. To record the 20 percent commission earned on the March sales of TV sets.

Consignment in—Jackson Manufacturing Company.......	800	
Commissions earned—consignment sales............		800

6. To record the remittance to accompany the March 31 account sales forwarded to the consignor.

Consignment in—Jackson Manufacturing Company....... 3,165
    Cash..   3,165

After the above entries are posted, the Consignment In account will appear as follows:

Consignment In—Jackson Manufacturing Company

March 1–31	Drayage	15	March 1–31	Ten TV sets sold	4,000
	Warranty adjustments	20			
	Commission	800			
March 31	Cash remitted	3,165			
		4,000			4,000

Modifications of Entries and Account Structure

On some occasions the consignee may remit cash to the consignor in advance of the sale of any of the consigned goods; such an advance should be debited to the Consignment In account (or a special receivable account) and should be used to abate subsequent remittances to the consignor. Additionally, if the consignor assumes the responsibility for credit sales (i.e., the consignee is not a *del credere agent*), the remittance accompanying the account sales may consist of both cash and transferred open accounts. Of course, if the ultimate purchasers of consigned goods remit directly to the consignor, it is probable that the account sales will reflect an amount due to the consignee.

Should there be but one monthly consignment transaction, or several transactions involving the same type of merchandise, there is little need for subsidiary account detail. Procedural variations may be required, however, to accommodate special or unique consignment arrangements. For example, if a second shipment of consigned merchandise of a different type is received from the Jackson Company, e.g., 20 black and white TV sets (Model SS-100), a more formal set of unit inventory records may be required. Additionally, the accumulation of cost and revenue data may be reflected in more detailed records as follows:

Controlling account: Consignment In Control—Jackson Manufacturing Company
Subsidiary accounts: Consignment In—Jackson Manufacturing Company
        (Model AK-320)
        Consignment In—Jackson Manufacturing Company
        (Model SS-100)

This type of account structure would facilitate the preparation of a *control account sales,* expressed in dollars only, supported by *subsidiary account sales* for each type of merchandise expressed in both units and dollar amounts.

Financial Statement Presentation

In the income statement of the consignee, the *commissions earned* should be reported as an item of operating income. A balance in the Consignment In account represents either a debt to or receivable from the consignor, and should be reported in the balance sheet as a current asset if a debit balance and as a current liability if a credit balance. Consignment In account balances which relate to different consignors should not, however, be offset; rather, the sum of the debit balances should be reported as an asset and the sum of the credit balances should be reported separately as a liability.

ACCOUNTING BY THE CONSIGNOR

The specific accounting procedures for the consignor depend upon the following two circumstances: (1) consignment transactions may be recorded in separate accounts, or merely entered in standard account classifications which accommodate both consignment and nonconsignment transactions; and (2) perpetual or periodic inventory methods may be used in the existing accounting system of the consignor. Whatever the basic format elected by the consignor, he must maintain a record, or set of records, reflecting consigned units shipped, sales of consigned goods and related expenses, and the status of his accountability with each consignee.

Consignment Out Account

In the event consignment transactions are commingled with other operating data, no unique accounting problems are presented. If it is desired to separate the regular and consignment sales, however, a special account, *Consignment Out,* is created in which are summarized the basic data concerning consignment transactions. The normal inclusions in the account are revealed as follows:

Consignment Out—(Name of Consignee)

Cost of goods shipped on consignment	Sales of consigned goods as reported by consignee on account sales
Expenses related to consignment, incurred by consignor	
Expenses related to consignment, incurred and reported by the consignee on the account sales	
Commissions earned on consigned goods sold by the consignee and reported on the account sales	
Debit (credit) adjustment to yield the correct end-of-period account balance—the cost of the inventory of goods held on consignment, and other deferred costs which relate thereto	

During the accounting period, the Consignment Out account effectively operates as a summary account in respect to all consignment transactions. At the end of the period, however, it is conventionally adjusted such that the residual balance represents the sum of the cost of unsold consigned goods and relevant deferred expenses. The relevant deferred expenses— including those of both the consignor and the consignee—may then be reallocated and separately identified as Deferred Consignment Costs in the accounts and/or balance sheet of the consignor. These capitalizable outlays include all expenditures incurred to place the goods in position for sale, e.g., freight charges, drayage costs, and shipping insurance; they do not include expenditures for advertising, commissions, or other direct selling costs.

Illustrative Entries—Perpetual Inventory

Illustration 23–2 presents in tabular form the entries made by the consignor (Jackson Manufacturing Company) for the transactions relative to the consignment arrangement reflected in the account sales in Illustration 23–1; additionally, the necessary period-end adjustments are illustrated. Entries are given under two assumptions: (1) a separate set of accounts is used for consignment sales and regular sales, and (2) one set of accounts is used for *both* regular and consignment sales. Under each assumption, a perpetual inventory system is used.

At the end of the period (the month of March), the Consignment Out account will appear as follows:

Consignment Out—Matthewson Retailers

Shipped 15 TV sets (Model AK-320)		2,250	Sale of 10 TV sets (Model AK-320)		4,000
Consignor's expenditures:					
Crating costs	45				
Freight-out	60	105			
Consignee's expenditures:					
Warranty adjustments	20				
Local freight	15				
Commissions	800	835			
Period-end adjustment (consignment profit)		1,600	Balance carried forward		790
		4,790			4,790
April 1 inventory—5 TV sets (Model AK-320) @ $158		790			

The assignment of costs for purposes of inventory valuation and the determination of profit on consignment sales is analyzed in detail in Illustration 23–3.

Inventoriable and Noninventoriable Costs

In respect to the tabular calculation in Illustration 23–3, it is important to note the fundamental distinction between inventoriable costs and noninventoriable costs. The inventoriable costs include the original merchandise costs and subsequent value increments; to the extent that these costs attach to unsold units, they are properly deferred to future periods to be matched against related revenues. Packing, freight, and drayage paid by the consignee are illustrative of expenditures usually regarded as increasing the value of the consigned units.

Contrariwise, the noninventoriable costs are those expenditures that fail to add value to the unsold consigned units, and are accordingly charged to expense in the period of outlay. In addition to the normal selling expenses of the consignee, there are frequently other, sometimes unusual, expenditures which are generally regarded as noninventoriable costs. In respect to transshipments of consigned goods, the ultimate valuation of the inventory should reflect costs of transportation which are not in excess of those normally incurred by direct shipment from the consignor; any additional transportation cost should be regarded as a current expense. Similarly, in the event that a portion of unsold consigned goods are returned to the consignor, they should be restored to the inventory account at their original acquisition cost, and the incremental expenditures, to the extent they are

Illustration 23–2

JOURNAL ENTRIES BY CONSIGNOR
(Perpetual Inventory Method)

	Separate Accounts Used for Consignment Transactions		Regular Accounts Used for Consignment Transactions	
(1)	To record cost of 15 TV sets shipped on consignment, at $150 per set:			
	Consignment out—Matthewson Retailers........ 2,250		Merchandise on consignment........ 2,250	
	Inventory........	2,250	Inventory........	2,250
(2)	To record crating costs, $45, incurred by the consignor on the above shipment:			
	Consignment out—Matthewson Retailers........ 45		Deferred consignment costs........ 45	
	Cash........	45	Cash........	45
(3)	To record $60 freight paid by the consignor on the shipment in (1):			
	Consignment out—Matthewson Retailers........ 60		Deferred consignment costs........ 60	
	Cash........	60	Cash........	60
(4)	To record transaction details reported in the account sales (Illustration 23–1):			
	Cash........ 3,165		Cash........ 3,165	
	Consignment out—Matthewson Retailers........ 835		Warranty expense........ 20	
	Consignment out—Matthewson Retailers........	4,000	Deferred consignment costs........ 15	
			Commissions........ 800	
			Sales........	4,000

Warranty adjustments (on sets sold)........ $ 20
Drayage on 15 sets........ 15
Commissions on sets sold........ 800
$835

(5) To adjust the balance in the Consignment Out account to the end-of-the-period capitalizable costs in respect to unsold goods, and to recognize profit on consignment sales:

Consignment out—Matthewson Retailers........ 1,600
    Consignment profit................................ 1,600

Inventoriable costs related to
15 sets:

Inventory value when		
shipped...............	$2,250	
Packing expense.........	45	
Freight-out..............	60	
Local freight—consignee...	15	
Total...............	$2,370	
Unit cost ($2,370 ÷ 15)........	$ 158	
Inventory valuation		
($158 × 5)...............	$ 790	
Preadjustment *Credit* balance in		
Consignment Out account	810	
Debit adjustment............	$1,600	

To adjust inventory account for the end-of-the period cost of goods held by the consignee:

*Cost of sales............................. 1,580
    Merchandise on consignment............ 1,500
    Deferred consignment costs............ 80

(6) To close:

Consignment profit........................ 1,600
    Income summary......................... 1,600

Sales.................................... 4,000
    Cost of sales......................... 1,580
    Warranty expense..................... 20
    Commissions........................... 800
    Income summary....................... 1,600

* The expired portion of deferred consignment costs, $80, may be identified as a separate expense in this entry.

Illustration 23–3

	Consigned Merchandise			Inventory		Profit and Loss		
	Units	Total Cost	Unit Cost	Units	Valuation	Units	Costs	Amounts
Sales (10 units @ $400)............								$4,000
Inventoriable costs:								
Incurred by consignor:								
Merchandise cost when shipped......	15	$2,250	$150	5	$750	10	1,500	
Packing expense.........	15	45	3	5	15	10	30	
Freight-out........	15	60	4	5	20	10	40	
Incurred by consignee:								
Local freight.........	15	15	1	5	5	10	10	1,580
								$2,420
Selling expenses incurred by consignee:								
Warranty adjustments........							$ 20	
Commissions........							800	820
Profit on consignment sales........								$1,600
Inventory valuation.......			$158	5	$790			

not recoverable from the consignee, should be reported as current expenses. Expenditures for repairs and other charges in respect to the care and safety of consigned goods are usually accounted for as period costs, and accordingly charged to expense in the period in which they are incurred.

Deferred Consignment Costs

It has been previously noted that there are several alternative methods of recording and disclosing the inventoriable value increments incurred in the consignment expenditures. The entries in Illustration 23–2 harmonize with the concepts of asset valuation and the matching of revenues and expenses under both assumptions; however, many variations are possible.

Even where the Consignment Out account is used to accumulate the inventoriable costs associated with the consignment arrangement, the consignor may elect to separately identify the additional value increments. These amounts are easily calculated by using the transaction details such as are depicted in Illustration 23–3. In the event that a Deferred Consignment Costs account is to be used in conjunction with a Consignment Out account, Entry No. 5 in Illustration 23–2 would be modified as follows:

Deferred consignment costs (5 units @ $8)	40	
Consignment out—Matthewson Retailers	1,560	
Consignment profit		1,600

The total capitalized value of consignment costs, as before, would consist of—

Inventory of goods on consignment:		
Consignment out—Matthewson		
Retailers (5 units @ $150)	$750	
Deferred consignment costs	40	
Total	$790	

The balance in the Deferred Consignment Costs account would remain $40 until the end of the succeeding accounting period, at which time it would require additional adjustment. Alternatively, the Deferred Consignment Costs account may be debited for each relevant cost when incurred, as in the procedure where "regular" accounts are used for both consignment and nonconsignment transactions. This procedure seems unnecessary, however, in view of the existence of the specially created Consignment Out account and the procedure outlined above for periodically identifying, by adjustment, the deferred consignment costs.

In those circumstances where separate accounts are not maintained, the entries in Illustration 23–2 may also be modified. In particular, the packing and freight expenditures may be charged directly to their standard expense classifications. If this practice were followed, the individual expense accounts would have to be adjusted at the end of the period to give effect to the $40 cost deferment in respect to unsold goods. In the opinion of the authors, the previously illustrated technique is preferable. If practical considerations compel the use of normal expense classifications, then materiality—a practical doctrine—may also indicate that it is unnecessary to defer the additional inventoriable expenditures.

Modification of Entries for Periodic Inventory Method

The entries in Illustration 23–2 assume that a perpetual inventory is maintained by the consignor. In the event that the periodic inventory method is followed, only minor modifications of the entries in this illustration are required.

When consignment transactions are recorded separately, Entry No. 1 takes the following form:

```
Consignment out—Matthewson Retailers................... 2,250
    Consigned shipments................................          2,250
```

The Consigned Shipments account is essentially a suspense credit to Purchases, and is created primarily to effect dollar control in respect to current shipments. No other changes are required except to close this account to Purchases at the end of the accounting period.

If the "regular" accounts are used to record consignment transactions, the changes are equally minor. Only a memorandum record is usually made of the shipment (Entry No. 1). Subsequent transactions are recorded as before. In the closing sequence, a Merchandise on Consignment account is created with a balance of $750, and the Deferred Consignment Costs account is adjusted to yield a residual balance of $40.

Financial Statement Presentation

In some cases the consignee may remit more or less than the amount due the consignor as reported on the account sales. If more is remitted than is due (or an advance is made), the excess remittance should be credited to a separate account, Payable to Consignee, rather than to the Consignment Out account. The balance in this account is properly reported as a current liability in the balance sheet of the consignor, as in most instances, it will be abated, or eliminated by offset, as amounts due are reported on subsequent account sales. If an advance is more permanent in nature, it should, of course, be reported as a long-term liability.

Where the consignee remits less than the reported amount due, the deficiency should be debited by the consignor to an asset account, Due from Consignee, and reported as a receivable under the current asset caption in the balance sheet. For example, if Matthewson Retailers (Illustration 23–2) remitted only $2,165 with the account sales, the consignor's entry to record the receipt would be as follows:

Cash..		2,165	
Due from consignee—Matthewson Retailers..................		1,000	
Consignment out—Matthewson Retailers....................		835	
Consignment out—Matthewson Retailers................			4,000

If, however, the $1,000 differential consists of trade accounts receivable transferred to the consignor by the consignee, the above entry should be modified to reflect this circumstance.

The balance in the Consignment Out account, after adjustment at the end of the accounting period, should be reported on the balance sheet of the consignor as follows:

Current Assets:
  Inventories:
    Merchandise on hand........... $12,500
    Consigned merchandise.........   790 $13,290

In the event a Deferred Consignment Costs account is used, it should be classified as a current asset—either in the inventory or prepaid expense category.

With respect to the income statement, the operating data for consignment transactions are often merged with other reported revenues and costs. However, a more prominent form of disclosure, and one that is especially appropriate if consignment sales are significant in respect to total revenues, is given in Illustration 23–4.

Illustration 23–4

THE BISHOP WHOLESALE CORPORATION
Income Statement
For Year Ended December 31, 1972

	Consignment Sales	Regular Sales	Total
Sales..............................	$40,000	$100,000	$140,000
Cost of sales.......................	24,000	58,000	82,000
Gross profit on sales................	$16,000	$ 42,000	$ 58,000
Operating expenses:			
Selling expenses..................	$ 8,000	$ 14,000	$ 22,000
Administrative expenses...........		25,000	25,000
Total operating expenses.........	$ 8,000	$ 39,000	$ 47,000
Net Income.......................	$ 8,000	$ 3,000	$ 11,000

A word of caution should be sounded in respect to the above type of presentation. The reported profit on consignment sales may be overstated, perhaps significantly, in view of the fact that the administrative costs are totally charged against the regular sales. Even if management desires to analyze the consignment transactions on a direct cost, or contribution margin, basis, this reporting implicitly assumes that *all* administrative costs are rigidly fixed or otherwise unrelated to the consignment activity. Manifestly, some effort should be made to allocate these costs, both on direct and absorption cost bases, in order to generate several useful indexes of each revenue-producing activity.

QUESTIONS

1. What is a consignment? Who are the parties to this business transaction?
2. Distinguish between a sale and a consignment.
3. How should one account for an inventory of consigned merchandise?
4. Do goods "sold" on consignment satisfy the revenue realization criterion? Explain.
5. In the absence of limiting arrangements, which party in the consignment is generally responsible for costs incurred which relate directly to the goods from date of shipment to the date of sale?
6. Under what circumstances would a consignment arrangement produce advantage to both the consignee and the consignor?
7. What is an "account sales" and what information does it normally include?
8. What data are recorded in the "Consignment In" account on the consignee's books? How is the balance (debit or credit) of this account presented on the balance sheet of the consignee?
9. How is the "Consignment Out" account balance reported on the balance sheet of the consignor?
10. What accounts arise as a result of the consignee remitting more or less than the amount due the consignor as reported on the account sales? How are these accounts classified on the balance sheet of the consignor?

PROBLEMS

Problem 23–1

Prepare all journal entries relating to the following transactions for the Smith Office Supply Company, consignor:

a) A consignment of 100 secretarial desks is sent to the Jones Company (a *del credere* agent). The cost of each desk is $62, and each is marked to sell for $100.
b) $150 freight on the above shipment is paid by the consignor.
c) The following account sales is received by the Smith Office Supply Company at the end of the fiscal year:

Desks received...............	100		
Unsold desks................	25		
Desks sold..................	75 @ $100		$7,500
Less:			
Commission...............		$750	
Advertising................		100	850
Amount remitted.............			$6,650

Problem 23–2

The Caps Manufacturing Company and Marks Retailers entered into a consignment agreement whereby the latter would sell sets of Columbian silverware on a consignment basis. The terms of the agreement provided that Marks would receive a commission of 25 percent on sales price and bill Caps for all expenses except 10 percent of advertising expenditures. Both firms close their books on December 31. Marks agreed to render an account sales at each year's end and remit all cash then due. Caps utilizes perpetual inventory procedures; both firms keep consignments separate from other merchandise transactions. Transactions were:

a) November 15, 1971. Caps shipped goods on consignment, 100 sets to sell at $30, cost $12 per set. Packing and freight costs, $200, were paid by the consignor.

b) December 31, 1971. An account sales was rendered by the consignee, reporting no sales but expenditures of $100 for local freight and $50 for advertising.

c) January–April, 1972. Consignee sold 90 sets at the agreed sales price.

d) April 30, 1972. Caps shipped goods on consignment, 200 sets to sell at $31, cost $13 per set. Packaging and freight costs, $400, were paid by the consignor.

e) April 30, 1972. Consignee paid $200 for local freight on the above shipment.

f) May, 1972. Consignee paid $300 for advertising, all of which related to consigned merchandise.

g) May–December, 1972. Consignee sold 110 sets at the agreed sales prices, which include the remainder of the sets from the first shipment.

h) December 31, 1972. An account sales was prepared; the required remittance was made.

Required:

(i) Prepare an account sales and give all entries on the books of the consignee for 1971 and 1972.

(ii) Give all entries on the books of the consignor for 1971 and 1972.

Problem 23–3

Sommerfeld, Inc., shipped 200 Super-X appliances to Jones Bros., retail distributors, for sale on a 15 percent *del credere* commission basis. The cost of each appliance was $83, with an additional payment of $2 per unit to crate and ship to the consignee. It was agreed that Sommerfeld would draw a sight draft on the consignee for 60 percent of the cost of the appliances, the advance to be recovered periodically by monthly deductions (based on units sold) from the remittances which accompany the account sales. All expenses of the consignee are deducted monthly as incurred.

The following account sales was rendered by the consignee at the conclusion of the first month's operations:

Sales of Super-X appliances (60 units @ $100).....		$6,000
Deductions for:		
Expenses paid by the consignee...............	$310	
Advance....................................	?	
Commission...............................	900	?
Remittance to consignor.......................		$?

Required:

(i) Give all entries on the books of the consignee.

(ii) Give entries for the month's transactions in the consignor's books assuming the use of a perpetual inventory and with the further assumption that:

   a) Consignment transactions are commingled with regular transactions.

   b) Consignment transactions are recorded separately.

Problem 23–4

The four journal entries which are shown below were used by a consignee to record the transactions arising out of a consignment of merchandise to him.

March 27, 1971

Consignment in..	24	
Cash...		24

April 25, 1971

Cash..	800	
Consignment in..		800

April 25, 1971

Consignment in..	200	
Commission earned.....................................		200

May 5, 1971

Consignment in..	576	
Cash...		576

Required:

(i) Describe fully the transactions which were recorded by the journal entries.

(ii) Prepare journal entries to record the consignment transactions *on the books of the consignor.* Assume that the consigned goods cost $400 and that the consignor keeps perpetual inventory records.

(iii) State how the facts should be presented on balance sheets of both the consignee and consignor as of April 30, 1971. Explain your reasons for such presentation.

(AICPA adapted)

Problem 23–5

In March, 1971, the Geis Company shipped 600 units of merchandise on consignment for sale to Overmeyer and Associates, total cost $4,200. Packing and shipping costs, paid by the Geis Company, amounted to $265. The shipment was recorded as follows:

Overmeyer and Associates.................................	6,000	
Transportation out.......................................	265	
Merchandise...		4,200
Cash..		265
Profit on consigned shipment............................		1,800

On December 28, 1971, the following account sales prepared by Overmeyer and Associates was received by the Geis Company:

Sales (400 units @ $10).................		$4,000
Costs and expenses:		
Insurance to December 31, 1971........	$220	
Drayage.............................	50	
Commission.........................	400	670
Check enclosed........................		$3,330

The account sales was recorded by the Geis Company with a debit to Cash and a credit to Overmeyer and Associates for $3,330.

On February 28, 1972, a second account sales was received by the consignor, although it has not yet been recorded, detailing the following:

Sales (150 units @ $10).................		$1,500
Costs and expenses:		
Insurance to February 28, 1972.........	$ 40	
Commission.........................	150	190
Balance due...........................		$1,310

The Geis Company closes its books December 31.

Required:

Make any appropriate entries to adjust and correct the books of the Geis Company through February 28, 1972, reflecting consignment profit realized to this date.

Problem 23–6

The Stans Corporation ships goods on consignment to Law Distributors, a consignee. The consignment contract provides that the consignor shall bear all expenses of the consignee which relate to the consignments; an agency commission of 30 percent of all consignment sales shall be paid to the consignee. The consignee is required to render an account sales at each year-end and to remit all cash due plus a $5,000 advance because of the existence of a considerable quantity of unsold merchandise. The accounts of the Stans Corporation showed the following balances at December 31, 1971 (end of the accounting period):

Cash.	$ 60,000	
Accounts receivable (net).	180,000	
Plant and equipment (net).	250,000	
Accounts payable.		$ 80,000
Advance from consignee.		5,000
Merchandise inventory (regular).	140,000	
Consignment out (valuation of goods on consignment at December 31, 1971, exclusive of deferred shipping costs).	30,000	
Deferred shipping costs—goods on consignment (paid by consignor).	2,000	
Commission on consignment sales.	30,000	
Deferred shipping costs—goods on consignment (paid by consignee).	1,000	
Advertising costs (paid by consignee).	13,000	
Sales, regular.		800,000
Sales, consignment.		100,000
Cost of goods sold, regular.	320,000	
Cost of goods sold, consignment.	40,000	
Selling expenses.	190,000	
Administrative expenses.	150,000	
Capital stock.		400,000
Retained earnings (January 1, 1971).		21,000
	$1,406,000	$1,406,000

Assume an income tax rate of 52 percent and that 20 percent of the tax liability is paid at the year's end; income taxes are not reflected by the above balances.

Required:

Based upon the above data prepare an income statement for 1971, reporting consignment transactions separately, and a balance sheet as of December 31, 1971.

Problem 23–7

Transactions are executed between a consignor and consignee under provisions of a contract stipulating that (*a*) the consignor will reimburse the consignee for all costs related to piano consignments except advertising costs, which are to be borne 60 percent by the consignor and 40 percent by the consignee; (*b*) the consignee's commission will be 20 percent of sales; and (*c*) receivables arising from consignment sales are to be carried on the books of the consignor.

Inventoriable expenditures incurred in addition to merchandise cost at shipment date are carried in a deferred cost account by the consignor. Both parties close their books at calendar year-end.

The transactions during the first accounting period were:
a) The consignor shipped 10 pianos to the consignee, cost $300 each, to sell at $700.
b) The consignor paid $150 for crating, freight, and insurance on the 10 pianos shipped on consignment.
c) The consignee paid $50 drayage upon receiving the above shipment of 10 pianos.
d) The consignee sold three pianos for $500 cash down payment (per piano), the balance to be paid at the end of 12 months.
e) The consignee paid $300 advertising costs relating to the pianos.
f) The consignee sold five pianos for cash at the agreed price.

g) The consignee submitted an account sales and remitted the cash due on the eight pianos sold. No collections had been made on the receivables.

h) The books were adjusted and closed.

Required:

(i) Prepare all entries for the period (including any memorandum entries) on the books of both the consignor and the consignee as indicated by the above information. Assume that both parties utilize perpetual inventory procedures and that consignment transactions are recorded separately.

(ii) Prepare the account sales.

Problem 23–8

The Stone Manufacturing Company closes its books annually on December 31. In making an investigation of the accounts of the company in respect to 1971, you discover the following facts:

a) During November and December, the company shipped stoves to two dealers, A and B, on a consignment basis. The consignment agreements provided that the stoves were to be sold by the consignee at a list price of $180 each. The consignee was to be allowed a 25 percent commission on each sale and was to be reimbursed for all expenses paid in connection with the stoves. Sales on account are at the risk of the consignee.

b) At the time of shipment, the consignor debited Trade Accounts Receivable and credited Sales $120 for each stove, this being the usual sale price received by the consignor on the basis of which a gross profit of 20 percent on cost is realized.

c) All cash received from these two consignees was credited to Trade Accounts Receivable. No other entries have been made in respect to these accounts.

d) Information as to all of the transactions with the consignees is given following:

(1) Stoves shipped out: to A—100, to B—40.

(2) Stoves unsold by consignees as of 12/31/71: A—35, B—25.

(3) Crating and shipping cost to consignor—$84.

(4) Freight paid by consignees: A—$130, B—$100.

(5) Cash advanced by A at date of receipt of the first 100 stoves— $4,000. Cash subsequently remitted by A—$5,395.

(6) Cash remitted by B—$575.

Required:

(i) Show, by entries in T-accounts, transactions completed and adjustments required by the Stone Company.

(ii) Prepare a trial balance of the accounts affected by these transactions and adjustments.

(AICPA adapted)

Problem 23–9

You are examining the December 31, 1971, financial statements of the Conol Sales Company, a new client. The company was established on January 1, 1970, and is a distributor of air-conditioning units. The company's income statements for 1970 and 1971 were as follows:

THE CONOL SALES COMPANY

Statements of Income and Expense
For Years Ended December 31, 1970 and 1971

	1971	1970
Sales.	$1,287,500	$1,075,000
Cost of sales.	669,500	559,000
Gross profit.	$ 618,000	$ 516,000
Selling and administrative expenses.	403,500	330,000
Net income before income taxes.	$ 214,500	$ 186,000
Provision for income taxes @ 50%.	107,250	93,000
Net Income.	$ 107,250	$ 93,000

Your examination disclosed the following:

a) Some sales were made on open account; other sales were made through dealers to whom units were shipped on a consignment basis. Both sales methods were in effect in 1970 and 1971. In both years, however, the company treated all shipments as outright sales.

b) The sales price and cost of the units were the same in 1970 and 1971. Each unit had a cost of $130 and was uniformly invoiced at $250 to open account customers and to consignees.

c) During 1971 the amount of cash received from consignees in payment for units sold by them was $706,500. Consignees remit for the units as soon as they are sold. Confirmations received from consignees showed that they had a total of 23 unsold units on hand at December 31, 1971. Consignees were unable to confirm the unsold units on hand at December 31, 1970.

d) The cost of sales for 1971 was determined by the client as follows:

		Units
Inventory on hand in warehouse, December 31, 1970.		1,510
Purchases.		4,454
Available for sale.		5,964
Inventory on hand in warehouse, December 31, 1971.		814
Shipments to: Open account customers.	3,008	
Consignee customers.	2,142	5,150

Required:

(i) Compute the total amount of the Conol Sales Company's inventory at—
   a) December 31, 1971.
   b) December 31, 1970.

(ii) Prepare the auditor's working paper journal entries to correct the financial statements for the year ended December 31, 1970.

(iii) Prepare the formal adjusting journal entries to correct the accounts at December 31, 1971. (The books have not been closed.)

(AICPA adapted)

Problem 23–10

The Winston Company, which manufactures and sells gas burners to be installed in coal-burning furnaces, arranged in September, 1971, to sell some of its product through three dealers to whom it consigned burners packed with their related parts and fixtures, each such package being identified as a burner. The contract with the consignee provides that:

a) He shall fix the sales price for all burners to be sold in his territory, such price to be approved by the Winston Company;

b) He shall pay all expenses incident to handling, selling, and collecting for the burners after delivery to him, except for repairs and expenses pertinent thereto, required because of defective production;

c) He shall retain as commission 25 percent of the amount for which he sells the burners, exclusive of installation charges;

d) He shall be responsible for the proper installation of burners sold and may make therefor suitable charges in which the Winston Company shall not participate;

e) He shall render, within 10 days after the end of each month, an account sales, accompanied by a check for the amount due the Winston Company as the result of transactions during the month to which the report relates.

A condensed trial balance of the Winston Company's accounts at September 30, 1971, follows:

Cash...	$ 58,910	
Accounts receivable.............................	241,964	
Inventories:		
Finished burners and related parts and fixtures.....	21,200	
Work in process, materials and supplies...........	42,271	
Prepaid expenses.................................	3,007	
Plant..	128,762	
Accounts payable................................		$ 31,742
Accrued liabilities...............................		138,798
Capital stock....................................		100,000
Retained earnings...............................		18,978
Sales..		643,947
Sales returns and allowances.....................	2,648	
Manufacturing...................................	129,384	
Selling expense..................................	139,637	
Administrative expense...........................	89,423	
Allowance for bad debts.........................		9,398
Accumulated depreciation........................		27,632
Nonoperating income.............................		318
Nonoperating expense............................	3,607	
Provision for income taxes.......................	110,000	
	$970,813	$970,813

All shipments charged to Accounts Receivable were credited to Sales.

Accounts receivable included accounts with the three consignees, which, upon examination, revealed the following:

HOLMES PLUMBING COMPANY

Debits:		
9/4/71	18 burners shipped on consignment...............	$3,600.00
9/20/71	Transportation charges paid on two burners returned as defective.......................................	22.00
9/27/71	Cost of repairing two burners returned as defective..	18.00
		$3,640.00
Credits:		
9/30/71	Cash received for 13 burners.....................	1,767.75
Balance, 9/30/71......		$1,872.25

LUNDEEN HEATING EQUIPMENT COMPANY

Debits:

9/6/71	6 burners shipped on consignment.................	$1,200.00
9/15/71	Transportation charges on one burner returned as defective.......................................	28.00
		$1,228.00

Credits:

9/15/71	1 burner returned as defective........	$200.00	
9/30/71	Cash received for 3 burners..........	544.50	744.50
Balance, 9/30/71...			$ 483.50

QUINCY FURNACE COMPANY

Debits:

9/5/71	12 burners shipped on consignment.................	$2,400.00
9/5/71	Freight prepaid on consigned burners..............	36.00
9/30/71	Commission on 9 burners.......................	450.00
		$2,886.00

Credits:

9/30/71	Cash received for 9 burners.....................	1,344.00
Balance, 9/30/71...		$1,542.00

Consignees reported burners on hand at 9/30/71 as follows:

> Holmes Plumbing Company..................... 3
> Lundeen Heating Equipment Company........... 2
> Quincy Furnace Company...................... 3

Shipping records show that on September 27, 1971, the Winston Company shipped burners, freight prepaid, to replace those returned by consignees, as follows:

> To: Holmes Plumbing Company.................. 2
>   Lundeen Heating Equipment Company....... 1

Burners on hand at the Winston Company's plant at September 30, 1971, numbered 212 and were inventoried at manufacturing cost. Inventories at the beginning of the period have been closed into Manufacturing while those at the end of the period have been closed out of Manufacturing. All normal adjusting entries have been made for the fiscal year ended September 30, 1971. Unpaid commissions on sales were credited to Accrued Liabilities.

Account sales for September, 1971, with related checks, were received by the Winston Company as follows:

> From: Holmes Plumbing Company................ October 7, 1971
>   Lundeen Heating Equipment Company...... October 12, 1971
>   Quincy Furnace Company................. October 9, 1971

Those from Holmes Plumbing Company and Lundeen Heating Equipment Company reflect payments of $36 and $18, respectively, for transportation charges which they paid upon receiving their consignments; that from Quincy Furnace Company includes a charge for the cost of repairs to a defective burner, in the amount of $6.

All entries in the Winston Company's accounts with the consignees which are dated September 30, 1971, were based on checks received and data recorded in their account sales received on the dates stated above.

Required:

From the data above prepare:

(i)   An account sales for September, 1971, as rendered by each of the three consignees.

(ii) Entries to correct the accounts of the Winston Company, as of September 30, 1971. (No adjustment of the provision for income taxes is required; assume consignment transactions are not separately recorded.)

(iii) An adjusted balance sheet of the Winston Company as of September 30, 1971.

(iv) A condensed income statement of the Winston Company for the year ended September 30, 1971.

(AICPA adapted)

Chapter 24

Installment Sales

Nature of Installment Sales

The installment sales contract is a special type of credit arrangement which provides for a schedule of predetermined, periodic collections from the sale of real estate, merchandise, or other personal property. In respect to the usual credit sale, the collection interval is comparatively short and title passes unconditionally to the buyer concurrent with the completion of the sale; however, installment sales contracts are more frequently characterized by (1) a cash down payment at the date of sale followed by periodic (frequently equal) payments over a relatively long period of time, and (2) a transfer of title which remains conditional until the debt is fully discharged.

In view of the typically long collection period, and the concomitant increase in risk, a variety of contractual arrangements are used to provide some additional measure of protection to the seller. Most of these agreements involve some form of title retention by the seller; among these are the following:

1. Conditional sales contracts, whereby the seller retains legal title of transferred property until the schedule of installment collections is completed.
2. Hire-purchase contracts, whereby the vendor, in effect, leases the property to the buyer until the final installment (rental) payment is made, at which time title is conveyed to the buyer for some nominal consideration.
3. Custodial arrangements, wherein legal title to property is vested in a third party (a trustee) until payment therefor is completed, at which time title transfers to the purchaser; this arrangement is primarily applicable to sales of realty.

In other types of agreements, title passes to the purchaser under a mortgage or lien arrangement. Such contracts enable the vendor to reclaim possession of transferred property in those instances where the purchaser is in default.

Despite these safeguards, losses from installment sales tend to be significantly larger than those from short-term credit sales. This may be attributed, in part, to such unique variables as the extended collection period, the relatively small value of many items of repossessed merchandise (whether due to physical deterioration, obsolescence, or depreciation), increased collection expenses, and necessary costs of repossession. Accordingly, the accountant must carefully appraise the measurement of net income where the amount of revenue from installment sales contracts is significant.

Criteria for Gross Profit Recognition

The accounting process of measuring net income from installment sales should theoretically follow the conventional treatment for ordinary credit sales, i.e., by relating gross sales of an accounting period with costs and expenses which appertain thereto. In this reckoning, provision must necessarily be made for the accrual of certain costs expected to be incurred in the future (e.g., those associated with collection) and for estimated losses due to uncollectible receivables. However, because of the prolonged period for liquidating receivable balances, losses in respect thereto are frequently large, and realistic estimates of other costs (or expenses) which relate to installment sales are often difficult to determine.

For these and other reasons, special methods of accounting for installment sales which accent cash collections have been developed. Among the various proposed income determination concepts, each of which focuses primarily on the recognition of gross profit, are the following:

1. Gross profit (sales less cost of goods sold) is not given account recognition until collections are equivalent in amount to the cost of the transferred property; all subsequent receipts are then recorded as realized gross profit. This deferral of gross profit until cost is totally recovered appeals to accounting conservatism. Perhaps a circumstance involving a one-time installment sale with an unusually high degree of risk may justify the application of this method; however, it appears to be an overly cautious criterion for income recognition when applied to a business regularly engaged in installment sales transactions.

2. Collections of receivable balances are first recognized as elements of gross profit; subsequent collections are accounted for as a return of cost. This approach essentially controverts the reason for a unique income determination concept, as the timing of revenue recognition closely parallels the preferred theoretical treatment for regular sales; consequently, it has gained very little support.

3. Each collection is regarded as a partial recovery of cost and a partial realization of gross profit, in the same proportion that these two elements are present in the original selling price. This treatment is known as the *installment sales method*. The frequency of its use derives importantly from the fact that it is approved for income tax purposes. Apropos of Section 453(a) of the Internal Revenue Code, "a person who regularly sells or

otherwise disposes of personal property on the installment plan may return as income therefrom in any taxable year that proportion of the installment payments actually received in that year which the gross profit, realized or to be realized when payment is completed, bears to the total contract price." This treatment is also extended to the sale of realty in Section 453(b).

The Installment Sales Method

With respect to regular sales, revenue is realized (or confirmed) upon completion of the sale transaction; accordingly, it is recognized in the accounting period when title transfers to the buyer. This identification of revenue with the period of sale appears reasonable in view of the fact that there is either an immediate recovery of the total sales price, or collection is made within a relatively short period of time. However, in the case of installment sales, the collection period is frequently an extended interval and the probability of loss because of uncollectible receivables is significantly greater than for regular sales; for this reason, attention is diverted from the date of sale to the process of collection. Under the installment sales method, revenue, or more precisely gross profit, is considered realized (confirmed) in the period of collection rather than in the period of sale. The amount of gross profit recognized in a given period depends upon the relevant gross profit rate and the collected amount of installment receivables.

To illustrate, assume an installment sale of property, the cost of which was $3,000, was made on December 31, 1970, for $5,000, with a cash down payment of $1,000 and 40 monthly payments of $100 scheduled thereafter. The total gross profit to the seller was $2,000 (40 percent of the selling price). Under the installment sales method, annual realized gross profit is recognized according to the following table:

Year	Cash Collected	Gross Profit Realized	
		Computations	Amount
1970	$1,000	$1,000/$5,000 × $2,000	$ 400
1971	1,200	1,200/ 5,000 × 2,000	480
1972	1,200	1,200/ 5,000 × 2,000	480
1973	1,200	1,200/ 5,000 × 2,000	480
1974	400	400/ 5,000 × 2,000	160
Totals	$5,000		$2,000

The deferral of gross profit recognition, which is the essence of the installment sales method, compels the accountant to examine the consistency of the treatment of related expenses. It is evident that the deferral of gross profit, in effect, constitutes a delayed recognition of both sales revenue *and* cost of goods sold. Significantly, however, other operating expenses—some of which relate directly to installment selling, such as distribution costs, collection expenses, and other administrative overhead —are accounted for as period costs. Accordingly, the matching of revenue from installment sales relates only to those product costs incident to, and directly associated with, the acquisition or manufacture of merchandise; the matching process in this application does not extend to other operating expenses. Advocates for the nondeferral of these expenses frequently argue (1) that conservatism is best served by this treatment, (2) that such expenses often have only a tenuous relationship to either the sales or collection patterns, (3) that realistic measurements for accruals are frequently difficult to estimate with dependable accuracy, and (4) that this method accords with income tax provisions. However, these arguments, at best, merely reflect pragmatic constraints on the more consistent, and preferable, bases of associating costs and revenues. Where the installment sales method is used, it would appear that the materiality doctrine is the only meaningful basis for a nondeferral of many conventional operating expenses.

The treatment of bad debt losses poses a special problem. The installment sales method is predicated upon somewhat uncertain collection prospects, and accordingly defers the recognition of profit. Additionally, it is frequently assumed that the repossession privilege affords the vendor an opportunity to recover the amount of uncollectible installment receivables, at least to the extent of the unrecovered costs of the reclaimed merchandise which are implicit in these balances. Under these circumstances, it would appear that provision for estimated bad debt losses is not required. However, when it becomes evident that the value of repossessed merchandise fails to compensate for corresponding losses of uncollectible accounts (viz., unrecovered cost and previously recognized gross profit), estimates of these losses should be made in the same manner as for other credit sales. Since the cost of the merchandise transferred at date of sale is often the principal component of the ultimate loss, the provision for bad debts is properly reported in the period of sale.

Interest on Unpaid Installment Receivable Balances

Because the collection period for installment sales is often prolonged and may involve large amounts of unliquidated receivable balances, interest is often charged on these unpaid balances. Where this condition prevails, each installment collection consists of (1) amounts applied in liquidation of the unpaid principal (receivable) balance and (2) interest income. The installment contract may expressly provide for an allocation of the scheduled payments, detailing that portion of each collection which shall relate to the debt principal and interest.

The interest requirement may follow one of several common patterns. These include the following:

1. Cash payments of equal amount are made each period. Each successive installment collection includes an *increased* reduction of principal and

a corresponding *decrease* in interest. This is the conventional method of payment on installment sales contracts and will be illustrated subsequently.

2. Each period's collection consists of a payment in reduction of principal, plus a payment for interest on the amount of the current principal reduction for the time period from the date of sale to the date of the current installment payment. The cash received increases each period as a consequence of an increasing interest charge. However, since conventional accounting calls for interest to be accrued on the unpaid balance of the principal, this method produces a difference between the amount accrued and the amount of interest actually collected. Uncollected interest should accordingly be reported on the balance sheet as Accrued Interest Receivable on Installment Sales Contracts.

3. Interest is charged on the receivable balance unpaid at the beginning of each period. Normally, where this approach is followed, there is a constant reduction of principal in each successive period. Also, the amount of cash received decreases with each collection as a consequence of a decreasing amount of interest.

The first approach is illustrated using the following data:

Installment sale made on January 1, 1970......................... $2,500.00
Cash down payment.. 500.00
Annual installment collection for 4 consecutive years (including 5 per-
cent interest)... *564.02
  * Computation of equal periodic payment:[1]
   Periodic payment = original unpaid receivable balance
      ÷ present value of an annuity of $1 for 4 periods
       at 5%
      = $2,000 ÷ 3.5459505
      = $564.02.

TABLE OF ENTRIES FOR PERIODIC COLLECTIONS

Date	Cash (Debit)	Interest Earned (Credit)	Installment Accounts Receivable (Credit)	Unpaid Balance
1/1/70				$2,500.00
1/1/70	$500.00		$500.00	2,000.00
1/1/71	564.02	(a) $100.00	464.02	1,535.98
1/1/72	564.02	(b) 76.80	487.22	1,048.76
1/1/73	564.02	(c) 52.44	511.58	537.18
1/1/74	*564.04	(d) 26.86	537.18	–0–

 (a) $2,000.00 × 5% = $100.00.
 (b) $1,535.98 × 5% = $ 76.80.
 (c) $1,048.76 × 5% = $ 52.44.
 (d) $ 537.18 × 5% = $ 26.86.
 * Adjusted to reflect the requirements of the terminal payment.

[1] See Appendix 1 for a summary description of compound interest fundamentals and related tables.

Although no further detailed illustrations are offered at this time, the third interest pattern described is illustrated subsequently with a journal entry sequence for the sale of realty on an installment basis.

Accounting Procedures for the Installment Sales Method

Various accounting procedures may be used to record transactions using the installment sales method. The sequence of entries described and illustrated in the following pages is essentially a distillate of current accounting practice.

Although there are no substantive differences in the several applications of this income concept, it is convenient to consider separately two basic types of property transfers, with their attendant procedural details:

1. Installment sales of items other than regular merchandise—realty and casual sales of personal property (see Illustration 24–1).
2. Installment sales of conventional merchandise (see Illustration 24–3).
   a) Perpetual inventory basis.
   b) Periodic inventory basis.

Entries for Installment Sale of Realty (and Other Casual Sales). The following installment sale transaction is assumed to occur on January 31, 1971.

Sales of realty (Plot 9)	$100,000
Cost of the realty	70,000
Gross profit on sale (30 percent of the sales price)	$ 30,000
Expenses of sale	$ 2,000
Collection schedule:	
Cash down payment at date of sale	20,000
Note secured by a mortgage lien on the realty. Liquidation is to be made by eight annual payments of $10,000. Six percent interest is payable each January 31 on the unpaid balance at the beginning of the year	80,000

In order to emphasize the special effect of the installment sales method on revenue recognition from the sale of realty, entries which indicate the recognition of gross profit under the installment method (i.e., ratably over the periods in which collections are made) are juxtaposed against entries determining net income by the conventional accrual method (i.e., in the period of sale) for a two-year period in Illustration 24–1. A comparative analysis of the annual amounts of recognized gross profit over the total time interval is given in Illustration 24–2.

Entries for Installment Sale of Merchandise. In application of the installment sales method to a merchandising operation, it is important that the accounting system be modified sufficiently to accommodate the neces-

Illustration 24–1

	Accrual (Conventional) Method (Gross Profit Recognized in Period of Sale)		Installment Sales Method (Gross Profit Recognized with the Progress of Collection)	
(1) January 31, 1971. Sale of Plot 9, cost $70,000, for $100,000, and collection of cash down payment of $20,000 (gross profit rate = 30%).				
Cash...................................	20,000		20,000	
Note receivable........................	80,000		80,000	
Real estate (Plot 9).................		70,000		70,000
Gain on sale of realty................		30,000		
Deferred gross profit on sale of realty..				30,000
(2) January 31, 1971. Payment of expenses related to sale.				
Expenses of realty sales...................	2,000		2,000	
Cash............................		2,000		2,000
(3) December 31, 1971. Realized gross profit on installment basis: $20,000 × 30% = $6,000.				
Deferred gross profit on sale of realty........			6,000	
Realized gross profit on sale of realty....				6,000
(4) December 31, 1971. Accrued interest income on note receivable for 11 months: $80,000 × 6% × 11/12 = $4,400.				
Interest receivable......................	4,400		4,400	
Interest earned.....................		4,400		4,400
(5) December 31, 1971. Year-end closing.				
Gain on sale of realty....................	30,000			
Realized gross profit on sale of realty........			6,000	
Interest earned........................	4,400		4,400	
Expenses of realty sales..............		2,000		2,000
Income summary..................		32,400		8,400
(6) January 1, 1972. Reversal of entry (4).				
Interest earned........................	4,400		4,400	
Interest receivable.................		4,400		4,400
(7) January 31, 1972. Receipt of first installment on note receivable and interest of $4,800 ($80,000 × 6%).				
Cash.................................	14,800		14,800	
Note receivable.....................		10,000		10,000
Interest earned....................		4,800		4,800
(8) December 31, 1972. Gross profit on installment basis: $10,000 × 30% = $3,000.				
Deferred gross profit on sale of reality.......			3,000	
Realized gross profit on sale of realty....				3,000

Illustration 24–1—Continued

	Accrual (Conventional) Method (Gross Profit Recognized in Period of Sale)		Installment Sales Method (Gross Profit Recognized with the Progress of Collection)	
(9) December 31, 1972. Accrued interest income on note receivable for 11 months: $70,000 × 6% × 11/12 = $3,850.				
Interest receivable..........................	3,850		3,850	
Interest earned......................		3,850		3,850
(10) December 31, 1972. Year-end closing.				
Realized gross profit on sale of realty........			3,000	
Interest earned.........................	4,250		4,250	
Income summary....................		4,250		7,250

Illustration 24–2

ACCRUAL AND INSTALLMENT METHODS COMPARED

Year	Collections	Uncollected Balance at Year-End	Recognized (Realized) Gross Profit on Sale of Realty		Deferred Gross Profit at Year-End	
			Accrual Method	Installment Method	Accrual Method	Installment Method
1971........	$ 20,000	$80,000	$30,000	$ 6,000	–0–	$24,000
1972........	10,000	70,000	–0–	3,000	–0–	21,000
1973........	10,000	60,000	–0–	3,000	–0–	18,000
1974........	10,000	50,000	–0–	3,000	–0–	15,000
1975........	10,000	40,000	–0–	3,000	–0–	12,000
1976........	10,000	30,000	–0–	3,000	–0–	9,000
1977........	10,000	20,000	–0–	3,000	–0–	6,000
1978........	10,000	10,000	–0–	3,000	–0–	3,000
1979........	10,000	–0–	–0–	3,000	–0–	–0–
Totals......	$100,000		$30,000	$30,000		

Note: Interest earned and period costs are accorded equivalent treatment under both methods, and thus are excluded from this analysis.

sary account detail and additional procedures. This involves many considerations, among which are the following:

1. Sales, accounts receivable, and cost of sales should be given separate account designations identifying them as either "regular" or "installment."

2. Hyphenated accounts should also be used for installment receivables, in which there should be an identification of the year of sale.

3. The journalizing process should accent gross profit deferral, either at the date of sale or in the period-end closing process. The latter is clearly preferable when installment sales represent a large amount of

the total revenue; additionally, it is the only feasible method when the periodic inventory method is used.

4. Gross profit should, as indicated before, be periodically recognized in porportion to the current collections of installment accounts receivable; this recognition becomes an essential part of the sequence of adjusting entries.

Recording procedures are also influenced, at least partially, by the method of inventory accounting used; accordingly, entries are presented in Illustration 24–3 based upon two assumptions: (1) that perpetual inventory records are maintained, and (2) that periodic inventory procedures are followed.

Assume the following data relate to the XY Corporation:

	1971	1972
Sales:		
Regular.....................................	$200,000	$220,000
Installment..................................	100,000	110,000
Merchandise inventory, January 1...................	10,000	20,000
Merchandise inventory, December 31...............	20,000	15,000
Purchases.....................................	185,000	189,900
Cost of sales:		
Regular.....................................	115,000	130,000
Installment..................................	60,000	64,900
Selling expenses................................	50,000	65,000
Provision for doubtful accounts (regular sales)........	1,000	1,100
Collections on account:		
Installment accounts receivable—1971.............	30,000	40,000
Installment accounts receivable—1972.............		50,000
Accounts receivable (regular)....................	180,000	230,000

These data are recorded in summary form for each of the two years in Illustration 24–3. Although the comparative interperiod effect of electing the installment sales method is not again calculated, it remains essentially consistent with the results derived in Illustration 24–2. Since sales of

Illustration 24–3

	Perpetual Inventory Method		Periodic Inventory Method	
(1) January–December, 1971. Regular and installment sales in 1971.				
Accounts receivable (regular)..........	200,000		200,000	
Installment accounts receivable—				
1971............................	100,000		100,000	
Sales (regular)...................		200,000		200,000
Installment sales................		100,000		100,000
(2) January–December, 1971. Purchases of merchandise in 1971.				
Merchandise inventory..............	185,000			
Purchases........................			185,000	
Accounts payable (cash)..........		185,000		185,000

Illustration 24–3—Continued

	Perpetual Inventory Method	Periodic Inventory Method
(3) January–December, 1971. Selling expenses and provision for doubtful accounts during 1971.		
Selling expenses..................... 50,000		50,000
Estimated loss on doubtful accounts.... 1,000		1,000
Accounts payable (Cash).........	50,000	50,000
Allowance for doubtful accounts...	1,000	1,000
(4) January–December, 1971. Collection of receivables during 1971.		
Cash............................. 210,000		210,000
Accounts receivable (regular)......	180,000	180,000
Installment accounts receivable— 1971.......................	30,000	30,000
(5) Determination of cost of sales for 1971:		
(a) January–December, 1971.		
Cost of sales (regular)........... 115,000		
Cost of installment sales......... 60,000		
Merchandise inventory......	175,000	
(b) December 31, 1971.		
*Cost of sales (regular)...........	115,000	
*Cost of installment sales.........	60,000	
Merchandise inventory..........	10,000	
Purchases................		185,000

* In view of the paucity of inventory detail under the periodic method, this cost allocation may be necessarily based on some estimating process in actual practice.

	Perpetual Inventory Method	Periodic Inventory Method
(6) December 31, 1971. Determination of 1971 deferred gross profit on installment sales. Gross profit rate = $40,000 ÷ $100,000 = 40%.		
Installment sales.................... 100,000		100,000
Cost of installment sales..........	60,000	60,000
Deferred gross profit on installment sales—1971.............	40,000	40,000
(7) December 31, 1971. Realized gross profit in 1971 on installment sales.		

Year of Sale	Gross Profit Rate	Collections	Realized Gross Profit
1971	40%	$30,000	$12,000

	Perpetual Inventory Method	Periodic Inventory Method
Deferred gross profit on installment sales—1971..................... 12,000		12,000
Realized gross profit on installment sales.................	12,000	12,000
(8) December 31, 1971. Year-end closing for realized gross profit.		
Realized gross profit on installment sales........................... 12,000		12,000
Income summary..............	12,000	12,000

Illustration 24–3—Continued

	Perpetual Inventory Method		Periodic Inventory Method	
(9) December 31, 1971. Year-end closing for other nominal accounts.				
Sales (regular)......................	200,000		200,000	
Cost of sales (regular)............		115,000		115,000
Estimated loss on doubtful accounts....................		1,000		1,000
Selling expenses................		50,000		50,000
Income summary...............		34,000		34,000
Income summary...................	46,000		46,000	
Retained earnings..............		46,000		46,000
(10) January–December, 1972. Regular and installment sales in 1972.				
Accounts receivable (regular).........	220,000		220,000	
Installment accounts receivable— 1972..........................	110,000		110,000	
Sales (regular).................		220,000		220,000
Installment sales...............		110,000		110,000
(11) January–December, 1972. Purchases of merchandise in 1972.				
Merchandise inventory.............	189,900			
Purchases.........................			189,900	
Accounts payable (Cash)........		189,900		189,900
(12) January–December, 1972. Selling expenses and provision for doubtful accounts during 1972.				
Selling expenses...................	65,000		65,000	
Estimated loss on doubtful accounts...	1,100		1,100	
Accounts payable (Cash)........		65,000		65,000
Allowance for doubtful accounts..		1,100		1,100
(13) January–December, 1972. Collection of receivables during 1972.				
Cash.............................	320,000		320,000	
Accounts receivable (regular).....		230,000		230,000
Installment accounts receivable —1971......................		40,000		40,000
Installment accounts receivable —1972....................		50,000		50,000
(14) Determination of cost of sales for 1972:				
(*a*) January–December, 1972.				
Cost of sales (regular)..........	130,000			
Cost of installment sales........	64,900			
Merchandise inventory.....		194,900		
(*b*) December 31, 1972.				
Cost of sales (regular)..........			130,000	
Cost of installment sales.......			64,900	
Merchandise inventory.....				5,000
Purchases..............				189,900

Illustration 24–3—Continued

	Perpetual Inventory Method		*Periodic Inventory Method*	

(15) December 31, 1972. Determination of 1972 deferred gross profit on installment sales. Gross profit rate = $45,100 \div \$110,000 = 41\%$.

Installment sales....................	110,000		110,000	
Cost of installment sales.........		64,900		64,900
Deferred gross profit on installment sales—1972............		45,100		45,100

(16) December 31, 1972. Realized gross profit in 1972 on installment sales.

Year of Sale	Gross Profit Rate	Collec- tions	Realized Gross Profit
1971	40%	$40,000	$16,000
1972	41%	50,000	20,500

Deferred gross profit on installment sales—1971.....................	16,000		16,000	
Deferred gross profit on installment sales—1972.....................	20,500		20,500	
Realized gross profit on installment sales..................		36,500		36,500

(17) December 31, 1972. Year-end closing for realized gross profit.

Realized gross profit on installment sales..........................	36,500		36,500	
Income summary..............		36,500		36,500

(18) December 31, 1972. Year-end closing for other nominal accounts.

Sales (regular).....................	220,000		220,000	
Cost of sales (regular)..........		130,000		130,000
Estimated loss on doubtful accounts....................		1,100		1,100
Selling expenses..............		65,000		65,000
Income summary..............		23,900		23,900
Income summary..................	60,400		60,400	
Retained earnings..............		60,400		60,400

merchandise on the installment basis often extend over many periods of business operations, however, calculations of net income under the conventional accrual method and the installment sales method will eventually tend to converge.

Financial Statement Presentation

Transactions involving installment sales introduce several problems in respect to informative reporting. As with other special types of transactions, adequacy of disclosure is a compelling consideration. Significantly, however, informative reporting may be accomplished in a number of ways. The preferable statement format will depend upon the characteristics of each particular situation. For this reason, various alternative approaches are illustrated in the following pages using the data contained in Illustration 24–3.

Income Statement. With respect to the income statement, the degree of detail to be reported frequently will vary, depending upon the magnitude of installment sales revenues in relation to total sales. For example, if installment sales are relatively insignificant in amount, the type of presentation in Illustration 24–4 may be appropriate.

Illustration 24–4

THE XY CORPORATION

Income Statement

For Year Ended December 31, 1972

(Installment Sales Are Not Significant in Amount)

Sales..	$220,000
Cost of goods sold...........................	130,000
Gross profit.................................	$ 90,000
Realized gross profit on installment sales...	36,500
Total gross profit...........................	$126,500
Expenses....................................	66,100
Net Income.................................	$ 60,400

Alternatively, should installment sales represent a material segment of the total revenues of a business enterprise, additional detail may be required for a full and informative disclosure. In this event, the accountant may elect one of two basic approaches, viz.:

1. The presentation of details concerning installment transactions may be integrated, but separately identified, in the income statement, supported as necessary with appropriate footnotes (see Illustration 24–5).
2. The presentation of details concerning installment transactions may be principally disclosed in one or more separate schedules which support a summarized income statement (see Illustrations 24–6 and 24–7).

Manifestly, many other variants on these illustrative statement forms are available.

Balance Sheet. With respect to balance sheet presentation, installment accounts receivable from the sale of merchandise are usually classified as current assets and shown as follows:

ASSETS

Current Assets:		
Notes receivable.........................	$25,000	
Accounts receivable......................	60,000	
	$85,000	
Less: Allowance for doubtful accounts.....	5,000	$ 80,000
Installment accounts receivable:		
From 1971 sales.........................	$50,000	
From 1972 sales.........................	90,000	140,000

Illustration 24–5

THE XY CORPORATION
Income Statement
For Year Ended December 31, 1972
(Installment Sales Are Significant in Amount)

		Total	Sales Regular	Installment
Sales		$330,000	$220,000	$110,000
Cost of goods sold:				
Merchandise inventory January 1	$ 20,000			
Purchases	189,900			
	$209,900			
Merchandise inventory, December 31	15,000			
Total		194,900	130,000	64,900
Accrual-basis gross profit on 1972 sales		$135,100	$ 90,000	$ 45,100
Less: Gross profit to be deferred on 1972 installment sales		24,600		24,600
		$110,500		$ 20,500
Add: Realized gross profit in 1972 on installment sales of prior year—1971		16,000		16,000
Total gross profit realized in 1972 on installment sales (Note 1)				$ 36,500
Total realized gross profit		$126,500		
Expenses (detailed)		66,100		
Net Income		$ 60,400		

Note 1: Approximately one third of the sales of the XY Corporation are represented by installment sales, for which the average collection period is three years. Gross profit on these sales is deferred until realized (or confirmed) through collection of receivable balances. This procedure is used for both financial accounting and income tax purposes.

Illustration 24–6

THE XY CORPORATION
Income Statement
For Year Ended December 31, 1972
(Installment Sales Are Significant in Amount)

Sales		$220,000
Cost of goods sold:		
Merchandise inventory, January 1, 1972	$ 20,000	
Purchases	189,900	
	$209,900	
Less: Shipment of merchandise on installment basis—1972 (Schedule 1)	64,900	
	$145,000	
Less: Merchandise inventory, December 31, 1972	15,000	130,000
Gross profit on regular sales		$ 90,000
Add: Realized gross profit on installment sales (Schedule 1)		36,500
Total gross profit		$126,500
Expenses (detailed)		66,100
Net Income		$ 60,400

Illustration 24–7

SCHEDULE 1
THE XY CORPORATION
Calculation of Realized Gross Profit on Installment Sales
For Year Ended December 31, 1972

Realized gross profit on 1972 installment sales:

Installment sales—1972	$110,000	
Cost of installment sales—1972	64,900	
Gross profit on installment sales—1972 (41% of sales)	$ 45,100	
Collections on 1972 installment sales	$ 50,000	
Rate of gross profit in 1972	41%	
Gross profit realized in 1972 on 1972 sales		$20,500
Realized gross profit on 1971 installment sales:		
Collections on 1971 installment sales in 1972	$ 40,000	
Rate of gross profit in 1971	40%	
Gross profit realized in 1972 on 1971 sales		16,000
Total gross profit realized in 1972 (Note 1)		$36,500

Note 1: Gross profit on installment sales is regarded as realized in the accounting period in which installment accounts receivable are collected.

This treatment accords with the accepted notion of current assets as consisting of "cash and other assets or resources commonly identified as those which are reasonably expected to be realized in cash or sold or consumed during the normal operating cycle of the business."[2] Installment transactions generate an operating cycle, at least for one segment of the enterprise's operations, which by definition includes the *collection* of these accounts. On the other hand, it would be difficult to justify this classification for an installment contract, or contracts, resulting from a transaction which is unrelated to normal operations (e.g., the infrequent sale of land held either for expansion or investment); consequently, receivable balances which derive from such a source should be reported in the "investments" or the "other assets" section of the balance sheet.

The balance of Deferred Gross Profit on Installment Sales at the end of an accounting period is frequently classified as a current liability and reported as follows:

LIABILITIES

Current Liabilities:
  Deferred revenues:
    Deferred gross profit on installment sales—
      1971 .... $28,000
    Deferred gross profit on installment sales—
      1972 .... 42,000 $70,000

Differences of opinion exist, however, concerning the most desirable balance sheet classification of this account. At least six different viewpoints can be identified:

[2] American Institute of Certified Public Accountants, *Accounting Research and Terminology Bulletins, Final Edition* (New York, 1961), p. 20.

1. Deferred gross profit on installment sales should be reported as a current liability, although identified separately as a deferred revenue, as illustrated on page 826. This approach has been accorded the widest acceptance because of its simplicity and because it prudently compromises other views with respect to the several issues involved.

2. The balance of deferred gross profit should be reported in the enumeration of other current liability items without separate subclassification. A common argument often made against this classification is that there is no commitment, now or in the future, for the use of the firm's resources.

3. Such balances should be identified in a separate classification between liabilities and stockholders' equity. This position has gained some measure of approval, although it patently begs the question of a precise classification within the enumeration of conventional equity interests.

4. Deferred gross profit is a valuation adjustment of the related Installment Accounts Receivable. Although this produces a conservative valuation of the receivable, the amount of deferred gross profit has no inherent relationship with the estimated collectible value of the accounts receivable. The authors therefore reject this position.

5. Deferred gross profit should be reported as a separate designation in the stockholders' equity section of the balance sheet. The strength of this position is to be found in the argument that installment sales have actually given rise to profits in the same manner as have regular sales; realization of profits in both cases is contingent upon the receivables collection. The varying time periods involved in the collection process are recognized in the form of different classes of "accumulated" earnings. Notwithstanding these arguments, this classification has gained very little following to date.

6. Such balances consist essentially of three basic elements which should be classified as follows:

    a) That portion of the deferred gross profit that is equivalent to the estimated income tax liability to be eventually paid when the sales are reported as realized revenue should be reported as an estimated current liability.

    b) That portion of the deferred gross profit estimated as being necessary to offset collection expenses and possible bad debt and repossession losses should be reported on the balance sheet as a deduction from installment accounts receivable.

    c) The residual balance of deferred gross profit represents net income associated with installment sales and should be reported as net income from installment sales, restricted as to dividend availability, in the retained earnings statement.

As collections progress, these elements must be appropriately reclassified. Although this proposal synthesizes the best features of (2), (4), and (5) above, it essentially represents a commitment to a new concept of income determination, controverting the notion of profit deferral.

Additionally, it generates little practical support because of the difficult problem of allocating deferred gross profit as between the three basic elements.

Defaults and Repossessions

If one who has purchased goods on an installment contract defaults in any of the scheduled payments, the vendor may repossess or reclaim the units sold to satisfy the residual indebtedness. Normally, the goods repossessed are subsequently resold, either in their reclaimed condition or after costs have been incurred to restore them to a more marketable state. Default and repossession requires that the vendor (1) record the repossessed item in an appropriate inventory account at its market value at date of repossession; (2) eliminate, or remove, the uncollected receivable balance of the defaulted account; (3) write off the amount of deferred gross profit implicit in the above receivable balance; and (4) enter the resulting gain or loss on repossession.

Assume the following data in respect to a default and concurrent repossession on April 15, 1971:

Installment accounts receivable—1969...............	$1,000
Deferred gross profit on installment sales—1969 (gross profit rate 30 percent of selling price)........	300
Estimated market value of item repossessed in its reclaimed condition............................	600

The entry for repossession on April 15, 1971, is made as follows:

Inventory of repossessed merchandise.........................	600	
Deferred gross profit on installment sales—1969................	300	
Loss on defaults (repossessions).............................	100	
Installment accounts receivable—1969.....................		1,000

Costs of restoration which relate to repossessed merchandise should be accounted for as a cost increment to the Inventory of Repossessed Merchandise account; resale of repossessed merchandise should be accounted for in the conventional manner for regular or installment sales transactions.

With respect to the valuation of repossessed merchandise (or other property), the above entry assumes that *fair market value* in present condition at date of repossession is appropriate. This value is the estimated cash purchase price of the repossessed units as established in the local used-goods, or wholesale, market. Subsequent calculations of net income for the used-goods department of the business are then relatively reliable indexes of operating efficiency. Arguments are also made for several other valuation bases:

1. The value of repossessed property should be the *book value* of the unliquidated indebtedness, i.e., the uncollected balance of the relevant installment account receivable reduced by the amount of deferred gross profit which relates thereto. Clearly, the actual value of repossessed

goods may have little relationship to the book value of the indebtedness. The seller is compelled to reclaim the merchandise to minimize a potential loss; the magnitude of that loss should be determined preferably by a comparison of the used-goods replacement cost of the item repossessed and the book value of the indebtedness. Accordingly, the residual net book value of uncollected receivables has gained comparatively little support as a valuation basis for repossessed merchandise.

2. No value should be assigned to the repossessed asset; rather, a loss at date of repossession should be recognized in the amount of the book value of the indebtedness. Upon resale of the repossessed item, the total sales price is regarded as revenue. This treatment, which fails to ascribe *any* value to repossessed property, can be justified only on the grounds of conservatism; consequently, it is seldom used in accounting practice.

3. The value of repossessed property should be that amount which will allow the recognition of a "normal profit" on its resale. This approach is deficient in several important respects. Primarily, it violates the cost principle in respect to asset valuation and accordingly incorrectly measures the loss on repossession; it effectively capitalizes profits (at an arbitrary rate) which are yet to be realized; and it invokes the practical problem of estimating future costs to repair, to resell, and, conceivably, to repossess again.

As a consequence of the above considerations, the use of the used-goods replacement cost value as an inventory valuation basis for repossessed goods is generally subscribed to by most accountants.

The above entry for the repossession of goods on defaulted contracts assumes a relatively simple circumstance with complete knowledge of all relevant data. In the case of a one-time sale of realty, this condition is often satisfied. However, in regard to the sale of merchandise in the normal course of business, more careful consideration should be given to the timing of the repossession. If the default and repossession occur in an accounting period subsequent to the period of sale, the applicable gross profit rate is established, and a certain proportion of the total gross profit has been previously recognized in the accounts. Consequently, the repossession entry may be recorded as illustrated earlier, wherein the debit to Deferred Gross Profit is based upon the amount of unrealized gross profit implicit in the uncollectible balance; this requires a subsequent recognition, in the normal period-end closing process, of realized gross profit on collections during the current year prior to the default. Alternatively, the debit to Deferred Gross Profit may be based upon the balance of the receivable at the beginning of the period. This type of entry denies the existence of realized gross profit on current period collections prior to the default, and reduces the repossession loss by the same amount. In effect, this represents a movement in the direction of the concept of total cost recovery prior to the recognition of any gross profit; it approximates the *ex post facto* analysis of "bad debt" losses as the sum of unrecovered cost— calculated as the difference between merchandise cost and total collections on account—plus previously recognized gross profit. However, since the method is retroactively applied only to the beginning of the period, the measurement of repossession loss still includes a composite of the two factors.

If the repossession of merchandise occurs in the period of sale, the gross profit rate (a composite) is not yet determinable. Therefore, recording the repossession must necessarily be accomplished in two steps. On the date of repossession, one may conceive of the original transaction as essentially abrogated and reverse the original entry of sale; to the extent of prior collections on the account, a value is established in a special nominal account—Revenue from Defaulting Customers. Additionally, the repossessed merchandise is recorded in an appropriate account, with a corresponding credit to Loss on Repossessions. When the average gross profit rate for the period is established, the cost of installment sales which are currently in default is closed to the Loss on Repossessions account. If these two nominal accounts are subsequently combined, there results a correct measure of the unrecovered cost. Alternatively, only the repossession may be recorded on the date of default, with a credit to Loss on Repossessions. After the gross profit rate is established at the end of the period, the receivable and the associated deferred gross profit may be written off to Loss on Repossessions, and gross profit realized on collections received prior to default. In essence, these methods reflect the same two basic concepts which are applicable to repossessions in accounting periods subsequent to the period of sale.

These entries are modified to a relatively minor extent depending upon the inventory procedures (perpetual or periodic) that are followed. It is usually not feasible to calculate a gross profit rate prior to the end of the accounting period, notwithstanding perpetual inventory records, as a composite rate for the period is often desirable. Therefore, the previously illustrated differences between these two methods remain applicable. Apropos of repossessed merchandise, it is usual to record the appropriate value(s) in an inventory account (Repossessed Merchandise Inventory) under a perpetual inventory system, and in a nominal account (Repossessed Goods), analogous to Purchases, where periodic inventory procedures prevail.

The balance in the Repossessed Merchandise Inventory account is usually reported on the balance sheet as a current asset; gain or loss on repossessions is reported variously in the income statement either as an adjustment to realized gross profit on installment sales, as a separately identified item of gain or loss, or as an addition to, or deduction from, the loss on doubtful accounts. Alternatively, if a provision has been previously made for losses on doubtful accounts which included an allowance for installment sales, the loss on repossessions may be charged to Allowance for Doubtful Accounts (regular and installment sales).

QUESTIONS

1. Distinguish between installment sales and regular credit sales. Do the differences between these types of credit arrangement generate different bases for the recognition of gross profit?

2. Why do credit losses on installment sales transactions tend to be larger than those from other forms of credit sales?

3. What underlying process is involved in the "installment sales method" of revenue recognition?

4. What special problem do bad debt losses present with respect to installment sales? How is this difficulty resolved under the "installment sales method"?

5. List and briefly describe three interest plans frequently referred to in installment sales contracts.

6. To what extent are variations in the form and content of income statements introduced by the presence of installment sales which are material in amount?

7. List several different balance sheet classifications for "Deferred Gross Profit on Installment Sales." Which classification is most widely accepted?

8. What steps must a vendor take to record a default and repossession of goods which have been sold on an installment basis?

9. What elections are available to the accountant in recording the valuation of repossessed merchandise? Which method is most frequently used?

10. Outline the procedural sequence for recording the repossession of merchandise *in the period of sale*. In periods *subsequent to* the period of sale.

PROBLEMS

Problem 24–1

The Cox Realty Company sold a plot of real estate for $80,000 designated as the Baker Addition. The property originally cost $25,000, and $35,000 was subsequently spent for grading, drainage, and other similar costs. Expenses incident to sale were $6,000. The terms of the sale were: 20 percent down payment and a note specifying five annual payments (at year-end) including a constant reduction in principal *and* 6 percent interest per annum on the unpaid balance at the start of each year.

Required:

(i) Prepare a schedule of payments.

(ii) Prepare journal entries through the second installment assuming the installment sales method is used.

(iii) Indicate how the amounts relating to the second period should be reported on the income statement and balance sheet.

Problem 24–2

The Oyster Bay Sales Company balance sheet on January 1, 1971, reported the following:

Cash......................	$ 20,000	Accounts payable............	$ 30,000
Merchandise inventory.......	120,000	Deferred gross profit on install-	
Accounts receivable		ment sales—1969...........	12,000
(regular).................	11,000	Deferred gross profit on install-	
Allowance for doubtful ac-		ment sales—1970...........	29,400
counts...................	[1,000]	Capital stock................	203,000
Installment accounts receivable		Retained earnings............	75,600
—1969....................	30,000		
Installment accounts receivable			
—1970....................	70,000		
Various assets...............	100,000		
	$350,000		$350,000

Transactions during 1971 were (summarized):

Sales:
Regular (on credit)........................	$300,000
Installment..............................	100,000
Purchases of merchandise (cash)..............	238,000
Ending inventory (periodic basis)..............	130,000
Cost of installment sales....................	57,000
Selling expenses............................	105,000
Allowance for doubtful accounts..............	¼ of 1% of regular sales

Collections on installment receivables:
1969 accounts............................	$ 20,000
1970 accounts............................	40,000
1971 accounts............................	55,000
Regular accounts.........................	280,000

Required:

(i)   Compute gross profit rates for 1969, 1970, and 1971.
(ii) Prepare journal entries for 1971, including adjusting and closing entries at December 31.
(iii) Prepare an income statement for 1971.
(iv) Prepare a balance sheet as of December 31, 1971.

Problem 24–3

On January 2, 1971, the ABC Company purchased display equipment under the following terms: $2,000 to be paid upon installation, plus five annual payments of $1,000, the first payment to be made on December 31, 1971. Title to the display equipment was retained by the seller until the final payment was made. It is estimated that the display equipment will be used for 10 years with no residual value.

This same display equipment was available at a cash price of $6,600.

Ignore income tax aspects of the transaction.

Required:

Prepare all accounting entries relating to the display equipment as of January 2 and December 31, 1971, and as of December 31, 1972. For each entry, give your supporting reasons.

(AICPA adapted)

Problem 24–4

The following is the preclosing trial balance of the Gamma Company on December 31, 1971:

Cash	$100,000	
Installment accounts receivable—1970	40,000	
Installment accounts receivable—1971	60,000	
Installment sales		$100,000
Cost of installment sales	70,000	
Deferred gross profit—1970		30,000
Capital stock		80,000
Retained earnings		60,000
	$270,000	$270,000

Required:

(i) Prepare journal entries on December 31, 1971, to record the gross profit realized in 1971 and complete the closing of the accounts. The rate of gross profit on sales in 1970 was 25 percent.

(ii) On February 10, 1972, a customer defaults on his payments and the merchandise is repossessed. Prepare the journal entry for the repossession given the following information:

Original sale	$500
Date of sale	July, 1970
Collections to date	$300
Estimated market value of repossessed	
goods	$100

Problem 24–5

On October 1, 1971, the Television Company sold a set costing $400 to Jones for $600. Jones made a down payment of $150 and agreed to pay $25 the first of each month for 18 months thereafter.

The first two installments due on November 1 and December 1, 1971, were paid. In 1972, five payments were made by Jones, who then defaulted on the balance of his payments. The set was repossessed on November 1, 1972. The company closes its books on December 31.

Required:

(i) Give three different amounts that might be shown as realized gross profit for 1971 and indicate the circumstances under which each of these amounts would be acceptable.

(ii) Assuming that the repossessed television set has a wholesale value of $50 and a retail value of $75, prepare a journal entry to record the repossession under the "installment method" of accounting. Explain fully the reasoning applicable to your entry.

(AICPA adapted)

Problem 24–6

On April 1, 1971, the Kiley Department Store sold an item of furniture which cost $160, for $280. A down payment of $30 was made with the provision that additional payments of $25 be made monthly thereafter. Interest was to be charged the customer at a monthly rate of 1 percent on the unpaid contract balance; the monthly remittance was to apply first to the accrued interest and the balance to the principal.

After completing four monthly payments, the customer defaulted and the furniture was reclaimed; the replacement value of the furniture (used) was estimated to be $75.

The Kiley Department Store maintains a perpetual inventory with respect to major appliances and furniture.

Required:

Make all journal entries for the installment sale, from April 1, 1971, through September 1, 1971.

Problem 24–7

Pitts-Marvel Sales Corporation sells goods and accounts for such sales on the installment basis. At the end of each year it takes up gross profit on the basis of the year(s) of collection rather than the year of sale; accordingly, each collection consists of cost and gross profit elements.

The balances of the control accounts for Installment Accounts Receivable at the beginning and end of 1972 were:

	January 1, 1972	December 31, 1972
Installment accounts receivable—1970......	$ 24,020	–0–
Installment accounts receivable—1971......	344,460	$ 67,440
Installment accounts receivable—1972......		410,090

As collections are made, the company debits Cash and credits Installment Accounts Receivable. During 1972, upon default in payment by customers, the company repossessed merchandise having an estimated wholesale value of $1,400. The sales had been made in 1971 for $5,400, and $3,200 had been collected prior to default. The company recorded the default and repossession by a debit to Inventory of Repossessed Merchandise and a credit to Installment Accounts Receivable—1971 for the uncollected receivable balance.

The company's sales and cost of sales for the three years involved are summarized below:

	1970	1971	1972
Net sales...................	$380,000	$432,000	$602,000
Cost of sales...............	247,000	285,120	379,260

Required:

(i) Prepare journal entries to record at December 31, 1972, the recognition of profits and any other adjustments arising from the above data. Give complete explanations in support of your entries.

(ii) Give one acceptable alternate method of handling the repossession and discuss the relative merits of it as compared to the method you used in (i).

(AICPA adapted)

Problem 24–8

The Jones Company sells furniture on the installment plan. For its federal income tax returns, it reports its profit from sales on the "installment basis." For its financial reports, it considers the entire profit to be earned in the year of sale.

Required:

(i) Discuss the relative merits of the two methods of reporting income.
(ii) Explain the installment basis as used for income tax purposes.
(iii) Discuss the effects of the use of these two bases by the Jones Company on the significance of its reported annual net income.

(AICPA adapted)

Problem 24–9

A specialty appliance distributor selling on the installment basis was organized as a retail sales outlet on January 1, 1968. Reorganization was begun, however, after three and one-half years operations, on July 1, 1971. Operating data for this interim period was summarized following:

Year	Sales	Cost of Sales	Expenses*
1968	$ 60,000	$36,000	$15,000
1969	100,000	61,000	16,000
1970	120,000	75,600	17,500
1971	70,000	32,900	14,000

* Excludes gains or losses from defaulted accounts.

Year of Sale	Collections				Accounts Defaulted		
	1968	1969	1970	1971	1969	1970	1971
1968	$40,000	$19,000			$1,000		
1969		80,000	$ 18,000			$2,000	
1970			100,000	$15,000			$5,000
1971				68,000			2,000

Repossessed merchandise is assumed to have no value.

Required:

Prepare an analysis of net income for each year (or fractional year) contrasting the differences when—

(i) Net income is computed using the installment method of accounting for sales revenue.

(ii)   Net income is computed on the assumption that revenue is recognized at the time of sale, and bad debts are charged to expense as they occur.

Problem 24–10

The Jones Appliance Store started business on January 1, 1970. Separate accounts were set up for installment and cash sales, but no perpetual inventory record was maintained. On the installment sales, a down payment of one third was required, with the balance payable in 18 equal monthly installments. A Deferred Gross Profit account was created at each year-end in respect to the current year's installment sales. When contracts were defaulted, the unpaid balances were charged to Bad Debt Expense, and sales of repossessed merchandise were credited to this account. The expense account was adjusted at the year-end to reflect the actual loss.

A summary of the transactions of the Jones Appliance Store for 1970 and 1971 follows:

	1970	1971
Sales:		
New merchandise for cash......................	$ 21,348	$ 29,180
New merchandise on installment (including one-third		
cash down payment)........................	188,652	265,320
Sales of repossessed merchandise.................	600	700
Purchases....................................	154,000	173,585
Physical inventories at December 31:		
New merchandise at cost......................	36,400	48,010
Repossessions at realizable (market) value.........	150	160
Unpaid balances of installment contracts defaulted:		
1970 sales..................................	2,865	3,725
1971 sales..................................		3,010
Cash collections on installment contracts, exclusive of		
down payments:		
1970 sales..................................	42,943	61,385
1971 sales..................................		55,960

Required:

(i)   Compute the gross profit rates for the years 1970 and 1971.
(ii)   In T-account form, reproduce the ledger accounts for installment accounts receivable.
(iii)   Calculate the net loss on defaulted accounts for the year 1970; it is assumed that realizable value is an appropriate value basis for repossessed merchandise.
(iv)   Prepare a schedule showing the realized gross profit for the year 1971 that would be reported on the income statement.

(AICPA adapted)

Problem 24–11

The Installment Jewelry Company has been in business for five years but has never had an audit of its financial statements. Engaged to make an audit for 1971, you find that the company's balance sheet carries no allowance for doubtful accounts, doubtful accounts having been expensed as written off and recoveries credited to income as collected. The company's policy is to write off at December 31 of each year those accounts on which no collections have been received for three months. The installment contracts generally are for two years.

Upon your recommendation the company agrees to revise its accounts for 1971 to give effect to doubtful account treatment on the "estimated allowance" basis. The allowance is to be based on a percentage of sales which is derived from the experience of prior years.

Statistics for the past five years are as follows:

	Credit Sales	Accounts Written Off and Year of Sale			Recoveries and Year of Sale
1967	$100,000	(1967) $ 550			
1968	250,000	(1967) 1,500	(1968) $1,000		(1967) $100
1969	300,000	(1967) 500	(1968) 4,000	(1969) $1,300	(1968) 400
1970	325,000	(1968) 1,200	(1969) 4,500	(1970) 1,500	(1969) 500
1971	275,000	(1969) 2,700	(1970) 5,000	(1971) 1,400	(1970) 600

Accounts receivable at December 31, 1971, were as follows:

1970 sales......................	$ 15,000
1971 sales......................	135,000
	$150,000

Required:

Prepare the adjusting journal entry or entries as of December 31, 1971, with appropriate explanations to set up the allowance for Doubtful Accounts.

(AICPA adapted)

Problem 24–12

The Johnson Appliance Company started business on January 1, 1971. Separate accounts were established for installment and cash sales, but no perpetual inventory record was maintained.

On installment sales, the price was 106 percent of the cash sale price. A standard installment contract was used whereby a down payment of one fourth of the installment price was required, with the balance payable in 15 equal monthly installments. (The interest charge per month is 1 percent of the unpaid cash sale price equivalent at each installment.)

Installments receivable and installment sales were recorded at the contract price. When contracts were defaulted, the unpaid balances were charged to bad debt expense. Sales of default merchandise were credited to bad debt expense.

Sales:

Cash sales..	$126,000
Installment sales................................	265,000
Repossessed sales...............................	230
Inventory, January 1, 1971:	
Merchandise inventory.........................	58,060
Purchases, 1971:	
New merchandise...............................	209,300
Inventories, physical, December 31, 1971:	
New merchandise...............................	33,300
Repossessed inventory.........................	180
Cash collections on Installment Contracts, 1971:	
Down payments................................	66,250
Subsequent installments........................	79,341

(Average six monthly installments on all contracts except on defaulted contracts)

Five contracts totaling $1,060 were defaulted, in each case after three monthly installments were paid.

Interest should be recognized in the period earned.

Required:

(i) A computation of the gross profit rate for 1971.

(ii) A schedule showing, by payment for the first seven months: the cash sale price equivalent, the contract balance, the amount of interest earned, and the cash collected on a $1,060 installment sale contract.

(iii) A computation of the net gain or loss on defaulted contracts during 1971.

(iv) A computation of the realized gross profit for 1971.

(AICPA adapted)

analysis, it is obvious that the amount accumulated at the end
ods (S) will be

$$S = \$1(1.02)^4 \, ,$$

rally, the amount of \$1 after n periods at i rate of interest
given by the formula

$$S = \$1(1 + i)^n \, .$$

t of the general formula is independent of the fact that only
. If a larger amount, $\$K$, were invested, the amount to
rs would accumulate after n periods at i rate of interest

$$S = \$K(1 + i)^n \, .$$

putational difficulty relates to the determination of
gly, tables are available which give the *amount of \$1*
ations of interest periods and interest rates (see page
consider the following. To what amount will \$5,000
years at 4 percent annual interest, compounded semi-
n is easily determined as follows:

$$
\begin{aligned}
S &= \$5,000(1.02)^{20} \\
&= \$5,000(1.48594740) \\
&= \$7,429.74 \, .
\end{aligned}
$$

1 to be received, or delivered, a given number of
lated directly to the concept of the amount of \$1.
be received two years in the future, its present
derives from the fact that some smaller amount,
e invested currently such that it will accumulate
ears. Assuming the current interest rate is 4
nnually, the time-scale analysis of this concept

Interest Periods
(2 Percent Interest per Period)

example and the previous one is evident.
f an unknown current investment of P is
he previous formula, the present value, P,

$$P(1.02)^4 \, ,$$
$$\$1(1.02)^{-4} \, ,$$

APPENDIXES

Appendix 1

Mathematical

COMPOUND INTEREST

The concepts and underlying assum
measure of the cost of using, or forego
in Chapter 1. This brief review of
directed at the four basic forms that
and the application of standard tabl

Amount of $1

If $1 were invested currently
one may ask to what amount this
number of interest periods. The
periods at i rate of interest per

For example, if $1 were i
pounded semiannually, the a
volves four periods of comp
nature of the accumulation
the aid of a time-scale ana

$1
|——————|—
0   1

I
(2 Perce

If $1 is invested at th
it will be increased b
it will have accumu
be directly calcula

i.e., $1 increase
percent interes
period, viz.,

were $(1.02)^{-4}$ measures the present value of $1 to be received, or de-livered, four periods in the future, discounted at 2 percent per period. In fact, the present value of $1 is the reciprocal of the amount of $1 for the same number of periods at the same rate of interest. Similarly, the present value (P) of some larger amount, $$K$, may be computed as follows:

$$P = \$K(1 + i)^{-n} .$$

Again, numeric tables for the present value of $1, $(1 + i)^{-n}$, are readily available (see page 847). For example, if $5,000 is to be received 10 years in the future and the current annual interest rate is 4 percent, com-pounded semiannually, the present value of this future receipt is calculated:

$$P = \$5,000(1.02)^{-20}$$
$$= \$5,000(0.67297133)$$
$$= \$3,364.86 .$$

Amount of Annuity of $1

An *annuity* is a series of equal payments, or rents, which are invested, or received, at the end of each period for a given number of interest periods. In the case of an annuity which represents an investment, one may be interested in the amount to which the rents will accumulate at a given rate of interest. If the amount of each of four rents is $1 and the rate of interest each period is 2 percent, the procedure for calculating the *amount of an annuity of $1* may be reflected on a time scale as follows:

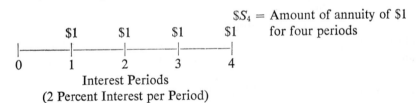

$$S_4$$ = Amount of annuity of $1 for four periods

It is manifest that the amount of an annuity of $1 is merely the summation of the amount of $1 for each individual rent. In this case, the amount of the four-period annuity, at 2 percent interest per period, is

$$S_{\overline{4}|} = \$1(1.02)^3 + \$1(1.02)^2 + \$1(1.02)^1 + \$1$$
$$= s_{\overline{4}|2\%},$$

where $s_{\overline{4}|2\%}$ is a symbolic abbreviation of the formula which results from an algebraic manipulation of the first equation. Tables for the amount of an annuity of $1 for n periods at i percent, denoted $s_{\overline{n}|i\%}$, are available (see page 848). As before, if rents are given for some arbitrary amount, $$K$, the amount of this annuity (S_n) may be calculated as follows:

$$S_n = \$K(s_{\overline{n}|i\%}) .$$

For example, if $10,000 is invested each year for 10 years at 4 percent, compounded annually, the amount of the annuity, S_{10}, is

$$S_{10} = \$10,000(s_{\overline{10}|\,4\%})$$
$$= \$10,000(12.0061071)$$
$$= \$120,061.07 .$$

Present Value of Annuity of $1

If the individual rents represent future inflows, it may be useful to measure the present value of these receipts. For example, if rents of $1 are to be received at the end of each of four periods and the effective rate of interest is 2 percent per period, the process of determining the *present value of annuity of $1* is implicit in the time-scale representation following:

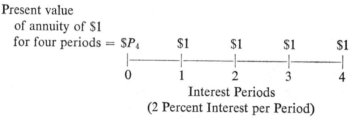

Present value
of annuity of $1
for four periods = P_4 $1 $1 $1 $1

0   1   2   3   4

Interest Periods
(2 Percent Interest per Period)

In a manner analogous to the previous computation (the amount of an annuity), the present value of this annuity is the summation of the present values of each individual rent. In this case,

$$P_4 = \$1(1.02)^{-1} + \$1(1.02)^{-2} + \$1(1.02)^{-3} + \$1(1.02)^{-4}$$
$$= a_{\overline{4}|2\%},$$

where $a_{\overline{4}|2\%}$ is a symbolic abbreviation of the formula resulting from an algebraic simplification of the first equation. Tables for the present value of an annuity of $1 for n periods at i percent, denoted $a_{\overline{n}|i\%}$, are also available (see page 849). If the rents of some arbitrary amount are given, K, the present value of this annuity (P_n) is calculated

$$P_n = \$K(a_{\overline{n}|i\%}) .$$

For example, if $10,000 is to be received at the end of each of 10 years and the effective interest rate is 4 percent, compounded annually, the present value of this annuity, P_{10}, is

$$P_{10} = \$10,000(a_{\overline{10}|\,4\%})$$
$$= \$10,000(8.1108958)$$
$$= \$81,108.96 .$$

Linear Interpolation to Approximate Interest Rates

If the interest rate that is relevant to a problem is not included in a table but is interposed between two interest rates which are included therein, it is possible to *approximate* the correct value by *linear interpolation*. For example, one may approximate the present value of $1 for 10 periods at 2½ percent in the following manner:

Present value of \$1 for 10 periods at 2%	= 0.82034830
Present value of \$1 for 10 periods at 3%	= 0.74409391
Difference attributable to 1%	= 0.07625439
Approximation to $\frac{1}{2}$% difference	
(0.07625439 ÷ 2)	= 0.038127195
Estimate of present value of \$1 for 10 periods	
at $2\frac{1}{2}$% = 0.74409391 + 0.038127195	= 0.782221105

The error introduced by this estimating process results from the assumption that the difference between 2 percent and 3 percent is uniformly allocable over the 1 percent difference. This form of interpolation, however, is usually satisfactory for most applications.

MATRICES

The Matrix Structure

A matrix is a rectangular array of elements—numbers, functions, etc. —which can be used to describe problems involving *relations* between these elements. Although operations such as addition and multiplication can be performed on matrices, the matrix itself is not evaluated quantitatively. A matrix A may be represented

$$A = \begin{bmatrix} a_{11} \, a_{12} \cdots a_{1n} \\ a_{21} \, a_{22} \cdots a_{2n} \\ \cdots \cdots \\ a_{m1} \, a_{m2} \cdots a_{mn} \end{bmatrix}.$$

In the above expression, the first subscript for a given element indicates the *row* in which it appears and the second subscript denotes the *column*. Such a matrix with m rows and n columns is normally referred to as an $m \times n$ *matrix*, or a matrix of *order* (m, n).

Matrix Operations

Once the elements are ordered, it is then appropriate to refer to *operations* on the matrix. For example, a matrix *sum* may be formed by adding corresponding elements of matrices of the same order; also it is appropriate to multiply a given matrix by a scalar or by another matrix. In scalar multiplication, each element of the matrix is multiplied by a real number. Where one matrix is to be multiplied by a second matrix, however, multiplication is possible only where the matrices are conformable for multiplication, i.e., where the number of columns in the first matrix is equal to the number of rows in the second. Given the 2×3 matrix A and the 3×2 matrix B, the matrix product AB, a 2×2 matrix is given following:

$$AB = \begin{bmatrix} a_{11} \, a_{12} \, a_{13} \\ a_{21} \, a_{22} \, a_{23} \end{bmatrix} \begin{bmatrix} b_{11} \, b_{12} \\ b_{21} \, b_{22} \\ b_{31} \, b_{32} \end{bmatrix}$$

Table A
(Amount of 1): $(1 + i)^n$

Period	1-1/2%	2%	2-1/2%	3%	3-1/2%	4%	5%	6%	8%
0	1.	1.	1.	1.	1.	1.	1.	1.	1.
1	1.015	1.02	1.025	1.03	1.035	1.04	1.05	1.06	1.08
2	1.0302 25	1.0404	1.0506 25	1.0609	1.0712 25	1.0816	1.1025	1.1236	1.1664
3	1.0456 7838	1.0612 08	1.0768 9063	1.0927 27	1.1087 1788	1.1248 64	1.1576 25	1.1910 16	1.2597 12
4	1.0613 6355	1.0824 3216	1.1038 1289	1.1255 0881	1.1475 2300	1.1698 5856	1.2155 0625	1.2624 7696	1.3604 8896
5	1.0772 8400	1.1040 8080	1.1314 0821	1.1592 7407	1.1876 8631	1.2166 5290	1.2762 8156	1.3382 2558	1.4693 2808
6	1.0934 4326	1.1261 6242	1.1596 9342	1.1940 5230	1.2292 5533	1.2653 1902	1.3400 9564	1.4185 1911	1.5868 7432
7	1.1098 4491	1.1486 8567	1.1886 8575	1.2298 7387	1.2722 7926	1.3159 3178	1.4071 0042	1.5036 3026	1.7138 2427
8	1.1264 9259	1.1716 5938	1.2184 0290	1.2667 7008	1.3168 0904	1.3685 6905	1.4774 5544	1.5938 4807	1.8509 3021
9	1.1433 8998	1.1950 9257	1.2488 6297	1.3047 7318	1.3628 9735	1.4233 1181	1.5513 2822	1.6894 7896	1.9990 0463
10	1.1605 4083	1.2189 9442	1.2800 8454	1.3439 1638	1.4105 9876	1.4802 4428	1.6288 9463	1.7908 4770	2.1589 2500
11	1.1779 4894	1.2433 7431	1.3120 8666	1.3842 3387	1.4599 6972	1.5394 5406	1.7103 3936	1.8982 9856	2.3316 3900
12	1.1956 1817	1.2682 4179	1.3448 8882	1.4257 6089	1.5110 6866	1.6010 3222	1.7958 5633	2.0121 9647	2.5181 7012
13	1.2135 5244	1.2936 0663	1.3785 1104	1.4685 3371	1.5639 5606	1.6650 7351	1.8856 4914	2.1329 2826	2.7196 2373
14	1.2317 5573	1.3194 7876	1.4129 7382	1.5125 8972	1.6186 9452	1.7316 7645	1.9799 3160	2.2609 0396	2.9371 9362
15	1.2502 3207	1.3458 6834	1.4482 9817	1.5579 6742	1.6753 4883	1.8009 4351	2.0789 2818	2.3965 5819	3.1721 6911
16	1.2689 8555	1.3727 8571	1.4845 0562	1.6047 0644	1.7339 8604	1.8729 8125	2.1828 7459	2.5403 5168	3.4259 4264
17	1.2880 2033	1.4002 4142	1.5216 1826	1.6528 4763	1.7946 7555	1.9479 0050	2.2920 1832	2.6927 7279	3.7000 1805
18	1.3073 4064	1.4282 4625	1.5596 5872	1.7024 3306	1.8574 8920	2.0258 1652	2.4066 1923	2.8543 3915	3.9960 1950
19	1.3269 5075	1.4568 1117	1.5986 5019	1.7535 0605	1.9225 0132	2.1068 4918	2.5269 5020	3.0255 9950	4.3157 0106
20	1.3468 5501	1.4859 4740	1.6386 1644	1.8061 1123	1.9897 8886	2.1911 2314	2.6532 9771	3.2071 3547	4.6609 5714
21	1.3670 5783	1.5156 6634	1.6795 8185	1.8602 9457	2.0594 3147	2.2787 6807	2.7859 6259	3.3995 6360	5.0338 3372
22	1.3875 6370	1.5459 7967	1.7215 7140	1.9161 0341	2.1315 1158	2.3699 1879	2.9252 6072	3.6035 3742	5.4365 4041
23	1.4083 7715	1.5768 9926	1.7646 1068	1.9735 8651	2.2061 1448	2.4647 1554	3.0715 2376	3.8197 4966	5.8714 6365
24	1.4295 0281	1.6084 3725	1.8087 2595	2.0327 9411	2.2833 2849	2.5633 0416	3.2250 9994	4.0489 3464	6.3411 8074
25	1.4509 4535	1.6406 0599	1.8539 4410	2.0937 7793	2.3632 4498	2.6658 3633	3.3863 5494	4.2918 7072	6.8484 7520

Table B
(Present Value of 1): $(1 + i)^{-n}$

Period	1-1/2%	2%	3%	4%	5%	6%	8%
1	0.9852 2167	0.9803 9216	0.9708 7379	0.9615 3846	0.9523 8095	0.9433 9623	0.9259 2593
2	0.9706 6175	0.9611 6878	0.9425 9591	0.9245 5621	0.9070 2948	0.8899 9644	0.8573 3882
3	0.9563 1699	0.9423 2233	0.9151 4166	0.8889 9636	0.8638 3760	0.8396 1928	0.7938 3224
4	0.9421 8423	0.9238 4543	0.8884 8705	0.8548 0419	0.8227 0247	0.7920 9366	0.7350 2985
5	0.9282 6033	0.9057 3081	0.8626 0878	0.8219 2711	0.7835 2617	0.7472 5817	0.6805 8320
6	0.9145 4219	0.8879 7138	0.8374 8426	0.7903 1453	0.7462 1540	0.7049 6054	0.6301 6963
7	0.9010 2679	0.8705 6018	0.8130 9151	0.7599 1781	0.7106 8133	0.6650 5711	0.5834 9040
8	0.8877 1112	0.8534 9037	0.7894 0923	0.7306 9021	0.6768 3936	0.6274 1237	0.5402 6888
9	0.8745 9224	0.8367 5527	0.7664 1673	0.7025 8674	0.6446 0892	0.5918 9846	0.5002 4897
10	0.8616 6723	0.8203 4830	0.7440 9391	0.6755 6417	0.6139 1325	0.5583 9478	0.4631 9349
11	0.8489 3323	0.8042 6304	0.7224 2128	0.6495 8093	0.5846 7929	0.5267 8753	0.4288 8286
12	0.8363 8742	0.7884 9318	0.7013 7988	0.6245 9705	0.5568 3742	0.4969 6936	0.3971 1376
13	0.8240 2702	0.7730 3253	0.6809 5134	0.6005 7409	0.5303 2135	0.4688 3902	0.3676 9792
14	0.8118 4928	0.7578 7502	0.6611 1781	0.5774 7508	0.5050 6795	0.4423 0096	0.3404 6104
15	0.7998 5150	0.7430 1473	0.6418 6195	0.5552 6450	0.4810 1710	0.4172 6506	0.3152 4170
16	0.7880 3104	0.7284 4581	0.6231 6694	0.5339 0818	0.4581 1152	0.3936 4628	0.2918 9047
17	0.7763 8526	0.7141 6256	0.6050 1645	0.5133 7325	0.4362 9669	0.3713 6442	0.2702 6895
18	0.7649 1159	0.7001 5937	0.5873 9461	0.4936 2812	0.4155 2065	0.3503 4379	0.2502 4903
19	0.7536 0747	0.6864 3076	0.5702 8603	0.4746 4242	0.3957 3396	0.3305 1301	0.2317 1206
20	0.7424 7042	0.6729 7133	0.5536 7575	0.4563 8695	0.3768 8948	0.3118 0473	0.2145 4821
21	0.7314 9795	0.6597 7582	0.5375 4928	0.4388 3360	0.3589 4236	0.2941 5540	0.1986 5575
22	0.7206 8763	0.6468 3904	0.5218 9250	0.4219 5539	0.3418 4987	0.2775 0510	0.1839 4051
23	0.7100 3708	0.6341 5592	0.5066 9175	0.4057 2633	0.3255 7131	0.2617 9726	0.1703 1528
24	0.6995 4392	0.6217 2149	0.4919 3374	0.3901 2147	0.3100 6791	0.2469 7855	0.1576 9934
25	0.6892 0583	0.6095 3087	0.4776 0557	0.3751 1680	0.2953 0277	0.2329 9863	0.1460 1790

Table C
(Amount of Annuity of 1): $[(1 + i)^n - 1]/i$

Period	2-1/4%	3%	3-1/2%	4%	4-1/2%	5%	6%	8%
1	1.	1.	1.	1.	1.	1.	1.	1.
2	2.0225	2.030	2.035	2.040	2.045	2.050	2.060	2.080
3	3.0680 0625	3.090 9000	3.1062 25	3.121 6000	3.1370 25	3.152 5000	3.183 6000	3.246 4000
4	4.1370 3639	4.183 6270	4.2149 4288	4.246 4640	4.2781 9113	4.310 1250	4.374 6160	4.506 1120
5	5.2301 1971	5.309 1358	5.3624 6588	5.416 3226	5.4707 0973	5.525 6313	5.637 0930	5.866 6010
6	6.3477 9740	6.468 4099	6.5501 5218	6.632 9755	6.7168 9166	6.801 9128	6.975 3185	7.335 9290
7	7.4906 2284	7.662 4622	7.7794 0751	7.898 2945	8.0191 5179	8.142 0085	8.393 8377	8.922 8034
8	8.6591 6186	8.892 3361	9.0516 8677	9.214 2263	9.3800 1362	9.549 1089	9.897 4679	10.636 6276
9	9.8539 9300	10.159 1061	10.3684 9581	10.582 7953	10.8021 1423	11.026 5643	11.491 3160	12.487 5578
10	11.0757 0784	11.463 8793	11.7313 9316	12.006 1071	12.2882 0937	12.577 8925	13.180 7949	14.486 5625
11	12.3249 1127	12.807 7957	13.1419 9192	13.486 3514	13.8411 7879	14.206 7872	14.971 6426	16.645 4875
12	13.6022 2177	14.192 0296	14.6019 6164	15.025 8055	15.4640 3184	15.917 1265	16.869 9412	18.977 1265
13	14.9082 7176	15.617 7905	16.1130 3030	16.626 8377	17.1599 1327	17.712 9829	18.882 1377	21.495 2966
14	16.2437 0788	17.086 3242	17.6769 8636	18.291 9112	18.9321 0937	19.598 6320	21.015 0659	24.214 9203
15	17.6091 9130	18.598 9139	19.2956 8088	20.023 5876	20.7840 5429	21.578 5636	23.275 9699	27.152 1139
16	19.0053 9811	20.156 8813	20.9710 2971	21.824 5311	22.7193 3673	23.657 4918	25.672 5281	30.324 2830
17	20.4330 1957	21.761 5877	22.7050 1575	23.697 5124	24.7417 0689	25.840 3664	28.212 8798	33.750 2257
18	21.8927 6251	23.414 4354	24.4996 9130	25.645 4129	26.8550 8370	28.132 3847	30.905 6526	37.450 2437
19	23.3853 4966	25.116 8684	26.3571 8050	27.671 2294	29.0635 6246	30.539 0039	33.759 9917	41.446 2632
20	24.9115 2003	26.870 3745	28.2796 8181	29.778 0786	31.3714 2277	33.065 9541	36.785 5912	45.761 9643
21	26.4720 2923	28.676 4857	30.2694 7068	31.969 2017	33.7831 3680	35.719 2518	39.992 7267	50.422 9214
22	28.0676 4989	30.536 7803	32.3289 0215	34.247 9698	36.3033 7795	38.505 2144	43.392 2903	55.456 7552
23	29.6991 7201	32.452 8837	34.4604 1373	36.617 8886	38.9370 2996	41.430 4751	46.995 8277	60.893 2956
24	31.3674 0338	34.426 4702	36.6665 2821	39.082 6041	41.6891 9631	44.501 9989	50.815 5774	66.764 7592
25	33.0731 6996	36.459 2643	38.9498 5669	41.645 9083	44.5652 1015	47.727 0988	54.864 5120	73.105 9400

Table D

(Present Value of Annuity of 1): $[1 - (1 + i)^{-n}]/i$

Period	1-1/2%	2%	2-1/2%	3%	3-1/2%	4%	5%	6%	8%
1	0.985 2217	0.980 3922	0.975 6098	0.970 8738	0.9661 8357	0.961 5385	0.952 3810	0.943 3962	0.9259 2593
2	1.955 8834	1.941 5609	1.927 4242	1.913 4697	1.8996 9428	1.886 0947	1.859 4104	1.833 3927	1.7832 6475
3	2.912 2004	2.883 8833	2.856 0236	2.828 6114	2.8016 3698	2.775 0910	2.723 2480	2.673 0120	2.5770 9699
4	3.854 3847	3.807 7287	3.761 9742	3.717 0984	3.6730 7921	3.629 8952	3.545 9505	3.465 1056	3.3121 2684
5	4.782 6450	4.713 4595	4.645 8285	4.579 7072	4.5150 5238	4.451 8223	4.329 4767	4.212 3638	3.9927 1004
6	5.697 1872	5.601 4309	5.508 1254	5.417 1914	5.3285 5302	5.242 1369	5.075 6921	4.917 3243	4.6228 7966
7	6.598 2140	6.471 9911	6.349 3906	6.230 2830	6.1145 4398	6.002 0547	5.786 3734	5.582 3814	5.2063 7006
8	7.485 9251	7.325 4814	7.170 1372	7.019 6922	6.8739 5554	6.732 7449	6.463 2128	6.209 7938	5.7466 3894
9	8.360 5173	8.162 2367	7.970 8655	7.786 1089	7.6076 8651	7.435 3316	7.107 8217	6.801 6923	6.2468 8791
10	9.222 1846	8.982 5850	8.752 0639	8.530 2028	8.3166 0532	8.110 8958	7.721 7349	7.360 0871	6.7100 8140
11	10.071 1178	9.786 8481	9.514 2087	9.252 6241	9.0015 5104	8.760 4767	8.306 4142	7.886 8746	7.1389 6426
12	10.907 5052	10.575 3412	10.257 7646	9.954 0040	9.6633 3433	9.385 0738	8.863 2516	8.383 8439	7.5360 7802
13	11.731 5322	11.348 3738	10.983 1850	10.634 9553	10.3027 3849	9.985 6479	9.393 5730	8.852 6830	7.9037 7594
14	12.543 3815	12.106 2488	11.690 9122	11.296 0731	10.9205 2028	10.563 1229	9.898 6409	9.294 9839	8.2442 3698
15	13.343 2330	12.849 2635	12.381 3777	11.937 9351	11.5174 1090	11.118 3874	10.379 6580	9.712 2490	8.5594 7869
16	14.131 2641	13.577 7093	13.055 0027	12.561 1020	12.0941 1681	11.652 2956	10.837 7696	10.105 8953	8.8513 6916
17	14.907 6493	14.291 8719	13.712 1977	13.166 1185	12.6513 2059	12.165 6689	11.274 0663	10.477 2597	9.1216 3811
18	15.672 5609	14.992 0313	14.353 3636	13.753 5131	13.1896 8173	12.659 2970	11.689 5869	10.827 6035	9.3718 8714
19	16.426 1684	15.678 4620	14.978 8913	14.323 7991	13.7098 3742	13.133 9394	12.085 3209	11.158 1165	9.6035 9920
20	17.168 6388	16.351 4333	15.589 1623	14.877 4749	14.2124 0330	13.590 3263	12.462 2103	11.469 9212	9.8181 4741
21	17.900 1367	17.011 2092	16.184 5486	15.415 0241	14.6979 7420	14.029 1600	12.821 1527	11.764 0766	10.0168 0316
22	18.620 8244	17.658 0482	16.765 4132	15.936 9166	15.1671 2484	14.451 1153	13.163 0026	12.041 5817	10.2007 4366
23	19.330 8615	18.292 2041	17.332 1105	16.443 6084	15.6204 1047	14.856 8417	13.488 5739	12.303 3790	10.3710 5895
24	20.030 4054	18.913 9256	17.884 9858	16.935 5421	16.0583 6760	15.246 9631	13.798 6418	12.550 3575	10.5287 5828
25	20.719 6112	19.523 4565	18.424 3764	17.413 1477	16.4815 1459	15.622 0799	14.093 9446	12.783 3562	10.6747 7619

$$= \begin{bmatrix} a_{11}b_{11} + a_{12}b_{21} + a_{13}b_{31} & a_{11}b_{12} + a_{12}b_{22} + a_{13}b_{32} \\ a_{21}b_{11} + a_{22}b_{21} + a_{23}b_{31} & a_{21}b_{12} + a_{22}b_{22} + a_{23}b_{32} \end{bmatrix}.$$

Substituting an integer for each symbolic element of the two matrices, the matrix product takes the following form:

$$AB = \begin{bmatrix} 7 & 0 & -2 \\ 1 & 5 & -3 \end{bmatrix} \begin{bmatrix} 0 & 2 \\ -1 & 3 \\ 0 & 4 \end{bmatrix} = \begin{bmatrix} 0 & 6 \\ -5 & 5 \end{bmatrix}.$$

Matrix Inverse

The square matrix A, if it has an inverse, has a unique *inverse,* denoted A^{-1}, such that $AA^{-1} = A^{-1}A = I$, where I denotes the *identity* matrix (a square matrix with ones on the main diagonal and all other elements zero). This inverse may be computed as follows:

1. Set up a tableau with the coefficient matrix to be inverted on the left and an identity matrix on the right. For example, a 3 × 3 matrix A would produce the following tableau:

$$\begin{bmatrix} a_{11} & a_{12} & a_{13} & 1 & 0 & 0 \\ a_{21} & a_{22} & a_{23} & 0 & 1 & 0 \\ a_{31} & a_{32} & a_{33} & 0 & 0 & 1 \end{bmatrix}.$$

2. By the elementary operations of (*a*) multiplying a row (including the elements in all six columns) by a constant, (*b*) by adding a row, or a multiple of a row, to another row, or (*c*) by interchanging two rows, reduce the 3 × 3 matrix on the left to the identity matrix.

3. After this transformation, the inverse of the original 3 × 3 matrix will be in the 3 × 3 matrix on the right.

For example, assume that the following matrix A is given:

$$A = \begin{bmatrix} 5 & 0 & 0 \\ 0 & 20 & 1 \\ 0 & 10 & 0 \end{bmatrix}.$$

In determining the inverse of this matrix, the following series of operations are performed:

1. Set up the tableau with the matrix to be inverted on the left and the identity matrix on the right:

$$\begin{bmatrix} 5 & 0 & 0 & 1 & 0 & 0 \\ 0 & 20 & 1 & 0 & 1 & 0 \\ 0 & 10 & 0 & 0 & 0 & 1 \end{bmatrix}.$$

2. Divide all of the elements of row 1 by 5:

$$\begin{bmatrix} 1 & 0 & 0 & \tfrac{1}{5} & 0 & 0 \\ 0 & 20 & 1 & 0 & 1 & 0 \\ 0 & 10 & 0 & 0 & 0 & 1 \end{bmatrix}.$$

Note that only the six elements in row 1 are changed.

3. Subtract two times row 3 from row 2:

$$\begin{bmatrix} 1 & 0 & 0 & | & \frac{1}{5} & 0 & 0 \\ 0 & 0 & 1 & | & 0 & 1 & -2 \\ 0 & 10 & 0 & | & 0 & 0 & 1 \end{bmatrix}.$$

4. Divide row 3 by 10:

$$\begin{bmatrix} 1 & 0 & 0 & | & \frac{1}{5} & 0 & 0 \\ 0 & 0 & 1 & | & 0 & 1 & -2 \\ 0 & 1 & 0 & | & 0 & 0 & \frac{1}{10} \end{bmatrix}.$$

5. Interchange the positions of row 2 and row 3:

$$\begin{bmatrix} 1 & 0 & 0 & | & \frac{1}{5} & 0 & 0 \\ 0 & 1 & 0 & | & 0 & 0 & \frac{1}{10} \\ 0 & 0 & 1 & | & 0 & 1 & -2 \end{bmatrix}.$$

6. Since the identity matrix is now on the left, the inverse of A, denoted A^{-1}, is to be found on the right side of the tableau, viz.,

$$A^{-1} = \begin{bmatrix} \frac{1}{5} & 0 & 0 \\ 0 & 0 & \frac{1}{10} \\ 0 & 1 & -2 \end{bmatrix}.$$

7. The accuracy of these calculations may be verified by multiplying A and A^{-1} to produce the identity matrix (i.e., $AA^{-1} = I$):

$$AA^{-1} = \begin{bmatrix} 5 & 0 & 0 \\ 0 & 20 & 1 \\ 0 & 10 & 0 \end{bmatrix} \begin{bmatrix} \frac{1}{5} & 0 & 0 \\ 0 & 0 & \frac{1}{10} \\ 0 & 1 & -2 \end{bmatrix}$$

$$= \begin{bmatrix} 1 & 0 & 0 \\ 0 & 1 & 0 \\ 0 & 0 & 1 \end{bmatrix}.$$

Verification of the fact that $A^{-1}A = I$ is left as an exercise for the reader. Although this example is very elementary, the essential computational procedures apply equally to any matrix. A larger and more complex matrix merely enlarges the number of elementary operations (row transformations) required to calculate its inverse.

Appendix 2

Summary of Recommended Accounting Principles (National Committee on Governmental Accounting)[1]

1. *Legal Compliance and Financial Operations.* A governmental accounting system must make it possible: (a) to show that all applicable legal provisions have been compiled with; and (b) to determine fairly and with full disclosure the financial position and results of financial operations of the constituent funds and self-balancing account groups of the governmental unit.

2. *Conflicts between Accounting Principles and Legal Provisions.* If there is a conflict between legal provisions and generally accepted accounting principles applicable to governmental units, legal provisions must take precedence. Insofar as possible, however, the governmental accounting system should make possible the full disclosure and fair presentation of financial position and operating results in accordance with generally accepted principles of accounting applicable to governmental units.

3. *The Budget and Budgetary Accounting.* An annual budget should be adopted by every governmental unit, whether required by law or not, and the accounting system should provide budgetary control over general governmental revenues and expenditures.

4. *Fund Accounting.* Governmental accounting systems should be organized and operated on a fund basis. A fund is defined as an independent fiscal and accounting entity with a self-balancing set of accounts recording cash and/or other resources together with all related liabilities, obligations, reserves, and equities which are segregated for the purpose of carrying on specific activities or attaining certain objectives in accordance with special regulations, restrictions, or limitations.

5. *Types of Funds.* The following types of funds are recognized and should be used in accounting for governmental financial operations as indicated.

(1) The General Fund to account for all financial transactions not properly accounted for in another fund;

(2) Special Revenue Funds to account for the proceeds of specific revenue sources (other than special assessments) or to finance specified activities as required by law or administrative regulation;

---

[1] National Committee on Governmental Accounting, *Governmental Accounting, Auditing, and Financial Reporting* (Chicago, 1968), pp. 3–14.

(3) Debt Service Funds to account for the payment of interest and principal on long-term debt other than special assessment and revenue bonds;

(4) Capital Projects Funds to account for the receipt and disbursement of moneys used for the acquisition of capital facilities other than those financed by special assessment and enterprise funds;

(5) Enterprise Funds to account for the financing of services to the general public where all or most of the costs involved are paid in the form of charges by users of such services;

(6) Trust and Agency Funds to account for assets held by a governmental unit as trustee or agent for individuals, private organizations, and other governmental units;

(7) Intergovernmental Service Funds to account for the financing of special activities and services performed by a designated organization unit within a governmental jurisdiction for other organization units within the same governmental jurisdiction;

(8) Special Assessment Funds to account for special assessments levied to finance public improvements or services deemed to benefit the properties against which the assessments are levied.

6. *Number of Funds.* Every governmental unit should establish and maintain those funds required by law and sound financial administration. Since numerous funds make for inflexibility, undue complexity, and unnecessary expense in both the accounting system and the over-all financial administration, however, only the minimum number of funds consistent with legal and operating requirements should be established.

7. *Fund Accounts.* A complete self-balancing group of accounts should be established and maintained for each fund. This group should include all general ledger accounts and subsidiary records necessary to reflect compliance with legal provisions and to set forth the financial position and the results of financial operations of the fund. A clear distinction should be made between the accounts relating to current assets and liabilities and those relating to fixed assets and liabilities. With the exception of Intragovernmental Service Funds, Enterprise Funds, and certain Trust Funds, fixed assets should not be accounted for in the same fund with the current assets, but should be set up in a separate, self-balancing group of accounts called the General Fixed Asset Group of Accounts. Similarly, except in Special Assessment, Enterprise, and certain Trust Funds, long-term liabilities should not be carried with the current liabilities of any fund, but should be set up in a separate, self-balancing group of accounts known as the General Long-term Debt Group of Accounts.

8. *Valuation of Fixed Assets.* The fixed asset accounts should be maintained on the basis of original cost, or the estimated cost if the original cost is not available, or, in the case of gifts, the appraised value at the time received.

9. *Depreciation.* Depreciation on general fixed assets should not be recorded in the general accounting records. Depreciation charges on such assets may be computed for unit cost purposes, provided such charges are recorded only in memorandum form and do not appear in the fund accounts.

10. *Basis of Accounting.* The accrual basis of accounting is recommended for Enterprise, Trust, Capital Projects, Special Assessment, and Intragovernmental Service Funds. For the General, Special Revenue, and Debt Service Funds, the modified accrual basis of accounting is recommended. The modified

accrual basis of accounting is defined as that method of accounting in which expenditures other than accrued interest on general long-term debt are recorded at the time liabilities are incurred and revenues are recorded when received in cash, except for material or available revenues which should be accrued to reflect properly the taxes levied and the revenues earned.

11. *Classification of Accounts.* Governmental revenues should be classified by fund and source. Expenditures should be classified by fund, function, organization unit, activity, character, and principal classes of objects in accordance with standard recognized classification.

12. *Common Terminology and Classification.* A common terminology and classification should be used consistently throughout the budget, the accounts, and the financial reports.

13. *Financial Reporting.* Financial statements and reports showing the current condition of budgetary and proprietary accounts should be prepared periodically to control financial operations. At the close of each fiscal year, a comprehensive annual financial report covering all funds and financial operations of the governmental unit should be prepared and published.

INDEX

Index

This book has been set in 10 and 9 point Times Roman, leaded 2 points. Unit numbers and unit titles are in 36 and 24 point Janson. Chapter numbers are in 18 point Janson and 30 point Caslon Oldstyle #337. Chapter titles are in 18 point Janson. The size of the type page is 27 by 46½ picas.